# THE ORDERING OF THE STOREHOUSE MODULES

| | Sight words (SW) | Word analysis (WA) | Information gathering (IG) | Manipulative thinking (MT) | Evaluative thinking (ET) |
|---|---|---|---|---|---|
| CLUSTER I | I·SW·1 Visual discrim.<br>I·SW·2 Visual memory<br>I·SW·3 Naming<br>I·SW·6 Visual sequencing<br>I·SW·17 Easily confused letters and words | I·WA·1 Auditory memory<br>I·WA·4 Auditory closure<br>I·WA·5 Auditory discrim.<br>I·WA·9 Sound-symbol<br>I·WA·14 Context/phonics | I·IG·1 Content words<br>I·IG·2 Affix meaning<br>I·IG·3 Function words/ relationships | I·MT·1 Classification<br>I·MT·2 Inference | I·ET·1 Judging content |
| CLUSTER II | II·SW·6 Sight words<br>II·SW·8 Language experience | II·WA·1 Auditory fusion<br>II·WA·18 Letter substitution<br>II·WA·25 Structural analysis | II·IG·4 Contextual prediction (context clues) | | |
| CLUSTER III | | | III·IG·4 Contextual prediction (word order)<br>III·IG·6 Factual recall | III·MT·2 Main idea | |
| CLUSTER IV | | | | | IV·ET·1 Assessing word choice |
| CLUSTER V | | | V·IG·4 Contextual prediction (punctuation) | | |
| CLUSTER VI | | VI·WA·1 Vowel generalizations | | | |
| CLUSTER VII | | VII·WA·1 Syllabication | VII·IG·5 Contextual prediction (intonation) | | |
| CLUSTER VIII | | | | | |

# SYSTEMATIC READING INSTRUCTION

# SYSTEMATIC READING INSTRUCTION

## SECOND EDITION

## GERALD G. DUFFY
## GEORGE B. SHERMAN
### MICHIGAN STATE UNIVERSITY

**HARPER & ROW, PUBLISHERS**
NEW YORK, HAGERSTOWN, SAN FRANCISCO, LONDON

89681

Sponsoring Editor: Michael E. Brown
Project Editor: Cynthia Hausdorff
Designer: Gayle Jaeger
Production Supervisor: Will C. Jomarrón
Compositor: V & M Typographical, Inc.
Printer and Binder: The Murray Printing Company
Art Studio: Vantage Art Inc.

Systematic Reading Instruction, Second Edition

Library of Congress Cataloging in Publication Data

Duffy, Gerald G.
    Systematic reading instruction.

    1.  Reading (Elementary)  I.  Sherman, George B.,
joint author.  II.  Title.
LB1573.D75   1977        372.4        76-14862
ISBN 0-06-041794-3

# CONTENTS

# PREFACE

We believe that a primary cause of reading failure is that teachers have not been adequately trained in the skills of reading. Because teachers do not know the skills, they are unable to teach them, and even when a teacher does know them, instruction is too frequently haphazard and inefficient because the instructor lacks a system for determining what skill each learner needs at any given moment and also lacks an instructional strategy for teaching that skill. Consequently, a resource tool for diagnosing and teaching basic reading skills is needed.

This book meets that need. It lists the basic skills of word recognition and comprehension needed to attain a level of functional literacy and provides a system for efficiently diagnosing and teaching these skills.

This book has a broad range of utility and can be a valuable supplement to almost any reading program. In a standard basal text program it can be used to systematize skill instruction. In partnership with a language experience approach or an individualized reading program, it can provide the necessary structure and sequencing for supportive skill development. It can be used with Head Start, kindergarten, and elementary age children; with remedial readers in the secondary school; and with adults. It can be used with individual learners in tutorial situations or with groups in a regular classroom. Finally, it is a resource for the experienced teacher and an invaluable guide for pre-service teachers and volunteer tutors.

It is distinctive from other books on reading instruction in five ways.

First, it focuses on the skills of reading, stating each of these in performance terms. Second, it provides brief but specific tests to determine quickly what skills must be learned. Third, its focus is on the teaching-learning act itself and not the theoretical considerations thereof. Fourth, it provides specific suggestions for using both modeling and discovery techniques for teaching each of the major skills. Finally, it provides an extensive resource of specific suggestions for reteaching, practicing, and applying the skills.

Although the book has a broad range of utility and a number of distinctive features, *it must not be viewed as a total reading program.* Instead its focus is limited to the skills (or the mechanics) of reading. Although skills are crucial, they represent only part of a good reading program. Teacher-pupil relationships, interests, attitudes of both the learner and the teacher, vital creative learning experiences, and the role of literature are also crucial and must be provided. Hence this book is a resource that contributes uniquely to one aspect of the total reading program—that of teaching the basic skills.

Gerald G. Duffy
George B. Sherman

# ONE

# THE METHOD

# THE ROLE OF SKILLS IN A READING PROGRAM

The average life span of the free schools has been nine months. Why do they fail so often?

Unfashionable and unromantic as it may appear, the major cause for failure in the free schools is our unwillingness or inability to teach the hard skills.[1]

JONATHAN KOZOL

In recent years increased emphasis has been placed on reading instruction. The federal government has made the achievement of literacy a priority goal, massive programs have been initiated to give every citizen the "right to read," and the public (as well as teachers) has become deeply concerned with reading instruction.

This is as it should be. Reading is the most crucial of the fundamental skills; a child's success or failure in both school and society depends largely upon the ability to read. Consequently, we must ensure that each child can read well enough to function adequately in society.

## THE SKILLS OF READING

To achieve the goal of functional literacy for all our citizens the reading programs in our schools must be comprehensive, reflecting all the complexities of the act of reading. These programs should provide different and

From "Free Schools Fail Because They Don't Teach," *Psychology Today,* **5,** April 1972, p. 30.

creative reading activities that use a variety of materials and that have a firm foundation in the basic skills, which are the most fundamental requirements for successful reading. Reading itself consists of a group of skills that extend from the simple to the complex. The successful reader uses each of these skills when reading; a person who is unable to read or who has difficulty reading lacks one or more of the basic skills needed to be a successful reader. Consequently, instruction in the basic skills of reading must be one of the major components of a good reading program.

There are literally thousands of different skills, but they fall into only four categories, of which only two are associated with basic literacy. These are skills of (1) oral language and reading comprehension and (2) word recognition. Beyond the level of functional literacy, the child learns the skills of efficient study (including study techniques, various rates of reading, and other skills associated with reading efficiency) and the skills of literary understanding (in which the learner interprets literary devices and does higher-level thinking).

The progression of skill development during the school years is simply described in the following chart. The four major categories of reading skills—word identification, comprehension, efficient study and literary understandings—are listed in four vertical streams representing a continuum from kindergarten through high school. The skills of word identification and comprehension are emphasized at the earliest stages, with the learner moving gradually to efficient study and finally to the skills of literary understanding in the later grades. Although some sophisticated skills of word identification and comprehension are taught in the high school years and some of the lower-level study and literary skills are taught in the

**The Reading Skills**

| Elementary school | Word Identification | Comprehension | Efficient Study | Literary Skills |
|---|---|---|---|---|
| K | Discriminating letters and sounds | Interpreting oral language | | |
| 1 | | | | |
| 2 | | Interpreting written language | | |
| 3 | Word recognition and analysis | | | |
| 4 | | | | |
| 5 | | | | |
| Middle school | | | Study techniques | |
| 6 | | | | |
| 7 | | | Rates of reading | |
| 8 | | | | |
| High school | | | | Interpreting literary devices |
| 9 | | | | |
| 10 | | | | |
| 11 | | | | Higher level thinking |
| 12 | | | | |

4 ●

early grades, the primary emphasis of skill instruction at these varying grade levels can be seen in the chart.

This book focuses on describing the word identification and comprehension skills needed to achieve functional literacy and a strategy for teaching them. Its foundation rests on assumptions about the reading program, the reading process, the learner, and the nature of instruction.

### The Reading Program

In this book reading instruction is viewed in terms of a means-ends relationship. The end or goal of reading instruction is that the child should read, and read widely—library books, textbooks, magazines, comics, recipes, directions, encyclopedias, job application forms, letters, and any other form of written communication. Such reading is an important element of the reading program.

However, many children do not achieve the ends of reading simply by surrounding them with books or by waiting for them to generalize to reading "naturally." Instead they must be taught the means by which one reads; they must be taught the individual skills that, when viewed collectively, represent the act of reading. These means, or skills, are the second element of a reading program.

Finally, since it is often difficult for children to transfer isolated skills to the actual reading act, children need a bridge that guides them to apply the learned skills in context. This bridge brings the means and ends together as seen in the following chart:

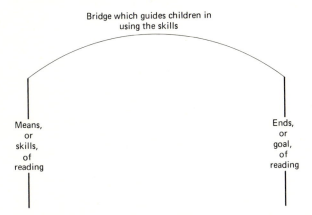

Bridge which guides children in using the skills

Means, or skills, of reading

Ends, or goal, of reading

In operation a reading program should include instruction on the means or skills that constitute the act of reading; it should include guided assistance in using these skills in contextual settings, and it should provide multiple opportunities for using the skills in the reading of meaningful and exciting material.

## The Reading Process

Because one of the main emphases of the reading program is the means, or skills, of reading, three points about the selection of these skills should be noted. First, although reading is a complex and lifelong activity in which many skills are used, this book emphasizes only the beginning stages of reading that are frequently encountered in the elementary school: the development of functional literacy or the ability to read fifth grade material. Second, this book views functional literacy as a balance between being able to identify the words and knowing what the words are saying —a balance between word recognition and comprehension. And finally, the skills taught in this book reflect a comprehensive view of the nature of reading and the reading process itself.

## The Individual Child

One cannot work for long as a teacher without facing the reality that children differ dramatically in the way they learn to read. Some children learn easily and need little systematic instruction, whereas others desperately need help. In any given grade or classroom some children may have achieved the ends of reading to the extent that they can read very difficult books and others may be unable to read any book at all. Some children learn the skills without much effort but others need considerable help in comprehension or word identification or both.

No reading instruction is effective unless it deals satisfactorily with this reality of individual differences. This book does so in two ways. First, it offers specific and concrete guidelines for diagnosing what the skill differences are; second, it provides specific guidelines for organizing a classroom, monitoring student progress, and simultaneously supervising the multiple and various classroom activities that accompany individualization.

## The Nature of Instruction

Once the program has been outlined, the skills identified and diagnosed, and the classroom management system established, learning must occur.

Some children learn to read with little or no direct instruction. They possess characteristics from their heredity and environment that makes it easy for them to learn. Such children are seldom a problem for most teachers; in fact, teaching these children is often simply a matter of keeping them pointed in the right direction.

Many other children, however, find reading a difficult task, a mysterious process with no apparent order to it. Giving such children a book or a basal text and hoping they will learn to read by reading is fruitless, and incidental instruction on skills often compounds the problem rather than easing it. Such children need a *systematic* program emphasizing both skills instruction and how these skills can be applied in reading. It is with these children in mind that this book is written.

Instruction is systematic if each of several criteria is met:

1. If the child is taught the precise skill he or she needs to learn next, not one already learned in the past or one for which necessary prerequisites are lacking.
2. If the teacher can do a task analysis of the skill to be learned and use that analysis in planning instruction.
3. If the teacher guides the child through a series of instructional steps until the task can be performed independently.
4. If the teacher makes sure that the learned task becomes a habit.
5. If, most importantly, the teacher makes sure that a learned skill is usefully applied to improve the child's reading of contextual material.

This book, then, is built on fundamental assumptions about the structure of the reading program, the nature of the reading process, the importance of individualization, and the nature of instruction. It views reading as a learned process realized through the systematic implementation of a sequential list of skills which reflect the nature of the reading process. It requires

1. Teachers who are sensitive, empathetic persons who care about each child.
2. Teachers who know how children differ in relation to reading, how the process of reading is structured, how to diagnose and instruct, and how to manage individual differences.
3. Teachers who do build a reading program in which each child moves at his or her optimum rate in learning and applying the skills associated with reading literacy.

## THE FOCUS OF THIS BOOK

The heart of the book, starting on page 87 and continuing through page 455, consists of a series of 218 skills, 150 of which focus on word identification and 68 of which focus on comprehension. These skills are essential for successful reading of fourth and fifth grade materials and they form the crucial foundation for continued growth in reading. Consequently, a person's success as a reader (and ultimately, in school and society) is dependent upon mastery and application of these fundamental skills. They must be carefully taught and thoroughly learned.

To ensure that they are taught and learned, each skill is described in a separate module. (Modules begin on page 87.) Each module includes a specific statement of the skill expressed in behavioral terms, a simple pretest for determining the learner's ability to perform the skill prior to instruction, guides for directing the learner's attention, both a modeling and a discovery strategy for teaching the skill, suggestions for reteaching the skill if the child does not learn it the first time, multiple suggestions for providing practice to habituate the skill, a simple posttest to make sure that instruction has resulted in learner mastery of the skill, and suggestions for making sure that the learner transfers the skill from the lesson to his or her daily reading.

The modules are organized to be used in a four-step sequence that emphasizes (1) precise appraisal of learner needs, (2) specific instruction, (3) demonstrated mastery of skills, and (4) application of the learned skill in actual reading materials.

In action the system works as follows. First, administer the pretest for the lowest-level skill in the hierarchy. If the learner performs at or above the stated criterion level for that pretest, assume the skill has already been mastered. Go on to the next skill, administering the pretest and comparing the learner's performance to the criterion level established for that skill. If the learner once again performs at or above the established criterion, assume this skill has been mastered and move on to the next. This process continues until the learner encounters a skill he or she cannot perform. Thus the first step in the strategy is that of data gathering, in which the series of simple pretests is used to determine what the learner can and cannot do. Time is not wasted teaching a skill already mastered and effort is not wasted teaching a skill that is too difficult.

The second step is to provide direct instruction to develop the skill. Here the skill module's suggestions for teaching and practice are used. The lessons are highly intensive and direct. There is no misunderstanding concerning what needs to be taught, nor is the skill left to develop "naturally" or as a result of generalized reading lessons. The objective for the lesson is clear; the instruction is specific.

The third step is the administration of the posttest to determine whether the instruction has been successful. This procedure is similar to the first step. If the learner performs at or above the stated criterion level, the instruction has been successful; the skill has been mastered and the learner can be moved to the next skill. If the child fails, however, one must assume that the instruction has not been successful and another lesson must be planned and taught using the provided suggestions for reteaching. Thus the third step in the system makes sure that each skill in the sequence is mastered in turn and that no learner is moved on too quickly, thus preventing the assumption that the skill was learned simply because it was taught.

Finally, in the fourth step the teacher helps the learner apply the newly learned skill in the real world of reading. The child is given a book having a readability level appropriate to his or her reading level and is shown how to use the skill when actually reading. This step ensures learner transfer of the skill to the ultimate act of reading and eliminates the possibility of teaching skills in isolation from the reading of books.

The system can be diagrammed in the following way:

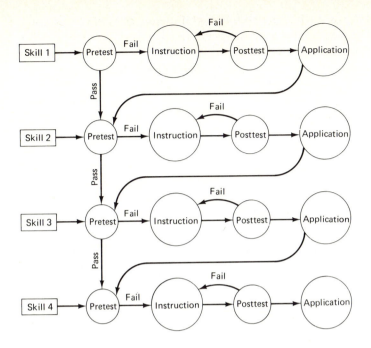

As can be seen, a learner proceeds through the skill hierarchy in a sequential fashion, from the simplest to the most complex. The structure for teaching reading skills is systematic. The pretest for each skill ensures that instructional time is spent only on what needs to be mastered; instruction for each skill is direct and specific; the posttests serve as checks so that no student moves from one skill to another until the prerequisite has been mastered; and application activities make sure that the skill will be used. Utilization of this test-teach-test-apply cycle of skill teaching ensures that each child receives the basic instruction needed to become functionally literate.

## WHY IS THIS BOOK NECESSARY?

Why is it necessary to have a separate resource book for teaching the basic reading skills? Does the teacher not already have, in the commercial reading materials available in the classroom, the resources for systematically teaching the skills? For the children who do not learn easily, the too frequent answer to this question is No, because such children do not learn to read simply by being "plugged in" to a set of materials.

To illustrate, we can look at the most widely used tool for teaching beginning reading—the basal reading textbook. A basal program consists of a graded series of books ranging in difficulty from pre-first to sixth grade. The basal textbook at each level contains stories considered appropriate, both in content and readabality, for a particular grade level. When the basal text is used the instruction focuses on these stories; the new words are identified and the story is introduced, read silently, and discussed. The teacher may then assign a page of skill work from the companion workbook. The premise of the basal text is essentially that children learn to read by reading, and the majority of the suggestions in the teacher's guide relate to the reading act itself rather than to the skills one must learn to be a better reader.

As a result, the typical basal text approach has five potential weaknesses. First, rather than teaching the learner the needed skills and then helping apply them in a reading situation, most basals first ask the child to read and then to learn the skills. Second, rather than having the skills specified in a definite sequence to guide the teacher's daily planning, many basals frequently leave gaps in the skills sequence or state the skills vaguely with little direction to the teacher regarding what skills have priority. Third, rather than providing specific pretests to determine skill needs, basals usually leave such diagnosis to the teacher. Fourth, rather than providing specific strategies for teaching each skill, basals often provide just a workbook page, with the implication that the child will learn the skill simply by completing the exercise. Finally, basals seldom provide the specific guidance needed for reteaching, practicing, and applying the skills. In short, then, the basal, although a valuable source of graded reading material in which children can apply learned skills, suffers from the assumption that all children will learn to read by being "plugged in" to that material. Such is not the case, and it is the child who does not learn easily who pays the price.

Other types of packaged commercial materials suffer from the same "plug them in and let them go" approach to instruction. Probably the most common of these are the various workbooks and kits that profess to emphasize skills. In reality, however, they seldom account adequately for transferring skills to the reading act; they do not often have a systematic listing of all the word recognition and comprehension skills, emphasizing instead a single aspect, such as phonetic analysis or word meaning; they seldom provide multiple strategies for teaching the skills, relying on the child to teach herself or himself; and they usually do not provide adequate suggestions for the task of reteaching. Although these workbooks and kits are often useful in providing practice material for skills that have already been taught, they fail to provide the comprehensive assistance needed to develop fully the basic skills for all readers.

Similar weaknesses are found in other approaches to reading, such as the language experience approach (in which children are taught to read materials they have written that reflect their own experiences) and the individualized reading approach (in which children select library books to be read at their own pace). Both approaches are valuable and useful because they provide meaningful materials for the learner to read; however, both are weak in skill development because they lack a structure for systematically developing the crucial fundamental skills.

In summary, there is no single panacea for the problems and difficulties of teaching reading. This is particularly true when teaching children who do not learn easily. To plug such children into one of the attractive new reading kits is not enough by itself; leading them page by page through a commercially published workbook series is not enough by itself; having them "read" each story in a new basal text is not enough by itself. In each case the missing ingredient is a caring teacher who provides direct assistance to the children who need it before asking them to complete a task. It is at this need that *Systematic Reading Instruction* is aimed.

## ● CHAPTER SUMMARY

This book provides a highly systematic and effective strategy for developing the skills needed for functional literacy. When used well it eliminates much wasted motion in skill teaching while ensuring a great measure of success among learners, particularly those who have difficulty learning to read.

One must not, however, think of this book as a total reading program or assume that functional literacy can be achieved simply by doing what is specified in the skill modules. Rather, this book should be considered a resource for specifying, diagnosing, and teaching the means or skills of reading to those children who do not learn to read easily. While using the book to plan instruction for such children, one must be sure also that the total program includes many activities that reflect the "ends" of reading, that appropriate instruction is provided for the children who learn to read easily, and, most important, that all children are reading.

# THE READING
# SKILL
# SEQUENCE

This is a story about Larry. Larry is a real boy. If you saw him during recess or art class, you would probably call him an average third grader. He is average—average intellect, average home life, average learning skills. However, Larry is different. He started school when he was four years old, and then had to spend an extra year in a "transition room" before going on to first grade. His teachers called him immature and found it difficult to help him learn to read. They tried. They drilled and directed and plugged him into the most popular packaged materials. When they became flustered and frustrated, they moved him into "remedial reading," where for two years Larry was subjected to games, rewards, threats, and the newest programs, but all for naught.

Larry cannot read. Everyone is stumped, even Larry. One day when he was asked to pronounce the words on the Dolch list, he summed up his dilemma and that of countless other children who have not been taught the skills that reflect the reading process when he said, "How do people know what these are?"

The skill sequence provided in Part Two of this book is built on some assumptions about reading and learning. In order to understand these assumptions and their relationship to helping a child learn to read, this chapter describes the model from which they were generated. It answers the basic question of *why* each skill is included in the hierarchy, because a professional teacher should know not only what he or she is teaching and how to teach it, but why.

The act of reading can be described or analyzed from any of a number of models. Obviously the teacher's model determines to a large extent his or her choice of teaching activities. If the teacher defines reading as an *interest,* a major component of instruction will be the motivation of children, through materials they have selected and shared interaction. Should the teacher define reading as a *language process,* the focus will be on such teaching devices as language experience, with much emphasis on the comprehension of what is read. The teacher who views reading as a *learned process* will usually emphasize skill development, with careful control of the learning conditions that influence mastery of each skill. A teacher who operates from a *cultural model* will be very careful to match children with material, to give attention to dialect differences, and to emphasize the oral-aural components of reading. Should he or she choose certain *linguistic models* of instruction, reading materials might emphasize both phonics, with such exercises as "Pat a fat cat, Matt," and the effect of oral language and intonation on reading. The point is that all reading programs grow to some extent from theoretical models that frame the act of reading and give scope and sequence to what is to be taught.

The reconciliation of these models is often very difficult. Disputes over the merits of any model and its success or failaure when compared to other models generate heated discussions and often create implacable enemies. With this in mind, the skill sequence presented in this book, although based on a view of reading as a learned process, draws from many models of reading. It reflects the belief that all models have some strengths that should be amalgamated into any instructional program.

## THE SRI READING MODEL

Reading is an act of communication. Someone has something to say and wants to be heard. Unfortunately there is no one to listen. The audience is absent. Therefore this person must resort to writing his or her message on paper and sending the paper to the audience. This system works extremely well *if* the audience can make the scribbles on paper give the same message the author intended.

This act of resurrection, of making the inscrutably silent scribbles speak, is the primary difference between reading and listening. The goal of each is to receive a message, but the reader must first decode the written page into language before the message can be understood.

Traditional reading methodology has labeled these two elements of the reading process "word recognition" and "comprehension." Although these two concepts do accurately represent the goals of instruction (first, making the message speak; second, understanding it), they tend to isolate the two elements from each other and to obscure the interactions that exist between them. These interactions are crucial and can be more readily seen by defining the reading process as a psycholinguistic guessing game or, more accurately, as three games played simultaneously by the reader. Each game consists of signals that help the reader predict the written message and that help in both the word recognition and comprehension acts. These signals can be described as the rules or skills of each game, and thus the rules or skills of reading. A good reader has these three sets of signals under control and uses each with appropriate speed and precision. The poor reader either lacks basic skill in one or more of the sets of signals or emphasizes or exaggerates one set to the exclusion of the other two. In either case reading growth suffers. The teacher's job is to help children learn to use the three sets of signals well and to develop a proper balance between them in the total act of reading.

## The Graphemic Signals

The first of the three very distinct but interrelated sets of signals comes from the printed letters and words. A child looks at these and reads because he or she can recognize and remember words from the way they are spelled. The child is cued to this identification through a series of signals embedded in the English spelling system. Knowledge of and skill with this system allow the child either to know or to predict a word identification. In this system letters represent, to some extent, speech sounds and the child reads by associating these sounds with their visual representatives. The rules of this game are fairly simple. The child learns how to look and what to look for; learns how to listen and what to listen for; and makes an association between what he or she sees and what he or she hears. When these skills are learned the child becomes an identifier of words. This area of skill is often called the graphemic or spelling process. Its application moves the words from the page and into the child's head.

## The Syntactic Signals

The second set of reading signals comes from the syntactic or grammatical structure of the English language. When words are grouped into phrases, sentences, or paragraphs, they are automatically arranged in accordance with the constraints of English grammar. As children translate the words from the page, they process them into English syntax and predict where the message is going and the words it will contain. The message leaps from the page in grammatical chunks rather than just limping along from word identification to word identification. Accurate word recognition and the push of grammatical convention produce a continuous loop of meaning. A recognized word triggers a grammatical prediction that produces another recognized word, which in turn produces further grammatical predictions, and so on through the message. The good reader "guesses" his or her way through the message, using spelling and syntactic codes, each of which helps to make the other prediction more precise.

## The Semantic Signals

The third guessing game is played at the meaning or semantic level. Words grouped in phrases, sentences, or paragraphs share not only grammatical structure but also common content. Each contributes to the message meaning, and as the child reads he or she is actively predicting what this meaning is. Constant feedback from the graphemic and syntactic systems allows children to verify or reject these predictions. The basic context of the message gives this insight. The better children's understanding of the content of the message, the better will be their predictions of future word identifications and grammatical forms. The better their predictions of future word identification and grammatical structures, the better will be their predictions of the message content. Again the interrelationship of word identification, syntactic constraints, and semantic prediction is apparent. The total process contains elements of both word recognition and comprehension, but these elements are never mutually exclusive in the *good* reader. Instead they blur together into three distinct but interrelated operations, each of which feeds and is fed by the other two. The good reader guesses or predicts his or her way through the message, using graphemic, syntactic, and semantic signals. The better the reader's ability to apply each of these codes simultaneously, the better his or her total reading development will be.

## Summary

Study the following chart. It should help clarify the relationships of the operations just described.

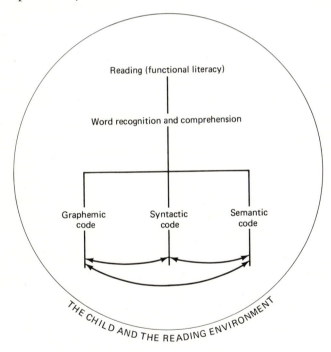

As the chart shows, developing reading to the level of functional literacy has the dual goals of word recognition and comprehension, which require emphasis on three coding systems: the graphemic, the syntactic, and the semantic. Although these can be arbitrarily separated for purpose of discussion and instruction, they actually interconnect and interrelate, as shown by the arrows at the bottom. Skills learned in each system blend not only into that system but also into the other two, creating a gradual but steady progression from nonreader to reading behavior. Finally, all considerations of the reading process must be viewed from within the context of the individual child (hence the encompassing circle), since the degree of emphasis on one operation or another varies from child to child, depending upon the background brought to the task of reading.

## OPERATIONALIZING THE MODEL

If readers can predict their way through a written message by appropriately using the spelling, grammar, and meaning cues embedded in it, a most logical and important question then becomes, "How do I, as a teacher, help a child use these cues?" Although there is some dispute over how this question should be answered, the overwhelming consensus is that the teacher must instruct the child in the various skills and knowledges that characterize these three coding systems. Hence the skill hierarchy found in this book provides you with both a listing of the skills that comprise the three coding systems and suggestions on how to teach these skills; it converts the elements of the reading process from a theoretical consideration into a teachable operation.

To help you understand how the process theory is translated into operational teaching objectives, the following sections describe in some detail the skills associated with each coding system. Consistent with the dual goals of reading instruction, our discussion is divided into two parts: word recognition and comprehension. Although the graphemic code is emphasized in word recognition and the syntactic and semantic codes are emphasized in comprehension, you are cautioned once again to remember how these three signaling systems work together in creating efficient readers. Further, as might be expected, the description of the reading process becomes more and more complex as we add more and more detail. We will update our process chart as we go along to help you create a more complete picture of the complex act of reading.

# READING SKILLS IN THE WORD RECOGNITION AREA

The skills in the graphemic system make a major contribution toward the generalized reading behavior we call word recognition. This is one of the major goals of reading skill instruction. Even a cursory comparison of good readers with poor ones yields very dramatic evidence of this fact. Good readers can recognize and name many words, whereas poor ones show a diminished recognition vocabulary, usually in proportion to their degree of disability. This difference is also reflected in the books children read and the groups they are taught in. The more words a child recognizes, the higher is his or her reading level and the more positive his or her group identification; the good readers we label "rabbits" or "bluebirds," the poor ones "turtles" or "sparrows." It is absolutely necessary for all teachers in all grades to recognize the importance of a child developing effective word recognition skills and to support this commitment with a sophisticated understanding of the learning tasks and instructional techniques that influence their acquisition.

The single most important aspect of word recognition for a teacher to remember is that it is a *dual,* not a *unitary,* skill. Two very separate and distinct learning tasks are involved. An example should help to make this clear. Little Joan is reading a page of her basal primer. The page has 34 separate words on it and she has learned to recognize 27 of them at sight. They are old friends from preceding pages and earlier books. These 27 words represent one kind of word recognition that can be very descriptively called *instant identification.* We could also say that this child recognizes these words *at sight;* they are part of her *sight vocabulary.*

But what of the seven words that are *not recognized?* As Joan reads, she comes to the first of these. She does not recognize the word because she has never seen it before. She stops and looks but nothing happens. There is no memory for a spoken word that connects to that set of squiggled letters. But as she looks at the word again and puzzles on it, she guesses that it must be the word **funny** because it begins with the word **fun** (a word that she can instantly recognize) and **funny** makes sense in the story being read. She is correct; the unknown word is **funny** and Joan has just performed the second and more difficult word recognition task; she has *figured out* or *analyzed* a word that was not instantly recognized. This can be very accurately called a *mediated identification.* Something (or a series of things) has helped solve the problem of that unknown word.

The dual tasks of instant recognition and mediated strategies, although two distinct learning tasks, share the common goal of developing fluency in word recognition. Mediated strategies serve as a bridge between not knowing words at all and recognizing them instantly. For instance, when children mediate an unknown word, they have identified it for the moment and are then able to continue reading. If they meet it again on the same page, they will seldom recognize it *instantly.* It is much more likely that they will again be forced to stop and think, to mediate. The time that they spend figuring it out will probably be less than the earlier recognition and the analysis strategies employed may be different, but the word is *not* instantly recognized on the second meeting and there is a break in fluency as some mediating behavior or skill is employed in order to recognize it. Children will continue to use mediating strategies to identify a word until, through the increased familiarity that comes from repetition, they learn to recognize it instantly. In this way the dual skills, although distinctly different acts, work together to create fluent recognizers of words.

This description of word recognition should serve as an introduction to both *instant* and *mediated* recognition. The following pages describe these two skills and their learning tasks.

## INSTANT RECOGNITION

One of the primary goals of word recognition instruction is the development of an ever-expanding sight vocabulary. In order to help a child in this task a teacher must have both a clear and a basic understanding of the nature of the learning involved and a store of appropriate instructional techniques. The first provides a theoretical framework on which to make instructional decisions; the second is the application of this decision in the actual teaching situation. The following gives an understanding of the task of instant recognition.

### Visual Prerequisites

Instant recognition is a visually based task. Children who learn sight words quickly and seemingly without effort are those who know how to use their eyes—how to look and what to look for. Although some children come to school already knowing these things, such children probably constitute, at best, a small majority of the total population of beginners. The remainder of a class must be very carefully taught those specific visual readiness skills that are prerequisite to future success in instantly recognizing words.

These visual prerequisites reflect an arbitrary set of conventions in the English spelling code that must be understood and applied if sight words are to be learned effectively. These conventions include (1) left-to-right progression of letters, (2) the visual representation (letters) of speech sounds, and (3) the left-to-right and top-to-bottom progression of words and sentences. Learning to operate within the framework of these conventions is probably more a conditioned activity than a cognitive one; that is, the child must develop the habit of taking in the visual signals from the page in accordance with these three conventions of English writing. To this end a teacher must help the child develop this restricted set of prerequisite visual behaviors. Only then will the child be able efficiently and accurately to apply the visual cues necessary for speedy and accurate reading.

DISCRIMINATION. By far the major learning task involved in these visual activities can be categorized as a discrimination skill. The child must learn to see (discriminate) the often subtle differences between letters and between similarly spelled words. Problems involving incomplete closure (**O, C,** and **G** have very similar configurations), rotations (**p, d, b, g; m, w, n, u,** and so on), and common elements (**j, i; t, f; R, B**) all must be solved before more sophisticated discrimination can be made. Similarly, children can be confused by the constant juggling of comparative and contrastive visual elements in whole words. They need to learn that words share common letters (e.g., **run** and **ran**) and that this commonality is a desirable and necessary part of an alphabet writing system, but they also need to understand that seeing only common letters leads to confusion and inaccuracy. They must know that each word has one or more distinctive letters that differentiate it from all other words and must learn to use both the common and the unique letters in making a word identification.

VISUAL SEQUENCE. The second visual prerequisite for successful reading achievement is the habitual response of seeing words from left to right, beginning to end. Although this is really a type of discrimination learning, the unwarranted confusions some children exhibit with "backward reading," "perceptual confusions," and "visual-motor disorientations" suggest that careful programming and instruction beyond the simple discrimination of letter and word differences are necessary. The goal of this instruction is to train the child to look at words in the same spatial direction in which they were written.

VISUAL MEMORY. The third prerequisite, visual memory, normally accrues as an adjunct to the visual discrimination and visual sequencing activities. However, in those few cases where this aptitude for remembering what the eyes have seen is not transferred as a result of discrimination and sequencing instruction, objectives that teach this skill are advisable. The goal of this instruction is once again to teach children how to use their eyes effectively and specifically to learn to remember what they have seen.

## Learning Sight Words

When children look at a word and instantly recognize it, they are performing a type of learning called *paired association*. As the name suggests, this learning has two elements that in some fashion become associated with each other. In learning sight words the visual spelling of the word is one element and its spoken form the other. Children learn to pair what is seen with what is said. In other words, they develop an association between a visual stimulus (a written word) and a spoken response (the name of that word).

This all seems simple enough but in reality children who make a correct identification have used their skill with the preceding visual prerequisites to perform three very difficult and specific activities. First, they *discriminated* the stimulus (the spelled word) as different from any other spelled word. If they use insufficient cues to make this discrimination (that is, if they see only the first and second letter or find some other partial component of the spelled words as the visual discriminator in this particular paired association), then they will continually miscall that word when they see other words that share this partial discriminator. For example, if a child looks at the word **run** but sees only the **r** and learns to say **run** each time he or she sees the **r**, then any other word beginning with **r** will also be identified as **run**. A paired association must begin with a discriminated stimulus.

Second, children make the connection or association between the discriminated stimulus and the spoken word. The key condition here is the contiguity in time between what their eyes see and their mouths or minds say. If, for example, they look at the word **run,** discriminate it in total, but then glance to the teacher's face or to a picture at the top of the page before saying or thinking **run,** there is little chance that the association between the written and spoken forms of this word will be paired. When learning an association, they must look and say or think simultaneously.

Finally, they *remember* this association. That they accurately discriminate the written word and respond on time with the spoken word is all for naught unless they remember that association the next time they see the word.

So the child who can read all the words in the preprimer has really learned a very complex task. He or she has learned to make a series of paired associations by (1) discriminating a precise visual array of letters that spell each word, (2) associating the spoken form of each word with its visual form, and (3) remembering this association.

## SUMMARY OF INSTANT RECOGNITION

Instant recognition is a crucial reading skill. With the mastery of a large stock of sight words, decoding becomes an automatic process, thereby freeing the reader to concentrate on syntactic and semantic considerations. However, instant recognition is not a natural phenomenon for most children. It requires both the mastery of certain prerequisite subskills that orient the child to the visual conventions of the graphemic system and the utilization of paired-association learning in building a large stock of sight words.

## MEDIATED RECOGNITION

The second category of skills in the graphemic system produces children who, when faced with a word that is not in their sight vocabulary, attack and recognize this word through a system of mediating strategies. It is the children's ability to use these strategies that allows them to figure out new and unknown words.

There are many things that children can do when they come to an unknown word. They can stop reading, skip the word and pretend it does not exist, ask someone else to identify it, sound it out, use the sense of the sentence in which it appears to guess its identity, examine it to see if it contains other known words or word parts on which to base a guess, or struggle with a dictionary and its pronunciation key. All these operations, however, are not necessarily valued equally as mediating strategies. Some are more appropriate than others; to discover which are effective, we must measure each against four criteria:

1. Is the mediating strategy *independent;* that is, can the child use it without outside help?

2. Is it *accurate?* It does little good to apply a mediating technique that produces a misidentification.
3. Is it *speedy?* It seems obvious that if it takes an inordinate amount of time to figure out a strange word, then the usefulness of the technique should be questioned.
4. Does the strategy *generalize* to other unknown words? This criterion suggests that the mediating strategy must be as useful on page 3 of the pre-primer as it is on page 67 of the sixth grade reader.

A very quick application of these criteria to the seven mediating strategies identified at the beginning of this section should help us to determine which of the preceding techniques are appropriate. Let us look first at those that fail to meet the criteria. For instance, children who stop reading entirely when they come to an unknown word are *not* using any analysis strategy. This behavior should be eliminated, not encouraged. In the second example, children who skip an unknown word are ignoring the need for accurately reproducing the written message and its information. Third, children who read only when someone else is there to help with the new words lack independence, although such a technique is certainly accurate, speedy, and useful at any time that help is at hand. Finally, searching for a word pronunciation in the dictionary can be done independently; it is accurate if the child knows how to use the pronunciation keys; but it is not speedy. In fact, only the rare child can sustain interest and understanding in a story that is constantly interrupted because of a need to look up a word in the dictionary. For this reason the dictionary as a mediating tool in word recognition is useless. This does not mean that a dictionary cannot be used for many other school or reading purposes; it means only that it is too cumbersome to be useful in figuring out a word that is not instantly recognized by a child.

Some mediating strategies do meet the criteria. For instance, the technique of sounding out a word (that is, applying the sound-symbol code) can be independent, speedy, and accurate for most words that a child reads. Not all words can be correctly identified by sounding them out, but this technique is a reflection of *one* of the *codes* or *guessing games* in the reading process and does generalize to most words in most sentences. Similarly, guessing a word identification by using the grammar and meaning in the sentence is also independent, speedy, and capable of generalization to other sentences on other pages. Although it is sometimes not totally accurate, accuracy can be improved by combining it with the sounding process. Because English words can be compounded, inflected, derived, and so on, teaching a child to search out known structure elements is also a useful mediating strategy. It is fast, is independent, can be generalized to other words, and is reasonably accurate, especially when combined with one or both of the sounding and contextual skills.

In summary, we find that only three strategies meet our criterion needs. Phonic (or letter-sound) mediators, structured (or morphemic) mediators, and context (or semantic-syntactic) mediators all offer a reasonable and realistic fit to our selection criteria. These are the mediating skills that, when applied singly or in tandem, produce readers who can accurately and effectively analyze and identify a word that is not instantly recognized. Also, although the mediating strategies are categorized with the graphemic system, it is important to note that both the structured and contextual mediators contain elements of the syntactic and semantic systems, illustrating once again that the three major sets of signals interrelate.

Before examining each of the mediating strategies in greater detail, one should consider two other important concerns. The first relates to the fact that mediating strategies frequently result only in approximations of the unknown word. Consider the task of figuring out an unrecognized word. It is difficult because it is a type of learning that almost involves problem solving. This suggests a much higher level of cognitive behavior than merely associating a written word with a spoken word. However, not only is the learning task more difficult or of a higher order, but not one of the mediating strategies of phonics, structure, or context has a set of rules that can always be relied on to deliver an accurate recognition of a strange word. To the contrary, any prediction that a child makes using these basic strategies has an element of error because the code system is only representative of the message and, as such, can only approximate that message.

For example, the three letters **d-o-g** represent the three phonemes we hear in the spoken word **dog.** But because the correspondence between the way these three letters can sound and the way they sound when a child simply speaks the word **dog** can be very different, learners must realize that turning letters into sounds and sounds into words will not always produce the word as they speak it. The letter sounds give an *approximation* of the word as it is usually spoken, but many times learners will need to say to themselves **d-ŏ-g** as in **hŏt,** but **dŏg** is really **dōg** or **dawg** or whatever other dialect difference exists in speech. The point is that written letters are *approximations* of the sounds made in normally spoken words, and although children may do a good job of generalizing a sound value and using that generalization to sound out a new word, they must always measure the resultant pronunciation against their own spoken language and be prepared to adjust the approximated sound value to that reality. The child who sounds the word **come** as **cōm** and then says, "Oh, that's **come,**" is telling you that she or he realizes the need for this adjustment of the spelling-sounding system to fit real spoken words. This same need to mediate a fit between the way a word is spelled and sounded and the way it is normally spoken becomes even more apparent as the child sounds out polysyllabic words that reflect both letter sound and *accent* problems. Here the need to test what is sounded "against the ear" is an absolute necessity.

Similarly, a word identification based on either semantic or syntactic context reflects a child's guess that the man who wrote the sentence was aiming it at a particular idea, using particular grammatical structure. Children identify an unknown word by again approximating what they feel the sentence meaning and grammar should finally be. In contextual behavior this approximation characteristic results from the almost infinite number of grammatical choices plus the almost infinite number of permutations of meaning possible in the experience of an idea. A single example should illustrate this.

A child is reading the sentence, "Tom gave his dog a _____." The blank represents a new and unrecognized word. Grammatically, any noun will produce a closure; that is, any noun will approximate a sentence sense. This fact eliminates the need for a child to predict any other part of speech for this identification. Semantically, he or she again have multiple choices. There are hundreds of things one can give a dog, from a kick to a crust of bread. Thus the sentence meaning and context do give hints of what the word identification might be, but these hints are only approximations and the child must be ready to juggle numerous word possibilities in the search for the correct identification. The sentence and its grammatical hints only approximate what the writer is saying. Is it any wonder that some children never seem to catch on to what is happening when they try to read?

In addition to the approximation reality of the mediating signals, you should also be aware of the need for balanced skill development in all three of the mediation strategies. Children who are taught to rely only on phonic mediators can develop into laboriously slow readers because reading for them is predominantly a visual-sounding activity. Likewise, the child who uses only minimal word identification and considerable contextual guessing can quickly lose sight of the need for getting the writer's message and instead go through the page quite unaware of what is actually happening. Instructional balance is imperative in the development of competent, mature readers.

In early stages of reading growth children usually need more attention on the graphemic code signals of the reading act, because this is really the basic difference between reading and any other communication medium. As skill with and understanding of this visual-aural process occur there should be a slow but steady shift toward the meaning, or contextual, element. Good third grade readers use the message sense more than the spelling code. As their eyes move across the page, they both receive and predict the message. This in turn allows them to spend less and less time examining single words or letters. It is only when the contextual prediction is unavailable (that is, the mental signal does not mesh with the visual one) that they resort to careful looking and sounding in order to establish a word identification that in turn starts a new set of contextual predictions. In order to reach this happy state readers must have learned the coding skills of phonics, structural and contextual prediction, and applied them to the messages found on the pages of a book.

## Phonetic Analysis as a Mediating Strategy

The letter-to-sound application of the English speaking system is the foundation skill for deciphering a strange word in print. It is a skill that should be learned and applied early in reading instruction, because one of the striking characteristics of good readers is their basic grasp of the letter-sound characteristics of the written lnguage. Although the way a word is spelled does not always reflect the way it is pronounced, the fact remains that our alphabet is a visual code based on a correspondence between speech sounds and printed letters, and an understanding and application of this phenomenon is necessary for even a modicum of success in learning to read. Although this understanding is sometimes generalized by the child without apparent overt instruction, most children must be taught this coding property of English writing.

AUDITORY PREREQUISITES. Whereas instant recognition is primarily a visually based skill, phonetic analysis relies heavily on auditory cues. Children who use phonetic mediators well know how to use both their eyes and their ears; they know how to listen, what to listen for, and how to associate the sounds they hear with the visual cues of the graphemic system. Learning to do this requires mastery of specific auditorily based readiness skills that are prerequisite to future success in analyzing words phonetically. These prerequisites include beginning and ending sound discrimination, letter-sound association, and sound blending as it is taught in both fusion and closure activites. With these skills children begin to generalize the concept of writing and reading as a phonemic-graphemic system rather than a visual-ideographic, or pictographic, process. With these skills under control they can examine written words that have never been seen before and, through his letter-sound competence, predict their identification. They know the spelling-grapheme code and how to use it to identify any written word.

AUDITORY DISCRIMINATION (BEGINNING, MEDIAL, AND ENDING SOUND). In many respects auditory discrimination is similar to visual discrimination. Both involve the manipulation of comparative and contrastive elements and both require instructional skill in determining what these elements are and how to show them to the child. The basic difference between discrimination of visual and auditory stimuli is that a visual array is created of spatial dimensions—height, length, depth—and can be referred to with two senses; it can be seen and felt. It remains constant for prolonged examination by these senses. Thus it can be more easily shown to the learner. In contrast, an auditory stimulus is temporal; that is, it exists momentarily and then disappears. Further, it can normally be perceived only by the ear. These time and single-sense qualities make it considerably more difficult to grasp and are the cause of much of the spelling code confusions that many children exhibit.

Despite its difficulty, however, auditory discrimination is an essential skill for phonetic analysis. Before children can associate a sound with a letter or otherwise use the phonemic-graphemic relationships of the system, they must be able to distinguish one sound from another. Consequently, auditory discrimination is the foundation of success in phonetic analysis.

SOUND BLENDING (FUSION AND CLOSURE). The purpose of teaching the auditory skills is to help readers use the graphemic system for analyzing written words. This is a two-stage process. First, they learn to make individual letters or groups of letters "speak"; second, they guess the total word. Sound-blending skills are designed to help readers in this second effort. As the name suggests, they help readers blend isolated letter sounds into familiar spoken words. Sounding out a word normally produces a string of sounds that barely approximate the word as it is really spoken. Readers must be able to compress these sounds into a closer approximation of the real word before they can recognize it. To help them do this, sound-blending skills called fusion and closure are taught.

Fusion skills give children practice in joining isolated strings of sound into spoken words. This is a prereading skill and in its simplest form, the teacher is modeling the process through which it is done. He or she might say, "Listen to what I can do. I can say r . . . u . . . n. Say it fast—**run.** Who else can do this?" A variation might be to pronounce the whole word first, produce its isolated letter sounds, and then say it fast. The point is that all sounds are first produced and then compressed into normal spoken cadence.

Closure skills have the same general purpose and format as fusion skills. They too give the reader practice in blending isolated sounds into recognizable spoken words. They differ in one respect only. In closure skills one or more sounds are left out of the string of isolated sounds. This creates a gap that must be filled, or clozed, in order to produce the spoken word. For example, a teacher might say, "Listen to me, I am going to say a word with some parts left out. See if you can hear what word I am saying and say it the way I really want to say it. Here is the word: **–eanutbutter.** What is the word I want to say?" Now the teacher waits to see if these *sounds* will be auditorialy clozed into the word **peanutbutter.** This skill recognizes that future sounding skills will not always produce an accurate pronunciation of a strange word. The child will make both sound distortions and omissions. Closure tasks are designed to prepare children for this and to give them both a confidence and a technique to ignore those gaps and arrive at an accurate spoken word from its sounded approximation.

LETTER-SOUND ASSOCIATION. The preceding auditory skills and the visual prerequisites described under instant recognition converge to create a series of skills of letter-sound association or sound-symbol connection. What the child has previously been taught to see and hear are now connected or associated with each other. "What you see is what you say," or, "What you say is what you visualize," might give an idea of the general direction of this learning.

The instructional key to teaching letter sounds is to realize the compound nature of the skill. It is simultaneously a discrimination skill (a letter must be seen and a sound heard), an association skill (what the ears hear or the mouth speaks must be paired with what the eyes are looking at), and a memory skill (the association or pairing between visual and auditory components must be remembered). This compounding of tasks demands an equal compounding of the attenders necessary for the learning. For instance, if you wish to teach children that **m** says the sound m-m-m, they must first know that **m** is not **w** or **n,** that it looks the same to them as it does to people who know how to read. Next, they must hear the sound of **m** as /m/, not **ng** or **n.** If these two conditions are met the teacher's next job is to be sure that his or her teaching tactics force children to look at the visual letter as they hear or say its sound value. They cannot be looking at the teacher's mouth or at their classmates. The eyes and ears must be tuned to the same letter for association to take place. Finally, the teacher's instructional tactic should also contain built-in memory strategies that cue a recall of the desired letter sound. And this is only half of the battle.

The letter-sound skills taught in this book are *not* taught in isolation. That is, each time these skills are taught, they are taught *as they occur in spoken or written words.* Although this adds another burden to the instructional problem, in the long run this forced application of what letter sounds are for and where they really live in real life will pay immeasurable dividends in the acquisition of more sophisticated word recognition and word analysis skills. A teacher who constantly teaches the sound properties of English spelling *in the context of the words in which they occur* will not produce children in third or fourth grade who know a myriad of generalizations about the spelling code but have no appreciation of or use for this information in reading words. Thus letter sounds must be taught in application, not isolation.

## The Sounding Skills

As children begin mastering the prerequisites, they should be taught the more sophisticated phonetic analysis skills. These include consonant sound skills, vowel sound skills, substitution skills, and syllabication skills.

CONSONANT SOUND SKILLS. The first letter-sound association skills in the phonics hierarchy teach children to associate regular consonant sounds with their appropriate letters. These include single consonants, consonant clusters in which each letter retains its single letter sound (**br, sl, str,** and so on), and consonant clusters in which new sounds are associated to familiar letters (**th, ch,** and so on). These skills are like miniature sight word skills in that they contain the same three task elements of discrimination, association, and memory. When children have accumulated a stock of consonant associations, they have a valuable first tool for sounding out new words. The predictable regularity of consonant sound values also helps to build a confidence in the code properties of English spelling.

The only real difficulty in this learning activity is the confusion many children have between a letter name and a letter sound. These are two distinct concepts and must be so understood if children are to make normal progress in letter sound acquisition and application. The sound value is the critical element. A letter name is interesting but it does not help the child assimilate and apply the graphemic code as a reading tool.

VOWEL SOUND SKILLS. Although consonants usually have a consistent sound, vowels do not. A vowel standing by itself can have a variety of sounds; an accurate sound value can only be predicted when it is seen in relation to the letters that suround it. Therefore vowel instruction focuses on vowel families or phonograms that have both a high frequency and a high predictability in English spelling.

The vowel skill objectives and their instructional techniques have been designed to focus the child on the operation of using *known sight words* having standard vowel characteristics and spelling patterns to predict *unknown words* having the same vowel characteristics but different surrounding consonants. The purpose of this instruction is twofold. First, it helps children learn to associate vowel sounds with the letter patterns that produce them; second, it fixes the knowledge that known words can be used to learn unknown ones. It highlights the fact that there is a system operating in the way a word is spelled. Children are led to see that the spelling of a word is not arbitrary but reflects the graphemic code properties of English writing.

SUBSTITUTION.  Substitution is the name given to the process of using *known words* to read *unknown words*. This might be called a transfer skill. As soon as children learn a sight word that contains a regular vowel phonogram, they learn to substitute other consonants, first at the beginning and then at the end, to create new words that can be recognized. For example, if a boy's name is Sam, the substitution skills should show him how to read **ham, bam, cram,** and even **ran.** The steps in this learning are (1) the recognition of –am as a vowel sound unit, and (2) the substitution of the consonants **h–, b–,** and **r–** and the cluster **cr–** in place of the **S** in **Sam,** and the substitution of –n for –m at the end to make the word **ran.** This activity teaches children to associate vowel sounds with the real spelling units that produce them. Initial substitutions are with first letters but as children become more skillful they can be expected to see and say a substitution of ending letters (**Sam** to **sat**) and even the vowel itself (**sat** to **sit**).

SYLLABICATION SKILLS.  Descriptively, a word that has three syllables is a word that also has three vowel phonograms. Identifying such a word through sounding out must begin with recognition of the three vowel phonograms that comprise its syllabic structure. Children who have a firm grasp of the vowel units described in the preceding section will have a relatively easy time grasping syllabication strategies and using them to sound out longer words.

To facilitate this behavior the skills program in this book includes a sequence of syllabication objectives. These objectives are designed to help children "see" vowel patterns already familiar to them from previous vowel instruction. Once seen, these patterns (syllables) are easily sounded. The only difficulty with sounding out longer words comes in helping children visually group the vowel units that comprise each syllable. The key is for a child to see syllabic divisions (vowel phonograms) that can then be sounded.

Traditionally, syllabication rules are taught as an aid in making syllabic divisions. Although rules can be given that reflect the varieties and vagaries of spelled syllables, few good readers can explain these rules that they apply so easily. Moreover, children taught such a list of rules seldom succeed in applying them as an analysis strategy. Such instruction seems more to clutter than to facilitate the attempt at sounding out words of more than one syllable.

Syllabication instruction should teach children two simple but reliable manipulations to be used when encountering a long word that they do not instantly recognize. The first of these helps to isolate probable syllabic units visually, first, by identifying vowels, and second, by arbitrarily assigning consonants to each. For example, examine the word **chocolate.** Step 1 would highlight each of the vowels visually, perhaps as follows: **chocolate.** Then, with simple dashes, the syllables are isolated: **cho–co–la–te.** Previous phonogram instruction has eliminated the final **e** configuration as a vowel unit, and the child is left with three phonograms (syllables if you prefer) to be sounded **cho-co-late.** These are then pronounced following the generalized patterns learned during vowel phonogram instruction, with this probable result: **chō-cō-lāte.** This division causes all vowels to be seen in their long environments. Next comes the second phase of syllabic instruction—turning the syllables thus sounded into a recognizable word. This second step is another reflection of the *approximation characteristic of English spelling.* Children are taught to "play with" the long vowel syllables in an attempt to discover the spoken word their identification approximates. Both their ears and syntactic-semantic contextual clues from the material being read should help them with this. Should they fail to identify the syllabicated word as **chocolate.** then they are taught simply to move their syllabic divisions one place to the right. This, in effect, makes the first two vowels short by putting them into a short vowel configuration. Now the word would look like **choc-ol-ate** and would be sounded **chŏc-ŏl-ăte.** Again children are told to pronounce the syllables and to see if they now approximate a known word. If the word identification remains a mystery (that is, if neither syllabic division gives the necessary clues to its real spoken character), then one of two things is wrong. Either the spelling does not give a reasonable approximation of the spoken word, in which case no sounding tactics will mediate an identification, or the word is not in a child's speaking or listening vocabulary. In the latter case the child should have been familiarized with the new words he or she was going to read prior to the lesson or should have been encouraged to *ask for help.* There is no way for children to analyze a word independently that is strange both in print and to the ear.

To summarize, the analysis and mediated recognition of longer words is approached through the application of previous vowel phonogram learnings. The child is taught to separate vowels visually from one another and then to sound the resulting divisions as vowel phonograms, using the resulting approximation as a basis for guessing the identity of the unknown word.

### Structural Analysis as a Mediating Strategy

The English language has both a tendency to compound and an inflected and derived grammatical system. These factors have produced a very repetitive and rather high frequency set of spelling structures that can be useful in mediating an unrecognized word.

Reading teachers usually refer to these skills as "structural attack" or "structural analysis" techniques. In many ways they combine elements of phonetic analysis with instant sight word recognition. They look like units that should be sounded but they are learned through instant identification.

The multitude of skill objectives taught as "structural mediators" are designed to show children how to recognize and manipulate only three basic systems: prefixes, suffixes, and compound words. As children gain familiarity with and can more quickly recognize these structural properties, unknown words containing them will be more accurately and speedily identified. For example, consider the word **unrecognized.** If children have learned to spot the common **un–** and **–ed** affixes, then identification of the word is reduced to the sounding of the internal root **recognize.** The number of problem-solving operations has been reduced by two and ultimate identification is normally achieved that much quicker. Structural analysis cuts down on the number and complexity of sounding operations. This, in turn, produces a faster mediation of an unrecognized word.

This happy event occurs because children have learned to isolate the structural units, their sounds and visual positions, for instant identification, leaving fewer unknowns to be syllabicated, sounded, and so on. These structural units can be isolated because their spelling and position are constant; that is, they transfer from word to word with a predictable regularity. This regularity allows children to learn them as they learn sight words.

To summarize, many words in English contain regularly spelled and positioned units called prefixes and suffixes. When sound and position of these units are memorized they can greatly diminish the unknowns in a word being analyzed.

Similarly, compounds can be more easily analyzed when they are recognized as compounds. Children who can instantly recognize **when** and **ever** but who go through some isolated sounding behavior when they meet the word **whenever** give a very strong signal of being unaware of the compounding process. By practicing an analysis of compound words this habit can be established. In many cases it produces faster and more efficient word identification.

## Contextual Analysis as a Mediating Strategy

The final mediating skill involves combining letter sounds with the syntax and semantics of spoken English. This mediation device might be labeled contextual and letter-sound analysis because it involves the anticipation of an unrecognized word through the simultaneous pressures created by the meaning of the sentence in which it occurs, the grammar of the sentence in which it occurs, and its recognized letter-sound properties.

Words in context offer an exceedingly powerful tool for mediating the identification of an unrecognized word. This results from the grammatical and semantic pressure to cloze, or complete, a structure or idea being experienced. As a sentence is read, the child allows the recognized words to direct his or her thinking into the same paths and modes as the author intended. The child who does such thinking as he or she reads allows the gestalt of syntax and meaning to cloze, thereby predicting the identification of any strange word. By combining this syntactical-semantic technique with an examination of the initial letter-sound properties of the unknown word, the child has an exceedingly powerful mediating strategy.

At the prerequisite or readiness level, a teacher's job is to get children in the habit of clozing, or finishing phrase and sentence structures by applying what they know about English grammar and the sense of the sentence meaning. The child who habitually uses this contextual meaning sense is the one who moves rapidly from the spelling (word-calling) components of reading into the more mature behaviors we often define as "thought gathering" or "reading for meaning."

Although the initial emphasis is on oral closure using syntactical and semantic clues almost exclusively, children should be directed to use their context skills in combination with known phonetic elements as they develop a sight word vocabulary. In this manner they gradually develop skill in using elements of the graphemic, syntactic, and semantic systems to mediate the identification of unknown words.

## SUMMARY OF WORD RECOGNITION

In a very real sense a good part of learning to read involves learning to decipher the graphemic code of English spelling. Mastery of this code gives the reader the skills of word recognition, both instant and mediated. These skills in turn produce a sight vocabulary that becomes the basis for making both syntactic and semantic predictions.

The skills of the graphemic system include visual and auditory tasks, association tasks, and problem-solving tasks. An understanding of each of these skill pieces and their place in the graphemic code is absolutely necessary if teachers are to help children master the word identification element of reading.

This view of word recognition creates some new elements for our process chart.

As can be seen, most of the skills in the area of word recognition reflect the graphemic code. Within the graphemic system, however, we find two streams of skills; one leads to instant recognition and the other leads to analyzing, or mediating, those words that are not immediately known. Within each stream are specific kinds of skills that contribute to the ultimate goals of either instant or mediated word recognition. An arrow goes from the mediated stream to the instant stream to reflect the fact that after an unknown word has been mediated several times, it ought to become a sight word. An additional arrow with points at either end goes between the word recognition and comprehension areas to reflect the interconnectedness and interrelatedness of the graphemic, syntactic, and semantic codes.

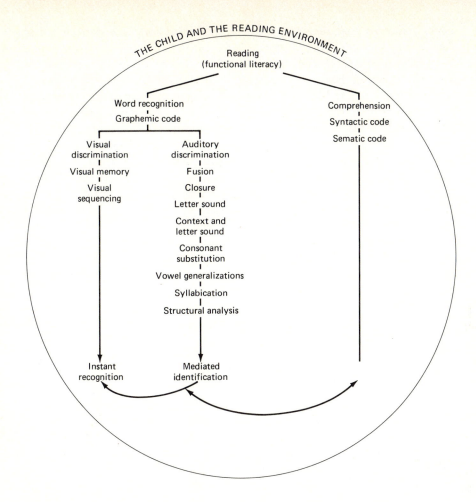

Reading
(functional literacy)

Word recognition
Graphemic code

Comprehension
Syntactic code
Sematic code

Visual
discrimination
Visual memory
Visual
sequencing

Auditory
discrimination
Fusion
Closure
Letter sound
Context and
letter sound
Consonant
substitution
Vowel generalizations
Syllabication
Structural analysis

Instant
recognition

Mediated
identification

Finally, the whole process continues to be encircled by the child and his or her environment, because whether a particular child will need more emphasis on instant or mediated strategies or on any particular skill within either of those streams depends upon the background brought to the task.

## READING SKILLS IN THE COMPREHENSION AREA

Learning to read is more than recognizing words and assimilating the coding system with which they are written. In its largest sense reading is a thought-gathering process; learning to recognize and remember the written word is only the first, albeit critical, step. Once the words are identified there remains the large and often difficult task of understanding what they say.

Comprehension appears to involve two stages. The first stage occurs during the actual reading activity. The reader examines the message and simultaneously recognizes words and meaning through skill with the graphemic, syntactic, and semantic systems. Understanding is *instantaneous* at this stage.

The second stage can occur any time during or following the first stage. This comprehension might best be described as a *reflective* activity. The written message has been translated or received and now can be subjected to a more thoughtful analysis. Surface understandings that were created at the instantaneous level can be examined with regard to their original accuracy or subjected to more complex mental operations.

Theoretically there must be an infinite number of mental operations that a reader makes in order to comprehend instantaneously and reflectively. It would seem to follow, then, that a reader needs to be taught an infinite number of comprehension skills in order to achieve this comprehension, but fortunately this is not the case. Through factor analysis long lists of what have traditionally been thought of as discreet comprehension skills have been found to be a limited number of skills used for varying purposes; a very small number of *operational skills* are used to understand an infinite variety of written messages. Although each message a child reads, be it an arithmetic story problem or a social studies lesson in American history, may be unique in its content, comprehension is realized through the application of these very few operational skills. The teacher's job becomes twofold: (1) to show children how to do these basic operations and (2) to ensure that they are transferred to the daily reading activities.

The operational skills can be classified into three subgroups. Each group defines a comprehension purpose or process. These are

1. Comprehension as an informational process.
2. Comprehension as a thinking or manipulative process.
3. Comprehension as an evaluative or judgmental process.

Comprehension as an informational process suggests that the readers are trying to learn something from reading. They are trying to learn the *factual content* of the message and want to know what the message says literally. To accomplish this they must have meaning for all the words read and a recognition of and memory for the facts they convey.

Comprehension as a thinking or manipulative process suggests that once the informational process is secure, readers can be expected to think about this information; they can explore its deeper implications and inferences. To do this they must be able to grasp the significance of various relationships based on their own past experiences and understanding of the more complex structures of English grammar.

Comprehension as an evaluative process suggests that after a message has been understood at both its information and manipulative levels, it can be acted upon. This action might consist of such varied activities as acceptance of the message and its commitment to memory, rejection of the message, or a searching out of more information to clarify a position or understanding.

Each of the three subgroups contains operational skills that are used to understand written messages. They include

1. Informational processes
   Word meaning skills
   Signalers of relationships
   Skills of contextual prediction
   Recognition and memory for factual content
2. Manipulative processes
   Classification and main idea thinking
   Inferential thinking
3. Evaluative processes
   Judging the validity of content
   Judging the author's purpose or point of view

The preceding skills of comprehension are hierarchical; that is, evaluative operations cannot exist without the manipulative thinking activities and manipulative thinking cannot exist unless there is something to think with and about (information). This means that a teacher *must* originate all comprehension activities at the information or literal level. When the teacher is certain that the basic information is understood, he or she can teach for manipulative thinking. With these two processes as a base the possibility of evaluative-judgmental levels of understanding exists and can be examined. An illustration might help make this developmental sequence clear. A fifth grade social studies class is reading a selection about the Boston Tea Party. The teacher is interested in using the selection to teach all three levels of comprehension. The teacher's first goal is to assure that each child has a basic understanding of the facts and details concerning the Boston Tea Party. He or she tests this by asking factual questions regarding word meanings, relationships, and factual content after the reading is completed. Satisfied that the basic information is understood by the class, the teacher proceeds to help them discover a relationship that is implicit but buried in the information. Finally, when he or she is satisfied that each child has made the desired inferences from the material, the teacher asks them to make judgments about alternative actions the colonists could have taken and how this historical event applies to today's society. Hence the cycle of comprehension goes from information to manipulation to evaluation.

## READING COMPREHENSION AS AN INFORMATION PROCESS

The mastery of four operational skills allows a child to obtain the basic information from the printed page. These include word meaning skills, understanding relationships, contextual prediction, and factual recall.

## Word Meaning Skills

Comprehension instruction begins at the word meaning level. A written message is made up of strings of words, all of which contain meanings. If these meanings are not within the experience of the reader, both minimal understanding and the higher levels of comprehension are thwarted.

In a larger sense word meaning is a problem of concept development. Words are the labels we give to concepts. The word **snow**, for example, names the concept of the cold, wet, white stuff we spin our wheels in during the winter. This concept is different from the cold, wet stuff we label "rain." Each is a separate concept with a separate label. Concepts and the words we use to label them are the core elements in comprehension. We comprehend as a response to the meanings that words carry. The meaning a word carries is that which our language assigns it. Thus if a learner does not have the *assigned* meaning for words, both written and oral communication become impossible and comprehension remains confined to the very limited and personal language of each learner. An understanding of this duality (the concept and the name or label for it) is critically important in expanding the word meaning capabilities of children.

The message in an English sentence comes from two kinds of words. Some can be thought of as carrying the *meaning* of the sentence. These words are usually called *content* words. Other words act as glue to connect the content words together into English grammatical structure and are called *function* words. For example, in the sentence, "We see the goblins on Halloween," the content words are **we, goblins,** and **Halloween.** If readers do not know what these words mean (that is, the concepts they stand for) they will not grasp the content of the sentence. The words **see, the,** and **on,** however, are function words; they signal the grammatical relationships that put **we, goblins,** and **Halloween** into a meaningful context. The functional relationships expressed by these three little words are as important to an understanding of the message as the content itself.

The teacher must ensure that learners have accurate concepts for both the words that carry the content of a message and the grammatical subtleties expressed by function words. This can be illustrated by the following true story. A teacher had a boy in her second grade class who went for weeks without making any answers on his seat work. Daily she would duplicate problem sheets so that the children could practice their addition and subtraction, but Art's paper never had any answers on it. When she finally questioned him about this, she found that he knew how to add and subtract but was confused by her directions: "Do your own paper and mark the answer under each problem." Art finally found enough courage to ask, "What is an answer?" His was a content word problem. **He** did not have a concept for the word **answer.** However, if Art had failed to do his work because he did not understand where to write his answer (had no meaning for the word **under**), he would have had a problem with function word meaning. He would have lacked the concept for the word **under.**

There are literally thousands of content words for which a learner needs meaning. Each subject area taught has its own content vocabulary of concepts related to that subject. The teacher is responsible for helping learners find both the concept and the label for it, because the content words carry an essential portion of the information in a message.

Function words, which are as important to comprehension as content words, cannot be discussed in isolation from the relationships they signal. Therefore they are placed under the following heading.

## Understanding Relationships

Children's function word vocabulary is of crucial concern. They must grasp the concepts signaled by such seemingly insignificant words as **on, or, if, because, while,** and **any,** because these words signal the syntactical relationships among the content words. For instance, to obtain the basic information from a passage, children must know the meaning of prepositions that signal both positional and time relationships; of pronouns that signal a relationship to an antecedent; and words that signal chronology, cause-effect, and compare-contrast relationships.

The meaning in an English sentence results from a partnership between content words and function words. In any sentence the learner not only must know the concepts associated with the content words but also must know the relationships between those content words as they are signaled by function words. Though the function words tend to be short, they are as important as and more subtle than the content words.

## Contextual Prediction

Contextual prediction involves fluency with English grammar and the predictive impulse it generates. As children listen to a communication, a portion of their understanding comes from their "sentence sense" that allows them simultaneously to know the idea of the message (its content) and to predict from both this knowledge and their grasp of grammatical relationships what word will follow what word and what idea will follow what idea. When children's grasp of the content and fluency of the grammar are equal to the message being read, they are not simply passive receivers of the message, but are actively moving ahead, anticipating what and how it will be said. As the eyes of fluent readers slide across the page identifying words, their minds race along with those ideas, unconsciously predicting where the ideas are going (the semantics of the message) and how they will get there (the syntax of the message). Influences on children's acquisition of this critical language skill are many. Social, cultural, and economic factors all play a part. Dialect differences can stifle its development. Even an overemphasis on word recognition in early reading instruction *without parallel commitment to an understanding of the message* can cause the skill to wither or be stunted. Therefore teachers face the responsibility of influencing as best they can the full range of a child's language. This is difficult. Peer pressures and habits that have been developed over years of preschool language activity are not easily modified. Traditional English classes involving such rote activities as learning the parts of speech, classes of words, types of sentences, and so on, are pathetically inadequate to the task. The let-the-child-talk program is usually too little and too late. On the other hand, the skill development emphasized in this book contains frequent *contextual* practice, which is oral at the beginning level and shifts to reading as quickly as a sight vocabulary is accumulated.

Two benefits accrue with this emphasis. First, children are helped to develop their language patterns to fit those they will need in order to read or listen with understanding to "standard English usage." Second, children become accustomed to the idea of thinking with the message and predicting what it will say and how it will say it. This instructional device should not be underestimated. It has the potential for alleviating many of the difficulties in comprehension found in later reading instruction.

### Recognizing and Recalling Factual Content

The ability to understand and retain the factual content of a message is built upon the skills of word meaning, comprehension of relationships, and contextual prediction. As children develop an expanded vocabulary of both content and function words and the ability to predict closure from the grammatical form and ideational content of a message, these skills are used to arrange and retain the factual information found in longer stories. This ability to see and remember the facts is of obvious importance in the informational part of comprehension.

The major emphasis in this skill is twofold. First, learners must be able to identify the important or relevant facts from among the mass of word meanings and relationships contained in the message. Second, they must be able to remember the facts. Hence the twin thrusts of this area are identification and memory.

### SUMMARY

Children can be expected to know what is in a message if they have the concepts for the function and content words, the set to think along with them in a contextual sense, and practice in "sifting and seeing" what facts they contain. Although only minimal thinking is involved, the basic information needed to perform higher-level manipulative operations is obtained. One cannot think without something to think about. Word meanings and sentence sense, and awareness of the informational value these two elements give to a communication, constitute the essence of thought and represent the basic informational content of a message.

### READING COMPREHENSION AS A MANIPULATIVE PROCESS

Once children have a firm control over the vocabulary, grammatical, and factual content of a selection, they can think about the information it contains. The problems involved in teaching children to think as they read are formidable, both for children and for the teacher. There are at least two major reasons for this. First, children respond to the words they read or hear from a very egocentric position. What they think about as they read or listen is the total of their own unique involvement with the ideas that come to them. They may or may not have had experiences to parallel those the author is reconstructing. What is real and relevant to the author may be irrelevant or meaningless to the child. The possibilities for error stagger the imagination.

The second difficulty, as confounding as the first, relates to a child's ability to process an input of thoughts and ideas. We know that thinking takes place in readers who understand what they read, but what takes place and how are open to conjecture. There are no certified road maps guaranteeing readers who can and will think. However, even though knowledge of the thinking process is theoretical and full of unknowns, experience suggests operational skills that produce thinking, even when we are not certain why.

These operational skills are manipulative in the sense that a message or communication contains multiple concepts that can be structured and restructured, categorized and recategorized—manipulated, in short. As children manipulate the ideas or concepts of a message, their comprehension of that message is made broader and deeper. They move from a literal to an inferential understanding. Memory is augmented by thought.

Two types of skills are manipulative. These are (1) classification–main idea thinking and (2) inferential reasoning.

### Classification–Main Idea Thinking

The skill of classification and main idea thinking allows children to classify ideas by discovering their relationships and then group them into sets on the basis of their shared properties. First, children are taught to discover how concepts can be related to other concepts, words to other words. These relationships can be causal, chronological, or logical, based on use, size, shape, position, and similar or dissimilar features (synonyms and antonyms), and they can exist between single words or in longer structures, such as phrases, sentences, paragraphs, and chapters.

This type of manipulation is the first step in finding the focus or point to a mass of information. At its highest level in reading comprehension, children are able to extract, through classification thinking, the main ideas of a sentence, paragraph, or larger selection. Having been taught to group and classify ideas automatically, they will be able to read hundreds of words and not lose sight of their point of focus. They will be able to see both the forest and the trees and know which is which.

### Inferential Reasoning

In addition to classification thinking, children are taught to think beyond the information level of a written communication by "reading between the lines." Factual information must be manipulated in order to discover both implications and inferences. This skill is based on logic and prediction. Children with this skill can use the facts of a selection and their experience background to generate more sophisticated levels of understanding; they can grasp what the facts imply and can then infer conclusions based on these implications.

Inferential reasoning is an important comprehension skill, because not all information worth obtaining is necessarily stated literally; much valuable information is found "between the lines." Obtaining it requires sophistication, however, because learners must simultaneously examine the factual information in a passage and compare it with their experiences related to the topic. Such thought is truly manipulative.

## SUMMARY

The manipulative level of comprehension contains two separate but related skills. First is the skill of seeing relationships or connections between facts that otherwise might be viewed as discreet and classifying these relationships into sets sharing common properties. Second is the skill of projected or logical implication or inference. With these types of mental operations, children can take the words and facts of a selection and think their way to understandings that are far beyond the literal meaning of the message.

## READING COMPREHENSION AS AN EVALUATIVE PROCESS

The third stream of comprehension skills involves drawing conclusions and making evaluative judgments. In the first stream comprehension was limited to information gathering. From this basic or literal understanding comprehension moves to the second or manipulative stream in which children are asked to think with and about the elements found in the first level. Now they are ready to act on this thought. This third action stage focuses on helping children make judgments about what they read.

Notice that this comprehension activity can only be valid if it follows both information and manipulative thinking. It is absurd to ask children to do such an activity without the prerequisites of comprehension found in the preceding factual and manipulative levels. The teacher's task is to help children develop the ability to move with logic from informational to manipulative to judgmental activities. In this way they learn to make judgments based on facts and thinking. Emotional or stereotyped conclusions are minimized, or at least identified for what they are when they do occur. By following this progression at each level, comprehension achieves a precision missing in any slapdash instructional approach.

Two types of operational skills can be taught to help children make evaluative judgments as they read. The first focuses on judging the content itself; the second examines the author's choice of language.

## Judging Content of Material

Occasionally one may read material that does not make sense in terms of one's personal experience, knowledge, or beliefs. In such cases one judges the material to be invalid. Children, however, do not always possess this ability. Indeed they sometimes exhibit a tendency to believe everything they read. This skill, then, is designed to teach children that they should use their experience, knowledge, and values to judge materials; that something is not necessarily true just because it appears in a book.

## Author's Choice of Language

The skill involving the author's choice of language teaches a learner to assess word choice for clues about an author's position on a topic. Careful examination of word choice is an important evaluative skill, because it is a major way in which learners make judgments about what they read.

Good readers can detect bias through the author's use of emotion-laden words, words that create bias or stereotype, mood words, propaganda devices, and other elements of word choice. Once the words cue the reader to author bias, he or she is able to judge the topic and is comprehending critically.

## SUMMARY

Comprehension in the informational and manipulative areas is passive in the sense that readers interpret what the author meant. At the evaluative level, however, readers assert themselves and strike out on their own, making a judgment that may or may not be what the author intended. In this sense evaluative comprehension may be the most important kind of thinking to be taught in a democratic society.

## SUMMARY OF COMPREHENSION

Although learning to read does demand emphasis on identifying words, it is essentially a communication process in which obtaining meaning is of primary importance. In this book the meaning-getting process is divided into three streams: informational, manipulative, and evaluative. Graphically, comprehension fits into our process chart as shown.

As can be seen, the skills of comprehension reflect the syntactic and semantic codes described at the beginning of this chapter. Within the syntactic-semantic area, however, we find three "streams" of skills; one helps obtain the basic information of a passage, one facilitates manipulation and thinking about that information, and one leads to making evaluations about what is read. Within each stream are specific kinds of operational skills that contribute to the ultimate goals of that stream. Arrows go from the informational to the manipulative streams and from the manipulative to the evaluative streams to indicate that manipulative thinking cannot be done without information and that evaluative thinking cannot

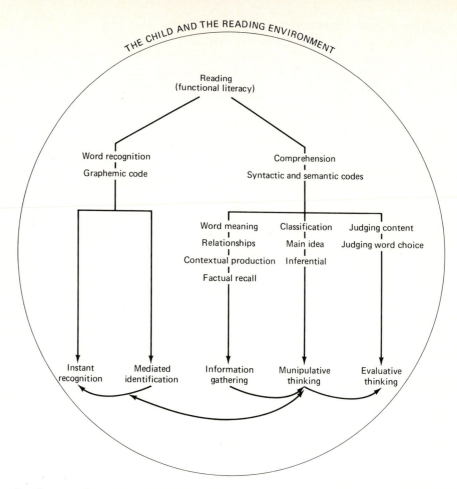

be done without previous manipulation of the facts. Similarly, an arrow with points at either end is found between word recognition and comprehension to indicate the continuing interrelatedness of the graphemic and syntactic-semantic codes. Finally, the whole process description is circled to represent the fact that a particular child from a particular environment will react differently from children who are from other environments and that therefore it may be necessary to emphasize different elements of the process with different children.

## ● CHAPTER SUMMARY

This chapter, we hope, has helped you to understand not only *what* reading skills to teach, but also *why* each of the major skills is included in the hierarchy and *how* each skill contributes to the child's total reading competence. In the process certain fundamental concepts about reading have become evident. They include the following:

1. The reading process is a complex interrelationship among the graphemic, syntactic, and semantic codes.
2. To be functionally literate in terms of reading, one must possess the basic skills of word recognition and comprehension.
3. Word recognition tends to reflect primarily the graphemic code and comprehension tends to reflect primarily the syntactic and semantic codes.
4. The skills of both word recognition and comprehension are divided into vertical "streams" according to the major goals of instruction, with word recognition having the dual goals of instant and mediated word identification and comprehension having the three goals of information gathering, manipulative thinking, and evaluative reasoning.
5. Each stream contains a limited number of operational skills that are taught in a variety of settings to achieve the ultimate goal of that stream.
6. The skills within a stream are organized in simple-to-complex hierarchies in which one skill tends to be prerequisite to the following one.
7. There are interrelationships between and among the various streams of skills as well as hierarchical relationships within a particular stream.
8. Any view of the reading process must be made from the individual child's standpoint, since instruction must reflect not only the elements of the process but also the child's particular strengths and weaknesses in terms of that process.

The final step in completing understanding of the reading process requires that you assimilate the preceding knowledge into an organizational schema which views skill hierarchies as "spiraling in levels." This means that the five vertical streams of skills (as they are presented in this book) are arbitrarily divided horizontally to create levels ranging from simple to complex. The child is then led through the hierarchy from stream to stream within a particular level and then moves on to the next level. This can be illustrated in our chart of the reading process.

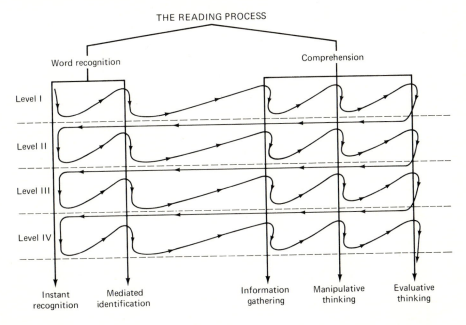

THE READING PROCESS

Theoretically, the progress of a child through the process would start with the instant recognition skills of the first level and continue to the mediated, the information-gathering, the manipulative, and the evaluative skills of the first level, it would continue on to the instant recognition and mediated skills of the second level, and so on through the hierarchy. In this way there is an orderly progression to the learning of the skills comprising the skill hierarchy.

This, then, is the reading process. Understanding its structure and its elements is the first step in preparing for effective instruction.

# AN INSTRUC-
# TIONAL MODEL
# FOR TEACHING
# SKILLS

. . . and then there is the story of the reading teacher who, after several visits to the psychiatrist, was told, "Your feelings of insecurity seem to have started when little Mary Smith said to you, 'Maybe I don't have a learning disability—maybe you have a teaching disability.' "

The basic structure of effective skill instruction, as described in Chapter 1, follows a test-teach-test-apply sequence. Testing is the easiest step to implement because specific tests and directions for their administration are provided in this book and because they can be rapidly and efficiently administered. Basically, the process involves giving learners the pretest and saying to them, "Can you do this?" If they can, the teacher goes to the next skill. If they cannot, the teacher teaches the skill and helps them apply it.

At the teaching and applying steps, however, the task becomes more difficult. Too many teachers simply continue testing and call it teaching. That is, they continue to ask children to do a task again, they give them a commercial workbook that asks them to do it again, or they play a game with them requiring that the task be done again without ever providing any assistance in how to do it. There is, however, a great deal of difference between testing, teaching, and applying. Anybody can test, pass out workbooks or kits and hope that the material will do the teaching, listen to children read orally from a basal reader, and get the advantaged children to read. It takes special skill, however, to create a skill competence in a child who formerly was totally unable to perform the task. Although testing and diagnosis are crucial, teaching and applying ultimately determine whether skills are mastered. Consequently, this chapter emphasizes techniques for teaching reading skills; the following chapter stresses strategies for helping children apply learned skills.

## THE DIFFERENCE BETWEEN TEACHING AND TESTING

To develop reading skills in children you must both test and teach effectively. However, because testing and teaching are two distinctly different types of teacher behavior, it is crucial that your work in the classroom reflect this difference.

### Testing

Testing is the diagnostic step, the point at which the teacher determines whether the learner can perform the desired skill. Normally testing occurs in two places: prior to teaching (pretest), to determine if the learner already knows the skill and therefore needs no instruction, and following teaching (posttest), to determine whether those who failed the pretest have now achieved mastery as a result of instruction.

Testing requires first specifying the skill to be assessed. This book provides this specification by stating each skill as a performance objective at the head of each skill module. Second, testing requires structuring a situation in which learners are forced to respond, that is, to perform the skill in its totality. It is not broken down or simplified. For example, if you are testing for sight words, the whole word is flashed to the learner, who is required to respond to the rapid exposure; if sound-symbol connection is being tested, you present the child with a sound and require him or her to identify the symbol; if you are testing for ability to analyze words by substituting initial consonants in phonograms, the learner is presented with a list of unknown words having the same phonogram element but different initial consonants and is required to pronounce them; and if you are testing for ability to identify the meaning of unknown words through the use of context, you give the learner a sentence using an unknown word and require him or her to state its meaning. In any case, testing requires little teacher effort beyond ensuring that the test does indeed assess the specified skill. In this book, of course, both the pretests and the posttests are provided.

### Teaching

Teaching is the instructional step, the point at which you provide the learners with the input that allows them to perform the task they were unable to perform on the pretest. Because a learner is unable to respond correctly during the test, it stands to reason that teaching requires more than simply asking him or her to respond again. The teacher must *directly assist* the learner in mastering the skill. The provision for directed assistance sets teaching apart from testing.

There are six specific ways to assist the learner directly, all of which should be present in one form or another in every instructional episode. These steps include creating a responsive set, directing attention, highlighting, diminishing the assistance, ensuring responses, and reinforcing.

### Creating a Responsive Set

Learning, by definition, requires a change in behavior. The act of teaching, then, is the act of changing behavior in specified ways. One of the greatest impediments to such change, however, is the expectation by society generally and by teachers particularly that everyone should succeed at everything the first time and that failure is bad. This expectation produces children who resist learning because of a fear of failing.

A more realistic view of learning accepts the fact that some frustration is associated with all learning and that it is alright to fail sometimes. When children understand this they become less resistant to learning because they know that they will not be viewed as abnormal or stupid if they do not master the task the first time; they know they can fail without jeopardizing their self-concept. The first directed assistance offered by the teacher should therefore be the sensitive acknowledgment of the difficulty of the task, thereby allowing learners to respond confidently without endangering their image of themselves.

As an example let us look at pie baking. Suppose I bake a pie and invite you to eat it with me. You taste the first bite and exclaim over the deliciousness of the pie and my skill at piebaking. "I wish I could bake a pie like this," you say. This is the point where the responsive-set principle comes into play.

If I am a poor teacher I will say to you, "Fine. Pie making isn't hard, so let's learn to make a pie." In my efforts to give you the necessary confidence to try I may even say, "Anyone can bake pies." With these two encouragements I have probably spoiled your opportunity to learn to be a successful pie baker by removing the challenge to learn pie baking. Let us see what happens.

You take the recipe and my directions and you proceed to bake a pie. When it is finished you take the first taste and the pie is delicious. You are a successful learner of piemaking. But wait. Is this anything to be proud of? Didn't I explain that pie baking was easy and anyone could do it? Do you feel like a successful pie baker when you know that the task is easy and that anyone can perform the skill? The answer is obvious.

Let us consider what happens if your first pie baking effort is a failure. You take the first bite and it tastes terrible. What can you say about yourself? The task, according to me, was easy, but you could not do it. What does this make you? "Anyone can bake a pie," I said. Does this make you less than anyone? Do you suppose you will try baking pies again? Probably not, because by failing to acknowledge the difficulty of the learning, I canceled your success as a learner. If you did the task successfully, it really was not worth doing in the first place because it was so easy, and if you failed the first time, it was because of a defect in you, since anyone else could do it. You lose either way.

In contrast, what does a more sensitive teacher do? When you indicate interest in baking a pie, the good teacher recognizes that pie baking is not easy. The teacher says, "I will give you the recipe and careful directions, but pie baking is not easy. You can do everything right and still not bake a good pie. Not everyone can bake a good pie the first time." The task is now made realistic; the difficulty of the task has been acknowledged.

What happens when you bake a pie and it is delicious? You feel that you have achieved considerable success as a pie baker. You will probably bake other pies and go on to other successful learning. The task was difficult, but you did it. Your self-concept as a learner receives great reinforcement.

But suppose the pie is poor, what happens then? Well, you had been forewarned that the task was not easy. You had been told that not everyone can bake a good pie the first time. Is this damaging to your self-concept? No. It was not you that was defective; the task itself was difficult. You can try again, knowing that failure is no stigma when the task is hard.

The recognition of the difficulty of learning and the sensitive acknowledgment of this difficulty are important aspects of any instruction. It is a wise teacher who recognizes that learning is seldom a one-time affair, that failure will probably occur as often as success, and that recognition of the difficulty of the task is essential if the learner is not to feel failure as a learner.

This principle is particularly relevant to teaching reading skills, where children are too often told that learning to discriminate between a **d** and a **b** or learning the sound associated with the **ch** digraph are easy tasks. Although they may be easy for the teacher, the children know they are not easy for them. After all, they may have just failed the pretests for those skills, demonstrating rather dramatically that it was difficult for them. They think the teacher is saying, "It *ought* to be easy for you. If it's not easy, you must be stupid." Naturally learners do not want to run the risk of being considered stupid, so they protect themselves by not responding at all.

You can counter this behavior and directly assist the children in their learning by stating that the task is difficult and that many perfectly normal people cannot do it the first time. By creating empathy in this way, you are making it possible for children to respond in the learning situation without endangering their self-concepts. With such empathy as the foundation, the lesson is off to a good start.

## Directing Attention

When we talk about attention in the instructional situation we do not necessarily mean sitting up straight in the seat with arms folded. Rather, we mean that learners must attend to the salient features of the task at hand. For instance, if they are learning to read their names, they must listen to the sound of the name and simultaneously look at its spelling. If they are not attending with these two senses simultaneously, pairing the name with its written form will only occur by accident. If a child is listening but looking at a fly on the window, he or she could conceivably pair his or her name with the fly. This is an exaggerated illustration but should serve as a warning that if you do not control the input to the learner's senses, both visual and aural, no learning of the desired pair can result.

As teachers we are always saying, "Now pay attention." Unfortunately this is all too often our total instructional repertoire for creating attending behavior. This is not enough, for it does not tell children what specifically they must attend to in order to master the task. Attention needs specific cues, both verbal and physical, that eliminate the uncertainty about what must be done to learn the task.

There are two ways to direct learners' attention. The first, and the simpler of the two, is to state what they are to learn. If they are to learn how to read their names, the teacher says, "Today you are going to learn how to read your name." If they are to learn to read the word **dinosaur** at sight, the teacher says, "Today you are going to learn how to recognize the word **dinosaur** instantly when I flash it to you." If they are to learn the sound-symbol connection for the **ch** digraph, the teacher says, "Today you are going to learn the sound that the **ch** makes at the beginning of words."

Although this technique may at first seem to be simplistic, it is actually a powerful way to direct attention. When children know what they are supposed to learn, the purpose of the learning becomes clear and they apply themselves more directly to the task. If they are unsure of what they are supposed to be learning, however, they are put in the position of trying to read the teacher's mind, which can easily cause confusion and frustration. Consequently, the teacher can directly assist children in their learning by clearly stating the purpose of the lesson at the outset.

The second and more complex technique for directing attention involves analyzing the skill performance to determine precisely what components of the task the learner must pay attention to in order to master the skill. As such, if children are learning to read their names, the teacher tells them to look at the printed form of the name as they simultaneously listen to its sound. If the children are learning to recognize at sight the easily confused words **was** and **saw,** they are directed to the left-to-right sequence of the letters in each word. If they are learning to identify the meaning of an unknown word through the use of context, they are directed to the words in the sentence that provide clues to the meaning of the unknown word.

Failure to direct attention to the task's salient features will result in the children not paying attention or paying attention to the wrong thing. They are again in the position of trying to guess what they are supposed to do to learn the task. Failure on the pretest indicates that a child is unable to guess successfully. If the teacher does not direct attention to the crucial features, confusion and frustration result. Consequently, you should directly assist the child in learning by specifying the salient features of the task.

You should use two techniques in directing attention. You should specify the task to be learned and should be precise in directing the learner to the crucial aspects of the task. Both techniques, when used well, will directly assist the child in learning the skill.

### Highlighting

Once the teacher has analyzed the skill and determined the salient features that are crucial for learning, one must dramatize or highlight these features so that the attending task is simplified. This can take the form of auditory emphasis, color coding, underlining, circling, use of flannelboard, or use of any other device that helps the learner to focus on the crucial features of the task.

In highlighting, the teacher is actually providing the learner with a crutch to help in the first few difficult steps in learning the skill. For instance, in teaching learners to analyze words by substituting initial consonants in phonograms, the teacher might highlight by presenting the words as follows:

$$\text{ⓒ a t}$$
$$\text{ⓑ a t}$$
$$\text{ⓡ a t}$$
$$\text{ⓕ a t}$$
$$\text{ⓢ a t}$$

In teaching learners to use left-to-right sequence in distinguishing the letters **d** and **b,** one might highlight by presenting the letters as follows:

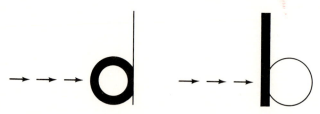

The type of highlighting used is not crucial as long as it succeeds in getting the learner to focus on the crucial elements of the task. Consequently, there is no particular advantage in using color coding rather than underlining or vice versa. What is crucial, however, is that some form of highlighting be provided in the early part of the lesson and that this highlighting focus on the correct component of the task. When this is the case the learner is directly assisted in learning and the teacher is providing good instruction.

## Diminishing the Assistance

Although learners are provided with highlighting devices early in the lesson to help in focusing attention and in ensuring successful responses, the ultimate goal is to have them respond without the assistance of crutches. Consequently, with each passing successful response, the highlighting is gradually diminished so that they have fewer and fewer crutches. Ultimately they respond without any highlighting assistance; at this point they have succeeded in performing the task as it was specified in the objective.

For instance, if auditory emphasis was used as a highlighter, the degree of auditory emphasis would be reduced gradually with each successful response until the word or sound was said normally, with no emphasis. If circling and underlining were used, the highlighting could be diminished in the following manner:

ⓒ a t
ⓑ a t
⒭ a t
⒡ a t
s a t

Just as it is crucial that highlighting be provided at the initial stages of instruction, so it is crucial that this highlighting be gradually diminished. If a crutch is provided and never taken away, learners are unable to perform the task in a real reading situation because they are helpless without the crutch. If it is removed too quickly they lose sight of what they are to attend to and become confused. The trick is to gauge, with each individual learner, the amount of highlighting needed and when to remove it. There is no formula for determining this in advance; the decision must be made by the teacher on the basis of the quality of the learner's response each time the use of a crutch is lessened.

## Response

As implied in the discussions of highlighting and diminished assistance, good instruction calls for frequent responses on the part of the learner. Learning does not take place without an expenditure of energy, and for the learner that energy is expended in making responses.

Good teachers call for frequent responses during a lesson, and since repetition is a necessary part of all learning, they find many ways to elicit responses without making them boring. Responses are called for in the initial stage when a maximum amount of highlighting is provided, and they are called for again each time the highlighting is diminished. In fact, the only way one knows whether to continue diminishing the amount of highlighting is by noting the quality of the learner's response. If learners respond correctly with a given amount of highlighting, the crutch can be diminished; if they do not, the crutch must be maintained and perhaps even strengthened.

There are basically two strategies for eliciting responses from learners. One is a modeling technique and the other is a discovery technique. In the first technique the teacher models, or demonstrates the performance of the task for the learner and has the children mimic the demonstration. This technique requires that a teacher "talk through" the steps in performing the task, directing learners to do as the teacher did. Through such imitation children learn to perform the skill.

The second model, in contrast, requires the teacher to set conditions so that learners can generalize. Rather than demonstrating and having the learner mimic, the teacher sets up a situation in which the principle to be learned is highlighted and through a series of questions leads the learners to discover the principle for themselves.

The two techniques can be contrasted by examining how each would be used to teach a skill, such as substituting initial consonants in known short-vowel phonograms. In both cases the teacher would create a responsive set, direct attention, use highlighting, and diminish assistance. The dialogue between teacher and student would differ, however. If the modeling strategy is used the dialogue might go somewhat as follows:

*Teacher:* Today we are going to learn to change the first letter in related words and pronounce the new words. This is not always easy, so I have listed some of the words on the board, circling the first letter of each word and underlying the parts of each word that are related. Watch me while I show you how to do this. I already know the first word is **cat**. Now I look at the second word. It has –**at** in it just like the first word. It must sound like the –**at** in **cat**. But the second word is not **cat** because it starts with the letter **b**. I'll get my mouth ready to make the **b** sound and say the new word. **B—at, bat.** Now let's look at the next word and do it together.

At this point the teacher directs the learner to the word **rat** and repeats the procedure, but with learner responses. The process continues with other words, with both the amount of teacher modeling and the highlighting being gradually diminished and learner response being increased until the child is able to substitute initial consonants independently in known vowel phonograms and pronounce the new words.

In contrast, the discovery strategy would go somewhat as follows:

*Teacher:* Today we are going to learn to change the first letter in related words and pronounce the new words. This is not always easy so I have listed some of the words on the board, circling the first letter and underlining the parts of each word that are related. We know the first word in the list because we learned it the other day as a sight word. What is it?

*Learner responds.*
*Teacher:* Let's look at all the words in the list. In what way do they all look alike?

*Learner responds.*
*Teacher:* In what ways do each of the words look different?

*Learner responds.*
*Teacher:* Let's go back to the first word again. We said we know that word because we learned it the other day. It is **cat.** It is like all the the other words on the list because it has –at at the end. It is different because it starts with a different first letter. Let's concentrate on the ending for a minute. I'm going to say **cat** slowly and I want you to listen and tell me what sound you hear at the end of the word. **C . . . at, cat.**

*Learner responds.*
*Teacher:* If the –at in **cat** says "at," what sound do you suppose you will hear at the end of the next word? And the word after that?

*Learner responds.*
*Teacher:* Okay, we can say that all the words in the list are related because they end with the same letters and the same sounds. They are different, however, because they have different beginnings. We have learned the sounds for these beginning letters, though, and if we "get our mouth ready" to say the beginning sound, say it, and then add the –at sound of the ending, we can say the word. Can you do that with the first word?

*Learner responds.*

This process is continued for other words, with the amount of highlighting being gradually diminished until the learner is able to substitute initial consonants independently in known vowel phonograms and pronounce the new words.

It can be seen, then, that both the modeling and the discovery techniques elicit learner response, and either strategy can be used in teaching. The modeling technique has the advantage of controlling more tightly the response pattern of the learner, whereas the discovery technique involves the learner more actively in the thinking process. One should use both strategies according to the needs and learning styles of the particular learner. In either technique, however, frequent responses must be elicited. Only when learners are actively involved in learning can they be effectively assisted in mastering the skill.

## Reinforcement

The final way to assist learning is through reinforcement. Reinforcement goes by many names. Some call it reward, others call it bribery. As teachers we too often view the condition of reward as an intrinsic state where success in the task is internalized by learners and they learn for learning's sake. This is fine for those who have such a reward system but unfortunately many children come to school without knowing what it means to be praised for doing something well. The successful learner has developed a reward system; the poor learner has not yet learned how to accept reinforcements. A teacher's first task in using reinforcement, consequently, is to judge each child individually and to choose reinforcers that are appropriate to the child's system.

At the lowest level these reinforcers are physical—an apple, a token that buys a toy plane at the end of the week, some candy, or a box of raisins. This may seem like bribery but it can be the start of a reward system.

The next step above physical rewards is a touch or movement reward. Here you pat a shoulder or shake a hand when the learning is properly closed. At a still higher level you gradually replace the touch or movement with a word or two of praise.

Your objective is to help learners find satisfaction in the learning task, moving them through the levels of reinforcers as they progress. As they progress you help them extinguish the lower rewards, which are replaced with words and gestures. To learners who ultimately develop sophisticated reinforcement systems, a smile or a nod is sufficient reward. In any case the reward or reinforcement must be appropriate to the learning and to the learner's reward system.

A second, and equally important consideration, is to provide the reward immediately following the correct response. Delayed rewards work only after the child has learned to delay them. At the early stages of learning especially, children need immediate feedback regarding their success, for the reinforcement is the learner's primary indication of success, just as the response is a teacher's primary indication of the learner's understanding.

Reinforcement, then, entails providing a reward for learners when they make the desired response. The reward must be appropriate to the learning and to the learners' reward systems. It should utilize levels of reinforcers with the intent of moving learners from "bribes" to intrinsic rewards and should immediately follow the correct response in order to provide feedback regarding success or failure. Such reinforcement, when used skillfully, directly assists children in their attempts to learn the skill.

## SUMMARY

Teaching is different from testing because one does not directly assist learners during a test but does provide such assistance during teaching. In this book six techniques are provided for directly assisting children in learning. In every skill lesson the teacher should ensure that the difficulty of the task is acknowledged, that the learner's attention is directed to the task to be learned and to its salient features, that these salient features are highlighted, that the highlighting is gradually diminished as the learner begins to respond correctly, that there is frequent opportunity to respond, and that the learner receives immediate reinforcement appropriate for his or her particular reward system.

Because the skill has been taught does not necessarily mean that it has been mastered or that learners are ready for a posttest. The teaching act itself only takes children to the point where they can perform the task independently on a particular day. Practice is necessary before we can be sure that they will remember the skill on future days.

Practice consists of numerous repetitions of the task. Its purpose is to help the learner solidify the skill response so that it becomes habitual. In many ways practice exercises are similar to tests in that they require frequent response to a task without any directed assistance from the teacher. A typical example of such practice would be a workbook page or Ditto exercise.

Practice is essential to effective learning because children retain what they have learned only if they have repeatedly performed the task. In fact, when children are taught a skill and seem to know it one day but are unable to do it two days later, the difficulty can almost always be traced to lack of practice. The more practice they receive, the easier it is for them to remember the skill.

Practice does not necessarily have to be boring and rote. There are many lively ways to provide multiple repetitions of a task. Games, audio-visual materials, reading machines, and various kits and workbooks are just some ways in which practice can be made enjoyable. Although many additional ideas are provided in the skill modules of this book, the only limit to innovative practice is the degree of creativeness and commitment brought to the task.

Regardless of whether you choose to use creative practice or more mundane methods such as workbooks and Ditto sheets, you must ensure that the practice meets certain minimum criteria. First, the practice exercise must provide multiple repetitions in the skill taught and not in some other skill. For instance, a practice activity in which children make up new –at phonogram words would not be appropriate following a lesson on pronouncing such words when they appear in print. If the skill taught was that of pronouncing –at phonogram words encountered in print, then the practice exercise should require multiple repetitions in pronouncing **–at** phonogram words encountered in print.

Second, the practice activity ought to be completed independent of you. That is, when the instruction is completed and the children have been taught how to do the task, you give the practice activity to them and they go to their seats or to some other location to complete the exercise. This frees you to begin instruction with other learners rather than spending valuable instructional time supervising practice activities.

Finally, as much as possible, the practice activity should allow self-checking. Because the children are doing the activity independently, you are not available to correct them and to ensure that they "stay on the track." Consequently, there is a danger that a child may complete an entire practice activity incorrectly, thereby making a habit out of the wrong response. By providing a way for learners to check themselves and by directing them to complete the activity only if they are making the correct responses, you are sure that the learner is solidifying the correct response.

Practice, then, is an integral part of the total instructional process. Without it children may not remember the skill when they need it. Practice is not, however, synonymous with teaching, because it does not provide learners with directed assistance. Consequently, you must ensure that the learner can do the skill before being given practice and you should avoid assigning practice materials (such as workbooks, worksheets, games, and so on) as teaching devices unless these materials provide directed assistance.

### ● CHAPTER SUMMARY

In its totality the instructional model for teaching reading skills can be described in terms of an hourglass such as the following:

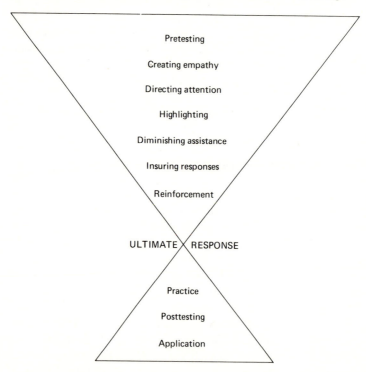

Pretesting

Creating empathy

Directing attention

Highlighting

Diminishing assistance

Insuring responses

Reinforcement

ULTIMATE RESPONSE

Practice

Posttesting

Application

At the top of the hourglass is the pretest, where children are tested on their ability to perform the skill. At the neck of the hourglass is the "ultimate response," the point at which children can perform the skill without any directed assistance. When they fail a pretest, you directly assist learners in mastering what they do not know. Thus the upper half of the hourglass, with the exclusion of the pretest, represents the teaching activity. Once the skill has been taught and the learner can perform it unassisted, the focus moves to the bottom half of the hourglass, where practice is provided, the posttest is administered, and guidance is given in applying the skill in real reading situations.

The instructional model can be illustrated by looking at a sample situation. The learner is Sam. The teacher has been taking Sam through the various pretests in the hierarchy of reading skills. On one pretest, he is unable to distinguish between the sight words **where** and **there**. Consequently, the teacher plans an appropriate instructional episode. She first states what Sam is to learn and acknowledges to him the difficulty of the task, explaining how hard it is, noting the difficulty that many children have with it, and generally creating empathy. Sam is then directed to the **wh** and **th** in the two words and is told that these are the features of the two words that must be particularly noted if they are to be distinguished and remembered. The **wh** and **th** are heavily highlighted early in the instructional sequence to help focus Sam's attention. Then, using either a modeling strategy or a discovery strategy, the teacher elicits frequent responses from the learner regarding the differences in the two words and the manner in which they can be distinguished. After each correct response Sam is reinforced and the amount of highlighting is gradually diminished. When the learner can identify **where** and **there** without any highlighting (the ultimate response), the teacher plans a practice activity that requires Sam to identify the words a large number of times. If the practice is completed satisfactorily, the teacher administers a posttest to ensure that the instruction has been successful. If the posttest indicates mastery, the teacher provides assistance in transfering the skill from the instructional situation to the reading of books and other materials, as described in the next chapter.

This, then, is the instructional model. This book assists in implementing the model, since each skill module contains a specific pretest; guides for directing the learner's attention; specific suggestions for highlighting, diminishing assistance, and eliciting responses with both a modeling and a discovery technique; multiple suggestions for developing practice activities for each skill; a specific posttest; suggestions for reteaching the skill if the learner fails the posttest; and suggestions for helping the learner apply the skill in his or her daily reading.

# HELPING CHILDREN APPLY LEARNED SKILLS

Having a reading program based on just diagnosis and prescription is like making a cake and not tasting it—
  Like notes of music on paper—
  Like a library with closed doors—
  Like a marriage by contract.

Explaining the rule for determining whether **g** is "hard" or "soft" is like outlining how to play jazz—
  Like instructing how to kiss—
  Like using a compass without a map—
  Like explaining a bad joke.

Reading is not a Forty-five Minute
Period of Instruction with Behavioral
Objectives and Predictable Outcomes.

Reading is enjoying, learning, feeling, becoming, sensing, laughing, crying, hating, deciding, loving, growing, sympathizing, listening.
  Reading is All Day—
    Being and Becoming—
    Growing and Growing.[1]

NANCY WHITELAW

The biggest danger in emphasizing skills is that we may become so busy teaching them that we neglect to develop readers. That is, we may produce learners who can perform the skills in isolation but who cannot use them

[1]Excerpts from "Some Negative and Positive Thoughts on Reading in School," *The Reading Teacher*, XXIX, November, 1975, 145.

in the real world of reading books. To avoid this we must provide a balance between skill instruction and meaningful reading activities, avoiding polar positions such as saying, on the one hand, that skills are the answer to everything or, on the other hand, that children learn to read by reading and that skills are just deadening mechanics. A balanced view recognizes that many children do need the skills and that they also need many reading activities in which to put their skills to work. Our task, then, is to create a learning situation in which children receive systematic instruction in the needed basic skills while also receiving abundant guidance in using all their skills in their reading.

## GUIDED APPLICATION IN BASAL TEXTBOOKS

There are two basic ways to help children transfer learned reading skills from the skill lesson to reading books. One involves teacher assistance and is called guided application. The other involves independent reading and is called independent application. In guided application, the skill is taught in a skill lesson and, once it is mastered, you give the child a specific piece of reading material in which the skill must be used. When giving the child this material you direct his or her attention to the skill or skills that ought to be applied. In some instances, particularly for those children who have difficulty making the transfer from the skill lesson to reading, you might even highlight certain sections, thereby directing the learner's attention to the fact that this is the place to put his or her newly learned skill to work. As the learner becomes more proficient, of course, this highlighting is gradually diminished until the learner can apply the skill unassisted.

The most useful material for guided application is the basal reading textbook. It has the advantage of being available in most classrooms, of containing a variety of stories that are graded in difficulty, and of having a teacher's guide that often provides clues to the skills required in particular stories. Although, as was mentioned in Chapter 1, the basal text is not a complete reading program, it is an extremely valuable source for guided application.

When using the basal text for guided application, you should first divide your instructional time into periods for skill teaching and periods for application. In the early grades, where two separate periods are frequently allocated for reading, you can use one for skills and the other for application. In the later grades you may wish to devote one day's reading period entirely to skill teaching and another day's period to guided application. In any case, during the time set aside for guided application, your learners are grouped according to reading level and you meet with each basal text group in turn. The standard format for a directed reading lesson is followed with each group except that, instead of using this time to teach new skills, previously learned skills are applied. The procedure usually is somewhat as follows: introduce the story, identify any new words;

specify the previously learned skills that the learners should be applying as they read; state any other appropriate aims; have the children read the story silently; and finally, be sure that the previously learned skill was applied.

In using guided application you will want to identify those learners who have the greatest difficulty in making the transfer from skill instruction to application, since they will need the greatest amount of guidance. Although many children apply the learned skills quite easily, it will be necessary to assist some children directly at this stage, sometimes even to the extent of modeling the application process and having the learner mimic your actions. However, once the learner gets the idea that he or she is not learning skills for their own sake but for their utility in improving reading, the learner will begin to make the transfer more readily. It is at this point that the learner is ready for independent application.

## INDEPENDENT APPLICATION IN RECREATIONAL READING

In independent application the learner applies reading skills in library books and other recreational reading materials without teacher assistance. Because the development of voracious readers who automatically use their skills in pursuing genuine and meaningful reading tasks is the ultimate goal of skill instruction, such recreational reading is a crucial part of good reading instruction.

Recreational reading is just what its name implies—reading for the fun of it. As such, it must be structured to make reading enjoyable. It should be presented as a respite from the rigors of the regular school day, as relaxation and as an activity having inherent value for the learner. It should never take on the connotation of work, nor should the learner ever be put in the position of reading a book simply to complete a book report assignment.

### DEVELOPING A RECREATIONAL READING PROGRAM

Implementing a recreational reading program as a vehicle for independent application requires conscious effort and commitment on your part. You must find the time, provide the materials, structure a supportive environment, and plan related activities.

Time is always a factor. There are so many things to teach and only so much time in the school day. However, we always find time for the important things and providing for independent application certainly is important. Consequently, we must "steal" the time, if necessary. A good way to do this is to schedule recreational reading first thing in the morning so that you *know* you will have time for it. Another technique is to use recreational reading as one of the independent activities that learners do when they are not working directly with you during the skill instruction period. However, you must always be careful not to relegate recreational reading to the status of something to be done when other work is finished, since this implies that everything else is more important.

Recreational reading must occur frequently. Although the time periods devoted to it can be short, they should be part of the regular schedule so the learners can anticipate them. Avoid the traditional practice of confining recreational reading to the last period on Friday, when the learners do not concentrate, and you should not view the recreational reading period as something you schedule only when you need to complete your attendance register or other pressing paperwork.

For independent application to succeed there must be something to read. Library books are obviously your major source of materials, but you should not confine yourself to books. Magazines, newspapers, comics, brochures, pamphlets, and any other printed matter having any interest to your learners should be provided. The collection should reflect a wide range of interests consistent with the assortment of individuals you are serving. Room libraries, consisting of books borrowed from the school library or from the local public library, should be on constant display in the room, with one collection of books frequently replacing another. Trade books should be used in the subject matter areas, and related fictional and informational books should be available. All this reading material is of little value, however, if the learner never has time to use it. Consequently, you must frequently encourage the learners to browse through and read the material being displayed.

Obtaining reading materials is frequently a problem. Schools rarely have the money these days to purchase them, so we must find alternate ways. The most obvious of these is the library system in your local community. Although librarians are a frequent target of abuse, most are anxious to help; when they are informed of what you are trying to do, most will gladly provide you with boxes and boxes of books. Paperback book clubs, which provide learners with the opportunity to purchase some of the best children's books at a very low cost, are another source. Each learner can then be encouraged to leave his or her books on the shelf in the room for reading by others. Another source is local newsstands, which frequently save torn copies of paperback books, magazines, and comics and happily donate them upon request. The learner's themselves can be involved in gathering materials by soliciting book and magazine donations from the neighborhood; by running cake sales, paper drives, or other fund-raising projects in which the proceeds are used to purchase reading materials; and by contributing the books they have at home to the room library. Finally, you must be a beggar, a borrower, and a saver yourself, collecting reading material from any source available and storing it in your classroom for use by your learners. In providing materials, the best guide is, "I can never have too much."

The classroom environment plays a crucial role in independent application. It should reflect the focus on books in many ways. Bulletin boards, for instance, should present recommended book lists, books on a single theme, information on the winners of book awards, the backgrounds of authors, children's art depicting book scenes, and children's evaluations of books they have read. Films and recordings of fables, folk tales, poetry, picture books, and so on, should be available. Finally, a place should be designated in the classroom for relaxed reading. This can be a corner of the room with an old rug, some throw pillows scattered about, and perhaps an old easy chair or rocker. The intent is to provide an appealing place in the room where children can relax with a book.

In the final analysis, however, the most important element of a supportive environment is you. If you want your learners to be readers, you must constantly seek to convey this attitude to the class. You should become familiar with all kinds of children's books, make frequent references to children's literature in your teaching, and show that it is important to you that learners enjoy their reading. Most important of all, you should make obvious your own enjoyment by reading a book of your choice when the learners are themselves engaged in recreational reading. Nothing will impress your learners more than your eagerness to practice what you preach regarding recreational reading.

The reading habit can also be developed through book-related activities. Two of the most profitable activities are oral reading by you and learner sharing of books they have read. The daily activities of all reading classes should include oral reading by you of children's literature, since such reading, especially when it emphasizes highly recommended books the learners are unlikely to read by themselves, is probably more effective than any other single technique in building a love of literature and in starting learners toward the reading habit. This activity requires some preparation on your part, however, since you must be familiar with the book and practice reading it aloud if you are to read it well. It should also be emphasized that this activity is designed to be enjoyable. Any discussion following the oral reading should be casual and nonintimidating, not a testing session.

Learner sharing of the books they have read also creates interest in reading and stimulates independent application. The emphasis, however, must be on sharing and not on reporting, since reporting has a coercive connotation we want to avoid. Consequently, the decision to share a book with others should be left to the learner. When a child reads a book he or she really enjoys, encourage him or her to share it as a means of getting others interested in reading it. Such sharing may take the form of book talks, audience reading, book fairs, puppetry, dramatization, book want ads, or any other activity in which learners discuss a book with the intention of interesting others in it.

## QUESTIONS REGARDING INDEPENDENT APPLICATION

Teachers rarely question the value of independent application itself. They do, however, frequently pose questions about particular aspects of recreational reading. Some questions and their answers follow.

1. *What kind of book should we encourage the learner to use for independent application?*

   There are really only two considerations regarding the kind of book a learner should read. The first is, "Does the child want to read it?" That is, does the book interest him or her? The second is, "Can the child read it?" That is, is he or she ready to apply the reading skills necessary to handle the book or is it too hard? If the child both wants to read the book and is able to read it, it is an appropriate book.

2. *How do we involve the very slow reader in independent application?*

   Because a learner is unable to read does not mean he or she cannot participate in the recreational reading program. The learner can be provided with picture books and picture magazines that interest him or her and are of the appropriate level. You can also make booklets out of interesting material cut from old editions of *My Weekly Reader, Jack and Jill, Children's Digest,* and other sources containing material commensurate with the child's ability. Comic books are another source for such learners. Using such easy material, the learner can read for relaxation in the same manner as more advanced learners and will not feel stupid unless your attitude *makes* him or her feel that way. If you accept the reading material as being worthwhile, so will the learner.

3. *Should we outlaw comic books in the classroom?*

   As has been implied earlier, we are not opposed to comic books per se. It is better for children having much difficulty with reading to read comic books than nothing at all. However, it is doubtful that comics help develop the reading habit, and learners should be weaned away from them and guided to books as soon as they possess the skills. These first books should possess the same characteristics of low readability, adventure, action, and colorful pictures that attract learners to comics. It is helpful to remember also that the most effective way to eliminate the appeal of comics is to make them readily available. As soon as you ban them they attain the aura of forbidden fruit and their appeal soars.

4. *Should we be concerned about the learner who only reads Dr. Seuss stories or who only reads horse stories?*

   Our primary concern is that of applying learned skills. Initially, any book will do as long as it calls for the use of previously learned skills and as long as the child *wants* to read it. Once the reading habit has become established, however, you will want to encourage learners to vary their interests and enrich their tastes.

5. *Should we have contests in our classroom to see who can read the most books?*

Definitely not. First, we want to encourage children to read because it is an enjoyable and rewarding act in itself, not because it will win a prize. Second, and more important, such contests motivate only those who need no motivating while frustrating those who need to be encouraged the most, since only the good readers have a chance to win the prize. If you feel that some form of reward is needed to encourage learners to begin reading books, make it a personal thing between you and the learners rather than a competition in which many learners have no chance to win.

## ● CHAPTER SUMMARY

Skills cannot be taught in isolation and then forgotten. Instead there must be a structured and systematic attempt to transfer these skills to the reading act, to put the skills to work with books. Guided application with basal texts and other graded material and independent application with a recreational reading program provide the means for such application. By providing application you acknowledge that the ultimate goal of reading instruction is the development of learners not only who are able to read but who do read.

# MANAGING IN-DIVIDUALIZED SKILL INSTRUCTION

And it came to pass that the fourth day being Thursday did fall upon me and I was sore afraid. For it was on this day that bedlam was my lot. It was the dark day of the "Great Collection" and of the mound of reports that flowed into the upper chambers.

And I did take from my desk drawer and laid thereon the faded money sack and the record sheet. I did also take the envelope for daily lunch collections, my daily attendance cards and the head count sheets that were past due; these I set before me wondering when—if ever—I would complete them. I then sayeth, "Forsooth, when doth I teach?"

(AUTHOR UNKNOWN)

Individualization is an integral part of effective skill instruction since not all children will need simultaneous instruction in a particular skill. On any pretest some children will fail and some will pass; consequently, the teacher will be working with some children at the very low levels and others at higher levels. How to organize and manage instruction in which different children receive different instruction on different skills is a major problem.

Historically, a great deal of lip service has been given to the idea that some form of individualized instruction is essential to meet the variety of reading needs found in a typical elementary classroom. For the most part, however, efforts have emphasized the need for individualization rather than how to accomplish it. In contrast, this chapter focuses on the practical concerns of creating an operational organization and management system.

# PREREQUISITES TO EFFECTIVE MANAGEMENT

You must initially possess a prerequisite mind-set. First, you must accept the fact that we cannot teach all learners the same reading skills at the same time and with the same materials. When a teacher persists in the myth of holding children to certain arbitrary standards, usually expressed in terms of grade levels, individualization is being rejected and no significant progress can be made.

Second, we must recognize that individualized instruction cannot be purchased in a commercial package. To the contrary, classroom organization and management is always the responsibility of the teacher, one that can be met only through commitment and diligence. There is no easy way to manage individualized instruction; it will always require much hard work and we can succeed only if we accept this fact.

Third, it must be agreed that *now* is the time to begin individualizing. It is always easy to find reasons for delaying difficult tasks. In individualization we can point to class size or to the lack of teacher aides or to an unsympathetic administrator. The fact is, however, that there are always reasons for delaying individualizing, and if they are accepted as valid, the job will not be started. We must individualize despite the problems. Teachers who want to are already doing it, and the rest of us can do likewise.

Fourth, we must define individualized instruction not as "one teacher teaching one child at a time," but as teaching however many children need a particular skill at any particular time. If, on Monday, nine children need instruction on identifying the main idea of a paragraph, then those nine children should be grouped together and taught the skill. Only when there is just one child who needs a skill should he or she be taught alone. Consequently, the crucial criterion is not the size of the group, but whether each child in the group can and should learn that skill at that time. Such a strategy is practical since it would be grossly inefficient to teach a skill nine times to nine different children when one could accomplish the same thing in a much shorter time by grouping the nine children together.

Finally, we must recognize that the core of management is not what we do with the group we are teaching at the moment, but what we do with those learners who are not under direct supervision. If you have 25 children in a class and you are teaching a skill to 5 of them, what do you do with the other 20? How do you make sure that they are not getting into trouble? How do you prevent them from causing multiple interruptions in the skill lesson? Failure to account for this variable is the primary reason that individualized instruction has frequently failed in the past.

# THE COMPONENTS OF MANAGING INDIVIDUALIZATION

Teaching is at least as much art as science, but management is one area that requires a particularly high degree of art. There is no foolproof formula for ensuring successful management; much depends upon the teacher's sensitivity, common sense, and diligence. However, six components can be identified as guidelines in establishing a system of grouping by common skill needs.

## Independent Activities

The solution to the problem of what to do with the children who are not in the skill group you are currently teaching lies in providing independent activities. While you are teaching the skill group, the rest of the children can be actively involved in work they complete by themselves. Such independent work usually relates to ongoing projects in the classroom and can include recreational reading, guided reading of basal textbooks, pursuit of social studies assignments, completion of science experiments, practice on previously taught reading and math skills, working on art projects, practicing handwriting, doing creative writing, and any other class-related activity that the learners can complete by themselves. To make independent activities work, however, the teacher must ensure that four conditions are met. These involve planning, ability level, directions, and relevance.

Individualized instruction is difficult because the planning load is doubled. Not only must the skill lessons be planned but so must the independent activities. Despite the added work, however, such planning is essential for success. With careful planning the children not receiving skill instruction can be meaningfully occupied, but careless planning results in frequent interruptions of skill lessons by learners who are confused about their independent work.

The second condition requires that the independent activities be geared to each child's ability level. Assigning independent reading of a fourth grade social studies book would be inappropriate for the child with a second grade reading level, who would be unable to complete the work alone. Independent work must be individualized just as skill work is individualized since there are few tasks that all the children can handle.

When the planning is complete, you must give children directions regarding their independent activities. This direction giving may be written or oral but it must be totally understood by the class. Each learner must know what to do and must be able to determine when the task has been accomplished. Given inadequate directions some learners will decide that they have finished after only a few minutes and, with time on their hands, will disrupt the class, particularly the skill group. Consequently, successful management requires thorough directions.

The final condition, relevance, describes the condition that is the opposite of busy-work. One must create independent work that does not involve doing a certain number of problems or filling in blanks. Such busy-work invariably creates disrupting behavior in children. Whatever the independent work, it must have a motivating relevance for children. If it does not it will fail to hold their attention and thereby cause a double failure, both leaving meaningless work undone and disrupting the skill group. Independent work is relevant when learners know why it is important or if it will be used in some important way. For instance, some teachers achieve relevance by sending independent material home regularly for parental inspection.

### Safety Valves

The first step in individualizing is creating independent activities for learners to pursue while the teacher is working with skill groups. However, children will not all finish their independent work at the same time. Some will be done before you have finished teaching the skill groups; if you have not anticipated this, disruption may result. Consequently, you should plan safety valve activities that children can fall back on when they finish their independent work.

Such safety valves usually take the form of learning centers or activities that children can participate in at any time. They are different from independent activities because they do not change daily, they are not always associated with the ongoing academic work in the classroom, and they tend to be viewed as fun. For instance, appropriate safety valves include a recreational reading corner, listening centers, vocabulary and math games, purely recreational games such as checkers and chess, art centers, a sandbox, a play house, or any other activity the learner could fall back on with little direction from the teacher.

An important criterion for safety valves is that the learner view them as rewarding. For this, two conditions should be present. First, there should be a variety of safety valves, to ensure that there is something to interest everybody. Second, children should help create safety valves, to make sure that these activities reflect the group's particular interests. When these conditions are met safety valves become an extremely effective management device.

### Physical Setting

The physical setting of the classroom is another crucial component. If the classroom is simultaneously to accommodate small group skill teaching, independent activities, and learning centers containing safety valves, the traditional arrangement of five rows with five children in a row will not be appropriate, because the rows of desks and chairs will take up all the floor space.

The best way to handle this dilemma is to rearrange the furniture, pushing the children's desks together in clusters of four in the middle of the classroom. This will provide desks where children can do independent activities and at the same time create new space around the edges of the classroom for a skill teaching corner and safety valve activities. Such a floor plan might look like the following:

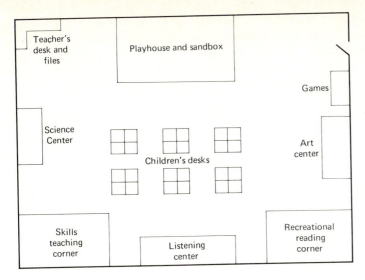

There is, of course, no single way to arrange the classroom. The only limitations are the particular dimensions of your room and the limits of your creativity in working within those dimensions. Some teachers, for instance, use large refrigerator boxes, portable screens, old furniture, large floor pillows, and hanging screens as part of the physical setting. Others accomplish the same result simply by moving furniture. Either approach is suitable as long as there is room for independent activities, safety valves, and skill teaching.

## Training

Individualized instruction requires that children often work by themselves or in small groups on independent activities and safety valves while the teacher is, for all practical purposes, isolated from them in the skill teaching corner. If the children are unprepared for such independence, they will be unable to handle it and the management system will collapse. Consequently, the teacher must orient the children to the system and train them to work independently.

This orientation and training should begin in September and continue until the children have adjusted. The time needed will vary from group to group, but generally the younger children who have not been exposed to any other kind of classroom organization will adjust very quickly, whereas older children, who may be used to a more traditional system allowing little independent movement or action, will sometimes require six weeks or more of training. The time is well spent, however, since it ensures the smooth operation of the reading program for the remainder of the year.

You should initiate the orientation and training with a full explanation of exactly how the reading program will be operated. Then the class should be involved in the development of procedures and rules that will expedite management. You can aid this process by setting up hypothetical situations, having the learners decide how they could be handled. For instance, one could pose questions such as the following:

1. What should we do if we have to move chairs around and a child is swinging a chair so carelessly as to hurt someone?
2. What should we do if you have to go to the bathroom or get a drink of water and the teacher is busy in the skill corner?
3. What should we do if two children want to use the listening center and there is only room for one at the moment?

To pose the right questions you must anticipate what might go wrong, thereby preventing the problem before it occurs. Despite such forethought, however, you can expect unanticipated problems during the year. This is natural and you must resign yourself to resolving these as they occur.

Once anticipated problems have been identified and procedures established, you should directly supervise the children as they try out independent activities and safety valves. You are then immediately available to develop appropriate independent behavior in the initial stages, when the routines have not yet been established. As children adjust to the system, you can gradually move into skill teaching, perhaps teaching only a single skill group on the first day and spending the balance of the period supervising, moving to the teaching of two skill groups the next day, and so on, until eventually the entire period is spent teaching skill groups while learners work entirely independently.

Some teachers insist that their particular students cannot work independently, that this system of organization and management might work for "good" children but will not work for theirs. The authors' experience does not support this position. All children can work independently *if* the teacher is sensitive to them, is committed to making the system work, and spends enough time in training.

Although such orienting and training are sometimes frustrating and boring, they are crucial to successful management of individualized teaching. Children cannot be expected to work independently just because teachers want them to. They must receive direct teacher assistance in how to work independently and in routinely handling the various problems that are likely to occur. Only then can teachers expect to create an efficient management system.

## Buffer

Despite good planning, individualized instruction can fail for lack of a mechanism for handling unanticipated routine matters. Such situations always develop when learners work independently. Your time, however, must be totally free to work with the small skills group. Consequently, you need to create a "buffer" between you and the children working independently—a person who handles unanticipated situations while you remain free to teach the skill group. Minor problems ranging from assignment directions to toilet turns become the buffer's responsibility.

In addition to handling unanticipated situations, the buffer can also supervise practice activities, play learning games with children, listen to children read, ensure that learners are applying previously learned skills in their reading, give pretests and posttests, assist with correcting papers and record keeping, and generally provide any needed kind of nonprofessional classroom assistance. The buffer should not teach, however, since this is a highly technical task requiring professional skills that most buffers do not possess.

Who is the buffer? It can be almost anyone. Most desirable would be a trained paraprofessional or teacher's aide. Almost as desirable would be buffers chosen from parents or senior citizens who have volunteered their time. The buffer could also be a high school student who is a member of the Future Teachers of America and who, consequently, can be released from school to perform such duties. Also available are students from higher grades in the same school, such as a sixth grader who helps the third grade teacher for an hour a day. Finally, and least desirable, the buffer can be a student from the teacher's own classroom who has been trained to assist.

Regardless of who performs the function, however, you must recognize that managing individualized instruction is very difficult, and although it can be done without assistance, the problems are much fewer with help. The buffer can provide that help and therefore makes it much easier to achieve the goal of individualized instruction.

**Record Keeping**

Because of the multitude of skills to be taught and the individual differences in children, keeping track of each child's progress is often a monumental task. It is essential therefore that you develop an efficient system for keeping records.

There are many ways to keep records efficiently. One the authors have used with success consists of a regular loose-leaf notebook and pages of quarter-inch graph paper. There are pages for each group (or cluster) of word recognition skills and for each group (or cluster) of comprehension skills. Along the left-hand side of the page, each pupil's name is recorded. Every quarter-inch square on the graph paper represents a single skill, as noted by name and number at the bottom and top of that column of squares. As you pretest each child, simply put a slash (/) in the square to indicate a failure to pass the test and color the square to indicate passing the test. A sample page might look like the one shown on page 70.

The notebook is kept in the skill teaching corner; by glancing at it you know immediately who must receive which skill instruction. For instance, starting from the first skill in the example, we see that Burt must be taught visual discrimination of geometric forms, that Sam and Mike can be grouped together for instruction in visual memory of geometric

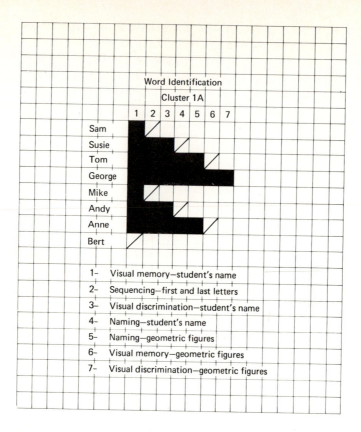

Word Identification

Cluster 1A

|  | 1 | 2 | 3 | 4 | 5 | 6 | 7 |
|---|---|---|---|---|---|---|---|
| Sam | | | | | | | |
| Susie | | | | | | | |
| Tom | | | | | | | |
| George | | | | | | | |
| Mike | | | | | | | |
| Andy | | | | | | | |
| Anne | | | | | | | |
| Bert | | | | | | | |

1– Visual memory—student's name
2– Sequencing—first and last letters
3– Visual discrimination—student's name
4– Naming—student's name
5– Naming—geometric figures
6– Visual memory—geometric figures
7– Visual discrimination—geometric figures

figures, that Susie and Andy need instruction in recognizing their names, that Tom and Anne are ready for a sequencing lesson on first and last letters, and that George has mastered all the skills in this particular cluster.

This is a good record-keeping device because it is not cumbersome, because it takes little time or effort to mark the results of tests, and because it provides an immediate visual picture of where each child is in the skills sequence and how they can be grouped for instruction. It is efficient for the task and is therefore a good tool.

Of course, a record-keeping device need not look like the one shown here. It can be modified for the teacher's particular needs, or a completely different system can be devised. Whatever the device, however, it must be manageable in size, be easy to use, and provide a good visual picture of the skill instruction needed. With such a record-keeping device, implementation of individualized instruction is greatly facilitated.

## SUMMARY

To teach reading skills effectively the teacher must provide each learner with instruction at his or her particular level. Consequently, instruction must be individualized, for it is extremely unlikely that a single class, regardless of the level, will be populated by students who all require the same skill instruction at the same time.

Individualization traditionally fails because of lack of attention to the mundane details of implementation. Any individualized instruction is complex, with many different things going on at once, and it cannot be realized through a casual approach or with minimum effort. To the contrary, it requires a consistent expenditure of teacher effort and time; even then it will not be perfect and will need constant adjustment. However, attention to the principles of independent activities, safety valves, physical setting, training, buffer, and record keeping significantly facilitates the task.

## ONE EXAMPLE OF THE MANAGEMENT SYSTEM IN ACTION

How does a classroom appear if the management system described in this book is being utilized? Let us examine one such classroom. The situation described is a fourth grade in a disadvantaged section of a midwestern city. There are 25 pupils in the class, all of whom are reading at the second grade level or below. The children have experienced three years of failure, and their attitude toward school in general and reading in particular is poor.

The children's attitude, as illustrated by their aggression and general behavior difficulties, is rooted in three sources. First, they are being asked to perform reading tasks that are too difficult for them. Like the beginning swimmer who develops a defensive attitude toward swimming instruction when thrown into an advanced swimming class, these beginning readers developed a defensive attitude toward reading instruction when required to perform at the fourth grade level with first and second grade tools. Second, their reading materials have little or no meaning for them. Finally, they have poor self-images and little confidence in their ability to handle any reading task independently, a fact attributable to their lack of reading skills.

We will examine the classroom in three ways. First, we will look at the teacher's overall strategy. Second, we will look at the physical setting. Finally, we will look at the whole class as it operates during the reading period.

### The Teacher's Overall Strategy

To meet the reading needs of the children in this class, the teacher instituted a three-step program. First, he determined the level at which each child was currently reading in order to provide reading matter suitable to individual abilities. Second, he provided each child with reading matter he or she was interested in and at the child's reading level. Finally, he instituted the program of systematic skill instruction developed in this book.

The teacher used a simple technique to determine each child's reading level. First, he selected representative passages from various basal texts, ranging in difficulty from a preprimer to a third grade level. He then asked each child to read these passages to him orally, noting the child's errors. If the child made fewer than one error in 20 words and if he or she could correctly answer four out of five questions about the passage after reading it, the teacher assumed that the child could adequately handle a book of that difficulty. If, however, the child made more than one error in 20 words *or* failed to answer at least four out of five comprehension questions, the teacher assumed material of that level was too difficult for the child.

Once the teacher had determined each child's reading level, he knew the range of material needed. In the class being described this material ranged from picture books to second grade level.

In selecting the material to be used the teacher operated from the view that children in school seldom have the opportunity to read what interests them and that, consequently, they do not learn that reading can be enjoyable. To eliminate this problem, material that children find stimulating, enjoyable, and important was begged, borrowed, and bought from all available sources and kept in the room. This material included comic books; selected stories cut from old basal texts and stapled together; old *Weekly Reader* stories; material written by the class regarding field trips, social studies projects, science investigations, and other activities; hard- and soft-bound easy-to-read books; popular magazines such as *Sport* and *Cycle;* materials written by the teacher; stories dictated or written by the pupils themselves; stories written by the children in higher grades; basal texts; and anything else that could be obtained that could possibly interest the children.

These materials were distributed around the room in an attractive fashion and children were urged to look at and read any that interested them. They were not tested on what they read, they were not required to make book reports, and they were not required to read everything they picked up. They were, however, encouraged to share a particularly good story with the rest of the class and time was provided to develop projects relating to the books they read, to prepare puppet plays, to dramatize particularly enjoyable stories, to make up scrapbooks relating to a particular theme in their reading, and generally to tell their peers whenever a particularly enjoyable piece of reading material was encountered. As a result, the class became enthusiastic about reading while also applying the skills they had learned.

Once the children started "reading" materials of their own choice, the teacher began systematically to teach the reading skills, following the procedures described in this book. Each child was pretested on the skills appropriate to his or her level and the results were recorded in a notebook. By looking in the notebook and noting which children had not yet successfully completed a particular skill, the teacher could select those children needing instruction. While the rest of the children were occupied with independent activities, the teacher would teach a 10- or 15-minute lesson on a particular skill for those children who needed it. For instance, he would get Sam and Mike together for a lesson on visually discriminating geometric figures. He would give a posttest following practice to determine which child had mastered the skill and which had not, noting the results in the notebook. In the next 10- or 15-minute time segment, the teacher would draw out another group needing instruction in another skill. This process continued except for those times when the teacher was helping children apply learned skills in their individual reading.

The teacher's strategy met the particular needs of this group of children. Having each child read individual material matched to his or her ability level eliminated the defensive attitude toward reading that had grown from frustration with material that was too hard. Having each child select material of interest to him or her provided a viable reason for reading and helped that child become more enthusiastic about reading generally. Teaching the skills in a systematic fashion provided children with the mechanics needed to read harder and harder material in the independent work and to improve their self-images and confidence in handling the reading act.

## The Physical Setting

The time is 8 A.M. We see the teacher in the classroom preparing for the reading period, which is the first activity for the morning. At this time he is both determining which children will need specific skill instruction by noting their progress in his recording device and planning the independent activities the other children will pursue while he is working with the skill groups.

As we enter the classroom we notice several safety valves. The west side of the room contains a number of science experiments. For instance, an aquarium is set up and there are a number of books about fish and fish care nearby, together with some specific instructions for experiments the children may wish to pursue dealing with fish life and care. Similarly, there is a terrarium and an incubator in the same section of the room, with easy books and dittoed instructions regarding specific reading activities to be completed that deal with these areas. Near the northwest corner there are a number of shoe boxes, each with the name of a child printed on the side. Inside these boxes are corrected papers and specific assignments the teacher has prepared for each child. These are used as part of the independent activities to be carried out by each child when he or she is not involved in a skill group.

The northeast corner of the room has been separated from the rest of the room by large bookcases, thereby leaving a space that is physically separated from the rest of the room. It is here that the reading skill lessons are taught.

Against the east wall there is a recreational reading center. It is composed of a small table with many attractive books scattered on it, a bulletin board describing favorite books, a small rug on the floor, and some throw pillows. Here the children can come to select and read books of their choice.

In the southeast corner and extending down the south wall is a long table and ten small chairs. On the table is a tape recorder and a set of ten earphones. Here the children come to do independent listening activities.

The children's desks are set up in irregular clusters in the center of the classroom. The teacher's desk is near the southwest corner of the room. Just behind the desk is an activity bulletin board relating to the class study of regional geography. This bulletin board also invites pupil participation, since specific directions are provided regarding independent activities relating to geography.

## The Reading Period

The children arrive at 8:45 A.M. Following the short opening exercises, the teacher begins the reading period. As the children enter the room they find on their desks packets of materials that the teacher has prepared in advance as part of the independent work to be completed while he teaches the skill groups. In the packets are such activities as mathematics and social studies. The packets of certain children may also contain some specific materials planned to provide practice with a skill taught to these children yesterday. In accordance with the management guidelines already described, the assignments have been carefully planned by the teacher and are relevant to the children.

The teacher first gives directions regarding the independent activities. He rapidly, but thoroughly, goes through the common material found in the packets and describes what should be done and what can be learned or practiced. He also provides instructions regarding any special assignments he may have included for specific individuals. He reminds the children of who the buffer is and indicates some of the safety valve activities available around the room, such as the ongoing projects in science, regional geography, listening, and recreational reading. He also reminds children that they may use this time to work on projects relating to the sharing of books they have been reading as well as checking their shoe boxes for the special activities included there.

The teacher then calls the names of Sam and Mike and takes them to the reading corner. He immediately begins to teach these children visual discrimination of geometric figures. Meanwhile, the rest of the children begin work on the independent work found in their packets. There is general movement around the room, but it is purposeful rather than aimless. If questions arise they are directed to the buffer. When a child comes in late the buffer quickly goes over to the latecomer and explains what is to be done in the independent activities. The children do their independent work in no particular order, but they work through it steadily. As they complete assignments, they select one of the many safety-valve activities and continue to work diligently.

## ● CHAPTER SUMMARY

The preceding illustration serves three purposes. First, it shows how this text's basic strategy regarding systematic skill instruction can be applied in the classroom. Second, it illustrates how the principles of classroom management can be implemented. Finally, it shows how a teacher structures a classroom situation to meet the specific needs of the children.

There are many variations, however, that could be employed in implementing this book. This particular example was effective in the situation described because it met the needs of the children and fit the desires and style of the teacher. Other teachers may wish to use the skills program with a basal text approach to instruction, with a language experience approach, or with some other approach that is suitable to the needs of the pupils and that fits the local teaching conditions and style of the teacher.

# 6
# USING THIS BOOK EFFECTIVELY

"The time has come," the Walrus said,
   "To talk of many things:
Of shoes—and ships—and sealing wax—
   Of cabbages—and kings—
And why the sea is boiling hot—
   And whether pigs have wings."

LEWIS CARROLL,
*"The Walrus and the Carpenter"*

This book is a resource tool for planning and teaching the basic reading skills; consequently, it contains numerous aids for systematically diagnosing and teaching the skills needed to achieve functional literacy. To reap its full benefits, however, you must be aware of the resources it offers and be oriented to their uses.

## THIS BOOK IN PERSPECTIVE

This book provides multiple resources for teaching the word recognition and comprehension skills that are essential for achieving functional literacy. Skill instruction, however, is only one aspect of a well-rounded reading program; the teacher must provide the other vital components. Although it is not the purpose here to describe these other components in detail, the following list suggests some activities that can be coordinated with this text to create a total reading program.

1. Provide for much oral sharing of experiences through activities such as Show-and-Tell.
2. Develop games that involve learners in oral language activities.
3. Read and discuss storybooks with children frequently.
4. Have many books and other reading matter of interest to the learners scattered about the room and encourage them to use these.
5. Take field trips and encourage children to share these experiences with each other.
6. Use films and other media to expand the learner's horizons and to develop new concepts.
7. Play games requiring learners to manipulate such concepts as up, down, big, small, tall, short, bright, dull, and so on.
8. Encourage learners to tell each other about the books they have particularly enjoyed.
9. Dramatize favorite stories.
10. Make puppets of favorite story characters or make up stories to go with the puppets.
11. Let learners make up and tell their own stories.
12. Do much reading of rhythmical, rhyming poetry.
13. Make up riddles and stories together and share these with each other.
14. Devise choral speaking activities, especially with rhyming poems, riddles, and so on.
15. Do a lot of role playing involving common social situations.
16. Re-create difficult human situations and discuss appropriate emotional responses for these situations.
17. Do a considerable amount of art work, especially that relating to reading (e.g., illustrate favorite stories or write and illustrate stories made up by individuals or by the class).
18. Plan activities to help children use effectively such parts of books as the table of contents, the glossary, and so on.
19. Help children develop study skills and study habits.
20. Create a total learning environment in which reading plays an integral role in all subject areas.

## THE ORGANIZATION OF THE SKILLS

The core of this text is made up of the skill modules that begin with the next chapter. Each module encompasses a single skill objective to be mastered on the road to functional literacy. Before using them, however, the reader should know how they are organized.

There are 218 modules representing both word identification and comprehension skills. They are divided into eight clusters or groups, with each cluster containing both word identification and comprehension skills of about the same difficulty level. The skills contained in Cluster I therefore are of the lowest level, whereas the skills in Cluster VIII are taught as the child nears functional literacy.

Within each cluster the skills are organized in "streams" consistent with the Chapter 2 description of the skill hierarchy. Consequently, every cluster contains sight word skills (SW) and word analysis skills (WA), both of which relate to the general category of word identification, and three streams of comprehension skills: information gathering (IG), manipulative thinking (MT), and evaluative thinking (ET).

Normally each cluster contains several skills in any given stream. For instance, in Cluster I there are eighteen sight word skills, twenty-one word analysis skills, and so on. Each skill in a stream is numbered in terms of its sequence, with the first skill being number 1, the second number 2, and so on. Each skill is then given an additional number to designate the cluster. Consequently, the skill numbered I-SW-1 is the first sight word skill in Cluster I, and III-MT-5 is the fifth manipulative thinking skill in Cluster III. The book's value will be enhanced if you can use the numbering system with understanding and confidence.

## THE RESOURCES OFFERED BY THIS BOOK

This book provides three basic kinds of resources. They are diagnostic aids, teaching suggestions, and general resources.

### The Diagnostic Aids

Two kinds of diagnostic aids are provided, a placement test and individual pre- and posttests. The placement test, which is found in Appendix C, consists of a teacher's edition and a pupil's edition. When used correctly it will help you get a quick idea of where each child is in the skill hierarchy. It is a time-saver that allows you to start pretesting each child at a point close to where the learner is likely to need help. This eliminates the necessity of starting at the beginning of the hierarchy and pretesting each and every skill until an unlearned skill is found. For instance, if you are teaching a third grade, you probably will have some children who are already at functional literacy or fairly close to it. If you were to follow a strict policy of pretesting each and every skill from the very beginning until each child's particular skill need was found, most of the school year might be spent just in pretesting. The placement test is designed to prevent this by cutting the pretest time to a manageable segment.

The placement test, unlike the individual pretests, is a group test that can be administered to all students in one or two sittings. It represents skills selected at random from each cluster of word identification skills and adjusted to accommodate a paper-and-pencil situation. It is administered by giving each child a pupil's edition of the test and having him or her respond to the directions you read aloud from the teacher's edition. The test is then corrected using the guidelines provided to determine approximately where each child lies in the skill hierarchy.

Let us consider an example. Sam, for instance, made the following pattern of errors on the placement test:

| | |
|---|---|
| Cluster I | 0 |
| Cluster II | 0 |
| Cluster III | 1 |
| Cluster IV | 1 |
| Cluster V | 3 |
| Cluster VI | 5 |
| Cluster VII | 8 |
| Cluster VIII | 9 |

Looking at the pattern of errors, we see that Sam had little or no difficulty with the items in Clusters I through IV. We can assume therefore that he probably already possesses the skills taught in those clusters and that we need not pretest him on these. Beginning in Cluster V, however, Sam exhibits a pattern of steadily increasing difficulty. Consequently, we can assume that Sam's skill proficiency takes him only through Cluster IV; we will have to pretest him on each separate word identification and comprehension skill beginning in Cluster V to determine his specific needs. The placement test therefore provides a quick and efficient way to minimize the amount of time spent pretesting. Therefore it is a valuable tool.

There are, however, warnings to be kept in mind when using the placement test. First, it is not a precise instrument, nor is it a standardized test. It is, rather, a guide that you should use flexibly and cautiously to decide where to begin pretesting. Second, because it is not a precise instrument, you should score the child low when there is doubt regarding his or her exact level of skill proficiency. For instance, if Sam's pattern of errors had included five errors in Cluster IV, with everything else remaining the same, the pretesting should probably begin with that cluster to make sure that he has indeed mastered each of these skills. It is always safer to go too low and be sure than to go too high and miss some crucial skills. Third, the placement test should be administered at a steady pace, with no assistance provided other than that specified in the directions. If certain children cannot keep pace and plead with you to slow down, you should begin pretesting them at the point where the pace became too swift for them. Such student behavior invariably signals the beginning of frustration; to determine that point is, after all, the purpose of the test. Fourth, because you are purposely scoring low, you may begin pretesting in a cluster that is too easy for the child. This is to be expected and is neither a cause for alarm nor a weakness in the test. The idea is to save time by not testing those clusters of skills we are sure the child knows but still to start low enough so that nothing essential is missed. Consequently, if a child pretests out of the cluster you begin with, simply go on to the next and pretest there. Fifth, and finally, you should not make diagnostic judgments regarding specific skill needs on the basis of the placement test. The placement test is designed only to help you know where to begin pretesting; its very design prohibits effective diagnosis for specific skill difficulty. Consequently, use it only to place children in clusters of skills; use the pretests to determine specific skill needs.

The placement test, then, is a time-saving device to help in placing children efficiently and quickly in the clusters of word identification and comprehension skills. Although it is not a precise diagnostic instrument, it is a handy tool for making an initial placement and should be used as such.

A second diagnostic aid is the individual pre- and posttests at the head of each skill module. Once you have determined a child's approximate skill level using the placement test, you start pretesting on the first skill in that cluster. If he or she performs at or above the criterion for mastery on that test, the next skill should be taken up. The process should be repeated until the child encounters an objective he or she is unable to perform satisfactorily. At this point the skill instruction for that child begins.

For each pretest the directions, criterion for mastery, and specific test items are specified. You need do little more than prepare the necessary materials and administer the test to the learner according to the directions. In this sense this text provides an invaluable diagnostic resource. Nevertheless several words of caution should be noted about pretesting. First, you should make the situation as nonintimidating as possible by explaining frankly that the aim is to find out how best to help each learner, by minimizing the tendency of learners to compare their performances with each other and by conducting the pretests in a routine, matter-of-fact manner. Second, the teacher should be sure that the pretest items are appropriate for the experience backgrounds and dialects of the learners. It is impossible to foresee all the situations in which the pretests will be used. Therefore you should not hesitate to use the pretest as a model for building another, more appropriate one if this seems necessary. Third, some pretests can be administered simultaneously to numbers of learners whereas most must be individually administered. Those administered to groups should be conducted to ensure that you are determining the learner's ability to perform the task and not his or her ability to follow the lead of another, more competent, peer. Finally, you are cautioned to take nothing for granted on the pretests. If you have any reason to doubt the learner's mastery of a particular task, it is always better to teach the skill and ensure mastery than to make a faulty assumption that will handicap the learner later when he or she encounters more sophisticated skills for which this one is a crucial prerequisite.

## The Teaching Suggestions

The teaching suggestions specified in each skill module constitute a major resource of this book. These include specifics for directing the learner's attention to the salient features of the skill task, descriptions of both a modeling and a discovery strategy for teaching the skill, multiple suggestions for helping the child practice the skill, techniques for reteaching any skill a learner fails to master in the first instructional situation, and suggestions for helping the child apply the skill in daily reading.

Using these suggestions effectively, however, requires an understanding of a storehouse objective. A storehouse objective is a skill module that contains a multitude of suggestions for teaching, reteaching, practicing, and applying a particular type of skill; it is a resource to be drawn on when teaching that type of skill.

The need for storehouse objectives arises because, although this book contains 218 objectives, there are only 30 distinctly different types of skills taught. For instance, in the visual stream of word identification, there are 55 objectives, but only 7 different types of skills: visual discrimination, visual memory, visual sequencing, naming letters, sight words, easily confused words, and language experience. To reprint the same multitude of instructional activities each time a higher-level visual discrimination skill appeared, for instance, would make for an extremely large book. Consequently, the first time a particular type of skill appears, all the instructional suggestions for teaching that skill are detailed. When the same type of skill appears again in later objectives, you are referred back to the original objective to select strategies and activities from the storehouse provided there. Although this system necessitates some flipping back and forth in the book, it is the only way to keep the book to a manageable size (and, more importantly, to a manageable cost). To help you understand the concept of storehouse modules, a complete list of storehouses is shown graphically in the chart on page 82 and inside the front cover; a list of all 218 objectives and the page location of their respective storehouse modules is provided in Appendix E; on the inside back cover is a list of the storehouse modules and their respective page numbers.

## General Resources

In addition to the diagnostic and teaching aids, this text also provides other kinds of resources.

As noted above, the chart of the storehouse modules is repeated inside the front cover and an index of the module page numbers is on the inside back cover.

The appendix provides other resources. Appendix A is a source list for obtaining workbooks, kits, and other useful practice material. Appendix B lists high-interest, easy-to-read books and sources of other lists for finding reading material that could be used independently. Appendix C contains the placement test described previously. Appendix D contains diagnostic charts of common reading skill difficulties and suggests which storehouse modules in this book could be used for correcting these deficiencies. As mentioned above, Appendix E lists all the skill modules and the location of their respective storehouses.

These resources are provided as a general support to your efforts to provide systematic skill instruction. It is hoped that they prove helpful.

# THE ORDERING OF THE STOREHOUSE MODULES

| | Sight words (SW) | Word analysis (WA) | Information gathering (IG) | Manipulative thinking (MT) | Evaluative thinking (ET) |
|---|---|---|---|---|---|
| CLUSTER I | I•SW•1 Visual discrim.<br>I•SW•2 Visual memory<br>I•SW•3 Naming<br>I•SW•6 Visual sequencing<br>I•SW•17 Easily confused letters and words | I•WA•1 Auditory memory<br>I•WA•4 Auditory closure<br>I•WA•5 Auditory discrim.<br>I•WA•9 Sound-symbol<br>I•WA•14 Context/phonics | I•IG•1 Content words<br>I•IG•2 Affix meaning<br>I•IG•3 Function words/relationships | I•MT•1 Classification<br>I•MT•2 Inference | I•ET•1 Judging content |
| CLUSTER II | II•SW•6 Sight words<br>II•SW•8 Language experience | II•WA•1 Auditory fusion<br>II•WA•18 Letter substitution<br>II•WA•25 Structural analysis | II•IG•4 Contextual prediction (context clues) | | |
| CLUSTER III | | | III•IG•4 Contextual prediction (word order)<br>III•IG•6 Factual recall | III•MT•2 Main idea | |
| CLUSTER IV | | | | | IV•ET•1 Assessing word choice |
| CLUSTER V | | | V•IG•4 Contextual prediction (punctuation) | | |
| CLUSTER VI | | VI•WA•1 Vowel generalizations | | | |
| CLUSTER VII | | VII•WA•1 Syllabication | VII•IG•5 Contextual prediction (intonation) | | |
| CLUSTER VIII | | | | | |

The resources of this book, coupled with the efforts of a sensitive, dedicated, and committed teacher, can result in highly effective skill instruction. The following step-by-step plan will aid in successfully implementing such instruction.

**Step 1.** The first step is to organize your class for efficient instruction, as described in Chapter 5. Unless the routines of effective management have been clearly established and both teacher and learners understand what is expected at any given time, skill instruction will bog down in aimless wandering and constant threats of disciplinary action. To avoid this you should take a considerable amount of time to establish firmly the needed routines and to acquaint the learners with how things are to be done. It is much better to delay the skills program for six weeks to be sure that it functions smoothly for the remaining 34 than to rush into it and then have it fall apart periodically because of management difficulties.

**Step 2.** The second step is to determine the level at which each learner is currently reading. It is essential to provide each learner with reading material commensurate with his or her ability. The skill program will fail if you demand that learners read material that is too difficult for them, since they will then become frustrated and build elaborate defense mechanisms justifying why they *should not* learn how to read. To determine reading levels use the suggestions in Chapter 5.

**Step 3.** Once you know the level at which each of the learners is currently reading, collect materials for a recreational reading program. The suggestions provided in Chapter 4 are helpful in this regard, as is the source list of appealing trade books found in Appendix B. As you gather these materials, create an enticing atmosphere in your classroom that reflects an emphasis on books and reading and begin implementing some of the Chapter 4 suggestions on activities that support the development of an interest in reading.

**Step 4.** As your classroom begins to get organized and as your recreational reading program gets underway, begin your skill diagnosis. Administer the placement test provided in Appendix C and, once you know each child's approximate skill level, begin pretesting each child at the appropriate cluster level.

**Step 5.** When you begin pretesting, you will need to have a record-keeping device ready. The suggestions provided in Chapter 5 will aid you in developing an efficient and manageable record system.

**Step 6.** When the initial pretests have been concluded and recorded, examine your record-keeping device to determine your initial skill groups. In the interest of efficiency you should strive for group instruction, rather than head-to-head instruction.

**Step 7.** You are now ready to initiate skill instruction. Using the skill groups identified in step 6, select one group for instruction. Locate in this book the page containing the objective that needs to be taught. Follow the suggestions provided in the skill modules and use the storehouse module to aid you in your planning.

**Step 8.** Once the child has finished practice, administer the posttest to ensure that he or she has now mastered the skill. The same guidelines outlined for the pretests in step 4 are appropriate for this task.

**Step 9.** Once the learner has successfully completed the posttest, you must ensure that he or she applies the skill in daily reading. This means that you must, in the days following the skill lesson, consciously structure experiences that help put the skill to work. For instance, the child can read a short story containing the skill or can be shown how it is used in today's social studies assignment. In any case the skill must be transferred from the isolated skill lesson to the learner's reading and the application suggestions provided in each skill module should be utilized.

**Step 10.** Any group will have some children who have mastered the skill and some who require more teaching. This poses a severe problem of organization since some learners are ready for the next skill and some are not. However, it is a problem you can handle. One alternative is to hold back the children who have mastered the skill until you have re-taught it to those needing extra help, at which time the whole group proceeds on together. Another alternative is to move ahead with those who have mastered the skill, holding back those who have not until the next group needing that skill comes along, at which time they join them. Finally, you can just form those who need extra help into a separate group. In any case, the situation requires considerable flexibility and organization. However, although it will seem a nuisance at times, the success of individualized skill instruction demands that each learner be taught what he or she needs to know at the time and not that you keep him or her with a particular group regardless of whether or not the skill has been mastered.

## A WEEK-BY-WEEK PLAN FOR IMPLEMENTATION

Because the implementation of individualized skill instruction is so complex, it is often helpful to think of it in terms of a week-by-week progression. Consequently, the following description may be helpful.

### Prior to the Opening of School

1. Develop many ongoing safety valve ideas.
2. Develop a basic plan for independent activity that will meaningfully involve the balance of the class while you are working with the skill groups.
3. Develop a system of record keeping that will ensure that the skill progress of each child is accurately recorded while not demanding an excess of teacher time.
4. Plan the physical organization of the room so that seating arrangement,

interest centers, and so on, effectively support your basic instructional plan.

5. Develop a plan for systematic positive reinforcement. How will pupils be rewarded for successful performances in reading?
6. Steal, beg, borrow, make, and buy any and all kinds of practice material; cut it up and file it according to skill objectives.
7. Steal, beg, borrow any and all types of reading material that could be used in a recreational reading program.

## The First Week of School

1. No formal reading instruction. Systematically teach the basic, general routines you want children to follow regularly and orient them to the management system you will be using.

## The Second Week of School

1. Teach children to use the safety valve activities independently.
2. Begin utilizing a buffer. Explain his or her function to pupils, supervise his or her work, and consciously strive to develop a positive class attitude toward the function of the buffer.
3. As the buffer gets used to his or her role. give the buffer the opportunity to operate independently while you administer the placement test.

## The Third Week of School

1. Initiate the basic plan of independent activities that will involve the pupils while you are working with skill groups. Isolate the routines upon which the success of the independent activities depend and systematically teach them.
2. Implement the plan for reinforcement.
3. Continue to develop the role of the buffer.
4. Encourage children to use the safety valve activities when they complete independent activities.
5. Determine each learner's current reading level.
6. Begin administering the pretests provided in this book. Be aware of the attention span of children and administer each day only as many pretests as the pupils can handle.

## The Fourth Week of School

1. Continue the previously established procedures relating to the basic independent activities, the safety valve activities, and the buffer.
2. Complete the pretests for the skill objectives.
3. Record the pretest performances on your record-keeping device. Determine the number of skill groups you will have initially.

4. Make sure that you are putting the recreational reading program into operation.

## The Fifth Week of School

1. On Monday teach one short skill group while the rest of the class does independent activities. Then spend the rest of the class supervising the independent activities. At the end of the class evaluate how the organization worked and plan necessary adjustments.
2. On Tuesday implement any adjustments in your management system resulting from the previous day's activity. Do not teach a skill group today. Concentrate on implementing the adjustments.
3. On Wednesday try another short skill lesson, evaluate, and make adjustments.

## The Sixth Week of School

1. If you feel that your organization is now thoroughly worked out, initiate the full program of independent activities and skill instruction. If the organization is not yet sound, continue to make adjustments until it is ready.

## ● A FINAL WORD

With the completion of this chapter you are ready to embark on the task of implementing skill instruction in reading. We hope that the resources of this book will assist you in this task. However, it is appropriate to point out once again that the success or failure of any reading program ultimately depends upon the manner in which a dedicated and sensitive teacher blends *all* resources together to forge a powerful program. We hope you use this book and other resources to create a program that

1. Accepts and capitalizes on the individual differences of children in a spirit of humanism.
2. Bases instruction on diagnosis of specific needs.
3. Ensures that each child acquires the basic reading skills needed to achieve functional literacy.
4. Provides direct and systematic instruction reflecting the principles of attending, highlighting, diminishing, responding, reinforcing, practicing, and applying.
5. Makes use of a variety of exciting and meaningful reading materials as a means for developing children who *do* read as well as children who *can* read.
6. Utilizes a classroom management system that expedites individualized instruction.

# THE SKILL MODULES

**TWO**

. . . there are always a certain number of children who learn
to read in much the same way that they learn to tell time,
navigate the streets of their own neighborhood or talk and play
games with each other. For these children, formal reading
methods are a waste of time. They tend merely to mechanize
and to devitalize the child's own creative power. *In most cases,
however, it is both possible and necessary to teach reading in
a highly conscious, purposeful and sequential manner.*[1]

JONATHAN KOZOL

[1]From "Free Schools Fail Because They Don't Teach," *Psychology Today*, **5**, April 1972, p. 30.

88 ●

# CLUSTER I

● **THE PERFORMANCE OBJECTIVE**

When given three geometric figures that are exactly alike and one that is clearly different, the learner will mark the one that is different.

● **THE PRETEST**

Direct the learner to indicate (mark or point to as appropriate) which figure in the following sets is different. The criterion for mastery is 80 percent.

| | | | |
|---|---|---|---|
| Set I | ○ ○ □ ○ | Set VI | ⬭ ⬭ ○ ⬭ |
| Set II | □ ○ □ □ | Set VII | ▽ △ △ △ |
| Set III | △ ○ ○ ○ | Set VIII | □ □ ▱ □ |
| Set IV | ○ ▱ ▱ ▱ | Set IX | ▱ ◇ ◇ ◇ |
| Set V | ○ ○ ○ ⬭ | Set X | ▭ □ □ ▭ |

● **DIRECTING THE LEARNER'S ATTENTION**

The purpose of this task is to teach the learner to discriminate visually among geometric forms. Much of a child's future success as a reader will depend upon his or her skill at spotting the visual characteristics that make one figure, letter, or word different from another. This objective is the first

● 89

in a series of visual discrimination tasks that ultimately will ensure that the learner can visually examine symbols and efficiently note the characteristics setting them apart.

To teach learners to discriminate visually among symbols, you must ensure that they have a concept for *different* and you must direct their attention by stating exactly what they are learning to do and by highlighting the visual characteristics that make one geometric form different from the others in any particular set. (In Set I, for instance, the points on the square could be highlighted to contrast with the curves of the circles.)

### • THIS IS A STOREHOUSE OBJECTIVE

The following instructional activities are your storehouse of techniques for developing skill in noting visual differences. This skill recurs in more sophisticated forms later in the skill hierarchy. The following activities are to be adapted and used with each of these as they occur.

### • TEACHING ACTIVITIES

*The modeling technique.* Draw enlarged forms of two of the figures (or letters or words) on a plain piece of paper, highlighting (with color or in some other way) the visual characteristics that set one symbol apart from the others in a set. Say, "These two figures are different. Watch me while I show you how I know that they are different." Point to each symbol in turn, direct the learner to the highlighting that emphasizes that symbol's unique visual characteristic, and say, "This one is different because it has . . . but this one does not." Have the learner mimic your actions and words with the first two symbols and with two new symbols that have the distinctive visual characteristics highlighted. If the child responds correctly, continue the process with other symbols included in the pretest, diminishing the amount of help you provide and the amount of highlighting with each sequence until he or she can respond successfully without any assistance.

*The discovery technique.* The principle to be discovered is that printed symbols have distinguishing visual characteristics that allow us to discriminate between them. Draw enlarged forms of the figures (or letters or words) on a plain piece of paper, highlighting (with color or in some other way) the visual characteristics that set one symbol apart from the others in a set. Point to the two symbols in turn and ask, "Does this look like this?" When the response is "No," say, "Look at each figure in turn and at the highlighting I have added and tell me *why* one is different." If the child responds correctly continue this questioning process with other symbols included in the pretest, diminishing the amount of highlighting with each sequence until he or she can respond successfully without any assistance. If the child does not respond correctly at any point, emphasize more directly the highlighting that distinguishes the visual forms and repeat the questioning process.

## • SUGGESTIONS FOR RETEACHING

If, after having been taught with either of the preceding techniques, the learner is unable to discriminate among the geometric forms, you should

1. Reteach the skill, using the alternate technique.
2. Be more specific in directing the learner's attention, ensuring that your highlighting is providing enough help in distinguishing the visual characteristics of each geometric figure.
3. Ensure that the learner has an adequate concept for the word *different*. If he or she does not, develop this concept using such three-dimensional objects as chairs, desks, balls, and blocks.
4. Go to I-SW-3 (naming geometric forms) and then return to this objective, because some learners who have trouble discriminating are aided if they know the names of the forms they are examining.

## • SUGGESTIONS FOR PRACTICE

Once discrimination of geometric forms has been taught successfully, use one or more of the following practice activities to solidify the skill.

1. Have learners match geometric forms, letters, and words. They draw a form, letter, or word from a grab bag and match it with individual cards in front of them.
2. Provide simple puzzles of forms, letters, or numerals or provide for experiences in assembling blocks to duplicate symbols.
3. Make up a jigsaw puzzle in which the pieces to be fitted are commonly confused forms, letters, or words. The learner must match the pieces to the appropriate place in the jigsaw puzzle.
4. Forms, letters, or words can be written on the chalkboard in arrangements similar to the following:

**b**    b   b   d   b

The learner is asked to find the one in the set that is different from the one to the left and to say how it is different.
5. The same activity as described in activity 4 can be varied by using different mediums for the activity. For instance, alphabet blocks, sandpaper letters, tagboard letters, and so on, can be used to give the learner the use of the tactile, as well as the visual, sense in assessing the differences between the letters.
6. Using two frequently confused forms, letters, or words, list them on the chalkboard in this fashion:

| | |
|---|---|
| was | saw |
| saw | was |
| saw | saw |
| was | was |
| was | saw |

Direct the learner to circle all the words in the two columns that are just like the first word in the left column and to draw a line under each word that is just like the first word in the right-hand column.

7. Use a list of words such as the following and direct the learner to draw a line under all the words in the list that are exactly alike except for the first letter:

cola    take    cook    make    sake    rake    fade

8. In an exercise similar to activity 7, use a list of words such as the following and direct the learner to draw a line under all the words on the list that are like the first word except for the letter at the end:

him    hat    hit    have    his

9. Have the learner find the form, letter, or word in a written series that is unlike the other words in the series.
10. Provide the learner with two parallel columns of words, letters, or forms in which the same words, letters, or forms are used but in a different order. Direct the learner to draw lines connecting the like words, forms, or letters in the two columns.

## • THE POSTTEST

The directions and criterion for mastery are the same as for the pretest.

| | | |
|---|---|---|
| Set I | □□○□ | |
| Set II | ○△△△ | |
| Set III | □□▽□ | |
| Set IV | ▭▭▭▭ | |
| Set V | ○◻◻◻ | |
| Set VI | △△△△ | |
| Set VII | △▽▽▽ | |
| Set VIII | ○○◯○ | |
| Set IX | □□◻□ | |
| Set X | ◇◇◇▱ | |

## • ENSURING TRANSFER

Learners will apply the skill in the more complex visual discrimination and visual memory tasks with which they work as they progress through the skill hierarchy. However, in addition to these applications, you should be sure that this visual discrimination skill is used during the routine daily activities of the classroom. Some suggested techniques are the following:

1. Have play blocks cut in the shape of forms, numerals, and letters; as the learner plays with these, ask him or her to pick out the different block from the group being played with.
2. During art have the learner work with paper cut in the shape of geometric forms, letters, or numerals and require that he or she pick out the different form from a group of forms.

### • THE PERFORMANCE OBJECTIVE

When given a few seconds to examine a geometric figure, the learner will reproduce from memory, to the satisfaction of the teacher, a figure just like it.

### • THE PRETEST

Prepare four flashcards, one with a square, one with a circle, one with a triangle, and one with a diamond. Flash each for the count of 1001, 1002, 1003. Then direct the learner to reproduce it. The criterion for mastery is teacher judgment concerning accuracy of lines and angles for each reproduction. Size is not a criterion. *Caution:* It is not necessary for the learner to name the geometric form.

### • DIRECTING THE LEARNER'S ATTENTION

The purpose of this task is to develop the learner's visual memory for geometric forms. Successful readers carry word images in their heads; they remember what words look like. This is the first in a series of objectives that create visual memory for printed symbols.

To teach a learner to remember the shape and form of geometric figures, you must be sure that he or she has mastered the previous skill on visual discrimination of geometric figures and you must direct the learner's attention by stating exactly what learning is to be done and by highlighting the visual characteristics of the geometric form to be remembered (see example in previous objective).

### • THIS IS A STOREHOUSE OBJECTIVE

The following instructional activities are your storehouse of techniques for developing skill in visual memory. This skill recurs in more sophisticated forms later in the hierarchy. The activities that follow are to be adapted and used with each of these as they occur.

### • TEACHING ACTIVITIES

*The modeling technique.* Start your instruction by using simpler forms and manipulative materials. For instance, use a one-line figure instead of a three-line figure and make the figures from clay, blocks, or other three-dimensional materials. Say, "I am going to look at this figure and try to remember its shape so that I can draw it when it is taken away. Watch me while I show you how I will remember this form." Point to the symbol's unique visual characteristics and say, "I am going to hold a picture in my mind of this form, remembering particularly that it has . . ." (state the visual characteristic). Then close your eyes, trace the form, and say out loud what it is about the form that you are trying to remember. Have the learner mimic your words and actions using the same figure. Then have the learner go through the same process with a different symbol. Repeat this process with additional symbols, with each symbol being a little more difficult. As the child begins to respond successfully, gradually replace the manipulative materials with symbols that have the visual characteristics highlighted with color. As the learner continues to respond successfully, diminish the color highlighting until she or he can remember the form without any assistance.

*The discovery technique.* Since this is a low-level memory skill, there is no principle to be discovered. However, you can use questions to help the learner determine a way to remember symbols. Start with the simpler symbols and manipulative materials just described. Say, "I am going to show you this figure (or letter or word), then I will take it away and I will ask you to draw it from memory. What will you have to remember about this symbol in order to draw it from memory?" If the child is unable to respond, direct attention to the visual characteristics of the form through the use of highlighting. Repeat the process as the learner proceeds from simple to more difficult figures, gradually diminishing the amount of highlighting and introducing two-dimensional figures until he or she is able to do the task as it is presented in the pretest.

### • SUGGESTIONS FOR RETEACHING

If, after having been taught with either of the preceding techniques, the learner is unable to reproduce the geometric forms, you should

1. Reteach the skill, using the alternate technique.
2. Simplify the early steps of instruction even more than you did and increase the amount of highlighting on the distinguishing characteristics that must be remembered.
3. Return to the previous skill and be sure that the learner has the prerequisite skill of being able to discriminate visually between geometric figures.

### • SUGGESTIONS FOR PRACTICE

Once memory of geometric forms has been taught successfully, use one or more of the following practice activities to solidify the skill.

1. Play a game with the learner in which you touch one object; she or he then touches that object and one more; the next learner touches both previous objects and one more; and so on, with each learner touching all the objects that were previously touched before adding a new object.
2. Play a game somewhat like television's Concentration, in which figures, letters, or words are placed on a table and covered up. The learner draws a card containing a figure, letter, or word from a box in front of him or her and must remember where the matching pair is located on the table. Begin simply, using just a few possibilities; add other figures, letters, or words as the learner becomes more proficient.

3. Put a group of figures, letters, or words on the chalkboard. Direct the learner to examine these and then to turn away from the board. You erase one figure. When the learner turns back, he or she must reproduce the figure, letter, or word you erased. Start simply, using just two possibilities, increasing the number as the learner becomes more proficient.

4. Using a tachistoscope or flashcards, show the learner a numeral and direct him or her to reproduce it from memory. If the learner can do that, repeat the process using two numerals in a sequence. Continue to increase the number of numerals the child is asked to reproduce as each level is met successfully.

## • THE POSTTEST
The pretest may be used as the posttest.

## • ENSURING TRANSFER
The learner will be applying this skill in learning the more complex visual memory tasks necessary for progress through the skill hierarchy. However, in addition to these applications, you should be alert for ways to point out the use of this visual memory skill during the routine daily activities of the classroom. Some suggested techniques follow:

1. Make visual memory a part of your art lessons by presenting learners with a visual stimulus (such as a geometric form, a letter, or a numeral) and having them reproduce these from memory, using a particular art technique (crayon, paint, paper cutout, collage, and so on).

2. When returning from a field trip or some other common activity, ask the learners to recall the shapes of what they saw, asking such questions as, "How many of you saw something that was shaped like the form I am holding up?"

## I•SW•3

## • THE PERFORMANCE OBJECTIVE
When shown a circle, square, triangle, diamond, and rectangle, the learner will point to and name each geometric form in turn.

## • THE PRETEST
Draw on separate cards a circle, a square, a triangle, a diamond, and a rectangle. Show each card to the learner in turn and ask him or her to give you the name for the form on the card. The criterion for mastery is 100 percent.

## • DIRECTING THE LEARNER'S ATTENTION
The purpose of this task is to teach the learner to associate a name with the various geometric forms. Later the child will be taught to associate names with numerals, letters, and, ultimately, words. At this stage of the reading process this skill is not nearly as crucial as visual discrimination

and visual memory, since it is possible to learn to read without having a name for the letters. Naming does, however, have two uses. First, knowing the names of the forms (or letters or numerals) is often an aid in discrimination. Second, communicating with the learner is easier if he or she knows the names of the forms (or letters or numerals) because you can simply name it rather than show which one you mean.

Naming is an association task in which the learner must connect the name with the visual form. To teach this skill you must be sure that the learner knows exactly what is to be learned and you must direct her or his attention by highlighting both the visual form and the sound of the name to which it is to be connected. (With a triangle, for instance, you might have the learner point to the three corners while simultaneously saying, "Triangle".)

## • THIS IS A STOREHOUSE OBJECTIVE

The following instructional activities are your storehouse of techniques for developing skill in naming symbols. This skill recurs in more sophisticated forms later in the skill hierarchy. The activities that follow are to be adapted and used with each of these as they occur.

## • TEACHING ACTIVITIES

*The modeling technique.* Using wooden block shapes of the geometric forms (or letters or numerals), tell the learner you are going to teach him or her to remember the name of each symbol and that you want him or her to watch and mimic your actions. Then pick up one of the symbols, point out its distinguishing visual characteristics (such as the three corners on the triangle or the two humps on the letter **m**,) and trace the symbol with your finger while simultaneously saying, "This is a triangle" (or, "This letter is **m**"). Have the learner mimic you, being sure that he or she is looking at the symbol while saying its name. This is a matter of rote learning and will require, for most learners, some degree of repetition. At each succeeding response, however, the amount of assistance should be diminished until the learner can do the task with an unhighlighted printed form of the symbol and without mimicking your actions. *Caution:* Symbols that are easily confused (such as the square and the rectangle or the letters **b** and **d**) should be taught initially at widely separate times. If the learner has persistent difficulty with these symbols, however, they can be taught together, with the strategy being one of highlighting the visual characteristics that set the two easily confused symbols apart (see Objective I-SW-17.

*The discovery technique.* Naming is basically a task of rote memory, with no real principle to be discovered. However, you can use questions to help the learner find a way to remember the names of the symbols. Start with the wooden block shapes already described. Say, "This is a _____. Look at the _____ as I say its name. Can you figure out a way to remember the name of this form (or letter or numeral)?" As the learner responds, direct attention to the visual characteristics of the form through the use of highlighting and be sure that he or she simultaneously looks at the symbol while saying its name. Move gradually from the wooden block shapes to printed forms of the symbol, diminishing the amount of highlighting until the learner is able to remember the symbol without assistance.

## • SUGGESTIONS FOR RETEACHING

If, after having been taught with either of the preceding techniques, the learner is unable to name the geometric figures, you should

1. Reteach the skill, using the alternate technique.
2. Emphasize more strongly the connection between the visual form and the sound of the name by ensuring that the learner is looking at the symbol while saying its name.
3. Emphasize the visual characteristics of the symbol by having the learner repeatedly trace the geometric form while saying its name.

## • SUGGESTIONS FOR PRACTICE

Once naming of geometric forms has been taught successfully, use one or more of the following practice activities to solidify the skill:

1. Games such as Climb the Ladder can be played, in which each rung has a symbol connected to it. The learner "climbs" the ladder rung by rung as he or she names each of the symbols in sequence.
2. Similar games can be devised that use other devices, such as adding cars to a train (each car having a new symbol) or putting leaves on a tree.
3. A form of the television game Concentration can be played in connection with this task. Prepare duplicate cards of five symbols. The ten cards are mixed and turned upside down. The learner turns over a card, names the symbol, and tries to match it by turning over the card that is its duplicate. *Caution:* Make sure the learner *names the symbol* when turning it over.
4. Games can be played in which symbols are placed on bowling pins. The learner rolls a ball at the pins, knocking down as many pins as possible. However, only those pins whose symbols the learner can name are counted in the score.
5. Place symbol cards on the seats of chairs arranged in a large circle. The learners march around the chairs in time to music, until the music stops. Then each must name the symbol on the seat of the chair next to where he or she stopped.
6. Seat the children in a circle, with one in the middle. Provide each learner with a symbol card. The child in the center calls out the names of two or three symbols and the learners having these letter cards change seats. The child in the middle also tries to get a seat; the one left standing calls the next symbol.

7. Make a pocket chart and provide the learners with symbol cards. Hold up a card (such as the letter a) and say, "This is the letter **a**. If you have a letter **a**, come place it in the same pocket where I put mine, and say the letter names as you do so." When all the pockets of the chart are filled, point to each pocket in turn, have the learner examine the symbol in that pocket, and have him or her name each symbol while looking at it.

8. Use the pupil's names to help practice letter names. For instance, place the names of the pupils on the chalkboard and say, "How many of our names have the letter **f** in them? Who can find a letter **f** in any of our names?" The learner goes to the board, underlines the letter **f** in as many names as he or she can find it, and says the letter name each time the letter is underlined.

## • THE POSTTEST

The pretest can be used as a posttest but the geometric forms should be shown in a different order.

## • ENSURING TRANSFER

The learner will be using this skill (particularly the naming of letters) while progressing through the skill hierarchy. However, in addition to these applications, you should be alert for ways to point out the use of the names during the routine daily activities of the classroom. Some suggested techniques follow:

1. Learners can be provided with symbol cards while waiting to be dismissed or while waiting to begin another activity; they proceed according to who has the symbol named by the teacher ("All those who have the letter **m** should go now").

2. Use the symbols as identifying marks around the room and direct children to these points by naming the symbol ("Jimmy, please get my book that has the triangle on the cover," or, "Mary, would you bring me the pile of papers that has the letter **m** on top?").

## I•SW•4

## • THE PERFORMANCE OBJECTIVE

When presented with a card having his or her name printed on it, the learner will point to and say his or her name.

## • THE PRETEST

Give the learner a card with his or her name printed on it. Tell him or her to point to the word printed on the card and to tell you what it says. The criterion for mastery is 100 percent.

## • DIRECTING THE LEARNER'S ATTENTION

The purpose of this task is to teach the learner to identify his or her name in print. This task will result in the child being able to read his or her own name, thereby providing the first word he or she can recognize and read instantly. This is basically the same task as I-SW-3, but focus is on the learner's name rather than on geometric figures. To teach this skill you must be sure that the learner knows exactly what is to be learned and you must direct attention by highlighting both the visual form of his or her name and the sound of the name to which it is to be connected. (With the name **Sue,** for instance, you might have the learner point out the sequence of letters while she simultaneously looks at the printed form and says, "Sue.")

### • TEACHING ACTIVITIES

This is a naming task similar to that described in I-SW-3, and you can adapt your teaching strategy from either the modeling technique or the discovery technique described in that objective.

### • SUGGESTIONS FOR RETEACHING

If, after having been taught with either the modeling or the discovery technique, the learner is unable to read his or her own name, you should

1. Reteach the skill, using the alternate technique.
2. Emphasize more heavily the connection between the visual form and the sound of the name by ensuring that the learner is looking at his or her name while saying it.
3. Emphasize the visual characteristics of the name by having the learner repeatedly trace his or her name while saying it.

### • SUGGESTIONS FOR PRACTICE

After teaching the learner to read his or her name, create practice activities to solidify the skill, using the suggestions provided in I-SW-3.

### • THE POSTTEST

The procedure and criterion for mastery are the same as for the pretest.

### • ENSURING TRANSFER

Although the learner will be reading his or her name frequently, you should use the suggestions in I-SW-3 to ensure that the learner is identifying the printed form of his or her name during the routine daily activities of the classroom.

## I•SW•5

### • THE PERFORMANCE OBJECTIVE

When given a list of five names of students in the class, the learner will identify her or his name by drawing a circle around it.

### • THE PRETEST

Prepare a multiple listing of pupil names in groups of five. Each learner is given a list containing his or her own name and is asked to point to it, say it, and draw a circle around it. The criterion for mastery is 100 percent.

### • DIRECTING THE LEARNER'S ATTENTION

The purpose of this task is to teach the learner to discriminate his or her name visually from other names. This is similar to I-SW-1 but with names rather than geometric forms. To teach this skill you must be sure that the learner knows exactly what is to be learned and you must direct attention by highlighting the visual characteristics that make the printed form of her or his name different from the printed form of other children's names. (For instance, the names **Meg** and **Margaret** can be discriminated by length, **Jack** and **Bill** can be discriminated by the different beginning letters, **John** and **June** can be discriminated by different last letters, and so on.)

### • TEACHING ACTIVITIES

This is a visual discrimination task similar to I-SW-1, and you can adapt your teaching strategy from either the modeling technique or the discovery technique described in that objective..

### • SUGGESTIONS FOR RETEACHING

If, after having been taught with either the modeling or the discovery technique, the learner is unable to discriminate his or her name from among other names, you should

1. Reteach the skill, using the alternate technique.
2. Be more specific in directing the learner's attention, being sure that your highlighting is providing enough help in distinguishing the visual characteristics of the learner's name.
3. Be sure that the learner recognizes his or her name in print and teach recognition of the name if he or she does not.
4. Return to earlier visual discrimination skills, being sure that the learner can do these tasks before asking him or her to discriminate among names.

### • SUGGESTIONS FOR PRACTICE

After successfully teaching the skill, create practice activities to solidify the skill, using the suggestions provided in I-SW-1.

### • THE POSTTEST

The pretest is repeated but the names are arranged in a different order.

### • ENSURING TRANSFER

Although the learner will be applying this visual discrimination skill while progressing to the more complex skills in the hierarchy, you should use the suggestions provided in I-SW-1 to be sure that the skill is used during the routine daily activities of the classroom.

● **THE PERFORMANCE OBJECTIVE**

When presented with a card having his or her name printed on it, the learner will point to the first letter and to the last letter in his or her name.

● **THE PRETEST**

Give the learner a card with his or her name printed on it. Direct the learner to point to the first letter and the last letter in the name. The criterion for mastery is 100 percent. *Caution:* You cannot expect the learner to name the letters, since the naming skill has not yet been taught.

● **DIRECTING THE LEARNER'S ATTENTION**

The purpose of this task is to teach the learner the left-to-right sequence of letters in words. To read successfully the learner must be oriented in terms of the visual sequence one follows when reading—from the front of the book to the back, from the top of the page to the bottom, and from the left of a word to the right. This is the first of a series of tasks that creates this sense of visual sequencing in reading.

To teach a learner to sequence visually from left to right, you must be sure that he or she has a concept for *first* and *last* and you must direct attention by stating exactly what is to be learned and by highlighting the left-to-right sequence of letters in the name. (With the name **Mary**, for instance, you might have the learner point to the first letter and then move his or her finger in a physical left-to-right sweep under the word until he or she is pointing to the last letter.)

● **THIS IS A STOREHOUSE OBJECTIVE**

The following instructional activities are your storehouse of techniques for developing skill in visual sequencing. This skill recurs in more sophisticated forms later in the hierarchy. The teaching activities that follow are to be adapted and used with each of these as they occur.

● **TEACHING ACTIVITIES**

*The modeling technique.* Draw an enlarged form of the learner's name on a plain piece of paper, highlighting (with color or in some other way) the first and last letters in her or his name and the left-to-right direction to be taken in examining it. Say, "We always look at words in the same way. We start here (point to the first letter) and move in this direction to here (point to the last letter). Watch me while I show you how my eyes move from the first letter in the word to the last letter in the word here and then I'll ask you to do the same thing." After demonstrating in this fashion, have the learner mimic your actions of moving your finger from the left of the word to the right as you point out the first and last letters. In subsequent sequences gradually diminish the amount of highlighting on the printed form of the learner's name and the amount of verbal assistance you provide until she or he is able to point out the first and last letters without any assistance.

*The discovery technique.* Provide the learner with an enlarged form of her or his name in which the visual sequence has been highlighted as already described. Say, "In the past when I have written words on the blackboard, I have always shown it to you by moving my finger under it like this (demonstrate a left-to-right movement). Now look at your name and the way in which I have highlighted certain things. As I say your name, I am going to move my finger under the word in this direction. Can you figure out why I do that?" Your intention here is for the learner, with the help of your questions and the highlighting you have provided on the word, to discover the principle that our eyes move from left to right in visually examining a word.

● **SUGGESTIONS FOR RETEACHING**

If, after having been taught with either the modeling or the discovery technique, the learner is unable to point to the first and last letters in his or her name, you should

1. Reteach the skill, using the alternate technique.
2. Be more specific in directing the learner's attention, being sure that your highlighting is providing enough help in directing him or her to the left-to-right sequence.
3. Ensure that the learner has an adequate concept for the words *first* and *last*, teaching these terms if he or she does not.
4. Teach the concept of *left* and *right* and then reteach this skill, using the newly learned terms as well as the highlighting techniques already described.

● **SUGGESTIONS FOR PRACTICE**

Once visual sequencing of the learner's name has been successfully taught, use one or more of the following practice exercises to solidify the skill.

1. Make separate cards for each letter in the learner's name. Scramble these and direct the learner to put them back in the right order to form his or her name while saying, "First letter, other letters, last letter."
2. Write a word on a card or on the chalkboard, leaving off either the first or last letter. The learner is directed to print the missing letter in the proper position, saying, "First letter . . ." or, "Last letter. . . ."
3. Use puzzles in which the learner must trace a pattern following numbers or letters. Always have the pattern in such activities move from top to bottom and from left to right to establish the sequencing responses desired.
4. Prepare a set of pictures in which direction is clearly indicated. Direct

the learners to find something in the pictures that is at the top, at the bottom, going down, going up, going from left to right, and so on.

5. Give the learner sets of pictures in which each picture tells part of a story. Comics are useful for this activity. Scramble the pictures and then direct the learner to arrange the pictures to tell the story. Be sure that he or she arranges the pictures in a top-to-bottom and left-to-right sequence.

### • THE POSTTEST

The procedure and criterion for mastery are the same as for the pretest.

### • ENSURING TRANSFER

The learner will be using this skill while progressing to the more complex visual skills in the hierarchy. However, in addition to these applications, you should be sure that this visual-sequencing skill is used during the routine daily activities in the classroom. Some suggested techniques follow:

1. Any time there is an opportunity to display art work or other learner products, place them on the chalkboard, starting at the left and moving to the right. When discussing these with learners, discuss the one at the left first and progress to the right, emphasizing that movement with a physical motion of your hand in the left-to-right direction.
2. When placing directions on the chalkboard or when writing charts with learners, emphasize both the top-to-bottom sequence and the left-to-right sequence by pointing these out to the learners. Look for opportunities for eliciting learner responses, such as having them go to the chart to point to the first word, the last word, the first letter in a certain word, the last letter in a certain word, and so on.
3. When reading stories to children or when sharing picture books with them, point out the front-to-back, top-to-bottom, left-to-right directions and look for ways to elicit learner responses to sequencing as they share these stories with you.
4. Make frequent use of a wall pocket chart in which the pockets are arranged in rows. Have children use the pocket chart, being sure that they always begin at the top and move to the right across the rows.
5. Use a calendar to apply the left-to-right system by marking off the days in each week.

## I•SW•7

### • THE PERFORMANCE OBJECTIVE

When given a few seconds to examine his or her name, the learner will reproduce it from memory to the satisfaction of the teacher.

### • THE PRETEST

Print the learner's name on a card, flash it to him or her for the count of three and direct the learner to reproduce it. The criterion for mastery is teacher judgment regarding the accuracy of the reproduction. Size is not a criterion.

● **DIRECTING THE LEARNER'S ATTENTION**

The purpose of this task is to develop the learner's visual memory for his or her name. This is similar to I-SW-2. To teach this skill you must be sure that the learner knows exactly what is to be learned and you must direct attention by highlighting the visual characteristics of the printed form of his or her name. (See the examples provided in the previous module.)

● **TEACHING ACTIVITIES**

This is a visual memory task similar to that described in I-SW-2, and you can adapt your teaching strategy from either the modeling technique or the discovery technique described in that objective.

● **SUGGESTIONS FOR RETEACHING**

If, after having been taught with either the modeling or the discovery techniques, the learner is unable to reproduce his or her name, you should

1. Reteach the skill, using the alternate technique.
2. Be more specific in directing the learner's attention, being sure that your highlighting is providing enough help in distinguishing the visual characteristics of the name to be remembered.
3. Return to the previous two skills and be sure that the learner recognizes his or her name in print and can discriminate the name from among other names before requiring the learner to complete the more complex task of reproducing his or her name in response to a visual stimulus.

● **SUGGESTIONS FOR PRACTICE**

After successfully teaching the learner how to reproduce his or her name, create practice activities to solidify the skill, using the suggestions provided in I-SW-2.

● **THE POSTTEST**

The pretest may be used also for the posttest.

● **ENSURING TRANSFER**

Although the learner will be writing his or her name from memory frequently while progressing through school, you should also use the suggestions provided in I-SW-2 to be sure that the learner is remembering the form of his or her name during the routine daily activities of the classroom.

# I•SW•8

● **THE PERFORMANCE OBJECTIVE**

When given three letters that are exactly alike and one that is clearly different, the learner will mark the one that is different.

## • THE PRETEST

Direct the learner to indicate (mark or point to as appropriate) which letter in the following sets is different. The criterion for mastery is 80 percent.

| Set I   | g | g | w | g |     | Set VI   | x | x | x | c |
|---------|---|---|---|---|-----|----------|---|---|---|---|
| Set II  | S | a | a | a |     | Set VII  | d | r | d | d |
| Set III | e | y | e | e |     | Set VIII | o | o | j | o |
| Set IV  | m | m | m | l |     | Set IX   | z | z | z | x |
| Set V   | b | v | b | b |     | Set X    | s | s | S | s |

## • DIRECTING THE LEARNER'S ATTENTION

The purpose of this task is to teach the learner to discriminate visually among clearly different letters. This is similar to I-SW-1, but with finer discriminators. To teach this skill you must be sure that the learner knows exactly what is to be learned and you must highlight the visual characteristics that make one letter different from others in any particular set. (In Set I, for example, the tails of the g's could be highlighted to contrast with the absence of tails on the **w**.)

## • TEACHING ACTIVITIES

This is a visual discrimination task similar to that described in I-SW-1, and you can adapt your teaching strategy from either the modeling technique or the discovery technique described in that objective.

## • SUGGESTIONS FOR RETEACHING

If, after having been taught with either the modeling or the discovery technique, the learner is unable to discriminate among the letters, you should

1. Reteach the skill, using the alternate technique.
2. Be more specific in directing the learner's attention, being sure that your highlighting is providing enough help in distinguishing the visual characteristics of each letter.
3. Return to I-SW-1, being sure that the learner has a clear understanding of the word *different* and that he or she can discriminate among geometric forms.
4. Go to I-SW-11 (naming letters) and then return to this objective, because some learners who have trouble discriminating are aided if they know the names of the letters they are examining.

## • SUGGESTIONS FOR PRACTICE

After successfully teaching how to discriminate among letters, create practice activities to solidify the skill, using the suggestions provided in I-SW-1.

## • THE POSTTEST

The directions and criterion for mastery are the same as for the pretest.

| Set I | t | t | T | t | | Set VI | v | b | b | b |
| Set II | b | b | b | i | | Set VII | l | l | l | m |
| Set III | u | u | j | u | | Set VIII | y | e | y | y |
| Set IV | r | d | r | r | | Set IX | w | w | q | w |
| Set V | c | c | c | x | | Set X | a | s | s | s |

### • ENSURING TRANSFER

Although the learner will be applying this visual discrimination skill while progressing to the more complex skills in the hierarchy, you should also use the suggestions provided in I-SW-1 to be sure that he or she is discriminating among letters during the routine daily activities of the classroom.

## I•SW•9

### • THE PERFORMANCE OBJECTIVE

When presented with a card having a letter printed on it, the learner will point to the left, right, top, and bottom parts of the letter.

### • THE PRETEST

Give the learner a card that has a large letter printed on it. Direct him or her to point in turn to the first (or left) part of the letter, to the last (or right) part, to the top part, and to the bottom part. The criterion for mastery is 100 percent. *Caution:* You cannot expect the learner to name the letters at this time, because the names of the letters have not yet been taught.

The letters to be tested are as follows:

g    d    m    j    s    y    u    b    p    o

### • DIRECTING THE LEARNER'S ATTENTION

The purpose of this task is to teach the learner how to examine letters, particularly in terms of left-to-right and top-to-bottom sequencing. This is a visual sequencing task similar to I-SW-6. To teach this skill you must be sure that the learner knows exactly what is to be learned and you must direct attention by highlighting the left, right, top, and bottom of each letter. (With the letter **d,** for instance, you would highlight the ball on the left, the stick on the right, where the ball rests on the line at the bottom, and the top of the stick.)

### • TEACHING ACTIVITIES

This is a visual sequencing task similar to that described in I-SW-6, and you can adapt your teaching strategy from either the modeling technique or the discovery technique that is described in that objective.

### • SUGGESTIONS FOR RETEACHING

If, after having been taught with either the modeling or the discovery technique, the learner is unable to point to the left, right, top, and bottom of the letters, you should

1. Reteach the skill, using the alternate technique.
2. Be more specific in directing the learner's attention, being sure that your highlighting is providing enough help in directing attention to the top, bottom, left, and right parts of the letters.
3. Be sure that the learner has an adequate concept for the words *top, bottom, left* and *right*.
4. Return to simpler tasks of visual sequencing to be sure that he or she can do these tasks before asking the learner to complete the more complex task described in this objective.

## • SUGGESTIONS FOR PRACTICE

After successfully teaching the learner to point to the left, right, top, and bottom of the letters, create practice activities to solidify the skill, using the suggestions provided in I-SW-6.

Do your pupils see you as a positive person?

## • THE POSTTEST

The pretest may also be used as the posttest, but the letters should be presented in a different order.

## • ENSURING TRANSFER

The learner will be using this visual sequencing skill while progressing through the hierarchy of skills. However, in addition to these applications, you should also use the suggestions provided in I-SW-6 to be sure that this visual sequencing skill is used during the routine daily activities in the classroom.

# I•SW•10

## • THE PERFORMANCE OBJECTIVE

When given a few seconds to examine a letter, the learner will reproduce the letter from memory, to the satisfaction of the teacher.

## • THE PRETEST

Prepare ten flashcards, with each card having one letter of the following sequence: q, s, a, e, y, m, l, v, b. Flash each for the count of three. Then direct the learner to reproduce it. The criterion for mastery is teacher judgment concerning the accuracy of each reproduction. Size is not a criterion. *Caution:* It is *not* necessary at this time for the learner to be able to name the letters, because naming is tested later.

## • DIRECTING THE LEARNER'S ATTENTION

The purpose of this task is to develop the learner's visual memory for clearly different letters. This is basically the same task as I-SW-2, but the learner is being asked to remember letters rather than geometric forms. To teach this skill you must be sure that the learner knows exactly what is to be learned and you must direct attention by highlighting the visual characteristics of the letter to be remembered. (See the example in the previous objective.)

• **TEACHING ACTIVITIES**

This is a visual memory task similar to that described in I-SW-2, and you can adapt your teaching strategy from either the modeling technique or the discovery technique described in that objective.

• **SUGGESTIONS FOR RETEACHING**

If, after having been taught with either the modeling or the discovery technique, the learner is unable to reproduce the letters, you should

1. Reteach the skill, using the alternate technique.
2. Be more specific in directing the learner's attention, being sure that your highlighting is providing enough help in distinguishing the visual characteristics to be remembered.
3. Return to the previous skill and be sure that the learner is able to discriminate visually between clearly different letters.
4. Return to I-SW-2 and reteach the simpler task of remembering geometric forms before requiring the learner to complete the more complex task of remembering letters.

• **SUGGESTIONS FOR PRACTICE**

After successfully teaching how to remember the form of letters, create practice activities to solidify the skill, using the suggestions provided in I-SW-2.

• **THE POSTTEST**

The pretest may be used also as the posttest.

• **ENSURING TRANSFER**

Although the learner will be applying this visual memory skill while progressing to the more complex skills in the hierarchy, you should also use the suggestions provided in I-SW-2 to be sure that the learner is remembering letter forms during the routine daily activities of the classroom.

## I•SW•11

• **THE PERFORMANCE OBJECTIVE**

When presented with a random group of alphabet letters in lower case, the learner will point to and name each letter in turn.

• **THE PRETEST**

Direct the learner to point to and name each of the following letters. The criterion for mastery is 100 percent, with the rationale being that if the learner can name each of the letters selected randomly, the chances are good that he or she knows all the letters. However, if you note that a learner does not know all the letters despite a 100 percent performance on this task, you should test for all the letters and teach those not known, using the following suggestions.

m t w a s e b r o y

### • DIRECTING THE LEARNER'S ATTENTION

The purpose of this task is to teach the learner to associate a name with the lower case letters of the alphabet. This is basically the same task as I-SW-3, but with letters rather than geometric forms. To teach this skill you must be sure that the learner knows exactly what is to be learned and you must direct attention by highlighting both the visual form of the letter and the sound of the name to which it is to be connected. (With the letter s, for instance, you might have the learner point out the curves of the letter while simultaneously looking at the letter and saying, "This is the letter s."

### • TEACHING ACTIVITIES

This is a naming task similar to that described in I-SW-3, and you can adapt your teaching strategy from either the modeling technique or the discovery technique described in that objective.

### • SUGGESTIONS FOR RETEACHING

If, after having been taught with either the modeling or the discovery technique, the learner is unable to name the letters, you should

1. Reteach the skill, using the alternate technique.
2. Emphasize more strongly the connection between the visual form of the letter and the sound of the name by being sure that the learner is looking at the letter while saying its name.
3. Emphasize the visual characteristics of the letter by having the learner repeatedly trace the letter while saying its name.

### • SUGGESTIONS FOR PRACTICE

After successfully teaching the naming of letters, create practice activities to solidify the skill, using the suggestions provided in I-SW 3.

### • THE POSTTEST

The procedure and criterion for mastery are the same as for the pretest.

a s d f e g u h j i

### • ENSURING TRANSFER

Although the learner will be using letter names frequently while progressing through the hierarchy, you should also use the suggestions provided in I-SW-3 to be sure that he or she is naming letters during the routine daily activities of the classroom.

• **THE PERFORMANCE OBJECTIVE**

Given three numerals from 1 to 10 that are exactly alike and one that is clearly different, the learner will mark the one that is different.

• **THE PRETEST**

Direct the learner to indicate (mark or point to as appropriate) which numeral in the following sets is different. The criterion for mastery is 80 percent.

| | | | | | | | | | |
|---|---|---|---|---|---|---|---|---|---|
| Set I | 2 | 2 | 1 | 2 | Set VI | 9 | 2 | 2 | 2 |
| Set II | 0 | 9 | 9 | 9 | Set VII | 6 | 6 | 6 | 7 |
| Set III | 8 | 3 | 8 | 8 | Set VIII | 5 | 4 | 5 | 5 |
| Set IV | 5 | 4 | 4 | 4 | Set IX | 0 | 3 | 3 | 3 |
| Set V | 1 | 1 | 1 | 6 | Set X | 7 | 7 | 1 | 7 |

• **DIRECTING THE LEARNER'S ATTENTION**

The purpose of this task is to teach the learner to discriminate among numerals. This is basically the same task as I-SW-1, but the learner is to note differences in numerals rather than in geometric forms. To teach this skill you must be sure that the learner knows exactly what is to be learned and you must direct his or her attention by highlighting the visual characteristics that make one numeral different from the others in a particular set. (In Set I, for instance, the curves in the 2 could be highlighted to contrast to the straight line in the 1).

• **TEACHING ACTIVITIES**

This is a visual discrimination task similar to that described in I-SW-1, and you can adapt your teaching strategy from either the modeling technique or the discovery technique described in that objective.

• **SUGGESTIONS FOR RETEACHING**

If, after having been taught with either the modeling or the discovery technique, the learner is unable to discriminate among the numerals, you should

1. Reteach the skill, using the alternate technique.
2. Be more specific in directing the learner's attention, being sure that your highlighting is providing enough help in distinguishing the visual characteristics of each numeral.
3. Return to the previous discrimination skills, being sure that the learner has a clear understanding of the term *different* and that he or she can discriminate among geometric forms and among clearly different letters.
4. Go to I-SW-15 (naming numerals) and then return to this objective, since some learners who have trouble discriminating are aided if they know the names of the numerals they are examining.

## • SUGGESTIONS FOR PRACTICE

After successfully teaching how to differentiate among numerals, create practice activities to solidify the skills, using the suggestions provided in I-SW-1.

## • THE POSTTEST

The procedure and criterion for mastery are the same as on the pretest.

| Set I   | 1 | 1 | 7 | 1 | Set VI   | 6 | 6 | 6 | 1 |
|---------|---|---|---|---|----------|---|---|---|---|
| Set II  | 3 | 0 | 0 | 0 | Set VII  | 4 | 5 | 5 | 5 |
| Set III | 4 | 5 | 4 | 4 | Set VIII | 3 | 8 | 3 | 3 |
| Set IV  | 7 | 7 | 7 | 6 | Set IX   | 9 | 0 | 0 | 0 |
| Set V   | 2 | 9 | 9 | 9 | Set X    | 1 | 1 | 2 | 1 |

## • ENSURING TRANSFER

Although the learner will be applying this visual discrimination skill while progressing to the more complex skills in the hierarchy, you should also use the suggestions provided in I-SW-1 to be sure that he or she is discriminating among numerals during the routine daily activities of the classroom.

# I•SW•13

## • THE PERFORMANCE OBJECTIVE

When given a few seconds to examine a numeral, the learner will reproduce it from memory, to the satisfaction of the teacher.

## • THE PRETEST

Prepare ten flashcards, with each card having one numeral in the sequence from 1 to 10. Flash each card in random order for the count of three and direct the learner to reproduce it. The criterion for mastery is teacher judgment concerning the accuracy of each reproduction. Size is not a criterion. *Caution:* It is not necessary for the learner to be able to name the numerals since naming is tested later in the hierarchy of skills.

## • DIRECTING THE LEARNER'S ATTENTION

The purpose of this task is to develop the learner's visual memory for numeral forms. This is basically the same task as I-SW-2, but the learner is being asked to remember numerals rather than geometric forms. To teach this skill you must be sure that the learner knows exactly what is to be learned and you must direct attention by highlighting the visual characteristics of the numeral to be remembered. (See the example in the previous objective.)

## • TEACHING ACTIVITIES

This is a visual memory task similar to that described in I-SW-2, and you can adapt your teaching strategy from either the modeling technique or the discovery technique described in that objective.

If, after having been taught with either the modeling or the discovery technique, the learner is unable to reproduce the numerals, you should

1. Reteach the skill, using the alternate technique.
2. Be more specific in directing the learner's attention, being sure that your highlighting is providing enough help in distinguishing the visual characteristics to be remembered.
3. Return to the previous skill and be sure that the learner is discriminating between numerals.
4. Return to I-SW-2 and reteach the simpler task of remembering geometric forms before requiring the learner to complete the more complex task of remembering numerals.

### • SUGGESTIONS FOR PRACTICE

After successfully teaching how to remember the form of numerals, create practice activities to solidify the skill, using the suggestions provided in I-SW-2.

### • THE POSTTEST

The pretest may also be used as the posttest.

### • ENSURING TRANSFER

Although the learner will be applying this visual memory skill while progressing to the more complex skills in the hierarchy, you should also use the suggestions provided in I-SW-2 to be sure that he or she is remembering numeral forms during the routine daily activities of the classroom.

## I•SW•14

### • THE PERFORMANCE OBJECTIVE

When presented with a card having a numeral printed on it, the learner will point to the left, right, top, and bottom parts of the numeral.

### • THE PRETEST

Give the learner a card that has a large numeral printed on it. Direct him or her to point in turn to the first (or left) part of the numeral, to the last (or right) part, to the top part, and to the bottom part. The criterion for mastery is 100 percent. *Caution:* You cannot expect the learner to name the numerals at this time, since the names of numerals have not yet been taught.

The numerals to be tested follow:

16   5   19   11   2   4   13   7   12   15

### • DIRECTING THE LEARNER'S ATTENTION

The purpose of this task is to teach the learner how to examine numerals, particularly in terms of left-to-right and top-to-bottom sequencing. This is a visual sequencing task similar to I-SW-6. To teach this skill you must be sure that the learner knows exactly what is to be learned and you must direct his or her attention by highlighting the left, right, top, and bottom of each numeral. (With the numeral 16, for instance, you might highlight the 1, the 6, the loop at the bottom of the 6, and the "flag" on the top of the 1.

## • TEACHING ACTIVITIES

This is a visual sequencing task similar to that described in I-SW-6, and you can adapt your teaching strategy from either the modeling technique or the discovery technique described in that objective.

## • SUGGESTIONS FOR RETEACHING

If, after having been taught with either the modeling or the discovery technique, the learner is unable to point to the left, right, top, and bottom of the numerals, you should

1. Reteach the skill, using the alternate technique.
2. Be more specific in directing the learner's attention, making sure that your highlighting is providing enough help in directing him or her to the top, bottom, left, and right parts of the numeral.
3. Be sure that the learner has an adequate concept for the words *top*, *bottom*, *left*, and *right*, teaching the meaning of these words if necessary.
4. Return to I-SW-6 and reteach the simpler task of pointing to the first and last letters in the child's name before asking for completion of the more complex task described in this objective.

## • SUGGESTIONS FOR PRACTICE

After successfully teaching the learner to point to the left, right, top, and bottom parts of numerals, create practice activities to solidify the skill, using the suggestions provided in I-SW-6.

## • THE POSTTEST

The pretest may also be used for the posttest but the numerals should be presented in a different order.

## • ENSURING TRANSFER

The learner will be using this visual sequencing skill while progressing through the hierarchy of skills. However, in addition to these applications you should also use the suggestions provided in I-SW-6 to make sure that this visual sequencing skill is used during the routine daily activities in the classroom.

# I•SW•15

## • THE PERFORMANCE OBJECTIVE

When presented with a random group of numerals, the learner will point to and name each numeral in turn.

## • THE PRETEST

Direct the learner to point to and name each of the following numerals. The criterion for mastery is 100 percent.

9  4  17  1  13  0  6  19  2  9

## • DIRECTING THE LEARNER'S ATTENTION

The purpose of this task is to teach the learner to associate a name with the numerals 1 through 20. This is similar to I-SW-3, but with numerals rather than geometric forms. To teach this skill you must be sure that the learner knows exactly what is to be learned and you must direct attention by highlighting both the visual form of the numeral and the sound of the name to which it is to be connected. (With the numeral 0, for instance, you might have the learner point to the roundness of the numeral while he or she simultaneously looks at the numeral and says, "Zero".)

## • TEACHING ACTIVITIES

This is a naming task similar to that described in I-SW-3, and you can adapt your teaching strategy from either the modeling technique or the discovery technique described in that objective.

## • SUGGESTIONS FOR RETEACHING

Have you ordered your practice material (see Appendix A)?

If, after having been taught with either the modeling or the discovery technique, the learner is unable to name the numerals, you should

1. Reteach the skill, using the alternate technique.
2. Emphasize more strongly the connection between the visual form and the sound of the name by being sure that he or she is looking at the numeral while saying its name.
3. Emphasize the visual characteristics of the numeral by having the learner repeatedly trace the numeral and at the same time say its name.

## • SUGGESTIONS FOR PRACTICE

After teaching the numeral names, create practice activities to solidify the skill, using the suggestions provided in I-SW-3.

## • THE POSTTEST

The procedure and criterion for mastery are the same as for the pretest.

20  3  5  16  13  2  6  9  10  11

## • ENSURING TRANSFER

Although the learner will be naming numerals frequently while progressing through the hierarchy, you should also use the suggestions provided in I-SW-3 to be sure that she or he is naming numerals during the routine daily activities of the classroom.

• **THE PERFORMANCE OBJECTIVE**

When given three letters that are exactly alike and one that is somewhat similar, the learner will mark the one that is different.

• **THE PRETEST**

Direct the learner to indicate (mark or point to as appropriate) which letter in each of the following sets is different. The criterion for mastery is 80 percent.

| | | | | | | | | | |
|---|---|---|---|---|---|---|---|---|---|
| Set I | m | n | m | m | Set VI | o | o | o | c |
| Set II | o | a | a | a | Set VII | l | l | h | l |
| Set III | q | q | g | q | Set VIII | p | q | p | p |
| Set IV | v | v | v | u | Set IX | w | w | w | v |
| Set V | b | d | b | b | Set X | i | i | j | i |

• **DIRECTING THE LEARNER'S ATTENTION**

The purpose of the task is to teach the learner to discriminate among the fine differences in letters. As such, the task is similar to I-SW-1, but with less obvious discriminators. To teach this skill you must be sure that the learner knows exactly what is to be learned and you must direct his or her attention by highlighting the visual characteristics that make one letter different from the others in a particular set. (In Set I, for instance, the two humps on the **m** could be highlighted to contrast with the single hump on the **n**.)

• **TEACHING ACTIVITIES**

This is a visual discrimination task similar to that described in I-SW-1, and you can adapt your teaching strategy from either the modeling technique or the discovery technique described in that objective.

• **SUGGESTIONS FOR RETEACHING**

If, after having been taught with either the modeling or the discovery technique, the learner is unable to discriminate among the similar letters, you should

1. Reteach the skill, using the alternate technique.
2. Be more specific in directing the learner's attention, being sure that your highlighting is providing enough help in distinguishing the unique visual characteristics of each like letter.
3. Return to the previous visual discrimination skills, ensuring that the learner is able to discriminate among visual forms that require gross discrimination before asking him or her to make the fine discriminations described in this objective.

After successfully teaching the learner to discriminate among like letters, create practice activities to solidify the skill, using the suggestions in I-SW-1.

• **THE POSTTEST**

Use the same directions and criterion for mastery as on the pretest.

| Set I   | l | l | i | l | Set VI   | t | l | t | t |
|---------|---|---|---|---|----------|---|---|---|---|
| Set II  | o | o | o | c | Set VII  | e | e | e | a |
| Set III | y | y | g | y | Set VIII | q | p | q | q |
| Set IV  | u | u | u | v | Set IX   | n | m | n | n |
| Set V   | d | b | d | d | Set X    | w | w | m | w |

• **ENSURING TRANSFER**

Although the learner will be applying this visual discrimination skill while progressing to the more complex skills in the hierarchy, you should also use the suggestions in I-SW-1 to be sure that the learner uses fine discrimination skills during the routine daily activities of the classroom.

# I·SW·17

• **THE PERFORMANCE OBJECTIVE**

Given a flash presentation of each of the following frequently confused letters, the learner will say the name of the letter within one second. The letters to be tested are

b   d   u   v   m   n   p   q   w   i   j

• **THE PRETEST**

Print each of the preceding letters on cards. Flash each card in turn to the learner, giving him or her only a second or less to examine the word before saying its name. The criterion for mastery is 100 percent. *Note:* Keep track of the letters missed on the pretest, since only the missed letters need to be taught. If letters other than the ones listed above are confused by the learner, they also should be noted and taught.

• **DIRECTING THE LEARNER'S ATTENTION**

The purpose of this task is to teach the learner to recognize instantly each of the above easily confused letters (plus any other letters that might be confusing) when they are presented on cards. For some learners progress in reading is impeded by persistent confusion over such letters as **d** and **b** and, at later stages, such words as was and saw, **then** and **when**. Such difficulties exist because the learner does not know how to examine printed symbols visually; particularly in relation to visually discriminating among fine differences and looking at words in the correct sequence (from left to right and from top to bottom). Consequently, instant recognition of easily confused letters and words combines elements of both visual discrimination and visual sequencing. This is the first in a series of objectives that creates skill in instantly recognizing frequently confused letters and words.

To teach this skill you must state exactly what is to be learned and you must highlight the visual discriminator in each pair that serves as the cue for contrasting the easily confused letters. (With **b** and **d**, for instance, the discriminator is the side of the stick the ball is sitting on; for **p** and **b** it is whether the stick goes up or down from the ball; and for **u** and **v** it is whether the letter is rounded or pointed at the bottom.)

- **THIS IS A STOREHOUSE OBJECTIVE**

The following instructional activities are your storehouse of techniques for developing skill in instantly recognizing easily confused letters and words. This skill recurs in more sophisticated forms throughout the hierarchy. The activities that follow are to be adapted and used with each of these as they occur.

- **TEACHING ACTIVITIES**

*The modeling technique.* Teach each pair of easily confused letters (or words) together. Tell the learner that you are going to help him or her remember two letters (or words) that are difficult to tell apart and that he or she should watch and mimic your actions. Write each pair of letters (or words) on a piece of paper with the discriminator highlighted (with color or some other technique). For instance, with **d** and **b** you might highlight the ball at the left side of the **d** and the stick at the left side of the **b**; with **u** and **v,** the rounded part of the bottom of the **u** and the pointed part of the **v** could be in a different color. Say, "I can tell the **d** and the **b** apart because when I look at them from left to right, I see the ball first with the **d** and I see the stick first with the **b**." Then point to each letter in turn and say, "This is a **d** because the ball is on the left and this is a **b** because the stick is on the left." Have the learner mimic you, being sure that he or she is noting the discriminator and is looking at the letter (or word) while saying its name. Repeat the procedure several times, diminishing the amount of highlighting on the discriminating cue until the learner can instantly recognize the letters (or words) without mimicking you and without highlighting.

*The discovery technique.* The principle to be discovered in this key objective is that each of the easily confused letters (or words) has a visual characteristic that serves as the discriminator for contrasting the pairs. Using the same type of highlighting as is described earlier, point to the two symbols in turn and ask, "Does this look like this?" When the response is "No," say, "Look at each letter (or word) in turn and at the highlighting I have added and tell me why one is different from the other." If the learner responds correctly, continue this questioning process with diminished amounts of highlighting until he or she can respond successfully without any assistance. If the learner does not respond successfully, emphasize more directly the highlighting that distinguishes the letters (or words) and repeat the questioning process.

## • SUGGESTIONS FOR RETEACHING

If, after having been taught with either of the preceding techniques, the learner is unable to recognize instantly the easily confused letters, you should

1. Reteach the skill, using the alternate technique.
2. Reexamine your attenders to be sure that the highlighting is directing the learner to the most utilitarian cue in discriminating among the letters.
3. Reteach the skill, using a more dramatic form of highlighting to assist the learner in visually examining the dieffrences between the letters.
4. Have the learner repeatedly trace the confusing letters while stating both the distinguishing visual characteristics and the letter name.
5. Return to previous visual discrimination and visual sequencing skills in the hierarchy to be sure that the learner possesses the prerequisite skill needed to perform this more complex task.

## • SUGGESTIONS FOR PRACTICE

Once the easily confused letters or words have been taught successfully, adapt and use a practice activity from those listed in either I-SW-3 (naming) or II-SW-6 (sight word recognition).

## • THE POSTTEST

The procedure and criterion for mastery are the same as for the pretest.

## • ENSURING TRANSFER

The learner will be using his or her skill in instantly recognizing easily confused letters while progressing through the skill hierarchy. However, in addition to these applications, you should be alert for ways to point out the use of instantly recognizing these letters during the daily activities of the classroom. The suggestions in I-SW-1 can be adapted for this purpose.

# I•SW•18

## • THE PERFORMANCE OBJECTIVE

When given a few seconds to examine a letter that is easily confused with other letters, the learner will reproduce the letter from memory, to the satisfaction of the teacher.

## • THE PRETEST

Prepare ten flashcards, each of which has one letter of the following sequence: g, a, m, v, b, o, p, h, w, i. Flash each for the count of three. Then direct the learner to reproduce it. The criterion for mastery is teacher judgment.

The purpose of this task is to develop the learner's visual memory for letters that are easily confused. This task is basically the same task as I-SW-2, but the learner is being asked to remember the letters he or she confuses rather than geometric forms. To teach this skill you must be sure that the learner knows exactly what is to be learned and you must direct attention by highlighting the visual discriminator that makes a letter different from the one with which it is confused. (See the examples in I-SW-17.)

• TEACHING ACTIVITIES

This is a visual memory task similar to that descriebd in I-SW-2, and you can adapt your teaching strategy from either the modeling technique or the discovery technique described in that objective.

• SUGGESTIONS FOR RETEACHING

If, after having been taught with either the modeling or the discovery technique, the learner is unable to reproduce the confused letters from memory, you should

1. Reteach the skill, using the alternate technique.
2. Highlight more carefully the distinguishing visual characteristics that must be remembered.
3. Return to the previous two skills of naming and discriminating among like letters and be sure that the learner is able to perform these tasks.
4. Return to earlier skill objectives on visual memory and reteach simpler tasks of remembering before requiring the learner to complete the more complex task of remembering like letters.

• SUGGESTIONS FOR PRACTICE

After successfully teaching how to remember like letters, create practice activities to solidify the skill, using the suggestions provided in I-SW-2.

• THE POSTTEST

The procedure and the criterion for mastery are the same as for the pretest. Use the following sequence of letters: **q, o, n, u, d, c, p, l, v, i.**

• ENSURING TRANSFER

Although the learner will be applying this visual memory skill while progressing to the more complex skills in the hierarchy, you should also use the suggestions provided in I-SW-2 to be sure that he or she is remembering like letters during the daily routine activities of the classroom.

**I•WA•1**

• THE PERFORMANCE OBJECTIVE

When directed to close his or her eyes and listen to rhythms tapped by the teacher, the learner will reproduce the rhythm.

Using a fist on a tabletop, produce the following rhythm patterns that correspond to regular Morse code signals. A tap followed by a pause is a dash; a tap without a pause is a dot. The criterion for mastery is 80 percent.

| Set I | dot-dot | Set VI | dot-dot-dash-dot |
| Set II | dash-dot | Set VII | dot-dash-dot-dot-dot |
| Set III | dot-dash-dot | Set VIII | dash-dot-dash-dot |
| Set IV | dash-dot-dot | Set IX | dot-dash-dash-dot |
| Set V | dot-dot-dot | Set X | dash-dash-dot-dot-dash-dot |

### • DIRECTING THE LEARNER'S ATTENTION

The purpose of this task is to help the learner create a memory both for sounds and for the sequence in which they are produced. This is a crucial skill since success as a reader depends, in part, on ability to remember sounds in a specific sequential order. For instance, the blended sounds of a word analyzed in print will be remembered and produced in a precise sequence from the first to the last sound. This objective is the first in a series of skills developing this skill.

In teaching this skill you must direct the learner's attention by stating exactly what is to be learned and by highlighting the pattern of the rhythms. (In Set I, for example, you might take the learner's hand and create the pattern while saying, "Dot dot.")

### • THIS IS A STOREHOUSE OBJECTIVE

The following instructional activities are your storehouse of techniques for developing skill in remembering sounds in sequence. This skill recurs in more sophisticated forms later in the skill hierarchy. The instructional activities that follow are to be adapted and used with each of these as they occur.

### • TEACHING ACTIVITIES

*The modeling technique.* Direct the learner to watch and listen as you clap your hands in a simple rhythm. Then take the learner's hands and repeat the same pattern with his or her hands and say, "Clap-clap," as you do so. Then have the learner repeat the process using more complex clapping patterns and gradually stop holding the learner's hands and saying the pattern as the learner responds more successfully. Once a child can remember a sequence of claps, do the same with tapping. Assist the learner at first by holding his or her hand and by providing an oral cue, as you did for the clapping. Gradually reduce this assistance until the child can reproduce the rhythms alone.

*The discovery technique.* Since this is a low-level auditory memory skill, there is no principle to be discovered. However, you can use a questioning technique to help the learner discover a technique for remembering the sequence of sounds. Start with the simpler clapping procedure just described and say, "I am going to clap my hands in a certain way and then I will ask you to do the same thing. Watch and listen while I do it once and then tell me what you will have to remember in order to do what I did." If the learner is unable to respond, guide his or her hands as he or she repeats a clapping pattern; then repeat the question. Diminish the amount of physical assistance provided until the learner is able to do both the clapping and the tapping unassisted.

### • SUGGESTIONS FOR RETEACHING

If, after having been taught the skill with either the modeling or the discovery technique, the learner is still unable to reproduce the tapped rhythms in sequence, you should

1. Reteach the skill, using the alternate technique.
2. Reexamine your attenders, being sure that the highlighting you have provided assists the learner in remembering the rhythmic patterns.
3. Use simpler activities that emphasize rhythm, such as clapping in time with music and reproducing rhythms with rhythm band instruments.

### • SUGGESTED PRACTICE ACTIVITIES

Once the skill has been taught successfully, use one or more of the following practice activities to solidify it.

1. Using a tape recorder, record patterns of sounds. When recording each set, give the pattern first, and then instruct the child to stop the recorder and repeat the sound pattern, and then to turn the recorder back on so that the sound pattern is repeated, thereby allowing the child to check himself or herself.
2. Play the Airport game with learners using a gameboard, a toy airplane, and someone to give the oral sound patterns to each child in turn. If the child reproduces it correctly, he or she moves the airplane one space down the runway. As each plane reaches the end, it may be flown briefly. The same technique can be used in reverse to return the airplanes to the hangar.
3. Play a game in which learners are paired and take turns clapping pairs of sound patterns to each other. The partner must respond to each pattern by identifying them as the same or different. The winner can be determined either by keeping track of the number each child gets right or by adapting the game to a game board like the one described in activity 2.
4. Play the game Monkey Hear, Monkey Do, using pairs of players and a gameboard. One child claps or says a sound pattern and the partner mimics it. If the partner is correct, he or she moves forward one space on the gameboard.
5. Play a Dot-to-Dot game, using any connect-the-dots picture. Learners are paired and one says or claps a sound pattern. The other mimics and,

if correct, connects as many dots in the picture as there are sound units in the pattern.

6. Play a remembering game in which one learner says a word, the next learner says that word and adds another, the third learner repeats the first two words and adds a third, and so on. Continue until one learner cannot remember the sequence. The object is to develop a sequence of words or sounds as long as possible.

### • THE POSTTEST

Procedure and criterion for mastery are the same as on the pretest.

| | | | |
|---|---|---|---|
| Set I | dot-dash-dot | Set VI | dot-dash-dot-dot |
| Set II | dot-dot | Set VII | dot-dot-dash-dot |
| Set III | dash-dot | Set VIII | dot-dash-dot-dash-dot |
| Set IV | dot-dot-dash-dot | Set IX | dot-dash-dash-dot |
| Set V | dot-dot-dot | Set X | dash-dash-dot-dot-dot |

### • ENSURING TRANSFER

The learner will be applying this skill in learning the more complex auditory memory tasks with which he or she will be working while progressing through the skill hierarchy. However, in addition to these applications you should also be alert for ways to point out the use of this auditory memory and sequencing skill during the routine daily activities of the classroom. Some suggested techniques follow.

1. As learners are waiting to be dismissed or to move to another activity, you can say, "If you can repeat this sequence of sounds, you can go."
2. Sing songs with learners that use an ever-increasing number of sound units that must be repeated in order. A typical example would be "The Twelve Days of Christmas."
3. Use choral speaking with children, choosing poems that require remembering sounds in a sequence.
4. Play playground games with children, such as rope skipping, which is done to the accompaniment of a repetitive song or chant.

## I•WA•2

### • THE PERFORMANCE OBJECTIVE

When directed to close his or her eyes and listen to three words spoken by the teacher, the learner will reproduce the words in the sequence in which they were given.

### • THE PRETEST

Direct the learner to close his or her eyes and listen to what you say. Say, "Listen carefully to the words I say. When I stop I want you to say them just like I did." Produce the sets of words in the following sequence. The criterion for mastery is 80 percent.

| Set I | school | bell | playground |
|-------|--------|------|------------|
| Set II | elephant | dog | cat |
| Set III | desk | chair | table |
| Set IV | pencil | pen | eraser |
| Set V | red | blue | yellow |
| Set VI | grass | house | rug |
| Set VII | ford | sky | donkey |
| Set VIII | window | hydrant | card |
| Set IX | fight | run | tree |
| Set X | laugh | church | sign |

### • DIRECTING THE LEARNER'S ATTENTION

The purpose of this task is to help the learner create a memory for sequenced words; as such, it is similar to storehouse module I-WA-1. To teach this skill you must be sure that the learner knows exactly what is to be learned and you must direct his or her attention by highlighting the sequence of the words. (In Set I, for example, you may provide oral assistance by saying, "The first word is **school**, then comes **bell**, and the last word is **playground**.")

### • TEACHING ACTIVITIES

In teaching this skill you can use either the modeling technique or the discovery technique described in I-WA-1, adjusting these to focus on remembering spoken words in sequence rather than tapped rhythms.

### • SUGGESTIONS FOR RETEACHING

If, after having been taught this skill with either the modeling or the discovery technique, the learner is still unable to reproduce the sequence of words, you should

1. Reteach the skill, using the alternate technique.
2. Reexamine your attenders, being sure that the highlighting you have provided assists the learner in remembering the sequence of words.
3. Return to I-WA-1 (or create other auditory memory activities) and be sure the learner can do simple tasks of auditory memory and sequencing before requiring him or her to reproduce a sequence of words. One way to simplify the task is to start with a single word and have the learner repeat it, then have him or her reproduce two words, and so on, until the complete task can be done.

### • SUGGESTIONS FOR PRACTICE

Once the skill has been taught successfully, create practice activities to solidify the skill, using the suggestions provided in I-WA-1.

### • THE POSTTEST

Use the same procedure and criterion for mastery as on the pretest. Repeat the pretest, reading each set backward.

Although the learner will be applying this auditory memory and sequencing skill while progressing to the more complex skills in the hierarchy, you should also use the suggestions provided in I-WA-1 to be sure that the skill is used during the routine daily activities of the classroom.

# I•WA•3

● **THE PERFORMANCE OBJECTIVE**

When directed to close his or her eyes and listen to three words spoken by the teacher, the learner will repeat the first word and the last word spoken by the teacher.

● **THE PRETEST**

Use the words provided in the previous pretest. Read each of the sets in turn, directing the learner to close his or her eyes and listen carefully. After each set ask the learner to tell what the first word was. If the response is corect ask him or her what the last word was. The criterion for mastery is 80 percent.

● **DIRECTING THE LEARNER'S ATTENTION**

The purpose of this task is to familiarize the learner with sound position in time (first and last); as such, it is similar to storehouse module I-WA-1. This is a difficult concept to teach because the last word provided is the closest to the child in time; consequently, the child often picks that one as the first word heard. To teach this skill you must be sure that the learner knows exactly what is to be learned and you must direct his or her attention by highlighting the first and last words spoken. (In Set I, for instance, you may say each set of words twice. On the second time say, "First word, **school**; last word, **playground**.")

● **TEACHING ACTIVITIES**

In teaching this skill you can use either the modeling technique or the discovery technique described in I-WA-1, adjusting these to focus on spoken words rather than tapped rhythms.

● **SUGGESTIONS FOR RETEACHING**

If, after having been taught this skill with either the modeling technique or the discovery technique, the learner is still unable to identify the first and last words spoken, you should

1. Reteach the skill, using the alternate technique.
2. Reexamine your attenders, being sure that the highlighting you have provided assists the learner in remembering the first and last words.
3. Be sure that the learner understands the meaning of the words *first* and *last* and teach these meanings if necessary.
4. Return to I-WA-1 (or create other auditory memory activities) and be

sure that the learner can do simple tasks of auditory memory and sequencing before requiring him or her to reproduce the first and last words in a spoken sequence.

## • SUGGESTIONS FOR PRACTICE

Once the skill has been taught successfully, create practice activities to solidify the skill, using the suggestions provided in I-WA-1.

## • THE POSTTEST

Use the words provided in the previous pretest, reversing the sequence in which they are spoken. Repeat the pretest procedures. The criterion for mastery remains 80 percent.

## • ENSURING TRANSFER

Although the learner will be applying this auditory memory and sequencing skill while progressing to the more complex skills in the hierarchy, you should use the suggestions provided in I-WA-1 to be sure that the skill is used during the routine daily activities of the classroom.

# I•WA•4

## • THE PERFORMANCE OBJECTIVE

Given a polysyllabic word spoken by the teacher in which the initial sound unit has been omitted, the learner will repeat the word correctly and supply the missing sound.

## • THE PRETEST

Direct the learner to listen carefully as you say a word. Explain that the word is one that he or she knows but that it will sound strange because you will not say all of it. Some part of the word will be left out. Ask the child to think of the word you want to say and to say it the way it really sounds. The criterion for mastery is 80 percent.

| | |
|---|---|
| —ish hook (fishhook) | Now you say what I want to say. |
| —ēanutbutter (peanut butter) | Now you say what I want to say. |
| —āseball (baseball) | Now you say what I want to say. |
| —ētween (between) | Now you say what I want to say. |
| —īolin (violin) | Now you say what I want to say. |
| —ŏtrod (hot rod) | Now you say what I want to say. |
| —ăckboard (blackboard) | Now you say what I want to say. |
| —ōtorcycle (motorcycle) | Now you say what I want to say. |
| —irthday (birthday) | Now you say what I want to say. |
| —elevision (television) | Now you say what I want to say. |

## • DIRECTING THE LEARNER'S ATTENTION

The purpose of this task is to help the learner develop the ability to *cloze*, or complete, a word identification even when the word is distorted by leaving out one important sound value. The need for this skill is based on the assumption that a reader often omits or distorts some letter sound while attempting to sound out a strange word. When this happens the learner must be ready to *guess* the word identification in spite of the fact that all the letter sounds are not there for help. What has been sounded is only an *approximation* of the real spoken word, and the child must develop the habit of ignoring the sound gaps or distortions and leaping to an identification by *testing* the ear for real words and matching them against the spoken approximation.

To facilitate this learning you must direct the child's attention to the realization that the strange word you pronounce is *a real word that he or she knows and can speak*. The child must be ready to search for real words instead of viewing this activity as a game played with made-up nonsense words.

### • THIS IS A STOREHOUSE OBJECTIVE

The following instructional techniques are your storehouse of activities for developing skill in clozing spoken word approximations into spoken real words. This skill recurs in more sophisticated forms in the skill clusters that follow. The instructional activities and suggestions that follow must be adapted and used with each of these as they occur.

### • TEACHING ACTIVITIES

*The modeling technique.* Clozure skills can be easily modeled. Say to the child, "I want to say the word **paper** but I forget to say the first part. Instead of **paper** I say **ā–per**. Is **āper** a word? No! But I'm smart, and I know how to listen to **āper** and say to myself, **aper** is really **paper**. Now, let's see you do this." You have modeled the total learning for the child; as the child discovers how you can guess a word even when parts of it are left out, he or she will start guessing the identification without needing your cue for the real word.

*The discovery technique.* The key to clozure skills is the learner's realization that what you are saying are *real* words that the learner can discover if he or she listens carefully and guesses accurately. You can help the child make this discovery by using this tactic. Say, "I'm going to say a word, but I will leave out one of its parts. It will sound funny. *The word I will say is either. . . .*" (Here you will name three words, one of which is the one you will want the child to cloze.) "Now listen carefully as I say one of the words, leaving part of it out. Can you discover which word I am saying?" In this case discovery is limited to only three choices. This technique allows the child to *discover* this closure technique by limiting the number of approximations that must be dealt with.

### • SUGGESTIONS FOR RETEACHING

If after multiple teaching activities, either modeled or discovery, the learner is still unable to cloze a spoken word that has its beginning sound omitted, you might

1. Reteach the skill, using the other presentation model. (Switch from modeled to discovery, or discovery to modeled cuing.)
2. Prepare a list of words *suggested by the learner* to use in this teaching. Five words are sufficient for the first effort. Explain that you are going to speak these five words, leaving off some part of them. The learner's task is to decide which word you are saying. Then proceed with the modeled presentation.
3. Select words that can be represented by a picture. Three to five are sufficient. Help the learner draw these words, each on a separate card or sheet. Direct the learner to point to each picture and speak its word. Repeat this activity, with you saying the word and omitting its first sound while the learner points. As quickly as you pronounce the distorted identification, have the child name the picture. Finally, when this can be done satisfactorily, you identify each picture at random, leaving off the first sound and ask the learner to point to the picture and identify it correctly.

- **SUGGESTIONS FOR PRACTICE**

Once this skill has been successfully taught and learned, use one or more of the following practice activities for retention.

1. During story time or reading time purposely distort some word in the story by leaving off its first sound. Stop and say, "Oh, I didn't say that word correctly! What should I have said?" This can be done during any daily oral activity.
2. Prepare a tape of spoken words that have their initial sound omitted. Collect pictures to represent each spoken word. Each picture will have a color cue on the back. Direct the learner to listen to the tape and select the picture of the word you are speaking. Have the tape direct the child to speak the word as it is normally spoken. Finally, tell him or her the color that should appear on its back and direct the learner to check his or her selection. All these directions can be taped with necessary directions, distorted words, pauses for learner response, and color cues to indicate learner accuracy.
3. Pair students with a suitable deck of picture cards. Let each select a card and speak its identification with the first sound omitted; the other learner then guesses the identification. A variation of this is to speak the word in its normal identification and then one learner tries to speak it, leaving off the first sound value.

- **THE POSTTEST**

The procedure and criterion for mastery are the same as for the pretest.

| | |
|---|---|
| —īrefly (firefly) | Now you say what I want to say. |
| —ŏnda (Honda) | Now you say what I want to say. |
| —ăsket (basket) | Now you say what I want to say. |
| —ĕncil sharpener (pencil sharpener) | Now you say what I want to say. |

—ŭmp truck (dump truck)          Now you say what I want to say.
—ōman (snowman)                  Now you say what I want to say.
—oolbus (schoolbus)              Now you say what I want to say.
—īce Krispies (Rice Krispies)    Now you say what I want to say.
—ănana (banana)                  Now you say what I want to say.
—āke (bake, rake, snake, etc.)   Now you say what I want to say.

## • ENSURING TRANSFER

As the learner develops more sophisticated phonetic analysis skills, those skills will be used to sound out many words that are strange in print. Often recognition of these sounded words will depend upon the child's ability to cloze the sounds into a familiar word. Transfer is at this stage. You can directly affect this transfer by constantly calling attention to the approximation characteristic of English spelling and the need to adjust sounds until they create recognizable spoken words.

# I•WA•5

## • THE PERFORMANCE OBJECTIVE

Given spoken pairs of words, the learner will say "Yes" if the words begin alike and will say "No" if they do not begin alike.

## • THE PRETEST

Using the following ten pairs of words, say each pair in turn. Direct the learner to say "Yes" if the pairs begin with the same sound and to say "No" if the pairs do not begin with the same sound. The criterion for mastery is 80 percent.

| Set I    | mine  | music | Set VI    | boy   | book  |
| Set II   | desk  | chair | Set VII   | happy | house |
| Set III  | cat   | cow   | Set VIII  | sand  | kiss  |
| Set IV   | dog   | dig   | Set IX    | chair | shoot |
| Set V    | lake  | last  | Set X     | this  | that  |

## • DIRECTING THE LEARNER'S ATTENTION

The purpose of this task is to teach the learner to discriminate by ear among the beginning sounds of words. Auditory discrimination is a crucial skill since ultimately the learner's ability to analyze and pronounce unknown words will depend upon success in hearing the various phonetic elements of words, particularly as they relate to beginning sounds. This is the first in a series of auditory discrimination skills designed to help the learner differentiate among the sounds used in the English spelling system.

To teach the learner to discriminate beginning sounds of words by ear, you must be sure that he or she has a concept for different as it relates to sounds and you must direct his or her attention by stating exactly what is being learned and by highlighting the beginning sound of each pair of words. (In Set I, for instance, you might say each word twice, exaggerating the beginning sound the first time and saying it normally the second time.)

- **THIS IS A STOREHOUSE OBJECTIVE**

The following instructional activities are your storehouse of techniques for developing skill in noting sound differences at the beginning, middle, and end of words. This skill recurs in more sophisticated form later in the hierarchy. The instructional activities that follow are to be adapted and used with each of these as they occur.

- **TEACHING ACTIVITIES**

*The modeling technique.* Say each word, using a say-it-slow, say-it-fast technique. Tell the learner that you are going to say each of the two words twice, once slowly and once at normal speed; have the learner listen to the first sound in both words and tell whether they are the same or different. "Say, "I'm going to say the first word slowly. **M—ine.** Now I'm going to say it fast. **Mine.** Now I'll say the second word slowly. **M—usic.** Now I'll say it fast. **Music.**" Then ask the learner if the sounds at the beginning of the two words were the same or different. If the child still has difficulty, highlight the first sound more by using the say-it-slow, say-it-fast technique with words that differ only at the beginning, such as **mine** and **line, bake** and **lake,** and so so on. For words like **bake,** in which the first sound cannot be said slowly, highlight by telling the learner to watch your mouth as you get ready to say the first sound and then exaggerate this mouth movement and have the learner mimic your actions. As the learner begins to respond satisfactorily with the highlighting, gradually diminish the amount of emphasis you place on the beginning sound until the learner is able to distinguish the sound differences when you say the words in a normal fashion only.

*The discovery technique.* The principle to be discovered is that spoken words have distinguishing auditory characteristics that allow us to distinguish one from another. In this particular objective the focus is on the distinctive beginning sounds, but subsequent objectives will focus on ending and middle sounds. Using words that differ only at the end and using highlighting such as the say-it-slow, say-it-fast technique or the get-your-mouth-ready-to-say technique just described, say a pair of words and ask the question, "Do the two words sound the same?" When the response is "No," say, "Listen to the two words as I say them again and tell me where the two words are different." If the learner responds by correctly identifying the beginning sounds as being different, continue this questioning process with other pairs of words, diminishing the amount of auditory emphasis with each sequence until he or she can respond successfully without any assistance. If the child does not respond correctly at any point, emphasize again the part of the word to be discriminated and repeat the questioning process.

- **SUGGESTIONS FOR RETEACHING**

If, after having been taught with either of the preceding techniques, the learner is unable to discriminate among the beginning sounds of words, you should

● 129

1. Reteach the skill, using the alternate technique.
2. Be more specific in directing the learner's attention, being sure that the learner is listening to the *beginning* sound and that your highlighting is emphatic enough to help distinguish the beginning sounds in the pairs of words.
3. If there is still difficulty, be sure that the learner has a concept for the word *different* as it relates to sounds. If there is not such a concept, develop it, using sounds with which the learner is familiar, such as bells, doors slamming, footsteps, dripping faucets, and so on.
4. Learners having extreme difficulty with the task can be helped by teaching them how the sound is formed with the mouth. For example, you can provide the learner with a mirror and help her or him to note how the sound heard at the beginning of **fish** is formed, as opposed to how the sound heard at the beginning of **dish** is formed.

## • SUGGESTIONS FOR PRACTICE

Once the skill has been taught successfully, use one or more of the following practice activities to solidify the skill.

1. Have learners bring to class pictures cut from magazines, with each picture or series of pictures showing something that has the same sound at the beginning (or end or middle).
2. Bring in a group of magazine pictures yourself, directing the learner to name what each picture shows and to sort the pictures according to the common beginning, middle, or ending sounds. For instance, all the pictures that begin with the same sound heard at the beginning of **kite** go in one pile, all the pictures that begin with the same sounds heard at the beginning of **top** go in another pile, and so on.
3. Paste a number of pictures on a large piece of tagboard. Direct the learner to match smaller pictures to the pictures on the tagboard on the basis of like sounds at the beginning, middle, or end.
4. A form of bingo can be played that will reinforce the learning of beginning, middle, or ending sounds. For instance, the learner can be provided with a bingolike playing card having pictures in the squares. Say, "Do you have a picture on your card that begins with the same sound you hear at the beginning of **dog**? If you do, you may cover that square with a marker." The first learner to have every picture in a row covered wins the game.
5. A group of picture cards can be placed on the table. Learners take turns matching pairs of pictures that begin with the same sound. Learners having the most pairs win. This activity can also be adapted to ending and middle sounds.
6. Provide learners with an oral listing of words, such as **boy, bat, ball, bingo, tall**. Direct the learner to name the word that has a different sound at the beginning (or end or middle).

7. Spread a group of pictures on the floor. Have the learner point to a picture that has the same sound you hear at the beginning (or end or middle) of the word you say.

8. Play games with learners that follow this pattern: "I'm thinking of something on your desk that begins with the same sound heard at the beginning of the word **pig.** What am I thinking of?" This activity can also be adapted to middle and ending sounds.

9. Play a fishing game with learners in which pictures are clipped or stapled to paper fish. Give the learner a pole with a magnet tied to the end. As the learner catches each fish, have her or him say, "I caught a fish that begins like _____." This activity can also be adapted to middle and ending sounds.

10. Pass out picture cards. Hold up another picture card yourself, saying, "Who has a picture whose name sounds the same at the beginning (or end or middle) as the name of my picture?" Direct the learner to hold up the card if he or she has such a picture.

11. Recite lines from familiar poems, leaving out the rhyming word in the second line of the couplet. Directions to the learner are, "What word goes here? What other word does it sound like? In what way does it sound like it?" Then you might say, "Can you think of another word that sounds like these two words at the end?"

12. You can play the game, I Am Going to Africa. You say, "I am going to Africa and I'm going to take a ring, and I will sing. Who can go to Africa with me?" The learner must respond with something he or she is going to take to Africa and that also ends with the –ing rhyme. For instance, if you are working with ending rhymes, the learner might say he or she is going to take a **swing.** If you are working with the ending **–ong** sound, the learner might say he or she is going to take a **song.** This activity can also be adapted to beginning and middle sounds.

13. You say, "Let's play a game with words." Choose a rhyming pattern and say two words, elongating the first sound, as in **b . . . at, s . . . at, c . . . .** Here (in the third instance) the learner completes the word. This activity can also be modified for use with both ending consonant sounds and middle sounds as well as rhymes.

14. You pronounce a word for the learner. He or she listens and then provides another word that has the same sound at the beginning or middle or end.

15. Construct a shallow box divided into four squares. Place a key picture in each of the top two squares. Provide the learner with a group of pictures, directing him or her to sort the pictures and place them in the square beneath the picture with the same sound at the beginning (or end or middle).

## ● THE POSTTEST

The procedure and criterion for mastery are the same as for the pretest.

| Set I | money | mama | Set VI | huddle | happen |
|-------|-------|------|--------|--------|--------|
| Set II | dip | tip | Set VII | hit | bit |
| Set III | dinosaur | doll | Set VIII | turtle | burp |
| Set IV | lamp | camp | Set IX | bicycle | boomerang |
| Set V | Sunday | ceiling | Set X | ring | water |

### • ENSURING TRANSFER

The learner will be applying this skill in the more complex word analysis tasks with which he or she will be working while progressing through the hierarchy. However, in addition to these applications, you should be sure that this auditory discrimination skill is also used during the routine daily activities of the classroom. Some suggested techniques follow.

1. Direct the learner to point to and name things in the classroom that have the same beginning (or ending or middle) sound as is heard in _____.
2. As learners are waiting to be dismissed or to move to another activity, you can say, "If you can tell me a word that sounds the same as _____ at the beginning (or the middle or the end), you can go."
3. After returning from a field trip or some other common activity, you can direct the learner to name all the things he or she saw that had the same sound at the beginning as _____. This activity can also be adapted to middle and ending sounds.
4. During Show-and-Tell, you can direct the learner to show something that has the same beginning (or ending or middle) sound as he or she hears in _____.

## I•WA•6

### • THE PERFORMANCE OBJECTIVE

Given words in pairs that either rhyme or do not rhyme, the learner will say "Yes" if the pair rhymes and will say "No" if the pair does not rhyme.

### • THE PRETEST

Using the following ten pairs of words, say each pair in turn. Direct the learner to say "Yes" if the pair rhymes and to say "No" if the pair does not rhyme. If the learner does not understand the concept of rhyming, modify the directions to say "sounds the same at the end." The criterion for mastery is 80 percent.

| Set I | house | boy | Set VI | store | more |
|-------|-------|-----|--------|-------|------|
| Set II | rug | hug | Set VII | grass | glass |
| Set III | apply | donkey | Set VIII | chick | church |
| Set IV | desk | chair | Set IX | flower | tower |
| Set V | book | look | Set X | quiet | quick |

### • DIRECTING THE LEARNER'S ATTENTION

The purpose of this task is to teach the learner to discriminate among the ending sounds of words in terms of those that rhyme and those that do not;

as such, it is similar to storehouse module I-WA-5. Next to beginning sounds, the most helpful cue to the reader who wishes to analyze and pronounce an unknown word is the ending sound. Typically, the reader will focus on the initial sound as the primary cue and then turn to the final sound as a secondary cue when needed. Consequently, the learner must be able to distinguish the various sounds of phonetic elements at the end of words as well as at the beginning.

To teach the learner to discriminate by ear among words that rhyme, you must be sure that he or she has a concept for the word *rhyme* and you must direct his or her attention by stating exactly what is to be learned and by highlighting the ending sounds in each pair of words. (In Set I, for instance, you may adapt the say-it-slow, say-it-fast technique described in I-WA-5 as a means for emphasizing the endings of words.)

### • TEACHING ACTIVITIES

In teaching this auditory discrimination skill you can use either the modeling technique or the discovery technique described in I-WA-5 adjusting the suggestions to focus on ending rather than beginning sounds.

### • SUGGESTIONS FOR RETEACHING

If, after having been taught with either the modeling or the discovery technique, the learner is still unable to discriminate by ear among words that rhyme, you should

1. Reteach the skill, using the alternate technique.
2. Reexamine your attenders, being sure that the learner is listening to the *ending* sound and that your highlighting is emphatic enough to help him or her distinguish the ending sounds in the pairs of words.
3. If there is still difficulty, be sure that the learner has a concept for the word *rhyme* and teach this concept if necessary.
4. Return to the previous skills of auditory memory and discrimination, being sure that the learner can do the simpler auditory tasks before requiring him or her to discriminate among ending sounds.

### • SUGGESTIONS FOR PRACTICE

Once the skill has been taught successfully, create practice activities to solidify it, using the suggestions provided in I-WA-5.

### • THE POSTTEST

The procedure and criterion for mastery are the same as for the pretest.

| Set I | pipe | table | Set VI | black | stack |
| Set II | book | sit | Set VII | pencil | pen |
| Set III | play | stay | Set VIII | thank | thumb |
| Set IV | jump | bump | Set IX | floor | flew |
| Set V | fly | sky | Set X | fishhook | bookend |

Although the learner will be applying this auditory discrimination skill while progressing to the more complex skills in the hierarchy, you should use the suggestions provided in I-WA-5 to be sure that the skill is used during the routine daily activities of the classroom.

# I•WA•7

### • THE PERFORMANCE OBJECTIVE

Given a polysyllabic word spoken by the teacher in which a medial sound unit has been omitted or distorted, the learner will repeat the word correctly supplying the missing sound.

### • THE PRETEST

Direct the learner to listen carefully as you say a word. Explain that the word is one he or she knows but that it will sound different because you have not said it correctly. The middle part has been changed. Ask the child to think of the word you want to say and say it the "way it really sounds." The criterion for mastery is 80 percent.

| | |
|---|---|
| rōo—beer (root beer) | Now you say what I want to say. |
| ha—urger (hamburger) | Now you say what I want to say. |
| T—m (Tim, Tom) | Now you say what I want to say. |
| vic—ory (victory) | Now you say what I want to say. |
| tel—phone (telephone) | Now you say what I want to say. |
| dru—store (drugstore) | Now you say what I want to say. |
| ōv—shoes (overshoes) | Now you say what I want to say. |
| dow—town (downtown) | Now you say what I want to say. |
| sl—pry (slippery) | Now you say what I want to say. |
| bēg—n (begin) | Now you say what I want to say. |

### • DIRECTING THE LEARNER'S ATTENTION

When a child fails a task, does he or she think the fault lies within him or her or in the difficulty of the task?

The purpose of this task is to teach a learner to cloze a word identification when a vital sound value in the center of the word is either omitted or distorted. The task demands that the child listen carefully to the distorted word and then test her or his ear against other words that share those sound properties, guessing which one most nearly fits the distorted approximation. The child's attention must first focus on the spoken word in its distorted form and then shift to all other words that share sound values. Finally, the child tests each to see where the best fit lies.

### • TEACHING ACTIVITIES

This is a closure task similar to the storehouse module I-WA-4, and you can build your teaching strategy using either the modeling or discovery techniques described there.

### • SUGGESTIONS FOR RETEACHING

Examine storehouse module I-WA-4 for suggestions on how to reteach this skill.

- **SUGGESTIONS FOR PRACTICE**

After teaching this skill, create practice activities as suggested in module I-WA-4.

- **THE POSTTEST**

The procedure and criterion for mastery are the same as for the pretest. Select ten new words and make a medial distortion, as done in the pretest.

- **ENSURING TRANSFER**

Transfer techniques are the same as in module I-WA-4; you should adapt those suggestions to this skill.

- **THE PERFORMANCE OBJECTIVE**

Given a stimulus word beginning with either **m** or **d** and a group of three other words one of which begins with **m** or **d,** the learner will pair the two words beginning with the same letter sound.

- **THE PRETEST**

Using the following words, say to the learner, "Here are three words. Listen carefully." (Say the three words.) "Which one sounds like (say the stimulus word) at the beginning?" Repeat the three original words. The criterion for mastery is five out of six correct.

| | | | |
|---|---|---|---|
| elephant | pencil | monkey | Which one sounds like **mouse** at the beginning? Repeat the three words. |
| milk bottle | coat | bicycle | Which one sounds like **mouse** at the beginning? Repeat the three words. |
| dinosaur | tree | baby | Which one sounds like **dog** at the beginning? Repeat the three words. |
| never | music | needle | Which one sounds like **mouse** at the beginning? Repeat the three words. |
| dive | plane | sky | Which one sounds like **dog** at the beginning? Repeat the three words. |
| baby | balloon | dump truck | Which one sounds like **dog** at the beginning? Repeat the three words. |

- **DIRECTING THE LEARNER'S ATTENTION**

The purpose of this task is to teach the learner to distinguish the **m** and **d** sounds from among other beginning consonant sounds. As such, it is similar to storehouse module I-WA-5. To teach this skill you must direct the learner's attention by stating exactly what is to be learned and by highlighting the beginning sounds of the words. (You might, for instance, say each word twice, exaggerating the beginning sound the first time, using the say-it-slow or the get-your-mouth-ready techniques described in I-WA-5 and saying the word normally the second time.)

## • TEACHING ACTIVITIES

In teaching this auditory discrimination skill you can use either the modeling technique or the discovery technique described in I-WA-5, adjusting the suggestions to focus on the sounds being taught.

## • SUGGESTIONS FOR RETEACHING

If, after having been taught this skill with either the modeling or the discovery techniques, the learner is unable to distinguish auditorily the m and d sounds from among other beginning consonant sounds, you should

1. Reteach the skill, using the alternate technique.
2. Reexamine your attenders, being sure that the learner is listening to the *beginning* sounds of the word and that your highlighting is emphatic enough to help him or her distinguish the beginning sounds of the words.
3. Return to the previous auditory discrimination skills, being sure that the learner has a concept for different as it relates to sounds and that he or she can do the simpler tasks of auditory discrimination before requiring the learner to perform this task.

## • SUGGESTIONS FOR PRACTICE

Once the learner can distinguish the m and d sounds from among other beginning consonant sounds, create practice activities to solidify the skill, using the suggestions provided in I-WA-5.

## • THE POSTTEST

The procedure and criterion for mastery are the same as for the pretest.

| can | sidewalk | did | Which one sounds like **dog** at the beginning? Repeat the three words. |
| book | mine | cloud | Which one sounds like **mouse** at the beginning? Repeat the three words. |
| dark | bird | shoot | Which one sounds like **dog** at the beginning? Repeat the three words. |
| sign | doctor | ball | Which one sounds like **dog** at the beginning? Repeat the three words. |
| moon | go | car | Which one sounds like **mouse** at the beginning? Repeat the three words. |
| mother | school | night | Which one sounds like **mouse** at the beginning? Repeat the three words. |

## • ENSURING TRANSFER

Although the learner will be applying this skill while learning to attach symbols to the sounds in subsequent objectives, you should also use the suggestions provided in I-WA-5 to be sure that the skill is used during the routine daily activities of the classroom.

## • THE PERFORMANCE OBJECTIVE

Given spoken words, beginning with **m** or **d** sounds, the learner will identify the beginning letter as **m** or **d**.

## • THE PRETEST

Give the learner two cards, one having the letter **m** printed on it and the other having the letter **d** printed on it. Say the following words, directing the learner to point to the letter card whose sound begins the words. The criterion for mastery is 80 percent with no letter sound being missed more than once.

| | | | | |
|---|---|---|---|---|
| menthol | deadeye | den | dial | match |
| mast | mammoth | design | may | duffel |

## • DIRECTING THE LEARNER'S ATTENTION

The purpose of this task is to teach the learner to establish a sound-symbol connection between the letters **m** and **d** and the sounds these letters make at the beginning of words. This is a particularly crucial task for the reader to learn, since ability to analyze or sound out such words as **man** and **dog** will depend to a large extent upon connecting the correct sound with the letter **m** at the beginning of **man** and with the letter **d** at the beginning of **dog**. As the learner progresses to subsequent skills, he or she will learn to connect sounds with letters at the middle and end of words as well as at the beginning and to connect sounds with vowels as well as with consonants.

To connect letters and their sounds the learner must use both visual and auditory skills, must be able to discriminate visually among and name the letters (as was taught in I-SW-11), and must be able to distinguish by ear the sounds of the letters being taught from other sounds. Consequently, you must be sure that the learner has mastered these prerequisite skills before asking her or him to perform this task.

To teach this skill you must (in addition to being sure that the learner possesses the prerequisites) direct attention by stating exactly what is being learned and by highlighting the sound heard at the beginning of the word and the form of the letter it is to be connected with. (With the word **men,** for instance, you might exaggerate the beginning sound heard in the word while simultaneously pointing to a cutout letter **m**.)

## • THIS IS A STOREHOUSE OBJECTIVE

The following instructional activities are your storehouse of techniques for developing skill in establishing connections between letters and the sounds they produce. This skill recurs for other letters later in the hierarchy. The

activities that follow are to be adapted and used with each of these as they occur.

• **TEACHING ACTIVITIES**

*The modeling technique.* Gather together a series of pictures or objects that have names beginning with the sound of the letter to be taught and cutouts of the letter. Direct the learner to watch you and to be ready to mimic your words and actions. Take one of the pictures or objects that begin wtih the letter m and say, 'This is a picture of a mouse. I'm going to say the word slowly and then fast so I can hear the beginning sound. **M-m-m-ouse. Mouse.** Now I'm going to put the picture down and put the letter m to the left of it. Now I will say the name. **Mouse.** Then I will say the name slowly, pointing to the letter m as I say the first sound. **M-m-m-ouse.** Then I'll say it fast. **Mouse.** The letter I hear at the beginning of **mouse** is m. I'm going to get my mouth ready to say another m word. **M-m-monkey.**" Then have the learner mimic your action, being sure that the child is both pointing to and looking at the letter while saying the beginning sound of the word so that the connection between the letter and its sound is made. As the learner responds successfully, repeat the procedure and gradually diminish the amount of help you provide until the learner is able to name the letter heard at the beginning of m words without either modeling your actions of exaggerating the sound as he or she points to the appropriate letter.

Is there a comfortable place in the classroom for children to stretch out and read?

*The discovery technique.* The principle to be discovered is that a particular sound at the beginning of words can be associated with a particular letter. Use pictures and cutout letters as described earlier. Show several of the pictures and say their names one after another, exaggerating the beginning sounds in the initial stages. Have the learner listen to the beginning sound and tell you whether all the beginning sounds in words are alike. If the learner responds "Yes", say, "The first word begins with the letter m. Watch and listen as I point to the letter m and say the word. **M-m-m-money. Money.** If the first word begins with m and all the words sound alike at the beginning, what letter do you suppose the other words begin with?" If the learner responds correctly, have him or her say each word in turn, pointing to the beginning letter while saying the beginning of each word. If the learner does not respond correctly, return to the first word, exaggerate again the sound as you point to the letter m, and say, 'The first letter in **money** is m. **Man** begins with the same sound as **money.** The first letter in **man** is also m. Listen to the next word. **Mouse.** Does it begin like **money** and **man**? If **money** and **man** begin with the letter m, what letter will **mouse** begin with?" If the learner responds correctly have him or her say the remaining words while pointing to the letter heard at the beginning.

• **SUGGESTIONS FOR RETEACHING**

If, after having been taught with either of the preceding techniques, the learner is unable to connect the letters m and d with the sounds they make at the beginning of words, you should

1. Reteach the skill, using the alternate technique.
2. Be more specific in directing the learner's attention, being sure that he or she is listening to the beginning sound while simultaneously looking at the letter.
3. Use more emphasis in highlighting the beginning sound, the letter, and the connection between them.
4. Return to the previous objective and be sure that the learner can distinguish the beginning **m** and **d** sounds before requiring him or her to connect the sound to a letter.
5. Return to the objectives on visually discriminating and naming letters to be sure that the learner has mastered these prerequisite skills.

● **SUGGESTIONS FOR PRACTICE**

Once the learner has successfully connected the **m** and **d** letters to the **m** and **d** sounds, use one or more of the following practice activities to solidify the skill:

1. Make a shutter device out of tagboard in which the opening of the shutter can be controlled by you. Insert a card that has the letter to be learned at the left, followed by a picture of an object with the sound of that letter at the beginning. Open the shutter to reveal first the letter and then the picture. Have the learner form the letter sound with his mouth and blend that sound into the picture name as it is exposed.
2. Use the same device as described in activity 1, but this time insert a picture first, then the letter, then the picture again. Have the learner say the picture name, then the letter sound heard at the beginning of the picture name, and then blend that sound into the picture name as it is exposed the second time.
3. Use flashcards containing the letters to be learned. Flash a letter to the learner and direct him or her to respond with a word that begins (or ends) with that letter sound.
4. To help the learner connect the letter and the sound, display pictures of common objects (dogs, money, and so on) with the letter the object begins with printed at the left. Encourage the learner to use these pictures when trying to remember the sound of a particular letter.
5. Make a box and label it with a large printed form of the letter you are teaching. Place in the box pictures and objects whose names begin (or end) with the letter to be practiced. Direct the learner to reach into the box, draw a picture or object, name it, and tell what letter the object begins with. Make sure the learner looks at the letter on the box while saying the object's name.
6. For learners who need review on a number of letters and their sound corespondence, you may modify the activity described in 5 above by putting several letters on the outside of the box and placing objects that begin with all these letters in the box. The learner then draws an object, names it, and points to the letter on the box that begins the object's name.

7. Give each learner a group of pictures, some of which begin with the letter to be worked on and some of which do not. Hold up a letter card and direct the learner to hold up any picture he or she has that begins (or ends) with the sound associated with that letter.

8. Using a flannel board or a pocket chart, place a letter card to the left and a row of three pictures to the right. Two of the pictures should begin with the sound associated with the letter at the left and one should not. Direct the learner to pick out the two pictures that begin with the sound associated with the letter at the left.

9. Make a bullein board or a large chart showing the letters to be learned in one part and having, next to them and under a flap, a picture whose name begins with the sound associated with that letter. When the learner cannot remember the sound of **m**, for instance, he or she can go to the bulletin board, look under the flap next to **m** and say to himself, "Oh, the sound of **m** is what we hear we hear at the beginning of **money**" (or whatever the picture is under the flap).

10. Make a tagboard chart with the letters to be learned listed down one side and pictures beginning (or ending) with the sounds of these letters listed down the other. Attach pieces of string to the letters and direct the learner to connect the string for each letter to an object that begins with the sound of that letter.

11. Provide the learner with a number of letters. Play a game in which you say, "I see a letter whose sound we hear at the beginning of the word **money**. What letter do I see?" The learner responds by holding up the proper letter card, looking at it, and saying, "**Money** begins with the letter **m**."

12. Make a set of picture cards for each letter sound. Teach the learner to play a card game in which several cards are dealt to each player. The learner tries to pair picture cards beginning with the same letter sound. Each player takes turns asking his or her opponents, "Do you have a picture card beginning with the letter **m**?" If a child has such a card, he or she gives the picture card to the learner requesting it and then has the opportunity to draw a card from the learner's hand in return. The learner having the most pairs at the end wins.

13. Give the learners a group of letter cards. Each learner takes turns saying, "I have a letter. **Money** starts with the sound of my letter. What letter do I have?" The learner who responds correctly is the next one to select a letter.

14. Play a dramatization game with learners in which you hold up a letter card and ask them to act out something that begins with the sound of that letter. Those who are not acting must try to guess what begins with the letter sound being dramatized.

## • THE POSTTEST

The procedure and criterion for mastery are the same as for the pretest.

| machine | deadly | dusty | demand | meter |
|---------|--------|-------|--------|-------|
| maple | magnet | delay | march | deputy |

## • ENSURING TRANSFER

The learner will be applying this skill in the more complex word analysis tasks with which he or she will be working while progressing through the hierarchy. However, in addition to these applications, you should be sure that this sound-symbol connection skill is also used during the routine daily activities of the classroom. Some suggested techniques follow.

1. Have the learner name objects around the classroom and tell what the beginning letter of that name would be.
2. Have the learner tell the beginning sound of a word you write on the blackboard or of one found in books he or she is reading.
3. When new words come up in class discussion, write them on the blackboard and say, "This word is _____. It starts with the letter **m** because it has the same sound at the beginning as (name another word the learner knows as beginning with **m**)."
4. When the child is reading and meets an unknown word beginning with **m** or **d,** encourage him or her to get his mouth ready to say the sound of the letter as an initial step in analyzing the word.

### I•WA•10

## • THE PERFORMANCE OBJECTIVE

When given a stimulus word beginning with either **l** or hard **c** and a group of four other words one of which begins with **l** or hard **c,** the learner will pair the two words beginning with the same letter.

## • THE PRETEST

Using the following words, say to the learner, "Here are three words. Listen carefully. (Say the three words.) Which one sounds like (say the stimulus word) at the beginning?" Repeat the three words. Criterion for mastery is five out of six correct.

| dog | pipe | list | Which one sounds like **lip** at the beginning? Then repeat the three words. |
|-----|------|------|------|
| last | tow | feel | Which one sounds like **lip** at the beginning? Then repeat the three words. |
| tall | bell | cake | Which one sounds like **can** at the beginning? Then repeat the three words. |
| hate | list | purr | Which one sounds like **lip** at the beginning? Then repeat the three words. |
| kite | book | hat | Which one sounds like **can** at the beginning? Then repeat the three words. |
| pen | flower | cup | Which one sounds like **can** at the beginning? Then repeat the three words. |

## • DIRECTING THE LEARNER'S ATTENTION

The purpose of this task is to teach the learner to distinguish the l and hard c sounds from other beginning consonant sounds. As such, this task is similar to storehouse module I-WA-5. To teach this skill you must direct the learner's attention by stating exactly what is to be learned and by highlighting the beginning sounds of the words as described in I-WA-5.

## • TEACHING ACTIVITIES

In teaching this auditory discrimination skill, you can use either the modeling technique or the discovery technique described in I-WA-5, adjusting the suggestions to focus on the l and hard c sounds.

## • SUGGESTIONS FOR RETEACHING

If, after having been taught this skill with either the modeling or the discovery technique, the learner is unable to distinguish by ear the l and hard c sounds from other beginning consonant sounds, you should

1. Reteach the skill, using the alternate technique.
2. Reexamine your attenders, being sure that the learner is listening to the *beginning* sounds of the word and that your highlighting is emphatic enough to help him or her distinguish the beginning sounds from other sounds.
3. Return to the previous auditory discrimination skills, being sure that the learner has a concept for different as it relates to sounds and that he or she can do the simpler tasks of auditory discrimination before requiring him or her to perform this task.

## • SUGGESTIONS FOR PRACTICE

Once the learner can distinguish the l and hard c sounds from other beginning consonant sounds, create practice activities to solidify the skill, using the suggestions provided in I-WA-5.

## • THE POSTTEST

The procedure and criterion for mastery are the same as for the pretest.

| bowl | table | like | Which one sounds like **lip** at the beginning? Then repeat the three words. |
| loop | pick | fall | Which one sounds like **lip** at the beginning? Then repeat the three words. |
| fell | leaf | come | Which one sounds like **can** at the beginning? Then repeat the three words. |
| far | lend | bush | Which one sounds like **lip** at the beginning? Then repeat the three words. |
| pat | dope | sell | Which one sounds like **can** at the beginning? Then repeat the three words. |
| car | sleep | cap | Which one sounds like **can** at the beginning? Then repeat the three words. |

## • ENSURING TRANSFER

Although the learner will be applying this skill while learning to attach symbols to the sounds in subsequent objectives, you should also use the suggestions provided in I-WA-5 to be sure that the skill is used during the routine daily activities of the classroom.

## • THE PERFORMANCE OBJECTIVE

When given spoken words beginning with l or hard c sounds, the learner will identify the beginning letters as l or c.

## • THE PRETEST

Give the learner two cards, one having the letter l printed on it and the other having the letter c printed on it. Say the following words, directing the learner to point to the letter card whose sound begins the word. The criterion for mastery is 80 percent.

| | | | | |
|---|---|---|---|---|
| loop | catch | cannon | custom | locket |
| lucky | loose | coupon | lamp | cover |

## • DIRECTING THE LEARNER'S ATTENTION

The purpose of this task is to teach the learner to establish a sound-symbol connection between the letters l and c and the sound those letters make at the beginning of words. As such, this task is similar to storehouse module I-WA-9. To teach this skill you must direct the learner's attention by stating exactly what is to be learned and by highlighting both the sound heard at the beginning of the word and the form of the letter it is to be connected with. (In the word **loop,** for instance, you might exaggerate the beginning sound heard in the word while simultaneously pointing to a cutout letter l.)

## • TEACHING ACTIVITIES

In teaching this sound-symbol connection skill you can use either the modeling technique or the discovery technique described in I-WA-9, adjusting the suggestions to focus on the letters l and c.

## • SUGGESTIONS FOR RETEACHING

If, after having been taught this skill with either the modeling or the discovery technique, the learner is unable to connect letter and sound for l and hard **c,** you should

1. Reteach the skill, using the alternate technique.
2. Be more specific in directing the learner's attention, being sure that he or she is listening to the beginning sound while simultaneously looking at the letter.
3. Use more emphasis in highlighting the beginning sound, the letter, and the connection between them.

4. Return to the previous objective and be sure that the learner can distinguish between the beginning l and hard c sounds before requiring him to connect the sound with a letter.

● **SUGGESTIONS FOR PRACTICE**

Once the learner has successfully connected the l and c letters to words beginning with the l or hard c sounds, create practice activities to solidify the skill, using the suggestions provided in I-WA-9.

● **THE POSTTEST**

The procedure and criterion for mastery are the same as in the pretest.

| | | | | |
|---|---|---|---|---|
| last | cabbage | costume | cardinal | lower |
| loaf | lady | carton | locust | carve |

● **ENSURING TRANSFER**

Although the learner will be applying this skill in subsequent skills in the hierarchy, you should also use the suggestions provided in I-WA-9 to be sure that the skill is used during the routine daily activities of the classroom.

## I•WA•12

● **THE PERFORMANCE OBJECTIVE**

When given a stimulus word with either s or h at the beginning and a group of three other words one of which begins with s or h, the learner will pair the two words beginning with the same letter.

● **THE PRETEST**

Using the following words, say to the learner, "Here are three words. Listen carefully. (Say the three words.) Which one sounds like (say the stimulus word) at the beginning?" Then repeat the three words. The criterion for mastery is five out of six correct.

| cow | luck | soon | Which one sounds like **sew** at the beginning? Then repeat the three words. |
|---|---|---|---|
| sit | roll | fall | Which one sounds like **sew** at the beginning? Then repeat the three words. |
| ball | pit | has | Which one sounds like **his** at the beginning? Then repeat the three words. |
| sock | bike | leg | Which one sounds like **sew** at the beginning? Then repeat the three words. |
| hit | glass | roof | Which one sounds like **his** at the beginning? Then repeat the three words. |
| paper | tall | hunt | Which one sounds like **his** at the beginning? Then repeat the three words. |

The purpose of this task is to teach the learner to distinguish the s and **h** sounds from other beginning consonant sounds. As such, this task is similar to storehouse module I-WA-5. To teach this skill, you must direct the learner's attention by stating exactly what is to be learned and by highlighting the beginning sound of the words as described in I-WA-5.

• **TEACHING ACTIVITIES**

In teaching this auditory discrimination skill you can use either the modeling technique or the discovery technique described in I-WA-5, adjusting the suggestions to focus on the s and **h** sounds.

• **SUGGESTIONS FOR RETEACHING**

If, after having been taught this skill using either the modeling or the discovery technique, the learner is unable to distinguish the s and **h** sounds by ear from other beginning consonant sounds, you should

1. Reteach the skill, using the alternate technique.
2. Reexamine your attenders, being sure that the learner is listening to the *beginning* sounds and that your highlighting is emphatic enough to help him or her distinguish the beginning sounds from other sounds.
3. Return to the previous auditory discrimination skills, being sure that the learner can perform those before requiring him or her to complete this objective.

• **SUGGESTIONS FOR PRACTICE**

Once the learner can distinguish the s and **h** sounds from other beginning consonant sounds, create practice activities to solidify the skill, using the suggestions provided in I-WA-5.

• **THE POSTTEST**

The procedure and criterion for mastery are the same as for the pretest.

| cash | loop | sip | Which one sounds like **sew** at the beginning? Then repeat the three words. |
| suck | rice | fish | Which one sounds like **sew** at the beginning? Then repeat the three words. |
| bill | past | hurt | Which one sounds like **his** at the beginning? Then repeat the three words. |
| sort | bill | lake | Which one sounds like **sew** at the beginning? Then repeat the three words. |
| horse | glue | row | Which one sounds like **his** at the beginning? Then repeat the three words. |
| past | teach | hand | Which one sounds like **his** at the beginning? Then repeat the three words. |

## • ENSURING TRANSFER

Although the learner will be applying this skill while learning to attach the sounds to letters in subsequent objectives, you should also use the suggestions provided in I-WA-5 to be sure that the skill is used during the routine daily activities of the classroom.

## I•WA•13

## • THE PERFORMANCE OBJECTIVE

When given spoken words beginning with s or h sounds, the learner will identify the beginning letter as being either s or h.

## • THE PRETEST

Give the learner two cards, one having the letter s printed on it and the other having the letter h printed on it. Say the following words, directing the learner to point to the letter card whose sound begins the word. The criterion for mastery is 80 percent.

| soap | silly | hippy | single | happy |
|------|-------|-------|--------|-------|
| house | hide | set | hick | sunny |

## • DIRECTING THE LEARNER'S ATTENTION

The purpose of this task is to teach the learner to establish a sound-symbol connection between the letters s and h and the sound these letters make at the beginning of words. As such, this task is similar to storehouse module I-WA-9. To teach this skill you must direct the learner's attention by stating exactly what is to be learned and by highlighting both the sound heard at the beginning of the word and the form of the letter it is to be connected with. (In the word soap, for instance, you might exaggerate the beginning sound heard in the word while simultaneously pointing to the cutout letter s.)

## • TEACHING ACTIVITIES

In teaching this sound-symbol connection skill you can use either the modeling technique or the discovery technique described in I-WA-9, adjusting the suggestions to focus on the letters s and h.

## • SUGGESTIONS FOR RETEACHING

If, after having been taught this skill with either the modeling or the discovery technique, the learner is unable to connect letter and sound for s and h, you should

1. Reteach the skill, using the alternate technique.
2. Be more specific in directing the learner's attention, being sure that he or she is listening to the beginning sound while simultaneously looking at the letter.
3. Use more emphasis in highlighting the beginning sound, the letter, and the connection between them.

4. Return to the previous objective and be sure that the learner can distinguish between the beginning **s** and **h** sounds before requiring him or her to connect the sound with a letter.

## • SUGGESTIONS FOR PRACTICE

Once the learner has successfully connected the **s** and **h** letters to words beginning with the **s** or **h** sounds, create practice activities to solidify the skill, using the suggestions provided in I-WA-9.

## • THE POSTTEST

The procedure and criterion for mastery are the same as in the pretest.

| settle | high | hill | hard | hurry |
|--------|------|------|------|-------|
| supper | same | hobby | soup | saddle |

## • ENSURING TRANSFER

Although the learner will be applying this skill in subsequent skills in the hierarchy, you should also use the suggestions provided in I-WA-9 to be sure that the skill is used during the routine daily activities of the classroom.

# I•WA•14

## • THE PERFORMANCE OBJECTIVE

When given an oral sentence with one word missing and being cued for the missing word with a card having printed on it the first letter of that word (**m, d, l, c, s, h**), the learner will say a word that fits the context and begins with that letter.

## • THE PRETEST

Make cards with the preceding letters printed on them. Say, "I am going to say a sentence with one word missing. You look at the card and say a word that begins with the letter on the card and that finishes what I want to say." Use the following sentences. Display the letter card only when you come to the blank. The criterion for mastery is 10 out of 12, with no letter being missed more than once. *Note:* If a sentence fails to match the learner's background or does not provide enough context clues to complete the sentence, you should alter the sentence accordingly. Sentence 1, for instance, could be changed to read, "We go to the bank to get some m_____" or "I earn most of my m_____ by mowing lawns."

1. I like to spend m_____.
2. I gave a bone to the d_____.
3. The hat looks pretty on the l_____.
4. A c_____ likes to drink milk.
5. The s_____ was shining bright.
6. The man was painting the h_____.
7. I have m_____ toys.

8. I like to d_____ when I swim.
9. I l_____ at the funny joke.
10. Can you c_____ me?
11. The mattress is s_____.
12. H_____ me find my pencil. It is lost.

### • DIRECTING THE LEARNER'S ATTENTION

The purpose of this task is to help the learner use his or her knowledge of letter-sound correspondence and context to identify unknown words. This skill recognizes the fact that word analysis should not be limited to simple sounding of letters. Rather, the learner should be encouraged also to use his or her understanding of language patterns and experience to make re-alistic guesses about the unknown word. By combining the learner's language sense and knowledge of initial consonant sounds, the learner systematizes his or her guessing, limiting the number of possibilities about the unknown word.

Ultimately, the learner will use this skill when reading. At this stage, however, there is little the learner can read independently. Consequently, the skill is introduced here as a listening activity. As the learner develops a sight word vocabulary in subsequent objectives in the hierarchy, this skill will be used in the reading situation.

To teach this skill you must direct the learner's attention by stating exactly what is to be learned and by highlighting the words in the sentence that provide clues to the identity of the unknown word, the letter that the unknown word begins with and the sound associated with that letter. (In the first sentence in the pretest, for instance, you might highlight the word **spend,** direct the learner to look at a large cutout **m,** and have the learner get his or her mouth ready to say the sound of this letter.)

### • THIS IS A STOREHOUSE OBJECTIVE

The following instructional activities are your storehouse of techniques for developing skill in using both context sense and letter-sound correspon-dence to identify unknown words. This skill recurs in more sophisticated forms later in the skill hierarchy. The activities that follow are to be adapted and used with each of these as they occur.

### • TEACHING ACTIVITIES

*The modeling technique.* Tell the learner that you are going to demon-strate how to find out what an unknown word is by using clues in the sen-tence and the sound of a letter he or she knows and that he or she should be ready to do as you do when you are done. Then say the sentence, "I like to spend m_____," holding up the letter **m** letter card when you come to the blank. Say, "I must figure out what the last word in the sen-tence is. I know it begins with the letter **m** and so the word must sound at the beginning like **monkey, milk,** and other **m** words. I also know that the word must be something that I *spend.* So I am going to say the sen-tence again, think about what I like to spend, and get my mouth ready to say an **m** word when I come to the blank." Say the sentence again, emphasizing the word **spend,** exaggerate the get-your-mouth-ready technique and say the word **monkey.** Say, "I have an **m** word in the blank but it does not make sense because we do not spend monkeys." Repeat the process but put in the word **money.** Say, "**Money** must be the right word because it is an **m** word and it is something that we like to spend." Repeat the same process with the second sentence, but after you have highlighted the clue word(s), the letter, and its sound, have the learner supply the word to complete the sentence. Continue through subsequent sentences, diminishing the amount of assistance you provide until the learner is able to perform the task without assistance.

*The discovery technique.* The principle to be discovered is that we can identify an unknown word by using the sense of the sentence and the sound value of the first letter. To help the learner discover this principle, do several of the pretest items for her or him, highlighting the clue word, the beginning letter of the unknown word, and its sound value as you do so. Then ask the learner to discover how you knew what the unknown word was, directing her or his attention with questions such as the following

> Why did I emphasize this word (the clue word) when I said the sentence?

> Why did I look at the letter and get my mouth ready to say its sound when I came to the blank in the sentence?

> How did I know the word in the first sentence wasn't **monkey?** How did I know it wasn't **dollars?**

Are your learners coming to school excited and eager to start a new day?

As the learner responds correctly, provide other examples but gradually diminish the amount of highlighting you provide and the number of questions you ask until the learner can perform the task without assistance.

## • SUGGESTIONS FOR RETEACHING

If, after having been taught with either the modeling or the discovery technique, the learner is unable to use context and letter-sound correspondence to identify the unknown word, you should

1. Reteach the skill, using the alternate technique.
2. Be more specific in directing the learner's attention, being sure that he or she is attending to the meaning of the clue word, to the beginning letter, and to that letter's sound value.
3. Use more emphasis in highlighting the clue word(s), the beginning letter, and its sound.
4. Be sure that the sentences and words being used match the learner's experience background, changing these appropriately when you find that he or she does not understand the context.
5. Return to the objectives where the sound-symbol connection for the

various letters were taught, being sure that the learner has mastered these skills before requiring him or her to perform this task.

6. If the difficulty lies with the learner's understanding of the process itself, reverse the roles described in the pretest and have the learner create the sentences with the teacher responding.

7. If the difficulty lies in a general deficiency in oral language, provide many sentence completion activities in which the learner orally finishes thoughts begun by the teacher without using letter-sound clues.

### • SUGGESTIONS FOR PRACTICE

Once the learner has successfully learned to identify unknown words by using the context and his or her previous knowledge of sound-symbol connections, use one or more of the following practice activities to solidify the skill:

1. Once the learner develops a sight word vocabulary, you can use those words to create sentences such as those in the pretest, asking the learner to read the sentence and to provide the missing word. If the learner cannot yet read independently, you can do the same thing as a listening activity, with the sentences being put on tape or being provided by another learner, an aide, or you.

2. Read a paragraph to the learner and state that you will stop reading every once in a while and hold up a letter card. Direct the learner to keep the paragraph in mind, to look at the letter on the card, to think of the sound associated with that letter, and to say a word that both begins with that letter sound and that fits the sense of the paragraph.

3. Play games with the learner that require him or her to use both context and sound-symbol connections. For instance, direct the learner to listen to a sentence such as "I went to the store and bought a mouse, a _____, a _____, and a _____." Hold up a letter card to indicate the beginning letter of the word to fill the missing space. The learner expands the sentence by adding words that begin with the sound associated with the letter you show.

4. Group your learners in pairs. Give each pair a supply of letter cards. Let each take a turn in making up a sentence in which one word is left out. The learner must hold up the beginning letter of the missing word at the appropriate spot in the sentence. His or her partner uses the sense of the sentence and the sound-symbol connection of the letter card to guess what word goes in the space. If the learner correctly identifies the missing word, it is his or her turn to make up a sentence.

5. Give learners riddles in which the context supplies only a minimum outline of what the missing word is. For instance, you could provide the sentence, "The swimmer dived into the _____." Elicit learner response, encouraging a variety of answers, such as **water, pool, lake, river,** and so on. Then place a letter card (such as the letter **w**) at the left of the blank space and say, "Now what word *must* go in the blank space?"

The procedure and criterion for mastery are the same as on the pretest.

1. The sun comes out in the daytime but the m_____ comes out at night.
2. The teacher said, "Shut the d_____."
3. It is dark. Turn on the l_____.
4. Don't eat c_____ before dinner.
5. Put your shoes and s_____ under the bed.
6. He put the h_____ on his head.
7. When you cross the street, you m_____ look both ways.
8. What do you d_____ on a rainy day?
9. I l_____ candy.
10. Will you c_____ to my party?
11. Wash your hands with s_____ and water.
12. I h_____ a new bicycle.

• ENSURING TRANSFER

This skill should be applied frequently during the daily routine activities of the classroom. During oral activities you should look for opportunities to start sentences and ask learners to complete them, giving as a clue the beginning letter of the word you are thinking of. During reading, the learner should be encouraged to analyze unknown words by using both the context and the sound value of the first letter to make a calculated guess regarding the identity of the word.

I•WA•15

• THE PERFORMANCE OBJECTIVE

When given a stimulus word beginning with the **t**, **b**, or **p** sounds and a group of three other words, one of which begins with the **t**, **b**, or **p** sounds, the learner will pair the two words beginning with the same sound.

• THE PRETEST

Using the following words, say to the learner, "Here are three words. Listen carefully. (Say the words.) Which one sounds like (say the stimulus word) at the beginning?" Repeat the three original words. The criterion for mastery is five out of six correct.

| dog | house | tooth | Which one sounds like **top** at the beginning? Repeat the three words. |
| bike | rock | frog | Which one sounds like **boy** at the beginning? Repeat the three words. |
| dance | fall | took | Which one sounds like **top** at the beginning? Repeat the three words. |
| push | run | rush | Which one sounds like **pat** at the beginning? Repeat the three words. |
| stand | band | like | Which one sounds like **boy** at the beginning? Repeat the three words. |
| art | list | part | Which one sounds like **pat** at the beginning? Repeat the three words. |

## • DIRECTING THE LEARNER'S ATTENTION

The purpose of this task is to teach the learner to distinguish the **t, b,** and **p** sounds from other beginning consonant sounds. As such, the task is similar to storehouse module I-WA-5. To teach this skill you must direct the learner's attention by stating exactly is what to be learned and by highlighting the beginning sound of the words as described in I-WA-5.

## • TEACHING ACTIVITIES

In teaching this auditory discrimination skill you can use either the modeling technique or the discovery technique described in I-WA-5, adjusting the suggestions to focus on the **t, b,** and **p** sounds.

## • SUGGESTIONS FOR RETEACHING

If, after having been taught this skill with either the modeling or the discovery technique, the learner is unable to distinguish by ear the **t, b,** and **p** sounds from other beginning consonant sounds, you should

1. Reteach the skill, using the alternate technique.
2. Reexamine your attenders, being sure that the learner is listening to the *beginning* sounds and that your highlighting is emphatic enough to help him or her distinguish the beginning sounds from other sounds.
3. Return to the previous auditory discrimination skills, being sure that the learner can perform those before requiring him to complete this objective.

## • SUGGESTIONS FOR PRACTICE

Once the learner can distinguish the **t, b,** and **p** sounds from other beginning consonant sounds, create practice activities to solidify the skill, using the suggestions provided in I-WA-5.

## • THE POSTTEST

The procedure and criterion for mastery are the same as for the pretest.

| | | | |
|---|---|---|---|
| rest | pass | last | Which one sounds like **pat** at the beginning? Repeat the three words. |
| box | fox | likes | Which one sounds like **boy** at the beginning? Repeat the three words. |
| ran | fan | pan | Which one sounds like **pat** at the beginning? Repeat the three words. |
| able | table | fall | Which one sounds like **top** at the beginning? Repeat the three words. |
| best | rest | first | Which one sounds like **boy** at the beginning? Repeat the three words. |
| fell | blue | tell | Which one sounds like **top** at the beginning? Repeat the three words. |

## • ENSURING TRANSFER

Although the learner will be applying this skill while learning to attach the sounds to letters in subsequent objectives, you should also use the suggestions provided in I-WA-5 to be sure that the skill is used during the routine daily activities of the classroom.

### • THE PERFORMANCE OBJECTIVE

When given spoken words beginning with the **t, b,** or **p** sounds, the learner will identify the beginning letters as **t, b,** or **p.**

### • THE PRETEST

Give the learner three cards, one having the letter **t** printed on it, another having the letter **b** printed on it, and a third having the letter **p** printed on it. Say the following words, directing the learner to point to the letter whose sound begins the word just spoken. The criterion for mastery is 80 percent, with no letter sound being missed more than once.

| | | | | |
|---|---|---|---|---|
| tuba | bench | bubble | busy | pencil |
| table | powder | task | tower | bunch |

### • DIRECTING THE LEARNER'S ATTENTION

The purpose of this task is to teach the learner to establish a sound-symbol connection between the letters **t, b,** and **p** and the sounds these letters make at the beginning of words. As such, the task is similar to storehouse module I-WA-9. To teach this skill you must direct the learner's attention by stating exactly what is to be learned and by highlighting both the sound heard at the beginning of the word and the form of the letter it is to be connected with. (In the word **tuba,** for instance, you might tell the learner to get his or her mouth ready to say the beginning sound heard in the word while simultaneously pointing to the cutout letter **t.**)

### • TEACHING ACTIVITIES

In teaching this sound-symbol connection skill you can use either the modeling technique or the discovery technique described in I-WA-9, adjusting the suggestions to focus on the letters **t, b,** and **p.**

### • SUGGESTIONS FOR RETEACHING

If, after having been taught this skill with either the modeling or the discovery technique, the learner is unable to connect letter and sound for **t, b,** and **p,** you should

1. Reteach the skill, using the alternate technique.
2. Be more specific in directing the learner's attention, being sure that he or she is listening to the beginning sound while simultaneously looking at the letter.
3. Use more emphasis in highlighting the beginning sound, the letter and the connection between them.

4. Return to the previous objective and insure that the learner can distinguish between the beginning **t, b,** and **p** sounds before requiring him to connect the sounds with letters.

● **SUGGESTIONS FOR PRACTICE**

Once the learner has successfully connected the **t, b,** and **p** letters to their beginning sounds, create practice activities to solidify the skill using the suggestions provided in I-WA-9.

● **THE POSTTEST**

The procedure and criterion for mastery are the same as for the pretest.

| banana | teeth | taxi | pastor | buzz |
|--------|-------|--------|--------|-------|
| pig | bush | beetle | buggy | teach |

● **ENSURING TRANSFER**

Although the learner will be applying this skill in subsequent skills in the hierarchy, you should also use the suggestions provided in I-WA-9 to be sure that the skill is used during the routine daily activities of the classroom.

# I•WA•17

● **THE PERFORMANCE OBJECTIVE**

When given a stimulus word beginning with the **w, r,** or **f** sounds and a group of three words, one of which begins with the **w, r,** or **f** sound, the learner will pair the two words beginning with the same sound.

● **THE PRETEST**

Using the following words, say to the learner, "Here are three words. Listen carefully. (Say the words.) Which one sounds like (say the stimulus word) at the beginning?" Repeat the three original words. The criterion for mastery is five out of six correct.

| test | man | wish | Which one sounds like **win** at the beginning? Repeat the three words. |
|------|-----|------|------------------------------------------------------------------------|
| fall | tall | note | Which one sounds like **fan** at the beginning? Repeat the three words. |
| nest | rest | box | Which one sounds like **run** at the beginning? Repeat the three words. |
| task | fast | look | Which one sounds like **fan** at the beginning? Repeat the three words. |
| fell | talk | well | Which one sounds like **win** at the beginning? Repeat the three words. |
| stone | reap | top | Which one sounds like **run** at the beginning? Repeat the three words. |

● **DIRECTING THE LEARNER'S ATTENTION**

The purpose of this task is to teach the learner to distinguish the **w, r,** and **f** sounds from other beginning consonant sounds. As such, this task is similar to storehouse module I-WA-5. To teach this skill you must direct the learner's attention by stating exactly what is to be learned and by highlighting the beginning sounds of the words as described in I-WA-5.

## • TEACHING ACTIVITIES

In teaching this auditory discrimination skill you can use either the modeling technique or the discovery technique described in I-WA-5, adjusting the suggestions to focus on the w, r, and f sounds.

## • SUGGESTIONS FOR RETEACHING

If, after having been taught this skill with either the modeling or the discovery technique, the learner is unable to distinguish the w, r, and f sounds by ear from other beginning consonant sounds, you should

1. Reteach the skill, using the alternate technique.
2. Reexamine your attenders, being sure that the learner is listening to the *beginning* sounds and that your highlighting is emphatic enough to help him or her distinguish the beginning sounds from other sounds.
3. Return to the previous auditory discrimination skills, being sure that the learner can perform those before requiring him or her to complete this objective.

## • SUGGESTIONS FOR PRACTICE

Once the learner can distinguish the w, r, and f sounds from other beginning sounds, create practice activities to solidify the skill, using suggestions provided in I-WA-5.

## • THE POSTTEST

The procedure and criterion for mastery are the same as for the pretest.

| real | true | big | Which word sounds like **run** at the beginning? Repeat the three words. |
| go | gate | wait | Which word sounds like **win** at the beginning? Repeat the three words. |
| wish | fish | stop | Which word sounds like **fan** at the beginning? Repeat the three words. |
| up | rope | hope | Which word sounds like **run** at the beginning? Repeat the three words. |
| fact | down | ran | Which word sounds like **fan** at the beginning? Repeat the three words. |
| fence | out | went | Which word sounds like **win** at the beginning? Repeat the three words. |

Although the learner will be applying this skill while learning to attach
the sounds to letters in subsequent objectives, you should also use the suggestions provided in I-WA-5 to be sure that the skill is used during the
routine daily activities of the classroom.

# I•WA•18

### • THE PERFORMANCE OBJECTIVE
When given spoken words beginning with the w, r, or f sounds, the learner
will identify the beginning letters as w, r, or f.

### • THE PRETEST
Give the learner three cards, one having the letter w printed on it, another
having the letter r printed on it, and a third having the letter f printed on
it. Say the following words, directing the learner to point to the letter whose
sound begins the word just spoken. The criterion for mastery is 80 percent,
with no letter sound being missed more than once.

| | | | |
|---|---|---|---|
| wash | rush | fool | rascal |
| fire | fasten | window | windy |

### • DIRECTING THE LEARNER'S ATTENTION
The purpose of this task is to teach the learner to establish a sound-symbol
connection between the letters w, r, and f and the sounds these letters
make at the beginning of words. As such, the task is similar to storehouse
module I-WA-9. To teach this skill you must direct the learner's attention
by stating exactly what is to be learned and by highlighting both the sound
heard at the beginning of the word and the form of the letter it is to be
connected with. (In the word **wash**, for instance, you might exaggerate the
beginning sound heard in the word while simultaneously pointing to the
cutout letter **w**.)

### • TEACHING ACTIVITIES
In teaching this sound-symbol connection skill you can use either the modeling technique or the discovery technique described in I-WA-9, adjusting
the suggestions to focus on the letters w, r, and f.

### • SUGGESTIONS FOR RETEACHING
If, after having been taught this skill with either the modeling or the discovery technique, the learner is unable to connect letter and sound for w,
r, and f, you should

1. Reteach the skill, using the alternate technique.
2. Be more specific in directing the learner's attention, being sure that he
   or she is listening to the beginning sound while simultaneously looking
   at the letter.
3. Use more emphasis in highlighting the beginning sound, the letter, and
   the connection between them.

4. Return to the previous objective and be sure that the learner can distinguish between the beginning **w**, **r**, and **f** sounds before requiring him or her to connect the sounds with letters.

## • SUGGESTIONS FOR PRACTICE

Once the learner has successfully connected the **w**, **r**, and **f** letters to sounds, create practice activities to solidify the skill, using the suggestions provided in I-WA-9.

## • THE POSTTEST

The procedure and criterion for mastery are the same as for the pretest.

| | | | | |
|---|---|---|---|---|
| ready | razor | fix | farmer | fence |
| wash | wider | weapon | rocket | water |

## • ENSURING TRANSFER

Although the learner will be applying this skill in subsequent skills in the hierarchy, you should also use the suggestions provided in I-WA-9 to be sure that the skill is used during the routine daily activities of the classroom.

## • THE PERFORMANCE OBJECTIVE

Given a stimulus word beginning with the hard **g**, **k**, **j**, or **n** sounds and a group of three other words one of which begins with the hard **g**, **k**, **j**, or **n** sounds, the learner will pair the two words beginning with the same sound.

## • THE PRETEST

Using the following words say to the learner, "Here are three words. Listen carefully. (Say the three words.) Which one sounds like (say stimulus word) at the beginning?" Repeat the original three words. The criterion for mastery is seven out of eight correct.

| | | | |
|---|---|---|---|
| fate | sun | gate | Which one sounds like **good** at the beginning? Repeat the three words. |
| kiss | look | miss | Which one sounds like **kite** at the beginning? Repeat the three words. |
| toy | jack | ask | Which one sounds like **joy** at the beginning? Repeat the three words. |
| keel | desk | floor | Which one sounds like **kite** at the beginning? Repeat the three words. |
| bet | fall | net | Which one sounds like **no** at the beginning? Repeat the three words. |
| golf | tape | bag | Which one sounds like **good** at the beginning? Repeat the three words. |
| food | bed | juice | Which one sounds like **joy** at the beginning? Repeat the three words. |
| night | day | grass | Which one sounds like **no** at the beginning? Repeat the three words. |

## • DIRECTING THE LEARNER'S ATTENTION

The purpose of this task is to teach the learner to distinguish the hard **g**, **k**, **j**, and **n** sounds from other beginning consonant sounds. As such, the task is similar to storehouse module I-WA-5. To teach this skill you must direct the learner's attention by stating exactly what is to be learned and by highlighting the beginning sound of the word as described in I-WA-5.

## • TEACHING ACTIVITIES

In teaching this auditory discrimination skill you can use either the modeling technique or the discovery technique described in I-WA-5, adjusting the suggestions to focus on the hard **g**, **k**, **j**, and **n** sounds.

## • SUGGESTIONS FOR RETEACHING

If, after having been taught this skill with either the modeling or the discovery technique, the learner is unable to distinguish by ear the hard **g**, **k**, **j**, and **n** sounds from other beginning consonant sounds, you should

1. Reteach the skill, using the alternate technique.
2. Reexamine your attenders, being sure that the learner is listening to the *beginning* sounds and that your highlighting is emphatic enough to help him or her distinguish the beginning sounds from other sounds.
3. Return to the previous auditory discrimination skills, being sure that the learner can perform those before requiring him or her to complete this objective.

## • SUGGESTIONS FOR PRACTICE

Once the learner can distinguish the hard **g**, **k**, **j**, and **n** sounds from other beginning consonant sounds, create practice activities to solidify the skill, using the suggestions provided in I-WA-5.

## • THE POSTTEST

The procedure and the criterion for mastery are the same as for the pretest.

| | | | |
|---|---|---|---|
| never | soon | fear | Which one sounds like **no** at the beginning? Repeat the three words. |
| bird | case | jockey | Which one sounds like **joy** at the beginning? Repeat the three words. |
| gas | comic | house | Which one sounds like **good** at the beginning? Repeat the three words. |
| pouch | clip | night | Which one sounds like **no** at the beginning? Repeat the three words. |
| kangaroo | bat | flower | Which one sounds like **kite** at the beginning? Repeat the three words. |

| | | | |
|---|---|---|---|
| folder | junk | bunk | Which one sounds like **joy** at the beginning? Repeat the three words. |
| king | many | best | Which one sounds like **kite** at the beginning? Repeat the three words. |
| down | hold | give | Which one sounds like **good** at the beginning? Repeat the three words. |

#### • ENSURING TRANSFER

Although the learner will be applying this skill while learning to attach sounds to letters in subsequent objectives, you should also use the suggestions provided in I-WA-5 to be sure that the skill is used during the routine daily activities of the classroom.

#### • THE PERFORMANCE OBJECTIVE

When given spoken words beginning with the hard **g**, **k**, **j**, or **n** sounds, the learner will identify the beginning letters as **g**, **k**, **j**, or **n**.

#### • THE PRETEST

Give the learner four cards, one having the letter **g** printed on it, another with **k**, another with **j**, and the last with **n**. Say the following words, directing the learner to point to the letter whose sound begins the word just spoken. The criterion for mastery is 10 out of 12 correct, with no letter sound being missed more than once.

| | | | | | |
|---|---|---|---|---|---|
| get | kite | jackrabbit | king | gone | jerk |
| goose | near | navy | jar | keep | neat |

#### • DIRECTING THE LEARNER'S ATTENTION

The purpose of this task is to teach the learner to establish a sound-symbol connection between the letters **g**, **k**, **j**, and **n** and the sounds these letters make at the beginning of words. As such, the task is similar to storehouse module I-WA-9. To teach this skill you must direct the learner's attention by stating exactly what is to be learned and by highlighting both the sound heard at the beginning of the word and the form of the letter to be connected with. (In the word **get**, for instance, you might tell the learner to get his or her mouth ready to say the beginning sound in the word while simultaneously pointing to the cutout letter **g**.)

#### • TEACHING ACTIVITIES

In teaching this sound-symbol connection skill you can use either the modeling technique or the discovery technique described in I-WA-9, adjusting the suggestions to focus on the letters **g**, **k**, **j**, and **n**.

## • SUGGESTIONS FOR RETEACHING

If, after having been taught this skill with either the modeling or the discovery technique, the learner is unable to connect letter and sound for **g, k, j,** and **n,** you should

1. Reteach the skill, using the alternate technique.
2. Be more specific in directing the learner's attention, being sure that he or she is listening to the beginning sound while simultaneously looking at the letter.
3. Use more emphasis in highlighting the beginning sound, the letter, and the connection between them.
4. Return to the previous objective and be sure that the learner can distinguish between the beginning hard **g, k, j,** and **n** sounds before requiring him or her to connect the sounds with letters.

## • SUGGESTIONS FOR PRACTICE

Once the learner has successfully connected the **g, k, j,** and **n** letters to their common sounds, create practice activities to solidify the skill, using the suggestions provided in I-WA-9.

## • THE POSTTEST

The procedure and criterion for mastery are the same as for the pretest.

| | | | | | |
|---|---|---|---|---|---|
| nest | ketch | judge | neighbor | none | gossip |
| jar | gobble | kill | june bug | kiss | guess |

## • ENSURING TRANSFER

Although the learner will be applying this skill in subsequent skills in the hierarchy, you should also use the suggestions provided in I-WA-9 to be sure that the skill is used during the routine daily activities of the classroom.

# I•WA•21

## • THE PERFORMANCE OBJECTIVE

When given an oral sentence with one word missing and cued for the missing word with a card having printed on it the first letter of the missing word (**t, b, p, w, r, f, g, k, j,** and **n**), the learner will say a word beginning with that letter that fits the context of the sentence.

## • THE PRETEST

Make cards with the preceding letters printed on them. Say, "I am going to say a sentence with one word missing. You look at the card and say a word that begins with the letter on the card and that finishes what I want to say." Use the following sentences. Display the letter card only when you come to the blank. The criterion for mastery is 80 percent, with no letter being missed more than once. *Note:* If a sentence fails to match the learner's background or does not provide enough context clues for him or her to complete the sentence, you should alter the sentence accordingly. Sentence 1, for instance, could be changed to read, "When we count, we say 'one, t_____, three.'"

1. After the number nine comes the number t_____.
2. The girl and b_____ were playing ball.
3. I wrote my name with a p_____.
4. I'm sick and don't feel very w_____.
5. In the game I r_____ very fast.
6. When playing, I tripped and f_____.
7. The car stopped. It was out of g_____.
8. I flew my k_____ today.
9. I will run and j_____ over the fence.
10. The sun doesn't shine at n_____.
11. When I play hard I get t_____.
12. I rode by b_____ to school.
13. I will p_____ the wagon.
14. I hope we w_____ the game.
15. I put the r_____ on my finger.
16. I lost the ball. Can you f_____ it?
17. On Halloween I saw a g_____.
18. I saw the k_____ and the queen.
19. I broke the glass j_____.
20. She had a necklace around her n_____.

*Have you trained your pupils to work independently or have you just expected it to happen naturally?*

### • DIRECTING THE LEARNER'S ATTENTION

The purpose of this task is to help the learner use his or her knowledge of letter-sound correspondence and context to identify unknown words. As such, the task is similar to storehouse module I-WA-14. To teach this skill you must direct the learner's attention by stating exactly what is to be learned and by highlighting the words in the sentences that provide clues to the identity of the unknown word, to the letter that the unknown word begins with, and the sound associated with that letter. (In the first sentence in the pretest, for instance, you might highlight the words **after** and **nine**, direct the learner to look at a large cutout **t** and to get his or her mouth ready to say the sound of that letter.)

### • TEACHING ACTIVITIES

In teaching this context–letter-sound skill you can use either the modeling technique or the discovery technique described in I-WA-14, adjusting the suggestions to fit the letter-sound associations being tested in this objective.

### • SUGGESTIONS FOR RETEACHING

If, after having been taught with either the modeling or the discovery technique, the learner is unable to use context–letter-sound correspondence to identify unknown words in this objective, you should reteach using the suggestions found in I-WA-14.

● 161

The procedure and criterion for mastery are the same as in the pretest.

1. The bike was n_____ to the house.
2. For breakfast I had some orange j_____.
3. My grandmother k_____ me on the cheek.
4. I looked for my friend, but he was g_____.
5. He can run very f_____.
6. He tied the package with a r_____.
7. I threw the paper in the w_____basket.
8. I cooked the meat in a frying p_____.
9. Sam is my b_____ friend.
10. The car had a flat t_____.
11. I want Ann to sit n_____ to me.
12. I will play with the ball and the b_____
13. I found it. Can I k_____ it?
14. I am g_____ to the store.
15. The f_____ was swimming in the pond.
16. In the fall I r_____ the leaves.
17. I w_____ I were very rich.
18. I want to go to the birthday p_____.
19. I cut my finger, so I put a b_____ on it.
20. Is it t_____ to go to school?

• ENSURING TRANSFER

Although the learner will be applying this skill in subsequent objectives, you should also use the suggestions provided in I-WA-14 to be sure that the skill is used during the routine daily reading activities of the classroom.

## I•IG•1

• THE PERFORMANCE OBJECTIVE

When given content words that have been identified by the teacher, the learner will use each word correctly in an oral sentence.

• THE PRETEST

The words to be tested are selected by the teacher. These may be words that appear in the basal text or in stories being read orally by the teacher or in class that are associated with the study of a particular content area. To test for the meaning of such words, say each word out loud to the child. Ask him or her to make up a sentence or to "send you a message" using that word. The criterion for mastery is 100 percent, since any word not used correctly will have to be taught.

The leaner is asked to identify the following words in print in the next cluster. You should be sure that he or she understands these words prior to that time.

| | | |
|---|---|---|
| saw | go | father |
| mother | good | make |
| girl | like | cat |
| look | jump | sit |
| get | little | hot |
| boy | dog | |

## • DIRECTING THE LEARNER'S ATTENTION

The purpose of this task is to teach content word meanings (or the meanings of words that have a referent in our culture). Since the ultimate goal of reading is obtaining meaning and since content words are the foundation upon which meaning is built, this is a crucial comprehension skill. Consequently, this is the first in a series of objectives that help you be sure that the learner understands the words he or she is expected to use.

To teach a content word meaning you must direct the learner's attention by (1) providing either direct or vicarious experience to form the basis for the concept; (2) identifying the characteristics of that concept; and (3) connecting the concept with its word label (for the word **dog**, for instance, you would show the learner a real dog, a model of a dog, or a picture of a dog; list the characteristics of "dogness" that form the concept; and connect this concept and the verbal label **dog**). For words having multiple meanings you must also direct the learner to the context in which the word is found. For instance, contextual setting becomes an important cue in the sentences, "The *dog* was looking for his bone." and "The soldier decided he would *dog* it for the rest of the day." *Note:* This objective focuses on meaning alone. The learner should not be asked to pronounce these words as they appear in print until after this skill has been mastered.

## • THIS IS A STOREHOUSE OBJECTIVE

The following instructional activities are your storehouse of techniques for teaching content word meaning. This skill recurs throughout the skill hierarchy as the learner encounters more and more words that must be understood. The activities that follow are to be adapted and used with each of these as they occur.

## • TEACHING ACTIVITIES

*The modeling technique.* To teach the meaning of the word **dog,** for instance, you must first select an appropriate experience or set of experiences. The more direct the experience, the better the learning will be, although vicarious experiences must be used when it is impossible to provide direct experience. In teaching the meaning for the word **dog** you would refer to an experience the learner has previously had with dogs or (if there was no such previous experience) bring a real dog or a model of a dog or a picture of a dog to class. Using the experience as a basis, identify the characteristics of "dogness" for the learner, having the learner mimic or otherwise attend you. Say, "This is a dog. I know it is a dog because it is an animal, it has four legs, it is larger than a cat but smaller than a horse, it makes a barking noise," and so on. Then connect this concept to the word label by saying, "This animal is called a dog." You should then repeat the process several times with different kinds of dogs. This will enrich and broaden the learner's understanding of the concept **dog** while also allowing you gradually to diminish the amount of modeling as the learner becomes more confident of the concept. When the learner is using the new word comfortably in his or her oral language, you can assume its meaning has been learned.

*The discovery technique.* The basic frame of the lesson is the same for discovery as it is for modeling. The major difference lies in the way you handle the second step—identifying the characteristics of "dogness." Rather than being highly directive in specifying the characteristics for the learners as you would in modeling, you encourage the learner to use his or her observation skills to identify the characteristics. Consequently, the dialogue might proceed as follows: "This is a dog. I know it is a dog because of certain things it has. Can you look at it and guess how I know it is a dog?" As the learner responds, you give encouragement and direct him or her to certain characteristics he or she may be overlooking. After the learner examines one example of a dog and lists its characteristics, direct him or her to another example, directing the learner to list its characteristics and helping him or her to consolidate observations into a solid concept of **dog**. As before, when the learner is using the new word in oral language, its meaning has been learned.

Have you taken a field trip lately?

## • SUGGESTIONS FOR RETEACHING

If, after having been taught with either of the preceding techniques, the learner is unable to use the new word in his or her oral language, you should

1. Reteach the skill, using the alternate technique.
2. Provide a more relevant and direct experience as the basis for building the concept.
3. Provide more direction and assistance in highlighting the characteristics of the concept.
4. Be sure that you are not using unknown words to explain the meaning of another unknown word. (For instance, do not say, "a dog is smaller than a horse" unless the learner already understands the meaning of both the word *horse* and the word *smaller*.

## • SUGGESTIONS FOR PRACTICE

Once the learner is using the new word in oral language, use one or more of the following practice activities to solidify the meaning.

1. Use exercises in which words are replaced with synonyms. Each learner can be encouraged to supply another word that means about the same

thing. Appropriateness to the concept can be judged by discussion of the group.

2. Teach word opposites. One way to discriminate a concept is by knowing not only what it is but what it is not. It is most appropriate at all stages of reading development to play word games in which learners supply words that are opposite in meaning.

3. Encourage learners to associate content words with mental pictures of that concept. Let each learner draw or describe his or her mental picture.

4. Have learners note on 3- by 5-inch cards the word meanings they have learned and the key characteristics and/or synonyms they have created. In this way you not only build meaning vocabulary but also a synonym source for use in writing assignments.

5. Combine known simple words to create either real compound words or new compounds and discuss the new concepts created when two simple words are made into one compound word.

## • THE POSTTEST

The procedures, directions, and criterion for mastery are the same as for the pretest.

## • ENSURING TRANSFER

You should be sure that the new word meanings are used in contextual settings during the routine daily language activities of the classroom. A good way to do this is to use the words yourself in conversations with children and to ask questions that require learners to use the new words in their responses. Further, the new words should be incorporated into listening comprehension activities such as the one provided in the final chapter.

I•IG•2

## • THE PERFORMANCE OBJECTIVE

When given words containing known roots and –ed, –ing, and –s endings, the learner will use each word correctly in an oral sentence.

## • THE PRETEST

Say each word to be tested out loud, asking the child to make up a sentence or "send a message" using the word you have just said. The criterion for mastery is 100 percent and any endings that are not used correctly will have to be taught. Other root words with which the learner is familiar can be used in place of or in addition to those following.

| liked | liking | likes | boys |
| looked | looking | looks | cats |
| jumped | jumping | jumps | girls |

## • DIRECTING THE LEARNER'S ATTENTION

The purpose of this task is to teach the learner the meanings of the inflectional endings –ed, –ing, and –s. Although the meanings of many words are learned as root words in the manner described in the previous objective, the learner increases the number of word meanings in his or her vocabulary when root words can be combined with various meaning units, such as prefixes, suffixes, and inflectional endings. It is particularly important that children using nonstandard English dialects understand these meanings, since word parts (particularly word endings) may be different in their normal dialect. Consequently, this is the first in a series of skills that will ultimately help the learner understand and use the common meaning units found in the English language.

To teach the meanings of the various inflectional endings you must be sure that the learner has a meaning for the root word and you must direct his or her attention to the inflectional ending and the meaning associated with that ending. (In the word **boys**, for instance, you must be sure that the learner understands the root word **boy**, that he or she is attending to the –s ending, and that he or she associates that ending with meaning *more than one*). *Note:* This objective focuses on meaning alone. The learner should not be asked to pronounce these words as they appear in print until after this skill has been mastered.

### • THIS IS A STOREHOUSE OBJECTIVE

The following instructional activities are your storehouse of techniques for developing meanings for word parts. This skill recurs as the learner encounters other meaning units later in the skill hierarchy. The activities that follow are to be adapted and used with each of these as they occur.

### • TEACHING ACTIVITIES

*The modeling technique.* Assume that you are teaching the meaning for the –s inflectional ending as it appears in words such as **boys**. After being sure that the learner has a meaning for the root word **boy**, direct attention to the two parts in the word **boys**. Say, "The word **boys** is made up of two parts. They are **boy** and s-s-s. Listen carefully for the two parts as I say the word slowly and then say it fast. **Boy** . . . s-s-s-. **Boys.** Now you do it." When you are sure that the child hears both parts of the word, direct attention to the meaning of the– s ending by saying, "When we add an –s to a word such as **boy**, we are saying that we now have more than one boy. The word **boys** means 'more than one boy.' What does **boys** mean?" Repeat the procedure with other words (such as **cats**), gradually diminishing the amount of emphasis used in identifying the two parts of the words and the amount of direct assistance in determining the meaning of the inflectional ending. Once the learner can comfortably use words with these endings in sentences, you can assume that the meaning of that word part has been mastered.

*The discovery technique.* As with the modeling technique, the discovery technique begins by being sure that the learner understands the meaning of the root word. Once this is established, however, you use questioning rather than making the direct statements found in modeling. For instance, the learner will be asked to listen to you say the words **boy** and **boys** and to tell how they are different, with emphasis being provided if the learner needs such highlighting. Then you can put the two words in matching sentences such as

The bike belongs to the *boy*.
The bike belongs to the *boys*.

Ask the learner to tell how the two sentences are different or to draw a picture that explains how the two are different. If the learner needs more assistance, you can draw pictures to accompany each sentence and ask him or her to tell you how the two sentences are different. Repeat the procedure with other words, gradually diminishing the amount of assistance you provide until the learner is comfortable using words containing the ending.

- **SUGGESTIONS FOR RETEACHING**

If, after having been taught with either of the preceding techniques, the learner is unable to use words with these endings in oral sentences, you should

1. Reteach the skill, using the alternate technique.
2. Be sure that the learner has a meaning for the root word.
3. Be more specific in highlighting the meaning unit to be sure that the learner is attending to the correct part of the word.
4. Place more emphasis on the connection between the word part and the meaning that unit carries.

- **SUGGESTIONS FOR PRACTICE**

Once the meaning of the word part has been taught successfully, use one or more of the following practice activities to solidify the meaning:

1. Provide the learner with content exercises in which he or she fills in the missing word in sentences such as the following:

The two ———— (boy, boys) went to the movie.

2. Print known roots and word parts on cards and place the cards into two piles. The learner chooses a word from each pile, puts them together, and tells the meaning of the root word and the word part together (if the child cannot yet read, say the roots and word parts aloud).
3. Make charts or worksheets in which roots are on one side and word parts are on the other. Attach strings to the elements in the left column and have the learner connect the string with a word in the right column so as to make a new word. Have the learner use the new word in a sentence to be sure that he or she has a meaning for it.
4. Make up crossword puzzles in which words composed of roots and word parts are used as answers.

5. Play a card game in which each player is dealt cards having known root words written on them. Another deck, containing only word parts the learner understands, is placed in the center of the table. The learners take turns drawing cards from the deck and trying to match the drawn card with one of the root words to form a new word. If a learner can do so, he or she lays the two cards down together and gives a meaning for the new word. If the child draws a card he or she cannot use, it must be put back in the bottom of the pile. The first player to get rid of all his or her cards is the winner.

### • THE POSTTEST

The procedures, directions, and criterion for mastery for the posttest are the same as for the pretest.

### • ENSURING TRANSFER

You should be sure that the newly learned word parts are used in contextual settings during the routine daily activities of the classroom. A good way to do this is to use the word parts yourself in conversations with children and to ask questions that will require learners to use the word parts in answering. Further, the word parts should be incorporated into listening comprehension activities such as the one provided in the final chapter.

## I•IG•3

### • THE PERFORMANCE OBJECTIVE

When given two objects and function words that signal position (**to, at, in, on, out, here, there, by, from, over, into, upon, away, near**), the learner will position the two objects in relation to each other according to the relationship signaled by the function words contained in the teacher's oral directions.

### • THE PRETEST

Give the learner two objects such as the inner cardboard tube from a roll of paper towels and a small wooden block. Tell him or her to follow your oral directions by placing the tube and block in the positions you state. The criterion for mastery is 100 percent with any missed function word being taught. Directions such as the following can be used:

> Put the block *in* the tube.
> Bring the tube *to* the block.
> Put the block *on* the tube.
> Take the block *out* of the tube.
> Move the block *at* the tube.
> Put the block *here* and the tube *here*.

### • DIRECTING THE LEARNER'S ATTENTION

The purpose of this task is to teach the relationship signaled by the function words specified in the objective. This is the first in a series of objectives dealing with function words. They include function words that signal the following five essential meaning relationships common to English sentences:

1. Prepositions that signal both positional and time relationships.
2. Pronouns and their antecedents.
3. Words that signal contrast-comparison relationships.
4. Words that signal chronological sequences.
5. Words that signal cause-effect relationships.

The meaning in an English sentence results from a partnership between content words (such as those taught in I-A-1) and function words. To gather the information contained in any sentence, the learner must know both the concepts associated with the content words used and the relationship between those content words as they are signaled by function words. Though the function words tend to be short, the relationships expressed by those little words are as important as and much more subtle and less definitive than the content words.

Teaching function word meaning is more difficult than teaching content words because the relationships signaled by function words are difficult to visualize. To teach these relationships you must direct the learner's attention by emphasizing the function word as it appears in oral context while simultaneously demonstrating the relationship signaled. (For the function word *in,* for instance, you could say, "I will put the block *in* the tube," emphasizing the word *in* as you simultaneously place the block in the tube.) *Note:* This objective focuses on meaning alone. The learner should not be asked to pronounce these words as they appear in print until after this skill has been mastered.

### • THIS IS A STOREHOUSE OBJECTIVE

The following instructional activities are your storehouse of techniques for teaching the relationships signaled by function words. This skill recurs throughout the hierarchy as the learner encounters more and more function words. The activities that follow are to be adapted and used with each function word objective as it occurs.

### • TEACHING ACTIVITIES

*The modeling technique.* To teach a function word meaning you must use the word in a sentence while simultaneously demonstrating its relationship. For the function word *in,* for instance, you could put the block in the tube as you say, "I'm putting the block *in* the tube," emphasizing the word as you say it. The learner watches you and mimics both your actions and your words. In subsequent sequences you would provide less modeling and fewer manipulative demonstrations until the learner is using the function word comfortably in his or her daily language.

*The discovery technique.* In using the discovery technique you substitute questioning procedures for the mimicry found in the modeling technique. For instance, you might use two sentences such as the following:

Put the block *in* the tube.
Put the block *on* the tube.

You say each sentence in turn, emphasizing the function words while simultaneously demonstrating the relationships. Then say, "What did I do differently in each case? What word tells you where to put the block in the first sentence? In the second sentence?" In subsequent sequences you provide less auditory emphasis on the function word and fewer manipulative demonstrations until the learner is using the function word comfortably in his or her daily language.

● **SUGGESTIONS FOR RETEACHING**

If, after having been taught with either of the preceding techniques, the learner is unable to use the function words correctly, you should

Success and motivation are forever entwined. Have you made sure that each of your pupils will succeed today?

1. Reteach the skill, using the alternate technique.
2. Increase the number of oral language activities in which the function word is used.
3. Provide more tangible manipulative demonstrations of the relationship being signaled.
4. Emphasize the function word more clearly to be sure that the learner is attending to the correct word in the sentence.

● **SUGGESTIONS FOR PRACTICE**

Once the learner is using the function word in his or her oral language, adapt and use one or more of the following activities to solidify the skill.

1. Give children oral sentences and ask them to identify words that answer questions you pose, such as the following:

   Which word tells where the boy is?
   Which word tells when the event happened?
   Which word tells who *she* is?

2. Put words on the chalkboard that signal certain relationships and have the learner think up sentences using these function words.
3. Play games in which you begin a sentence that begins or ends with a function word. The learner completes the sentence, using words appropriate to the relationship signaled by the function word. For instance, you might provide sentences such as the following:

   The book is on . . .
   Because Tommy was late . . .

4. Using paragraphs such as the following, have learners specify the different relationship meanings of each paragraph and identify the function words that signal these relationships.

During our visit to the museum we saw a collection of old silverware, an absorbing display of old-fashioned wedding gowns, a room filled with Indian relics, and the first Stars and Stripes ever carried in battle.

During our visit to the museum we saw the first Stars and Stripes ever carried in battle; after that we enjoyed a collection of old silverware and later wandered into the room filled with Indian relics. Finally we found ourselves absorbed in a display of old wedding gowns.

During our visit to the museum we enjoyed seeing the first Stars and Stripes ever carried in battle and the asorbinbg display of old-fashioned wedding gowns much more than we did the room filled with Indian relics and the collection of old silverware.

Because on our visit to the museum we had seen the first Stars and Stripes ever caried in battle, a room full of Indian relics, a display of old silverware, and a collection of old-fashioned wedding gowns, we were able to present a successful class program in which we compared relics of the past with their modern equivalents.[1]

## • THE POSTTEST

The procedures, directions, and criterion for mastery are the same as for the pretest.

## • ENSURING TRANSFER

You should be sure that the new function words are used in contextual settings during the routine daily language activities of the classroom. Further, these words should be incorporated into listening comprehension activities such as the one provided in the final chapter.

# I•MT•1

## • THE PERFORMANCE OBJECTIVE

When given pairs of words, the learner will state the way in which the two words are related.

## • THE PRETEST

Direct the learner to listen to the two words you say and to think about the way in which the words are related. Do the first one as a sample. The criterion for mastery is 80 percent. An appropriate relationship is provided in parentheses, but you should allow any relationship the learner can justify.

| | | |
|---|---|---|
| dog | cat | (animals) |
| boy | girl | (children) |
| hammer | nail | (you use one with the other) |
| go | gone | (same meaning; tense difference) |
| ball | circle | (same shape) |
| chicken | cow | (both live on a farm) |

[1] O. S. Niles, "Comprehension Skills," in William K. Durr (Ed.), *Reading Instruction: Dimensions and Issues.* Boston: Houghton Mifflin, 1967, pp. 130–131.

## • DIRECTING THE LEARNER'S ATTENTION

The purpose of this task is to teach the learner to find relationships between content words and to classify the words according to these relationships. It is designed to help the learner to observe and label the world not as disconnected and mutually exclusive objects and events, but as experiencd realities related to other realities that can be grouped according to selected similarities or excluded because of some unacceptable contrast. Manipulative thinking tasks such as this help the learner grasp the relationship of the part to the whole or the whole to the part; consequently, they are important prerequisites to teaching the learner to extract the main idea from paragraphs and selections. Therefore, this is the first in a series of objectives that help the learner classify content words according to concepts they have in common.

To teach classification of content words you must be sure that the learner understands the meaning of the words used and you must direct his or her attention by highlighting the concepts associated with each content word and then to the common denominator that allows them to be classified together. (For the words **cat** and **dog,** for instance, you would first list the concepts associated with each word and then show that some of these concepts are the same for both words, thereby making the words "related.")

## • THIS IS A STOREHOUSE OBJECTIVE

The following instructional activities are your storehouse of techniques for teaching classification. This skill recurs in more complex forms as the learner progresses through the skill hierarchy. The activities that follow are to be adapted and used with each of these as they occur.

## • TEACHING ACTIVITIES

*The modeling technique.* After making sure that the words to be related are in the learner's meaning vocabulary, you can list the words on the chalkboard as follows:

cat
dog

Say to the learner, "Each of these words describes something I know about. For instance, I know that a cat is an animal, is a pet, meows, and humps up its back when it is mad. A dog is an animal, is a pet, barks, and is sometimes used for hunting." As you say each characteristic, note it beside the word on the board. Then say, "I can look at the things I know about each word and I see that some of the things are the same for both words." As you say this draw lines between the common elements, as follows:

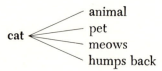

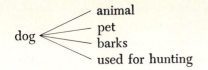

dog — animal
— pet
— barks
— used for hunting

Now say, "We can say that the words **cat** and **dog** are related because they are both pet animals. They would both fit together in a box for 'Pet Animals.' Dogs and cats are different in some ways and alike in other ways. The ways they are alike are the ways in which they are related." With subsequent pairs of words you can diminish the amount of modeling and decrease the amount of chalkboard highlighting you provide by listing concepts and drawing lines between common concepts until the learner is relating known contexts without assistance from you.

*The discovery technique.* As in the modeling technique, the discovery technique requires that you first be sure that the words to be related are in the learner's meaning vocabulary. Then you proceed in generally the same fashion, substituting questioning and learner response for the directed modeling used previously. For instance, after listing the words **dog** and **cat** on the board, you ask the learner to supply the characteristics to be listed for each word. Then you ask him or her to inspect the characteristics and find any common concepts, highlighting them by drawing lines between them as necessary. When the learner has identified the common concepts, ask why he or she thinks these words are related. Repeat the same procedure for subsequent pairs of words, gradually diminishing the listing and lines until the learner can relate the words without relying on such highlighting.

• **SUGGESTIONS FOR RETEACHING**

If, after having been taught with either of the preceding techniques, the learner is unable to classify the content words, you should

1. Reteach the skill, using the alternate technique.
2. Recheck to make sure the learner understands the meaning of the content words being related and follow the suggestions in I-IG-1 for any word not known.
3. Make sure that the meaning the learner has for the content word includes the concepts that form the common denominator between the words.
4. Provide more highlighting to emphasize the fact that the two words have concepts in common.
5. Simplify the task by using easier pairs of words and by creating an analogy between words that are related and family members that are related. (Each family member is different and yet each has something in common that makes them related.)

• **SUGGESTIONS FOR PRACTICE**

Once the learner is able to tell the way in which the words are related, use one or more of the following practice activities to solidify the skill.

1. Play games with learners in which you say words or show objects and the learners must tell how they are alike or which one does not belong.
2. Put pictures and/or words into a container. The learner classifies all the pictures and/or words and tells what each category has in common.
3. Create sentences like, "Jack collects many things, such as butterflies, rocks, matchbooks, model airplanes, and arrowheads" in a category titled "Things Jack Collects."
4. Play a bingo-type game in which squares on the board contain content words and the learner calls out other content words. Players put markers on words that can be related to the word called by the leader.
5. Play games in which one learner calls out a category (such as *groceries*) and another learner supplies as many things that would go in that category as possible.

### • THE POSTTEST

The directions and criterion for mastery are the same as for the pretest. Use the following pairs of words.

Are you planning ahead?

| | | |
|---|---|---|
| scissors | paper | (scissors are used to cut paper) |
| propeller | sail | (they both make something move) |
| zebra | elephant | (you could find both in a zoo) |
| teacher | janitor | (both work in a school) |
| corn | wheat | (both grow on a farm) |

### • ENSURING TRANSFER

You should be sure that relationships among content words are used as a thinking tool during the routine daily activities in the classroom. A good way to do this is to look for opportunities to ask such questions as, "How are those two things alike?" or, "Of the things we have talked about, which one is different and why?" Further, classifying of concepts should be incorporated into listening comprehension activities such as the ones provided in the final chapter.

## I•MT•2

### • THE PERFORMANCE OBJECTIVE

When given a short story problem read orally by the teacher, the learner will provide a solution that is implied but not stated.

### • THE PRETEST

Read each of the following paragraphs to the learner in turn, directing him or her to listen carefully because you are going to ask a question about it afterward. After you have read the story, ask the question that follows. The criterion for mastery is 100 percent.

Marie said, "I need to wash my aquarium. But I can't when the fish are inside. I've tried to get them in my hand, but they moved too fast."

174 ●

What should Marie use in getting out the fish?

Andy said, "I need to cut a little off the end of my kite tail. It is in my way when I'm running and trying to make the kite fly."

What should Andy use to cut the kite's tail?

### • DIRECTING THE LEARNER'S ATTENTION

The purpose of this task is to teach the learner to infer meanings implied in a passage. All information worth obtaining is not necessarily stated literally; much valuable data are found "between the lines." That is, the author may imply certain things without stating them explicitly. It is important, therefore, that the learner be able to do inferential thinking. This is the first in a series of objectives designed to teach this type of manipulative thinking.

In teaching inferential thinking three important points must be remembered. First, inferential thinking is based on the concepts, relationships, and facts found in the passage. Second, the learner cannot do inferential thinking about concepts or ideas he or she has not experienced. Third, the learner is not likely to do inferential thinking unless prodded by questions that force him or her to think "between the lines." Consequently, to teach inferential thinking you must be sure that the learner possesses a related background experience and the prerequisite skills of word meaning, factual recall, relationships, and classifying; you must pose questions that require the learner to examine what is implied; and you must direct the learner's attention to what the facts say and what experience has taught him or her about such concepts and ideas. (In the first pretest paragraph, for instance, you direct the learner to the facts regarding the problem of removing the fish from the aquarium and to his or her previous experience in moving fish from one place to another.)

### • THIS IS A STOREHOUSE OBJECTIVE

The following instructional activities are your storehouse of techniques for teaching inferential thinking. This skill recurs throughout the skill hierarchy as the learner encounters more and more complex material. The activities that follow are to be adapted and used with each of these as they occur.

### • TEACHING ACTIVITIES

*The modeling technique.* After making sure that the learner possesses the prerequisite word meaning, factual recall, relationship, and classification skills needed to determine the facts in the passage and after posing the inferential question, follow a procedure such as the following in helping the learner to do the thinking. Using the first paragraph as an illustration, say to the learner, "Listen to how I figure out the answer to that question. The story says that Marie needs to clean her aquarium but that she can't do it with the fish inside. The problem is to figure out how to get the fish out. I remember seeing a television program once where men used nets to move fish from the water to the boat. I'll bet that Marie could get the fish out of her aquarium with a net. I have used what I know from other places to help me answer this question. Can you do this?" Repeat the procedure with similar short story problems, gradually reducing the modeling help you provide as the learner begins to supply his or her own experiences and relate them to the problem.

*The discovery technique.* The procedure remains the same for the discovery technique except that you ask questions rather than having the learner model your thinking. For instance, you might ask, "What does the story say is happening? What is the problem? Have you ever had an experience similar to this one or have you ever seen anyone else have a similar experience? How was it solved in the other experience? Could you use that idea to solve the problem in this situation?" Repeat the procedure with subsequent story problems but gradually diminish the assistance you provide until the learner is able to answer the question without assistance.

### • SUGGESTIONS FOR RETEACHING

If, after having been taught with either of the preceding techniques, the learner is unable to supply the implied solution, you should

1. Reteach the skill, using the alternate technique.
2. Make sure that the learner has had experience with concepts similar to those in the story and supply that background if necessary.
3. Check to make sure that the learner has concepts for each of the words, reteaching word meanings where necessary.
4. Make sure that the learner has correctly interpreted the facts in the story.
5. Direct the learner more explicitly to the connection between the facts in the story and his or her related experiences that can be applied to this situation. One good way to do this is by following the inferential question with other questions that guide the learner to apply experience to the problem. For the first pretest paragraph, for instance, you might ask such questions as, "Have you seen other people cleaning aquariums? How did *they* remove the fish? How do you suppose Marie removed the fish?" Of course, if the learner's answer to the first question is No, you must provide such an experience background before going into the next two questions.

### • SUGGESTIONS FOR PRACTICE

Once the learner is able to supply the implied solution, adapt and use one or more of the following practice activities to solidify the skill.

1. Have the learner do workbook pages, Ditto sheets, and so on that offer numerous problems such as those found in the pretest.
2. Make up games in which learners must supply implied answers in order to achieve the goal or win the game.

3. Copy the first sentence from a story or factual selection. Direct the learner to read the sentence and then to hypothesize what the rest of the story is about. Building these hypotheses requires not only imagination but also inferential logic. This is a particularly good activity for learners who find it difficult to read for any purpose other than to remember the facts and details of a selection.

4. A good way to help learners infer meanings is to provide them with paragraphs and direct them to ask you, or each other, questions about the paragraph that do not have answers clearly stated in the passage itself. It is sometimes necessary to model such questions for learners at the early stages, but they soon are able to build their own. The more they build questions, the more they solidify the skill of inferential thinking.

## • THE POSTTEST

The procedure, directions, and criterion are the same as for the pretest. Use the following stories.

> Some workmen had just made a new sidewalk at Kari's house. They had left stones in the yard. Kari put lots of stones in a box. When she tried to move the box, she couldn't pull it.
>
> What should Kari use to take away the stones?
>
> The boys were in a tree house. Mike's mother came to the foot of the tree and called up to them.
> "I have some cookies for you," she said. "They are in this basket. But I can't bring them up to you."
>
> What should the boys use to pull up the basket?

## • ENSURING TRANSFER

You should make sure that the skill of inferential thinking is used during the routine daily activities of the classroom. One way to do this is to include inferential questions among those you ask during lessons in social studies, science, and so on. Further, the skill of inferential thinking should be incorporated into listening comprehension activities such as the one provided in the final chapter.

I•ET•1

## • THE PERFORMANCE OBJECTIVE

When given oral material containing factual and fanciful information with which the learner has experience, the learner will state whether the information is factual or fanciful and tell why.

## • THE PRETEST

The material to be tested should be selected by the teacher. It is imperative that the learner be familiar with the content of the material. Direct the learner to listen to each phrase you read and to decide whether what is described could really happen. The learner should say "Yes" for each statement that could really happen and "No" for each statement that is fanciful. Decisions for correctness of response depends upon the rationale of the learner. The criterion for mastery is 90 percent. The following are examples of phrases that could be used.

Sisters who look like each other
A dog who makes pies for himself
An animal who hides food for the winter
A kitten who puts on rubbers to go out in the rain
A bear in a store buying a winter coat
A basket as big as a building
A door banging in the wind
A cat climbing a tree
A car shouting, "Wait for me!"
A turtle sitting on a rock in a river

### • DIRECTING THE LEARNER'S ATTENTION

The purpose of this task is to teach the learner to judge whether material is fanciful or factual. Since one of the primary language goals is the development of evaluative thinking, this is a crucial comprehension skill. Consequently, this is a first in a series of objectives that help the learner make judgments about the content of the written material.

To teach the difference between factual and fanciful statements you must direct the learner's attention to whether the event could happen or not. This is done by using material that is in the learner's background experience. For instance, if you wanted the learner to judge if a turtle sitting on a rock were fact or fancy, the learner could decide it was a fact since he or she had seen or heard of such an event. It was real. Likewise, if the learner were to judge if a dog who makes cherry pies for himself were fact or fancy, the learner could decide it was fancy since he or she never saw or heard of a real dog making cherry pies.

### • THIS IS A STOREHOUSE OBJECTIVE

The following instructional activities are your storehouse of techniques for teaching how to judge the content of material. This skill will recur throughout the skill hierarchy as the learner encounters more and more complex materials. The activities that follow are to be adapted and used with each of these as they occur.

### • TEACHING ACTIVITIES

*The modeling technique.* To teach a learner how to decide if printed material is fact or fancy, you must first select material for which the learner has background, since this provides the basis for judging the content of the material. To highlight the decision you would need to model it. For example, the learner is asked to judge whether the phrase "sisters who look like each other" is fact or fancy. You would say, "This phrase is a fact since

I've seen two sisters who look alike." The learner then mimicks your decision. Repeat this procedure with other statements, diminishing the modeling as the learner gains confidence. Once the learner is successfully judging the content of the material, you can assume this skill has been mastered.

*The discovery technique.* The basic frame of the lesson remains the same for discovery as it is for modeling. The major difference lies in the second step of modeling. Rather than being highly directive in specifying the decision of fact or fancy and why, as you would in modeling, you allow the learner to discover the reasons for the factual or fanciful statement. For instance, the phrase could be "a kitten who puts on rubbers to go out in the rain." The dialogue could be, "Have you ever seen kittens wearing rubbers?" "No, I've never heard of a kitten who can do that." "So is it fact or fancy that a kitten can put rubbers on?" "It is fancy, since kittens can't put rubbers on." Repeat this procedure with other phrases, gradually diminishing your use of questions as the learner provides his or her own until the learner is doing the skill alone. At this time you can again assume that the learner has mastered the skill.

## • SUGGESTIONS FOR RETEACHING

If, after having been taught with either of the preceding techniques, the learner is unable to state whether phrases are factual or fanciful and why, you should

1. Reteach the skill, using the alternate techniques.
2. Be more specific in highlighting by modeling or questions.
3. Be sure that the learner has background experience for the printed or oral material.

Do you *teach* before the pupils' practice?

## • SUGGESTIONS FOR PRACTICE

Once the learner is able to judge the content of the material, adapt and use one or more of the following practice activities to solidify the skill.

1. Have the learner do workbook pages, Ditto sheets, and so on that offer numerous situations such as those found in the pretest.
2. Use any of the preceding exercises and attach any game board to it. A correct response for the exercise allows a turn for the game.
3. Have learners give situations that include factual and fanciful statements. The partner states whether it is fact or fancy and why.
4. Have factual or fanciful time. Either fact or fancy statements can only be said. Students try to reach as high a number as possible.

## • THE POSTTEST

The procedures, directions, and criterion are the same as for the pretest. You should select the items based on background experience.

### • ENSURING TRANSFER

You should make sure the skill of judging the content of material is used during the school day. One way is to incorporate this skill into the content area subjects. Social studies and science are ideal for this. The skill of judging the content of material should also be incorporated into listening comprehension activities such as the one found in the final chapter.

# CLUSTER II

● **THE PERFORMANCE OBJECTIVE**

When given a stimulus lower-case letter, the learner will match it with its upper-case counterpart.

● **THE PRETEST**

Prepare a duplicated handout as follows. Direct the learner to draw lines between the lower-case and upper-case forms of the same letters. The criterion for mastery is 100 percent.

a   s   e   d   c   g   n   i   o   p

C   A   G   D   P   O   S   I   N   E

● **DIRECTING THE LEARNER'S ATTENTION**

The purpose of this task is to teach the learner to associate a name with the upper-case letters of the alphabet. This task is similar to storehouse module I-SW-3. To teach this skill you must be sure that the learner knows exactly what he or she is to learn and you must direct his or her attention by highlighting both the visual form of the upper-case letter and the sound of the name to which it is connected while also, where appropriate, highlighting the similarity between the lower-case and upper-case forms of the

● 181

letter. (With the upper-case letter **S,** for instance, you might have the learner point out the curves of the letter and its similarity in form to the "little" s while simultaneously looking at the letter and saying, "This is a capital S"; with the upper-case **G,** you would do the same thing but note the differences between the upper, and the lower-case forms.)

### • TEACHING ACTIVITIES

This is a naming task similar to that described in I-SW-3, and you can adapt your teaching strategy from either the modeling technique or the discovery technique described in that objective.

### • SUGGESTIONS FOR RETEACHING

If, after having been taught with either the modeling or the discovery technique, the learner is unable to name the upper-case letters, you should

1. Reteach the skill, using the alternate technique.
2. Reteach the skill by pairing the lower-case letter with its upper-case counterpart, starting with those letters in which both forms are very much alike (such as **w-W, v-V,** and so on) and moving gradually to those letters that are quite different in form (such as **q-Q, r-R,** and so on).
3. Emphasize more heavily the connection between the visual form of the letter and the sound of the name by being sure that the learner is looking at the upper-case letter while saying its name.
4. Emphasize the visual characteristics of the letter by having the learner repeatedly trace the upper-case letter while saying its name.

### • SUGGESTIONS FOR PRACTICE

After successfully teaching the naming of the upper-case letters, create practice activities to solidify the skill, using the suggestions provided in I-SW-3.

### • THE POSTTEST

The procedure and criterion for mastery are the same as for the pretest.

q   w   r   t   y   u   i   m   v   b

Y   M   B   R   W   V   Q   U   T   I

### • ENSURING TRANSFER

Although the learner will be using upper-case letter names frequently while progressing through the hierarchy, you should also use the suggestions provided in I-SW-3 to be sure that he or she is naming upper case letters during the routine daily activities of the classroom.

## II•SW•2

### • THE PERFORMANCE OBJECTIVE

When given a few seconds to examine a word, the learner will pick out another word having the same initial consonant from a group of four words.

## • THE PRETEST

Prepare five flashcards, each of which has printed on it one of the words listed at the left in the sequence below. Give the child a duplicated list having printed on it the following five sets of four words. Flash each card for the count of three and direct the learner to mark the word in the set that has the same first letter. The criterion for mastery is 80 percent.

| Set I | Flash word: **love** | take | come | look | boy |
|---|---|---|---|---|---|
| Set II | Flash word: **kite** | kiss | card | board | pipe |
| Set III | Flash word: **hit** | paper | cat | hole | done |
| Set IV | Flash word: **men** | now | make | near | win |
| Set V | Flash word: **dig** | big | pig | did | gig |

## • DIRECTING THE LEARNER'S ATTENTION

The purpose of this task is to develop the learner's skill in visually noting and remembering the first letter in words. This is primarily a visual sequencing task focusing on the left-to-right order of words and is similar to storehouse module I-SW-6. To teach this skill you must be sure that the learner knows exactly what is to be learned and you must direct his or her attention by highlighting the first letter in the flash word and the first letters in each of the other four words. (In Set I, for instance, the l in **love** would be highlighted, as would the t in **take,** the c in **come,** the l in **look,** and the b in **boy.**)

## • TEACHING ACTIVITIES

This is a visual sequencing task similar to that described in I-SW-6, and you can adapt your teaching strategy from either the modeling technique or the discovery technique that is described in that objective.

## • SUGGESTIONS FOR RETEACHING

If, after having been taught with either the modeling or the discovery technique, the learner is unable visually to note and remember the first letter in words, you should

1. Reteach the skill, using the alternate technique.
2. Use more specific highlighting to direct the learner to the left-to-right sequence used in noting first letters.
3. Return to earlier visual sequencing skill objectives and reteach these simpler tasks before requiring the learner to perform the more complex task described in this objective.

## • SUGGESTIONS FOR PRACTICE

After successfully teaching the learner to note and remember the first letter in words, create practice activities to solidify the skill, using the suggestions provided in I-SW-6.

## • THE POSTTEST

The procedure and criterion for mastery are the same as for the pretest.

| Set I   | Flash word: **like**    | task  | cool     | love   | bang    |
|---------|-------------------------|-------|----------|--------|---------|
| Set II  | Flash word: **kitchen** | keep  | cord     | bottle | pasture |
| Set III | Flash word: **house**   | part  | candy    | harder | donkey  |
| Set IV  | Flash word: **mine**    | never | mask     | next   | window  |
| Set V   | Flash word: **doll**    | ball  | tall     | down   | fall    |

### • ENSURING TRANSFER

The learner will be using this skill of visual sequencing while progressing through the hierarchy. However, in addition to these applications, you should also use the suggestions provided in I-SW-6 to be sure that this skill is used during the routine daily activities of the classroom.

## II•SW•3

### • THE PERFORMANCE OBJECTIVE

When given three words that are exactly alike and one that is clearly different, the learner will mark the one that is different.

### • THE PRETEST

Direct the learner to indicate (mark or point to as appropriate) which word in each of the following sets is different. The criterion for mastery is 80 percent.

| Set I    | yes   | yes      | no   | yes   |
|----------|-------|----------|------|-------|
| Set II   | I     | and      | I    | I     |
| Set III  | the   | was      | was  | was   |
| Set IV   | in    | to       | to   | to    |
| Set V    | of    | of       | my   | of    |
| Set VI   | he    | elephant | he   | he    |
| Set VII  | here  | here     | at   | here  |
| Set VIII | come  | come     | come | of    |
| Set IX   | it    | he       | he   | he    |
| Set X    | up    | up       | up   | come  |

### • DIRECTING THE LEARNER'S ATTENTION

The purpose of this task is to teach the learner to discriminate visually among clearly different words. This is similar to storehouse module I-SW-1, but with more complex discriminators. To teach this skill you must be sure that the learner knows exactly what is to be learned and you must direct his or her attention by highlighting the visual characteristics that make one word different from the others in a particular set. (In Set I, for example, the tail of the y in yes could be highlighted to contrast with the absence of a tail in **no**.)

### • TEACHING ACTIVITIES

This is a visual discrimination task similar to that described in I-SW-1, and you can adapt your teaching strategy from either the modeling technique or the discovery technique described in that objective.

## • SUGGESTIONS FOR RETEACHING

If, after having been taught with either the modeling or the discovery technique, the learner is unable to discriminate among the words, you should

1. Reteach the skill, using the alternate technique.
2. Be more specific in directing the learner's attention, being sure that your highlighting is providing enough help in distinguishing the visual characteristics of each word.
3. Return to the previous visual discrimination skills, being sure that the learner has a clear understanding of the term **different** and that he or she can discriminate among visual forms that are less complex than words.

## • SUGGESTIONS FOR PRACTICE

After successfully teaching the learner to discriminate among clearly different words, create practice activities to solidify the skill, using the suggestions in I-SW-1.

## • THE POSTTEST

The directions and criterion for mastery are the same as for the pretest.

| | | | | |
|---|---|---|---|---|
| Set I | come | come | come | up |
| Set II | he | it | it | it |
| Set III | of | of | of | come |
| Set IV | at | at | here | at |
| Set V | elephant | he | elephant | elephant |
| Set VI | my | my | of | my |
| Set VII | to | in | in | in |
| Set VIII | was | the | the | the |
| Set IX | and | I | and | and |
| Set X | no | no | yes | no |

## • ENSURING TRANSFER

Although the learner will be applying this visual discrimination skill while progressing to the more complex skills in the hierarchy, you should also use the suggestions provided in I-SW-1 to be sure that the skill is immediately used during the routine daily activities of the classroom.

## II•SW•4

## • THE PERFORMANCE OBJECTIVE

When given three words that are exactly alike and one word that is somewhat similar, the learner will mark the word that is different.

## • THE PRETEST

Direct the learner to indicate (mark or point to as appropriate) which word in the following sets is different. The criterion for mastery is 80 percent.

| Set I | dog | dog | bog | dog |
| Set II | toy | boy | toy | toy |
| Set III | to | to | to | on |
| Set IV | ten | ten | net | ten |
| Set V | fox | box | box | box |
| Set VI | look | book | look | look |
| Set VII | like | lake | lake | lake |
| Set VIII | box | dox | box | box |
| Set IX | chair | chair | chair | char |
| Set X | saw | was | was | was |

### • DIRECTING THE LEARNER'S ATTENTION

Do your pupils like you?

The purpose of this task is to teach the learner to discriminate visually among similar words. This is similar to storehouse module I-SW-1, but with more complex discriminators. To teach this skill you must be sure that the learner knows exactly what is to be learned and you must direct his or her attention by highlighting the visual characteristics that make one word different from the others in a particular set. (In Set I, for instance, the initial consonant in **bog** could be highlighted to contrast with the different initial consonant in **dog**.)

### • TEACHING ACTIVITIES

This is a visual discrimination task similar to that described in I-SW-1, and you can adapt your teaching strategy from either the modeling technique or the discovery technique described in that objective.

### • SUGGESTIONS FOR RETEACHING

If, after having been taught with either the modeling or the discovery technique, the learner is unable to discriminate among the words, you should

1. Reteach the skill, using the alternate technique.
2. Be more specific in directing the learner's attention, making sure that your highlighting is providing enough help in distinguishing the visual characteristics of each word.
3. Return to the previous visual discrimination skills in the hierarchy, being sure that the learner can do those simpler tasks of visual discrimination before asking him or her to differentiate between like words.

### • SUGGESTIONS FOR PRACTICE

After successfully teaching the learner how to discriminate among like words, create practice activities to solidify this skill by using the suggestions in I-SW-1.

### • THE POSTTEST

The procedure and criterion for mastery are the same as for the pretest.

| Set I    | desk | desk | desk | best |
|----------|------|------|------|------|
| Set II   | long | song | long | long |
| Set III  | in   | in   | in   | in   |
| Set IV   | ban  | ban  | nab  | ban  |
| Set V    | mop  | top  | top  | top  |
| Set VI   | fish | wish | fish | fish |
| Set VII  | bake | bike | bike | bike |
| Set VIII | dog  | bog  | dog  | dog  |
| Set IX   | ship | ship | ship | shig |
| Set X    | on   | no   | on   | on   |

## • ENSURING TRANSFER

Although the learner will be applying this visual discrimination skill while beginning to learn sight words, you should also use the suggestions provided in I-SW-1 to be sure that the skill is immediately used during the routine daily activities of the classroom.

## • THE PERFORMANCE OBJECTIVE

When given a few seconds to examine a short word, the learner will reproduce the word from memory, to the satisfaction of the teacher.

## • THE PRETEST

Prepare ten flashcards, each of which has one word of the following sequence: **yes, no, and, the, was, in, to, of, my, he.** Flash each for the count of three. Then direct the learner to reproduce it. Criterion for mastery is teacher judgment regarding the accuracy of each reproduction. Size is not a criterion. *Caution:* it is not necessary for the learner to name the words at this time, since naming will be tested later in the skill hierarchy.

## • DIRECTING THE LEARNER'S ATTENTION

The purpose of this task is to develop the learner's visual memory for word forms. This is similar to storehouse module I-SW-2, but the learner is being asked to remember word forms rather than geometric figures. To teach this skill you must be sure that the learner knows exactly what is to be learned and you must direct his or her attention by highlighting the visual characteristics of the word to be remembered. (See the example in the previous objective.)

## • TEACHING ACTIVITIES

This is a visual memory task similar to that described in I-SW-2, and you can adapt your teaching strategy from either the modeling technique or the discovery technique described in that objective.

## • SUGGESTIONS FOR RETEACHING

If, after having been taught with either the modeling or the discovery technique, the learner is unable to reproduce the words, you should

1. Reteach the skill, using the alternate technique.
2. Be more specific in directing the learner's attention, being sure that your highlighting is providing enough help in distinguishing the visual characteristics to be remembered.
3. Return to the previous skill and be sure that the learner is discriminating between words.
4. Reteach the simpler tasks of remembering geometric forms and letters before requiring the learner to complete the more complex task of remembering words.

### • SUGGESTIONS FOR PRACTICE

After successfully teaching the skill, create practice activities to solidify the skill, using the suggestions provided in I-SW-2.

### • THE POSTTEST

The pretest may also be used as the posttest.

### • ENSURING TRANSFER

Although the learner will be applying this visual memory skill while progressing to the more complex skills in the hierarchy, you should also use the suggestions provided in I-SW-2 to be sure that the skill is used during the routine daily activities of the classroom.

# II•SW•6

### • THE PERFORMANCE OBJECTIVE

When given a fraction of a second to examine each of ten flashcards having printed on them words he or she selected as wanting to learn to read, the learner will pronounce each word within one second.

### • THE PRETEST

This is the first objective in which the learner is asked to recognize words. In future objectives the words to be recognized will be prescribed, but at this initial stage the learner is allowed to select the ten words he or she wants to learn, on the assumption that self-selected words will have a high association value to the learner and will therefore be easier for him or her to learn. Consequently, in preparing the pretest for this particular objective, you must first elicit from the learner the ten words he or she would like to learn to recognize. Once the learner selects the words, print each on separate flashcards. Then flash each word to the learner, giving only a second or less to examine the word. The criterion for mastery is 100 percent. *Note:* You should keep track of the words missed on the pretest, since it is only the missed words that need to be taught.

### • DIRECTING THE LEARNER'S ATTENTION

The purpose of this task is to teach the learner to recognize instantly and pronounce words when they are presented on flashcards. This is the first in a series of objectives in which the learner will be taught to recognize words instantly. This task is a crucial one for several reasons. First, our job is to develop fluent readers and not ones who must analyze and sound out each word in turn. Fluent readers are readers who instantly recognize words they are reading. Second, many of the words we read in the English language do not lend themselves to sounding out, since they do not follow the phonetic principles of the language. The only efficient way to teach such words is to teach the learner to recognize each at sight. Finally, to master the complete phonetic system of English is a laborious process and it would take too long if we were to wait until the learner had mastered this system before we let him or her read independently. By teaching the learner to read certain words instantly, we are allowing him or her to read many materials independently at a stage when he or she would otherwise be unable to do so.

The learning of words at sight is a visual task that draws heavily on the previously taught skills of visual discrimination, visual memory, and visual sequencing. In teaching this skill you must be sure that the learner has mastered the previous visual training skills, that he or she knows exactly what is to be learned, that the word being taught is in the learner's oral speaking vocabulary, and that you have directed his or her attention by highlighting the unique visual characteristics of the word (such as the initial and final letters, length, shape, double letters, and so on).

## • THIS IS A STOREHOUSE OBJECTIVE

The following instructional activities are your storehouse of techniques for developing skill in recognizing words instantly. This skill recurs in more sophisticated forms later in the skill hierarchy. The activities that follow are to be adapted and used with each of these as they occur.

## • TEACHING ACTIVITIES

*The modeling technique.* For every two words the learner needs to learn to recognize instantly, follow this procedure. First, make sure that the learner is familiar with the words by telling him or her what the words are and by having him or her use the words correctly in oral sentences. Once it is determined that the child is familiar with the words and can use them in oral language, say that you are going to demonstrate how to remember each of the words and that he or she is to watch and mimic your words and actions. Show the learner the printed forms of the words (in which the unique visual characteristics have been highlighted), saying, "This word says _____ and this word says _____. I can remember this word because it has . . . (specify and point to that word's unique visual form) and I can remember this word because . . . (specify and point to that word's unique visual form)." Have the learner mimic you and then show him or her how to connect the visual form of the word to the word name by saying, "I am going to look at the word; note its characteristics and say its name. Now you do the same." Provide for a number of repetitions in which the amount of modeling and highlighting is gradually diminished until the learner is able to recognize the word without assistance.

*The discovery technique.* The principle to be developed in teaching sight words is that every word has visual characteristics that serve to make it unique from all other words. Using pairs of words that are in the learner's oral vocabulary and that have been printed on cards with the distinguishing characteristics highlighted (as described earlier), ask questions designed to guide the learner to discover the way in which he or she will remember each word. For instance, place the two highlighted words before the learner and say, "This word says _____ and this word says _____. Look at each word and tell me how you will remember each word so that you will know it instantly when I flash it to you." Have the learner describe how he or she will remember, using your highlighting as a guide if the learner desires. Have the learner look at each word, note its characteristics, and then say the word. Provide for a number of repetitions in which the amount of highlighting and the number of cuing questions posed by you are gradually diminished until the learner is able to recognize the word instantly without assistance.

## • SUGGESTIONS FOR RETEACHING

If, after having been taught with either of the preceding techniques, the learner is unable to recognize the words instantly, you should

1. Reteach the skill, using the alternate technique.
2. Use the suggestions provided in I-SW-17 if the learner's problem is one of confusing words (saying **was** for **saw, where** for **there,** and so on).
3. Reexamine your analysis of the visual characteristics of the word to be sure that you are having the learner note the most helpful visual characteristics.
4. Reteach the skill, using a more dramatic form of highlighting to direct the learner more specifically to the unique visual characteristics of the word.
5. Recheck to make sure that the words are in the learner's oral vocabulary; if they are not, teach the learner to use the word orally before asking him or her to recognize it in print.
6. Use the VATK technique in which the visual, auditory, tactile, and kinesthetic senses are used to help the child remember the word by printing a large form of the word on paper, in sand, or on some other rough material and having him or her repeatedly trace the word with his or her index finger while simultaneously saying its name.
7. Have the learner temporarily use the initial sound of the word as a crutch (providing he or she has already mastered the sound-symbol connection for that letter) by telling him or her to look at the word and to get his or her mouth ready to say the first sound before actually saying the whole word.
8. If the word has a low association value (such as the words **the, through,**

and so on), teach the hard word in combination with another word with high association value (such as **dinosaur, astronaut,** and so on) by putting both words on a card together in a phrase (as in **the dinosaur**).

9. Have the learner repeatedly trace the word as he or she states both the distinguishing visual characteristics and the word name.
10. Return to previous visual discrimination, visual memory, and visual sequencing skills in the hierarchy to be sure that he or she possesses the prerequisite skills needed to perform this more complex visual task.

### • SUGGESTIONS FOR PRACTICE

Once you have taught the learner to recognize the words on the pretest instantly, use one or more of the following activities to help the learner solidify the skill.

1. Make up racing games in which learners progress in the race by pronouncing at sight the words to be learned. For instance, construct an auto racing course, dividing the track into equal-sized squares. Give each learner a toy racing car and provide yourself with a pack of cards upon which are printed the words you want the class to learn. Flash one word to each learner in turn. If the learner pronounces it instantly, he or she moves the racing car one square closer to the finish line. If the learner is unable to pronounce the word, his or her car does not move. The first learner to get his or her car to the finish line wins.
2. Help learners construct self-help references for the words they find difficult. For instance, each learner can be provided with a 3- by 5-inch file box and a supply of file cards. For every word that he or she has difficulty learning, the learner writes the word on the file card together with a picture or other aid to help remember the word. The learner refers to the file frequently to study the words and to remind himself or herself of what the word is if he or she is unable to identify it when meeting it in reading.
3. Place the words to be learned at sight on the chalkboard. One learner is sent out into the hall and another goes to the board and points to one of the words. The rest of the class pronounces the word to be sure that all the learners know it. Then the first learner is brought back into the room and he or she tries to guess which word has been pointed to. The learner points to one word and says, 'Is it _____?" The learner continues this way until he or she identifies the word.
4. Construct ladder games in which a paper ladder leads to a place where a reward of some kind is waiting. For instance, the ladder can be leading to the upper branches of a paper apple tree that has many paper apples on it. Each rung of the ladder has a sight word attached to it. The learner must instantly pronounce the word on each rung of the ladder. If he or she successfully reaches the top of the ladder, there is a reward, such as a real apple or a check on progress chart.
5. A multitude of games for building sight words can be devised based on

the idea of a trip. This trip may be a reconstruction of the adventures of some famous story character (such as Peter Rabbit), it may be a trip that the learners are actually going on, or it may be a trip that is completely imaginary (such as a trip to the moon, a trip to a distant city, and so on). In any case, a game board is constructed upon which is drawn the path to be followed in reaching the destination and the hazards to be overcome along the way. Each learner progresses on the trip by correctly pronouncing the words flashed when his or her turn comes up. The first learner to complete the trip wins the game.

6. A fishing game can be played in which the learner is given a pole constructed of a stick and a string having a magnet tied to the end. Paper fish having the words to be learned printed on them are placed in a box or in some other object that will serve as a pond. Attach a paper clip to each fish. Learners drop their line into the pond until the magnet attracts the paper clip on a fish. They pull the fish out and get to keep it if they can correctly pronounce the word printed on its side. The learner catching the most fish wins.

7. Make nine packs of ten cards each. The nine packs represent the nine holes of a golf course, and the word printed on the cards are the words to be learned at sight. The cards are shuffled and the player puts the pack for the first hole face down on his or her desk. The player turns each card over in turn, pronounces it, and goes on. Every time he or she is unable to pronounce a word correctly, a mark is placed on the scorecard and the number the learner gets wrong on the first hole (first pack of cards) is his or her score for that hole. The player continues in this manner through the nine packs of word cards, trying to get as small a score as possible. You should encourage the learner to keep a chart record of his or her score on this course so that the learner can note his or her progress in mastering the course. New courses offering new challenges can be constructed as new words need to be learned.

8. Put the words to be learned on cards, placing a numerical value in the upper right-hand corner of each card in accordance with its degree of difficulty in being remembered. For instance, **dinosaur** is a fairly easy word for learners to identify and would only be given a value of 1, but **the** is very difficult for young learners to recognize and would be given a value of 3. Learners take turns drawing the cards, reading the words and noting their scores. If they pronounce the word correctly, their score is the numerical value noted on the corner of the card. The learner with the most points at the end wins.

9. Play a treasure hunt game in which several packets of ten or more words each are hidden around the classroom. Give the learner the first packet and direct him or her to read each word. The learner goes through the words as quickly as possible and the last card will tell him where the next packet is hidden. The learner goes to that packet and repeats the process. The final packet will direct him or her to a spot in the classroom where the learner will receive a prize for having completed the game.

10. A variation of the television game Concentration can also be played. Place the words to be learned on cards and put them face down on the table. The learner must remember where there are two cards exactly alike and try to pick up matching pairs. As the player turns over each card, he or she must pronounce the word on the card. If the learner succeeds in picking up a word that matches the first word, he or she gets another turn. The learner with the most pairs at the end wins.

## • THE POSTTEST

The procedure and criterion for mastery are the same as for the pretest.

## • ENSURING TRANSFER

Once the learner has mastered the skill of instantly recognizing the words contained on the pretest, you should immediately provide for application of this skill by giving the child reading material containing the words he or she knows at sight. The following examples would be appropriate:

1. Make a class dictionary in which the sight words are printed in alphabetical order in a large notebook. The learners use old magazines to find pictures illustrating the word and are then encouraged to use this dictionary to look up a word any time they are reading.
2. Make a habit of sending short personal notes to your learners. For instance, when they come in the room before school in the morning, they may find on their desks a note from you saying, "Can you help me at my desk?" or, "How do you feel?" or even something as simple as, "I like you." In leaving these notes you should make sure that they utilize words that learners need to practice but that no words are used that the learners have not been exposed to. This is a highly motivating device for encouraging learners to master sight words.

*Are you teaching or testing?*

3. Place the learner in a basal textbook having a readability that matches his or her instructional reading level and have him or her read and discuss the stories. In doing so the learner will encounter many of the words learned at sight and will be using them in a contextual setting.
4. Write stories for the learner that feature the child as the central character and that utilize many of the words he or she has learned to recognize at sight. The child reads these stories for purposes specified ahead of time by the teacher and/or the child and, in the process, uses the sight words that have been taught.
5. Use the suggestions provided in the storehouse module II-SW-8 to help the learner create language experience stories in which he or she writes and reads his or her own stories as a means for using the words known at sight.
6. Encourage much recreational reading using library books, magazines, and other reading matter written at the learner's instructional reading level.

**• THE PERFORMANCE OBJECTIVE**

When given a fraction of a second to examine flashcards having printed on them the words **yes, no, I, and, the, a, to, was, in, it, of, my,** and **he,** the child will pronounce each word within one second.

**• THE PRETEST**

Print each of the preceding words on a flashcard. Flash each card to the learner giving less than one second to examine each word, and have him or her pronounce the word aloud. The criterion for mastery is 100 percent.

**• DIRECTING THE LEARNER'S ATTENTION**

The purpose of this task is to teach the learner to recognize instantly and pronounce the words contained in the pretest when they are printed on cards and flashed to him or her. This is a sight word recognition skill similar to storehouse module II-SW-6. To teach the skill you must be sure that the learner knows exactly what is to be learned, that the words being taught are in his or her oral speaking vocabulary and that you have directed his or her attention by highlighting the unique visual characteristics of each word (such as the initial and final letters, length, shape, double letters ,and so on).

**• TEACHING ACTIVITIES**

This is a sight word recognition skill similar to that described in II-SW-6. If the learner does not recognize the word in print, adapt your teaching strategy from either the modeling technique or the discovery technique described in that objective. If he or she confuses the word to be recognized with another word similar to it, adapt your strategy from the suggestions contained in I-SW-17.

**• SUGGESTIONS FOR RETEACHING**

If, after having been taught using the preceding techniques, the learner is unable to recognize instantly one or more of the words on the pretest, you should use the reteaching suggestions described in II-SW-6.

**• SUGGESTIONS FOR PRACTICE**

After successfully teaching the learner to recognize the words instantly on the pretest, create practice activities to solidify the skill, using the suggestions provided in II-SW-6.

**• THE POSTTEST**

The procedure and criterion for mastery are the same as for the pretest.

**• ENSURING TRANSFER**

To be sure that this skill is applied you must give the learner reading material containing the words he or she knows at sight and have him or her read. You may guide the learner's application by pointing out the words he or she has just learned to recognize or, as the learner becomes more proficient, you can encourage him or her to read independently. Any material that is at his or her instructional reading level and that contains the sight word he or she has learned would be appropriate. Additional suggestions for helping the learner use his or her known sight words in context are contained in II-SW-6.

### • THE PERFORMANCE OBJECTIVE

When given sentence frames created by the teacher and the words the learner recognizes at sight printed on cards, the learner will point to and name the word that completes the sentence frame.

### • THE PRETEST

Provide the learner with cards, each of which has printed on it a word he or she learned to recognize instantly in previous sight word objectives. Then use some of these words (plus others, if necessary) to construct a sentence frame, with each sentence having a blank space that can be filled by one of the other words the learner is able to recognize instantly. For instance, if one of the learner's words was **elephant,** a sentence such as the following could be constructed: "I went to the zoo and saw an ⎯⎯⎯⎯." Say each sentence frame to the learner, ask the learner to watch and listen carefully, and direct him or her to point to and name the word that "finishes what I want to say." The criterion for mastery is 100 percent.

### • DIRECTING THE LEARNER'S ATTENTION

The purpose of this task is to teach the learner to produce and read messages using the individual words he or she knows at sight. As such, it is an application technique making sure that the learner uses, in a contextual setting, the sight words he or she has mastered in previous objectives. This is an important objective since it accurately reflects the total language act; the message to be written is a product of thinking and is expressed first orally, with the oral message then being translated into written form by arranging the word cards to form a message that can be read and understood by others. As such, this task provides the learner with a tangible concept of what the reading-writing act is really all about. Because the emphasis is on the total language act and the message created is based on the learner's experience, this activity is known as "language experience."

Several things must be considered when teaching this objective. First, remember that your concern is not to teach recognition of the word itself (since it has already been taught in previous objectives) but to show the learner how to use, in the total context of the reading act, a word he or she may previously have only recognized on a card in isolated practice. Second, you must be sure that the learner knows exactly what is to be learned and you must direct his or her attention by highlighting the words in the sentence frame that give clues to what word should go in the blank space. (In the example given in the pretest, for instance, you highlight the words **zoo** and **saw** since the learner will use his experience regarding these concepts to put in the blank the name of something one would see in a zoo.)

● **THIS IS A STOREHOUSE OBJECTIVE**

The following instructional activities are your storehouse of techniques for creating language experience activities as a means for applying and using learned sight words. This activity recurs in more sophisticated forms throughout the hierarchy and you should adapt and use the following suggestions with each as they occur.

● **TEACHING ACTIVITIES**

*The modeling technique.* Place on a table ( so that they all can be seen) the cards having printed on them the words the learner recognizes at sight. Say, "I am going to show you how to use a word you know to send a written message that someone else can read." Then direct the learner to watch you as you arrange the word cards to make a sentence frame such as, "I went to the zoo and saw an ⎯⎯⎯." Highlight the words **zoo** and **saw** by having them printed larger, by pointing to them with cutout arrows, or in some other manner. Say the sentence frame out loud and then state, "I must now figure out which of my word cards goes in the blank spot (point to it). I am going to use the words **zoo** and **saw** to help me because the word that goes in the blank has to be something I would see at the zoo. Let's see. Would it be **astronaut**? No, you don't usually see astronauts at the zoo." Continue in this fashion, speaking out loud to model for the learner the thinking he or she must go through to determine which word goes in the blank. Finally, say, "Would it be **elephant**? Yes, it could be **elephant** because you can see an elephant at the zoo." Then have the learner mimic your actions with the same sentence. Continue the same procedure with subsequent sentence frames, gradually diminishing the amount of modeling you provide and the amount of highlighting on the clue words in the sentence frame until the learner can perform the task without assistance.

*The discovery technique.* Start with the cards spread out, a sentence frame constructed, and the key words highlighted just as you would for the modeling technique. Rather than modeling your thinking for the learner, however, ask a series of questions designed to help the learner discover that his or her experience with certain words in the sentence will help determine what word should go in the blank. A sample questioning procedure would be the following:

What words in the sentence frame are highlighted?

Do you know what a zoo is?

What do you see at a zoo?

What kind of animals do you see at the zoo?

What are the names of some of the animals you see at a zoo?

Can you look at your word cards and find the name of an animal that you would see at a zoo?

Repeat this questioning procedure with other sentence frames in which the key words have been highlighted. As the learner responds correctly, give him or her additional sentence frames in which the amount of highlighting on key words and the number of questions is gradually diminished until the learner can supply the missing word without assistance.

• **SUGGESTIONS FOR RETEACHING**

If, after having been taught with either the modeling or the discovery technique, the learner is unable to point to and name the word that goes in the blank, you should

1. Reteach the activity, using the alternate technique.
2. Reexamine your attenders, making sure that you are effectively highlighting the relationship between the learner's experience with the key words and the word that goes in the blank.
3. Check to make sure that the learner has experience with the concepts, changing the subject to match his or her experience, if necessary.
4. Recheck the learner's mastery of the sight words, reteaching them if he or she does not recognize them instantly.
5. Simplify the task further by having the learner choose one of the sight words and use it in a sentence first before you create with the word cards the sentence he or she said.

• **SUGGESTIONS FOR PRACTICE**

Once the learner has been taught to create messages, use one or more of the following practice activities to solidify the skill.

1. Provide the learner with intensive experiences in using oral language as a basis for communication. Use situations such as Show-and-Tell, dramatization, storytelling, games, message carrying, and any other situation to provide the learner with opportunities to communicate orally. As the child learns more reading skills, the communication emphasis can be shifted to include more written messages.
2. Make use of "experience charts" in which common experiences of the class are recorded on large chart paper following a sequence of steps such as the following. The learners first participate in an interesting and significant experience and discuss it with themselves and with you. Then you help them plan a title, the general content, and the exact sentences for the chart. The learners dictate the sentences to you and you print them on the chart. Be careful to use either words that the learners have been taught to recognize or that you have adequately identified for them.

You then read the chart to the learners, and they each take turns in reading the chart alone.

3. When an experience chart has been constructed, you can make individual word cards for each word that appears in the experience chart. Mix these up and give them to the learner, directing him or her to identify the words, sort them, and arrange the word cards to tell the same story as that told in the experience chart. The learner may use the large chart as a model from which to work.

4. An activity similar to that described in 3 above is one in which the learners are provided with sentence strips rather than with individual words. The sentences are then arranged to duplicate the story told on the experience chart. This is sometimes a helpful device if the learner seems to be stymied by the large number of word cards he must sort through in order to reconstruct the chart. By giving him the sentence strips, you are providing him with a transition step which he can go through before having to use the word cards.

### • THE POSTTEST

The procedure and criterion for mastery are the same as for the pretest.

### • ENSURING TRANSFER

This activity is, in and of itself, an application task since the learner is using in a contextual situation the sight words he or she has learned. Beyond this level, however, you should help the learner transfer the relationship between strings of words made from the sight word cards and the strings of words he or she finds printed in books, on the blackboard in the classroom, and in other familiar places. The ultimate goal here is to show the learner that writing or constructing sentences is a message-sending task and that reading is a message-getting task. The learner should begin to view reading as a communication process in which he or she can participate more and more as more and more words are learned.

## II•SW•9

### • THE PERFORMANCE OBJECTIVE

When given cards with words printed on them he or she has learned to pronounce at sight, the learner will, when directed to, point to the first letter and then to the last letter in each of these words.

### • THE PRETEST

Provide the learner with cards upon which are printed the words he or she recognizes at sight. The learner reads each word and when directed to point to the first and last letter in each of these words, he or she does so and names the first and last letters. The criterion for mastery is 100 percent.

### • DIRECTING THE LEARNER'S ATTENTION

The purpose of this task is to develop the learner's concept of left-to-right progression in visually examining words. This is a visual sequencing skill similar to the storehouse module I-SW-6. To teach this skill you must be sure that the learner knows exactly what is to be learned and you must direct his or her attention by highlighting the first and last letter in each of the words recognized at sight. (In the word **the,** for instance, you could color code the letter t and e and, as you show the learner the word, say, "First letter, **t.** Last letter **e.**")

### ● TEACHING ACTIVITIES

This is a visual sequencing skill similar to that described in I-SW-6, and you can adapt your teaching strategy from either the modeling technique or the discovery technique described in that objective.

### ● SUGGESTIONS FOR RETEACHING

If, after having been taught with either the modeling or the discovery technique, the learner is unable to point to the first and last letters in the words he or she recognizes at sight, you should

1. Reteach the skill, using the alternate technique.
2. Use more specific highlighting in directing the learner's attention to the first and last letters in words.
3. Return to earlier visual sequencing skills and reteach these simpler tasks before requiring the learner to perform the more complex task of picking out first and last letters in words.

### ● SUGGESTIONS FOR PRACTICE

After successfully teaching the learner to point to the first and last letters in words, create practice activities to solidify this skill, using the suggestions provided in I-SW-6.

### ● THE POSTTEST

The procedure and criterion for mastery for the posttest are the same as for the pretest.

### ● ENSURING TRANSFER

The learner will be using this visual sequencing skill while learning to remember additional words. In addition to these applications, however, you should be sure that this skill is used during the routine daily activities of the classroom by applying the suggestions provided in I-SW-6.

## II•SW•10

### ● THE PERFORMANCE OBJECTIVE

When given part of a sentence frame created by the teacher and the words he or she recognizes at sight printed on cards, the learner will place certain word cards in an order that completes the sentence and will read the sentence.

## • THE PRETEST

Provide the learner with cards, each of which has printed on it a word he or she learned to recognize instantly in previous sight word objectives. Use some of these words (plus others if necessary) to construct partial sentences with the end of the sentence being a blank that can be filled by using several of the words the learner is able to recognize instantly. For instance, you might create a partial sentence that says, "It was raining so I went _____" and the learner would use his or her sight words **in, the,** and **house** to complete the sentence with the phrase "in the house." You must be ready to accept any combination of words that make sense in the sentence, since you cannot always predict the precise words the learner will choose to use. The criterion for mastery is teacher judgment regarding both the quickness with which the task is performed and the quality of the sentence that results.

## • DIRECTING THE LEARNER'S ATTENTION

This is a language experience activity designed to teach the learner to produce and read messages using the individual words he or she knows at sight. As such, it is an application activity similar to storehouse module II-SW-8. To teach this activity you must be sure that the learner knows exactly what is to be learned and you must direct his or her attention by highlighting the words in the partial sentence that give clues to what should follow and the most likely key words in his or her sight word list. (In the example given, for instance, you might highlight **raining** and **went** in the partial sentence and words such as **house** in his sight word list, directing the learner to use his or her experience to determine where he or she would go if it was raining.)

## • TEACHING ACTIVITIES

This is a language experience activity similar to that described in II-SW-8. You should use the modeling and discovery techniques described in that objective as a basis for planning and teaching this task.

## • SUGGESTIONS FOR RETEACHING

If, after having been taught with either of the techniques described in the key objective, the learner is unable to use his or her sight words to complete the partial sentence, you should

1. Reteach the activity, using the alternate technique.
2. Reexamine your attenders to be sure that you are effectively highlighting the relationship between experience with the key words and the words that complete the sentence.
3. Be sure that the content of the sentence reflects the learner's experience, changing the subject to match his or her experience if necessary.
4. Recheck the learner's mastery of the sight words, reteaching them if necessary.

5. Return to the previous language experience objective and be sure that the learner can do that simpler task before requiring him or her to complete this objective.

## • SUGGESTIONS FOR PRACTICE

Once the learner has been taught to use sight words to complete and read a sentence, create practice activities to solidify this skill, adapting the suggestions made in II-SW-8.

## • THE POSTTEST

The procedure and criterion for mastery for the posttest are the same as for the pretest.

## • ENSURING TRANSFER

This objective is an application activity designed to help the learner use sight words in context. In addition to the applications specified here, however, you should use the suggestions provided in II-SW-8 to make sure that the learner uses his or her sight words in other contextual situations.

# II•SW•11

## • THE PERFORMANCE OBJECTIVE

When given a fraction of a second to examine flashcards having printed on them the color words (**white, black, red, blue, green,** and **yellow**), the learner will pronounce each word within one second.

## • THE PRETEST

Print each of the preceding words on a flashcard. Flash each card to the learner, giving less than one second to examine each word before he or she pronounces it. The criterion for mastery is 100 percent.

## • DIRECTING THE LEARNER'S ATTENTION

The purpose of this task is to teach the learner to recognize instantly and pronounce the color words listed in the pretest and is a sight word recognition skill similar to storehouse module II-SW-6. To teach this skill you must be sure that the learner knows exactly what is to be learned, that the words being taught are in his or her speaking vocabulary, and that you have directed his or her attention by highlighting the unique visual characteristics of each word (such as the initial and final letters, length, shape, double letters, and so on).

## • TEACHING ACTIVITIES

This is a sight word recognition skill similar to that described in II-SW-6. If the learner does not recognize the word in print, adapt your teaching strategy from either the modeling technique or the discovery technique described in that objective. If the learner confuses the word with another word similar to it, adapt your strategy from the suggestions contained in I-SW-17.

## • SUGGESTIONS FOR RETEACHING

If, after having been taught with either of the techniques suggested in the key objective, the learner is unable to recognize instantly one or more of the color words on the pretest, you should use the reteaching suggestions described in II-SW-6.

## • SUGGESTIONS FOR PRACTICE

After successfully teaching the learner to recognize instantly the words on the pretest, create practice activities to solidify this skill, using the suggestions provided in II-SW-6.

## • THE POSTTEST

The procedure and criterion for mastery for the posttest are the same as for the pretest.

## • ENSURING TRANSFER

To be sure that this skill is applied, you must give the learner reading material that contains the words he or she knows at sight and have the learner read. The suggestions described in II-SW-6 are appropriate.

# II•SW•12

## • THE PERFORMANCE OBJECTIVE

When given a fraction of a second to examine flashcards having printed on them the number words from **one** to **ten,** the learner will pronounce each word within one second.

## • THE PRETEST

Print each of the preceding words on a flashcard. Flash each card to the learner, giving less than one second to examine each word before he or she pronounces it. The criterion for mastery is 100 percent.

## • DIRECTING THE LEARNER'S ATTENTION

The purpose of this task is to teach the learner to recognize instantly and pronounce the number words listed in the pretest and is a sight word recognition skill similar to that described in II-SW-6. To teach this skill you must be sure that the learner knows exactly what is to be learned, that the words being taught are in his or her speaking vocabulary, and that you have directed his or her attention by highlighting the unique visual characteristics of each word (such as the initial and final letters, length, shape, double letters, and so on).

## • TEACHING ACTIVITIES

This is a sight word recognition skill similar to storehouse module II-SW-6. If the learner does not recognize the word in print, adapt your teaching strategy from either the modeling technique or the discovery technique described in that objective. If the learner confuses the word with another word similar to it, adapt your strategy from the suggestions contained in I-SW-17.

### • SUGGESTIONS FOR RETEACHING

If, after having been taught with either of the techniques suggested in the key objective, the learner is unable to recognize instantly one or more of the number words on the pretest, you should use the reteaching suggestions described in II-SW-6.

### • SUGGESTIONS FOR PRACTICE

After successfully teaching the learner to recognize instantly the words on the pretest, create practice activities to solidify the skill, using the suggestions provided in II-SW-6.

### • THE POSTTEST

The procedure and criterion for mastery for the posttest are the same as for the pretest.

### • ENSURING TRANSFER

To be sure that this skill is applied, you must give the learner reading material that contains the words he or she knows at sight and have him or her read. The suggestions described in II-SW-6 are appropriate.

# II•SW•13

### • THE PERFORMANCE OBJECTIVE

When given five known sight words in which the first letter is printed in lower case, the learner will match each word with the same word when the first letter is printed in upper case.

Does the environment of your room invite an interest in reading?

### • THE PRETEST

Prepare five cards on which previously taught sight words are printed. Then prepare a duplicate set on which are printed the same words with the first letters in upper case. Direct the learner to pronounce each word printed in lower case. The learner then looks through his or her second group of cards, finds the same word that has the first letter printed in upper case, and says that word.

### • DIRECTING THE LEARNER'S ATTENTION

The purpose of this task is to teach the learner to recognize known sight words when the first letter is printed in either lower case or upper case. As such, this skill is a combination of storehouse modules I-SW-3 (naming letters) and II-SW-6 (sight word recognition). To teach this skill you must be sure that the learner knows exactly what is to be learned and that you have directed his or her attention by highlighting the initial letter of the word in both its lower and upper case forms. (In the word **help,** for instance, you would highlight the lower case **h** in **help** and the upper case **H** in **Help.**)

## • TEACHING ACTIVITIES

The learner's success in performing this task depends upon both his or her ability to match upper- and lower-case letters and in remembering sight words. If the learner's difficulty lies with matching upper- and lower-case letters, use the teaching suggestions described in I-SW-3. If his or her difficulty lies with remembering the sight word when it is printed with the first letter in upper case, use the suggestions described in II-SW-6.

## • SUGGESTIONS FOR RETEACHING

If, after you have provided instruction, the learner is still unable to pass the posttest, you should return to the objectives for matching upper- and lower-case letters (II-SW-1) and remembering sight words (II-SW-6), using the reteaching techniques suggested there to help the learner develop the prerequisite skills he or she needs to perform the task described in this objective successfully.

## • SUGGESTIONS FOR PRACTICE

After successfully teaching the learner to recognize instantly words having either upper- or lower-case letters in the initial position, create practice activities to solidify this skill, using the suggestions provided in II-SW-6.

## • THE POSTTEST

The procedure and criterion for mastery for the posttest are the same as for the pretest.

## • ENSURING TRANSFER

To be sure that this skill is applied you must give the learner reading material that contains sight words printed with both upper- and lower-case letters in the initial position. The suggestions provided in II-SW-6 are appropriate.

# II•SW•14

## • THE PERFORMANCE OBJECTIVE

When given a fraction of a second to examine flash cards having printed on them the words **here, fast, to, me, at, come, see, help, home, work, down,** and **up,** the learner will pronounce each within one second.

## • THE PRETEST

Print each of the preceding words on a flashcard. Flash each to the learner, giving less than one second to examine each word before he or she pronounces it. The criterion for mastery is 100 percent.

## • DIRECTING THE LEARNER'S ATTENTION

The purpose of this task is to teach the learner to recognize instantly and pronounce the words contained in the pretest when they are printed on cards and flashed to him or her. This is a sight word recognition skill like that described in II-SW-6. To teach the skill you must be sure that the learner knows exactly what is to be learned, that the words being taught are in his or her speaking vocabulary, and that you have directed his or her attention by highlighting the unique visual characteristics of each word (such as the initial and final letters, length, shape, double letters, and so on).

## • TEACHING ACTIVITIES

This is a sight word recognition skill similar to that described in II-SW-6. If the learner does not recognize the word in print, adapt your teaching strategy from either the modeling technique or the discovery technique described in that objective. If he or she confuses the word with another word similar to it, adapt your strategy from the suggestions contained in I-SW-17.

## • SUGGESTIONS FOR RETEACHING

If, after having been taught with the technique suggested, the learner is unable to recognize instantly one or more of the words on the pretest, you should use the reteaching suggestions described in II-SW-6.

## • SUGGESTIONS FOR PRACTICE

After successfully teaching the learner to recognize instantly the words on the pretest, create practice activities to solidify the skill, using the suggestions provided in II-SW-6.

## • THE POSTTEST

The procedure and criterion for mastery for the posttest are the same as for the pretest.

## • ENSURING TRANSFER

To be sure that this skill is applied, you must give the learner reading material containing the words he or she knows at sight and have him or her read. You may guide the learner's application by pointing out the words he or she has just learned to recognize or, as the learner becomes more proficient, you can encourage him or her to read and apply the newly learned words independently. Any material that is at the learner's instructional reading level and that contains the sight words he or she has learned would be appropriate. Additional suggestions for helping the learner use known sight words in context are contained in II-SW-6.

## II•SW•15

## • THE PERFORMANCE OBJECTIVE

When given a page of writing and directed to point to the first word and last word in a line of print and to the first word and last word on a page, the learner will instantly do so.

## • THE PRETEST

Open a book to a page that has a solid block of writing. *Caution:* Do not use title pages, glossaries, table of contents, and so on. Direct the learner to look at the page and point to the first word on a specified line and/or page. Give similar directions for the last word of a line or page. The learner must respond immediately with 100 percent accuracy.

### • DIRECTING THE LEARNER'S ATTENTION

The purpose of this task is to help the learner approach the reading of a printed page from left to right and from top to bottom. This is a visual sequencing skill similar to the storehouse module on page I-SW-6. To teach this skill you must be sure that the learner knows exactly what is to be learned and you must direct his or her attention by highlighting the first and last word in a line of print and by highlighting the first and last word on a page. (For instance, you could color code the appropriate words and run your finger first from left to right and then from top to bottom as you say, "The first word on this line is _____ and the last word on this line is _____; the first word on this page is _____ and the last word on this page is _____.")

### • TEACHING ACTIVITIES

This is a visual sequencing skill similar to that described in I-SW-6, and you can adapt your teaching technique from either the modeling technique or the discovery technique described in that objective.

### • SUGGESTIONS FOR RETEACHING

If, after having been taught with either the modeling or the discovery technique, the learner is unable to point to the first and last letters in the words he or she recognizes at sight, you should

1. Reteach the skill, using the alternate technique.
2. Use more specific highlighting in directing the learner's attention to the first and last words on a line and page.
3. Return to easier visual sequencing skills and reteach these simpler tasks before requiring the learner to perform the more complex task of picking out first and last words on a line and on a page.

### • SUGGESTIONS FOR PRACTICE

After successfully teaching the learner to point to the first and last words on a line and a page, create practice activities to solidify this skill, using the suggestions provided in I-SW-6.

### • THE POSTTEST

The procedure and criterion for mastery for the posttest are the same as for the pretest.

### • ENSURING TRANSFER

The learner will be using this visual sequencing skill as soon as he or she begins reading pages of print. In addition to these applications, however, you should be sure that the skill is used during the routine daily activities of the classroom by applying the suggestions provided in I-SW-6.

### • THE PERFORMANCE OBJECTIVE

When given a fraction of a second to examine flashcards having printed on them the following words, the learner will pronounce each within one second.

| that | is   | go     | we   | have | what      | dog  |
| had  | are  | you    | did  | ride | something | ball |
| out  | not  | little | make | said | do        | with |
| look | who  | funny  | for  | this | want      | will |

### • THE PRETEST

Print each of the preceding words on a flashcard. Flash each to the learner, giving him or her less than one second to examine each word before pronouncing it. The criterion for mastery is 100 percent.

### • DIRECTING THE LEARNER'S ATTENTION

The purpose of this task is to teach the learner to recognize instantly and pronounce the words contained in the pretest when they are printed on cards and flashed to him. This is a sight word recognition skill like the storehouse module described in II-SW-6. To teach this skill you must be sure that the learner knows exactly what is to be learned, that the words being taught are in his or her speaking vocabulary, and that you have directed his or her attention by highlighting the unique visual characteristics of each word (such as the initial and final letters, length, shape, double letters, and so on).

### • TEACHING ACTIVITIES

This is a sight word skill similar to that described in II-SW-6. If the learner does not recognize the word in print, adapt your teaching strategy from either the modeling technique or the discovery technique described in that objective. If he or she confuses one word with another similar to it, adapt your strategy from the suggestions contained in I-SW-17.

### • SUGGESTIONS FOR RETEACHING

If, after having been taught with either the modeling or the discovery technique, the learner is unable to recognize instantly one or more of the words on the pretest, you should use the reteaching suggestions provided in II-SW-6.

### • SUGGESTIONS FOR PRACTICE

After successfully teaching the learner to recognize the words on the pretest instantly, create practice activities to solidify the skill, using suggestions provided in II-SW-6.

The procedure and criterion for mastery for the posttest are the same as for the pretest.

### • ENSURING TRANSFER

To be sure that this skill is applied, you must give the learner reading material containing the words he or she knows at sight and have him or her read. You may guide the learner's application by pointing out the words he or she has just learned to recognize or, as the learner becomes more proficient, you can encourage him or her to read and apply the newly learned words independently. Any material that is at the learner's instructional reading level and that contains the sight words he or she has learned would be appropriate. Additional suggestions for helping the learner apply known sight words in context are contained in II-SW-6.

## II•WA•1

### • THE PERFORMANCE OBJECTIVE

When given a word spoken by the teacher in which each of the syllabic units has been isolated, the learner will recognize and repeat the word by fusing these units together into a normally spoken cadence.

### • THE PRETEST

Direct the learner to listen carefully as you say a word. Explain that the word is one that he or she knows but that it will sound strange because you are going to say it very slowly. Ask the learner to listen and "think of the word I am saying, then say it the way we really do." The criterion for mastery is 80 percent.

| | |
|---|---|
| pa . . . ja . . . ma (pajama) | Now you say the real word. |
| Chev . . . ro . . . lā (Chevrolet) | Now you say the real word. |
| cheez . . . bur . . . ger (cheeseburger) | Now you say the real word. |
| Hal . . . o . . . ween (Halloween) | Now you say the real word. |
| di . . . no . . . saur (dinosaur) | Now you say the real word. |
| In . . . di . . . an (Indian) | Now you say the real word. |
| jack . . . o . . . lan . . . tern (jack-o'-lantern) | Now you say the real word. |
| bas . . . ket . . . ball (basketball) | Now you say the real word. |
| Min . . . ne . . . so . . . ta (Minnesota) | Now you say the real word. |
| kang . . . ga . . . roo (kangaroo) | Now you say the real word. |

### • DIRECTING THE LEARNER'S ATTENTION

The purpose of this task is to help the learner develop the ability to blend or fuse a word identification when its individual phonemes are sounded in isolation. As phonics skills develop, the learner will find that he or she often needs to sound out a word that is strange in print and that this sounding will fragment the word into a string of isolated sounds. When this happens, the learner must be ready to test this string of sounds against a real spoken word and guess its identity. To do this successfully, he or she must train himself or herself to realize that the spelling-sounding process yields only an *approximation* of a word the way it is really spoken (in this case, the cadence or time aspect is distorted) and that the learner must be ready to ignore this distortion and let his or her ear be the guide to a correct identification. To help the learner in this task, you must direct him or her to the realization that *the elongated word that you pronounce is a real word that he or she knows and can speak.* It is this realization that will help the learner search the sound cues and blend them into a known word.

### • THIS IS A STOREHOUSE OBJECTIVE

The following instructional techniques are your storehouse of activities for developing skill in fusing isolated sounds into real spoken words. This skill will recur in more sophisticated forms in the skill clusters that follow. Adapt these instructional activities and suggestions to the later objectives.

### • TEACHING ACTIVITIES

*The modeling technique.* Fusion skills can be easily demonstrated through modeling. Say to your learner, "I will speak the word **run,** but I will speak it very slowly, **r . . . u . . . n . . .** What word did I say? Yes, I said **run.** I can say it fast, **run,** and I can say it slow, **r . . . u . . . n.** Either way, I know what the word is. It is **run.** Now, let's see if you can do this." You have modeled the total activity for the child and as he or she learns how to guess a word when its sounds are detached into separate elements, he or she will also learn to make the identification without your first cuing him or her with the word spoken in its normal cadence.

*The discovery technique.* The key to helping a child discover how to fuse isolated sound elements into a real spoken word is in his or her understanding of the task itself. The child must be led to realize that the sounds you make can be compressed into a word that he or she knows. You can help the learner discover this by saying, "I am going to say a word that you know, but it will sound strange because I will speak very slowly. The word I will say is either . . . (here you will name two words, one of which is the one you want the child to fuse). Now listen carefully as I say one of these words very slowly. See if you can tell me which word I am saying." In this example discovery is limited to two choices. By limiting the number of possibilities to two, you can almost be sure that both the word and the fusion process will be discovered. As the child develops skill in this activity you will include more choices, and ultimately the child will be left to fuse the sounds from a choice of *all* words that are in his or her speaking vocabulary. The child will be given no clues other than the sounds to be fused.

### • SUGGESTIONS FOR RETEACHING

If after multiple learning opportunities, either modeled or discovered, the learner is still unable to fuse isolated sounds into a real, spoken word, you might

1. Reteach the skill, using the other presentation model. (Switch from modeled to discovery cuing, or vice versa.)
2. Have the learner select words that you will say slowly. Demonstrate with only one word at a time, so that the process is emphasized. Explain that you will speak the learner's word slowly and that he or she must, on cue, say it fast.
3. Reverse the role of teacher. You give the learner a word, direct him or her to say it slowly, and then you identify it by saying it fast.
4. Select words that can be pictured. Have the learner draw these words, each on a separate card. Arrange three cards in a row and have the learner speak the word as you point to each picture in turn. Now repeat this activity, but this time you speak the word "by sound" as the learner points to its picture. Cue the learner to immediately say the word fast. Finally, you can simply speak the word by sound, directing the learner to point to the picture that identifies the word and say it fast.

### • SUGGESTIONS FOR PRACTICE

Once this skill has been successfully performed, use one or more of the following practice activities to ensure retention.

1. During storytime purposely sound out some word instead of speaking it in normal cadence. Say, "Oh, that is a lazy word. How should I have said it?" This can be done during any oral activity.
2. Prepare a tape of spoken words that are sounded in isolation. Collect pictures that represent each spoken word and cue the identification with some color on the back. Direct the learner to listen to the tape and select the picture of the word he or she hears. Have the learner say it fast, and then check his or her response by looking at the color on the back. The tape can tell the learner the color he or she should see.

*Are your pupils creating some of the safety valves?*

### • THE POSTTEST

The procedure and criterion for mastery are the same as for the pretest.

| | |
|---|---|
| d . . . esk (desk) | Now you say the real word. |
| pu . . . py (puppy) | Now you say the real word. |
| wh . . . ere (where) | Now you say the real word. |
| mo . . . vie (movie) | Now you say the real word. |
| tea . . . cher (teacher) | Now you say the real word. |
| kang . . . ga . . . ro (kangaroo) | Now you say the real word. |
| Hal . . . o . . . ween (Halloween) | Now you say the real word. |
| s . . . ee (see) | Now you say the real word. |
| o . . . ver (over) | Now you say the real word. |
| r . . . ead (read) | Now you say the real word. |

### • ENSURING TRANSFER

As the learner develops more sophisticated phonetic-analysis skills, he or she will use these skills to sound out words that are strange in print. Many times the learner's recognition of these sounded words will depend upon ability to blend or fuse the isolated sound elements into a recognizable spoken word. Transfer occurs at this time. If the learner is comfortable with fusing tactics at this stage, he or she will easily transfer this skill when sounding out new words.

## • THE PERFORMANCE OBJECTIVE

When given a word spoken by the teacher in which each of the letter sound units have been isolated, the learner will recognize and repeat the word by fusing the isolated sounds together into a normal spoken cadence.

## • THE PRETEST

Direct the learner to listen carefully as you speak a word. Explain that the word is one that he or she knows but that it will sound strange because you are going to say it very slowly. Ask the learner to listen carefully and think of the word you are saying, then say it the way it really sounds. The criterion for mastery is 80 percent.

| | |
|---|---|
| r . . . u . . . n (run) | Now you say the real word. |
| p . . . or . . . ch (porch) | Now you say the real word. |
| bi . . . cy . . . cle (bicycle | Now you say the real word. |
| c . . . an . . . dy (candy) | Now you say the real word. |
| l . . . a . . . soo (lasso) | Now you say the real word. |
| sw . . . im (swim) | Now you say the real word. |
| o . . . pen (open) | Now you say the real word. |
| b . . . e . . . d (bed) | Now you say the real word. |
| w . . . in . . . ter (winter) | Now you say the real word. |
| thr . . . o (throw) | Now you say the real word. |

## • DIRECTING THE LEARNER'S ATTENTION

The purpose of this task is to help the learner blend or fuse a word identification when the individual syllables are sounded in isolation. As phonics skills are developed, the learner will find that he or she often guesses a word identification by sounding out its phoneme or phonogram units. Such sounding activity usually results in a disconnected approximation of the real spoken word. In order to recognize what has been sounded, the learner must blend these sounds together into a closer approximation of the normally spoken word. To help in this task you must direct the learner to the realization that *the separated sounds that you produce are a real spoken word that the learner knows and can speak.* This directed attention toward a normally spoken word will help in each of the sound cues and ultimate blending skill.

## • TEACHING ACTIVITIES

This is a fusion task similar to storehouse objective II-WA-1, and you can build your teaching strategies, using either modeling or discovery techniques described there.

## • SUGGESTIONS FOR RETEACHING

Examine storehouse objective II-WA-1 for suggestions on how to reteach this skill.

## • SUGGESTIONS FOR PRACTICE

After teaching this skill, create practice activities as suggested in objective II-WA-1.

## • THE POSTTEST

The procedure and criterion for mastery are the same as for the pretest. Select new words and separate syllables, as was done in the pretest.

## • ENSURING TRANSFER

Transfer techniques are the same as those found in objective II-WA-1 and you should adapt these suggestions to this skill.

# II•WA•3

## • THE PERFORMANCE OBJECTIVE

When given stimulus words ending with the **m, d, l,** or voiceless **s** sound and a group of three other words one of which ends with the **m, d, l,** or voiceless **s** sound, the learner will pair the two words ending with the same sound.

## • THE PRETEST

Using the following words, say to the learner, "Here are three words. Listen carefully. (Say the three words.) Which one sounds like (say the stimulus word) *at the end?*" Repeat the three words. The criterion for mastery is seven out of eight correct.

| | | | |
|---|---|---|---|
| Sam | ran | are | Which word sounds like **same** at the end? Repeat the three words. |
| had | want | rain | Which word sounds like **mad** at the end? Repeat the three words. |
| chair | hid | soon | Which word sounds like **mad** at the end? Repeat the three words. |
| book | floor | ball | Which word sounds like **hill** at the end? Repeat the three words. |
| picture | lamps | know | Which word sounds like **miss** at the end? Repeat the three words. |
| steal | rat | waste | Which word sounds like **hill** at the end? Repeat the three words. |
| limb | book | flower | Which word sounds like **same** at the end? Repeat the three words. |
| top | recess | belt | Which word sounds like **miss** at the end? Repeat the three words. |

## • DIRECTING THE LEARNER'S ATTENTION

The purpose of this task is to teach the learner to distinguish the final **m,
d, l,** and voiceless s sounds from other final consonant sounds, As such,
this task is similar to storehouse module I-WA-5 except that the focus is on
ending sounds rather than beginning sounds. To teach this skill you must
direct the learner's attention by stating exactly what is to be learned and
by highlighting the *ending* sound of the words. (You might, for instance,
say each word twice, exaggerating the ending sound the first time and saying the word normally the second time.)

## • TEACHING ACTIVITIES

In teaching this auditory discrimination skill you can use either the modeling technique or the discovery technique described in I-WA-5, adjusting
the suggestions to focus on the ending rather than the beginning sounds.

## • SUGGESTIONS FOR RETEACHING

If, after having been taught this skill with either the modeling or the discovery technique, the learner is unable to distinguish by ear the ending
**m, d, l, or** voiceless s sounds from other final consonant sounds, you should

1. Reteach the skill, using the alternate technique.
2. Reexamine your attenders, making sure that the learner is listening to
   the *ending* sounds and that your highlighting is emphatic enough to help
   him or her distinguish the ending sounds from other sounds.

## • SUGGESTIONS FOR PRACTICE

Once the learner can distinguish the ending **m, d, l,** and voiceless s sounds
from other final consonant sounds, create practice activities to solidify the
skill, using the suggestions provided in I-WA-5.

## • THE POSTTEST

The procedure and criterion for mastery are the same as for the pretest.

| | | | |
|---|---|---|---|
| not | if | seem | Which word sounds like **same** at the end? Repeat the three words. |
| key | said | any | Which word sounds like **mad** at the end? Repeat the three words. |
| all | painted | book | Which word sounds like **mad** at the end? Repeat the three words. |
| begin | word | maul | Which word sounds like **hill** at the end? Repeat the three words. |
| football | to | have | Which word sounds like **hill** at the end? Repeat the three words. |

| | | | |
|---|---|---|---|
| sew | paint | walrus | Which word sounds like **miss** at the end? Repeat the three words. |
| bomb | after | pen | Which word sounds like **same** at the end? Repeat the three words. |
| like | difference | it | Which word sounds like **miss** at the end? Repeat the three words. |

### • ENSURING TRANSFER

Although the learner will be applying this skill while learning to attach the ending sounds to letters in subsequent objectives, you should also use the suggestions provided in I-WA-5 to be sure that the skill is used during the daily activities of the classroom.

# II•WA•4

### • THE PERFORMANCE OBJECTIVE

When given spoken words ending with **m, d, l,** and voiceless **s** sounds, the learner will identify the ending letters as **m, d, l,** or **s.**

### • THE PRETEST

Give the learner four cards, one having the letter **m** printed on it, another with **d,** another with **l,** and the last with **s.** Say the following words, directing the learner to point to the letter whose sound *ends* the word just spoken. The criterion for mastery is 10 out of 12 correct, with no letter sound being missed more than once.

| | | | |
|---|---|---|---|
| came | dad | hippopotomus | red |
| repeal | walks | shall | skill |
| assume | cream | desks | watered |

### • DIRECTING THE LEARNER'S ATTENTION

The purpose of this task is to teach the learner to establish a sound-symbol connection between the letters **m, d, l,** and **s** and the sound these letters make at the end of words. As such, this task is similar to storehouse module I-WA-9 except that the focus is on the ending rather than the beginning letter sounds. To teach this skill you must direct the learner's attention by stating exactly what is to be learned and by highlighting both the sound heard at the end of the word and the form of the letter it is to be connected with. (In the word **came,** for instance, you might exaggerate the ending sound heard in the word while simultaneously pointing to the cut-out letter **m.**)

### • TEACHING ACTIVITIES

In teaching this sound-symbol connection skill you can use either the modeling technique or the discovery technique described in I-WA-9, adjusting the suggestions to focus on the ending letter sounds.

## • SUGGESTIONS FOR RETEACHING

If, after having been taught this skill with either the modeling or the discovery technique, the learner is unable to connect the letters m, d, l, and s with their ending sounds, you should

1. Reteach the skill, using the alternate technique.
2. Be more specific in directing the learner's attention, making sure that he or she is listening to the *ending* sound while simultaneously looking at the letter.
3. Use more emphasis in highlighting the ending sound, the letter, and the connection between them.
4. Return to the previous objective and be sure that the learner can distinguish the ending m, d, l, and voiceless s sounds before requiring him or her to connect the sounds with letters.

## • SUGGESTIONS FOR PRACTICE

Once the learner has successfully connected the m, d, l, and s letters to words ending with the m, d, l, and voiceless s sounds, create practice activities to solidify the skill, using the suggestions provided in I-WA-9.

## • THE POSTTEST

The procedure and criterion for mastery are the same as for the pretest.

| rhinoceros | pull | find | fell |
|------------|-------|-------|--------|
| this | mad | chase | random |
| flame | child | him | bell |

## • ENSURING TRANSFER

Although the learner will be applying this skill in subsequent skills in the hierarchy, you should use the suggestions provided in I-WA-9 to be sure that the skill is used during the routine daily activities of the classroom.

# II•WA•5

## • THE PERFORMANCE OBJECTIVE

When given stimulus words ending with b, f, g, n, p, t, or v and a group of three other words, one of which ends with the b, f, g, n, p, t, or v sound, the learner pairs the two words ending with the same sound.

## • THE PRETEST

Using the following words, say to the learner, "Here are three words. Listen carefully. (Say the three words.) Which one sounds like (say the stimulus word) at the end?" Repeat the three original words. The criterion for mastery is 12 out of 14 correct, with no one letter sound being missed more than once.

| | | | |
|---|---|---|---|
| dodge | dub | mad | Which word sounds like **lob** at the end? Repeat the three words. |
| save | lap | enough | Which word sounds like **laugh** at the end? Repeat the three words. |
| bad | lug | stun | Which word sounds like **bag** at the end? Repeat the three words. |
| sin | lime | fudge | Which word sounds like **fun** at the end? Repeat the three words. |
| lot | pup | lock | Which word sounds like **stop** at the end? Repeat the three words. |
| hit | tog | look | Which word sounds like **fat** at the end? Repeat the three words. |
| half | save | rob | Which word sounds like **have** at the end? Repeat the three words. |
| lock | fit | top | Which word sounds like **fat** at the end? Repeat the three words. |
| lug | love | loaf | Which word sounds like **have** at the end? Repeat the three words. |
| loop | post | rest | Which word sounds like **stop** at the end? Repeat the three words. |
| pest | rum | pin | Which word sounds like **fun** at the end? Repeat the three words. |
| flew | get | flag | Which word sounds like **bag** at the end? Repeat the three words. |
| fan | soup | miff | Which word sounds like **laugh** at the end? Repeat the three words. |
| fib | **box** | five | Which word sounds like **lob** at the end? Repeat the three words. |

## • DIRECTING THE LEARNER'S ATTENTION

The purpose of this task is to teach the learner to distinguish the final **b**, **f**, **g**, **n**, **p**, **t**, and **v** sounds from other final consonant sounds. As such, it is similar to the storehouse module I-WA-5 except that the focus is on ending sounds rather than beginning sounds. To teach this skill you must direct the learner's attention by stating exactly what is to be learned and by highlighting the *ending* sound of the words. (You might, for instance, say each word twice, exaggerating the ending sound the first time and saying the word normally the second time.)

## • TEACHING ACTIVITIES

In teaching this auditory discrimination skill you can use either the modeling technique or the discovery technique described in I-WA-5, adjusting the suggestions to focus on the ending rather than the beginning sounds.

## • SUGGESTIONS FOR RETEACHING

1. Reteach the skill, using the alternate technique.
2. Reexamine your attenders, making sure that the learner is listening to the *ending* sounds and that your highlighting is emphatic enough to help him or her distinguish the ending sounds from other sounds.

3. Return to the previous auditory discrimination skills, being sure that the learner can perform them before requiring him or her to complete this objective.

## • SUGGESTIONS FOR PRACTICE

Once the learner can distinguish the ending **b**, **f**, **g**, **n**, **p**, **t**, and **v** sounds from other final consonant sounds, create practice activities to solidify the skill, using the suggestions provided in I-WA-5.

## • THE POSTTEST

The procedure and criterion for mastery are the same as for the pretest.

| | | | |
|---|---|---|---|
| block | tried | stab | Which word sounds like **lob** at the end? Repeat the three words. |
| fake | staff | lake | Which word sounds like **laugh** at the end? Repeat the three words. |
| guess | bust | beg | Which word sounds like **bag** at the end? Repeat the three words. |
| plain | nest | fail | Which word sounds like **fun** at the end? Repeat the three words. |
| lip | stage | pull | Which word sounds like **stop** at the end? Repeat the three words. |
| fast | tag | flute | Which word sounds like **fat** at the end? Repeat the three words. |
| stove | pal | loaf | Which word sounds like **have** at the end? Repeat the three words. |
| stock | slit | far | Which word sounds like **fat** at the end? Repeat the three words. |
| blown | singe | strive | Which word sounds like **have** at the end? Repeat the three words. |
| pun | flop | stale | Which word sounds like **stop** at the end? Repeat the three words. |
| plan | next | new | Which word sounds like **fun** at the end? Repeat the three words. |
| egg | boast | gas | Which word sounds like **bag** at the end? Repeat the three words. |
| stuff | flesh | look | Which word sounds like **laugh** at the end? Repeat the three words. |
| lack | flab | basket | Which word sounds like **lob** at the end? Repeat the three words. |

Was that last Ditto sheet you assigned the best you could come up with?

## • ENSURING TRANSFER

Although the learner will be applying this skill while learning to attach the ending sounds to letters in subsequent objectives, you should also use the suggestions provided in I-WA-5 to be sure that the skill is used during the daily activities of the classroom.

### • THE PERFORMANCE OBJECTIVE

When given spoken words ending with **b, f, g, n, p, t,** or **v** sounds, the learner will identify the ending letters as **b, f, g, n, p, t,** or **v.**

### • THE PRETEST

Give the learner four cards, one having the letter **b** printed on it, another having the letter **f,** another having the letter **g,** and so on, for the letters being tested. Say the following words, directing the learner to point to the letter whose sound *ends* the word just spoken. The criterion for mastery is 12 out of 14 correct, with no letter sound being missed more than once.

| | | | | |
|---|---|---|---|---|
| cab | groove | invent | tent | flop |
| log | tough | scarf | scab | believe |
| rip | airplane | begin | slug | |

### • DIRECTING THE LEARNER'S ATTENTION

The purpose of this task is to teach the learner to establish a sound-symbol connection between the letters **b, f, g, n, p, t,** and **v** and the sounds these letters make at the end of words. As such, it is similar to the storehouse module I-WA-9 except that the focus is on the ending rather than the beginning letter sounds. To teach this skill you must direct the learner's attention by stating exactly what is to be learned and by highlighting both the sound heard at the end of the word and the form of the letter it is to be connected with. (In the word **cab,** for instance, you might exaggerate the ending sound heard in the word while simultaneously pointing to the cutout letter **b.**)

### • TEACHING ACTIVITIES

In teaching this sound-symbol connection skill you can use either the modeling technique or the discovery technique described in I-WA-9, adjusting the suggestions to focus on the ending letter sounds.

### • SUGGESTIONS FOR RETEACHING

If, after having been taught this skill with either the modeling or the discovery technique, the learner is unable to connect the letters **b, f, g, n, p, t,** and **v** with words that end with these sounds, you should

1. Reteach the skill, using the alternate technique.
2. Be more specific in directing the learner's attention, making sure that he or she is listening to the *ending* sound while simultaneously looking at the letter.
3. Use more emphasis in highlighting the ending sound, the letter, and the connection between them.
4. Return to the previous objective and be sure that the learner can distinguish the ending **b, f, g, n, p, t,** and **v** sounds before requiring him or her to connect sounds to letters.

- **SUGGESTIONS FOR PRACTICE**

Once the learner has successfully connected the **b, f, g, n, p, t,** and **v** letters to words ending with these sounds, create practice activities to solidify the skill, using the suggestions provided in I-WA-9.

- **THE POSTTEST**

The procedure and criterion for mastery are the same as for the pretest.

| | | | | |
|------|----------|------|-------|-------|
| tub | shove | flat | great | trap |
| plug | enough | leaf | scrub | sleeve |
| slap | superman | this | tag | |

- **ENSURING TRANSFER**

Although the learner will be applying this skill in subsequent skills in the hierarchy, you should also use the suggestions provided in I-WA-9 to make sure that the skill is used during the routine daily activities of the classroom.

# II•WA•7

- **THE PERFORMANCE OBJECTIVE**

When given a stimulus word beginning with the **q, v, y,** or **z** sounds, and a group of three other words one of which begins with the **q, v, y,** and **z** sounds, the learner will pair the two words beginning with the same sound.

- **THE PRETEST**

Using the following words, say to the learner, "Here are three words. Listen carefully. (Say the words.) Which one sound like (say the stimulus word) at the beginning?" Repeat the three original words. The criterion for mastery is seven out of eight corect.

| | | | |
|--------|------|-------|---|
| basket | veil | fall | Which one sounds like **vote** at the beginning? Repeat the three words. |
| cane | top | quack | Which one sounds like **queen** at the beginning? Repeat the three words. |
| zip | lip | size | Which one sounds like **zoo** at the beginning? Repeat the three words. |
| quiet | cap | king | Which one sounds like **queen** at the beginning? Repeat the three words. |
| joke | fell | yell | Which one sounds like **yes** at the beginning? Repeat the three words. |
| vain | fool | win | Which one sounds like **vote** at the beginning? Repeat the three words. |
| hole | yak | when | Which one sounds like **yes** at the beginning? Repeat the three words. |

| | | | |
|---|---|---|---|
| sand | zero | pale | Which one sounds like **zoo** at the beginning? Repeat the three words. |

### • DIRECTING THE LEARNER'S ATTENTION

The purpose of this task is to teach the learner to distinguish the **q, v, y,** and **z** sounds from other beginning consonant sounds. As such, the task is similar to the storehouse module I-WA-5. To teach this skill you must direct the learner's attention by stating exactly what is to be learned and by highlighting the beginning sound of the words as described in I-WA-5.

### • TEACHING ACTIVITIES

In teaching this auditory discrimination skill you can use either the modeling technique or the discovery technique described in I-WA-5, adjusting the suggestions to focus on the **q, v, y,** and **z** sounds.

### • SUGGESTIONS FOR RETEACHING

If, after having taught this skill with either the modeling or the discovery technique, the learner is unable to distinguish by ear the **q, v, y,** and **z** sounds from other beginning consonant sounds, you should

1. Reteach the skill, using the alternate technique.
2. Reexamine your attenders, making sure that the learner is listening to the *beginning* sounds and that your highlighting is emphatic enough to help him or her distinguish the beginning sounds from other sounds.
3. Return to the previous auditory discrimination skills, making sure that the learner can perform those before requiring him to complete this objective.

### • SUGGESTIONS FOR PRACTICE

Once the learner can distinguish the **q, v, y,** and **z** sounds from other beginning consonant sounds, create practice activities to solidify the skill, using the suggestions provided in I-WA-5.

### • THE POSTTEST

The procedure and criterion for mastery are the same as for the pretest. Use the following words.

| | | | |
|---|---|---|---|
| get | zombie | juice | Which one sounds like **zoo** at the beginning? Repeat the three words. |
| hide | yarn | whip | Which one sounds like **yes** at the beginning? Repeat the three words. |
| vat | note | whip | Which one sounds like **vote** at the beginning? Repeat the three words. |

| | | | |
|---|---|---|---|
| tub | fake | yellow | Which one sounds like **yes** at the beginning? Repeat the three words. |
| quite | seen | case | Which one sounds like **queen** at the beginning? Repeat the three words. |
| zone | lie | sip | Which one sounds like **zoo** at the beginning? Repeat the three words. |
| cap | tale | quick | Which one sounds like **queen** at the beginning? Repeat the three words. |
| bike | vice | fox | Which one sounds like **vote** at the beginning? Repeat the three words. |

## • ENSURING TRANSFER

Although the learner will be applying this skill as he or she learns to attach the sounds to letters in subsequent objectives, you should also use the suggestions provided in I-WA-5 to make sure that the skill is used during the routine daily activities of the classroom.

## II•WA•8

## • THE PERFORMANCE OBJECTIVE

When given spoken words beginning with the **q**, **v**, **y**, or **z** sounds, the learner will identify the beginning letter as **q**, **v**, **y**, or **z**.

## • THE PRETEST

Give the learner four cards, one having the letter **q** printed on it, another the **v**, another the **y**, and finally the **z**. Say the following words, directing the learner to point to the letter whose sound begins the word. The criterion for mastery is 80 percent, with no letter sound being missed more than once.

| | | | | | |
|---|---|---|---|---|---|
| quite | vast | yard | quiet | zone | vest |
| yankee | voice | quake | zoom | zipper | young |

## • DIRECTING THE LEARNER'S ATTENTION

The purpose of this task is to teach the learner to establish a sound-symbol connection between the letters **q**, **v**, **y**, and **z** and the sounds these letters make at the beginning of words. As such, the task is similar to storehouse module I-WA-9. To teach this skill you must direct the learner's attention by stating exactly what is to be learned and by highlighting both the sound heard at the beginning of the word and the form of the letter it is to be connected with. (In the word **quite**, for instance, you might exaggerate the beginning sound heard in the word while simultaneously pointing to the cutout letter **q**.)

## • TEACHING ACTIVITIES

In teaching this sound-symbol connection skill you can use either the modeling technique or the discovery technique described in I-WA-9, adjusting the suggestions to focus on the letters q, v, y, and z.

## • SUGGESTIONS FOR RETEACHING

If, after having been taught this skill with either the modeling or the discovery technique, the learner is unable to connect letter and sound for q, v, y, and z, you should

1. Reteach the skill, using the alternate technique.
2. Be more specific in directing the learner's attention, making sure that he or she is listening to the beginning sound while simultaneously looking at the letter.
3. Use more emphasis in highlighting the beginning sound, the letter, and the connection between them.
4. Return to the previous objective and be sure that the learner can distinguish between the beginning q, v, y, and z before requiring him to connect the sounds with letters.

## • SUGGESTIONS FOR PRACTICE

Once the learner has successfully connected the q, v, y, and z letters to their respective beginning sounds, create activities to solidify the skill, using the suggestions provided in I-WA-9.

## • THE POSTTEST

The procedure and criterion for mastery are the same as for the pretest. Use the following words.

| van | valve | quad | quarter |
| zero | question | zither | zebra |
| yoke | yet | you | vase |

## • ENSURING TRANSFER

Although the learner will be applying this skill in subsequent skills in the hierarchy, you should also use the suggestions provided in I-WA-9 to make sure that the skill is used during the routine daily activities of the classroom.

## II•WA•9

## • THE PERFORMANCE OBJECTIVE

When given an oral sentence with one word missing and cued for the missing word with a card having printed on it the first letter of that word (q, v, y, or z), the learner will say a word beginning with that letter that fits the context of the sentence.

Make cards with the preceding letters printed on them. Say, "I am going to say a sentence with one word missing. You look at the card and say a word that begins with the letter on the card and that finishes what I want to say." Use the following sentences. Display the letter card only when you come to the blank. The criterion for mastery is 10 out of 12 correct, with no letter being missed more than once. *Note:* If a sentence fails to match the learner's background or does not provide enough context clues for him or her to complete the sentence, you should alter it accordingly. Sentence 1, for instance, you could change to read, "We see wild animals such as the elephants, tigers and monkeys in the z _____."

1. I see the animals in the z_____.
2. When the teacher asked me if I wanted any candy, I said "_____."
3. The king and the princess were looking for the q_____.
4. In the election I v_____ for Sally.
5. The z_____ broke on my jacket.
6. I am going to play in my back y_____.
7. I didn't understand so I asked a q_____.
8. I don't want to go to bed because I'm not tired y_____.
9. The animal with the stripes is called a z_____.
10. I fell against the table and knocked over my mother's new v_____.
11. I'm too tied to play anymore. I'm going to q_____.
12. Mary has a beautiful singing v_____.

• DIRECTING THE LEARNER'S ATTENTION

The purpose of this task is to help the learner use his or her knowledge of letter-sound correspondence and context to identify unknown words. As such, the task is similar to that described in I-WA-14. To teach this skill you must direct the learner's attention by stating exactly what is to be learned and by highlighting the words in the sentence that provide clues to the identity of the unknown word, to the letter the unknown word begins with, and to the sound associated with that letter. (In the first sentence in the pretest, for instance, you might highlight the words **I, see,** and **animals**; direct the learner to look at a large cutout **z** and to get his mouth ready to say the sound of the **z**.)

• TEACHING ACTIVITIES

In teaching this context-letter-sound skill you can use either the modeling technique or the discovery technique described in I-WA-14, adjusting the suggestions to fit the letter-sound associations being tested in this objective.

• SUGGESTIONS FOR RETEACHING

If, after having been taught with either the modeling or the discovery technique, the learner is unable to use context–letter-sound correspondence to identify unknown words in this objective, you should reteach, using the suggestions found in I-WA-14.

Once the learner has successfully identified unknown words by using context and letter-sound correspondence tested in this objective, create practice activities to solidify the skill, using the suggestions provided in I-WA-14.

• THE POSTTEST

The procedure and criterion for mastery are the same as on the pretest.

1. I want to be healthy so I take my v_____ every morning.
2. It is too noisy in here. We must be q_____.
3. From the top of the mountain, we went down into the v_____.
4. It was very cold. On the thermometer it was below z_____.
5. Her dress was blue but mine was y_____.
6. You are too slow. You must do the work more q_____.
7. She wants to go with me, but I want to go with y_____.
8. My airplane z_____ through the air.
9. I play a guitar, but he plays a v_____.
10. I can't go yet. I'm not q_____ done.
11. I am very old, but you are y_____.
12. I saw a lion in the z_____.

• ENSURING TRANSFER

Although the learner will be applying this skill in subsequent objectives, you should also use the suggestions provided in I-WA-14 to make sure that the skill is used during the routine daily reading activities of the classroom.

# II•WA•10

• THE PERFORMANCE OBJECTIVE

When given a stimulus word beginning with the **sh** or voiceless **th** digraphs and a group of three other words one of which begins with the **sh** or voiceless **th** sound, the learner will pair the two words beginning with the same sound.

• THE PRETEST

Using the following words, say to the learner, "Here are three words. Listen carefully. (Say the words.) Which one sound like (say the stimulus word) at the beginning?" Repeat the three words. The criterion for mastery is five out of six correct.

| paint | leaf | shoe | Which one sounds like **ship** at the beginning? Repeat the three words. |
| trip | shell | black | Which one sounds like **ship** at the beginning? Repeat the three words. |
| first | thank | page | Which one sounds like **thick** at the beginning? Repeat the three words. |

| | | | |
|---|---|---|---|
| shine | chip | train | Which one sounds like **ship** at the beginning? Repeat the three words. |
| thirsty | when | who | Which one sounds like **thick** at the beginning? Repeat the three words. |
| car | thud | street | Which one sounds like **thick** at the beginning? Repeat the three words. |

## • DIRECTING THE LEARNER'S ATTENTION

The purpose of this task is to teach the learner to distinguish the **sh** and the voiceless **th** sounds from other beginning consonant sounds. As such, the task is similar to storehouse module I-WA-5. To teach this skill you must direct the learner's attention by stating exactly what is to be learned and by highlighting the beginning sound of the words as described in I-WA-5.

## • TEACHING ACTIVITIES

In teaching this auditory discrimination skill you can use either the modeling technique or the discovery technique described in I-WA-5, adjusting the suggestions to focus on the **sh** and voiceless **th** sounds.

## • SUGGESTIONS FOR RETEACHING

If, after having been taught this skill with either the modeling or the discovery technique, the learner is unable to distinguish by ear the **sh** and voiceless **th** sounds from other beginning consonant sounds, you should

Are you being specific in directing your learner's attention?

1. Reteach the skill, using the alternate technique.
2. Reexamine your attenders, being sure that the learner is listening to the *beginning* sound and that your highlighting is emphatic enough to help him or her distinguish the beginning sounds from other sounds.
3. Return to the previous auditory discrimination skills, making sure that the learner can perform those before requiring him or her to complete this objective.

## • SUGGESTIONS FOR PRACTICE

Once the learner can distinguish the **sh** and voiceless **th** sounds from other beginning consonant sounds, create practice activities to solidify the skill, using the suggestions provided in I-WA-5.

## • THE POSTTEST

The procedure and criterion for mastery are the same as for the pretest.

| | | | |
|---|---|---|---|
| think | block | fall | Which one sounds like **thick** at the beginning? Repeat the three words. |

| | | | |
|---|---|---|---|
| bed | storm | thumb | Which one sounds like **thick** at the beginning? Repeat the three words. |
| throw | shot | blue | Which one sounds like **ship** at the beginning? Repeat the three words. |
| show | snow | flow | Which one sounds like **ship** at the beginning? Repeat the three words. |
| third | green | tall | Which one sounds like **thick** at the beginning? Repeat the three words. |
| clip | trial | shop | Which one sounds like **ship** at the beginning? Repeat the three words. |

## • ENSURING TRANSFER

Although the learner will be applying this skill while learning to attach the sounds to letter combinations in subsequent objectives, you should also use the suggestions provided in I-WA-5 to make sure that the skill is used during the routine daily activities of the classroom.

# II•WA•11

## • THE PERFORMANCE OBJECTIVE

When given spoken words beginning with the **sh** or voiceless **th** sounds, the learner will identify the beginning letter as **sh** or **th**.

## • THE PRETEST

Give the learner two cards, one having the digraph **sh** and the other the digraph **th** printed on it. Say the following words, directing the learner to point to the letter whose sound begins with the word just spoken. The criterion for mastery is 80 percent with no letter sound being missed more than once.

| | | | | |
|---|---|---|---|---|
| shove | thigh | shout | thirty | short |
| shirt | thought | think | shack | thimble |

## • DIRECTING THE LEARNER'S ATTENTION

The purpose of this task is to teach the learner to establish a sound-symbol connection between the digraphs **sh** and **th** and the sounds these letters make at beginning of words. As such, it is similar to storehouse module I-WA-9. To teach this skill you must direct the learner's attention by stating exactly what is to be learned and by highlighting both the sound heard at the beginning of the word and the form of the digraph it is to be connected with. (In the word **shove**, for instance, you might exaggerate the beginning **sh** sound heard in the word while simultaneously pointing to the cutout letters **sh**.)

## • TEACHING ACTIVITIES

In teaching this sound-symbol connection skill you can use either the modeling technique or the discovery technique described in I-WA-9, adjusting the suggestions to focus on the digraphs **sh** and **th.**

## • SUGGESTIONS FOR RETEACHING

If, after having been taught this skill with either the modeling or the discovery technique, the learner is unable to connect letters and sound for the **sh** and **th,** you should

1. Reteach the skill, using the alternate technique.
2. Be more specific in directing the learner's attention, making sure that he or she is listening to the beginning sound while simultaneously looking at the letters.
3. Use more emphasis in highlighting the beginning sound, the letters, and the connection between them.
4. Return to the previous objective and make sure that the learner can distinguish between the beginning **sh** and voiceless **th** sounds before requiring him or her to connect the sounds with letters.

## • SUGGESTIONS FOR PRACTICE

Once the learner has successfully connected the **sh** and **th** digraphs to their respective beginning sounds, create practice activities to solidify the skill, using the suggestions provided in I-WA-9.

## • THE POSTTEST

The procedure and criterion for mastery are the same as for the pretest.

| | | | | |
|---|---|---|---|---|
| shower | thorn | thaw | shift | thin |
| shut | shy | theater | shock | thump |

## • ENSURING TRANSFER

Although the learner will be applying this skill in subsequent skills in the hierarchy, you should also use the suggestions provided in I-WA-9 to make sure that the skill is used during the routine daily activities of the classroom.

## II•WA•12

## • THE PERFORMANCE OBJECTIVE

When given an oral sentence with one word missing and cued for the missing word with a card having printed on it the **sh** or **th** digraphs, the learner will say a word beginning with that digraph that fits the context of the sentence.

## • THE PRETEST

Make cards with the preceding digraphs printed on them, Say, "I am going to say a sentence with one word missing. You look at the card and say a word which begins with the letters on the card and which finishes what I want to say." Use the following sentences. Display the letter card only when you come to the blank. The criterion for mastery is 80 percent, with no letter being missed more than once. *Note:* If a sentence fails to match the learner's experience background or does not provide enough context clues for him to complete the sentence, you should alter it accordingly. Sentence 1, for instance, could be changed to read, "First, the little girl put on her socks and then she put on her sh_____."

1. The little girl learned to tie her sh_____.
2. We went across the ocean on a sh_____.
3. The boy didn't eat much, and he was very th_____.
4. I was second in line and she was th_____.
5. I want to th_____ you for the present.
6. It was hot. I took off my sh_____.
7. There was no water fountain and I was th_____.
8. I am tall but he is sh_____.
9. He has a gun. He might sh_____ it.
10. On our hands we have four fingers and a th_____.

### • DIRECTING THE LEARNER'S ATTENTION

The purpose of this task is to help the learner use his or her knowledge of letter-sound correspondence and context to identify unknown words. As such, the task is similar to the storehouse module I-WA-14. To teach this skill you must direct the leaner's attention by stating exactly what is to be learned by highlighting the words in the sentence that provide clues to the identity of the unknown word, to the letter combination with which the unknown word begins, and to the sound associated with that letter combination. (In the first sentence in the pretest, for instance, you might highlight the words **girl, learned,** and **tie;** direct the learner to look at a large cutout **sh** and to get his or her mouth ready to say the sound of the **sh.**)

### • TEACHING ACTIVITIES

In teaching this context-letter-sound skill you can use either the modeling technique or the discovery technique described in I-WA-14, adjusting the suggestions to fit the letter-sound associations being tested in this objective.

### • SUGGESTIONS FOR RETEACHING

If, after having been taught with either the modeling or the discovery technique, the learner is unable to use context–letter-sound correspondence to identify unknown words in this objective, you should reteach, using the suggestions found in I-WA-14.

### • SUGGESTIONS FOR PRACTICE

Once the learner has successfully identified unknown words by using context and the letter-sound correspondences tested in this objective, create practice activities to solidify the skill, using the suggestions provided in I-WA-14.

## ● THE POSTTEST

The procedure and criterion for mastery are the same as for the pretest.

1. That little girl is very bashful and sh_____.
2. The paper is thin but the door is th_____.
3. Please don't sh_____. You are making too much noise.
4. Don't fall into those rose bushes or you will get a th_____ in your finger.
5. When you come in the house, be sure that you sh_____ the door.
6. You have twenty pieces of candy but I have th_____.
7. When you want to know how hot it is, you look at the th_____.
8. Sometimes I can't do anyth_____ right.
9. I know where it is. I'll sh_____ you.
10. I dug a big hole with my sh_____.

## ● ENSURING TRANSFER

Although the learner will be applying this skill in subsequent objectives, you should also use the suggestions provided in I-WA-14 to make sure that the skill is used during the routine daily reading activities of the classroom.

# II•WA•13

## ● THE PERFORMANCE OBJECTIVE

When given a stimulus word beginning with the **ch, wh,** or voiced **th** sounds and a group of three other words, one of which begins with the **ch, wh,** or the voiced **th** sounds, the learner will pair the two words beginning with the same sound.

## ● THE PRETEST

Using the following words, say to the learner, "Here are three words. Listen carefully. (Say the words.) Which one sounds like (say the stimulus word) at the beginning?" Repeat the three original words. The criterion for mastery is five out of six correct.

| | | | |
|---|---|---|---|
| church | curb | look | Which one sounds like **chug** at the beginning? Repeat the three words. |
| where | this | then | Which one sounds like **whip** at the beginning? Repeat the three words. |
| tip | those | whose | Which one sounds like **this** at the beginning? Repeat the three words. |
| wind | shoe | when | Which one sounds like **whip** at the beginning? Repeat the three words. |

| | | | |
|---|---|---|---|
| third | them | miss | Which one sounds like **this** at the beginning? Repeat the three words. |
| ship | chop | catch | Which one sounds like **chug** at the beginning? Repeat the three words. |

### • DIRECTING THE LEARNER'S ATTENTION

The purpose of this task is to teach the learner to distinguish the **ch, wh,** and voiced **th** sounds from other beginning consonant sounds. As such, the task is similar to the storehouse module I-WA-5. To teach this skill you must direct the learner's attention by stating exactly what is to be learned and by highlighting the beginning sound of the words as described in I-WA-5.

### • TEACHING ACTIVITIES

In teaching this auditory discrimination skill you can use either the modeling technique or the discovery technique described in I-WA-5, adjusting the suggestions to focus on the **ch, wh,** and voiced **th** sounds.

### • SUGGESTIONS FOR RETEACHING

If, after having been taught this skill with either the modeling or the discovery technique, the learner is unable to distinguish by ear the **ch, wh,** and voiced **th** sounds from other beginning consonant sounds, you should

1. Reteach the skill, using the alternate technique.
2. Reexamine your attenders, making sure that the learner is listening to the *beginning* sound and that your highlighting is emphatic enough to help him or her distinguish the beginning sounds from other sounds.
3. If the difficulty is in confusing sounds (such as interchanging the **sh** and **ch** sounds or the **wh** and **w** sounds), pair the confused sounds together and reteach, highlighting the differences in the sounds being interchanged.
4. Return to the previous auditory discrimination skills, making sure that the learner can perform those before requiring him or her to complete this objective.

### • SUGGESTIONS FOR PRACTICE

Once the learner can distinguish the **ch, wh,** and voiced **th** sounds from other beginning consonant sounds, create practice activities to solidify the skill, using the suggestions provided in I-WA-5.

### • THE POSTTEST

The procedure and criterion for mastery are the same as for the pretest. Use the following words.

| | | | |
|---|---|---|---|
| then | when | ten | Which word sounds like **this** at the beginning? Repeat the three words. |
| show | charm | cat | Which word sounds like **chug** at the beginning? Repeat the three words. |
| win | shop | why | Which word sounds like **whip** at the beginning? Repeat the three words. |
| tin | these | think | Which word sounds like **this** at the beginning? Repeat the three words. |
| what | won | then | Which word sounds like **whip** at the beginning? Repeat the three words. |
| chore | core | shine | Which word sounds like **chug** at the beginning? Repeat the three words. |

## • ENSURING TRANSFER

Although the learner will be applying this skill while learning to attach the sounds to letter combinations in subsequent objectives, you should also use the suggestions provided in I-WA-14 to make sure that the skill is used during the routine daily reading activities in the classroom.

## • THE PERFORMANCE OBJECTIVE

When given spoken words beginning with the **ch**, **wh**, or voiced **th** sounds, the learner will identify the beginning letters as **ch**, **wh**, or **th**.

## • THE PRETEST

Give the learner cards with **ch**, **wh**, or **th** printed on them. Say the following words, directing the learner to point to the letter whose sound begins the word just spoken. The criterion for mastery is eight out of nine correct, with no letter sound being missed more than once.

| | | |
|---|---|---|
| church | when | this |
| where | chop | them |
| those | why | chose |

## • DIRECTING THE LEARNER'S ATTENTION

The purpose of this task is to teach the learner to establish a sound-symbol connection between the digraphs **ch**, **wh**, and **th** and the sounds these letters make at the beginning of words. As such, it is similar to the storehouse module I-WA-9. To teach this skill you must direct the learner's attention by stating exactly what is to be learned and by highlighting both the sound heard at the beginning of the word and the form of the digraph it is to be connected with. (In the word **church**, for instance, you might exaggerate

● 231

the beginning **ch** sound heard in the word while simultaneously pointing to the cutout letters **ch.**)

### • TEACHING ACTIVITIES

In teaching this sound-symbol connection skill you can use either the modeling technique or the discovery technique described in I-WA-9, adjusting the suggestions to focus on the digraphs **ch, wh,** and **th.**

### • SUGGESTIONS FOR RETEACHING

If, after having been taught this skill with either the modeling or the discovery technique, the learner is unable to connect letters and sound for the **ch, wh,** and **th,** you should

1. Reteach the skill, using the alternate technique.
2. Be more specific in directing the learner's attention, making sure that he or she is listening to the *beginning* sound while simultaneously looking at the letters.
3. Use more emphasis in highlighting the beginning sound, the letters, and the connection between them.
4. Return to the previous objective and be sure that the learner can distinguish between the beginning **ch, wh,** and voiced **th** before requiring him or her to connect the sounds with the letters.

### • SUGGESTIONS FOR PRACTICE

Once the learner has successfully connected the **ch, wh,** and **th** digraphs to words beginning with the **ch, wh,** and voiced **th** sounds, create practice activities to solidify the skill, using the suggestions provided in I-WA-9.

### • THE POSTTEST

The procedure and criterion for mastery are the same as for the pretest. Use the following words.

| | | |
|---|---|---|
| them | which | child |
| whirl | charge | that |
| chirp | wheat | these |

### • ENSURING TRANSFER

Although the learner will be applying this skill in subsequent skills in the hierarchy, you should also use the suggestions provided in I-WA-9 to make sure that the skill is used during the routine daily reading activities of the classroom.

## II•WA•15

### • THE PERFORMANCE OBJECTIVE

When given an oral sentence with one word missing and cued for the missing word with a card having printed on it the digraph with which the word begins (**ch, wh,** or **th**), the learner will say a word beginning with that digraph that fits the context of the sentence.

## • THE PRETEST

Make cards with the preceding digraphs printed on them. Say, "I am going to say a sentence with one word missing. You look at the card and say a word that begins with the letters on the card and that finishes what I want to say." Use the following sentences. Display the letter card only when you come to the blank. Criterion for mastery is seven out of nine correct, with no digraph being missed more than once. *Note:* If a sentence fails to match a learner's background or does not provide enough context clues for him or her to complete the sentence, you should alter it accordingly. Sentence 1, for instance, could be changed to read, "On Sunday we go to ch_____ to pray."

  1. On Sunday we go to ch_____.
  2. It isn't here. It is over th_____.
  3. I can't find it. Wh_____ is it?
  4. I don't want to go with you. I want to go with th_____.
  5. Mice like to eat ch_____.
  6. The front wh_____ on my bicycle broke when I fell off.
  7. They aren't going with anybody. They're going all by th_____.
  8. The old man had long white wh_____ on his face.
  9. For lunch I like to have ch_____ noodle soup.

## • DIRECTING THE LEARNER'S ATTENTION

The purpose of this task is to help the learner use his or her knowledge of letter-sound correspondence and context to identify unknown words. As such, the task is similar to storehouse module I-WA-14. To teach this skill you must direct the learner's attention by stating exactly what is to be learned and by highlighting the words in the sentence that provide clues to the identity of the unknown word, the letter combination with which the unknown word begins, and the sound associated with the letter combination. (In the first sentence in the pretest, for instance, you might highlight the words **Sunday, we** and **go**; direct the learner to look at a large cutout **ch** and to get his or her mouth ready to say the sound of the **ch**.)

Do you *deserve* your learner's attention?

## • TEACHING ACTIVITIES

In teaching this context–letter-sound skill you can use either the modeling technique or the discovery technique described in I-WA-14, adjusting the suggestions to fit the letter-sound associations being tested in this objective.

## • SUGGESTIONS FOR RETEACHING

If, after having been taught with either the modeling or the discovery technique, the learner is unable to use context–letter-sound correspondence to identify unknown words in this objective, you should reteach, using the suggestions found in I-WA-14.

Once the learner has successfully identified unknown words using context and letter-sound correspondence tested in this objective, create practice activities to solidify the skill, using the suggestions provided in I-WA-14.

• THE POSTTEST

The procedure and criterion for mastery are the same as for the pretest. Use the following sentences.

1. My coat was yellow but yours is wh_____.
2. They aren't here. They are over th_____.
3. My big brother can't sing but he can wh_____ through his teeth.
4. The teacher was writing on the blackboard with ch_____.
5. When she came in from outdoors, her face was red and she had rosy ch_____.
6. I don't want this one. I want th_____ one.
7. The man wanted the horse to run faster, so he wh_____ him.
8. They are nice people. I like th_____.
9. I got my pants all wet in the snow and I will have to ch_____ them.

• ENSURING TRANSFER

Although the learner will be applying this skill in subsequent objectives, you should also use the suggestions provided in I-WA-14 to make sure that the skill is used during the routine daily reading activities of the classroom.

## II•WA•16

• THE PERFORMANCE OBJECTIVE

When given a stimulus word having a short **a, e, i, o,** or **u** as the medial sound and a group of three other words one of which has a short **a, e, i, o,** or **u** as the medial sound, the learner will pair the two words having the same medial sound.

• THE PRETEST

Using the following words, say to the learner, "Here are three words. Listen carefully. (Say the words.) Which one sounds like (say the stimulus word) at the beginning?" Repeat the three words. Criterion for mastery is 80 percent with no sound being missed more than once.

| gosh | had | with | Which one sounds like **cat** in the middle? Repeat the three words. |
|------|-----|------|---|
| this | set | love | Which one sounds like **sit** in the middle? Repeat the three words. |
| best | little | cave | Which one sounds like **get** in the middle? Repeat the three words. |
| beg | hat | bog | Which one sounds like **hot** in the middle? Repeat the three words. |

| | | | |
|---|---|---|---|
| bat | mud | lot | Which one sounds like **but** in the middle? <br> Repeat the three words. |
| sob | hill | rat | Which one sounds like **hot** in the middle? <br> Repeat the three words. |
| fix | bug | late | Which one sounds like **but** in the middle? <br> Repeat the three words. |
| lit | got | less | Which one sounds like **get** in the middle? <br> Repeat the three words. |
| wit | met | said | Which one sounds like **sit** in the middle? <br> Repeat the three words. |
| bed | bib | bath | Which one sounds like **cat** in the middle? <br> Repeat the three words. |

## • DIRECTING THE LEARNER'S ATTENTION

The purpose of this task is to teach the learner to distinguish the short vowel sounds from other medial sounds in words. As such, it is similar to storehouse module I-WA-5. To teach this skill you must direct the learner's attention by stating exactly what is to be learned and by highlighting the middle sound of the words. (For instance, you could exaggerate or prolong the vowel sound in each of the words.)

## • TEACHING ACTIVITIES

In teaching this auditory discrimination skill you can use either the modeling technique or the discovery technique described in I-WA-5, adjusting the suggestions to focus on the medial short vowel sounds.

## • SUGGESTIONS FOR RETEACHING

If, after having been taught this skill with either the modeling or the discovery technique, the learner is unable to distinguish by ear the short vowel sounds from other medial sounds in words, you should

1. Reteach the skill, using the alternate technique.
2. Reexamine your attenders, being sure that the learner is listening to the *middle* sounds and that your highlighting is emphatic enough to help him or her distinguish the middle sounds from other sounds.
3. If the difficulty is in confusing sounds (such as interchanging the short **e** and **short** i sounds), pair the confused sounds together and reteach, highlighting the differences of the sounds being interchanged.
4. Return to the previous auditory discrimination skills, making sure that the learner can perform them before requiring him or her to complete this objective.

## • SUGGESTIONS FOR PRACTICE

Once the learner can distinguish the short vowel sounds from other medial sounds, create practice activities to solidify the skill, using the suggestions provided in I-WA-5.

The procedure and criterion for mastery are the same as for the pretest. Use the following words.

| | | | |
|---|---|---|---|
| wet | grass | wish | Which one sounds like **cat** in the middle? Repeat the three words. |
| tin | lobe | sell | Which one sounds like **sit** in the middle? Repeat the three words. |
| like | lit | beg | Which one sounds like **get** in the middle? Repeat the three words. |
| horse | lock | bag | Which one sounds like **hot** in the middle? Repeat the three words. |
| such | bad | hat | Which one sounds like **but** in the middle? Repeat the three words. |
| hiss | sock | rise | Which one sounds like **hot** in the middle? Repeat the three words. |
| mud | lot | fish | Which one sounds like **but** in the middle? Repeat the three words. |
| guess | miss | give | Which one sounds like **get** in the middle? Repeat the three words. |
| sell | said | with | Which one sounds like **sit** in the middle? Repeat the three words. |
| cut | laugh | sit | Which one sounds like **cat** in the middle? Repeat the three words. |

• **ENSURING TRANSFER**

Although the learner will be applying this skill while learning to attach the short vowel sounds to vowel letters in subsequent objectives, you should also use the suggestions provided in I-WA-5 to be sure that the skill is used during the routine daily reading activities in the classroom.

# II•WA•17

• **THE PERFORMANCE OBJECTIVE**

When given spoken words with either the sound of the short vowel **a**, **e**, **i**, **o**, or **u** in the middle, the learner will identify the middle letters as **a**, **e**, **i**, **o**, or **u**.

• **THE PRETEST**

Give the learner cards, each of which has a different vowel letter printed on it. Say the following words, directing the learner to point to the letter whose sound is heard in the middle of the word just spoken. The criterion for mastery is 80 percent, with no vowel letter being missed more than once.

| | | | | |
|---|---|---|---|---|
| chat | lip | drop | flag | slid |
| must | nest | fish | bud | trod |

• **DIRECTING THE LEARNER'S ATTENTION**

The purpose of this task is to teach the learner to establish a sound-symbol connection between the vowel letters and the short vowel sounds. As such, the task is similar to the storehouse module I-WA-9. To teach this skill you must direct the learner's attention by stating exactly what is to be learned and by highlighting both the sound heard in the middle of the word and the form of the vowel letter it is to be connected with. (In the word **chat**, for instance, you might exaggerate the medial short a sound while simultaneously pointing to the cutout letter **a**.)

### • TEACHING ACTIVITIES

In teaching this sound-symbol connection skill you can use either the modeling technique or the discovery technique described in I-WA-9, adjusting the suggestions to focus on the short vowels.

### • SUGGESTIONS FOR RETEACHING

If, after having been taught this skill with either the modeling or the discovery technique, the learner is unable to connect the vowel letters with the short vowel sounds, you should

1. Reteach the skill, using the alternate technique.
2. Be more specific in directing the learner's attention, making sure that he or she is listening to the middle sound while simultaneously looking at the letter.
3. Use more emphasis in highlighting the middle sound, the letter, and the connection between them.
4. Return to the previous objective and make sure that the learner can distinguish between the short vowel sounds before requiring him or her to connect the sounds with vowel letters.

### • SUGGESTIONS FOR PRACTICE

Once the learner has successfully connected vowel letters to words having short vowel sounds in the medial position, create practice activities to solidify the skill, using the suggestions in I-WA-9.

### • THE POSTTEST

The procedure and criterion for mastery are the same as for the pretest. Use the following words.

| | | | | |
|---|---|---|---|---|
| plod | buck | did | dot | flush |
| flick | glad | bless | nip | flap |

### • ENSURING TRANSFER

Although the learner will be applying this skill in subsequent skills in the hierarchy, you should also use the suggestions provided in I-WA-9 to make sure that the skill is used during the routine daily reading activities of the classroom.

• **THE PERFORMANCE OBJECTIVE**

Given known words composed of the vowel consonant phonograms –at, –et, –it, –ot, –ut, the learner replaces the first consonant in each known word with another consonant or digraph and pronounces the new word.

• **THE PRETEST**

Use the following lists of words. The first word in each list has been previously taught as a sight word. Read the first word in the list and ask the learner to pronounce the remaining words in each list. The criterion for mastery is 35 out of 39 correct with no initial consonant or digraph being missed more than once. *Caution:* If the learner knows at sight any of the words other than the first word in each list, you may not know whether he or she can analyze in terms of the short vowel pattern. Consequently, each list contains two nonsense words that the child *must* analyze since there will have been no previous opportunity to learn them by sight.

| cat | get | sit | hot | but |
|-----|-----|-----|-----|-----|
| fat | met | fit | got | cut |
| hat | set | hit | lot | nut |
| pat | wet | bit | shot | shut |
| sat | let | kit | pot | rut |
| that | bet | wit | bot | lut |
| rat | whet | thit | fot | dut |
| bat | net | vit | | |
| chat | pet | | | |
| shat | chet | | | |
| zat | det | | | |

• **DIRECTING THE LEARNER'S ATTENTION**

The purpose of this task is to help the learner recognize the regular short vowel spelling patterns used in English and to teach him or her to substitute initial consonants in these patterns to identify unknown words. This is a crucial analyzing skill for the reader to learn since it provides him or her with a problem-solving technique to use when trying to determine the pronunciation of an unknown word or syllable that contains the short vowel phonogram.

To teach learners to use this problem-solving technique you must direct his or her attention to the task by stating exactly what is to be learned to do and by highlighting both the vowel phonogram that is common from word to word and the letter sound of the beginning consonant. (In the word **fat**, for instance, you might circle and pronounce the –at phonogram and tell the learner to get his or her mouth ready to say the beginning sound.)

• **THIS IS A STOREHOUSE OBJECTIVE**

The following instructional activities are your storehouse of techniques for developing skill in using letter substitution as a means for analyzing un-

known words. This skill recurs in more sophisticated forms later in the skill hierarchy. The teaching techniques that follow are to be adapted and used with each of these as they occur.

● **TEACHING ACTIVITIES**

*The modeling technique.* Use a known sight word that illustrates the vowel pattern being taught. Print this word on the chalkboard and ask the learner to read it. Then print another word having the same pattern directly underneath the first, highlighting with color the common vowel phonogram. Then say, "I can read the first word. It is **cat.** I see that the new word has an **at** in it just like the first word. It must sound like the **at** in **cat.** But the second word is not **cat** because it starts with the letter **b.** I'll get my mouth ready to make the **b** sound and say the new word **b . . . at, bat.**" Then put up another word of the same pattern, diminish the color cue, and repeat the preceding procedure but with learner participation. Gradually diminish the assistance on subsequent words until the learner can complete the process himself.

*The discovery technique.* Place a list of words on the blackboard, each word having the same vowel phonogram. Pose a series of questions in which you use the learner's responses to lead him or her to note that all the words in the list have the letter **at** in them. *Caution:* Although you may provide cues by highlighting the common phonogram, do not tell the learner what you want him or her to discover. When the learner has noted the visual similarities in the words, have him or her note the sound similarities either by having the learner read whatever words in the list he or she can identify or by reading one or two of the words yourself. Auditory highlighting of those sounds should be done at this time so that the learner knows that what he or she sees and what he or she hears are related. Finally, ask questions that direct the learner to the sound of the first letter in each of these words. Both auditory and visual highlighting, such as pointing to the key element and directing the learner to get his or her mouth ready to say this sound would be appropriate. If the learner can then pronounce the remaining words on the list, he or she has discovered the sound of the short vowel phonogram and the technique of consonant substitution.

● **SUGGESTIONS FOR RETEACHING**

If, after having been taught with either the modeling or discovery technique, the learner is unable to substitute initial consonants in common phonogram words and pronounce the new words, you should

1. Reteach the skill, using the alternate technique.
2. Reexamine your attenders to be sure that you are providing enough highlighting on the common vowel phonogram and the varying initial consonants.
3. Return to the prerequisite vowel and consonant sound-symbol connection skills to be sure that the learner can produce the necessary sound value for each letter.

Once the learner can substitute initial consonants in short vowel phonograms and pronounce the new words, use the following suggestions to create
practice activities to solidify the skill.

A useful device to help learners master this task is the word wheel. You
can construct word wheels by cutting two circles from tagboard, one
slightly larger than the other. On the larger wheel print words in which
the initial element is missing, starting each about the same distance from
the center and progressing toward the outer edge like the spokes of a
wheel. On the smaller circle put a slot of the size and position to expose
only one word ending at a time, printing the consonant letter, blend, digraph to be used to the left of the slot. Fasten the two circles together
with a paper fastener. As you rotate the lower circle, the letters on the
upper circle will make a new word as it is combined with each ending
on the lower circle. This same principle can be reversed so that the ending remains constant and the beginning changes.

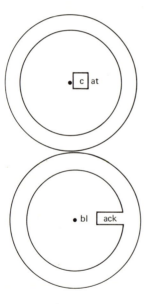

2. A similar device is the slip card, in which the phonogram pattern being
   worked on is written on a wide piece of tagboard and the letters to be

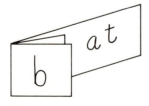

substituted are written on narrower cards and attached to the larger piece in a manner that allows one letter at a time to be shown with the spelling pattern.

3. Use activities in which you provide the learner with a key word and a sentence in which one word is missing. Direct him or her to supply a word to fill the blank. This word must be related to the key word. For instance, give the key word **cat** and the sentence, "Hit the ball with the _____." The learner must supply *and pronounce* the word **bat**.

4. Play games in which you start with a common spelling pattern written on the board. The learner changes either the initial or final letter, substitutes another, and pronounces the new word. The next learner must change it again and pronounce the new word. The pattern of words might look something like this:

> **cat** is changed to **bat**
> **bat** is changed to **bag**
> **bag** is changed to **bad**
> **bad** is changed to **had**
> **had** is changed to **has**

5. Have one learner write on the chalkboard a word illustrating a common phonogram pattern. He or she must then pronounce the word and make up a sentence using that word. The next learner goes to the chalkboard, changes either the initial or final consonant in the word, pronounces the new word, and uses it in a new sentence. At first you may want to accept any sentence the learners produce. As they become more skillful, however, you can modify the activity by having them produce successive sentences that are related to each other and that tell a story. For instance, the sentence might proceed in this manner:

> The **cat** is in the house.
> He is sleeping near the **bat**.
> A man put the cat in a **bag**.
> He must be a **bad** man.

6. Make word cards using words incorporating the common phonogram patterns you have been working on. Include also a number of cards that have the word *changeover* written on them. Deal each learner five cards. One learner starts by laying down any word card and naming it. If the learner cannot play, he or she draws from the deck until finding a word to play or drawing three cards. If the learner has the *changeover* card, he or she can play that and name the new related word that can be played on it. The first person out of cards wins the game.

7. Play a variation of Crazy Eights by making a deck of 40 cards that have printed on them words containing the phonogram patterns you have been working on. Make six cards with the numeral 8 on them. Each

learner gets four cards, with the rest of the cards placed in the center of the table. The first learner lays down a card from his or her hand that contains the same word element or an 8 card. If the learner has neither a word card that fits nor an 8 card, he or she must draw a card from the deck. The first person out of cards is the winner.

8. A variation of bingo can be played in which the game card has the common spelling patterns you have been working on printed in the squares. The learner has a number of consonant letters, blends, and digraphs in his or her possession. The leader holds up a letter card, the learner sees if the letter is in his or her pile. If it is, the learner tries to combine it with one of the spelling patterns on his or her game card. When all the words in a row are formed, the learner can call, "Bingo." If the learner can then pronounce each word he or she has formed in the row, he or she wins the game.

### • THE POSTTEST

The pretest can be used also for the posttest. The procedure and criterion for mastery are the same.

### • ENSURING TRANSFER

Once the learner has practiced this analysis technique, you must be sure that he or she is given reading material that calls for the use of this skill and that you guide the learner in applying this technique when he or she meets such unknown words in daily reading. Suitable application situations include basal textbooks, library books, language experience stories, magazines, comic books, and any other reading material in which the learner encounters unknown words that can be analyzed through consonant substitution.

## II•WA•19

### • THE PERFORMANCE OBJECTIVE

When given words he or she pronounced in the previous objective, the learner replaces the final consonant of the known word with another consonant or digraph and pronounces the new word.

### • THE PRETEST

Use the following lists of words. The first word in each list has been previously taught as a sight word or as one of the words analyzed in the previous objective. Read the first word in the list and ask the learner to pronounce the remaining words in each list. The criterion for mastery is 65 out of 69 correct. *Caution:* If the learner knows at sight any of the words other than the first word in the list, you may not know whether he or she can analyze in terms of substituting the final consonant. Consequently, each list contains two nonsense words that the learner *must* analyze, since there will have been no previous opportunity to learn them at sight.

| | | | | | | | | |
|---|---|---|---|---|---|---|---|---|
| **cat** | **hat** | **bat** | **rat** | **chat** | **met** | **bet** | **set** | **bit** |
| cap | had | bad | rash | chap | men | bed | sex | big |
| can | has | bag | rad | chad | mesh | beg | sed | bid |
| cas | hab | bath | rax | chan | med | bex | sesh | bib |
| cab | han | bab | | | meg | beb | | bim |
| | | bas | | | | | | bik |

| | | | | | | | |
|---|---|---|---|---|---|---|---|
| **fit** | **hit** | **sit** | **hot** | **lot** | **got** | **but** | **rut** |
| fish | his | sip | hop | lob | God | bus | rub |
| fid | hid | sib | hon | lon | gosh | bug | rud |
| fig | hib | sim | hov | losh | gol | buzz | ruk |
| fix | hin | sin | | | gok | bun | |
| fib | | | | | | bub | |
| fin | | | | | | bux | |
| fim | | | | | | | |

## • DIRECTING THE LEARNER'S ATTENTION

The purpose of this task is to teach the learner to substitute final consonants in regular short vowel spelling patterns and to identify the unknown words. As such, the task is similar to storehouse module II-WA-18. To teach this skill you must direct the learner's attention by stating exactly what is to be learned and by highlighting both the word part that is common from word to word and the sound of the ending consonant. (In the word **cap**, for instance, you might circle and pronounce the **ca–** element and tell the learner to get his or her mouth ready to say the final consonant sound.)

## • TEACHING ACTIVITIES

In teaching this consonant substitution skill you can use either the modeling technique or the discovery technique described in II-WA-18, adjusting the suggestions to focus on the ending consonant.

## • SUGGESTIONS FOR RETEACHING

If, after having been taught with either the modeling or the discovery technique, the learner is unable to substitute final consonants in common phonogram words and pronounce the new words, you should

1. Reteach the skill, using the alternate technique.
2. Reexamine your attenders, making sure that you are providing enough highlighting on the common parts of the words and the varying final consonants.
3. Return to the prerequisite vowel and consonant sound-symbol connection skills to make sure that the learner can produce the necessary sound value for each letter.

## • SUGGESTIONS FOR PRACTICE

Once the learner can substitute final consonants in common phonogram words, create practice activities to solidify the skill, using the suggestions provided in II-WA-18.

### • THE POSTTEST

The pretest can be used also for the posttest. The procedure and criterion for mastery remain the same.

### • ENSURING TRANSFER

You should use the suggestions provided in II-WA-18 to be sure that the learner uses the skill in pursuing daily reading activities.

# II•WA•20

### • THE PERFORMANCE OBJECTIVE

When given key words either introduced in the previous two objectives or identified during the course of this objective, the learner will change either the beginning or the ending of the words and pronounce the new words.

### • THE PRETEST

Use the following list of words. The first word in each list has been previously taught or is a word the learner has pronounced previously in this objective. Read the first word in the list and ask the learner to read the remaining words in each list. The criterion for mastery is 80 out of 84 correct. *Caution:* If the learner knows at sight any of the words other than the first word in the list, you may not know whether he or she can analyze in terms of letter substitution. Consequently, each list contains two nonsense words that the learner *must* analyze, since there will have been no previous opportunity to learn them at sight.

| cap | can | cab | had | bad |
|-----|-----|-----|-----|-----|
| sap | ran | gab | lad | mad |
| tap | than | gas | lax | mab |
| tad | man | bas | shax | shab |
| nad | mab | bap | | |
| | wab | | | |

| men | bed | beg | big | wit |
|-----|-----|-----|-----|-----|
| hen | fed | leg | dig | with |
| hess | led | leb | pig | wish |
| heb | red | deb | pid | shish |
| | rep | | nid | chid |
| | chep | | | |

| fish | fix | fin | sip | hop |
|------|-----|-----|-----|-----|
| dish | six | sin | tip | shop |
| dib | sib | sim | tid | pop |
| pid | chib | shim | chid | top |
| | | | | tod |
| | | | | chod |

| lob | bun | rub | cub | sub |
|------|-------|------|------|------|
| bob | fun | cub | cup | sud |
| box | run | tub | cuff | mud |
| fox | sun | sub | puff | much |
| dob | shun | sug | pud | such |
| shob | shush | chup | nud | sush |
| | rush | | | mush |
| | rud | | | |
| | shud | | | |

- **DIRECTING THE LEARNER'S ATTENTION**

The purpose of this task is to teach the learner to substitute both initial and final consonants in regular vowel spelling patterns and to identify the unknown words. As such, the task is similar to storehouse module II-WA-18. To teach this skill you must direct the learner's attention by stating exactly what is to be learned and by highlighting both the word part that is common from word to word and the letter sound of the varying consonant.

- **TEACHING ACTIVITIES**

In teaching this consonant substitution skill you can use either the modeling technique or the discovery technique described in II-WA-18, adjusting the suggestions to focus on both the initial and ending consonants.

- **SUGGESTIONS FOR RETEACHING**

If, after having been taught with either the modeling or the discovery technique, the learner is unable to substitute initial and final consonants in common phonograms and pronounce the new words, you should

1. Reteach the skill, using the alternate technique.
2. Reexamine your attenders, making sure that you are providing enough highlighting on the common parts of the words and the varying consonants.
3. Return to the prerequisite skills in consonant substitution and in vowel and consonant sound-symbol connection to be sure that the learner can produce the necessary sound value for each letter and can substitute that sound value in the initial and final positions.

Are you using dramatics, choral speaking, artwork, music, and other creative projects to support your reading program?

- **SUGGESTIONS FOR PRACTICE**

Once the learner can substitute both initial and final consonants in phonograms, create practice activities to solidify the skill, using the suggestions provided in II-WA-18.

- **THE POSTTEST**

The pretest can be used also as the posttest. The criterion for mastery and the procedure are the same.

You should see the suggestions in II-WA-18 to make sure that the learner uses the skill in pursuing daily reading activities.

# II•WA•21

### ● THE PERFORMANCE OBJECTIVE

When given words the learner has previously learned to recognize at sight, he or she will change the medial vowel in a short vowel phonogram and pronounce the new word.

### ● THE PRETEST

Use the following lists of words. The first word in each list has been previously taught as a sight word. Read the first word on the list and ask the learner to read the remaining words. The criterion for mastery is 36 out of 40 correct. *Caution:* Some of the words in the lists are nonsense words, which are included so that the learner *must* use analysis techniques rather than sight recognition.

| cat | get | sit | hot | but |
|------|------|-----|------|-----|
| cut | got | sat | hop | bat |
| cot | gat | set | hap | bet |
| chot | git | sot | hep | bit |
| chep | gut | sut | hip | bot |
| chip | chut | nut | hup | lot |
| ship | chot | net | chup | lit |
| shap | chat | nat | chap | let |
| shup | chet | not | chep | lat |

### ● DIRECTING THE LEARNER'S ATTENTION

The purpose of this task is to teach the learner to substitute medial vowels in regular short vowel spelling patterns and to identify the unknown words. As such, it is similar to storehouse module II-WA-18. To teach this skill you must direct the learner's attention by stating exactly what is to be learned and by highlighting both the letter sounds that are common from word to word and the letter sound of the varying vowel. (In the word **cut**, for instance, you might circle the **c** and the **t** as being the same sounds as found in the previous word and exaggerate the medial vowel sound.)

### ● TEACHING ACTIVITIES

In teaching this letter substitution skill you can use either the modeling technique or the discovery technique described in II-WA-18, adjusting the suggestions to focus on the medial vowel.

### ● SUGGESTIONS FOR RETEACHING

If, after having been taught with either the modeling or the discovery technique, the learner is unable to substitute medial vowels in short vowel phonograms, you should

1. Reteach the skill, using the alternate technique.
2. Reexamine your attenders, making sure that you are providing enough highlighting on the common parts of the words and on the varying vowel letters.
3. Return to the prerequisite letter substitution and sound-symbol connection skills to be sure that the learner can both produce the necessary letter sounds and substitute letter sounds into vowel phonograms.

● **SUGGESTIONS FOR PRACTICE**

Once the learner can substitute medial vowels into short vowel phonograms, create practice activities to solidify the skill, using the suggestions provided in II-WA-18.

● **THE POSTTEST**

The pretest can be used also for the posttest. The procedure and criterion for mastery are the same.

● **ENSURING TRANSFER**

You should use the suggestions in II-WA-18 to make sure that the learner uses the skill in pursuing daily reading activities.

● **THE PERFORMANCE OBJECTIVE**

When given a stimulus word ending with the **ck** sound and a group of three other words one of which ends with the **ck** sound, the learner will pair the two words that end with the **ck** sound.

● **THE PRETEST**

Using the following words, say to the learner, "Here are three words. Listen carefully. (Say the three words.) Which one sounds like (say the stimulus word) at the end?" Repeat the three words. The criterion for mastery is four out of five correct.

| | | | |
|---|---|---|---|
| land | band | back | Which word sounds like **neck** at the end? Repeat the three words. |
| sick | sit | Ned | Which word sounds like **neck** at the end? Repeat the three words. |
| love | luck | tube | Which word sounds like **neck** at the end? Repeat the three words. |
| lot | shot | rock | Which word sounds like **neck** at the end? Repeat the three words. |
| nut | miss | stick | Which word sounds like **neck** at the end? Repeat the three words. |

● **DIRECTING THE LEARNER'S ATTENTION**

The purpose of this task is to teach the learner to distinguish the **ck** sound from other ending consonant sounds. As such, the task is similar to storehouse module I-WA-5. To teach this skill you must direct the learner's attention by stating exactly what is to be learned and by highlighting the ending sound of the words. (For the word **neck,** for instance, you might use a say-it-slow, say-it-fast technique to emphasize the ending, as in **ne—ck**).

## • TEACHING ACTIVITIES

In teaching this auditory discrimination skill you can use either the modeling technique or the discovery technique described in I-WA-5, adjusting the suggestions to focus on the ending sound of the words.

## • SUGGESTIONS FOR RETEACHING

If, after having been taught this skill with either the modeling or the discovery technique, the learner is unable to distinguish by ear the –ck ending sound from other ending sounds, you should

1. Reteach the skill, using the alternate technique.
2. Reexamine your attenders, making sure that the learner is listening to the *ending* sound and that your highlighting is emphatic enough to help him or her distinguish the ending sound from other sounds.
3. Return to the previous auditory discrimination skills, making sure that the learner can perform those before requiring him or her to complete this objective.

## • SUGGESTIONS FOR PRACTICE

Once the learner can distinguish the –ck ending sound from other ending sounds, create practice activities to solidify the skill, using the suggestions in I-WA-5.

## • THE POSTTEST

The procedure and criterion for mastery are the same as for the pretest.

| | | | |
|---|---|---|---|
| pill | pit | pick | Which word sounds like **neck** at the end? Repeat the three words. |
| sack | sill | sash | Which word sounds like **neck** at the end? Repeat the three words. |
| dove | duck | nest | Which word sounds like **neck** at the end? Repeat the three words. |
| lot | net | lock | Which word sounds like **neck** at the end? Repeat the three words. |
| check | net | check | Which word sounds like **neck** at the end? Repeat the three words. |

## • ENSURING TRANSFER

Although the learner will be applying this skill while learning to attach letters to the –ck ending sound in subsequent objectives, you should also use the suggestions provided in I-WA-5 to make sure that the skill is used during the routine daily reading activities in the classroom.

### • THE PERFORMANCE OBJECTIVE

When given a spoken word, the learner will point to the letters **ck** if the word ends in the **ck** sound.

### • THE PRETEST

Give the learner a card having the letters **ck** printed on it. Say the following words, directing the learner to point to the **ck** card each time a word is spoken that ends with that sound. The criterion for mastery is eight out of ten correct.

| | | | | |
|---|---|---|---|---|
| bat | rock | back | chest | duck |
| pick | much | luck | cast | neck |

### • DIRECTING THE LEARNER'S ATTENTION

The purpose of this task is to teach the learner to establish a sound-symbol connection between the **ck** letter combination and the sound this combination makes at the end of words. As such, the task is similar to storehouse module I-WA-9. To teach this skill you must direct the learner's attention by stating exactly what is to be learned and by highlighting both the sound heard at the end of the word and the form of the **ck** letter combination to which the sound is to be connected. (In the word **pick,** for instance, you might exaggerate the **ck** sound heard at the end of the word while simultaneously pointing to the cutout letters **ck.**)

### • TEACHING ACTIVITIES

In teaching this sound-symbol connection skill you can use either the modeling technique or the discovery technique described in I-WA-9, adjusting the suggestions to focus on the ending **ck.**

### • SUGGESTIONS FOR RETEACHING

If, after having been taught this skill with either the modeling or the discovery technique, the learner is unable to connect letters and sound for the ending **–ck,** you should

1. Reteach the skill, using the alternate technique.
2. Be more specific in directing the learner's attention, making sure that he or she is listening to the ending sound while simultaneously looking at the letters.
3. Use more emphasis in highlighting the ending sound, the **ck** letters, and the connection between them.
4. Return to the previous objective and be sure that the learner can distinguish between the ending **–ck** and other ending sounds before requiring him or her to connect the sound with letters.

## • SUGGESTIONS FOR PRACTICE

Once the learner has successfully connected the **ck** letters with words ending with the **ck** sound, create practice activities to solidify the skill, using the suggestions in I-WA-9.

## • THE POSTTEST

The procedure and criterion for mastery are the same as for the pretest.

| | | | | |
|---|---|---|---|---|
| sack | bet | shell | sick | back |
| flab | pack | lock | buck | camp |

## • ENSURING TRANSFER

Although the learner will be applying this skill in subsequent skills in the hierarchy, you should also use the suggestions provided in I-WA-9 to make sure that the skill is used during the routine daily reading activities in the classroom.

# II•WA•24

## • THE PERFORMANCE OBJECTIVE

When given words he or she pronounced in previous objectives, the learner will replace the final consonant sound in these words with the **ck** and pronounce the new word.

## • THE PRETEST

Use the following lists of words. The first word in each list has been previously taught as a sight word or as one of the words analyzed in previous objectives. Read the first word in the list and ask the learner to read the remaining words in each list. The criterion for mastery is 28 out of 32 correct. *Note:* Some of the words in the lists are nonsense words, which are included to make sure that the learner must use analysis techniques rather than recognize them at sight.

| bat | bet | sit | lot | but |
|---|---|---|---|---|
| back | beck | sick | lock | buck |
| rack | neck | kick | shock | luck |
| hack | check | chick | hock | muck |
| shack | meck | pick | rock | shuck |
| pack | sheck | hick | mock | chuck |
| sack | | thick | chock | duck |
| mack | | shick | | |
| chack | | | | |

## • DIRECTING THE LEARNER'S ATTENTION

The purpose of this task is to teach the learner to pronounce new words that are created by substituting **ck** for the ending letter of words he knows. As such, the task is similar to storehouse module II-WA-18. To teach this skill you must direct the learner's attention by stating exactly what is to be learned and by highlighting both the letter sounds that are common from word to word and the sound value of the ck ending. In the word back, for instance, you might circle the ba– as being the same as found in the previous word and exaggerate the sound of the –ck ending.)

## • TEACHING ACTIVITIES

In teaching this letter substitution skill you can use either the modeling technique or the discovery technique described in II-WA-18, adjusting the suggestions to focus on the ending consonant sound.

## • SUGGESTIONS FOR RETEACHING

If, after having been taught with either the modeling or the discovery technique, the learner is unable to pronounce new words after substituting the ck in the ending position, you should

1. Reteach the skill, using the alternate technique.
2. Reexamine your attenders, to make sure that you are providing enough highlighting on the common parts of the word and on the –ck ending.
3. Return to the prerequisite consonant substitution and sound-symbol connection skills to make sure that the learner can both produce the necessary letter sounds and substitute letter sounds into vowel phonograms.

## • SUGGESTIONS FOR PRACTICE

Once the learner can pronounce new words after substituting the ck in the ending position, create practice activities to solidify the skill, using the suggestions provided in II-WA-18.

## • THE POSTTEST

The pretest can be used also for the posttest. The procedure and criterion for mastery are the same.

## • ENSURING TRANSFER

You should use the suggestions provided in II-WA-18 to make sure that the learner uses this skill in pursuing daily reading activities.

## • THE PERFORMANCE OBJECTIVE

When given words he or she has previously analyzed or learned to recognize at sight, the learner will add the structural ending –ed, –ing, or –s and pronounce the new words.

## • THE PRETEST

Use the following lists of words. Have the learner pronounce each word in each list in turn. The criterion for mastery is 37 correct out of 40, with no structural ending being missed more than once.

| like | fish | back | rack | pack | kick |
|------|------|------|------|------|------|
| likes | fished | backs | racks | packs | kicks |
| liked | fishing | backed | racked | packed | kicked |
| liking | | backing | racking | packing | kicking |

| pick | lock | duck | rock | shock | go |
|------|------|------|------|-------|-----|
| picks | locks | ducks | rocks | shocks | going |
| picked | locked | ducked | rocked | shocked | |
| picking | locking | ducking | rocking | shocking | it |
| | | | | | its |

| boy | hat | cat | sit | cut | rub |
|-----|-----|-----|-----|-----|-----|
| boys | hats | cats | sits | cuts | rubs |

## • DIRECTING THE LEARNER'S ATTENTION

The purpose of this task is to teach the learner to pronounce new words that are composed of a known root word and the –ed, –ing, or –s endings. As such, the task is one of a number of skills in which the learner identifies unknown words by looking at word parts or word structure. For instance, the learner identifies the parts in prefixed words such as **un-happy,** in suffixed words such as **back-ing,** and in compound words such as **snow-man.** (*Caution:* This skill is not the same as syllabication, which divides words into parts on the basis of *sound units* rather than on the basis of *meaning units* as is done here.) Analyzing by structure is another problem-solving technique the learner can use when meeting a word he or she does not know at sight. For instance, if the learner is unable to pronounce the word **back-ing** but already knows the word **back** and the sound produced by the –ing ending, he or she can say, "I know that b-a-c-k is pronounced **back** and I know the sound the –ing makes at the ends of words, so **back** and –ing must say **backing.**" This is a particularly efficient skill since it allows for rapid identification of the unknown word. *Caution:* Do not teach the learner to look for the little word in the big word, since this process is not helpful in analyzing words that are not compounds. (For instance, it is of little help to look for the little word **at** in **boat** or the little word **fat** in **father**).

In teaching this skill you must direct the learner's attention by stating exactly what is to be learned and by highlighting the previously seen root word and the visual and sound components of the new structural ending. (In the word **likes,** for instance, you might underline the known root word **like,** circle the unknown structural ending –s, and exaggerate the ending –s sound when pronouncing the word for the learner.)

## • THIS IS A STOREHOUSE OBJECTIVE

The following instructional activities are your storehouse of techniques for developing skill in analyzing words in terms of meaning units or structural analysis. This skill recurs in more sophisticated forms later in the hierarchy. The instructional activities that follow are to be adapted and used with each of these as they occur.

*The modeling technique.* When teaching a structural analysis skill such as this one, first print one root word on the board and make sure the child is able to pronounce it. Next, directly underneath the first word, print the word again, adding the structural ending. Underline the root word and circle or otherwise highlight the structural element. Next, point to the first word and say, "I know that this word is **like** because I have seen and pronounced it before. When I look at the word directly underneath it, I see that it has **like** in it (point to the underlined root word) and I see that it has an −s ending (point to the circled **s**)." Then pronounce the new word, using the say-it-slow, say-it-fast technique (see I-WA-5) as a means for auditory highlighting of the sound value of the structural ending. Have the learner model your behavior. Repeat this procedure with other words in the objective, gradually reducing the modeling and highlighting assistance until the learner can pronounce the words alone.

*The discovery technique.* Place a list of word pairs on the blackboard, with each pair having a root word and the root word with a common structural ending. (For instance, you might place on the board the words **like** and **likes, back** and **backs,** and so on.) Pose a series of questions in which you use the learner's responses to lead him or her to note that all the words in the list have the −s ending. Although you may provide cues by highlighting the common structural element, do not tell the learner what you want him or her to discover. When the learner has noted the visual similarities in the words, have him or her note the sound similarities, either by the learner reading whatever words in the list he or she can identify or by reading one or two of the words yourself. Auditory highlighting of the common structural elements should be done at this time, using the say-it-slow, say-it-fast technique (see I-WA-5). Direct the learner then to say the root word he or she knows and to add the ending. As he begins to respond correctly, you may diminish the amount of assistance provided by gradually removing the highlighting on the root word and structural element and by diminishing the amount of auditory highlighting on the sound value of the structural element.

• SUGGESTIONS FOR RETEACHING

If, after having been taught with either the modeling or discovery techniques, the learner is unable to pronounce words made up of a known root and the −ed, −ing, or −s ending, you should

1. Reteach the skill, using the alternate technique.
2. Examine your attenders, making sure that you are providing enough highlighting on the known root word and the new structural element.
3. If the learner's difficulty is in being able to remember the root word, redirect him or her to the objective where the word was originally taught and provide the learner with additional instruction in identifying the word.

4. If the learner's difficulty is in being able to associate a sound element with any particular structural element, you should use the suggestions provided in I-WA-9 to teach the child to develop a sound-symbol connection between the structural element and its sound value.
5. If the learner's difficulty is in differentiating the sounds of the structural elements, use the suggestions provided in I-WA-5 to teach the child to discriminate by ear among the sounds of the structural elements.

### • SUGGESTIONS FOR PRACTICE

Once the learner can pronounce words made up of known root words and the –ed, –ing, or –s endings, use the following suggestions to create practice activities to solidify the skill.

1. The word wheel and word slips techniques can be adapted for use in teaching the blending of structural elements to known words. A description of the construction and use of word wheels and word slips is contained in the storehouse of suggestions provided in II-WA-18.
2. Context activities can be used to develop this skill. Provide the learner with sentences in which one word is missing, giving him or her a choice of a root word or a root and its structural ending to fill the space. For instance, a sample sentence might be, "The two _____ (boy, boys) went to the store." The learner chooses the correct word word to fill the blank, pronounces it, and tells why that word is the correct one. *Caution:* The successful use of this technique presupposes that the learner already knows orally the correct form of the word. Certain dialects will not contain many of these inflected and derived forms of words. Teach these as oral responses prior to the activity.

*If a pupil does not learn a skill the first time, are you using the reteaching suggestions to help him or her the second time around?*

3. It is sometimes helpful to reverse the process described in the model teaching activity. That is, ask the learner to *create* words having prefixes, suffixes, or compound words. In such a case you should print the known words and word parts on separate cards, scramble them up, and have the learner choose one. Then the learner must choose another word card that would go with that word, making it either a prefixed word, a suffixed word, or a compound word. Be sure, however, that you have the learner pronounce the word he or she has created.
4. Make a chart or a worksheet in which root words or parts of compounds are listed down the left side and suffixes or the second part of the compound is listed down the right side. Attach strings to the words on the left-hand column and direct the learner to connect the string with the suffix or other part of the compound listed at the right so as to make a new word.
5. Make up crossword puzzles in which only compound words and/or prefixed and suffixed words can be used as answers.
6. Play a card game in which each player is dealt cards having root words written on the cards. The deck, containing just prefixes and/or suffixes, is placed in the center of the table. The learners take turns drawing

cards from the deck and trying to match the drawn card with one of the root words to form a new word. If he or she can do so, the learner lays the two cards down together and pronounces the new word. If the learner draws a card he or she cannot use, it is put back on the bottom of the pile. The first player to get rid of all his or her cards is the winner.

7. Give context experiences in which the learner must complete a series of sentences using the same root word in each. For instance, you might provide the learner with the root word **play** and tell him or her to use it together with suffixes to complete the following sentences (see *caution* in activity 2):

He is a baseball _____.
He is _____ in the game.
Yesterday he _____ football.
When he _____ he is happy.

## • THE POSTTEST

The pretest can be used as the posttest. The procedure and criterion for mastery are the same.

## • ENSURING TRANSFER

Once the learner has practiced this structural analysis skill, you must make sure that he or she is given reading material that calls for the use of the skill and that you guide him or her in applying this technique in reading words containing the structural elements. Suitable application situations include basal textbooks, library books, language experience stories, magazines, comic books, and any other reading materials in which the learner encounters words containing the structural elements.

# II•IG•1

## • THE PERFORMANCE OBJECTIVE

When given content words identified by the teacher, the learner will use each word correctly in an oral sentence.

## • THE PRETEST

The words to be tested are selected by the teacher. These may be words that appear in the basal text or in stories being read orally by the teacher in class or that are associated with the study of a particular content area. To test for the meaning of such words, say each word out loud to the learner. Ask him or her to make up a sentence or to "send a message" using that word. The criterion for mastery is 100 percent, since any word not used correctly will have to be taught.

The learner is asked to identify the following words in print in the next cluster of skills. You should include these words among those to be tested to make sure that he or she knows their meaning before having to pronounce them.

| | | | |
|---|---|---|---|
| new | want | pull | gone |
| said | went | long | pretty |
| baby | door | laugh | surprise |
| house | dog | ball | water |
| woman | word | write | |

### • DIRECTING THE LEARNER'S ATTENTION

The purpose of this task is to teach the learner the meaning of new words he or she will be encountering. The task is similar to storehouse module I-IG-1, but different words are being taught. To teach this skill you must direct the learner's attention by (1) providing either a direct or a vicarious experience to form the basis for the concept, (2) identifying the characteristics of that concept, and (3) connecting the concept to its word label. *Note:* This objective focuses on meaning alone. The learner should not be asked to pronounce these words as they appear in print until after this skill has been mastered.

### • TEACHING ACTIVITIES

This is a word meaning task similar to the storehouse module I-IG-1, and you can adapt your teaching strategy from either the modeling or the discovery technique described in that objective.

### • SUGGESTIONS FOR RETEACHING

If, after having been taught with either the modeling or the discovery technique, the learner does not understand the meaning of any of the words in this objective, you should adapt and use the suggestions in storehouse module I-IG-1 to reteach the skill.

### • SUGGESTIONS FOR PRACTICE

After teaching the learner the meaning of these words, create practice activities to solidify the skill, using the suggestions provided in module I-IG-1.

### • THE POSTTEST

The procedure and criterion for mastery are the same as for the pretest.

### • ENSURING TRANSFER

You should use the suggestions in I-IG-1, and listening comprehensive activities such as those included in the final chapter to make sure that the learner applies the new word meanings during the routine daily language activities in the classroom.

## II•IG•2

### • THE PERFORMANCE OBJECTIVE

When given the compound words he or she will be asked to identify in print in the next cluster of skills, the learner will use each correctly in an oral sentence.

## • THE PRETEST

Pronounce each compound for the learner and direct him or her to make up a sentence or "send a message" using the word you have just said. The criterion for mastery is 100 percent, with any word not used correctly being taught. The words to test are the following:

another anyone anything without into

## • DIRECTING THE LEARNER'S ATTENTION

The purpose of this task is to teach the learner the meaning of the compound words he or she will soon be asked to identify in print. This is similar to storehouse objective I-IG-2, but compounds are being taught rather than word endings. To teach this skill you must direct the learner's attention to the meaning of each separate part of the compound and to their meanings in combination.

## • TEACHING ACTIVITIES

This is a meaning unit task similar to the storehouse module I-IG-2, and you can adapt your teaching strategy from either the modeling or the discovery technique described in that objective.

## • SUGGESTIONS FOR RETEACHING

If, after having been taught with either the modeling or the discovery technique, the learner does not understand the meaning of the words in this objective, you should adapt and use the suggestions in I-IG-2 to reteach the skill.

## • SUGGESTIONS FOR PRACTICE

After teaching the learner the meaning of the words, create practice activities to solidify the skill, using the suggestions provided in I-IG-2.

## • THE POSTTEST

The procedure and criterion are the same as for the pretest.

## • ENSURING TRANSFER

You should use the suggestion in I-IG-2 and listening comprehension activities such as those included in the final chapter to make sure that the learner applies the new word meanings during the routine language activities in the classroom.

**II•IG•3**

## • THE PERFORMANCE OBJECTIVE

When given oral sentences containing the function words **she, some, you, we, they, who, me, I, my, he, it, him, us, her, the, his, our, any, your,** and **their,** the learner identifies the antecedent for each pronoun.

## • THE PRETEST

Direct the learner to listen to you carefully as you say a word and then use that word in a sentence. Tell the learner to listen for the word in the sentence and then to tell you who the word refers to in the sentence. Do the first one as an example. The criterion for mastery is 100 percent, with any missed pronoun being taught. Sentences such as the following may be used.

| | |
|---|---|
| she | I knew Mother was happy because **she** was singing. |
| some | We bought a bag of apples and ate **some.** |
| you | Mary looked at John and said, "**You** can sit here, John." |
| we | I went to the movie with Susie and Tom. **We** had fun. |
| they | We saw Marie and Anne. **They** were running. |
| who | Sam is the one **who** did it. |
| me | "I want you to go with **me,**" said the man. |
| I | "**I** need some milk and bread," said Mother. |
| my | Jackie was crying. "Don took **my** bike," he said. |
| he | Mike was in the race and **he** was running very fast. |
| it | The school was big and **it** had a playground. |

## • DIRECTING THE LEARNER'S ATTENTION

The puropse of this task is to teach the learner the relationship signaled by the function words specified in this objective. This is similar to the storehouse module I-IG-3. To teach this skill you must direct the learner's attention by emphasizing the function word as it appears in oral context while simultaneously demonstrating the relationship signaled.

## • TEACHING ACTIVITIES

This is an information-gathering task similar to the storehouse module I-IG-2, and you can adapt your teaching strategy from either the modeling or the discovery technique described in that objective.

## • SUGGESTIONS FOR RETEACHING

If, after having been taught with either the modeling or the discovery technique, the learner does not understand the use of these function words, you should adapt and use the suggestions in I-IG-3 to reteach the skill.

## • SUGGESTIONS FOR PRACTICE

After teaching the learner the uses of these function words create practice activities to solidify the skill, using the suggestions provided in I-IG-3.

## • THE POSTTEST

The procedure and criterion for mastery are the same as for the pretest.

## • ENSURING TRANSFER

You should use the suggestions in I-IG-3 and listening comprehensive activities such as those included in the final chapter to make sure that the learner applies the use of function words in contextual settings during the routine language activities in the classroom.

**• THE PERFORMANCE OBJECTIVE**

When given an oral sentence containing a word unknown in meaning and a direct definition clue to the word's meaning, the learner will state the meaning of the unknown word.

**• THE PRETEST**

State the unknown word, telling the child that you are going to use the word in a sentence that will give a clue to the word's meaning. After stating the sentence ask the child for the meaning of the word. The criterion for mastery is 80 percent.

| | |
|---|---|
| biplane | A **biplane**, an airplane with two wings, flies very fast. |
| jester | The **jester**, a man who tried to make people laugh, was very old. |
| escalator | An **escalator** is like a moving staircase and is fun to ride. |
| larder | The **larder**, a storage place for food, was large and cool. |
| figs | The king was eating **figs**, a sweet fruit grown in faraway lands. |

**• DIRECTING THE LEARNER'S ATTENTION**

The purpose of this task is to teach the learner to determine the meaning of an unknown word by using clues provided in the surrounding context. This skill of contextual prediction is crucial since learners must have means for learning new word meanings other than the direct instructional techniques described in I-IG-1. Using the syntactic and semantic clues found in the context is a major way of doing this. There are several different types of context clues, each of which should be taught. The first, which is taught in this objective, is the direct definition clue. Others taught in subsequent objectives are the following:

experience clues
example clues
synonym and antonym clues
inference clues
mood clues
summary clues

In determining word meaning through context clues, the learner makes use of several previously learned comprehension skills. For instance, the learner must know (1) the meanings of the words around the unknown word if he or she is to use them as clues, (2) certain of the signalers of relationships, (3) how concepts can be related, and (4) how to do some inferential thinking. With direct definition of context clues you must be sure that the learner has mastered the prerequisite comprehension skills in the hierarchy and you must direct his or her attention to the unknown word, to the commas that set off the explanatory phrase, and to the words within the phrase that explain the meaning of the unknown word. (In the first sentence of the pretest, for example, you would direct the learner's attention to the word **biplane,** the commas after **biplane** and **wings,** and to the words **airplane** and **two wings** within the phrase.) *Note:* The focus of this objective is to find meaning. If the learners cannot pronounce the unknown words, you should pronounce them for them.

### • THIS IS A STOREHOUSE OBJECTIVE

The following instructional activities are your storehouse of techniques for developing skill in contextual prediction. This skill recurs in more sophisticated forms later in the hierarchy. The instructional activities that follow are to be adapted and used with each of them as they occur.

### • TEACHING ACTIVITIES

*The modeling technique.* After making sure that the learner possesses the prerequisites, you would teach him or her to use direct definition context clues by placing highlighted sentences such as the following on the chalkboard:

A biplane, an airplane with two wings, flies very fast.

You could then say to the learner, "If I do not know the meaning of **biplane** in this sentence, I could figure out its meaning by looking for clues in the sentence. There are two kinds of clues in this sentence. The commas are the first clue and tell me that the author is providing me with extra information. When I see commas setting off words in this way, I want to examine the words between commas for clues. These words are the second kind of clue. In this case I find the words **airplane** and **two wings** between the commas. These words help me understand that a biplane is an airplane with two wings." In subsequent sentences you would ask the learner to assume more and more of the description of the thinking process while you provide fewer and fewer clues in the form of underlining, circling, and arrows. When the learner is able to determine independently the meaning of unknown words in such sentences, you can assume that he or she has learned the skill.

*The discovery technique.* As in the modeling technique, you could still make use of a sentence in which clues have been highlighted with circling, underlining, and arrows. Instead of directly modeling the thinking process, however, you could direct the learner's attention with questions. For instance, you could direct the learner to the commas and say, "Why do you suppose the author added the words within the commas? What words within the commas give us clues to the meaning of the word **biplane**?" In subsequent sentences you could gradually diminish both the circling, underlining, and arrows and the questioning until the learner is able to use direct definition context clues without assistance.

## • SUGGESTIONS FOR RETEACHING

If, after having been taught with either of the preceding techniques, the learner is unable to use direct definition context clues to discover the meaning of unknown words, you should

1. Reteach the skill, using the alternate technique.
2. Reassess the prerequisite comprehension skills to make sure that he or she has the background to perform this task.
3. Provide additional highlighting on the commas and the words within the commas that provide clues.
4. Make sure that the learner understands the meaning of the clue words within the comma.

## • SUGGESTIONS FOR PRACTICE

Once the learner is able to use direct definition context clues to determine the meaning of unknown words, you should provide practice activities to solidify this skill. The best way to do this is to give the learner exercises that offer multiple opportunities to use the skill. Ditto sheets, workbook pages, and similar activities would be appropriate.

Are you captivating your learners, or are they just captive?

## • THE POSTTEST

The procedures, directions, and criterion for mastery are the same for the posttest as they were for the pretest. Use the following sentences.

The **poplar,** a long and thin tree, is very pretty.
**Erosion,** the wearing away of land, is a very sad thing to watch.
I stood at the **pier,** a walkway going out into the lake, and watched the waves.
The **buoy,** a floating light that warns ships of danger, was red and white.
The **cardinal,** a bright red bird, was sitting on the wire.

## • ENSURING TRANSFER

You should make sure that direct definition context clues are used in the routine daily language activities of the classroom. One way to do this is to provide such clues every time you introduce new words in science and social studies lessons. Further, such clues should be incorporated into listening comprehension activities such as the one in the final chapter.

## II•MT•1

## • THE PERFORMANCE OBJECTIVE

When given a list of four words, the learner will group together those that belong together and explain his or her system for classifying them.

## • THE PRETEST

Direct the learner to listen to each word as you say it. Tell him or her that three of the four words you say can be grouped together and that one of the words does not belong with the group. Do the first one as an example and then have the learner complete the rest; have the learner tell you orally why the three words he or she chose go together. Criterion for mastery is eight out of ten correct.

| | | | |
|---|---|---|---|
| 1. **ear** | **nose** | **bump** | **arm** |
| 2. blue | wise | yellow | green |
| 3. after | front | back | side |
| 4. six | awake | two | eleven |
| 5. medicine | duck | chicken | hen |
| 6. love | shoe | coat | hat |
| 7. aunt | daughter | uncle | mother |
| 8. wind | rain | sad | snow |
| 9. year | minute | day | happy |
| 10. shout | scream | splash | yell |

### • DIRECTING THE LEARNER'S ATTENTION

The purpose of this task is to teach the learners how to group things together and explain their system. This is similar to storehouse objective I-MT-1. To teach this skill you must direct the learner's attention to the relationships that are used to classify and the system that is used to classify.

### • TEACHING ACTIVITIES

This is a manipulative task similar to storehouse module I-MT-1, and you can adapt your teaching strategy from either the modeling or the discovery technique described in that objective.

### • SUGGESTIONS FOR RETEACHING

If, after having been taught with either the modeling or the discovery technique, the learner does not understand how to use relationships to classify, you should adapt and use the suggestions in I-MT-1 to reteach the skill.

### • SUGGESTIONS FOR PRACTICE

After teaching the learner the classifying skill, create practice activities to solidify the skill, using the suggestions provided in I-MT-1.

### • THE POSTTEST

The procedure and criterion for mastery are the same as for the pretest, although you may want to substitute new material.

### • ENSURING TRANSFER

You should use the suggestions in I-MT-1 and in listening comprehension activities such as those in the final chapter to make sure that the learner applies classifying of concepts during the routine language activities in the classroom.

- **THE PERFORMANCE OBJECTIVE**

When given a short story read orally by the teacher and three possibilities about what will happen next, the learner will select the most likely outcome.

- **THE PRETEST**

Read each of the following paragraphs to the learner, directing him or her to listen carefully because you are going to ask questions about what happens after the story ends. After you have read the story ask each of the following questions. The criterion for mastery is 100 percent.

> Father had a surprise for Tom.
> He would not tell Tom what it was.
> He said it carried people on water.
> Tom guessed and guessed.
> Then Father said, "Open the box, Tom."

> What did Tom see in the box?
> > a gate   a boat   a book

> Mother put a surprise in a box.
> It was something good for the children to eat.
> They ate and ate.
> But they could not eat it all.

> What was still in this box?
> > a basket   a cake   a cookie

> Jack has a pet in a box.
> It is the pet he likes best.
> He will put his pet in water.

> What pet will Jack see when he opens the box?
> > a bunny   a turtle   a kitten

- **DIRECTING THE LEARNER'S ATTENTION**

The purpose of this task is to teach the learner how to predict what will come next. This is similar to storehouse objective I-MT-2. To teach this skill you must direct the learner's attention to the elements of the story that imply what will happen at the end of the story.

- **TEACHING ACTIVITIES**

This is a manipulative task similar to storehouse module I-MT-2, and you can adapt your teaching strategy from either the modeling or the discovery technique described in that objective.

- **SUGGESTIONS FOR RETEACHING**

If, after having been taught with either the modeling or the discovery technique, the learner does not understand how to predict outcomes, you should adapt and use the suggestions in I-MT-2 to reteach the skill.

## • SUGGESTIONS FOR PRACTICE

After teaching the learner how to predict outcomes, create practice activities to solidify the skill using the suggestions provided in I-MT-2.

## • THE POSTTEST

The procedure and criterion for mastery are the same as for the pretest, although you may want to substitute new material.

## • ENSURING TRANSFER

You should use the suggestions in I-MT-2 and listening comprehension activities such as those in the final chapter to make sure that the learner applies predicting outcome skills during the routine language activities in the classroom.

# II•ET•1

## • THE PERFORMANCE OBJECTIVE

When given the beginning of an oral sentence and three oral phrases with which to complete the sentence, the learner will choose the phrase that makes the most sense.

## • THE PRETEST

Direct the learner to listen to the first part of each sentence and to select an ending for the sentence that would make the most sense from the three choices provided orally. The criterion for mastery is 80 percent. (Readability: Second grade.)

> An apple could
> > say "Hi."
> > climb a tree.
> > be round.
>
> A cookie could
> > run into the barn.
> > have nuts on top of it.
> > play ball with you.
>
> A toy train could
> > be black and red.
> > push an airplane.
> > cry.
>
> A big wind could
> > cry because it is so cold.
> > blow open the door.
> > get sleepy.
>
> A big fat hen could
> > be in a store.
> > tell you to be good.
> > ask you for corn.

## • DIRECTING THE LEARNER'S ATTENTION

The purpose of this task is to teach the learner how to judge the best ending of a sentence. This is similar to the storehouse objective I-ET-1. To teach this skill you must direct the learner's attention to which ending best fits the sentence according to his or her knowledge of the subject material.

## • TEACHING ACTIVITIES

This is an evaluative task similar to storehouse module I-ET-1, and you can adapt your teaching strategy from either the modeling or the discovery technique described in that objective.

## • SUGGESTIONS FOR RETEACHING

If, after having been taught with either the modeling or the discovery technique, the learner does not understand how to evaluate and select the best ending, you should adapt and use the suggestions in I-ET-1 to reteach the skill.

## • SUGGESTIONS FOR PRACTICE

After teaching the learner how to judge and select the best ending for a sentence, create practice activities to solidify the skill, using the suggestions provided in I-ET-1.

## • THE POSTTEST

The procedure and criterion for mastery are the same as for the pretest, although you may want to substitute new material.

## • ENSURING TRANSFER

You should use the suggestions in I-ET-1 and listening comprehension activities such as those in the final chapter to make sure that the learner applies judgment skills for the endings of sentences during the routine language activities in the classroom.

# CLUSTER III

● **THE PERFORMANCE OBJECTIVE**

When given a fraction of a second to examine flashcards having printed on them the following words, the learner will pronounce each within one second.

| | | | | | | |
|------|-------|--------|----------|------|-------|--------|
| show | know | too | hot | like | saw | ask |
| car | paint | take | from | but | then | on |
| get | word | around | your | went | us | father |
| cat | she | tree | birthday | away | about | new |
| all | sit | good | soon | book | fun | house |

● **THE PRETEST**

Print each of the preceding words on a flashcard. Flash each to the learner, giving him or her less than one second to examine each word before pronouncing it. The criterion for mastery is 100 percent.

● **DIRECTING THE LEARNER'S ATTENTION**

The purpose of this task is to teach the learner to recognize instantly and pronounce the words contained in the pretest when they are presented on flashcards. This is a sight word recognition skill like that described in

II-SW-6. To teach the skill you must make sure that the learner knows exactly what is to be learned, that the words being taught are in the child's speaking vocabulary, and that you have directed his or her attention by highlighting the unique visual characteristics of each word (such as the initial and final letters, length, shape, double letters, and so on.)

### • TEACHING ACTIVITIES

This is a sight word recognition skill similar to that described in II-SW-6. If the learner does not recognize the word in print, adapt your teaching strategy from either the modeling technique or the discovery technique described in that objective. If the child confuses the word with another word similar to it, adapt your strategy from the suggestions contained in I-SW-17.

### • SUGGESTIONS FOR RETEACHING

If, after having been taught using the suggested technique, the learner is unable to recognize instantly one or more of the words on the pretest, use the reteaching suggestions described in II-SW-6.

### • SUGGESTIONS FOR PRACTICE

After successfully teaching the learner to recognize instantly the words on the pretest, create practice activities to solidify the skill, using the suggestions provided in II-SW-6.

### • THE POSTTEST

The procedure and criterion for mastery for the posttest are the same as for the pretest.

### • ENSURING TRANSFER

To be sure that this skill is applied, you must give the learner reading material containing the words now known at sight and have him or her read. You may guide the application by pointing out the words the child just learned to recognize or, as he or she becomes more proficient, you can encourage independent reading of the newly learned words. Any material at the child's instructional reading level that contains the learned sight words would be appropriate. Additional suggestions for helping the learner use known sight words in context are contained in II-SW 6.

## III•SW•2

### • THE PERFORMANCE OBJECTIVE

When given a flash presentation of words the learner frequently confuses, he or she will pronounce each word correctly within one second.

### • THE PRETEST

You will note whether the learner is confusing words any time you test him or her on sight words or listen to him or her read. If, during either of these activities, the learner says one word for another (such as **was** for **saw**), you should pair the words together and teach them, using the suggestions provided in this objective. No specific list of words is provided since various learners will confuse various words. As with other sight word objectives, the criterion for mastery is 100 percent, with any pair of confused words being taught.

#### • DIRECTING THE LEARNER'S ATTENTION

The purpose of this task is to teach the learner to recognize instantly pairs of words he or she has tended to confuse in the past. As such, this task is similar to that described in I-WA-17. To teach this skill you must be sure that the learner has mastered the previous visual training skill, that he or she knows exactly what is to be learned, that the words being taught are in his or her speaking vocabulary, and that you have directed his attention by highlighting the discriminator that sets one word apart from the other (such as the first letters in **was** and **saw**).

#### • TEACHING ACTIVITIES

In teaching this skill you can use either the modeling technique or the discovery technique described in I-WA-17, adjusting the suggestions to focus on the particular words the learner is confusing.

Do you threaten and scream or do you manage instruction efficiently?

#### • SUGGESTIONS FOR RETEACHING

If, after having been taught with either the modeling or the discovery technique, the learner continues to confuse the words, the reteaching suggestions provided in I-WA-17 should be used.

#### • SUGGESTIONS FOR PRACTICE

Once the learner can instantly recognize the words that were previously being confused, create practice activities to solidify the skill, using the suggestions provided in I-WA-17.

#### • THE POSTTEST

The procedure and criterion for mastery are the same as for the pretest.

#### • ENSURING TRANSFER

Once the learner can recognize the easily confused words you should immediately provide opportunities to apply this skill by supplying reading material containing the words now known at sight. For specific suggestions on such application activities see II-SW-6.

## III•SW•3

#### • THE PERFORMANCE OBJECTIVE

When given words that he or she recognizes instantly, the learner will create and read a single-sentence story using these words.

## • THE PRETEST

Provide cards, each of which has printed on it a word the learner instantly recognizes. Say to the learner, "Today we are going to do something that is very hard. We are going to send messages. Look at the cards you have in front of you. Each card has a word on it that you know. Can you send me a message using the words you have there? If you want to send a message using a word you don't have on a card, tell me and I will make a card for you with that word on it." The criterion for mastery is the combination of any number of words in a way that is grammatically accurate and that makes sense. When the learner has formed a sentence, reinforce the value of the effort by reading it aloud yourself.

## • DIRECTING THE LEARNER'S ATTENTION

This is a language experience activity designed to teach the learner to produce and read messages using individual words he or she knows at sight. As such, it is an application activity similar to that described in II-SW-8. To teach this activity you must be sure that the learner knows exactly what is to be learned and you must direct attention to the idea that is to be conveyed, to what the message will sound like when spoken, to what printed word cards she or he will need to "write" the message, and to the order in which the words must be placed. You might highlight by asking a series of questions such as, "What did you do yesterday after school that you could tell me about? Can you make a sentence about that and say it to me? What words did you use to say your sentence to me? How many of those words do you already have on cards and which ones will we have to make for you? What word will come first in your written message?"

## • TEACHING ACTIVITIES

This is a language experience activity similar to that described in II-SW-8, and the modeling and discovery techniques described in that objective can be used as a basis for planning and teaching this task.

## • SUGGESTIONS FOR RETEACHING

If, after having been taught with either of the techniques described in the key objective, the learner is unable to create a single-sentence message using his or her sight words, you should

1. Reteach the activity, using the alternate technique.
2. Be more specific in eliciting the idea the learner wishes to convey.
3. See that the learner expresses the message first in oral form and understands that the written message will say the same thing as the oral message.
4. Be sure that the content of the message matches the learner's experience, changing the subject to match his or her experience if necessary.
5. Recheck the learner's mastery of the sight words, reteaching any that have not yet been completely mastered.

6. Return to the previous language experience objectives and make sure the learner can do these simpler tasks before asking him or her to create entire sentences.

## • SUGGESTIONS FOR PRACTICE

Once the learner has been taught to use sight words to create and read sentences, devise practice activities to solidify this skill, adapting the suggestions provided in II-SW-8.

## • THE POSTTEST

The procedure and criterion for mastery for the posttest are the same as for the pretest.

## • ENSURING TRANSFER

This objective is an application activity designed to help the learner use sight words in context. In addition to the application specified here, however, you should use the suggestions in II-SW-6 to make sure that the learner uses the sight words in other contextual situations.

# III•WA•1

## • THE PERFORMANCE OBJECTIVE

When given a stimulus word beginning with one of the consonant blends **br, cr, dr, fr, gr, tr,** or **pr** and a group of three other words, one of which begins with a blend **br, cr, dr, fr, gr, tr,** or **pr,** the learner will pair the two words beginning with the same consonant blend.

## • THE PRETEST

Using the following words, say to the learner, "Here are three words. Listen carefully. (Say the words.) Which one sounds like (say the stimulus word) at the beginning?" Repeat the three words. The criterion for mastery is 13 out of 14 correct.

| | | | |
|---|---|---|---|
| dress | pray | think | Which one sounds like **press** at the beginning? Repeat the three words. |
| bread | drink | shirt | Which one sounds like **bring** at the beginning? Repeat the three words. |
| cap | come | cross | Which one sounds like **crash** at the beginning? Repeat the three words. |
| doll | drink | think | Which one sounds like **drop** at the beginning? Repeat the three words. |
| from | for | thumb | Which one sounds like **friend** at the beginning? Repeat the three words. |

| | | | |
|---|---|---|---|
| three | gas | grape | Which one sounds like **grow** at the beginning? Repeat the three words. |
| true | tee | tiger | Which one sounds like **tree** at the beginning? Repeat the three words. |
| glue | grass | gone | Which one sounds like **grow** at the beginning? Repeat the three words. |
| pin | pest | prize | Which one sounds like **press** at the beginning? Repeat the three words. |
| top | truck | luck | Which one sounds like **tree** at the beginning? Repeat the three words. |
| crop | cow | kite | Which one sounds like **crash** at the beginning? Repeat the three words. |
| bake | brave | blue | Which one sounds like **bring** at the beginning? Repeat the three words. |
| drum | dive | hive | Which one sounds like **drop** at the beginning? Repeat the three words. |
| fish | fine | free | Which one sounds like **friend** at the beginning? Repeat the three words. |

## • DIRECTING THE LEARNER'S ATTENTION

The purpose of this task is to teach the learner to distinguish the **r** blends from among other beginning consonant sounds. As such, the task is similar to storehouse module I-WA-5. To teach this skill you must direct the learner's attention by stating exactly what she or he is learning and by highlighting the beginning **r** blend of the words, as described in I-WA-5.

## • TEACHING ACTIVITIES

In teaching this auditory discrimination skill you can use either the modeling technique or the discovery technique described in I-WA-5, adjusting the suggestions to focus on the **r** blends.

## • SUGGESTIONS FOR RETEACHING

If, after having been taught this skill with either the modeling or the discovery technique, the learner is unable to distinguish by ear the **r** blends from among other beginning consonant sounds, you should

1. Reteach the skill, using the alternate technique.
2. Reexamine your attenders, making sure the learner is listening to the *beginning* sounds and that your highlighting is emphatic enough to help in distinguishing the beginning **r** blend from among other sounds.

3. Return to the previous auditory discrimination skills, being sure that the learner can distinguish single consonant sounds before going on to distinguish the **r** blends.

## • SUGGESTIONS FOR PRACTICE

Once the learner can distinguish the **r** blends from other beginning consonant sounds, create practice activities to solidify the skill, using the suggestions provided in I-WA-5.

## • THE POSTTEST

The procedure and criterion for mastery are the same as for the pretest. Use the following lists of words.

| | | | |
|---|---|---|---|
| freeze | fight | fly | Which one sounds like **friend** at the beginning? Repeat the three words. |
| drill | dish | dip | Which one sounds like **drop** at the beginning? Repeat the three words. |
| bat | bread | black | Which one sounds like **bring** at the beginning? Repeat the three words. |
| creep | keep | cash | Which one sounds like **crash** at the beginning? Repeat the three words. |
| tail | train | twist | Which one sounds like **tree** at the beginning? Repeat the three words. |
| pine | prune | pail | Which one sounds like **press** at the beginning? Repeat the three words. |
| glass | get | great | Which one sounds like **grow** at the beginning? Repeat the three words. |
| trade | tale | free | Which one sounds like **tree** at the beginning? Repeat the three words. |
| thank | gave | grease | Which one sounds like **grow** at the beginning? Repeat the three words. |
| fry | try | fly | Which one sounds like **friend** at the beginning? Repeat the three words. |
| desk | dream | mop | Which one sounds like **drop** at the beginning? Repeat the three words. |
| call | clash | creep | Which one sounds like **crash** at the beginning? Repeat the three words. |

| bright | bless | big | Which one sounds like **bring** at the beginning? Repeat the three words. |
| drug | price | pen | Which one sounds like **press** at the beginning? Repeat the three words. |

## • ENSURING TRANSFER

Although the learner will be applying this skill while learning to attach the sounds to letters in subsequent objectives, you should also use the suggestions provided in I-WA-5 to make sure that the skill is used during the routine daily reading activities of the classroom.

## III•WA•2

## • THE PERFORMANCE OBJECTIVE

When given spoken words beginning with the **br, cr, dr, fr, gr, tr,** or **pr** sounds, the learner will identify the beginning letters in each word.

## • THE PRETEST

Give the learner seven cards, each of which has printed on it one of the blends being tested (**br, cr, dr, fr, gr, tr,** and **pr**). Say the following words, directing the learner to point to the letters whose sound begins the word. The criterion for mastery is 13 out of 14 correct.

| pretty | braid | fresh | frog | crowd |
| grade | cradle | prove | brain | drug |
| tractor | dragon | ground | trick | |

## • DIRECTING THE LEARNER'S ATTENTION

The purpose of this task is to teach the learner to establish a sound-symbol connection between the letters **br, cr, dr, fr, gr, tr,** and **pr** and the sounds the combinations make at the beginning of words. As such, the task is similar to storehouse module I-WA-9. To teach this skill you must direct the learner's attention by stating exactly what is to be learned and by highlighting both the sound heard at the beginning of the word and the form of the letter combination with which it is to be connected. (In the word **pretty,** for instance, you might exaggerate the beginning sound of the **pr** blend while simultaneously pointing to the cutout letters **pr.**)

## • TEACHING ACTIVITIES

In teaching this sound-symbol connection skill you can use either the modeling technique or the discovery technique described in I-WA-9, adjusting the suggestions to focus on the beginning r blends.

## • SUGGESTIONS FOR RETEACHING

If, after having been taught this skill with either the modeling or the discovery technique, the learner is unable to connect letter and sound for the r blends, you should

1. Reteach the skill, using the alternate technique.
2. Be more specific in directing the learner's attention to listening to the beginning sound while simultaneously looking at the letter combination.
3. Use more emphasis in highlighting the beginning sound, the letter, and the connections between them.
4. Return to the previous objective and make sure that the learner can distinguish the r blend sounds from among other beginning consonant sounds before requiring him or her to connect the sound with a letter combination.

## • SUGGESTIONS FOR PRACTICE

Once the learner has successfully connected the r blend letter combinations to words beginning with these sounds, create practice activities to solidify the skill, using the suggestions provided in I-WA-9.

## • THE POSTTEST

The procedure and criterion for mastery are the same as for the pretest. Use the following words.

| brake | trap | prince | front | cream |
|-------|------|--------|-------|-------|
| crack | draw | print | gray | brat |
| grab | free | drive | trigger | |

## • ENSURING TRANSFER

The learner will be applying this skill in subsequent skills in the hierarchy, but you should also use the suggestions provided in I-WA-9 to make sure that the skill is used during the routine daily reading activities of the classroom.

## • THE PERFORMANCE OBJECTIVE

When given an oral sentence with one word missing and cued for the missing word with a card having printed on it the blend with which the word begins (br, cr, dr, fr, gr, tr, pr), the learner will say a word beginning with that letter blend that fits the context of the sentence.

## • THE PRETEST

Make cards with the preceding letters printed on them. Say, "I am going to say a sentence with one word missing. You look at the card and say a word that begins with the letter blend on the card and that finishes what I I want to say." Use the following sentences. The criterion for mastery is 12 out of 14, with no letter blend being missed more than once. *Note:* If a sentence fails to match a learner's experience background or does not provide enough context for him or her, you should alter the sentence accordingly. Sentence 1, for instance could be changed to read, "The minister in church told us to say our pr_____."

1. We go to church to pr_____.
2. The person who is in charge of the school is called a pr_____.
3. I like to dr_____ pictures.
4. We didn't have to pay any money because it was fr_____.
5. In our backyard the gr_____ is green.
6. At Halloween we play a lot of tr_____.
7. I would like to play the dr_____ in the band.
8. I like to put milk and fr_____ on my cereal.
9. I like to watch the tr_____ go down the tracks.
10. I'm going to be a baseball player when I gr_____ up.
11. The baby was sleeping in her cr_____.
12. I like to eat jelly on my br_____.
13. There were lots and lots of people in the cr_____.
14. In order to get over the river, we had to build a br_____.

What skills are you teaching tomorrow for your *best* readers?

### • DIRECTING THE LEARNER'S ATTENTION

The purpose of this task is to teach the learner to use his or her knowledge of **r** blend letter-sound correspondence and context to identify unknown words. As such, this task is similar to storehouse module I-WA-14. To teach this skill you must direct the learner's attention by stating exactly what is to be learned and by highlighting the words in the sentence that provide clues to the identity of the unknown word, the letter combination the unknown word begins with, and the sound associated with that letter combination. (In the first sentence of the pretest, for instance, you might highlight the word **church** and direct the learner to look at the large cutout **pr** and get his or her mouth ready to say the sound of the letter combination.)

### • TEACHING ACTIVITIES

In teaching this context–letter-sound skill you can use either the modeling technique or the discovery technique described in I-WA-14, adjusting the suggestions to focus on the **r** blend letter combinations.

### • SUGGESTIONS FOR RETEACHING

If, after having been taught with either the modeling or the discovery technique, the learner is unable to use context and **r** blends to identify unknown words, you should use the reteaching suggestions provided in I-WA-14.

### • SUGGESTIONS FOR PRACTICE

Once the learner has successfully used the **r** blends and context to identify unknown words, create practice activities to solidify the skill, using the suggestions provided in I-WA-14.

### • THE POSTTEST

The procedure and criterion for mastery are the same as for the pretest. Use the following sentences.

1. The sun was so br_____ that it hurt my eyes.
2. The lines he drew are not straight. They are cr_____.
3. I have a sister who is in the third gr_____ in school.
4. The farmer was sitting on his big tr_____.
5. I was thirsty so I got a dr_____.
6. My mother put the ice cream in the fr_____ so it wouldn't melt.
7. It was my birthday so I got a pr_____.
8. It was so cold that I nearly fr_____ my toes off.
9. The little girl wore a new dr_____.
10. I won a pr_____ because I was first in the race.
11. The cat ran up into the big tr_____.
12. The shirt was brown and gr_____.
13. The house was made out of wood and br_____.
14. Always look both ways before you cr_____ the busy street.

- **ENSURING TRANSFER**

You should use the suggestions provided in I-WA-14 to make sure that this skill is used during the daily reading activities of the classroom.

- **THE PERFORMANCE OBJECTIVE**

When given words he or she has learned previously, the learner will substitute the blends **br**, **cr**, **dr**, **fr**, **gr**, **tr**, and **pr** in the initial position and pronounce the new word.

- **THE PRETEST**

Use the following lists of words. The first word in each list has been previously taught as a sight word or has been previously analyzed. Read the first word in each list and ask the learner to pronounce the remaining words in the list. The criterion for mastery is 28 out of 31 correct, with no blend being missed more than once. *Note:* Some of the words listed are nonsense words which are included so that the learner must use analysis techniques rather than sight recognition.

| cap | fed | sip | top | tub | cab |
|------|------|------|------|------|------|
| trap | tred | drip | drop | drub | drab |
| drap | Fred | grip | prop | grub | crab |
| | pred | trip | crop | | grab |
| | | brip | frop | | prab |

| cat | buck | rush | bib | mess |
|------|-------|-------|------|-------|
| brat | truck | crush | crib | press |
| crat | bruck | brush | drib | dress |
| | | drush | | tress |

- **DIRECTING THE LEARNER'S ATTENTION**

The purpose of this task is to teach the learner to substitute r blends in the initial position of known short vowel phonograms and pronounce the new

- 277

word. As such, the task is similar to storehouse module II-WA-18. To teach this skill you must direct the learner's attention by stating exactly what is to be learned and by highlighting the initial **r** blend and the letters that are common from word to word. (In the word **trap**, for instance, you might circle the initial **tr** blend, underline the **ap**, and have the learner use the say-it-slow, say-it-fast technique (see I-WA-5) in pronouncing the word.)

### • TEACHING ACTIVITIES

In teaching this letter substitution skill you can use either the modeling technique or the discovery technique described in II-WA-18, adjusting the suggestion to focus on the **r** blends in the initial position.

### • SUGGESTIONS FOR RETEACHING

If, after having been taught this skill with either the modeling or the discovery technique, the learner is unable to substitute **r** blends in the initial position of known short vowel phonograms and pronounce the new words, you should use the reteaching suggestions provided in II-WA-18.

### • SUGGESTIONS FOR PRACTICE

Once the learner can substitute **r** blends in the initial position of known short vowel phonograms, create practice activities to solidify the skill, using the suggestions provided in II-WA-18.

### • THE POSTTEST

The pretest can also be used as the posttest. The procedure and criterion for mastery are the same.

### • ENSURING TRANSFER

You should use the suggestions provided in II-WA-18, to make sure that this skill is used by the learner during daily reading activities in the classroom.

## III•WA•5

### • THE PERFORMANCE OBJECTIVE

When given an oral presentation of a stimulus word beginning with the consonant blends **bl, cl, fl, pl, gl,** or **sl** and a group of three other words, one of which begins with the blends **bl, cl, fl, pl, gl,** or **sl,** the learner will pair the two words beginning with the same consonant blend.

### • THE PRETEST

Using the following words, say to the learner, "Here are three words. Listen carefully. (Say the words.) Which one sounds like (say the stimulus word) at the beginning?" Repeat the three words. The criterion for mastery is 11 out of 12 correct.

| | | | |
|---|---|---|---|
| sheep | keep | slab | Which one sounds like **sleep** at the beginning? Repeat the three words. |
| grab | glee | me | Which one sounds like **glad** at the beginning? Repeat the three words. |
| click | quick | cry | Which one sounds like **cliff** at the beginning? Repeat the three words. |
| pray | plank | pan | Which one sounds like **plow** at the beginning? Repeat the three words. |
| my | friend | fluff | Which one sounds like **fly** at the beginning? Repeat the three words. |
| sack | brown | blink | Which one sounds like **black** at the beginning? Repeat the three words. |
| glum | grow | got | Which one sounds like **glad** at the beginning? Repeat the three words. |
| prize | plump | hunt | Which one sounds like **plow** at the beginning? Repeat the three words. |
| sweep | sweet | slant | Which one sounds like **sleep** at the beginning? Repeat the three words. |
| flint | from | try | Which one sounds like **fly** at the beginning? Repeat the three words. |
| crime | clad | kiss | Which one sounds like **cliff** at the beginning? Repeat the three words. |
| bloom | broom | boom | Which one sounds like **black** at the beginning? Repeat the three words. |

• **DIRECTING THE LEARNER'S ATTENTION**

The purpose of this task is to teach the learner to distinguish the l blend sounds from other beginning consonant sounds. As such ,the task is similar to storehouse module I-WA-5. To teach this skill you must direct the learner's attention by stating exactly what is to be learned and by highlighting the beginning l blend sounds of the words as described in I-WA-5.

• **TEACHING ACTIVITIES**

In teaching this auditory discrimination skill you can use either the modeling technique or the discovery technique described in I-WA-5, adjusting the suggestions to focus on the l blend sounds.

If, after having been taught this skill with either the modeling or the discovery technique, the learner is unable to distinguish the l blend sounds from other beginning consonant sounds, you should

1. Reteach the skill, using the alternate technique.
2. Reexamine your attenders, making sure that the learner is listening to the *beginning* sounds of the word and that your highlighting is emphatic enough to help him or her distinguish the beginning sounds from other sounds.
3. Return to the previous auditory discrimination skills, making sure that the child can discriminate simpler consonant sounds before requiring completion of this task.

• SUGGESTIONS FOR PRACTICE

Once the learner can distinguish the l blends from other beginning consonant sounds, create practice activities to solidify the skill, using the suggestions provided in I-WA-5.

• THE POSTTEST

The procedure and criterion for mastery are the same as for the pretest. Use the following lists of words.

| | | | |
|---|---|---|---|
| blond | brown | black | Which one sounds like **black** at the beginning? Repeat the three words. |
| crowd | cloth | cold | Which one sounds like **cliff** at the beginning? Repeat the three words. |
| flour | from | fry | Which one sounds like **fly** at the beginning? Repeat the three words. |
| stump | creep | slump | Which one sounds like **sleep** at the beginning? Repeat the three words. |
| pride | plume | flower | Which one sounds like **plow** at the beginning? Repeat the three words. |
| gleam | grow | got | Which one sounds like **glad** at the beginning? Repeat the three words. |
| bright | buy | bleach | Which one sounds like **black** at the beginning? Repeat the three words. |
| fresh | find | fleet | Which one sounds like **fly** at the beginning? Repeat the three words. |

| | | | |
|---|---|---|---|
| prove | plod | poor | Which one sounds like **plow** at the beginning? Repeat the three words. |
| clerk | cross | come | Which one sounds like **cliff** at the beginning? Repeat the three words. |
| grace | glance | mad | Which one sounds like **glad** at the beginning? Repeat the three words. |
| shot | sweet | slum | Which one sounds like **sleep** at the beginning? Repeat the three words. |

## • ENSURING TRANSFER

The learner will be applying this skill while learning to attach symbols to the l blends in subsequent objectives, but you should also use the suggestions provided in I-WA-5 to make sure that the skill is used by the child during the routine daily reading activities of the classroom.

## • THE PERFORMANCE OBJECTIVE

When given spoken words beginning with the **bl, cl, fl, pl, gl,** and **sl** sounds, the learner will identify the beginning letters in each word.

## • THE PRETEST

Give the learner six cards, each of which has printed on it one of the blends being tested (**bl, cl, fl, pl, gl,** and **sl**). Say the following words, directing the learner to point to the letters whose sound begins the word. The criterion for mastery is 11 out of 12 correct.

| | | | |
|---|---|---|---|
| blare | gland | glow | blend |
| claim | pluck | plunge | clear |
| flannel | slash | slot | flush |

## • DIRECTING THE LEARNER'S ATTENTION

The purpose of this task is to teach the learner to establish a sound-symbol connection between the **bl, cl, fl, pl, gl,** and **sl** blends and the sounds these combinations make at the beginning of words. As such, this task is similar to storehouse module I-WA-9. To teach this skill you must direct the learner's attention by stating exactly what is to be learned and by highlighting both the sound heard at the beginning of the word and the form of the letter blend it is to be connected with. (In the word **blare,** for instance, you might exaggerate the beginning sound while simultaneously pointing to the cutout letter blend **bl.**)

## • TEACHING ACTIVITIES

In teaching this sound-symbol connection skill you can use either the modeling technique or the discovery technique described in I-WA-9, adjusting the suggestions to focus on the l blends.

● 281

### • SUGGESTIONS FOR RETEACHING

If, after having been taught this skill with either the modeling or the discovery technique, the learner is unable to connect letter and sound for the l blends, you should

1. Reteach the skill, using the alternate technique.
2. Be more specific in directing the learner's attention, making sure that he or she is listening to the beginning sound while simultaneously looking at the letter blend.
3. Use more emphasis in highlighting the beginning sound, the letter blend, and the connection between them.
4. Return to the previous objective and make sure that the learner can distinguish between the simpler consonant sounds before requiring completion of this objective.

### • SUGGESTIONS FOR PRACTICE

Once the learner has successfully connected the l blend letters to their respective sounds, create practice activities to solidify the skill, using the suggestions provided in I-WA-9.

### • THE POSTTEST

The procedure and criterion for mastery are the same as in the pretest. Use the following words.

| | | | |
|---|---|---|---|
| slate | flop | glare | flesh |
| plenty | clever | plastic | clam |
| glow | blank | slacks | blab |

### • ENSURING TRANSFER

Although the learner will be applying this skill in subsequent skills in the hierarchy, you should also use the sugestions provided in I-WA-9 to make sure that the skill is used by the child during the routine daily reading activities of the classroom.

## III•WA•7

### • THE PERFORMANCE OBJECTIVE

When given an oral sentence with one word missing and cued for the missing word with a card having printed on it the blend with which the word begins (**bl, cl, fl, pl, gl,** or **sl**), the learner will say a word beginning with the letter blend that fits the context of the sentence.

### • THE PRETEST

Make cards with the preceding letter blends printed on them. Say, "I am going to say a sentence with one word missing. You look at the card I hold up and say a word that begins with the letter blend on the card and that finishes what I want to say." Use the following sentences. The criterion for mastery is 10 out of 12, with no letter blend being missed more than once. *Note:* If a sentence fails to match a learner's experience background or does not provide enough context for him, you should alter the sentence accordingly. Sentence 1, for instance, could be changed to read, "I cut my finger and put a Band-Aid on it to stop the bl_____."

1. I cut my finger and it started to bl_____.
2. After the movie we all cl_____ our hands.
3. One of the first things we do each day in school is stand and salute the fl_____.
4. I drank my milk out of a gl_____.
5. After school we went outside to pl_____.
6. Because he was mad, he sl_____ the door as he left the room.
7. The preacher said, "God bl_____ you.'
8. We take a bath so that we will be cl_____.
9. We went close to the vase so we could smell the pretty fl_____.
10. It was cold outside so I put on my gl_____.
11. My mother put my food on my pl_____.
12. I slid down the hill on my sl_____.

## • DIRECTING THE LEARNER'S ATTENTION

The purpose of this task is to teach the learner to use his or her knowledge of l blend letter-sound correspondence and context to identify unknown words. As such, this task is similar to storehouse module I-WA-14. To teach this skill you must direct the learner's attention by stating exactly what is to be learned and by highlighting the words in the sentence that provide clues to the identity of the unknown word, the letter combination the unknown word begins with, and the sound associated with that letter combination. (In the first sentence of the pretest, for instance, you might highlight the words **cut, finger,** and **started** and direct the learner to look at the large cutout **bl** and to get his or her mouth ready to say the sound of the letter combination.)

## • TEACHING ACTIVITIES

In teaching this context–letter-sound skill you can use either the modeling technique or the discovery technique described in I-WA-14, adjusting the suggestions to focus on the l blend letter combinations.

## • SUGGESTIONS FOR RETEACHING

If, after having been taught this skill with either the modeling or the discovery technique, the learner is unable to use context and l blends to identify unknown words, you should use the reteaching suggestions provided in I-WA-14.

## • SUGGESTIONS FOR PRACTICE

Once the learner has successfully used the l blends and context to identify unknown words, create practice activities to solidify the skill, using the suggestions provided in I-WA-14.

The procedure and criterion for mastery are the same as for the pretest. Use the following sentences.

1. The baby sat on the floor and played with his bl_____.
2. To find out what time it is, the man looked at the cl_____.
3. I wish I could fl_____ like a bird.
4. I am so tired I could sl_____ all day.
5. I like all kinds of fruit, including pears, peaches, and pl_____.
6. The vase fell and broke, but we used gl_____ to put it back.
7. I dropped my pencil on the fl_____.
8. The big bird picked up the little animal with his cl_____.
9. The wind was so strong it made my hat bl_____ off.
10. I am real gl_____ to see that you are all better.
11. The teacher said, "Two pl_____ two equals four."
12. Be careful that you don't sl_____ on the ice!

### ● ENSURING TRANSFER

You should use the suggestions provided in I-WA-14 to make sure that the child uses this skill during the daily reading activities of the classroom.

# III•WA•8

### ● THE PERFORMANCE OBJECTIVE

When given words previously learned, the learner will substitute the blends **bl, cl, fl, pl, gl,** and **sl** in the initial position and pronounce the new words.

### ● THE PRETEST

The first word in each of the following lists has been previously taught as a sight word or has been previously analyzed. Read the first word in the list and ask the learner to pronounce the remaining words in each list. The criterion for mastery is 30 out of 36 correct, with no blend being missed more than once. *Note:* Some of the words listed are nonsense words which are included so that the learner **must** use analysis rather than sight recognition.

| **cap** | **bed** | **tip** | **hop** | **rub** | **mad** | **neck** |
|------|------|------|------|------|------|------|
| clap | fled | clip | flop | club | glad | fleck |
| slap | sled | flip | plop | blub | | pleck |
| glap | bled | slip | slop | | | |
| | | blip | glop | | | |

| **bib** | **rock** | **luck** | **shush** | **fat** | **mess** | **back** |
|------|------|------|------|------|------|------|
| glib | block | pluck | flush | flat | bless | black |
| flip | clock | cluck | blush | flag | pless | clack |
| slib | flock | bluck | | | | |

## • DIRECTING THE LEARNER'S ATTENTION

The purpose of this skill is to teach the learner to substitute l blends in the initial position of known short vowel phonograms and pronounce the new word. As such, this task is similar to storehouse module II-WA-18. To teach this skill you must direct the learner's attention by stating exactly what is to be learned and by highlighting the initial l blend and the letters that are common from one word to another. (In **clap,** for instance, you might circle the initial **cl** blend, underline the **–ap** and have the learner use the say-it-slow, say-it-fast technique (see I-WA-5) in pronouncing the word.)

## • TEACHING ACTIVITIES

In teaching this letter substitution skill you can use either the modeling technique or the discovery technique described in II-WA-18, adjusting the suggestions to focus on the l blends in the initial position.

## • SUGGESTIONS FOR RETEACHING

If, after having been taught this skill with either the modeling or the discovery technique, the learner is unable to substitute l blends in the initial position of known short vowel phonograms and pronounce new words, you should use the reteaching suggestions provided in II-WA-18.

## • SUGGESTIONS FOR PRACTICE

Once the learner can substitute l blends in the initial position of known short vowel phonograms, create practice activities to solidify the skill, using the suggestions provided in II-WA-18.

## • THE POSTTEST

The pretest can also be used for the posttest. The procedure and criterion for mastery are the same.

## • ENSURING TRANSFER

You should use the suggestions provided in II-WA-18 to make sure that this skill is used by the learner during the daily reading activities in the classroom.

# III•WA•9

## • THE PERFORMANCE OBJECTIVE

When given a spoken stimulus word ending with the **ng** sound and a group of three other words one of which ends with the **ng** sound, the learner will pair the two words that both end with the **ng** sound.

## • THE PRETEST

Using the following lists of words, say to the learner ,"Here are three words. Listen carefully. (Say the three words.) Which one sounds like (say the stimulus word) at the end?" Repeat the three words. The critrion for mastery is four out of five correct.

| | | | |
|---|---|---|---|
| land | back | sling | Which one sounds like **sang** at the end? Repeat the three words. |
| bang | bag | block | Which one sounds like **sang** at the end? Repeat the three words. |
| big | bring | help | Which one sounds like **sang** at the end? Repeat the three words. |
| finger | tick | fling | Which one sounds like **sang** at the end? Repeat the three words. |
| ran | rang | rag | Which one sounds like **sang** at the end? Repeat the three words. |

## • DIRECTING THE LEARNER'S ATTENTION

The purpose of this task is to teach the learner to distinguish the **ng** sound from among other ending consonant sounds. As such, the task is similar to storehouse module I-WA-5. To teach this skill you must direct the learner's attention by stating exactly what is to be learned and by highlighting the ending –**ng** sound of the words as described in I-WA-5.

## • TEACHING ACTIVITIES

In teaching this auditory discrimination skill you can use either the modeling technique or the discovery technique described in I-WA-5, adjusting the suggestions to focus on the –**ng** ending.

## • SUGGESTIONS FOR RETEACHING

Are you reading poems and stories to your learners every day?

If, after having been taught this skill with either the modeling or the discovery technique, the learner is unable to distinguish by ear the –**ng** ending from other ending consonant sounds, you should

1. Reteach the skill, using the alternate technique.
2. Reexamine your attenders, ensuring that the learner is listening to the *ending* sounds and that your highlighting is emphatic enough to help him distinguish the ending –**ng** from other ending sounds.
3. Return to the previous auditory discrimination skills, making sure that the learner can distinguish single consonants in an ending position before requiring him or her to distinguish the **ng** sound.

## • SUGGESTIONS FOR PRACTICE

Once the learner can distinguish the **ng** sound from other ending consonant sounds, create practice activities to solidify the skill, using the suggestions provided in I-WA-5.

## • THE POSTTEST

The procedure and criterion for mastery are the same as for the pretest. Use the following words.

| | | | |
|---|---|---|---|
| flake | sand | fang | Which one sounds like **sang** at the end? <br> Repeat the three words. |
| task | bring | sack | Which one sounds like **sang** at the end? <br> Repeat the three words. |
| wing | wig | wise | Which one sounds like **sang** at the end? <br> Repeat the three words. |
| tag | tang | tan | Which one sounds like **sang** at the end? <br> Repeat the three words. |
| swig | swim | swing | Which one sounds like **sang** at the end? <br> Repeat the three words. |

**• ENSURING TRANSFER**

Although the learner will be applying this skill while learning to attach the sound to letters in subsequent objectives, you should also use the suggestions provided in I-WA-5 to be sure that the skill is used by the child during the routine daily reading activities of the classroom.

**• THE PERFORMANCE OBJECTIVE**

When given a spoken word, the learner will point to the letters **ng** if the word ends in the **ng** sound.

**• THE PRETEST**

Give the learner a card having the letters **ng** printed on it. Say the following words, directing the learner to point to the **ng** card each time a word is spoken that ends with that sound. The criterion for mastery is four out of five correct.

tag     bang     pick     thing     sing

**• DIRECTING THE LEARNER'S ATTENTION**

The purpose of this task is to teach the learner to establish a sound-symbol connection between the letters **ng** and the sound these letters make at the end of words. As such, this task is similar to storehouse module I-WA-9. To teach this skill you must direct the learner's attention by stating exactly what is to be learned and by highlighting both the sound heard at the end of the word and the form of the **ng** letters. (In the word **bang**, for instance, you might exaggerate the ending sound of the **ng** while simultaneously pointing to the cutout letters **ng**.)

**• TEACHING ACTIVITIES**

In teaching this sound-symbol connection skill you can use either the modeling technique or the discovery technique described in I-WA-9, adjusting the suggestions to focus on the ending **ng** sound.

If, after having been taught this skill with either the modeling or the discovery technique, the learner is unable to connect letter and sound for the **–ng** ending, you should

1. Reteach the skill, using the alternate technique.
2. Be more specific in directing attention, making sure that the learner is listening to the ending sound while simultaneously looking at the letter combination.
3. Use more emphasis in highlighting the ending sound, the letter combination, and the connection between them.
4. Return to the previous objective and make sure that the learner can distinguish the **ng** sound from other ending consonant sounds before requiring him or her to connect the sound with the letter combination.

● **SUGGESTIONS FOR PRACTICE**

Once the learner has successfully connected the **ng** letter combination to the sound these letters make at the end of words, create practice activities to solidify the skill, using the suggestions provided in I-WA-9.

● **THE POSTTEST**

The procedure and criterion for mastery are the same. Use the following words.

> sting    flag    fig    strong    tongue

● **ENSURING TRANSFER**

Although the learner will be applying this skill in subsequent skills in the hierarchy, you should also use the suggestions provided in I-WA-9 to make sure that the child uses the skill during the routine daily reading activities of the classroom.

## III•WA•11

● **THE PERFORMANCE OBJECTIVE**

When given words pronounced in previous objectives, the learner replaces the final consonant sounds in these words with the **ng** sound, substitutes initial sounds he or she knows, and pronounces the new words.

● **THE PRETEST**

The first word in each of the following lists has been previously taught as a sight word or as one of the words analyzed in previous objectves. Read the first word in the list and ask the learner to read the remaining words in each list. The criterion for mastery is seven out of eight correct. *Note:* Some of the words listed are nonsense words, which are included so that the learner *must* use analysis rather than sight recognition.

| | |
|---|---|
| **bag** | **sit** |
| bang | sing |
| sang | wing |
| fang | thing |
| shang | ching |

● **DIRECTING THE LEARNER'S ATTENTION**

The purpose of this skill is to teach the learner to substitute the **ng** in the final position of known short vowel phonograms and to pronounce the new words. As such, the task is similar to storehouse module II-WA-18. To teach this skill you must direct the learner's attention by stating exactly what is to be learned and by highlighting the final **ng** and the letters that are common from word to word. (In the word **bang**, for instance, you might circle the –ng ending, underline the **ba**– and have the learner use the say-it-slow, say-it-fast technique (see I-B-5) in pronouncing the word.)

● **TEACHING ACTIVITIES**

In teaching this letter substitution skill you can use either the modeling technique or the discovery technique described in II-WA-18, adjusting the suggestions to focus on the **ng** in the final position.

● **SUGGESTIONS FOR RETEACHING**

If, after having been taught this skill with either the modeling or the discovery technique, the learner is unable to substitute the **ng** in the final position of known short vowel phonograms and pronounce the new words, you should use the reteaching suggestions provided in I-WA-18, adapting them to the final **ng**.

Are your independent activities differentiated according to ability?

● **SUGGESTIONS FOR PRACTICE**

Once the learner can substitute the **ng** in the final position of known short vowel phonograms, create practice activities to solidify the skill, using the sugestions provided in I-WA-18.

● **THE POSTTEST**

The pretest can also be used for the posttest. The procedure and criterion for mastery are the same.

● **ENSURING TRANSFER**

You should use the suggestions provided in I-WA-18 to make sure that this skill is used by the learner during the daily reading activities in the classroom.

**III•WA•12**

● **THE PERFORMANCE OBJECTIVE**

When given compound words composed of two known words, the learner will pronounce the compound words.

## • THE PRETEST

Print the following words on cards. Present each card to the learner one at a time, encouraging him or her to analyze each word and pronounce it. The criterion for mastery is 100 percent. The words are as follow:

another    anyone    anything    without    into

## • DIRECTING THE LEARNER'S ATTENTION

The purpose of this task is to teach the learner to pronounce compound words composed of two known words. As such, this task is similar to storehouse module II-WA-25. To teach this skill you must direct the learner's attention by stating exactly what is to be learned and by highlighting both of the known words. (In the word **another,** for instance, you might circle both **an** and **other.**)

## • TEACHING ACTIVITIES

In teaching this structural analysis skill you can use either the modeling or the discovery technique described in II-WA-25, adjusting the suggestions to focus on compound words.

## • SUGGESTIONS FOR RETEACHING

If, after having been taught with either the modeling or the discovery techniques, the learner is unable to pronounce compound words composed of two known words, you should use the reteaching suggestions provided in II-WA-25.

## • SUGGESTIONS FOR PRACTICE

Once the learner can pronounce compound words composed of two known words, create practice activities to solidify the skill using the suggestions provided in II-WA-25.

## • THE POSTTEST

The pretest can be used as the posttest. The procedure and criterion for mastery are the same.

## • ENSURING TRANSFER

You should use the suggestions provided in II-WA-25 to be sure that the learner uses this skill during daily reading activities.

## III•IG•1

## • THE PERFORMANCE OBJECTIVE

When given content words that have been identified by the teacher, the learner will use each word correctly in an oral sentence.

## • THE PRETEST

The words to be tested are selected by the teacher. These may be words that appear in the basal text or in stories being read in class or that are associated with the study of a particular content area. To test for the meaning of such words, say each word out loud to the learner. Ask him or her to make up a sentence or to "send a message" using that word. The criterion for mastery is 100 percent since any word that is not used correctly will have to be taught.

The learner is asked to identify the following words in print in the next cluster of skills. You should include these words among those you test to be sure that he or she knows their meaning before pronouncing them.

| please | day | apple | tell | horse |
|--------|--------|--------|----------|--------|
| old | bigger | talk | children | orange |
| chair | know | today | walk | keep |
| push | put | child | wash | table |
| song | busy | take | full | guess |

## • DIRECTING THE LEARNER'S ATTENTION

The purpose of this task is to teach the learner the meaning of new words he or she will be encountering. This task is similar to storehouse module I-IG-1, but different words are being taught. To teach this skill you must direct the learner's attention by (1) providing either a direct or vicarious experience to form the basis for the concept, (2) identifying the characteristics of the concept, and (3) connecting the concept to its word label. *Note:* This objective focuses on meaning alone. The learner should not be asked to pronounce these words as they appear in print until after this skill has been mastered.

## • TEACHING ACTIVITIES

This is a word meaning skill similar to storehouse module I-IG-1, and you can adapt your teaching strategy from either the modeling or the discovery techniques described in that objective.

## • SUGGESTIONS FOR RETEACHING

If, after having been taught with either the modeling or the discovery technique, the learner does not understand the meaning of any of the words in this objective, you should adapt and use the suggestions in I-IG-1 to reteach the skill.

## • SUGGESTIONS FOR PRACTICE

After teaching the learner the meaning of these words, create practice activities to solidify the skill, using the suggestions provided in I-IG-1.

## • THE POSTTEST

The procedure and criterion for mastery are the same as for the pretest.

## • ENSURING TRANSFER

You should use the suggestions in I-IG-1 and comprehension activities such as those found in the final chapter to be sure that the learner applies the new word meanings during the routine daily listening language activities of the classroom.

# III•IG•2

● **THE PERFORMANCE OBJECTIVE**

When given the contractions he or she will be asked to identify in print in the next cluster of skills, the learner will use each contraction correctly in an oral sentence and name the words from which each contraction is derived.

● **THE PRETEST**

Say each contraction out loud, asking the learner to use the word in a sentence. Once the child has composed the sentence, ask him or her to tell you the words from which the contraction is derived. The criterion for mastery is 100 percent, with each missed contraction being taught.

The contractions to be tested are as follows:

| | | | |
|---|---|---|---|
| I'm | I'll | he's | you've |
| can't | don't | it's | we've |
| won't | isn't | I've | let's |

● **DIRECTING THE LEARNER'S ATTENTION**

The purpose of this task is to teach the learner the meaning of the contractions he or she will soon be asked to identify in print. This is similar to storehouse module I-IG-2. To teach this skill you must direct the learner's attention to the meaning of the contraction and of the two words from which the contraction is formed.

● **TEACHING ACTIVITIES**

This is a meaning unit task similar to storehouse module I-IG-2, and you can adapt your teaching strategy from either the modeling or the discovery technique described in that objective.

● **SUGGESTIONS FOR RETEACHING**

If, after having been taught with either the modeling or the discovery technique, the learner does not understand the meaning of the words in this objective, you should adapt and use the suggestions in I-IG-2 to reteach the skill.

● **SUGGESTIONS FOR PRACTICE**

After teaching the learner the meaning of the words, create practice activities to solidify the skill, using the suggestions provided in I-IG-2.

● **THE POSTTEST**

The procedure and criterion are the same as for the pretest.

## • ENSURING TRANSFER

You should use the suggestion in I-IG-2 and comprehension activities such as those in the final chapter to be sure that the learner applies the new word meanings during the routine listening language activities in the classroom.

## • THE PERFORMANCE OBJECTIVE

When given function words that signal various relationships, the learner will use each correctly in an oral sentence.

## • THE PRETEST

Say each word to be tested out loud to the learner, asking him or her to make up a sentence or to "send a message" using the word you have just said. The criterion for mastery is 100 percent with any word not used correctly being taught. The following function words should be tested:

| | | | | | | |
|---|---|---|---|---|---|---|
| before | off | again | am | are | may | should |
| with | most | how | also | more | does | done |
| when | which | very | will | would | could | only |
| as | | | | | | |

## • DIRECTING THE LEARNER'S ATTENTION

The purpose of this task is to teach the learner the relationships signaled by function words specified in this objective. This task is similar to storehouse module I-IG-3. To teach this skill you must direct the learner's attention by emphasizing the function word as it appears in oral context while simultaneously demonstrating the relationship signaled.

## • TEACHING ACTIVITIES

This is an information-gathering task similar to storehouse module I-IG-3, and you can adapt your teaching strategy from either the modeling or the discovery technique described in that objective.

## • SUGGESTIONS FOR RETEACHING

If, after having been taught with either the modeling or the discovery technique, the learner does not understand how to use function words correctly, you should adapt and use the suggestions in I-IG-3 to reteach the skill.

You have to love children to teach them. Does your love show through?

## • SUGGESTIONS FOR PRACTICE

After teaching the learner how to use function words correctly, create practice activities to solidify the skill, using the suggestions provided in I-IG-3.

## • THE POSTTEST

The procedure and criterion for mastery are the same as for the pretest.

• ENSURING TRANSFER

You should use the suggestions in I-IG-3, and listening comprehension activities such as those included in the final chapter to be sure that the learner applies use of function words in contextual settings during the routine language activities in the classroom.

## III•IG•4

• THE PERFORMANCE OBJECTIVE

When given oral sentences with words or phrases out of position, the learner will orally repeat the sentence with all words in the correct position.

• THE PRETEST

The sentences to be tested are selected by the teacher and should reflect the learner's background. Their length and complexity depends on the oral meaning level of the learner. Five sentences is the suggested number to be given. To test for understanding of word position in sentences, say the sentences with words out of position, as shown in the following set of sentences, and ask the learner to restate the sentence with all the words in their correct positions. The criterion for mastery is 80 percent, since the learner may misunderstand some sentences or the teacher may select some sentences containing words that the learner is not familiar with. Any positioning of words that makes sense is correct.

> Book new I got a yesterday.
> Our new car shiny and green is.
> He is the fastest class in the runner.
> Television saw a movie on we.
> For recess said it was time the teacher.

• DIRECTING THE LEARNER'S ATTENTION

The purpose of this task is to teach how positions of words in sentences signal relationships in our language. It is particularly important that multilingual children understand this type of signal since the patterning of words in their native language may be different. Since word position in sentences can be developed from simple to complex in terms of length and complexity, this is the first in a series of objectives directing you to be sure that the learner gains understanding from the position of words within sentences.

To teach word positioning in sentences, you must direct the learner's attention by providing a direct or vicarious experience. This means the learner does an action with real objects or vicarious objects such as pictures and then verbalizes what was done. The teacher then provides an incorrect positioning of words in the same sentence to show a contrast. The incorrect word may have auditor highlighting. Since there are many ways to position words in sentences, it is imperative that the switched words clearly be in wrong positions.

## • THIS IS A STOREHOUSE OBJECTIVE

The following instructional activities are your storehouse of techniques for teaching word positions in sentences. This skill will reoccur throughout the skills hierarchy as the learner encounters longer and more complex sentences first in oral and later in printed form. The activities that follow are to be adapted and used with each positioning-in-sentence objective that occurs.

## • TEACHING ACTIVITIES

*The modeling technique.* To teach word positioning in sentences you must provide experiences that allow the learner to create sentences or thought units. This will help control the background variable. The more concrete the experience is, the better the learning is. When it is impossible to provide concrete experiences, use vicarious experiences. After the learner has said a sentence about the experience, provide an example of wrong positioning using the same sentence. Use auditor highlighting with the incorrect word positions. For instance, if the learner said the following sentence, "I put two blocks in the box," you could say, "I put two box in the blocks," emphasizing **box** and **blocks.** The teacher then states what is wrong about the sentence by pointing out that the two words, **blocks** and **box** are out of position and restate the correct sentence as created by the learner. The learner then models the thought procedure of the teacher. You should repeat the process diminishing the use of modeling, auditory emphasis, and concrete experiences until the learner can correctly restate oral sentences containing words in incorrect positions. You can now assume the learner has learned correct positioning of words in sentences.

*The discovery technique.* The basic frame of the lesson is the same for discovery as it is for modeling. The major difference lies in the way you handle the correcting of the incorrect example that you provide. Rather than being highly directive in specifying which words are in incorrect positions as you would in modeling, you encourage the learner to identify the words in incorrect positions. Auditory emphasis can still be used as the teacher restates the sentence with incorrect positioning. Consequently, the dialogue might proceed as follows: "Here are some figures of people. Put the figures in the toy gas station and tell me about it." After the learner says a sentence, you restate it, incorrectly positioning some of the words and auditorily emphasizing those words that are in incorrect positions. Ask the learner to tell you which words are in the wrong position and then have her or him say the sentence the right way. As before, when the learner can pick out words that are in incorrect positions and restate the sentence correctly, you can assume that she or he has learned correct positioning of words in sentences.

## • SUGGESTIONS FOR RETEACHING

If, after having been taught with either of the preceding techniques, the learner is unable to use correctly positioned words in sentences, you should

1. Reteach the skill, using the alternative technique.
2. Provide a more relevant and direct experience as the basis for developing the skill.
3. Simplify the task by incorrectly positioning just one or two words in any one sentence.
4. Provide more direction and assistance in highlighting the characteristics of the skill.
5. Be sure that the learner understands words used in the directions, such as *sentence*.
6. Be sure that the learner understands all words and concepts used.

## • SUGGESTIONS FOR PRACTICE

Once the learner is using the skill of word positions in sentences, use one or more of the following activities to solidify the skill.

1. Use exercises where oral sentences have words in incorrect positions. The learner corrects the positioning.
2. Attach any game board such as football, baseball, or checkers, to the preceding exercises. A correct response allows a turn with the game.
3. Have learners work in pairs with concrete objects. One learner manipulates the objects and makes a sentence. The other learner restates the sentence changing some of the word positions. The first learner corrects the restated sentence.
4. Use the preceding exercise but have the learner manipulate the objects and make a sentence with the words in incorrect positions. The second learner corrects the sentence.
5. Use exercises in which a string of words are orally stated to the learner. The learner then creates sentences using those words. Appropriateness is determined by correct positioning of the words in the created sentences.

## • THE POSTTEST

The procedures, directions, and criterion for mastery are the same as for the pretest.

## • ENSURING TRANSFER

You should be sure of the correct positioning of words in sentences during the routine daily activities of the classrooms. A good way to do this is to have children listen for incorrect positioning of words. The teacher or other students could provide the incorrect positioning. The learner notes the error and then corrects it. Furthermore, word position sentences provide the basis for the later learning of specialized relationship thinking, as when the word signals cause-and-effect relationships in sentences.

# III•IG•5

## • THE PERFORMANCE OBJECTIVE

When given an oral sentence containing a word unknown in meaning and an experience clue to the word's meaning, the learner states the meaning of the unknown word.

State the unknown word, telling the child that you are going to use the word in a sentence that will give a clue to the word's meaning. Using sentences such as the following, ask the child for the meaning of the word. The criterion for mastery is 80 percent.

| | |
|---|---|
| feeble | I saw an old man crossing the street with a cane. He was going so slowly because he was **feeble.** |
| fumed | Alex dropped his mother's favorite glass jar and broke it. She was angry and when she saw Alex she **fumed** at him. |
| collide | If a driver drives his car without looking where he is going, he will probably **collide** with another car. |
| lingered | The circus was so much fun that Mary **lingered** in her seat even after the show was over. She just did not want to leave. |
| obliged | Because he broke the window, Sam felt that he was **obliged** to pay for it. |

## • DIRECTING THE LEARNER'S ATTENTION

The purpose of this task is to teach the learner how to determine the meaning of an unknown word by using clues in the surrounding context and background. This is similar to storehouse module II-IG-4. To teach this skill you must direct the learners' attention to the unknown word, the surrounding words that indicate the meaning, and their own background.

## • TEACHING ACTIVITIES

This is an information-gathering task similar to storehouse module II-IG-4, and you can adapt your teaching strategy from either the modeling or the discovery technique described in that objective.

## • SUGGESTIONS FOR RETEACHING

If, after having been taught with either the modeling or the discovery technique, the learner does not understand how to use experience clues to figure out the meaning of the unknown word, you should adapt and use the suggestions in II-IG-4 to reteach the skill.

## • SUGGESTIONS FOR PRACTICE

After teaching the learner how to use contexts that have experience as clues for the meaning of an unknown word, create activities to solidify the skill, using the suggestions provided in II-IG-4.

## • THE POSTTEST

The procedure and criterion for mastery are the same as for the pretest, although you may want to substitute new material.

## • ENSURING TRANSFER

You should use the suggestions in II-IG-4 and listening comprehension activities such as those included in the final chapter to be sure that the learner continues to use experience clues to figure out the meaning of an unknown word during the routine language activities in the classroom.

## III•IG•6

### • THE PERFORMANCE OBJECTIVE

When given a short oral paragraph, the learner will recall details about the paragraph in response to the teacher's oral questions.

### • THE PRETEST

Read a paragraph like the following one to the learner, directing him or her to listen carefully because you are going to ask questions about it afterward. After you have read the story, ask each of the following questions. The criterion for mastery is 100 percent.

> Every morning a boy and his friends went to a high, grassy hill. Every morning the boys jumped and skipped to the top of the hill. When they got to the top, they ate their lunches until they were full.

> Where did the boys go?
> How did they get to the top of the hill?
> How long did the boys eat?

### • DIRECTING THE LEARNER'S ATTENTION

The purpose of this task is to teach the learner to recall factual information. Reading has many purposes but one of the most important is to gather information. Without knowledge gained from factual input, either through reading or listening, response to the world becomes a function of chance rather than reason; options for behavior disappear and are replaced by either passive indifference or emotional tantrums. Therefore one of your important jobs in teaching language is to help your learners gain factual knowledge through reading.

Factual recall is more remembering than thinking; more a function of memory than of cognition. The learner must note and *remember* those words or phrases that answer questions posed. The learner will remember best when he or she knows the meaning of the words used and knows what you are looking for. Hence to teach factual recall you must be sure that the learner knows the meaning of the words in the passage to be recalled and you must direct attention by setting specific purposes that serve as cues to the learner regarding what to note and remember while reading and listening. (For example, in the pretest the questions to be asked might be posed *before* the child listens to the passage so he or she will know what you expect him or her to note and remember.)

### • THIS IS A STOREHOUSE OBJECTIVE

The following instructional activities are your storehouse of techniques for teaching factual recall. This skill will recur throughout the skill hierarchy as the learner encounters more difficult and complex material. The activities that follow are to be adapted and used with each of these as they occur.

## • TEACHING ACTIVITIES

*The modeling technique.* The pretest paragraph can be used to illustrate how to recall factual information. After making sure that the learner knows the meaning of each word, say, "To answer questions about details and facts in a story, you must first know what the question is and then you must find and remember the words that answer the question." Show the learner the pretest but alter it so that the first question precedes the paragraph, the phrase *high, grassy hill* is underlined, and an arrow is drawn from the question to the underlined phrase. Say, "The first question asks where the boys went. In the first sentence of the story, it says the boys went to a **high grassy hill.** So, to answer the first question, I must remember the phrase *high, grassy hill.* Repeat the same procedure with subsequent questions in this and other paragraphs, gradually diminishing your modeling and the highlighting arrows and underlining until the learner is able to recall factual information in a paragraph at this level without assistance from you.

*The discovery technique.* The procedure for the discovery technique is basically the same as the preceding technique, but you substitute questioning for modeling. For instance, still using a paragraph altered as described, you would ask questions such as, "Why do you think the question to be answered is put first? Why is the phrase *high, grassy hill* underlined? Why is there an arrow from the question to the underlined phrase? What must you try to do when you have to answer questions about details and facts in a story?" This procedure should be repeated with other questions and other paragraphs as your questioning and highlighting devices are gradually diminished.

## • SUGGESTIONS FOR RETEACHING

If, after having been taught with either of the preceding techniques, the learner is unable to recall factual information, you should

1. Reteach the skill, using the alternate technique.
2. Be sure that the learner knows the meaning of each of the words being used in the selection.
3. Reteach the skill, using simplified material in which the answers to questions are more obvious.
4. Highlight more clearly both the question posed, the answer in the selection, and the connection between them.

## • SUGGESTIONS FOR PRACTICE

Once the learner is able to recall factual information, use one or more of the following practice activities to solidify the meaning.

1. Before reading a selection from a textbook or reader, put the following purpose-setting formula on the board:

Who?     Where?     When?     How many?     What happens?

Ask the learner to use this formula as a guide in his reading. Such a guide invariably will produce the details of a selection.

2. Before directing a learner to read a selection, set a purpose by asking the child how many things he or she can learn while reading. Direct the learner to make a tally mark on a paper as he or she reads, each mark standing for something learned while reading. Each mark will usually stand for a factual detail in the selection.

3. Before assigning a reading lesson, list key words from the selection on the board. Set the purpose by directing the learner to "find information about these words."

4. Prior to assigning a specific reading task, list several factual questions on the chalkboard as purpose setters. Direct the learner to find the answers to these specific questions while reading.

5. Teach learners how to set purposes for themselves by asking their own questions as they read. In the pretest selection on the Monarch butterfly, for example, train learners to anticipate factual information by listing for themselves some questions that they think they should be able to answer after having read the selection. At the conclusion of reading, they check to see how many of their questions they can answer, how many were not answeerd by the selection, and how many facts they had not anticipated in their questions.

6. Teach learners to use the SQ3R technique. This is a systematic purpose-setting study technique that is particularly effective with content textbooks. The five steps are:

*Survey, Question, Read, Recite, Review*

Before beginning their reading, learners are taught to *survey* a chapter or selection to get an idea of what it is about. They then examine the material, particularly the headings and subheadings, and pose *questions* for themselves that they should be able to answer when they have finished reading. They then *read* to answer their questions, *recite* to see whether they are now able to answer the questions, and *review* to find information relative to any question they were unable to answer. The first two steps in this technique, survey and question, are particularly appropriate to purpose setting because learners are actively involved in determining what they are trying to learn. They set the goals. It is *their* questions that guide their reading. This creates a relevance for learning that can be missing from other types of purpose setting.

## • THE POSTTEST

The procedure, directions, and criterion for mastery are the same for the posttest as for the pretest. Use the following paragraph and questions.

Next to the school there was a yard that had a big steam shovel in it. There was a fence around the yard and a sign on the fence said, "Stay out!" When the boys played ball, the ball went over the fence and they couldn't get it back. So a worker would pick up the ball with the steam shovel and drop it back into the school yard.

Where was the steam shovel?
What did the sign on the fence say?
How did the boys get their ball back when it went over the fence?

## • ENSURING TRANSFER

You should be sure that the learner uses factual recall skills during the routine daily activities of the classroom. For instance, during science and social studies lessons, factual questions should be posed and learners encouraged to use their skill to answer such questions. Further, factual recall should be incorporated into listening comprehension activities such as the one provided in the final chapter.

## • THE PERFORMANCE OBJECTIVE

Given an oral list of 12 words, the learner will classify each word according to three categories provided by the teacher.

## • THE PRETEST

Direct the learner to listen to the following list of words and to put each word into one of the following categories: sports, tools, farming. If any of these words are unfamiliar, select words that are part of the learner's background. The criterion for mastery is 17 out of 18 correct.

| home run | drill | skates | hammer | saw | crop |
| plowing | pitcher | hoe | football | fertilizer | screwdriver |
| touchdown | marbles | tractor | ax | harvester | barn |

## • DIRECTING THE LEARNER'S ATTENTION

The purpose of this task is to teach the learner how to classify words and determine a label for each category. This is similar to storehouse module I-MT-1. To teach this skill you must direct the learner's attention by highlighting the concepts associated with each content word and then the common denominator that allows them to be classified together. This common denominator leads to the labeling of the category.

## • TEACHING ACTIVITIES

This is a manipulative task similar to storehouse module I-MT-1, and you can adapt your teaching strategy from either the modeling or the discovery technique described in that objective.

## • SUGGESTIONS FOR RETEACHING

If, after having been taught with either the modeling or the discovery technique, the learner does not understand how to classify words and label concepts, you should adapt and use the suggestions in I-MT-1 to reteach the skill.

### • SUGGESTIONS FOR PRACTICE

After teaching the learner to classify, create practice activities to solidify the skill, using the suggestions provided in I-MT-1.

### • THE POSTTEST

The procedure and criterion for mastery are the same as for the pretest, although you may want to substitute new material.

### • ENSURING TRANSFER

You should use the suggestions I-MT-1 and listening comprehension activities such as those included in the final chapter to be sure that the learner applies classifying during the routine language activities in the classroom.

## III•MT•2

### • THE PERFORMANCE OBJECTIVE

When given a short oral paragraph, the learner will select an appropriate title for the paragraph from among three choices.

### • THE PRETEST

Read paragraphs like the following to the learner. After each, have the learner select the best title from among the three choices you read. The criterion for mastery is 100 percent.

> Some children went to the sea. They walked on the wet sand. They picked up colored stones and little starfish.
> Sam said, "It is fun to find things by the sea."

> What is the best title for this story?
> Sam Watched the Parade
> Mary and the Big Stone
> Finding Things by the Sea

> Dick and Mike liked to race on the wet sand. They would run to an old boat on the sand. Father watched them to see who would win the race.

> What is the best title for this story?
> A Big Stone
> A Race on the Sand
> The Airplane Race

### • DIRECTING THE LEARNER'S ATTENTION

The purpose of this task is to teach the learner to pick out the main idea in a paragraph. It is a manipulative thinking skill similar to classifying since both tasks require the learner to find the common focus of a group of words or concepts; both require that the learner use a categorizing procedure to extract the common denominator. This is a crucial comprehension skill since main idea thinking allows the learner to listen to or read hundreds and hundreds of words about a subject and identify the point of it all after finishing. Consequently, this is the first in a series of objectives that help the learner determine main ideas.

To teach main idea thinking you must be sure that the topic reflects the learner's background, that he or she knows the meaning of each word in the selection, and that he or she has mastered the prerequisite classifying skills. Then you must direct the learner's attention to the facts in the paragraph, to the common denominator of these facts that allows them to be categorized together, and to the one title of the three offered that reflects this category. (In the first pretest paragraph, for instance, you might highlight phrases such as *went to the sea, walked on wet sand, picked up colored stones and little starfish,* and *find things by the sea;* categorize them as looking for things by the sea; and then match that category to the title "Finding Things by the Sea.")

### • THIS IS A STOREHOUSE OBJECTIVE

The following instructional activities are your storehouse of techniques for teaching main ideas. This skill will recur in more sophisticated form as the learner progresses through the skill hierarchy. The activities that follow are to be adapted and used with each of these as they occur.

### • TEACHING ACTIVITIES

*The modeling technique.* After making sure that the prerequisite experiences, word meanings, and classifying skills are present, provide the learner with a paragraph such as the first pretest selection in which the key facts have been highlighted. Say to the learner, "The facts of the paragraph deal with the sea, walking on the sand, picking up colored stones and starfish, and finding things by the sea. If I were to put all these facts together, I could say they are all related because they all have something to do with looking for things by the sea. Now I look at the three suggested titles. Only the third title has anything to do with looking for things by the sea, so this would be the best title. Now let's look at the next paragraph and see if you can do as I did." Repeat the procedure in subsequent paragraphs, gradually reducing the amount of highlighting and the modeling until the learner is doing the main idea thinking alone.

*The discovery technique.* For this technique retain the paragraph with highlighted facts but substitute questioning for modeling, as follows. Say, "Look at the facts of the paragraph. Using your previously learned classifying skills, how would you group these facts together? How would you label the category in which all these facts would fit?" Once the learner has decided upon a category, have him examine the three possible titles, saying, "Now look at the titles you must choose from. Which of these describes a category that is almost the same as the one you described?" Repeat this procedure with other paragraphs, gradually reducing the highlighting on the facts and the amount of direction you provide through questioning until the learner is able to do the thinking independently.

## • SUGGESTIONS FOR RETEACHING

If, after having been taught with either of the preceding techniques, the learner is unable to find the main idea of a paragraph, you should

1. Reteach the skill, using the alternate technique.
2. Recheck to make sure that the learner possesses the prerequisite experience, word meanings, and classifying skills.
3. Simplify the task by substituting paragraphs in which the main idea is more clearly obtained through classification.
4. Increase the highlighting on the facts and the way in which they can be related or cataloged to form a main idea.

## • SUGGESTIONS FOR PRACTICE

Once the learner is able to pick out the main idea, adapt and use one or more of the following practice activities to solidify the skill.

1. Select a well-written informational paragraph. Put the paragraph's individual phrases on the chalkboard, direct each learner to examine each phrase and use their classifying skills to make their own phrase that expresses the part common to the others, as in the following example.

> Can your learners do today the skill you taught them last week?

    Brushing teeth regularly
    Bathing frequently
    Eating well-balanced meals
    Getting enough rest
    Getting regular exercise

   The main idea might be **Good Health Habits.**

2. Use the "telegram" technique. Direct your learners to read the paragraph and decide what words could be omitted without losing the meaning. Explain that they are going to send the paragraph as a telegram and will have to pay for each word. What is left will be a selection of the main idea and essential supporting details.
3. Make "stand-up" paragraphs. They can be fun and they can teach main idea and detail skills. Select a learner to stand in front of the class and think up a key topic sentence. (This might have to be supplied at first.) Other members of the class think up details that elaborate on the topic sentence. As each adds an important detail, the child stands behind the learner who made the topic sentence. The paragraph becomes a row of learners starting at the front of the room. When all the "sentences" have taken their places, have them repeat their sentences one after the other and then construct the paragraph. Don't be afraid to have sentences rearranged or even omitted if they do not belong.
4. Ask a question: "Did you have a good time over the weekend?" Answers should be either oral or written, giving reasons one, two, three, and so forth. The sentence that answers the question is the main idea, and the listed reasons are the supporting detail.

5. Teach learners to anticipate where the main idea is likely to occur. For example, at the lower reading levels the main idea is invariably the first or last sentence. If the structure of such paragraphs is analyzed and graphically illustrated for learners, they will have a strategy for finding the main idea. That is, they will look at the first and last sentences and see if this communicates the point of it all in the paragraph. One good way to illustrate paragraph structure graphically is to compare paragraphs to triangles; paragraphs with the main idea first are structured as $\triangle$ and those with the main ideas last are structured as $\triangledown$.

### • THE POSTTEST
The procedure, directions, and criterion are the same as for the pretest. Use the following paragraphs.

> Ann made a sand house with a little stone walk. Then the sea came and splashed over the house. It covered the sand house and took it away.

> What is the best name for this story?
> > Ann's Sand House
> > A Little Stone Walk
> > A Garden in the Sand

> Joe watches the children. He does not like to swim. He does not like the big splash of the sea. Joe does not like to get wet. The children laugh to see Joe run away from the sea.

> What is the best name for this story?
> > Joe Likes to Swim
> > Joe at the Sea
> > Joe Runs to the Water

### • ENSURING TRANSFER
You should be sure that main idea thinking is used as a thinking tool during the routine daily activities of the classroom. At the earliest stages of reading your learners can be directed, "There are three important ideas in this social studies lesson. See if you can use main idea thinking to find them as you read." Further, main idea thinking should be incorporated in listening comprehension activities found in the final chapter.

## III•MT•3

### • THE PERFORMANCE OBJECTIVE
When given an oral paragraph and a question about the paragraph that requires inferential thinking, the learner will supply details that are implied but not stated in the paragraph.

### • THE PRETEST
Direct the learner to listen to each of the following paragraphs and to complete the final sentence in each paragraph by choosing one of the three oral

answers provided. The criterion for mastery is 75 percent. (Readability: Second grade.)

Three men bought plane tickets. They bought tickets for three different places. Each one wanted to see for himself what the world was like.

Each man was going to ———.
    fly to a different place
    sell airplane tickets
    fly to the same place

The man flew in a white plane. The plane landed in a flat white field of snow. The wind blew. It was very cold. The man buttoned his coat.

This man said, "———."
    The world is warm
    The world is a cold place
    The wind is very warm

The man's plane flew high across the sky. It landed in a quiet place. A boy was watching his sheep. All around were fields of green grass.

This man said, "———."
    The world is cold
    The world is not quiet
    The world is quiet

The last man took a short trip in a seaplane. The plane landed on the water. The man looked around. There was nothing but water as far as he could see.

This man said, "———."
    The world is round
    The world is not water
    All the world is water

### • DIRECTING THE LEARNER'S ATTENTION

The purpose of this task is to teach the learner how to supply details that are inferred but not stated. This is similar to storehouse module I-MT-2. To teach this skill you must direct the learner's attention to the elements of the material that imply other details not directly stated.

### • TEACHING ACTIVITIES

This is a manipulative task similar to storehouse module I-MT-2, and you can adapt your teaching strategy from either the modeling or the discovering technique described in that objective.

### • SUGGESTIONS FOR RETEACHING

If, after being taught with either the modeling or the discovery technique, the learner does not understand how to supply inferred details, you should adapt and use the suggestions in I-MT-2 to reteach the skill.

## • SUGGESTIONS FOR PRACTICE

After teaching the learner how to supply inferred details, create practice activities to solidify the skill, using the suggestions provided in I-MT-2.

## • THE POSTTEST

The procedure and criterion for mastery are the same as for the pretest, although you may want to substitute new material.

## • ENSURING TRANSFER

You should use the suggestions in I-MT-2 and listening comprehension activities such as those included in the final chapter to be sure that the learner applies the skill of supplying inferred details during the routine language activities in the classroom.

# III•ET•1

## • THE PERFORMANCE OBJECTIVE

When given a short oral story containing an unlikely reference to time and sequence, the learner will identify the event that does not fit and tell why.

## • THE PRETEST

Direct the learner to listen to each paragraph and to tell you what happens in the story that does not make sense or that could not really happen. Criterion for mastery is 100 percent. (Readability: Second grade.)

> The pioneer was getting ready to go hunting. He was about to leave his log cabin. Then he remembered. He had forgotten his gun. He went back to get it. Then he got into his car and started off.

> The pioneer hunted all day long. He shot a deer and two squirrels. He started to go home. He was thinking about the good supper he would cook for himself. As he came close to his log cabin, he saw that the sun was just coming up in the east. "What a good day this has been," he said.

> The pioneer began to clean the deer and squirrels so that he could cook them for his supper. Then he saw that he didn't have enough wood to build a fire to cook with. So the pioneer picked up the telephone and called the store for more wood.

## • DIRECTING THE LEARNER'S ATTENTION

The purpose of this task is to teach the learner how to judge which event does not fit in a story and why. This is similar to storehouse module I-ET-1. To teach this skill you must direct the learner's attention to the event that does not fit the story to other elements that signal why it does not fit.

## • TEACHING ACTIVITIES

This is an evaluative thinking task similar to storehouse module I-ET-1, and you can adapt your teaching strategy from either the modeling or the discovery technique described in that objective.

## ● SUGGESTIONS FOR RETEACHING

If, after having been taught with either the modeling or the discovery technique, the learner does not understand how to judge the event that does not fit, you should adapt and use the suggestions in I-ET-1 to reteach the skill.

## ● SUGGESTIONS FOR PRACTICE

After teaching the learner the skill of judging which event does not fit the story, create practice activities to solidify the skill, using the suggestions provided in I-MT-1.

## ● THE POSTTEST

The procedure and criterion for mastery are the same as for the pretest, although you may want to substitute new material.

## ● ENSURING TRANSFER

You should use the suggestions in I-MT-1 and listening comprehension activities such as those included in the final chapter to be sure that the learner applies this thinking skill.

# CLUSTER IV

- **THE PERFORMANCE OBJECTIVE**

When given a fraction of a second to examine flashcards having printed on them the following words, the learner will pronounce each within one second.

| | | | |
|---|---|---|---|
| girl | by | bear | them |
| turn | as | please | cage |
| picture | boy | their | there |
| any | balloon | which | day |
| talk | before | her | pull |
| after | how | build | tomorrow |
| head | off | old | again |
| eye | been | am | our |

- **THE PRETEST**

Print each of the words in the preceding list on a flashcard. Flash each to the learner, giving him or her less than one second to examine each word before pronouncing it. The criterion for mastery is 100 percent.

- **DIRECTING THE LEARNER'S ATTENTION**

The purpose of this task is to teach the learner to recognize instantly and pronounce the words contained in the pretest when they are presented on flashcards. This is a sight word recognition skill like that described in II-SW-6. To teach the skill you must make sure that the learner knows exactly what is to be learned, that the words being taught are in the child's speaking vocabulary, and that you have directed his or her attention by highlighting the unique visual characteristics of each word (such as the initial and final letters, length, shape, double letters, and so on.)

• TEACHING ACTIVITIES

This is a sight word recognition skill similar to that described in II-SW-6. If the learner does not recognize the word in print, adapt your teaching strategy from either the modeling technique or the discovery technique described in that objective. If the child confuses the word with another word similar to it, adapt your strategy from the suggestions contained in I-SW-17.

• SUGGESTIONS FOR RETEACHING

If, after having been taught with the suggested technique, the learner is unable to recognize instantly one or more of the words on the pretest, use the reteaching suggestions described in II-SW-6.

• SUGGESTIONS FOR PRACTICE

After successfully teaching the learner to recognize instantly the words on the pretest, create practice activities to solidify the skill using the suggestions provided in II-SW-6.

• THE POSTTEST

The procedure and criterion for mastery for the posttest are the same as for the pretest.

• ENSURING TRANSFER

To be sure that this skill is applied, you must give the learner reading material containing the words now known at sight and have him or her read. You may guide the application by pointing out the words the child has just learned to recognize or, as he or she becomes more proficient, you can encourage independent reading of the newly learned words. Any material at the learner's instructional reading level that contains the learned sight words would be appropriate. Additional suggestions for helping the learner use known sight words in context are contained in II-SW-6.

# IV•SW•2

• THE PERFORMANCE OBJECTIVE

When given a flash presentation of words the learner frequently confuses, he or she will pronounce each word correctly within one second.

• THE PRETEST

You will note whether the learner is confusing words any time you test him or her on sight words or listen to him or her read. If, during either of these activities, the learner says one word for another (such as **father** for **after**), you should pair the words together and teach them, using the suggestions provided in this objective. No specific list of words is provided since various learners will confuse various words. As with other sight word objectives, the criterion for mastery is 100 percent, with any pair of confused words being taught.

### • DIRECTING THE LEARNER'S ATTENTION

The purpose of this task is to teach the learner to recognize instantly pairs of words he or she has tended to confuse in the past. As such, this task is similar to that described in I-SW-17. To teach this skill you must be sure that the learner has mastered the previous visual training skill, that he or she knows exactly what is to be learned, that the words being taught are in his or her speaking vocabulary, and that you have directed his attention by highlighting the discriminator that sets one word apart from the other (such as the left-to-right letter sequence in **after** and **father.**)

### • TEACHING ACTIVITIES

In teaching this skill you can use either the modeling technique or the discovery technique described in I-SW-17, adjusting the suggestions to focus on the particular words the learner is confusing.

What do you have planned for today that is really exciting and different?

### • SUGGESTIONS FOR RETEACHING

If, after having been taught this skill with either the modeling or the discovery technique, the learner continues to confuse the words, you should use the reteaching suggestions provided in I-SW-17.

### • SUGGESTIONS FOR PRACTICE

Once the learner can instantly recognize the words that were previously being confused, create practice activities to solidify the skill, using the suggestions provided in I-SW-17.

### • THE POSTTEST

The procedure and criterion for mastery are the same as for the pretest.

### • ENSURING TRANSFER

Once the learner can recognize the easily confused words, you should immediately provide opportunities to apply this skill by giving the child reading material containing the words now known at sight. For specific suggestions regarding such application activities, see II-SW-6.

## IV•SW•3

### • THE PERFORMANCE OBJECTIVE

Given words that he or she recognizes instantly, the learner creates and reads a single-sentence story using these words.

## • THE PRETEST

Provide cards each of which has printed on it a word the learner instantly recognizes. Say to the learner, "Today, we are going to do something that is very hard. We are going to send messages. Look at the cards you have in front of you. Each card has a word on it that you know. Can you send me a message using the words you have there? If you want to send a message using a word you don't have on a card, tell me and I will make a card for you having that word on it." The criterion for mastery is the combination of any number of words in a way that is grammatically accurate and that makes sense. When the learner has formed his sentence, reinforce the value of the effort by reading it aloud yourself.

## • DIRECTING THE LEARNER'S ATTENTION

This is a language experience activity designed to teach the learner to produce and read messages using individual words he or she knows at sight. As such, it is an application activity similar to that described in II-SW-8. To teach this activity you must be sure that the learner knows exactly what is to be learned and you must direct attention to the idea that is to be conveyed, to what the message will sound like when spoken, to what printed word cards he or she will need to "write" the message, and to the order in which the words must be placed. You might highlight by asking a series of questions such as, "What did you do yesterday after school that you could tell me about? Can you make a sentence about that and say it to me? What words did you use to say your sentence to me? How many of those words do you already have on cards and which ones will we have to make for you? What word will come first in your written message?"

## • TEACHING ACTIVITIES

This is a language experience activity similar to that described in II-SW-8. You should use the modeling and discovery techniques described in that objective as a basis for planning and teaching this task.

## • SUGGESTIONS FOR RETEACHING

If, after having been taught with either of the techniques described in the key objective, the learner is unable to create a single-sentence message using his or her sight words, you should

1. Reteach the activity, using the alternate technique.
2. Be more specific in eliciting the idea the learner wishes to convey.
3. Be sure that the learner expresses the message first in oral form and understands that the written message will say the same thing as the oral message.
4. Be sure that the content of the message matches the learner's experience, changing the subject to match the child's experience if necessary.
5. Recheck the learner's mastery of the sight words, reteaching any that have not yet been completely mastered.

6. Return to the previous language experience objectives and make sure the learner can do those simpler tasks before asking him or her to create entire sentences.

## • SUGGESTIONS FOR PRACTICE

Once the learner has been taught to use sight words to create and read sentences, devise practice activities to solidify this skill, adapting the suggestions provided in II-SW-8.

## • THE POSTTEST

The procedure and criterion for mastery for the posttest are the same as for the pretest.

## • ENSURING TRANSFER

This objective is an application activity designed to help the learner use the sight words in context. In addition to the application specified here, however, you should use the suggestions in II-SW-6 to make sure that the learner uses the sight words in other contextual situations.

## • THE PERFORMANCE OBJECTIVE

Given a known word composed of the vowel-consonant phonograms –en, –in, or –an, the learner will replace the initial consonant in each word with another consonant, digraph, or blend he or she knows and pronounce the new word.

## • THE PRETEST

Use the following lists of words. The first word in each list has been previously taught as a sight word or has been previously analyzed. Read the first word in each list and ask the learner to pronounce the remaining words in each list. The criterion for mastery is 18 out of 21 correct with no initial consonant, digraph, or blend being missed more than once. *Note:* Some of the words listed are nonsense words, which are included so that the learner *must* use analysis rather than sight recognition.

| ten | | in | | | can | | |
|-----|-----|-----|-----|-----|-----|-----|-----|
| men | when | tin | chin | thin | fan | bran | plan |
| then | slen | fin | grin | shin | tan | clan | shan |
| | | sin | win | drin | than | gran | |

## • DIRECTING THE LEARNER'S ATTENTION

The purpose of this task is to teach the learner to use his knowledge of letter substitution and short vowels to pronounce words ending in –en, –in, and –an. As such, this task is similar to storehouse module II-WA-18. To teach this skill you must direct the learner's attention by stating exactly what is to be learned and by highlighting the initial sound and the common ending. (In the word **men,** for instance, you might circle the **–en** and underline the initial **m,** having the learner use the say-it-slow, say-it-fast technique (see I-WA-5) in pronouncing the word.)

● **TEACHING ACTIVITIES**

In teaching this letter substitution skill you can use either the modeling technique or the discovery technique described in II-WA-18, adjusting the suggestions to focus on the **–en, –in,** and **–an** endings.

● **SUGGESTIONS FOR RETEACHING**

If, after having been taught this skill with either the modeling or the discovery technique, the learner is unable to substitute **–en, –in,** and **–an** endings and pronounce new words, you should use the reteaching suggestions provided in II-WA-18.

● **SUGGESTIONS FOR PRACTICE**

Once the learner can substitute **–en, –in,** and **–an** and pronounce the new words, you should create practice activities to solidify the skill, using the suggestions provided in II-WA-18.

● **THE POSTTEST**

The pretest can also be used as the posttest. The procedure and criterion for mastery are the same.

● **ENSURING TRANSFER**

You should use the suggestions provided in II-WA-18 to make sure that the learner uses this skill in the daily reading activities.

# IV•WA•2

● **THE PERFORMANCE OBJECTIVE**

Given a stimulus word beginning with the consonant blends **sk, sw, sm, sn, sp,** or **st** and a group of three other words, one of which begins with **sk, sw, sm, sn, sp,** or **st,** the learner will pair the two words beginning with the same sound.

● **THE PRETEST**

Using the following lists, say to the learner, "Here are three words. Listen carefully. (Say the words.) Which one sounds like (say the stimulus word) at the beginning?" Repeat the three words. Criterion for mastery is 11 out of 12 correct.

| slip | skim | sin | Which one sounds like **sky** at the beginning? Repeat the three words. |

| | | | |
|---|---|---|---|
| swan | sun | skip | Which one sounds like **swing** at the beginning?<br>Repeat the three words. |
| some | fall | smack | Which one sounds like **small** at the beginning?<br>Repeat the three words. |
| swap | sneak | smart | Which one sounds like **snake** at the beginning?<br>Repeat the three words. |
| space | save | soon | Which one sounds like **spoon** at the beginning?<br>Repeat the three words. |
| slap | staff | snow | Which one sounds like **stick** at the beginning?<br>Repeat the three words. |
| smooth | some | snob | Which one sounds like **small** at the beginning?<br>Repeat the three words. |
| sell | sew | swell | Which one sounds like **swing** at the beginning?<br>Repeat the three words. |
| soon | skit | fly | Which one sounds like **sky** at the beginning?<br>Repeat the three words. |
| sun | bake | snort | Which one sounds like **snake** at the beginning?<br>Repeat the three words. |
| stock | block | sick | Which one sounds like **stick** at the beginning?<br>Repeat the three words. |
| still | spot | soap | Which one sounds like **spoon** at the beginning?<br>Repeat the three words. |

Does your skill instruction end with the skill group or do you make sure that your learners apply these skills in their daily reading?

- **DIRECTING THE LEARNER'S ATTENTION**

The purpose of this task is to teach the learner to distinguish the s blends from among other beginning consonant sounds. As such, the task is similar to storehouse module I-WA-5. To teach this skill you must direct the learner's attention by stating exactly what is to be learned and by highlighting the beginning s blend in the words as described in I-WA-5.

- **TEACHING ACTIVITIES**

In teaching this auditory discrimination skill you can use either the modeling technique or the discovery technique described in I-WA-5, adjusting the suggestions to focus on the s blends.

- **SUGGESTIONS FOR RETEACHING**

If, after having been taught this skill with either the modeling or the discovery technique, the learner is unable to discriminate by ear the s blends from among other beginning consonant sounds, you should

1. Reteach the skill, using the alternate technique.
2. Reexamine your attenders, making sure that the learner is listening to the *beginning* sounds and that your highlighting is emphatic enough to help him or her distinguish the beginning s blend from other sounds.
3. Return to the previous auditory discrimination skills, making sure that the learner can distinguish single consonant sounds before requiring him or her to distinguish the s blends.

#### • SUGGESTIONS FOR PRACTICE

Once the learner can distinguish the s blends from among other beginning consonant sounds, create practice activities to solidify the skill, using the suggestions provided in I-WA-5.

#### • THE POSTTEST

The procedure and criterion for mastery are the same as for the pretest.

| | | | |
|---|---|---|---|
| skeleton | speed | sun | Which one sounds like **sky** at the beginning? Repeat the three words. |
| sag | snag | stag | Which one sounds like **sky** at the beginning? Repeat the three words. |
| pear | soon | spice | Which one sounds like **spoon** at the beginning? Repeat the three words. |
| swamp | slip | sing | Which one sounds like **swing** at the beginning? Repeat the three words. |
| sell | smash | tall | Which one sounds like **small** at the beginning? Repeat the three words. |
| sand | stand | span | Which one sounds like **stick** at the beginning? Repeat the three words. |
| see | clear | sneer | Which one sounds like **snake** at the beginning? Repeat the three words. |
| spoil | soil | stiff | Which one sounds like **spoon** at the beginning? Repeat the three words. |
| slick | stool | spool | Which one sounds like **stick** at the beginning? Repeat the three words. |
| suds | fudge | smudge | Which one sounds like **small** at the beginning? Repeat the three words. |
| stitch | sling | switch | Which one sounds like **swing** at the beginning? Repeat the three words. |

| sketch | stretch | sweat | Which one sounds like **sky** at the beginning? Repeat the three words. |

### • ENSURING TRANSFER

Although the learner will be applying this skill as he learns to attach the sounds to letters in subsequent objectives, you should also use the suggestions provided in I-WA-5 to make sure that the learner uses the skill during his daily reading activities in the classroom.

### • THE PERFORMANCE OBJECTIVE

When given spoken words beginning with the **sk, sw, sm, sn, sp,** and **st** sounds, the learner will identify the beginning letters in each word.

### • THE PRETEST

Give the learner six cards, with each card having printed on it one of the blends being tested (**sk, sw, sm, sn, sp,** or **st**). Say the following words, directing the learner to point to the letter card whose sound begins the word. The criterion for mastery is 11 out of 12 correct.

| snarl | stain | swat | skull | swift | stuff |
| spark | skid | small | snob | spy | smother |

### • DIRECTING THE LEARNER'S ATTENTION

The purpose of this task is to teach the learner to establish a sound-symbol connection between the letters **sk, sw, sm, sn, sp,** and **st** and the sound heard at the beginning of words beginning with these letter combinations. As such, this task is similar to storehouse module I-WA-9. To teach this skill you must direct the learner's attention by stating exactly what is to be learned and by highlighting both the sound heard at the beginning of the word and the form of the letter combination with which it is to be connected. (In the word **snarl,** for instance, you might exaggerate the beginning sound of the **sn** blend while simultaneously pointing to the cutout letters **sn.**)

### • TEACHING ACTIVITIES

In teaching this sound-symbol connection skill you can use either the modeling technique or the discovery technique described in I-WA-9, adjusting the suggestions to focus on the beginning s blends.

### • SUGGESTIONS FOR RETEACHING

If, after having been taught this skill with either the modeling or the discovery technique, the learner is unable to connect letter and sound for the s blends, you should

1. Reteach the skill using the alternate technique.
2. Be more specific in directing attention, making sure that the learner is listening to the beginning sound while simultaneously looking at the letter combination.
3. Use more emphasis in highlighting the beginning sound, the letter, and the connection between them.
4. Return to the previous objective and make sure that the learner can distinguish the s blends from among other beginning consonant sounds before requiring him or her to connect the sound with a letter combination.

● **SUGGESTIONS FOR PRACTICE**

Once the learner has successfully connected the s blend letter combination to the appropriate sounds, create practice activities to solidify the skill, using the suggestions in I-WA-9.

● **THE POSTTEST**

The procedure and criterion for mastery remain the same as for the pretest. Use the following words.

| | | | | | |
|---|---|---|---|---|---|
| stake | swim | snail | smoke | skip | speech |
| smart | spade | skill | swap | steam | snap |

● **ENSURING TRANSFER**

Although the learner will be applying this skill in subsequent skills in the hierarchy, you should also use the suggestions provided in I-WA-9 to be sure that the learner uses the skill during his routine daily reading activities.

**IV•WA•4**

● **THE PERFORMANCE OBJECTIVE**

When given an oral sentence with one word missing and cued for the missing word with a card having printed on it the blend with which the word begins (sk, sw, sm, sn, sp, or st), the learner will say a word beginning with the letter blend that fits the context of the sentence.

● **THE PRETEST**

Make cards with the preceding letter blends printed on them. Say, "I am going to say a sentence with one word missing. You look at the card and say a word that begins with the letter blend on the card and that finishes what I want to say." Use the following sentences. The criterion for mastery is 10 out of 12 correct, with no letter blend being missed more than once. *Note:* If a sentence fails to match a learner's background or does not provide enough context for him, you should alter the sentence accordingly. Sentence 1, for instance could be changed to read, "We saw the hockey players sk_____ around the ice rink."

1. When it is cold and the pond freezes, we like to go sk_____.
2. I used the broom to sw_____ the floor.
3. You could tell the girl was happy because she was sm_____.
4. It was cold outside and there was a lot of sn_____ on the ground.
5. I knocked over the glass and the milk sp_____.
6. When the bell rang, I ran up the st_____ into school.
7. The bug was so sm_____ that you could hardly see it.
8. When you sleep, do you sn_____ and make other noises?
9. The candy was sticky and sw_____.
10. Most people don't like the smell of a sk_____.
11. I am sick and I am going to have to st_____ at home.
12. Baseball is my favorite sp_____.

### • DIRECTING THE LEARNER'S ATTENTION

The purpose of this task is to teach the learner to use his or her knowledge of s blend letter-sound correspondence and context to identify unknown words. As such, the task is similar to storehouse module I-WA-14. To teach this skill you must direct the learner's attention by stating exactly what is to be learned and by highlighting the words in the sentence that provide clues to the identity of the unknown word, the letter combination the unknown word begins with, and the sound associated with that letter combination. (In the first sentence of the pretest, for instance, you might highlight the words **pond, freezes,** and **like,** and direct the learner to look at the large cutout **sk** and "get his mouth ready to say" the sound of the letter combination.)

### • TEACHING ACTIVITIES

In teaching this context-letter-sound skill you can use either the modeling technique or the discovery technique described in I-WA-14, adjusting the suggestions to focus on the s blend letter combinations.

### • SUGGESTIONS FOR RETEACHING

If, after having been taught this skill with either the modeling or the discovery technique, the learner is unable to use context and s blends to identify unknown words, you should use the reteaching suggestions provided in WA-14.

### • SUGGESTIONS FOR PRACTICE

Once the learner has successfully used the s blends and context to identify unknown words, create practice activities to solidify the skill, using the suggestions provided in I-WA-14.

### • THE POSTTEST

The procedure and criterion for mastery are the same as for the pretest. Use the following sentences.

1. My mother is baking cookies and they sm_____ good.
2. The policeman chased the man and made him st_____.
3. The young Indian warrior threw his sp_____ at the charging buffalo.
4. I can run faster when I have my new sn_____ on.
5. It was so hot outside that the sw_____ was dripping down my face.
6. In the wintertime we like to sk_____ down the big hill.
7. I ate so much that my st_____ was full.
8. The fly got caught in the cobweb and was eaten by the sp_____.
9. The little girl was frightened by the sn_____ she saw in the grass.
10. The boy got all the answers right because he is so sm_____.
11. He loves to go to the pool to sw_____.
12. The girl wore her new blouse and sk_____ to school.

## • ENSURING TRANSFER

You should use the suggestions provided in I-WA-14 to be sure that the learner uses the skill during the daily reading activities in the classroom.

# IV•WA•5

## • THE PERFORMANCE OBJECTIVE

When given key words learned in previous objectives, the learner will replace the initial consonants with an s-blend and pronounce the new words.

## • THE PRETEST

Use the following lists of words. The first word in each list has been previously taught. Read the first word in the list and ask the learner to pronounce the remaining words in each list. The criterion for mastery is 28 out of 31 correct. *Note:* Some of the words listed are nonsense words, which are included so that the learner *must* use analysis rather than sight recognition.

| bit | in | sip | back | crock | cap |
|------|------|-------|-------|-------|-------|
| skit | skin | skip | smack | smock | snap |
| slit | spin | snip | smash | spock | snack |
| | | spick | swash | | smack |
| | | sniff | | | slack |
| | | swiff | | | |

| not | tan | top | sun | him |
|------|------|------|-------|------|
| snot | span | stop | stun | swim |
| spot | stan | snop | stuck | stim |
| smot | | | snuck | |
| | | | skuck | |

## • DIRECTING THE LEARNER'S ATTENTION

The purpose of this skill is to teach the learner to substitute s blends in the initial position of known short vowel phonograms and to pronounce the new words. As such, this task is similar to storehouse module II-WA-18. To teach this skill you must direct the learner's attention by stating exactly what is to be learned and by highlighting the initial s blend and the letters that are common from word to word. (In the word **skit,** for instance, you might circle the **sk** blend, underline the **–it,** and have the learner use the say-it-slow, say-it-fast technique (see I-WA-5) in pronouncing the word.)

● **TEACHING ACTIVITIES**

In teaching this letter substitution skill you can use either the modeling technique or the discovery technique described in II-WA-18, adjusting the suggestions to focus on the s blends in the initial position.

● **SUGGESTIONS FOR RETEACHING**

If, after having been taught this skill with either the modeling or the discovery technique, the learner is unable to substitute s blends in the initial position of known short vowel phonograms and pronounce the new words, you should use the reteaching suggestions provided in II-WA-18.

● **SUGGESTIONS FOR PRACTICE**

Once the learner can substitute s blends in the initial position of known short vowel phonograms, create practice activities to solidify the skill, using the suggestions provided in II-WA-18.

● **THE POSTTEST**

The pretest can also be used as the posttest. The procedure and criterion for mastery are the same.

● **ENSURING TRANSFER**

You should use the suggestions provided in II-WA-18 to be sure that this skill is used by the learner during the daily reading activities in the classroom.

# IV•WA•6

● **THE PERFORMANCE OBJECTIVE**

When given a spoken stimulus word ending with the st sound and a group of three words one of which ends with the st sound, the learner will pair the two words that end with the st sound.

● **THE PRETEST**

Using the following words, say to the learner, "Here are three words. Listen carefully. (Say the three words.) Which one sounds like (say the stimulus word) at the end?" Repeat the three words. The criterion for mastery is four out of five correct.

| | | | |
|---|---|---|---|
| land | back | nest | Which one sounds like **lost** at the end?<br>Repeat the three words. |
| crust | crush | truck | Which one sounds like **lost** at the end?<br>Repeat the three words. |
| fall | bat | blast | Which one sounds like **lost** at the end?<br>Repeat the three words. |
| chess | close | chest | Which one sounds like **lost** at the end?<br>Repeat the three words. |
| fuss | loss | just | Which one sounds like **lost** at the end?<br>Repeat the three words. |

### • DIRECTING THE LEARNER'S ATTENTION

The purpose of this task is to teach the learner to distinguish the **st** ending sound from other ending consonant sounds. As such, this task is similar to storehouse module I-WA-5. To teach this skill you must direct the learner's attention by stating exactly what is to be learned and by highlighting the ending **st** sound of the words as described in I-WA-5.

### • TEACHING ACTIVITIES

Do you have a good working relationship with your librarian?

In teaching this auditory discrimination skill you can use either the modeling technique or the discovery technique described in I-WA-5, adjusting the suggestions to focus on the **st** ending.

### • SUGGESTIONS FOR RETEACHING

If, after having been taught this skill with either the modeling or the discovery technique, the learner is unable to distinguish by ear the –st ending from among other ending consonant sounds, you should

1. Reteach the skill, using the alternate technique.
2. Reexamine your attenders, making sure that the learner is listening to the *ending* sounds and that your highlighting is emphatic enough to help him or her distinguish the ending –st from among other sounds.
3. Return to the previous auditory discrimination skills, making sure that the learner can distinguish between other ending sounds before requiring completion of this objective.

### • SUGGESTIONS FOR PRACTICE

Once the learner can distinguish the ending –st sound from other ending consonant sounds, create practice activities to solidify the skill, using the suggestions provided in I-WA-5.

### • THE POSTTEST

The procedure and criterion for mastery are the same as for the pretest. Use the following words.

| | | | |
|---|---|---|---|
| thrust | throw | truck | Which one sounds like **lost** at the end? Repeat the three words. |
| fact | last | back | Which one sounds like **lost** at the end? Repeat the three words. |
| crush | crest | crunch | Which one sounds like **lost** at the end? Repeat the three words. |
| best | bet | let | Which one sounds like **lost** at the end? Repeat the three words. |
| mud | luck | must | Which one sounds like **lost** at the end? Repeat the three words. |

### • ENSURING TRANSFER

Although the learner will be applying this skill while learning to attach the sounds to letters in subsequent objectives, you should also use the suggestions provided in I-WA-5 to be sure that the learner uses the skill in daily reading activities in the classroom.

### • THE PERFORMANCE OBJECTIVE

When given a spoken word, the learner will point to the letters **st** if the word ends in the **st** sound.

### • THE PRETEST

Give the learner a card having the letters **st** printed on it. Say the following words, directing the learner to point to the **st** card each time a word is spoken that ends with that sound. The criterion for mastery is four out of five correct.

> desk    best    fast    least    lease

### • DIRECTING THE LEARNER'S ATTENTION

The purpose of this task is to teach the learner to establish a sound-symbol connection between the letters **st** and the sound these letters make at the end of words. As such, this task is similar to storehouse module I-WA-9. To teach this skill you must direct the learner's attention by stating exactly what is to be learned and by highlighting both the sound heard at the end of the word and the form of the letter combination with which it is to be connected. (In the word **best**, for instance, you might exaggerate the ending sound of –st while simultaneously pointing to the cutout letters **st**.)

### • TEACHING ACTIVITIES

In teaching this sound-symbol connection skill you can use either the modeling technique or the discovery technique described in I-WA-9, adjusting the suggestions to focus on the ending –st sounds.

### • SUGGESTIONS FOR RETEACHING

If, after having been taught this skill with either the modeling or the discovery technique, the learner is unable to connect letter and sound for the ending –st, you should

● 323

1. Reteach the skill, using the alternate technique.
2. Be more specific in directing the learner's attention, making sure that he or she is listening to the *ending* sound while simultaneously looking at the letter combination.
3. Use more emphasis in highlighting the ending sound, the letter, and the connection between them.
4. Return to the previous objective and make sure that the learner can distinguish the –st ending sound from among other ending sounds before requiring him or her to connect the sound to a letter combination.

## • SUGGESTIONS FOR PRACTICE

Once the learner has successfully connected the **st** letter combination to the appropriate sound, create practice activities to solidify the skill, using the suggestions provided in I-WA-9.

## • THE POSTTEST

The procedure and criterion for mastery are the same as for the pretest. Use the following words.

flesh    chest    cast    flask    test

## • ENSURING TRANSFER

Although the learner will be applying this skill in subsequent skills in the hierarchy, you should also use the suggestions provided in I-WA-9 to be sure that the learner uses the skill during daily reading activities in the classroom.

# IV•WA•8

## • THE PERFORMANCE OBJECTIVE

When given words pronounced in previous objectives, the learner will replace the final consonant sound with the **st** sound, substitute initial sounds he or she knows, and pronounce the new words.

## • THE PRETEST

Use the following word lists. The first word in each list has been previously taught as a sight word or has been analyzed in previous objectives. Read the first word in each list and ask the learner to pronounce the remaining words. The criterion for mastery is 12 out of 14 correct. *Note:* Some of the words listed are nonsense words, which are included so that the learner *must* use analysis rather than sight recognition.

| mud | bet | | lad |
|------|------|------|------|
| must | best | nest | last |
| just | rest | chest | blast |
| blust | test | crest | crast |
| | west | shest | |

## • DIRECTING THE LEARNER'S ATTENTION

The purpose of this skill is to teach the learner to use his knowledge of letter substitution and short vowel patterns to pronounce unknown words with the ending –st. As such, the task is similar to storehouse module II-WA-18. To teach this skill you must direct the learner's attention by stating exactly what is to be learned and by highlighting the final –st and the letters that are common from word to word. (In the word *must*, for instance, you might circle the –st ending and underline the –mu having the learner use the say-it-slow, say-it-fast technique (see I-WA-5) in pronouncing the word.)

## • TEACHING ACTIVITIES

In teaching this letter substitution skill you can use either the modeling technique or the discovery technique described in II-WA-18, adjusting the suggestions to focus on the ending –st.

Do any of your pupils need a special reinforcement system?

## • SUGGESTIONS FOR RETEACHING

If, after having been taught this skill with either the modeling or the discovery technique, the learner is unable to substitute the st in the final position or known short vowel phonograms and pronounce the new words, you should use the reteaching suggestions provided in II-WA-18.

## • SUGGESTIONS FOR PRACTICE

Once the learner can substitute the st in the final position of known short vowel phonograms and pronounce the new words, create practice activities to solidify the skill, using the suggestions provided in II-WA-18.

## • THE POSTTEST

The pretest can also be used as the posttest. The procedure and criterion for mastery are the same.

## • ENSURING TRANSFER

You should use the suggestions provided in II-WA-18 to be sure that this skill is used by the learner during daily reading activities in the classroom.

# IV•WA•9

## • THE PERFORMANCE OBJECTIVE

When given the contractions **I'm, can't, won't, I'll, don't, isn't, he's, it's, I've, you're, we've,** and **let's** printed on cards, the learner will pronounce each contraction and identify the two words that make up the contraction.

## • THE PRETEST

Using cards that have one of the preceding contractions printed on them, direct the learner to look at each card in turn. Ask him or her to say the contraction printed on each card and then to say the two words that make up the contraction. For instance, for the word **I'm**, show the learner the card that has **I'm** printed on it. The learner responds by saying **I'm** and the two words (**I** and **am**) that make up the contraction. The criterion for mastery is 100 percent. *Note:* Keep track of each one the learner gets wrong since only the ones missed on the pretest will have to be taught.

### • DIRECTING THE LEARNER'S ATTENTION

The purpose of this task is to teach the learner to pronounce the most common contractions when they are shown in print. As such, this is a structural analysis task similar to storehouse module II-WA-25. To teach this skill you must direct the learner's attention by stating exactly what is to be learned and by highlighting the two words that make up the contraction, the placement of the apostrophe, and the letter(s) omitted from each contraction. (In the word **I'm**, for instance, you might separate cards for the **I**, the **a**, the **m**, and the apostrophe, use the cards to form the words **I am**, and then replace the **a** card with the apostrophe, having the learner pronounce the contraction after you have modeled it.)

### • TEACHING ACTIVITIES

In teaching this structural analysis skill you can use either the modeling technique or the discovery technique described in II-WA-25, adjusting the suggestions to focus on contractions.

### • SUGGESTIONS FOR RETEACHING

If, after having been taught with either the modeling or the discovery technique, the learner is unable to pronounce the most common contractions, you should use the reteaching suggestions provided in II-WA-25, adjusting them to fit the concept of contractions.

### • SUGGESTIONS FOR PRACTICE

Once the learner can pronounce the contractions, create practice activities to solidify the skill, using the suggestions provided in II-WA-25.

### • THE POSTTEST

The pretest can be used as the posttest. The procedure and criterion for mastery are the same.

### • ENSURING TRANSFER

You should use the suggestions provided in II-WA-25 to be sure that the learner uses this skill in daily reading activities in the classroom.

## IV•IG•1

### • THE PERFORMANCE OBJECTIVE

When given content words identified by the teacher, the learner will use each word correctly in an oral sentence.

### • THE PRETEST

The words to be tested are selected by the teacher. These may be words that appear in the basal text or in stories being read in class or that are associated with the study of a particular content area. To test for the meaning of such words, say each word out loud to the learner. Ask him or her to make up a sentence or to "send a message" using that word. The criterion for mastery is 100 percent since any word that is not used correctly will have to be taught.

The learner is asked to identify the following words in print in the next cluster of skills. You should include these words among those you test to make sure that the learner knows their meaning before he or she must pronounce them.

| | | | | |
|---|---|---|---|---|
| give | street | milk | friend | end |
| find | family | doll | ready | brother |
| many | funny | good-bye | hurry | ask |
| sure | bread | morning | store | quiet |
| color | | | | |

### • DIRECTING THE LEARNER'S ATTENTION

The purpose of this task is to teach the learner the meaning of new words he or she will be encountering. This is similar to storehouse module I-IG-1 but different words are being taught. To teach this skill you must direct the learner's attention by (1) providing either a direct or a vicarious experience to form a basis for the concept, (2) identifying the characteristics of this concept, and (3) connecting the concept to its word label. *Note:* This objective focuses on meaning alone. The learner should not be asked to pronounce these words as they appear in print until after this skill has been mastered.

### • TEACHING ACTIVITIES

This is a word meaning skill similar to module I-IG-1, and you can adapt your teaching strategy from either the modeling or the discovery techniques described in that objective.

### • SUGGESTIONS FOR RETEACHING

If, after having been taught with either the modeling or the discovery technique, the learner does not understand the meaning of any word in this objective, you should adapt and use the suggestions in I-IG-1 to reteach the skill.

### • SUGGESTIONS FOR PRACTICE

After teaching the learner the meaning of these words, create practice activities to solidify the skill, using the suggestions provided in I-IG-1.

### • THE POSTTEST

The procedure and criterion for mastery are the same as for the pretest.

### • ENSURING TRANSFER

You should use the suggestions in I-IG-1 and listening comprehension activities such as those found in the final chapter to be sure that the learner applies the new word meanings during the routine daily language activities of the classroom.

## IV•IG•2

### • THE PERFORMANCE OBJECTIVE

When given words containing the suffixes –'s, –est, –ly, –er, and –y, the learner will use each word correctly in an oral sentence.

### • THE PRETEST

Say each word to be tested out loud, asking the child to make up a sentence using the word you have just said. The criterion for mastery is 100 percent. Words like the following can be used:

> boy's    tallest    older    quietly    tricky

### • DIRECTING THE LEARNER'S ATTENTION

The purpose of this task is to teach the learner the meaning of the suffixes listed in the objectives since he or she will be asked to identify in print words containing these suffixes in the next cluster of skills. This is similar to storehouse module I-IG-2 but different meaning units are used. To teach this skill you must be sure that the learner has a meaning for the root word and you must direct his attention to the suffix, its meaning, and the way the suffix alters the meaning of the root word.

### • TEACHING ACTIVITIES

This is a meaning unit task similar to storehouse module I-IG-2, and you can adapt your teaching strategy from either the modeling or the discovery techniques described in that objective.

### • SUGGESTIONS FOR RETEACHING

Are you supplying new books for use in your recreational reading program?

If, after having been taught with either the modeling or the discovery technique, the learner does not understand the meaning of the words in this objective, you should adapt and use the suggestions in I-IG-2 to reteach the skill.

### • SUGGESTIONS FOR PRACTICE

After teaching the learner the meaning of the words, create practice activities to solidify the skill, using the suggestions provided in I-IG-2.

### • THE POSTTEST

The procedure and criterion are the same as for the pretest.

### • ENSURING TRANSFER

You should use the suggestions in I-IG-2 and listening comprehension activities such as those included in the final chapter to be sure that the learner applies the new word meanings during the routine language activities in the classroom.

## • THE PERFORMANCE OBJECTIVE

When given a short paragraph with four happenings signaled by the function words **first, next, then,** and **finally,** the learner will number the four statements in the order in which they happened in the story.

## • THE PRETEST

Direct the learner to read a story like the following one and to number the following events in the order in which they happened in the story. Criterion for mastery is 100 percent. (Readability: Second grade.)

> Mother had to go to work. She left Sid and Judy alone. She told them they had to go to bed at eight o'clock. But she said that they could have some food to eat just before going to bed. First, after Mother left, Sid and Judy played some games. Next they watched television. Then they sat down at the table to wait for eight o'clock to come. They wanted to have the snack. They got very, very tired. But still the clock did not say eight o'clock. Finally they fell asleep at the table. When Mother came home she found Sid and Judy asleep at the table. The clock still did not say eight o'clock. Mother saw that the clock had stopped.

_____ Sid and Judy fell asleep at the table.
_____ Sid and Judy played some games.
_____ Sid and Judy sat down at the table to wait for eight o'clock to come.
_____ Sid and Judy watched television.

## • DIRECTING THE LEARNER'S ATTENTION

The purpose of this task is to teach the learner how the sequence of the story is signaled by function words. This is similar to storehouse module I-IG-3. To teach this skill you must direct the learner's attention to the function words that signal the sequence of events and to the statements that are ordered by these function words.

## • TEACHING ACTIVITIES

This is an information-gathering task similar to storehouse module I-IG-3, and you can adapt your teaching strategy from either the modeling or the discovery technique described in that objective.

## • SUGGESTIONS FOR RETEACHING

If, after having been taught with either the modeling or the discovery technique, the learner does not understand how to sequence statements by using function words, you should adapt and use the suggestions in I-IG-3 to reteach the skill.

## • SUGGESTIONS FOR PRACTICE

After teaching the learner how to sequence events, create practice activities to solidify the skill, using the suggestions provided in I-IG-3.

## • THE POSTTEST

The procedure and criterion for mastery are the same as for the pretest, although you may want to substitute new material.

## • ENSURING TRANSFER

You should use the suggestions in I-IG-3 and reading comprehension activities such as those included in the final chapter to be sure that the learner applies sequencing skills during the routine language activities in the classroom.

# IV•IG•4

## • THE PERFORMANCE OBJECTIVE

When given a sentence containing an unknown word and in which a clue to the word's meaning is provided by an example, the learner will state the meaning of the unknown word.

## • THE PRETEST

State the unknown word, telling the child that the word is used in the sentence he or she is to read, together with a clue to the word's meaning. Using sentences like the following, ask the child to state the meaning of the word. The criterion for mastery is 80 percent. (Readability: First grade.)

| | |
|---|---|
| respite | Jim took a **respite** from the hard work. He knew that a rest would be good for him. |
| absurd | Eating your shoes is **absurd**! It is silly. In fact, it is the silliest thing I have ever heard of. |
| endure | The man wanted the ring to last forever. "How can I make it **endure**?" |
| chuckled | Sam **chuckled** at what the man said. He often laughed softly in that way. |
| inquire | Jim decided to **inquire** about the job. He wrote a letter to ask about it. |

## • DIRECTING THE LEARNER'S ATTENTION

The purpose of this task is to teach the learner how to determine the meaning of an unknown word by using a synonym provided in the surrounding context. This is similar to storehouse module II-IG-4. To teach this skill you must direct the learner's attention to the unknown word and to the synonym that explains its meaning.

## • TEACHING ACTIVITIES

This is an information-gathering task similar to storehouse module II-IG-4, and you can adapt your teaching strategy from either the modeling or the discovery technique described in that objective.

## • SUGGESTIONS FOR RETEACHING

If, after having been taught with either the modeling or the discovery technique, the learner does not understand how to determine the meaning of an unknown word by using a synonym in the sentence, you should adapt and use the suggestions in II-IG-4 to reteach the skill.

## • SUGGESTIONS FOR PRACTICE

After teaching the learner the skill of using a synonym to determine the meaning of an unknown word, create practice activities to solidify the skill, using the suggestions provided in II-IG-4.

## • THE POSTTEST

The procedure and criterion for mastery are the same as for the pretest, although you may want to substitute new material.

## • ENSURING TRANSFER

You should use the suggestions in II-IG-4 and reading comprehension activities such as those included in the final chapter to be sure that the learner applies context clues using synonyms during the routine language activities in the classroom.

## • THE PERFORMANCE OBJECTIVE

When given a four-part analogy frame in which the first two words are related and the third word is paired with a blank, the learner will complete the frame by supplying a word that relates the second pair of words in the same way the first two words are related.

## • THE PRETEST

Direct the learner to read the phrase in the first column, to think about the relationship being described, and to complete the phrase in the second column to show the same relationship. The criterion for mastery is 80 percent. (The following phrases are illustrative.)

| | |
|---|---|
| night is to day as | cold is to _____ (heat) |
| wing is to bird as | arm is to _____ (man) |
| thick is to thin as | full is to _____ (empty) |
| paintbrush is to wall as | pencil is to _____ (paper) |
| food is to hungry as | sleep is to _____ (tired) |

## • DIRECTING THE LEARNER'S ATTENTION

The purpose of this task is to teach the learner to find a relationship between one pair of words and use that same relationship to select a word that fits into a second pair of words. This is similar to the storehouse module I-MT-1. To teach this skill you must direct the learner's attention to the relationship between the first set of words and indicate how that relationship signals what word to choose for the second set of words.

Do you smile?

## • TEACHING ACTIVITIES

This is a manipulative task similar to storehouse module I-MT-1, and you can adapt your teaching strategy from either the modeling or the discovery technique described in that objective.

## • SUGGESTIONS FOR RETEACHING

If, after having been taught with either the modeling or the discovery technique, the learner does not understand how to use relationships to determine analogies, you should adapt and use the suggestions in I-MT-1 to reteach the skill.

## • SUGGESTIONS FOR PRACTICE

After teaching the learner the skill of using relationships to determine analogies, create practice activities to solidify the skill, using the suggestions provided in I-MT-1.

## • THE POSTTEST

The procedure and criterion for mastery are the same as for the pretest, although you may want to substitute new material.

## • ENSURING TRANSFER

You should use the suggestions in I-MT-1 and reading comprehension activities such as those included in the final chapter to be sure that the learner applies the skill of using relationships to determine analogies during the routine language activities in the classroom.

# IV•MT•2

## • THE PERFORMANCE OBJECTIVE

Given a sentence to read, the learner matches the sentence with a title that expresses the main idea of the sentence.

## • THE PRETEST

Direct the learner to read each sentence and to draw a line from the sentence that tells what is in the book to the title at the right that goes with the statement. The criterion for mastery is five out of six correct.

| | |
|---|---|
| A book about peanuts, oranges, honey, and other foods. | Our Pets |
| A book about fires. | Foods We Eat |
| A book about cats, dogs, and pet birds. | Farm Friends |
| A book about ducks, cows, and hens. | Firemen |
| A book about where sick people get better. | Big City |
| A book about many buildings, cars, and people. | The Hospital |

## • DIRECTING THE LEARNER'S ATTENTION

The purpose of this task is to teach the learner how to select the main idea of a sentence that is read. This is similar to storehouse module III-MT-2. To teach this skill you must direct the learner's attention to the facts in the sentence, to the common denominator of these facts that allows them to be categorized together, and to the title that best reflects the category.

## • TEACHING ACTIVITIES

This is a manipulative task similar to storehouse module III-MT-2, and you can adapt your teaching strategy from either the modeling or the discovery technique described in that objective.

## • SUGGESTIONS FOR RETEACHING

If, after having been taught with either the modeling or the discovery technique, the learner does not understand how to select the best title of a sentence, you should adapt and use the suggestions in III-MT-2 to reteach the skill.

## • SUGGESTIONS FOR PRACTICE

After teaching the learner the skill of selecting the main idea of a sentence, create practice activities to solidify the skill, using the suggestions provided in III-MT-2.

## • THE POSTTEST

The procedure and criterion for mastery are the same as for the pretest, although you may want to substitute new material.

## • ENSURING TRANSFER

You should use the suggestions in III-MT-2 and reading comprehension activites such as those included in the final chapter to be sure that the learner applies the skill of finding the main idea of sentences during the routine language activities in the classroom.

# IV•MT•3

## • THE PERFORMANCE OBJECTIVE

When given a paragraph to read and three possibilities about what happened next in the story, the learner will select the most likely outcome.

## • THE PRETEST

Direct the learner to read paragraphs like the following and to answer the question about what happened next by choosing one of the three answers provided. The criterion for mastery is 75 percent. (Readability: Second grade.)

> Two kittens were playing near the big dog's dish. The big dog did not want the kittens to go near his food. The big dog ran to his dish of food.

> What happened next?
> The kittens ran away.
> The kittens ate the food.
> The big dog climbed a ladder.

The kittens saw a big frog. The frog sat on a log in a pond. The kittens jumped on the log. Then the log turned over.

What happened next?
    The kittens fell in the pond.
    The kittens had a race.
    The kittens flew home.

Grandfather and Paul went out to catch a fish for supper. They sat in the rowboat and waited for a fish to come. Soon they each had a big fish.

What happened next?
    The fish went for a swim.
    Grandfather milked the cows.
    They rowed to the shore.

John saw a big basket. He opened the basket. He saw five kittens inside. Then John went away and left the basket open.

What happened next?
    John rode home on a bus.
    The kittens jumped out.
    The kittens sailed away.

### • DIRECTING THE LEARNER'S ATTENTION

The purpose of this task is to teach the learner how to select the most likely outcome for the story. This is similar to storehouse module I-MT-2. To teach this skill you must direct the learner's attention to what the facts say and to what he or she knows about such concepts and ideas.

Use this guide as you teach: Tell me, I forget; show me, I remember; let me do, I understand.

### • TEACHING ACTIVITIES

This is a manipulative task similar to storehouse module I-MT-2, and you can adapt your teaching strategy from either the modeling or the discovery technique described in that objective.

### • SUGGESTIONS FOR RETEACHING

If, after having been taught with either the modeling or the discovery technique, the learner does not understand how to select the most likely outcome, you should adapt and use the suggestions in I-MT-2 to reteach the skill.

### • SUGGESTIONS FOR PRACTICE

After teaching the learner the skill of selecting the most likely outcome, create practice activities to solidify the skill, using the suggestions provided in I-MT-2.

### • THE POSTTEST

The procedure and criterion for mastery are the same as for the pretest, although you may want to substitute new material.

## ● ENSURING TRANSFER

You should use the suggestions in I-MT-2 and reading comprehension activities such as those included in the final chapter to be sure that the learner applies the skill of selecting the most likely outcome during the routine language activities in the classroom.

## ● THE PERFORMANCE OBJECTIVE

When given pairs of sentences that are identical except for one word, the learner will state whether the different word in the sentence makes him feel more positive or more negative about the topic being discussed.

## ● THE PRETEST

The teacher should be sure that the test material is familiar to the learner. Direct the learner to read two sentences and to tell whether the second sentence makes him or her feel more positive or more negative toward the topic. Criterion for mastery is 100 percent. Sentences such as the following should be used:

He **quickly** put away his books.
He **frantically** put away his books.

The **excited** boy ran to his mother.
The **frenzied** boy ran to his mother.

The **new** gadget was on the table.
The **newfangled** gadget was on the table.

## ● DIRECTING THE LEARNER'S ATTENTION

The purpose of this task is to teach the learner to assess word choice for clues regarding an author's position on a topic. Good readers can detect bias through an author's use of emotion-laden words, words that create bias or stereotype, mood words, or other elements of word choice. Careful examination of word choice is an important evaluative thinking skill since it is a major way in which the reader makes judgments about the validity of what he or she is reading. Consequently, this is the first in a series of objectives that help the learner assess word choice as a means for determining an author's position on a topic.

To teach this skill you must direct the learner's attention to the key word that signals the author's position and to the connotation associated with that word. (In the first pair of sentences in the pretest, for instance, you would highlight the word **frantically** and the aura of panic often associated with that word.)

## ● THIS IS A STOREHOUSE OBJECTIVE

The following instructional activities are your storehouse of techniques for teaching learners to assess word choice for clues regarding an author's

position on a topic. This skill recurs throughout the skill hierarchy as the learner encounters more sophisticated material. The activities that follow are to be adapted and used with each as they occur.

### • TEACHING ACTIVITIES

*The modeling technique.* Use the first pair of sentences from the pretest, writing them on the chalkboard one under the other. Highlight the different word. Orally describe a scenario from the learner's experience in which lines such as the pretest items might be used. Say, "An author has opinions and feelings about things just like everyone else. When he is writing, he often signals his opinions and feelings to us by using certain words. For instance, in the first pair of sentences, he would use the word **frantically** if he wanted the reader to know that the person was not very cool (or was a bit panicked) about putting away his books and he would use **quickly** if he felt either neutral or positive about the way he put his books away." Create another pair of sentences using the same words and have the learner model your thought process in describing how the key words reflect an author's feelings. Repeat the same procedure with other sentences and other key words, gradually diminishing the highlighting and the amount of modeling until the learner is able to judge an author's position by examining the choice of words.

*The discovery technique.* In the discovery technique you still use the sentences with the key word highlighted and create a scenario to provide an experiential context for the sentences. You then ask questions that lead the learner to discover the significance of the single variant word. Such questions might include the following: "Do you suppose an author sometimes has feelings regarding the topics he writes about? How might a writer reveal those feelings? Looking at the two sentences on the chalkboard, why might a writer use **frantically** instead of **quickly** in that sentence? What does the writer's use of **frantically** tell you regarding the author's opinion?" Repeat the process with other sentences and other words, gradually diminishing the highlighting of the key word and the amount of questioning until the learner is able to determine an author's feelings through his or her choice of words.

### • SUGGESTIONS FOR RETEACHING

If, after having been taught with either of the preceding techniques, the learner is unable to determine an author's position by examining his word choice, you should

1. Reteach the skill, using the alternate technique.
2. Make sure that you are using sample sentences that reflect the learner's background.
3. Be more specific in directing the learner's attention to the key word and its connotation.

4. Use role-playing, information patterns, or other devices to highlight the emotion associated with the key connotative word.

### ● SUGGESTIONS FOR PRACTICE

Once the learner is able to make judgments on the basis of the author's word choice, adapt and use one or more of the following practice activities to solidify the skill.

1. Create practice exercises similar to the pretest that offer multiple opportunities for the learner to make judgments about key words used by the author.
2. Play games in which one learner creates a sentence and another changes one word or phrase to indicate a change in emotion.
3. Create Ditto exercises in which the learner fills in a blank with a word that signals a negative position on the part of the writer.

### ● THE POSTTEST

The procedure, directions, and criteria for mastery are the same as for the pretest.

### ● ENSURING TRANSFER

You should be sure that the learner uses his or her skill of judging material on the basis of word choice during the routine language activities of the classroom. You can do this by pointing out the ways the learners use connotative words in their own daily encounters and the ways in which connotative language is reflected in the daily reading they do in such places as newspapers and so on. Further you should be sure that this critical thinking skill is incorporated into comprehension activities such as those found in the final chapter.

# CLUSTER V

● **THE PERFORMANCE OBJECTIVE**

When given a fraction of a second to examine flashcards having printed on them the following words, the learner will pronounce each within one second.

| | | | | |
|---|---|---|---|---|
| give | money | would | oh | shoe |
| color | turtle | more | many | animal |
| hurry | were | read | could | people |
| should | find | miss | own | into |
| hair | does | thought | hello | friend |
| push | store | feet | took | bird |
| right | next | good-bye | over | nothing |
| street | every | school | morning | song |
| ready | an | catch | | |

● **THE PRETEST**

Print each of the preceding words on a flashcard. Flash each to the learner, giving him or her less than one second to examine each word before pronouncing it. The criterion for mastery is 100 percent.

### • DIRECTING THE LEARNER'S ATTENTION

The purpose of this task is to teach the learner to recognize instantly and pronounce the words contained in the pretest when they are presented on flashcards. This is a sight word recognition skill like that described in II-SW-6. To teach the skill you must make sure that the learner knows exactly what is to be learned, that the words being taught are in the child's speaking vocabulary, and that you have directed his or her attention by highlighting the unique visual characteristics of each word (such as the initial and final letters, length, shape, double letters, and so on).

### • TEACHING ACTIVITIES

This is a sight word recognition skill similar to that described in II-SW-6. If the learner does not recognize the word in print, adapt your teaching strategy from either the modeling technique or the discovery technique described in that objective. If the child confuses the word with another word similar to it, adapt your strategy from the suggestions contained in I-SW-17.

### • SUGGESTIONS FOR RETEACHING

If, after having been taught with the suggested technique, the learner is unable to recognize instantly one or more of the words on the pretest, use the reteaching suggestions described in II-SW-6.

### • SUGGESTIONS FOR PRACTICE

After successfully teaching the learner to recognize instantly the words on the pretest, create practice activities to solidify the the skill using the suggestions provided in II-SW-6.

### • THE POSTTEST

The procedure and criterion for mastery for the posttest are the same as for the pretest.

### • ENSURING TRANSFER

To be sure that this skill is applied, you must give the learner reading material containing the words now known at sight and have him or her read. You may guide the application by pointing out the words the child has just learned to recognize or, as he or she becomes more proficient, you can encourage independent reading of the newly learned words. Any material at the learner's instructional reading level that contains the sight words would be appropriate. Additional suggestions for helping the learner use known sight words in context are contained in II-SW-6.

## V•SW•2

### • THE PERFORMANCE OBJECTIVE

When given a flash presentation of words the learner frequently confuses, he or she will pronounce each word correctly within one second.

## • THE PRETEST

You will note whether the learner is confusing words whenever you test on sight words or listen to him or her read. If, during either of these activities, the learner says one word for another (such as **ever** for **every**), you should pair the words together and teach them, using the suggestions provided in this objective. No specific list of words is provided since various learners will confuse various words. As with other sight word objectives, the criterion for mastery is 100 percent, with any pair of confused words being taught.

## • DIRECTING THE LEARNER'S ATTENTION

The purpose of this task is to teach the learner to recognize instantly pairs of words he or she has tended to confuse in the past. As such, this task is similar to that described in I-SW-17. To teach this skill you must be sure that the learner has mastered the previous visual training skill, that he or she knows exactly what is to be learned, that the words being taught are in his or her oral speaking vocabulary, and that you have directed attention by highlighting the discriminator that sets one word apart from another (such as the **y** in **every**).

## • TEACHING ACTIVITIES

In teaching this skill you can use either the modeling technique or the discovery technique described in I-SW-17, adjusting the suggestions to focus on the particular words the learner is confusing.

## • SUGGESTIONS FOR RETEACHING

If, after having taught this skill with either the modeling or the discovery techniques, the learner continues to confuse the words, you should use the reteaching suggestions provided in I-SW-17.

## • SUGGESTIONS FOR PRACTICE

Once the learner can instantly recognize the words that he was previously confusing, create practice activities to solidify the skill, using the suggestions provided in I-SW-17.

## • THE POSTTEST

The procedure and criterion for mastery are the same as for the pretest.

## • ENSURING TRANSFER

Once the learner can recognize the easily confused words, you should immediately provide for application of this skill by giving the child reading material containing the words now known at sight. For specific suggestions regarding such application activities, see II-SW-6.

# V•SW•3

## • THE PERFORMANCE OBJECTIVE

When given words he or she recognizes instantly, the learner will create and read a single-sentence story using these words.

## • THE PRETEST

Provide the learner with cards each of which has printed on it a word he instantly recognizes. Say to the learner, "Today, we are going to do something that is very hard. We are going to send messages. Look at the cards you have in front of you. Each card has a word on it that you know. Can you send me a message using the words you have there? If you want to send a message using a word you don't have on a card, tell me and I will make a card for you having that word on it." The criterion for mastery is the combination of any number of words in a way that is grammatically accurate and that makes sense. When the learner has formed his or her sentence, reinforce the value of the effort by reading it aloud yourself.

## • DIRECTING THE LEARNER'S ATTENTION

This is a language experience activity designed to teach the learner to produce and read messages, using the individual words he or she knows at sight. As such, this is an application activity similar to that described in II-SW-8. To teach this activity you must be sure that the learner knows exactly what is to be learned and you must direct attention to the idea he wishes to convey, to what the message would sound like when spoken, what printed word cards will be needed to "write" the message, and the order in which the words must be placed. You might highlight by asking a series of questions such as, "What did you do yesterday after school that you could tell me about? Can you make a sentence about that and say it to me? What words did you use to say your sentence to me? How many of those words do you already have on cards and which ones will we have to make for you? What word will come first in your written message?"

*Too much to do? Why not get a mother to act as a buffer?*

## • TEACHING ACTIVITIES

This is a language experience activity similar to that described in II-SW-8. You should use the modeling and discovery techniques described in that objective as a basis for planning and teaching this task.

## • SUGGESTIONS FOR RETEACHING

If, after having been taught with either of the techniques described in the key objective, the learner is unable to create a single-sentence message using his sight words, you should

1. Reteach the activity, using the alternate technique.
2. Be more specific in eliciting from the learner the idea he or she wishes to convey.
3. Be sure that the learner expresses the message first in oral form and that he or she understands that the written message will say the same thing as the oral message.
4. Be sure that the content of the message matches the learner's experience, changing the subject to match the experience if necessary.
5. Recheck the learner's mastery of the sight words, reteaching any that have not yet been completely mastered.

6. Return to the previous language experience objectives and make sure that the child can do those simpler tasks before asking for the creation of entire sentences.

### • SUGGESTIONS FOR PRACTICE

Once the learner has been taught to use sight words to create and read sentences, devise practice activities to solidify this skill, adapting the suggestions provided in II-SW-8.

### • THE POSTTEST

The procedure and criterion for mastery for the posttest are the same as for the pretest.

### • ENSURING TRANSFER

This objective is an application activity designed to help the learner use his sight words in context. In addition to the application specified here, however, you should use the suggestions in II-SW-6 to be sure that the learner uses the sight words in other contextual situations.

### • THE PERFORMANCE OBJECTIVE

When given a known word composed of the phonograms –and, –end, –ight, –old, and –ind, the learner will replace the initial consonant with another consonant, consonant blend, or digraph and pronounce the new word.

### • THE PRETEST

Use the following lists of words. The first word in each list has been previously taught as a sight word or has been previously analyzed. Read the first word in the list and ask the learner to pronounce the remaining words. The criterion for mastery is 27 out of 29 correct, with no initial consonant, digraph, or blend being missed more than once. *Note:* Some of the words listed are nonsense words, which are included so that the learner *must* use analysis rather than sight recognition.

| and | end | right | | old | | find |
|-----|-----|-------|---|-----|---|------|
| sand | send | fight | flight | sold | cold | blind |
| bland | bend | tight | bright | told | hold | mind |
| stand | lend | slight | fright | bold | gold | bind |
| chand | blend | might | blight | fold | brold | chind |
| | swend | | | | | |

### • DIRECTING THE LEARNER'S ATTENTION

The purpose of this skill is to teach the learner to use his knowledge of letter substitution to pronounce words ending in –and, –end, –ight, –old, and –ind. As such, the task is similar to storehouse module II-WA-18. To teach this skill you must direct the learner's attention by stating exactly what is to be learned and by highlighting the initial sound and the common ending. (In the word **sand,** for instance, you might circle the –**and** ending and underline the initial **s,** having the learner use the say-it-slow, say-it-fast technique (see I-WA-5) in pronouncing the word.)

- **TEACHING ACTIVITIES**

In teaching this letter substitution skill you can use either the modeling technique or the discovery technique described in II-WA-18, adjusting the suggestions to focus on the –**and,** –**end,** –**ight,** –**old,** and –**ind** endings.

- **SUGGESTIONS FOR RETEACHING**

If, after having been taught this skill with either the modeling or the discovery technique, the learner is unable to use his knowledge of letter substitution to pronounce words ending in –**and,** –**end,** –**ight,** –**old,** and –**ind,** you should use the reteaching suggestions provided in II-WA-18.

- **SUGGESTIONS FOR PRACTICE**

Once the learner can substitute the endings presented in this objective and pronounce the new words, you should create practice activities to solidify the skill, using the suggestions provided in II-WA-18.

- **THE POSTTEST**

The pretest can also be used as the posttest. The procedure and criterion for mastery are the same.

- **ENSURING TRANSFER**

You should use the suggestions provided in II-WA-18 to be sure that the learner uses this skill in daily reading activities in the classroom.

# V•WA•2

- **THE PERFORMANCE OBJECTIVE**

When given a known word containing a double **e** in the medial position, the learner will replace either the initial or final letter with other letters and pronounce the new words.

- **THE PRETEST**

Use the following word lists. The key words (**feet** and **keep**) have been previously learned as sight words. Have the learner identify the key words in each list and then ask him to pronounce the remaining words in the list. The criterion for mastery is 15 out of 17 correct. *Note:* Some of the words listed are nonsense words, which are included so that the learner *must* use analysis rather than sight recognition.

| **feet** | **feet** | **keep** | | **keep** |
|------|------|------|------|------|
| feel | meet | deep | sleep | keed |
| feed | sweet | peep | weep | keen |
| feek | breet | sheep | beep | keel |
| | fleet | | | keet |

## • DIRECTING THE LEARNER'S ATTENTION

The purpose of this task is to teach the learner to use his or her knowledge of letter substitution to pronounce words having a double **e** in the medial position. As such, the task is similar to storehouse module II-WA-18. To teach this skill you must direct the learner's attention by stating exactly what is to be learned and by highlighting the letters that are common from word to word and the letters that are different. (In the word **feel**, for instance, you might circle the **l** and underline the **fee**, having the learner use the say-it-fast, say-it-slow technique (see I-WA-5) in pronouncing the word.)

## • TEACHING ACTIVITIES

In teaching this letter substitution skill you can use either the modeling technique or the discovery technique described in II-WA-18, adjusting the suggestions to focus on words having a double **e** in the medial position.

## • SUGGESTIONS FOR RETEACHING

If, after having taught this skill with either the modeling or the discovery technique, the learner is unable to use his or her knowledge of letter substitution to pronounce words having a double **e** in the medial position, you should use the reteaching suggestions provided in II-WA-18.

## • SUGGESTIONS FOR PRACTICE

Once the learner can pronounce words having a double **e** in the medial position, you should create practice activities to solidify the skill, using the suggestions provided in II-WA-18.

## • THE POSTTEST

The pretest can also be used as the posttest. The procedure and criterion for mastery are the same.

## • ENSURING TRANSFER

You should use the suggestions provided in II-WA-18 to be sure that the learner uses this skill in daily reading activities in the classroom.

## V•WA•3

## • THE PERFORMANCE OBJECTIVE

When given a known one-syllable word containing the –ay combination, the learner will replace the initial consonant with another letter and pronounce the new word.

## • THE PRETEST

Use the following list of words. The first word (**day**) has been previously taught as a sight word. Have the learner identify this word and then ask him to pronounce the remaining words in the list. The criterion for mastery is 14 out of 16 correct. *Note:* Some of the words listed are nonsense words which are included so that the learner *must* use analysis rather than sight recognition.

|      |     | day  |      |
|------|-----|------|------|
| pay  | may | bray | clay |
| say  | lay | dray | tray |
| way  | hay | play | gray |
| slay | gay | stay | sway |

### ● DIRECTING THE LEARNER'S ATTENTION

The purpose of this task is to teach the learner to use his knowledge of letter substitution to pronounce words ending with the –ay combination. As such, the task is similar to storehouse module II-WA-18. To teach this skill you must direct the learner's attention by stating exactly what is to be learned and by highlighting the letters that are common from word to word and the letters that differ. (In the word **pay**, for instance, you might circle the **p** and underline the **ay**, having the learner use the say-it-slow, say-it-fast technique (see I-WA-5) in pronouncing the word.)

### ● TEACHING ACTIVITIES

In teaching this letter substitution skill you can use either the modeling technique or the discovery technique described in II-WA-18, adjusting the suggestions to focus on words ending with the –ay combination.

### ● SUGGESTIONS FOR RETEACHING

If, after having been taught this skill with either the modeling or the discovery technique, the learner is unable to use his or her knowledge of letter substitution to pronounce words ending with the –ay combination, you should use the reteaching suggestions provided in II-WA-18.

### ● SUGGESTIONS FOR PRACTICE

Once the learner can pronounce words having the –ay combination in the ending position, create practice activities to solidify the skill, using the suggestions provided in II-WA-18.

### ● THE POSTTEST

The pretest can also be used as the posttest. The procedure and criterion for mastery are the same.

### ● ENSURING TRANSFER

You should use the suggestions provided in II-WA-18 to be sure that the learner uses this skill in daily reading activities in the classroom.

## V•WA•4

### ● THE PERFORMANCE OBJECTIVE

When given a known one-syllable word ending in –ell or –ill, the learner will replace the initial consonant with another letter and pronounce the new word.

## • THE PRETEST

Use the following lists of words. The first word in each list has been previously taught as a sight word. Have the learner identify the first word in each list and then ask him or her to pronounce the remaining words in the list. The criterion for mastery is 19 out of 21 correct. *Note:* Some of the words listed are nonsense words, which are included so that the learner *must* use analysis rather than sight recognition.

| **well** | | | **will** | | |
|------|------|------|------|------|------|
| tell | bell | smell | hill | chill | skill |
| fell | shell | swell | kill | drill | spill |
| sell | spell | brell | fill | frill | still |
|      |      |      | bill | grill | shill |

## • DIRECTING THE LEARNER'S ATTENTION

The purpose of this task is to teach the learner to use his or her knowledge of letter substitution to pronounce words ending with the –el or –ill combinations. As such, this task is similar to storehouse module II-WA-18. To teach this skill you must direct the learner's attention by stating exactly what is to be learned and by highlighting the letters that are common from word to word and the letters that differ. (In the word **tell,** for instance, you might circle the **t** and underline the **ell,** having the learner use the say-it-slow, say-it-fast technique (see I-WA-5) in pronouncing the word.)

When today are your pupils going to read just for the fun of it?

## • TEACHING ACTIVITIES

In teaching this letter substitution skill you can use either the modeling technique or the discovery technique described in II-WA-18, adjusting the suggestions to focus on words ending with the –ell or –ill combinations.

## • SUGGESTIONS FOR RETEACHING

If, after having been taught this skill with either the modeling or the discovery technique, the learner is unable to use his or her knowledge of letter substitution to pronounce words ending in –ell or –ill, you should use the reteaching suggestions provided in II-WA-18.

## • SUGGESTIONS FOR PRACTICE

Once the learner can pronounce words having the –ell or –ill ending combinations, create practice activities to solidify the skill, using the suggestions provided in II-WA-18.

## • THE POSTTEST

The pretest can also be used as the posttest. The procedure and criterion for mastery remain the same.

## • ENSURING TRANSFER

You should use the suggestions provided in II-WA-18 to be sure that the learner uses this skill in daily reading activities in the classroom.

• **THE PERFORMANCE OBJECTIVE**

When given a known one-syllable ending in –all, the learner will replace the initial consonant with another letter and pronounce the new word.

• **THE PRETEST**

Use the following list of words. The first word (all) has been previously taught as a sight word. Have the learner identify **all** and then ask him to pronounce the remaining words in the list. The criterion for mastery is eight out of nine correct. *Note:* Some of the words listed are nonsense words, which are included so that the learner *must* use analysis rather than sight recognition.

| **all** | call | fall | mall | stall |
|---------|------|------|-------|-------|
| ball    | hall | tall | small | skall |

• **DIRECTING THE LEARNER'S ATTENTION**

The purpose of this task is to teach the learner to use his or her knowledge of letter substitution to pronounce words ending with the –all combination. As such, this task is similar to storehouse module II-WA-18. To teach this skill you must direct the learner's attention by stating exactly what is to be learned by highlighting the letters that are common from word to word and the letters that differ. (In the word **ball**, for instance, you might circle the **b** and underline the **all**, having the learner use the say-it-slow, say-it-fast technique (see I-WA-5) in pronouncing the word.)

• **TEACHING ACTIVITIES**

In teaching this letter substitution skill you can use either the modeling technique or the discovery technique described in II-WA-18, adjusting the suggestions to focus on words ending with the –all combination.

• **SUGGESTIONS FOR RETEACHING**

If, after having been taught this skill with either the modeling or the discovery technique, the learner is unable to use his or her knowledge of letter substitution to pronounce words ending in the –all combination, you should use the reteaching suggestions provided in II-WA-18.

• **SUGGESTIONS FOR PRACTICE**

Once the learner can pronounce words having the –all ending combination, create practice activities to solidify the skill, using the suggestions provided in II-WA-18.

• **THE POSTTEST**

The pretest can also be used as the posttest. The procedure and criterion for mastery are the same.

## • ENSURING TRANSFER

You should use the suggestions provided in II-WA-18 to be sure that the learner uses this skill in daily reading activities in the classroom.

## • THE PERFORMANCE OBJECTIVE

When given words he or she has previously analyzed or learned to recognize at sight, the learner will add the structural endings –'s, –est, –ly, –er, and –y and pronounce the new words.

## • THE PRETEST

Use the following list of words. Have the learner pronounce each word in each list in turn. The criterion for mastery is nine out of ten correct.

| | | | | |
|---|---|---|---|---|
| boy's | deepest | player | chilly | quietly |
| your's | tallest | older | jumpy | newly |

## • DIRECTING THE LEARNER'S ATTENTION

The purpose of this task is to teach the learner to pronounce words composed of a known root and the structural endings –'s –est, –ly, –er, and –y. As such, this is a structural analysis skill similar to storehouse module II-WA-18. To teach this skill you must direct the learner's attention by stating exactly what is to be learned and by highlighting both the known root and the structural ending. (In the word **boy's**, for instance, you might underline the word **boy**, circle the structural ending 's, and have the learner pronounce the new word after you model it.)

## • TEACHING ACTIVITIES

In teaching this structural analysis skill you can use either the modeling technique or the discovery technique described in II-WA-25, adjusting the suggestions to focus on the endings specified in this objective.

## • SUGGESTIONS FOR RETEACHING

If, after having been taught with either the modeling or the discovery technique, the learner is unable to pronounce known roots having –s, –est, –ly, –er, and –y added, you should use the reteaching suggestions provided in II-WA-25, adjusting them to fit these particular structural elements.

Can your pupils *see* the daily progress they make through the skill hierarchy?

## • SUGGESTIONS FOR PRACTICE

Once the learner can pronounce the words having the structural endings added, create practice activities to solidify the skill, using the suggestions provided in II-WA-25.

### ● THE POSTTEST

The procedure and criterion for mastery are the same. Use the following words.

|          |          |        |       |          |
|----------|----------|--------|-------|----------|
| brother's | sweetest | walker | milky | gladly   |
| girl's    | fastest  | flyer  | tricky | friendly |

### ● ENSURING TRANSFER

You should use the suggestions provided in II-WA-25 to be sure that the learner uses this skill in daily reading activities in the classroom.

## V·IG·1

### ● THE PERFORMANCE OBJECTIVE

When given content words identified by the teacher, the learner will use each word correctly in an oral sentence.

### ● THE PRETEST

The words to be tested are selected by the teacher. These may be words that appear in the basal text or in stories being read in class or that are associated with the study of a particular content area. To test for the meaning of such words, say each word out loud to the learner. Ask him or her to make up a sentence or to "send a message" using that word. The criterion for mastery is 100 percent, since any word used incorrectly will have to be taught.

The learner is asked to identify the following words in print in the next cluster of skills. You should include these words among those you test to be sure that the learner knows their meaning before he or she must pronounce them.

|        |        |        |         |          |
|--------|--------|--------|---------|----------|
| read   | break  | ride   | air     | believe  |
| school | wild   | listen | careful | catch    |
| own    | drink  | money  | felt    | ear      |
| car    | slow   | tried  | heavy   | lion     |
| shoe   | match  | miss   | love    | point    |
| bird   | mice   | nice   | poor    | together |

### ● DIRECTING THE LEARNER'S ATTENTION

The purpose of this task is to teach the learner the meaning of new words he or she will be encountering. This is similar to the storehouse module I-IG-1 but different words are being taught. To teach this skill you must direct the learner's attention by (1) providing either a direct or a vicarious experience to form a basis for the concept, (2) identifying the characteristics of this concept, and (3) connecting the concept to its word label. *Note:* This objective focuses on meaning alone. The learner should not be asked to pronounce these words as they appear in print until after this skill has been mastered.

## • TEACHING ACTIVITIES

This is a word meaning skill similar to storehouse module I-IG-1, and you can adapt your teaching strategy from either the modeling or the discovery techniques described in that objective.

## • SUGGESTIONS FOR RETEACHING

If, after having been taught with either the modeling or the discovery technique, the learner does not understand the meaning of any word in this objective, you should adapt and use the suggestions in I-IG-1 to reteach the skill.

Do your pupils *share* books or do they report on them?

## • SUGGESTIONS FOR PRACTICE

After teaching the learner the meaning of these words, create practice activities to solidify the skill, using the suggestions in I-IG-1.

## • THE POSTTEST

The procedure and criterion for mastery are the same as for the pretest.

## • ENSURING TRANSFER

You should use the suggestions in I-IG-1 and reading comprehension activities such as those found in the final chapter to be sure that the learner applies the new word meanings during the routine daily language activities of the classroom.

# V•IG•2

## • THE PERFORMANCE OBJECTIVE

When given words containing the prefixes **dis–** and **un–**, the learner uses each word correctly in an oral sentence.

## • THE PRETEST

Say each word to be tested out loud, asking the child to make up a sentence using the word you have just said. The criterion for mastery is 100 percent. Words such as the following can be used.

| | | | |
|---|---|---|---|
| dislike | unkind | discolor | unlike |
| unhappy | displease | unjust | distrust |

## • DIRECTING THE LEARNER'S ATTENTION

The purpose of this task is to teach the learner the meaning of the prefixes **dis–** and **un–** since he will be asked to identify in print words containing these prefixes in the next cluster of skills. This is similar to storehouse module I-IG-2. To teach this skill you must be sure that the learner knows the meaning of the root word and you must direct his attention to the prefix, its meaning, and the way the prefix alters the meaning of the root word.

● 351

This is a meaning unit task similar to storehouse module I-IG-2, and you can adapt your teaching strategy from either the modeling or the discovery techniques described in that objective.

• SUGGESTIONS FOR RETEACHING

If, after having been taught with either the modeling or the discovery technique, the learner does not understand the meaning of the words in this objective, you should adapt and use the suggestions in I-IG-2 to reteach the skill.

• SUGGESTIONS FOR PRACTICE

After teaching the learner the meaning of the words, create practice activities to solidify the skill, using the suggestions provided in I-IG-2.

• THE POSTTEST

The procedure and criterion are the same as for the pretest.

• ENSURING TRANSFER

You should use the suggestions in I-IG-2 and reading comprehension activities such as those included in the final chapter to be sure that the learner applies the new word meanings during the routine language activities in the classroom.

## V•IG•3

• THE PERFORMANCE OBJECTIVE

When given a sentence that states a cause-effect relationship and in which a function word has been omitted, the learner selects the appropriate function words from two choices that are provided.

• THE PRETEST

Direct the learner to read sentences like the following and to fill the blank with one of the two words provided so that the sentence will make sense. The criterion for mastery is 80 percent. (Readability: Second grade.)

The monkey was very excited _____ he saw that Sam had some peanuts.

    so      because

Al found the most eggs in the game _____ he was given the prize.

    so      because

The robber worked quickly _____ he knew that he would get caught if he did not.

    so      because

Jane would not have been in trouble _____ she had not broken the dish.

and     if

Mom got home. There was no cake left _____ the boys had eaten it.

if     because

## • DIRECTING THE LEARNER'S ATTENTION

The purpose of this task is to teach the learner how to select the best function word to fit a cause and effect sentence. This is similar to storehouse module I-IG-3. To teach this skill you must direct the learner's attention to the elements of the sentence that state the cause, to the elements of the sentence that state the effect, and to the function words that best signal that cause and effect relationship.

## • TEACHING ACTIVITIES

This is an information-gathering task similar to storehouse module I-IG-3, and you can adapt your teaching strategy from either the modeling or the discovery technique described in that objective.

## • SUGGESTIONS FOR RETEACHING

If, after having been taught with either the modeling or the discovery technique, the learner does not understand how to select the correct function word to signal a cause and effect relationship, you should adapt and use the suggestions in I-IG-3 to reteach the skill.

## • SUGGESTIONS FOR PRACTICE

After teaching the learner the skill of using function words to signal cause-and-effect relationships, create practice activities to solidify the skill, using the suggestions provided in I-IG-3.

## • THE POSTTEST

The procedure and criterion for mastery are the same as for the pretest, although you may want to substitute new material.

## • ENSURING TRANSFER

You should use the suggestions in I-IG-3 and reading comprehension activities such as those included in the final chapter to be sure that the learner applies the skill of function words that signal cause-and-effect relationships during the routine language activities in the classroom.

## V•IG•4

## • THE PERFORMANCE OBJECTIVE

When given a series of sentences containing ending punctuation, the learner orally reads each sentence with the correct voice intonation and states the varying meanings signaled by punctuation at the end of each sentence.

## • THE PRETEST

Direct the learner to read sentences like the following orally and to say what each ending punctuation means. The criterion for mastery is 100 percent with each incorrect punctuation mark being taught.

> The house is on fire!
> The house is on fire.
> The house is on fire?

## • DIRECTING THE LEARNER'S ATTENTION

The purpose of this task is to teach the relationships signaled by the punctuation marks at the end of sentences. This is the first in a series of three objectives focusing on punctuation as signalers of relationships. The others are (1) commas (a) as identifiers (as when the person spoken to is set off by commas in a sentence like, "Mike, you should go home"), (b) for items listed in a series, and (c) in parenthetical phrases; and (2) relationships signaled by quotation marks.

Although much of the meaning in the English language is tied to the concepts associated with the words, a significant portion of English meaning is conveyed by intonation patterns or the *way* something is said. A major way to signal such relationships is through the use of punctuation. Consequently, if the learner is to obtain full meaning from a passage, he or she should be able to interpret and use the punctuation that signals various relationship meanings.

To teach punctuation as signalers of relationships, you must be sure that the learner possesses meaning for each of the words used and you must direct his or her attention to the punctuation mark, the associated intonation pattern, and the meaning that punctuation mark gives the words around it. (In the first pretest item, for instance, you must direct the learner to the exclamation point at the end, to the oral interpretation of the sentence, and to the aura of excitement that is signaled by the exclamation point.)

## • THIS IS A STOREHOUSE OBJECTIVE

The following instructional activities are your storehouse of techniques for teaching the relationships signaled by punctuation. This skill will recur in other forms later in the hierarchy. The activities that follow are to be adapted and used with each punctuation objective as it occurs.

## • TEACHING ACTIVITIES

*The modeling technique.* Using the first sentence of the pretest as an illustration, you could teach this skill by following these procedures. Write out the first pretest sentence with the exclamation point highlighted. Then say each sentence with the correct intonation, saying, "Because this sentence ends with an exclamation point, I know the writer wants the sentence said with excitement. Therefore, when I read the sentence, I say it like this. . . ." After orally reading the sentence, say, "When a sentence ends with this punctuation mark, it is signaling excitement to me and I should read it that way. Can you read that sentence as I did?" Repeat the procedure with other sentences that end in exclamation points as well as with other ending punctuation marks, gradually diminishing the highlighting in the ending punctuation and your modeling of the oral intonation until the learner is able to apply the correct intonations and meanings without assistance from you.

***The discovery technique.*** When using the discovery technique, you could still make use of sentences with the punctuation highlighted. However, rather than taking one sentence at a time, you could read the first sentence and then the second sentence, saying, "Listen as I say these two sentences. Does my voice sound the same in both sentences? How is my voice different? What am I saying different in each sentence by the *way* I say the sentence? How do you think I knew how to make my voice different in each sentence?" After doing the first two sentences, proceed to other pairs of sentences, gradually diminishing the highlighting on the punctuation marks and the number of questions asked until the learner can do the task without any help.

### • SUGGESTIONS FOR RETEACHING

If, after having been taught with either of the preceding techniques, the learner is unable to interpret the meaning signaled by ending punctuation, you should

1. Reteach the skill, using the alternate technique.
2. Provide an increased amount of oral language activities with these kinds of sentences before interpreting such sentences as they are written.
3. Be sure that the sentences used reflect the learner's experience.
4. Exaggerate the highlighting on the ending punctuation and the oral intonation you provide when reading the sentences.

Evaluate your day: How much of what you did was really professional and how much could have been done by a babysitter?

### • SUGGESTIONS FOR PRACTICE

Once the learner is correctly interpreting the meaning signaled by the punctuation, adapt and use one or more of the following activities to solidify the skill:

1. Play games in which the learner progresses toward a goal by orally reading sentences printed on cards. To receive credit the learner must use intonation that reflects the meaning signaled by the punctuation.
2. Create short plays in which the learner takes various parts and must read lines with intonation that reflects the punctuation.
3. Provide unpunctuated sentences for the learner. Have him or her punctuate each sentence several times, using different punctuation each time. Then have the learner read each sentence, using the correct information according to the punctuation he or she supplied.
4. Give the learner descriptions of happenings and a choice of three statements made by participants in the happening. The learner chooses the statement with punctuation that reflects the situation.

The procedure, directions, and criterion are the same for the posttest as for the pretest. Use the following sentences:

> She can see the ship.
> She can see the ship?
> She can see the ship!

### • ENSURING TRANSFER

You should ensure that the learner's understanding of the meanings signaled by punctuation is used in the daily routine activities of the classroom. One good way to do this is by providing *realistic* and *meaningful* oral reading situations in which one child reads to share information with others who do not have access to that information. Further, the learner should be using such punctuation in interpreting comprehension activities such as those provided in the final chapter.

## V•IG•5

### • THE PERFORMANCE OBJECTIVE

When given sentences containing a word unknown in meaning and in which a clue to the word's meaning is provided by either a synonym or an antonym, the learner will state the meaning of the unknown word.

### • THE PRETEST

State the unknown word for the child, telling him or her that the word appears in the sentences to be read, together with a clue to the word's meaning. Using sentences like the following, ask the child to state the meaning for the word. The criterion for mastery is 80 percent. (Readability: Third grade.)

| | |
|---|---|
| surrender | The captain gave up. The crew had to **surrender** too. |
| gallant | "You are so brave," the girl said when the **gallant** man saved her from danger. |
| feeble | The **feeble** boy tried to fight off the wild bear. But he was not strong enough. |
| mimic | The boys liked to **mimic** Tom. No matter what Tom did, all the boys did just the same thing. |
| laden | The table was **laden** with all kinds of good things to eat at Thanksgiving. The table was so full with food that the family could not eat it all. |

### • DIRECTING THE LEARNER'S ATTENTION

The purpose of this task is to teach the learner to determine the meaning of an unknown word by using clues provided in the surrounding context. This is similar to storehouse module II-IG-4. To teach this skill you must direct the learner's attention to the unknown word and the synonym or antonym in the surrounding context that explains the meaning of the unknown word.

## • TEACHING ACTIVITIES

This is an information-gathering task similar to storehouse module II-IG-4, and you can adapt your teaching strategy from either the modeling or the discovery technique described in that objective.

## • SUGGESTIONS FOR RETEACHING

If, after having been taught with either the modeling or the discovery technique, the learner does not understand how synonyms or antonyms in the surrounding context explain the meaning of an unknown word, you should adapt and use the suggestions in II-IG-4 to reteach the skill.

## • SUGGESTIONS FOR PRACTICE

After teaching the learner to use antonym and synonym context clues to determine the meaning of unknown words, create practice activities to solidify the skill using the suggestions in II-IG-4.

## • THE POSTTEST

The procedure and criterion for mastery are the same as for the pretest, although you may want to substitute new material.

## • ENSURING TRANSFER

You should use the suggestions in II-IG-4 and reading comprehension activities such as those included in the final chapter to ensure that the learner applies context clues usage during the routine language activities in the classroom.

## V•IG•6

## • THE PERFORMANCE OBJECTIVE

When given a paragraph to read in which the details can be classified together, the learner will recall the details from the story in response to questions from the teacher.

## • THE PRETEST

Direct the learner to read a paragraph like the following one. Then ask him or her to answer orally the questions that follow the paragraph. The criterion for mastery is 80 percent. (Readability: Second grade.)

> Once there was a little dog. She was so little. All the children called her Tiny. Tiny was brown with little white spots. Tiny looked happy. But she was not happy. No one knew why she was unhappy. Mother guessed that Tiny was lonely. So she got another dog to be Tiny's friend. Then Tiny was really happy!
>
> How big was the dog?
> What was the dog's name?
> What color was the dog?
> Was the dog happy or unhappy?
> What did Mother do to make Tiny happy?

Have you asked your
learners to think
today?

● **DIRECTING THE LEARNER'S ATTENTION**

The purpose of this task is to teach the learners to remember details as they
read. This is similar to storehouse module III-IG-6. To teach this skill you
must direct the learner's attention by setting purposes that serve as cues to
the learner regarding what to note and remember as he reads.

● **TEACHING ACTIVITIES**

This is an information-gathering task similar to storehouse module III-IG-6,
and you can adapt your teaching strategy from either the modeling or the
discovery technique described in that objective.

● **SUGGESTIONS FOR RETEACHING**

If, after having been taught with either the modeling or the discovery technique, the learner does not understand how to remember details, you should
adapt and use the suggestions in III-IG-6 to reteach the skill.

● **SUGGESTIONS FOR PRACTICE**

After teaching the learner the skill of recalling details, create practice
activities to solidify the skill using the suggestions in III-IG-6.

● **THE POSTTEST**

The procedure and criterion for mastery are the same as for the pretest,
although you may want to substitute new material.

● **ENSURING TRANSFER**

You should use the suggestions in III-IG-6 and reading comprehension
activities such as those included in the final chapter to be sure that the
learner applies the recalling details skill during the routine language activities in the classroom.

# V•MT•1

● **THE PERFORMANCE OBJECTIVE**

When given a list of phrases, the learner will sort the phrases into three
categories and label each category.

● **THE PRETEST**

Direct the learner to read phrases like the following and to classify them
into three categories. The three categories should be things that are
pointed, things that are soft, and things that are heavy. The criterion for
mastery is seven out of nine correct.

> the end of a pin
> a pile of feathers
> a truckload of steel
> a snowbank
> a pillow

the teeth of a rake
an armload of big books
a newly sharpened pencil
carrying your teacher on your back

## • DIRECTING THE LEARNER'S ATTENTION

The purpose of this task is to teach the learner to find relationships between phrases and to classify these phrases according to these relationships. This is similar to storehouse module I-MT-1. To teach this skill you must direct the learner's attention by highlighting the concepts associated with each phrase and then to the common denominator that allows them to be classified together.

## • TEACHING ACTIVITIES

This is a manipulative task similar to storehouse module I-MT-1, and you can adapt your teaching strategy from either the modeling or the discovery technique described in that objective.

## • SUGGESTIONS FOR RETEACHING

If, after having been taught with either the modeling or the discovery technique, the learner does not understand how to classify phrases, you should adapt and use the suggestions in I-MT-1 to reteach the skill.

## • SUGGESTIONS FOR PRACTICE

After teaching the learner the classifying of phrases skill, create practice activities to solidify the skill, using the suggestions in I-MT-1.

## • THE POSTTEST

The procedure and criterion for mastery are the same as for the pretest, although you may want to substitute new material.

## • ENSURING TRANSFER

You should use the suggestions in I-MT-1 and reading comprehension activities such as those included in the final chapter to ensure that the learner applies the classifying of phrases skill during the routine language activities in the classroom.

# V•MT•2

## • THE PERFORMANCE OBJECTIVE

When given a list of words and four possible story titles, the learner will sort the phrases into three categories and select one title that would be appropriate for all three categories.

## • THE PRETEST

Direct the learner to read words like the following and to divide them into three categories, labeling each category. Then tell him or her to select one title that would fit all three categories from the three provided. The three categories should be farm animals, wild animals, and pets. The criterion for mastery is 100 percent.

cows   pigs      cats
dogs   horses   squirrels
deer   raccoons  sheep

Possible titles:   At the Zoo
                 Animals We Know
                 In the Woods
                 What We See in the Woods

### • DIRECTING THE LEARNER'S ATTENTION

The purpose of this task is to teach the learner to find relationships between words and to select the title by classifying the words. This is similar to storehouse module I-MT-1. To teach this skill you must direct the learner's attention by highlighting the concepts associated with each word, to use those relationships to select categories, and then to use those categories to select a best title for all three categories.

### • TEACHING ACTIVITIES

This is a manipulative task similar to storehouse module I-MT-1, and you can adapt your teaching strategy from either the modeling or the discovery technique described in that objective.

### • SUGGESTIONS FOR RETEACHING

If, after having been taught with either the modeling or the discovery technique, the learner does not understand how to select a title from categories created by relationships between words, you should adapt and use the suggestions I-MT-1 to reteach the skill.

### • SUGGESTIONS FOR PRACTICE

After teaching the learner the skill of selecting titles from categories that came from word relationships, create practice activities to solidify the skill, using the suggestions provided in I-MT-1.

### • THE POSTTEST

The procedure and criterion for mastery are the same as for the pretest, although you may want to substitute new material.

### • ENSURING TRANSFER

You should use the suggestions in I-MT-1 and reading comprehension activities such as those included in the final chapter to ensure that the learner applies titling categories of words during the routine language activities in the classroom.

● **THE PERFORMANCE OBJECTIVE**

When given a paragraph in which the mood is implied and in which a word has been omitted, the learner will select a word that describes the mood from a choice of two words provided.

● **THE PRETEST**

Direct the learner to read paragraphs like the following and to complete the final sentence in each paragraph by choosing one of the three words provided. The criterion for mastery is 100 percent. (Readability: Second grade.)

> The wind was strong. It blew leaves from the trees and dust into people's eyes. Because it was so strong, the wind felt
> frightened   tiny   important

> The boy was hurrying home with a bowl of flour. His mother needed the flour for supper. The wind blew the flour away. The boy was afraid his mother would be
> proud   angry   glad

> The wind saw what it had done. When it thought of the poor mother and the boy who would be hungry, it felt
> sorry   good   angry

● **DIRECTING THE LEARNER'S ATTENTION**

The purpose of this task is to teach the learner to infer mood implied in the paragraph. This is similar to storehouse module I-MT-2. To teach this skill you must direct the learner's attention to what the facts say and what his or her experience has taught about such concepts and ideas.

● **TEACHING ACTIVITIES**

This is a manipulative task similar to storehouse module I-MT-2, and you can adapt your teaching strategy from either the modeling or the discovery technique described in that objective.

● **SUGGESTIONS FOR RETEACHING**

If, after having been taught with either the modeling or the discovery technique, the learner does not understand how to infer the mood of a paragraph, you should adapt and use the suggestions in I-MT-2 to reteach the skill.

Do you *teach* reading or do you just plug your pupils into the newest commercial program?

● **SUGGESTIONS FOR PRACTICE**

After teaching the learner to infer mood, create practice activities to solidify the skill, using the suggestions provided in I-MT-2.

● **THE POSTTEST**

The procedure and criterion for mastery is the same as for the pretest, although you may want to substitute new material.

- **ENSURING TRANSFER**

You should use the suggestions in I-MT-2 and reading comprehension activities such as those included in the final chapter to ensure that the learner applies the skill of determining mood by inference during the routine language activities in the classroom.

# V•ET•1

- **THE PERFORMANCE OBJECTIVE**

When given a paragraph and the main idea, the learner will identify the details in the paragraph that are irrelevant.

- **THE PRETEST**

Direct the learner to read paragraphs like the following and to cross out the sentence in each paragraph that does not make sense. The criterion for mastery is 75 percent. (Readability: Second grade.)

> The shoemaker walked across the room. He opened the blue door of his inner workshop. Inside were rows of new shoes and neatly wrapped packages. He chose one of the packages. He placed it in Ann's lap. The baker pulled two loaves of freshly baked bread from the oven.

> Tom sat alone. The teacher looked at him. Some boys turned around and shook their fists at him. One boy walked by Tom's desk. The boy bumped him. Tom knew he would be happy in his new school.

> He did not look at all like a king. He was short. He was very shy. He was bald. And he had lost most of his teeth. He was a good example of a wise ruler. His pale blue eyes were close together and watery. His nose had a wart on it. His ears stuck out like small cups. His arms were too long. His legs were too short. He looked like a scarecrow in winter.

> I live in Big Valley, a town 50 miles from New York City. We live in a house with trees and a large lot. I used to live with my family in the city. We lived near Fifty-fifth Street and Third Avenue. When my parents were first married they lived in a very large apartment.

- **DIRECTING THE LEARNER'S ATTENTION**

The purpose of this task is to teach the learner to judge whether material is relevant or irrelevant. This is similar to storehouse module I-ET-1. To teach this skill you must direct the learner's attention to whether the details are relevant to the paragraph or not relevant.

- **TEACHING ACTIVITIES**

This is a evaluative thinking task similar to storehouse module I-ET-1, and you can adapt your teaching strategy from either the modeling or the discovery technique described in that objective.

- **SUGGESTIONS FOR RETEACHING**

If, after having been taught with either the modeling or the discovery technique, the learner does not understand how to judge whether details are relevant or irrelevant, you should adapt and use the suggestions in I-ET-1 to reteach the skill.

### ● SUGGESTIONS FOR PRACTICE

After teaching the learner the skill of judging details as relevant or irrelevant, create practice activities to solidify the skill, using the suggestions provided in I-ET-1.

### ● THE POSTTEST

The procedure and criterion for mastery are the same as for the pretest, although you may want to substitute new material.

### ● ENSURING TRANSFER

You should use the suggestions in I-ET-1 and reading comprehension activities such as those included in the final chapter to ensure that the learner applies the skill of judging relevant and irrelevant during the routine language activities in the classroom.

# CLUSTER VI

● **THE PERFORMANCE OBJECTIVE**

When given a fraction of a second to examine flashcards having printed on them the following words, the learner will pronounce each within one second.

| even | window | write | chair | behind | pony |
|------|--------|-------|-------|--------|------|
| wagon | woman | along | bee | pocket | TV |
| zoo | airplane | penny | picnic | toy | letter |
| under | food | stopped | story | live | enough |
| dress | sister | party | lost | open | boy |
| rocket | peanut | maybe | grass | better | rabbit |
| began | never | | | | |

● **THE PRETEST**

Print each of the preceding words on a flashcard. Flash each to the learner, giving him or her less than one second to examine each word before pronouncing it. The criterion for mastery is 100 percent.

● **DIRECTING THE LEARNER'S ATTENTION**

The purpose of this task is to teach the learner to recognize instantly and pronounce the words contained in the pretest when they are presented on

● 365

flashcards. This is a sight word recognition skill like that described in II-SW-6. To teach the skill you must make sure that the learner knows exactly what is to be learned, that the words being taught are in the child's speaking vocabulary, and that you have directed his or her attention by highlighting the unique visual characteristics of each word (such as the initial and final letters, length, shape, double letters, and so on.)

#### • TEACHING ACTIVITIES

This is a sight word recognition skill similar to that described in II-SW-6. If the learner does not recognize the word in print, adapt your teaching strategy from either the modeling technique or the discovery technique described in that objective. If the child confuses the word with another word similar to it, adapt your strategy from the suggestions contained in I-SW-17.

#### • SUGGESTIONS FOR RETEACHING

If, after having been taught with the suggested technique, the learner is unable to recognize instantly one of more of the words on the pretest, use the reteaching suggestions described in II-SW-6.

#### • SUGGESTIONS FOR PRACTICE

After successfully teaching the learner to recognize instantly the words on the pretest, create practice activities to solidify the skill, using the suggestions provided in II-SW-6.

#### • THE POSTTEST

The procedure and criterion for mastery for the posttest are the same as for the pretest.

#### • ENSURING TRANSFER

To make sure that this skill is applied, you must give the learner reading material containing the words now known at sight and have him or her read. You may guide the application by pointing out the words the child has just learned to recognize or, as he or she becomes more proficient, you can encourage independent reading of the newly learned words. Any material at the learner's instructional reading level and that contains the sight words would be appropriate. Additional suggestions for helping the learner use known sight words in context are contained in II-SW-6.

## VI•SW•2

#### • THE PERFORMANCE OBJECTIVE

When given a flash presentation of words that the learner frequently confuses, he or she will pronounce each word correctly within one second.

#### • THE PRETEST

You will note whether the learner is confusing words any time you test on sight words or listen to him or her read. If, during either of these activities, the learner says one word for another (such as **woman** for **women**), you should pair the words together and teach them, using the suggestions provided in this objective. No specific list of words is provided since various learners will confuse various words. As with other sight word objectives, the criterion for mastery is 100 percent, with any pair of confused words being taught.

## • DIRECTING THE LEARNER'S ATTENTION

The purpose of this task is to teach the learner to recognize instantly pairs of words that he or she has tended to confuse in the past. As such, it is similar to that described in I-SW-17. To teach this skill you must make sure that the learner has mastered the previous visual training skill, that he or she knows exactly what is to be learned, that the words being taught are in the learner's speaking vocabulary, and that you have directed the child's attention by highlighting the discriminator that sets one word apart from another (such as the **a** in **woman** and the **e** in **women.**)

Is your record-keeping device efficient?

## • TEACHING ACTIVITIES

In teaching this skill you can use either the modeling technique or the discovery technique described in I-SW-17, adjusting the suggestions to focus on the particular words the learner is confusing.

## • SUGGESTIONS FOR RETEACHING

If, after having been taught this skill with either the modeling or the discovery technique, the learner continues to confuse the words, you should use the reteaching suggestions provided in I-SW-17.

## • SUGGESTIONS FOR PRACTICE

Once the learner can instantly recognize the words that he or she was previously confusing, create practice activities to solidify the skill, using the suggestions provided in I-SW-17.

## • THE POSTTEST

The procedure and criterion for mastery are the same as for the pretest.

## • ENSURING TRANSFER

Once the learner can recognize the easily confused words, you should immediately provide for application of this skill by giving the child reading material containing the words he or she now knows at sight. For specific suggestions regarding such application activities see II-SW-6.

**VI•SW•3**

## • THE PERFORMANCE OBJECTIVE

When given the words he or she recognizes instantly, the learner will create and read a single-sentence story using these words.

## • THE PRETEST

Provide the learner with cards, each of which has printed on it a word he or she instantly recognizes. Say to the learner, "Today we are going to do something that is very hard. We are going to send messages. Look at the cards you have in front of you. Each card has a word on it that you know. Can you send me a message using the words you have there? If you want to send a message using a word you don't have on a card, tell me and I will make a card for you with that word on it." The criterion for mastery is the combination of any number of words in a way that is grammatically accurate and that makes sense. When the learner has formed his sentence, reinforce the value of his effort by reading it aloud yourself.

## • DIRECTING THE LEARNER'S ATTENTION

This is a language experience activity designed to teach the learner to produce and read messages using the individual words known at sight. As such, it is an application activity similar to that described in II-SW-8. To teach this activity you must make sure that the learner knows exactly what is to be learned and you must direct his or her attention to the idea the learner wishes to convey, to what his or her message will sound like when spoken, what printed word cards will be needed to "write" the message, and the order in which the words must be placed. You might highlight by asking a series of questions, such as, "What did you do yesterday after school that you could tell me about? Can you make a sentence about that and say it to me? What words did you use to say your sentence to me? How many of those words do you already have on cards and which ones will we have to make for you? What word will come first in your written message?"

## • TEACHING ACTIVITIES

This is a language experience activity similar to that described in II-SW-8. You should use the modeling and discovery techniques described in that objective as a basis for planning and teaching this task.

## • SUGGESTIONS FOR RETEACHING

If, after having been taught with either of the techniques described in the key objective, the learner is unable to create a single sentence message using his or her sight words, you should

1. Reteach the activity, using the alternate technique.
2. Be more specific in eliciting from the learner the idea he or she wishes to convey.
3. Be sure that the learner expresses his or her message first in oral form and that he or she understands that the written message will say the same thing as the oral message.
4. Be sure that the content of the message matches the learner's experience and change the subject to match his or her experience if necessary.

5. Recheck the learner's mastery of the sight words and reteach any that have not yet been completely mastered.
6. Return to the previous language experience objectives and make sure that the learner can do those simpler tasks before asking him or her to create entire sentences.

## • SUGGESTIONS FOR PRACTICE

Once the learner has been taught to use sight words to create and read sentences, devise practice activities to solidify this skill, adapting the suggestions provided in II-SW-8.

## • THE POSTTEST

The procedure and criterion for mastery for the posttest are the same as for the pretest.

## • ENSURING TRANSFER

The procedure and criterion for mastery for the posttest are the same as sight words in context. In addition to the application specified here, however, you should use the suggestions in II-SW-6 to make sure that the learner uses sight words in other contextual situations.

# VI•WA•1

## • THE PERFORMANCE OBJECTIVE

When given a known word illustrating the silent **e** vowel principle, the learner will correctly pronounce other words illustrating the silent **e** principle.

## • THE PRETEST

Use the following list of words. The first word in the list has been taught previously as a sight word. Have the learner identify the first word and then ask him or her to pronounce the remaining words. The criterion for mastery is 45 out of 50 correct. *Note:* Some of the words listed are nonsense words, which are included so that the learner *must* use analysis rather than sight recognition.

| | | | | | | |
|---|---|---|---|---|---|---|
| **ride** | woke | game | joke | name | shine | shese |
| hide | bake | gate | late | nose | side | blose |
| nive | wide | gave | like | note | skate | use |
| fake | cake | mile | live | plate | slide | ate |
| wake | dame | same | smade | rake | smile | line |
| wave | rope | hole | shake | drode | stone | shake |
| while | drive | shome | save | time | take | smoke |
| shite | fine | | | | | |

## • DIRECTING THE LEARNER'S ATTENTION

The purpose of this task is to teach the learner to pronounce words illustrating the silent **e** principle. This principle, together with others taught in subsequent objectives, provides the learner with problem-solving techniques to use when trying to determine the pronounciation of unknown words that do not fit any of the letter substitution skills previously taught. Although the learner could learn to pronounce such words by looking for patterns and substituting initial consonants (as in **ride, hide, wide,** and so on), as has been illustrated in previous objectives, the strategy here is first to try teaching the child to generalize to the principle, with the letter substitution technique being reserved for reteaching if it becomes necessary. Armed with both substitution skills and generalizations of the major vowel principles, the learner is equipped to analyze most of the vowel patterns he or she is likely to encounter in his reading.

To teach this (or any other) principle you should follow a three-step sequence in which first the words are represented orally, then the words are represented visually, and finally the principle is modeled. For this particular principle you would, after stating exactly what is to be learned, direct the child's attention by first using auditory highlighting of the long vowel sound in the middle of the words, then visually highlighting the medial vowel and silent **e** in each of the words and, finally modeling the principle itself. (With such words as **ride, wide,** and **hide,** for instance, you would first say each word while exaggerating the long **i** sound in the middle, then write each word with the medial **i** and the final **e** circled, and finally model the effect the final **e** has on the medial vowel.)

*Caution:* All vowel principles have exceptions. Consequently, you must be careful to point out that the principle is generally but not universally true, citing examples of exceptions to support the point. For the silent **e** principle, for instance, you might illustrate with such common exceptions as **come** and **have.**

- **THIS IS A STOREHOUSE OBJECTIVE**

The following instructional activities are your storehouse of techniques for developing skill in using various vowel principles in analyzing unknown words. This skill recurs with other vowel principles in subsequent objectives in the hierarchy. The instructual suggestions that follow are to be adapted and used with each of these as they occur.

- **TEACHING ACTIVITIES**

*The modeling technique.* Rearrange the words provided in the pretest so that the long **a** words are together, the long **i** words are together, and so on. Start with the **a** words. Say the word, using the say-it-slow, say-it-fast technique (see I-WA-5) to exaggerate the sound of the medial vowel. Say, "I am going to say a word slowly and then fast and I am going to listen carefully to the sound I hear in the middle. Here is the word. **L . . . a-a . . . te. Late.** The sound I hear in the middle is **a.**" Repeat the process with other words, gradually diminishing the modeling you do and the exaggeration you provide on the medial sound until the learner is able to identify the sound in the middle. Then write on the board the same words you just used, circling the medial **a** and the silent **e**. Say, "Here are the words we were just listening to. We said that the sound we heard in the middle was **a**. I am going to look at the first word. What letter does it have in the middle? It is an **a**. I heard an **a** sound and the letter in the middle is an **a**. But now let's look at the last letter in the word. The last letter is an **e**. We did not hear an **e** in the word but it has one at the end." Continue this process with subsequent **a** words, gradually diminishing the assistance you provide until the learner is independently identifying the visual pattern of the letters in the words. Then model the principle for the learner, saying, "Let's look at the words we have. In each word we heard an **a** sound and we saw an **a** letter in the middle and an **e** which did not make any sound on the end of the word. It looks like we can expect a word that ends in an **e** to have a middle letter that says its own name and that the final **e** will be silent. Let's look at some of the other words to make sure." Repeat basically the same procedure with words having other medial letters, diminishing the assistance you provide auditorily, and visually and in verbalizing the principle. You can go on to practice when the learner can look at a word illustrating the silent **e** principle and accurately predict the pronounciation of the word.

*The discovery technique.* As in the modeling technique, arrange the pretest words according to common medial sounds and start with **a** words. Direct the learners to listen carefully to the middle sounds of the words you are going to say and to tell you what letter sound he or she heard. Use the say-it-slow, say-it-fast technique (see I-WA-5) to highlight the medial sound, gradually diminishing the assistance as the learner responds correctly. When the learner has established that the sound in the middle is an **a** sound, direct him or her to look at the list of words you have on the board and to tell you what they have in common. You may circle (or otherwise highlight) the medial letter and the final **e** to direct the learner's attention to the visual features you want him or her to note, diminishing such assistance as the child begins to recognize the visual pattern. Then pronounce the first few words for the learner, stating that they are the same words the learner had been listening to you say earlier. As you pronounce the words encourage the child to hypothesize regarding how he or she could predict the sound of the middle and final letters in each of the subsequent words in the list. Provide as much assistance as necessary initially, gradually diminishing this as the learner begins to see the effect the silent **e** has on the preceding vowel. Repeat the process with the other lists of words, providing less and less help each time. Once the learner can accurately predict the pronounciation of words illustrating the silent **e** principle, he or she is ready for practice.

Remember, not all children need systematic skill instruction. Let those who blossom by themselves do so!

## • SUGGESTIONS FOR RETEACHING

If, after having been taught with either the modeling or the discovery technique, the learner is unable to pronounce words illustrating the silent **e** principle, you should

1. Reteach the skill, using the alternate technique.
2. Reexamine your attenders, making sure that you are providing enough highlighting on the vowel sound and on the visual pattern of medial vowel and final **e**.
3. Reteach the skill as a task of letter substitution, arranging the words according to common final endings (such as **ride, wide,** and **hide**) and using the teaching suggestions provided in II-WA-18.

● **SUGGESTIONS FOR PRACTICE**

Once the learner can pronounce words illustrating the silent **e** principle, use the following suggestions to create practice activities to solidify the skill.

1. Using pairs of words such as the following, play games with the learner that require pronouncing each pair of words and explaining the effect of the silent **e**.

   | not | Tim | mad | hid | shin | rid | rod | slid |
   |-----|-----|-----|-----|------|-----|-----|------|
   | note | time | made | hide | shine | ride | rode | slide |

2. Using words such as those listed in the preceding item, construct a word wheel or a slip card (see II-WA-18) in which a word is first pronounced without the final **e** and then is pronounced with the final **e**.
3. Make up short stories for the learner to read, making sure that each story has many opportunities to recognize and use the silent **e** principle (as in "**Tim** did **not** get the **note** on **time**.")
4. Make up nonsense words that illustrate the principle and have the learner read these or use nonsense words found in poems such as Lewis Carroll's "Jabberwocky" and have the learner read such lines as, "Twas brillig and the slithy **toves**. . . ."
5. Play a variation of bingo in which one-syllable words with no silent **e** are printed in each square. The learner calls out a one-syllable word with a short medial vowel and the learner looks for this word on the card. If the learner has the word **and** if he or she can correctly pronounce the new word that is made by adding an **e** at the end, the learner can cover it with a marker. When the learner has all the words in a row covered, he or she can call "Bingo." If the learner can then pronounce each word on the card *and* what each word would be if an **e** were added at the end, he or she wins the game.
6. Play a game with the learner using a construction paper spider web and a deck of cards that have vowel generalizations printed on them. The learner picks a card from the pile, puts the vowel generalization with one of the beginning letters in the spider web, and pronounces the new word. If the learner pronounces the word correctly, he or she fills that space in the spider web with a construction paper fly. When the spider web is filled with flies, the game is over.

7. Play a form of the card game Fish with the learner. Each player is dealt a group of playing cards that have either beginning consonants or endings that include a vowel generalization printed on them. The object is to get rid of all your cards by pairing beginnings with endings and correctly pronouncing the word. Each player asks the player to his or her right for a specific letter or letter combination. If that player has the requested card, he or she must give it up and the first player can use it to complete a word and discard those cards. If a requested card is not available, however, the first player must draw from the pile.

8. Play a variation of a ring toss game with the learner. On each ring print a beginning consonant letter or combination and on each hook print an ending that illustrates a vowel generalization. The players throw the rings in an attempt to put the ring on the hook. If successful, the learner gets an additional point if he or she can also pair the beginning sound on the ring with the ending on the hook and pronounce the new word.

9. A variation of baseball can be played with the learner. The batter is given four examples of vowel generalization (such as **i–e** or **o–a**.) The pitcher "throws" the batter two consonants for each generalization, which the learner must then combine with the vowels; then the learner must pronounce the word. For each word completed correctly, the learner receives one base; if all four words are correctly done, it is a home run.

10. Play a variation of Scrabble with the learner in which some of the vowel letter combinations, such as **oa, ow, ee,** and so on, are used and other word blocks are consonants. For each word constructed the learner must provide an accurate pronunciation in order to receive the credit.

### • THE POSTTEST
The pretest can be used also for the posttest. The procedure and criterion for mastery are the same.

### • ENSURING TRANSFER
Once the learner has practiced this analysis technique, you must be sure that he or she is given reading material that call for the use of the skill and that you guide him or her in applying the technique when such unknown words are met in daily reading. Suitable application situations include basal textbooks, library books, language experience stories, magazines, comic books, and any other reading material in which the learner encounters unknown words that can be analyzed through application of the silent **e** principle.

## VI•WA•2

### • THE PERFORMANCE OBJECTIVE
When given a known word illustrating the two-vowels-together principle, the learner will correctly pronounce other words illustrating this principle.

Use the following list of words. The first word in the list has been previously taught as a sight word. Have the learner identify the first word and then ask him to pronounce the remaining words. The criterion for mastery is 22 out of 26 correct. *Note:* Some of the words listed are nonsense words, which are included so that the learner *must* use analysis rather than sight recognition.

| **read** | peat | nail | seat | wheat |
|---|---|---|---|---|
| moat | suit | paint | tail | rain |
| clean | train | plain | teach | fruit |
| coat | leaves | road | wait | goat |
| each | mail | seap | weak | trail |
| east | meat | | | |

### • DIRECTING THE LEARNER'S ATTENTION

The purpose of this task is to teach the learner to pronounce words illustrating the two-vowels-together principle. As such, the task is similar to storehouse module VI-WA-1. To teach this skill you should direct the learner's attention by stating exactly what is to be learned and by highlighting the medial sound, the vowel pattern, and the resultant principle. (For words such as **tail, nail,** and **trail,** for instance, you would first say each word while exaggerating the long a sound in the middle, then write each word that the **ai** circled, and finally model the effect of two vowels together by pronouncing the words for the learner.)

### • TEACHING ACTIVITIES

In teaching this vowel generalization you can use either the modeling or the discovery technique described in VI-WA-1, adjusting the suggestions to focus on the two-vowels-together principle.

### • SUGGESTIONS FOR RETEACHING

If, after having been taught with either the modeling or the discovery technique, the learner is unable to pronounce words illustrating the two-vowels-together principle, you should

1. Reteach the skill, using the alternate technique.
2. Reexamine your attenders, making sure that you are providing enough highlighting on the medial sound and the visual pattern of two vowels together.
3. Reteach the skill as a task of letter substitution, arranging the words according to common final endings (such as **tail, nail,** and **trail**) and using the teaching suggestions provided in II-WA-18.

### • SUGGESTIONS FOR PRACTICE

Once the learner can pronounce words illustrating the two-vowels-together principle, create practice activities to solidify the skill, using the suggestions provided in VI-WA-1.

### • THE POSTTEST

The pretest can be used also as the posttest. The procedure and criterion for mastery are the same.

### • ENSURING TRANSFER

You should use the suggestions provided in VI-WA-1 to be sure that the learner uses the skill in pursuing his or her daily reading activities.

### • THE PERFORMANCE OBJECTIVE

When given a known one-syllable word ending in a vowel, the learner will correctly pronounce other syllable units ending in a vowel.

### • THE PRETEST

Use the following lists of words. The first word in each list has been previously taught as a sight word or as a word previously analyzed. Read the first word in the list and ask the learner to pronounce the remaining words. The criterion for mastery is 13 out of 15 correct. *Note:* Some of the words listed are nonsense words, which are included so that the learner *must* use analysis rather than sight recognition.

| me | no | | my |
|----|----|----|----|
| we | so | by | sky |
| be | go | why | dry |
| de | bo | cry | try |
| | ho | fly | sly |

### • DIRECTING THE LEARNER'S ATTENTION

The purpose of this task is to teach the learner to pronounce words illustrating the open-syllable principle, in which a vowel ending a syllable or a word is pronounced long. As such, the task is a vowel generalization similar to storehouse module VI-WA-1. To teach this skill you should direct the learner's attention by stating exactly what is to be learned and by highlighting the ending letter, the ending sound, and the resultant principle. (For words such as **me, we,** and **be,** for instance, you would circle the ending **e** and exaggerate the long **e** sound heard at the end.)

### • TEACHING ACTIVITIES

In teaching this vowel generalization you can use either the modeling technique or the discovery technique described in VI-WA-1, adjusting the suggestions to focus on one-syllable words ending in a vowel.

### • SUGGESTIONS FOR RETEACHING

If, after having been taught with either the modeling or the discovery technique, the learner is unable to pronounce one-syllable words ending in a vowel, you should

1. Reteach the skill, using the alternate technique.
2. Reexamine your attenders, making sure that you are providing enough highlighting on the sound of the ending vowel and the visual form of the ending vowel.
3. Reteach the skill as a task of letter substitution, arranging the words according to common final endings (such as **me, we, be**) and using the teaching suggestions provided in II-WA-18.

### • SUGGESTIONS FOR PRACTICE

Once the learner can pronounce one-syllable words ending in a vowel, create practice activities to solidify the skill, using the suggestions provided in VI-WA-1.

### • THE POSTTEST

The pretest can also be used as the posttest. The procedure and criterion for mastery are the same.

### • ENSURING TRANSFER

You should use the suggestions provided in VI-WA-1 to make sure that the learner uses the skill in pursuing daily reading activities.

# VI•WA•4

### • THE PERFORMANCE OBJECTIVE

When given a known word illustrating the two-vowels-together principle as it applies to the **ow** combination, the learner will correctly pronounce other words illustrating this principle.

### • THE PRETEST

Use the following list of words. The first word in the list has been previously taught as a sight word. Have the learner identify the first word and then ask him or her to pronounce the remaining words. The criterion for mastery is seven out of eight correct.

**slow**

| | | | |
|---|---|---|---|
| row | mow | flow | crow |
| show | grow | snow | blow |

### • DIRECTING THE LEARNER'S ATTENTION

The purpose of this task is to teach the learner to pronounce words illustrating the two-vowels-together principle as it relates to the **ow** combination. As such, the task is similar to storehouse module VI-WA-1. To teach this skill you should direct the learner's attention by stating exactly what is to be learned and by highlighting the medial sound, the **ow** pattern, and the resultant principle. (For words such as **row**, for instance, you would first say the word while exaggerating the long **o** in the middle, then write the word with the **ow** circled, and finally model the effect of the principle by pronouncing the word for the learner.)

### • TEACHING ACTIVITIES

In teaching this vowel generalization you can use either the modeling or the discovery technique described in VI-WA-1, adjusting the suggestions to focus on the two-vowels-together principle as it applies to the **ow** combination.

### • SUGGESTIONS FOR RETEACHING

If, after having been taught with either the modeling or the discovery technique, the learner is unable to pronounce words illustrating the two-vowels-together principle as it applies to the **ow** combination, you should

1. Reteach the skill, using the alternate technique.
2. Reexamine your attenders, making sure that you are providing enough highlighting on the medial sound and the **ow** letter combination.
3. Reteach the skill as a task of letter substitution using the teaching suggestions provided in II-WA-18.

Are you directly assisting the pupils who have difficulty learning to read?

### • SUGGESTIONS FOR PRACTICE

Once the learner can pronounce words illustrating the two-vowels-together principle as it applies to **ow** words, create practice activities to solidify the skill, using the suggestions provided in VI-WA-1.

### • THE POSTTEST

The pretest can be used also as the posttest. The procedure and criterion for mastery are the same.

### • ENSURING TRANSFER

You should use the suggestions provided in VI-WA-1 to be sure that the learner uses the skill in pursuing daily reading activities in the classroom.

## VI•WA•5

### • THE PERFORMANCE OBJECTIVE

When given words containing the **ou** and **ow** diphthongs, the learner will correctly pronounce other words containing these diphthongs.

### • THE PRETEST

Use the following lists of words. The first word in each of the two lists has been taught previously as a sight word. Have the learner identify the first word in the list and then have him or her pronounce the succeeding words. The criterion for mastery is 11 out of 13 correct, with no more than one error in each list. *Note:* Some of the words listed are nonsense words, which are included so that the learner must use analysis techniques rather than sight recognition.

| out | | how | |
|------|-------|-------|-------|
| mouse | mouth | bow | town |
| count | clout | low | drown |
| loud | bloud | clown | slowt |
| | | frown | |

• DIRECTING THE LEARNER'S ATTENTION

The purpose of this task is to teach the learner to pronounce words containing the **ou** and **ow** diphthongs. As such, the task is similar to storehouse module VI-WA-1. To teach this skill you should direct the learner's attention by stating exactly what is to be learned and by highlighting the sound of the diphthong, the **ou** or **ow** letters, and the resultant principle. (In words such as **mouse,** for instance, you would first say the word while exaggerating the sound in the middle, then write the word with the **ou** circled, and finally model the principle by pronouncing the word for the learner.)

• TEACHING ACTIVITIES

In teaching this vowel generalization you can use either the modeling or the discovery technique described in VI-WA-1, adjusting the suggestions to focus on the **ou** and **ow** diphthongs.

• SUGGESTIONS FOR RETEACHING

If, after having been taught with either the modeling or the discovery technique, the learner is unable to pronounce words containing the **ou** or **ow** diphthongs, you should

1. Reteach the skill, using the alternate technique.
2. Reexamine your attenders, making sure that you are providing enough highlighting on the sound of the diphthong and the **ou** and **ow** letter combination.
3. Reteach the skill as a task of letter substitution, using the teaching suggestions provided in II-WA-18.

• SUGGESTIONS FOR PRACTICE

Once the learner can pronounce words containing the **ou** and **ow** diphthongs, create practice activities to solidify the skill, using the suggestions provided in VI-WA-1.

• THE POSTTEST

The pretest can be used also as the posttest.. The procedure and criterion for mastery are the same.

You should use the suggestions provided in VI-WA-1 to be sure that the learner uses the skill in pursuing daily reading activities in the classroom.

• **THE PERFORMANCE OBJECTIVE**

When given spoken stimulus words ending with either the –nd, the –nt, or the –nk sounds and a group of three other words of which one ends with either the –nd, the –nt, or the –nk sounds, the learner will pair the two words that end in the same sound.

• **THE PRETEST**

Using the following words, say to the learner, "Here are three words. Listen carefully. (Say the three words.) Which one sounds like (say the stimulus word at the end?" Repeat the three words. The criterion for mastery is five out of six correct.

| | | | |
|---|---|---|---|
| bank | pond | best | Which one sounds like **land** at the end? Repeat the three words. |
| thin | rack | pink | Which one sounds like **tank** at the end? Repeat the three words. |
| sent | send | spent | Which one sounds like **hunt** at the end? Repeat the three words. |
| take | think | tanned | Which one sounds like **tank** at the end? Repeat the three words. |
| plant | plate | plan | Which one sounds like **hunt** at the end? Repeat the three words. |
| last | found | flank | Which one sounds like **land** at the end? Repeat the three words. |

• **DIRECTING THE LEARNER'S ATTENTION**

The purpose of this task is to teach the learner to distinguish the –nd, –nt, and –nk sounds from other ending consonant sounds. As such, the task is similar to storehouse module I-WA-5. To teach this skill you must direct the learner's attention by stating exactly what is to be learned and by highlighting the ending –nd, –nt, and –nk sounds of the words as described in I-WA-5.

• **TEACHING ACTIVITIES**

In teaching this auditory discrimination skill you can use either the modeling technique or the discovery technique described in I-WA-5, adjusting the suggestions to focus on the –nd, –nt, and –nk ending sounds.

• **SUGGESTIONS FOR RETEACHING**

If, after having been taught this skill with either the modeling or the discovery technique, the learner is unable to discriminate auditorily the –nd, –nt, and –nk sounds from other ending consonant sounds, you should

1. Reteach the skill, using the alternate technique.
2. Reexamine your attenders, making sure that the learner is listening to the *ending* sounds and that your highlighting is emphatic enough to help him or her distinguish the ending –nd, –nt, and –nk sounds from among ending sounds.
3. Return to the previous auditory discrimination skills, making sure that the learner can distinguish single consonants in an ending position before requiring him or her to distinguish the –nd, –nt, and –nk ending sounds.

### • SUGGESTIONS FOR PRACTICE

Once the learner can distinguish the –nd, –nt, and –nk sounds from other ending consonant sounds, create practice activities to solidify the skill, using the suggestions provided in I-WA-5.

### • THE POSTTEST

The procedure and criterion for mastery are the same as the for the pretest. Use the following words.

| | | | |
|---|---|---|---|
| wink | wind | lamp | Which one sounds like **land** at the end? Repeat the three words. |
| tent | hug | hunk | Which one sounds like **hunt** at the end? Repeat the three words. |
| blind | blink | blimp | Which one sounds like **tank** at the end? Repeat the three words. |
| meant | mark | hurt | Which one sounds like **hunt** at the end? Repeat the three words. |
| stick | stink | stand | Which one sounds like **tank** at the end? Repeat the three words. |
| lank | found | flake | Which one sounds like **land** at the end? Repeat the three words. |

### • ENSURING TRANSFER

Although the learner will be applying this skill while learning to attach the sound to letters in subsequent objectives, you should also use the suggestions provided in I-WA-5, to make sure that the skill is used by the child during the routine daily reading activities of the classroom.

## VI•WA•7

### • THE PERFORMANCE OBJECTIVE

When given three cards that have the letters **nd** printed on one, the letters **nt** on another, and the letters **nk** on the third and a spoken stimulus word that ends in either the –nd, the –nt, or the –nk sounds, the learner will point to the letter card having printed on it the letters with which the word ends.

### • THE PRETEST

Give the learner three cards having printed on them either the letters **nd**, **nt**, or **nk.** Say the following words, directing the learner to point to the letter card that has printed on it the letters with which the spoken word ends. The criterion for mastery is five out of six correct.

    stand   pink   plant   round   thank   sent

## • DIRECTING THE LEARNER'S ATTENTION

The purpose of this task is to teach the learner to establish a sound-symbol connection between the letter combinations **nd, nt,** and **nk** and the sounds these combinations make at the end of words. As such, this skill is similar to storehouse module I-WA-9. To teach this skill you must direct the learner's attention by stating exactly what is to be learned and by high-lighting both the sound heard at the end of the word and the form of the letter combinations at the end of the words. (In the word **stand,** for instance, you might exaggerate the ending sound of the −nd while simultaneously pointing to the cutout letters **nd.**)

## • TEACHING ACTIVITIES

In teaching this sound-symbol connection skill you can use either the model-ing technique or the discovery technique described in I-WA-9, adjusting the suggestions to focus on the ending −nd, −nt, and −nk sounds.

*Are you using your basal textbook or is your basal textbook using you?*

## • SUGGESTIONS FOR RETEACHING

If, after having been taught this skill with either the modeling or the dis-covery technique, the learner is unable to connect letter and sound for the −nd, −nt, and −nk endings, you should

1. Reteach the skill, using the alternate technique.
2. Be more specific in directing the learner's attention, making sure that he or she is listening to the ending sound while simultaneously looking at the letter combination.
3. Use more emphasis in highlighting the ending sound, the letter combina-tion, and the connection between them.
4. Return to the previous objective and make sure that the learner can dis-tinguish the **nd, nt,** and **nk** sounds from other ending consonant sounds before requiring him or her to connect the sound with the letter com-bination.

## • SUGGESTIONS FOR PRACTICE

Once the learner has successfully connected the **nd, nt,** and **nk** letter com-bination to the sounds these combinations make at the end of words, create practice activities to solidify the skill, using the suggestions provided in I-WA-9.

## • THE POSTTEST

The procedure and criterion for mastery are the same as for the pretest. Use the following words.

    hunt   think   found   bent   stink   sand

Although the learner will be applying this skill in subsequent skills in the hierarchy, you should also use the suggestions provided in I-WA-9 to make sure that the child uses the skill during the daily reading activities of the classroom.

## VI•WA•8

• THE PERFORMANCE OBJECTIVE

When given words he or she pronounced in previous objectives, the learner will replace the final consonant sound of these words with the –nd, the –nt, or the –nk sound and pronounce the new words.

• THE PRETEST

Use the following word list. The first word in each list has been previously taught. Have the learner identify the first word in each list and then ask him or her to pronounce the remaining words in each list. Criterion for mastery is 20 out of 22 correct, with no ending sound being missed more than once. *Note:* Some of the words listed are nonsense words, which are included so that the learner *must* use analysis techniques rather than sight recognition.

| sat | pot | wit | mouse | thank | ten |
|------|-------|------|--------|-------|-------|
| sand | pond | wind | mound | think | tent |
| land | shond | | sound | drink | sent |
| band | | | found | pink | bent |
| stand | | | bound | stink | went |
| | | | ground | blink | blent |

• DIRECTING THE LEARNER'S ATTENTION

The purpose of this skill is to teach the learner to substitute the **nd, nt,** and **nk** letter combinations in the final position of known vowel phonograms and pronounce the new words. As such, the task is similar to storehouse module II-WA-18. To teach this skill you must direct the learner's attention by stating exactly what is to be learned and by highlighting the final letter combination and the letters that are common from word to word. (In the word **sand,** for instance, you might circle the **–nd** ending, underline the **sa,** and have the learner use the say-it-slow, say-it-fast technique (see I-WA-5) in pronouncing the word.)

• TEACHING ACTIVITIES

In teaching this letter substitution skill you can use either the modeling technique or the discovery technique described in II-WA-18, adjusting the sugestions to focus on the **nd, nt,** and **nk** in the final position of the words.

• SUGGESTIONS FOR RETEACHING

If, after having been taught this skill with either the modeling or the discovery technique, the learner is unable to substitute the **nd, nt,** and **nk** letter combinations in the final position of known vowel phonograms and pronounce the new words, you should use the reteaching suggestions provided in II-WA-18, adapting them to fit this objective.

### • SUGGESTIONS FOR PRACTICE

Once the learner can substitute the **nd, nt,** and **nk** in the final position of known vowel phonograms and pronounce the new words, create practice activities to solidify the skill, using the suggestions provided in II-WA-18.

### • ENSURING TRANSFER

You should use the suggestions provided in II-WA-18 to make sure that this skill is used by the learner during daily reading activities in the classroom.

### • THE PERFORMANCE OBJECTIVE

When given known sight words, the learner will pronounce these words when they are prefixed by **dis–** and **un–**.

### • THE PRETEST

Use the following lists of words. Have the learner identify the first word in each list, first without the prefix and then with it added. Next, direct him or her to pronounce the other words in the list. The criterion for mastery is 7 out of 8 correct.

| please | displease | happy | unhappy |
|--------|-----------|-------|---------|
|        | dislike   |       | unjust  |
|        | discolor  |       | unkind  |
|        | distrust  |       | unlike  |

### • DIRECTING THE LEARNER'S ATTENTION

The purpose of this task is to teach the learner to pronounce words that are composed of a known root word and the prefix **dis–** or **un–**. As such, this skill is similar to storehouse module II-WA-25. To teach this skill you must direct the learner's attention by stating exactly what is to be learned and by highlighting both the known root word and the prefix. (In the word **dislike,** for instance, you might circle both **like** and **dis.**)

### • TEACHING ACTIVITIES

In teaching this structural analysis skill you can use either the modeling technique or the discovery technique described in II-WA-25, adjusting the suggestions to focus on the prefixes **dis–** and **un–**.

### • SUGGESTIONS FOR RETEACHING

If, after having been taught with either the modeling or the discovery technique, the learner is unable to pronounce words composed of a known root and the prefix **dis–** or **un–**, you should use the reteaching suggestions provided in II-WA-25.

● **SUGGESTIONS FOR PRACTICE**

Once the learner can pronounce words composed of known root words and the prefix **dis–** and **un–**, create practice activities to solidify the skill, using the suggestions provided in II-WA-25.

● **THE POSTTEST**

The pretest can be used for the posttest. The procedure and criterion for mastery are the same.

● **ENSURING TRANSFER**

You should use the suggestions provided in II-WA-25 to make sure the learner uses this skill in pursuing daily reading activities.

# VI•IG•1

● **THE PERFORMANCE OBJECTIVE**

When given content words identified by the teacher, the learner will use each word correctly in an oral sentence.

● **THE PRETEST**

The words to be tested are selected by the teacher. These may be words that appear in the basal text or in stories being read in class that are associated with the study of a particular content area. To test for meaning of such words, say each word out loud to the learner. Ask him or her to make up a sentence or to "send a message" using that word. The criterion for mastery is 100 percent, since any word not used correctly will have to be taught.

The learner is asked to identify the following words in print in the next cluster of skills. You should include these words among those you test to make sure that he or she knows their meaning before pronouncing them.

| post | held | fire | uncle | quite |
|------|------|------|-------|-------|
| voice | quick | hello | egg | animal |
| war | roar | hair | hurt | every |
| warm | arrow | honey | climb | turn |
| wonder | bump | piece | end | kept |
| breakfast | country | roll | circus | large |
| feather | elephant | turtle | kind | noise |
| umbrella | board | move | floor | else |
| nothing | caught | both | clothes | already |
| field | early | bowl | paw | always |

● **DIRECTING THE LEARNER'S ATTENTION**

The purpose of this task is to teach the learner the meaning of new words. This is similar to the storehouse module I-IG-1 but different words are being taught. To teach this skill you must direct the learner's attention by (1) providing either a direct or a vicarious experience to form a basis for the concept, (2) identifying the characteristics of this concept, and (3) connecting the concept to its word label. *Note:* This objective focuses on meaning alone. The learner should not be asked to pronounce these words as they appear in print until after this skill has been mastered.

## • TEACHING ACTIVITIES

This is a word meaning skill similar to module I-IG-1, and you can adapt your teaching strategy from either the modeling or the discovery techniques described in that objective.

## • SUGGESTIONS FOR RETEACHING

If, after having been taught with either the modeling or the discovery technique, the learner does not understand the meaning of any word in this objective, you should adapt and use the suggestions in I-IG-1 to reteach the skill.

## • SUGGESTIONS FOR PRACTICE

After teaching the learner the meaning of these words, create practice activities to solidify the skill, using the suggestions provided in I-IG-1.

## • THE POSTTEST

The procedure and criterion for mastery are the same as for the pretest.

## • ENSURING TRANSFER

You should use the suggestions in I-IG-1 and comprehension activities such as those found in the final chapter to be sure that the learner applies the new word meanings during the routine daily language activities of the classroom.

## VI•IG•2

## • THE PERFORMANCE OBJECTIVE

When given words containing the prefixes **im–**, **in–**, and **re–**, the learner will use each word correctly in an oral sentence.

## • THE PRETEST

Say each word to be tested out loud for the child, asking him or her to make up a sentence using the word you have just said. The criterion for mastery is 100 percent. Words such as the following can be used.

impossible   inability   reopen   repave   impolite

## • DIRECTING THE LEARNER'S ATTENTION

The purpose of this task is to teach the learner the meaning of the prefixes **im–**, **in–**, and **re–**. To teach this skill you must be sure that the learner has a meaning for the root word and you must direct his or her attention to the prefix, its meaning, and the way the prefix alters the meaning of the root word.

## • TEACHING ACTIVITIES

This is a meaning unit task similar to storehouse module I-IG-2, and you can adapt your teaching strategy from either the modeling or the discovery techniques described in that objective.

## • SUGGESTIONS FOR RETEACHING

If, after having been taught with either the modeling or the discovery technique, the learner does not understand the meaning of the words in this objective, you should adapt and use the suggestions in I-IG-2 to reteach the skill.

## • SUGGESTIONS FOR PRACTICE

After teaching the learner the meaning of the words, create practice activities to solidify the skill, using the suggestions provided in I-IG-2.

## • THE POSTTEST

The procedure and criterion are the same as for the pretest.

## • ENSURING TRANSFER

You should use the suggestions in I-IG-2 and comprehension activities such as those in the final chapter to make sure that the learner applies the new word meanings during the routine language activities in the classroom.

## VI•IG•3

## • THE PERFORMANCE OBJECTIVE

When given a paragraph containing a compare-contrast relationship, the learner identifies both the relationship and the function words that signal the relationship.

## • THE PRETEST

Direct the learner to read paragraphs like the following and to select the ideas that are being compared (or contrasted) in each and the word that signals the relationship. The criterion for mastery is 75 percent. (Readability: Third grade).

Pretend that your mother wanted some meat to eat. She would go to the refrigerator to get it. If she had no meat she could go to a store to buy some. But if a pioneer wanted meat to make a stew, he or she would have to hunt for it.

If your mother told you to put some potatoes on to boil, you would probably put them into a pan. You would cover the potatoes with water. Then you would put the pan on a stove. Pioneers boiled potatoes in another way. They had to boil them in a kettle. The kettle was in the fireplace.

It is easy to get books today. Bookstores have exciting and colorful books. Boys and girls want to read them. Some schools have libraries. Boys and girls can borrow books from them. Many towns and cities have libraries too. However, it was much harder for a pioneer to get a book.

People today live in many kinds of homes. Some people live in houses made of sawed lumber, bricks, metal, stone, or other things. Some people live in house trailers. Some live in big apartment buildings. However, pioneers would not picture the many kinds of houses today. Their homes were all built with whatever materials they could find.

### • DIRECTING THE LEARNER'S ATTENTION

The purpose of this task is to teach the learner the compare and contrast relationship and the function words that signal this relationship. This is similar to storehouse module I-IG-3. To teach this skill you must direct the learner's attention by emphasizing the comparison and contrast relationship and the function word that signals the relationship.

Some children do not easily transfer learned skills. Are you planning guided application activities. for these pupils?

### • TEACHING ACTIVITIES

This is an information-gathering task similar to storehouse module I-IG-3, and you can adapt your teaching strategy from either the modeling or the discovery technique described in that objective.

### • SUGGESTIONS FOR RETEACHING

If, after having been taught with either the modeling or the discovery technique, the learner does not understand compare and contrast relationship, you should adapt and use the suggestions in I-IG-3 to reteach the skill.

### • SUGGESTIONS FOR PRACTICE

After teaching the learner the compare and contrast relationship skill, create practice activities to solidify the skill, using the suggestions provided in I-IG-3.

### • THE POSTTEST

The procedure and criterion for mastery are the same as for the pretest, although you may want to substitute new material.

### • ENSURING TRANSFER

You should use the suggestions in I-IG-3 and reading comprehension activities such as those included in the final chapter to make sure that the learner applies the skill of compare and contrast relationship during the routine language activities in the classroom.

● **THE PERFORMANCE OBJECTIVE**

When given a group of sentences containing direct quotations, the learner will read only the words to be said by the speaker.

● **THE PRETEST**

Direct the learner to read sentences like the following to himself and then to read out loud to you only those words spoken by the characters in the story. The criterion for mastery is 100 percent. (Readability: First grade.)

> Ned was telling everyone about the baseball game. "I wish you could have seen it," he said. Timmy asked, "Who won the game?" "I don't know," said Ned. "I was too busy eating hot dogs!"

● **DIRECTING THE LEARNER'S ATTENTION**

The purpose of this task is to teach the learner the relationships signaled by the quotation marks. This is similar to storehouse module V-IG-4. To teach this skill you must direct the learner's attention to the quotation marks, since they signal the words spoken directly by the speaker.

● **TEACHING ACTIVITIES**

This is an information-gathering task similar to storehouse module V-IG-4, and you can adapt your teaching strategy from either the modeling or the discovery technique described in that objective.

● **SUGGESTIONS FOR RETEACHING**

If, after having been taught with either the modeling or the discovery technique, the learner does not understand the relationship that quotation marks signal, you should adapt and use the suggestions in V-IG-4 to reteach the skill.

● **SUGGESTIONS FOR PRACTICE**

After teaching the learner the relationship signaled by quotation marks, create practice activities to solidify the skill, using the suggestions provided in V-IG-4.

● **THE POSTTEST**

The procedure and criterion for mastery are the same as for the pretest, although you may want to substitute new material.

● **ENSURING TRANSFER**

You should use the suggestions in V-IG-4 and reading comprehension activities such as those included in the final chapter to make sure that the learner applies quotation marks to determine direct spoken words during the routine language activities in the classroom.

• **THE PERFORMANCE OBJECTIVE**

When given written sentences in which the subject and predicate phrases are out of order, the learner will arrange the phrases in the correct order and orally read the sentence.

• **THE PRETEST**

The sentences to be tested are selected by the teacher and should reflect the learner's background experience. Length and complexity of the sentences will depend upon the learner's oral language level. To test the learner's skill write several sentences, some of which have the subject and predicate phrases out of order. Have the learner read the sentences to you with the phrases in the correct order. The criterion for mastery is 80 percent. Use sentences such as the following one:

Will eat the farmer's carrots/even a tiny rabbit.

• **DIRECTING THE LEARNER'S ATTENTION**

The purpose of this task is to teach the learner how the position of words in sentences signals relationships in our language. This is similar to storehouse module III-IG-4. To teach this skill you must direct the learner's attention to the meaning of the phrases and how they best relate to each other in order to make sense.

• **TEACHING ACTIVITIES**

This is an information-gathering task similar to storehouse module III-IG-4, and you can adapt your teaching strategy from either the modeling or the discovery technique described in that objective.

• **SUGGESTIONS FOR RETEACHING**

If, after having been taught with either the modeling or the discovery technique, the learner does not understand how to position words correctly in sentences, you should adapt and use the suggestions in III-IG-4 to reteach the skill.

• **SUGGESTIONS FOR PRACTICE**

After teaching the learner the skill of word positions in sentences, create practice activities to solidify the skill, using the suggestions provided in III-IG-4.

• **THE POSTTEST**

The procedure and criterion for mastery are the same as for the pretest, although you may want to substitute new material.

• **ENSURING TRANSFER**

You should use the suggestions in III-IG-4 and reading comprehension activities such as those included in the final chapter to make sure that the learner applies correct positioning of words in sentences during the routine language activities in the classroom.

• **THE PERFORMANCE OBJECTIVE**

When given a sentence containing a word unknown in meaning to the learner and in which a clue to the word's meaning is provided through inference, the learner will state the meaning of the unknown word.

• **THE PRETEST**

State the unknown word for the child, telling him or her that the word appears in the sentence the learner is going to read, together with a clue to the word's meaning. Using sentences such as the following, ask the child to state the meaning of the word. The criterion for mastery is 80 percent. (Readability: Third grade.)

| | |
|---|---|
| vapid | After dinner, the man said, "That wasn't a very good meal. It was blah—just **vapid**." |
| flickered | The flame of the candle **flickered**. But it did not go out when the wind came through the open door. |
| screeched | Sue was very frightened when she saw the ghost. "Help!" she **screeched**. |
| stoop | The opening to the cave was so small. The man had to **stoop** to get in. |
| occupied | The president **occupied** the seat at the head of the table. |

• **DIRECTING THE LEARNER'S ATTENTION**

The purpose of this task is to teach the learner to determine the meaning of an unknown by using inference clues provided in the surrounding context. This is similar to storehouse module II-IG-4. To teach this skill you must direct the learner's attention to the unknown words and to the other words in the sentence that infer the meaning of the unknown word.

• **TEACHING ACTIVITIES**

This is an information-gathering task similar to storehouse module II-IG-4, and you can adapt your teaching strategy from either the modeling or the discovery technique described in that objective.

Is every child reading a book that he or she can handle easily?

• **SUGGESTIONS FOR RETEACHING**

If, after having been taught with either the modeling or the discovery technique, the learner does not understand how to determine word meaning through inference, you should adapt and use the suggestions in II-IG-4 to reteach the skill.

• **SUGGESTIONS FOR PRACTICE**

After teaching the learner the skill of determining word meaning through inference, create practice activities to solidify the skill, using the suggestions provided in II-IG-4.

## • THE POSTTEST

The procedure and criterion for mastery are the same as for the pretest, although you may want to substitute new material.

## • ENSURING TRANSFER

You should use the suggestions in II-IG-4 and reading comprehension activities such as those included in the final chapter to make sure that the learner applies definition by inference context clues during the routine language activities in the classroom.

## • THE PERFORMANCE OBJECTIVE

When given a paragraph containing details about who, what, when, and where, the learner will recall these details from the story in response to questions from the teacher.

## • THE PRETEST

Direct the learner to read a paragraph like the following one and to be ready to answer your questions about the details of the paragraph. The criterion for mastery is 75 percent. (Readability: Third grade.)

### The Train Trip

Once there was a train that got stuck on the top of a mountain. The engine was broken. It could not move. Because it was wintertime, other trains could not get through the snow to push the broken train down from the mountain. Finally, Tom Brown was able to plow the snow off the tracks. Then another engine pushed the broken train off the mountain where it was stuck.

Who plowed the snow off the track?
What was stuck at the top of the mountain?
When did this story take place?
Where did this story take place?

## • DIRECTING THE LEARNER'S ATTENTION

The purpose of this task is to teach the learner to recall factual information. This is similar to storehouse module III-IG-6. To teach this skill you must direct the learner's attention by setting specific purposes that serve as cues to the learner regarding what to note and remember while reading.

## • TEACHING ACTIVITIES

This in an information-gathering task similar to storehouse module III-IG-6, and you can adapt your teaching strategy from either the modeling or the discovery technique described in that objective.

## • SUGGESTIONS FOR RETEACHING

If, after having been taught with either the modeling or the discovery technique, the learner is unable to recall factual information, you should adapt and use the suggestions III-IG-6 to reteach the skill.

After teaching the learner the skill of recalling factual information, create practice activities to solidify the skill, using the suggestions provided in III-IG-6.

### • THE POSTTEST

The procedure and criterion for mastery are the same as for the pretest, although you may want to substitute new material.

### • ENSURING TRANSFER

You should use the suggestions in III-IG-6 and reading comprehension activities such as those included in the final chapter to make sure that the learner applies his factual recall skill during the routine language activities in the classroom.

## VI•MT•1

### • THE PERFORMANCE OBJECTIVE

When given three stories, the learner will answer correctly the teacher's questions regarding relationships between the central characters in the three stories.

### • THE PRETEST

Direct the learner to read stories like the following and to answer the questions that follow. The criterion for mastery is 100 percent. (Readability: Third grade.)

> Every day during the summer, Mike took Ann to the beach. They went swimming. Ann did not know how to swim. Mike would take her by the hand. He would try to get her to go in the water. He wanted to teach her to swim. Every time they got near the water, Ann would cry. She would run to play in the sand. Finally, on the last day of the season, Mike said, "It's no use trying to teach Ann to swim this year."
>
> Don was working on his coin collection. He had found a penny several days ago and he was trying to look it up in the coin book he had. He had looked at the coin carefully. He had tried to find a coin like it in the book. But he could not. "I'm just not going to be able to find out about this coin," he said. Just then his friend John came in. He said, "You've been working so hard on your coin collection. Let me help you."
>
> Mary did not like mice. Every time she saw one, she would scream and jump up on a chair to get away. This was a real problem in her house because Mary's sister raised mice in the cellar and some of them got loose quite often. Finally, Mary's sister said, "Mary, why don't you help me raise the mice? If you knew what they were like, you wouldn't be afraid of them."
>
> In story 1, Ann was like _____ in story 3.
> In story 3, Mary's sister was like _____ in story 2.
> In story 2, Don was like _____ in story 1.

## • DIRECTING THE LEARNER'S ATTENTION

The purpose of this task is to teach the learner the relationships between characters in stories. This is similar to storehouse module I-MT-1. To teach this skill you must direct the learner's attention by highlighting the concepts associated with each main character and then direct attention to the common denominator that shows the relationship between the main characters.

## • TEACHING ACTIVITIES

This is a manipulative task similar to storehouse module I-MT-1, and you can adapt your teaching strategy from either the modeling or the discovery technique described in that objective.

## • SUGGESTIONS FOR RETEACHING

If, after having been taught with either the modeling or the discovery technique, the learner does not understand the relationships between the main characters in stories, you should adapt and use the suggestions in I-MT-1 to reteach the skill.

## • SUGGESTIONS FOR PRACTICE

After teaching the learner the way the main characters are related, create practice activities to solidify the skill, using the suggestions provided in I-MT-1.

## • THE POSTTEST

The procedure and criterion for mastery are the same as for the pretest, although you may want to substitute new material.

## • ENSURING TRANSFER

You should use the suggestions in I-MT-1, and reading comprehension activities such as those included in the final chapter to make sure that the learner applies the skill of determining relationships between main characters during the routine language activities in the classroom.

## VI•MT•2

## • THE PERFORMANCE OBJECTIVE

When given the title of a possible story and a series of possible details, the learner will select the details that would be appropriate for the title and explain his or her reason for classifying them with the title.

## • THE PRETEST

Direct the learner to read words like the following and then to classify each word underneath the title where the word belongs. The criterion for mastery is 14 out of 16 correct.

| | | | |
|---|---|---|---|
| pigs | squirrel | bus | peanuts |
| football | dog | corn | duck |
| car | ice cream | baseball | train |
| golf | oranges | airplane | tennis |

*How to Travel    Good Things to Eat    Favorite Games    Animal Friends*

_____    _____    _____    _____

_____    _____    _____    _____

_____    _____    _____    _____

_____    _____    _____    _____

- **DIRECTING THE LEARNER'S ATTENTION**

The purpose of this task is to teach the learner how to select appropriate details for a title and explain why. This is similar to storehouse module III-MT-2. To teach this skill you must direct the learner's attention to the common denominator of these facts that allows them to be categorized with the title.

- **TEACHING ACTIVITIES**

This is a manipulative task similar to storehouse module III-MT-2, and you can adapt your teaching strategy from either the modeling or the discovery technique described in that objective.

- **SUGGESTIONS FOR RETEACHING**

If, after having been taught with either the modeling or the discovery technique, the learner does not understand how to classify details under a title, you should adapt and use the suggestions in III-MT-2 to reteach the skill.

- **SUGGESTIONS FOR PRACTICE**

After teaching the learner the skill of classifying details under a title, create practice activities to solidify the skill, using the suggestions provided in III-MT-2.

- **THE POSTTEST**

The procedure and criterion for mastery are the same as for the pretest, although you may want to substitute new material.

- **ENSURING TRANSFER**

You should use the suggestions in III-MT-2 and reading comprehension activities such as those included in the final chapter to ensure that the learner applies classifying details under a title during the routine language activities in the classroom.

## VI•MT•3

- **THE PERFORMANCE OBJECTIVE**

When given a paragraph in which the character's emotional reaction is implied, the learner will select the correct emotion from a choice of three.

## • THE PRETEST

Direct the learner to read paragraphs like the following and to complete the last sentence in the paragraph by selecting one of the three words provided. The criterion for mastery is 80 percent. (Readability: Third grade.)

The man got off the telephone. He had news. He said, "The president of the United States is coming to our town!" "Wonderful," cried Sam's mother. "He is a fine man." She felt _____.
terrible   joyful   tearful

One evening James was helping his mother with the dishes. The rest of the family was watching television. They were not expecting visitors. The family was _____.
surprised   wise   sad

Eddie was playing baseball at the playground. He noticed a man watching him. Somebody said, "That's Henry Aaron, the baseball player." Eddie ran up to the man. He got his autograph. Eddie was _____.
cross   quiet   thrilled

One day Jan was a bad girl in school. She was scolded by her teacher. She was scolded by the principal. "Oh, I hope they don't tell my mother," she said. Jan was _____.
proud   cheerful   worried

The children were playing hide and seek in the back yard. Mary and Nancy were looking for a place to hide. Suddenly Mary saw a big cardboard box near the garage. "Let's both hide in that box," she said. Nancy said, "We can try. I don't know if we both can fit." Nancy was _____.
angry   uncertain   eager

## • DIRECTING THE LEARNER'S ATTENTION

The purpose of this task is to teach the learner to infer a character's emotional reaction. This is similar to storehouse module I-MT-2. To teach this skill you must direct the learner's attention to what the facts say and what experience has taught him or her about such concepts and ideas.

## • TEACHING ACTIVITIES

This is a manipulative task similar to storehouse module I-MT-2, and you can adapt your teaching strategy from either the modeling or the discovery technique descriedb in that objective.

Can you look your pupils in the eye and tell them *why* you taught them the skill you did today?

## • SUGGESTIONS FOR RETEACHING

If, after having been taught with either the modeling or the discovery technique, the learner is unable to supply a character's emotional reaction when it is implied, you should adapt and use the suggestions in I-MT-2 to reteach the skill.

### • SUGGESTIONS FOR PRACTICE

After teaching the learner to supply the implied character's emotional reaction, create practice activities to solidify the skill, using the suggestions provided in I-MT-2.

### • THE POSTTEST

The procedure and criterion for mastery are the same as for the pretest, although you may want to substitute new material.

### • ENSURING TRANSFER

You should use the suggestions in I-MT-1 and reading comprehension activities such as those included in the final chapter to make sure that the learner applies inferring a character's emotional reaction during the routine language activities in the classroom.

# VI·ET·1

### • THE PERFORMANCE OBJECTIVE

When given a series of advertising claims, the learner will identify the propaganda words used in each advertisement.

### • THE PRETEST

Direct the learner to read advertising claims such as the following and to identify the words that influence him or her to buy the product being advertised. The criterion for mastery is 100 percent. (Readability: Second grade.)

> Buy Glard! It is the best headache pill in the world!
>
> Everybody's using Blubo! Don't be left out—you get some too!
>
> I'm no doctor. In fact, I'm just a common farmer. But we farmers know that Lidlo is the best there is.
>
> In a leading survey of doctors three out of four of those who responded said that they would recommend Rudex for a common backache.

### • DIRECTING THE LEARNER'S ATTENTION

The purpose of this task is to teach the learner to assess word choice for clues regarding the author's attempt to influence the readers. This is similar to storehouse module IV-ET-1. To teach this skill you must direct the learner's attention to the key words that signal the author's attempt to influence the reader.

### • TEACHING ACTIVITIES

This is an evaluative thinking task similar to storehouse module IV-ET-1, and you can adapt your teaching strategy from either the modeling or the discovery technique described in that objective.

## • SUGGESTIONS FOR RETEACHING
If, after having been taught with either the modeling or the discovery technique, the learner does not understand how to identify propaganda techniques, you should adapt and use the suggestions in IV-ET-1 to reteach the skill.

## • SUGGESTIONS FOR PRACTICE
After teaching the learner the skill of identifying propaganda techniques, create practice activities to solidify the skill, using the suggestions provided in IV-ET-1.

## • THE POSTTEST
The procedure and criterion for mastery are the same as for the pretest, although you may want to substitute new material.

## • ENSURING TRANSFER
You should use the suggestions in IV-ET-1 and reading comprehension activities such as those included in the final chapter to make sure that the learner applies the skill of identifying propaganda techniques during the routine language activities in the classroom.

# CLUSTER VII

**• THE PERFORMANCE OBJECTIVE**

When given a fraction of a second to examine flashcards having printed on them the following words, the learner will pronounce each within one second.

| | | | | |
|---|---|---|---|---|
| only | today | also | end | felt |
| bigger | full | sure | listen | lion |
| table | poor | quiet | air | bread |
| done | draw | slow | triad | Mrs. |
| love | doll | match | ear | apple |
| wild | break | wash | family | careful |
| brother | near | keep | Mr. | heavy |
| once | child | believe | most | together |
| busy | orange | upon | because | milk |

**• THE PRETEST**

Print each of the preceding words on a flashcard. Flash each to the learner, giving him or her less than one second to examine each word before pronouncing it. The criterion for mastery is 100 percent.

## • DIRECTING THE LEARNER'S ATTENTION

The purpose of this task is to teach the learner to recognize instantly and pronounce the words contained in the pretest when they are presented on flashcards. This is a sight word recognition skill like that described in II-SW-6. To teach the skill you must make sure that the learner knows exactly what is to be learned, that the words being taught are in the child's speaking vocabulary, and that you have directed his or her attention by highlighting the unique visual characteristics of each word (such as the initial and final letters, length, shape, double letters, and so on).

## • TEACHING ACTIVITIES

This is a sight word recognition skill similar to that described in II-SW-6. If the learner does not recognize the word in print, adapt your teaching strategy from either the modeling technique or the discovery technique described in that objective. If the child confuses the word with another word similar to it, adapt your strategy from the suggestions contained in I-SW-17.

## • SUGGESTIONS FOR RETEACHING

If, after having been taught with the suggested technique, the learner is unable to recognize instantly one or more of the words on the pretest, use the reteaching suggestions described in II-SW-6.

## • SUGGESTIONS FOR PRACTICE

After successfully teaching the learner to recognize instantly the words on the pretest, create practice activities to solidify the skill, using the suggestions provided in II-SW-6.

## • THE POSTTEST

The procedure and criterion for mastery for the posttest are the same as for the pretest.

## • ENSURING TRANSFER

To be sure that this skill is applied, you must give the learner reading material containing the words now known at sight and have him or her read. You may guide the application by pointing out the words the child has just learned to recognize or, as he or she becomes more proficient, you can encourage independent reading of the newly learned words. Any material at the child's instructional reading level that contains the learned sight words would be appropriate. Additional suggestions for helping the learner use known sight words in context are contained in II-SW-6.

# VII•SW•2

## • THE PERFORMANCE OBJECTIVE

When given a flash presentation of words that the learner frequently confuses, he or she will pronounce each word correctly within one second.

- **THE PRETEST**

You will note whether the learner is confusing words any time you test him or her on sight words or listen to him or her read. If, during either of these activities, the learner says one word for another (such as **quite** for **quiet**), you should pair the words together and teach them, using the suggestions provided in this objective. No specific list of words is provided since various learners will confuse various words. As with other sight word objectives, the criterion for mastery is 100 percent, with any pair of confused words being taught.

- **DIRECTING THE LEARNER'S ATTENTION**

The purpose of this task is to teach the learner to recognize instantly pairs of words he or she has tended to confuse in the past. As such, this task is similar to that described in I-SW-17. To teach this skill you must make sure that the learner has mastered the previous visual training skill, that he or she knows exactly what is to be learned, that the words being taught are in his or her speaking vocabulary and that you have directed attention by highlighting the discriminator that sets one word apart from another (such as the position of the **e** in **quite** and **quiet**).

Do you make sure that your learners use their learned reading skills in social studies? In science? In math?

- **TEACHING ACTIVITIES**

In teaching this skill you can use either the modeling technique or the discovery technique described in I-SW-17, adjusting the suggestions to focus on the particular words the learner is confusing.

- **SUGGESTIONS FOR RETEACHING**

If, after having been taught this skill with either the modeling or the discovery technique, the learner continues to confuse the words, you should use the reteaching suggestions provided in I-SW-17.

- **SUGGESTIONS FOR PRACTICE**

Once the learner can instantly recognize the words that he or she was previously confusing, create practice activities to solidify the skill, using the suggestions provided in I-SW-17.

- **THE POSTTEST**

The procedure and criterion for mastery are the same as for the pretest.

- **ENSURING TRANSFER**

Once the learner can recognize the easily confused words, you should immediately provide for application of this skill by giving the child reading material containing the words now known at sight. For specific suggestions regarding such application activities, see II-SW-6.

**VII·SW·3**

- **THE PERFORMANCE OBJECTIVE**

When given words he or she recognizes instantly, the learner will create and read a single-sentence story using these words.

## • THE PRETEST

Provide the learner with cards, each of which has printed on it a word he or she instantly recognizes. Say to the learner, "Today we are going to do something that is very hard. We are going to send messages. Look at the cards you have in front of you. Each card has a word on it that you know. Can you send me a message using the words you have there? If you want to send a message using a word you don't have on a card, tell me and I will make a card for you having that word on it." The criterion for mastery is forming a combination of any number of words in a way that is grammatically accurate and makes sense. When the learner has formed a sentence, reinforce the value of the effort by reading it aloud yourself.

## • DIRECTING THE LEARNER'S ATTENTION

This is a language experience activity designed to teach the learner to produce and read messages using the individual words he or she knows at sight. As such, it is an application activity similar to that described in II-SW-8. To teach this activity, you must be sure that the learner knows exactly what is to be learned and you must direct attention to the idea he or she wishes to convey, to what the message will sound like when spoken, to what printed word cards will be needed to "write" the message, and to the order in which the words must be placed. You might highlight by asking a series of questions such as, "What did you do yesterday after school that you could tell me about? Can you make a sentence about that and say it to me? What words did you use to say your sentence to me? How many of those words do you already have on cards and which ones will we have to make for you? What word will come first in your written message?"

## • TEACHING ACTIVITIES

This is a language experience activity similar to that described in II-SW-8. You should use the modeling and discovery techniques described in that objective as a basis for planning and teaching this task.

## • SUGGESTIONS FOR RETEACHING

If, after having been taught with either of the techniques described in the key objective, the learner is unable to create a single-sentence message using the sight words, you should

1. Reteach the activity using the alternate technique.
2. Be more specific in eliciting from the learner the idea he or she wishes to convey.
3. Be sure that the learner expresses the message first in oral form and that he or she understands that the written message will say the same thing as the oral message.
4. Be sure that the content of the message matches the learner's experience, changing the subject to match the experience if necessary.
5. Recheck the learner's mastery of the sight words, reteaching any that have not yet been completely mastered.

6. Return to the previous language experience objectives and be sure that the child can do those simpler tasks before asking for the creation of entire sentences.

## • SUGGESTIONS FOR PRACTICE

Once the learner has been taught to use sight words to create and read sentences, devise practice activities to solidify this skill, adapting the suggestions provided in II-SW-8.

## • THE POSTTEST

The procedure and criterion for mastery for the posttest are the same as for the pretest.

## • ENSURING TRANSFER

This objective is an application activity designed to help the learner use sight words in context. In addition to the application specified here, however, you should use the suggestions in II-SW-6 to be sure that the learner uses the sight words in other contextual situations.

## VII•WA•1

## • THE PERFORMANCE OBJECTIVE

When given a known word that illustrates the vowel-consonant–consonant-vowel principle of syllabication and in which both medial consonants are heard, the learner will correctly pronounce other words illustrating the principle.

## • THE PRETEST

Use the following list of words. The first word in the list has been previously taught as a sight word. Have the learner identify the first word and then ask him to pronounce the remaining words. The criterion for mastery is eight out of nine correct. *Note:* Some of the words listed are nonsense words, which are included so that the learner *must* use analysis rather than sight recognition.

| | | | | |
|---|---|---|---|---|
| **after** | basket | window | kitchen | niktop |
| almost | picnic | until | public | wankep |

## • DIRECTING THE LEARNER'S ATTENTION

The purpose of this task is to help the learner analyze and pronounce two-syllable words that illustrate the vowel-consonant–consonant-vowel principle. This is the first of a series of objectives designed to help the learner identify unknown words of more than one syllable. This is a crucial task to master in order to become an independent reader, since many of the words the learner encounters will be long and will require the use of syllabication principles to break them down into familiar sound units.

Although it is crucial to continued reading success, syllabication is an extremely difficult skill to learn. This is so because of its complexity. To identify multisyllable words accurately, the learner must be able to isolate each syllable visually, sound it by applying generalized vowel principles, adjust accent, whether primary, secondary, or tertiary, insert a schwa sound where appropriate, and finally pronounce the word. For most beginning readers this is too complex a task to be mastered all at once. Consequently, the strategy presented here is simplified.

To teach syllabication skills at this stage of the learner's development, this and subsequent objectives emphasize only three principles: visually isolating the discrete syllables, assigning the standard vowel sounding to each according to the arrangement of consonants and vowels, and saying the word with the understanding that the resultant pronunciation will be an *approximation* of the real word, which the learner will then have to verify through context and/or his or her own speaking vocabulary. For instance, after completing all the syllabication objectives, the learner would approach the unknown word *millimeter* by dividing it into syllables according to the visual pattern of consonants and vowels (mil–li–me–ter), pronouncing the syllables by assigning each vowel a "short" sound if it is followed by a consonant and a "long" sound if it is the last letter in a syllable, and then pronouncing the word and trying to match that approximation with a previous heard word. (For instance, the learner might pronounce it as **mil-lie-me-ter** and then say, "Oh, I know that word. We talked about it in math. It's **millimeter**.") If this first attempt does not work for the learner (that is, if the child does not recognize the word that is created), he or she is encouraged to move the syllable divisions one letter to the right (mill–im–et–er) and repeat the process. If neither process results in an approximation that the learner can tie to a word he or she has heard or said before, the learner has no recourse other than asking the teacher to pronounce the word.

To teach syllabication use the following sequence. First, present the words visually to be sure that the learner visually distinguishes the pattern of vowels and consonants that provides the cue for determining where the syllable break occurs. This can be easily illustrated (highlighted) by putting a dot under each vowel or vowel combination and then examining the consonants that stand between each pair of dots. If there are two consonants between vowels (dots), split them so that each vowel gets a consonant (for example, **af–ter**). Then model the pronunciation of each vowel according to whether it comes at the end of a syllable or just before a consonant. (**af** is the short vowel family similar to **at** or **am**; **ter** is the r-controlled vowel family and is easily predicted.) Finally you must show that the resultant pronunciation is an approximation, requiring the child to use his or her experience to identify the word precisely.

● **THIS IS A STOREHOUSE OBJECTIVE**

The following instructional activities are your storehouse of techniques for developing skill in pronouncing multisyllable words. This skill recurs in various forms in subsequent objectives in the hierarchy and the instructional suggestions that follow are to be adapted and used with each of these as they occur.

- **TEACHING ACTIVITIES**

*The modeling technique.* Using the list of pretest words, say to the learner, "I am going to say a word slowly and see if I can tell how many syllables I hear. **Af–ter.** I heard two syllables, **af** and **ter.** Now, I am going to say another word slowly and you see if you can tell me how many syllables you hear." Say other words for the learner, gradually diminishing the amount of help you provide by saying each succeeding word a little faster until you are saying the words normally. Then write the words on the board one under another, labeling the vowel-consonant–consonant–vowel arrangement and the syllable division as follows:

| *vc  cv* | *vc  cv* | *vc  cv* |
|----------|----------|----------|
| al–most  | bas–ket  | pic–nic  |

Say to the learner, "Look at the first word. It is **al–most.** We hear two syllables in the word. We also hear two syllables in **bas–ket** and **pic–nic.** I have written the words on the board showing the syllable break. I have also labeled an arrangement of vowels and consonants in the word because the syllable division in these words comes between the two consonants. If I see a vowel-consonant–consonant-vowel arrangement like this in a big word, I can divide it between the consonants and figure out how to say it." Demonstrate this with the three words, modeling the sound of the vowel when it comes before a consonant. Then write another word on the board; highlight the syllable break, the arrangement of vowels and consonants, and the vowel sound; and help the learner to pronounce the word. Repeat with other words, gradually diminishing the amount of help you provide in identifying the syllable break and letter pattern until the learner is able to identify each word without help. As the child pronounces each word, emphasize that his or her pronunciation may be an approximation that will require thinking of a familiar word that is close to the attempted pronunciation.

*The discovery technique.* Using the same words as in the preceding technique, pronounce each word slowly for the learner, directing him or her to tell you the number of syllables heard. As the child responds correctly, diminish the amount of exaggeration used in dividing the syllables until he or she is able to tell you the number of syllables as you say words normally. Then list the words on the board with the same highlighting as is described in the modeling technique. Say to the learner, "Look at this list of words. They are the words we just listened to, but now I have shown you where the syllable division is. Also, I have labeled a pattern of vowels and consonants that appears in each word. Can you look at the arrangement of vowel-consonant–consonant-vowel in each of these words and tell me how you might know where to make the syllable division in other words like these?" Provide whatever additional highlighting is necessary to help the learner see that the division comes between the consonants. Then provide other words and gradually diminish your assistance as the learner is able to identify the syllable break. Then show the learner that the resultant syllables are like the small words he or she has worked with before in letter substitution objectives and that when the vowel comes before a consonant, it makes a "short" sound. Have the child pronounce each of the words, providing as much help as is necessary until he or she is able to pronounce the words unassisted. As he or she pronounces the words, remind the learner that the pronunciation may only be an approximation that he or she will have to relate to a word in his or her oral vocabulary.

### • SUGGESTIONS FOR RETEACHING

If, after having been taught with either the modeling or the discovery technique, the learner is unable to pronounce words illustrating the vowel-consonant–consonant-vowel principle of syllabication, you should

1. Reteach the skill, using the alternate technique.
2. Reexamine your attenders to be sure you are providing enough highlighting on the sound units heard, on the pattern of vowels and consonants, on the sound produced by the vowel in each syllable and on tying the resultant pronunciation to a word in the child's oral vocabulary.
3. If the learner is having difficulty in hearing the sound units, return to objectives such as I-WA-4 and II-WA-1 and provide the necessary auditory discrimination background.
4. If the learner is having difficulty in identifying the sounds produced by the vowels in each syllable, return to appropriate letter substitution and vowel generalization objectives and provide additional instruction on the short vowel sound in closed vowel positions and the long vowel sound in open vowel positions.

### • SUGGESTIONS FOR PRACTICE

Once the learner can pronounce words that illustrate the vowel-consonant–consonant-vowel principle of syllabication, use the following suggestions to create practice activities to solidify the skill.

1. Provide the learner with a list of multisyllable words. Have him or her pronounce each word correctly to you or to a fellow classmate who already knows the words.
2. Play games with the learner in which aspects of syllabication must be used. For instance, use a gameboard device in which a learner progresses space by space toward some goal. Progress along the board toward the goal is dependent upon ability to tell you how many sound units are heard in the word you say orally or upon ability to pronounce correctly a word utilizing one or more of the syllable principles you have taught.

3. Play riddle games with children in which syllabication plays a part. For instance, you could ask the following:

I am a big animal. I have a trunk and tusks. You see me in the zoo. I have three syllables in my name. Who am I?

4. Play a variation of dominoes with the learner in which the usual rules of dominoes are used, but the dominoes have printed on them words that illustrate the various principles of syllabication. Each player has several dominoes and places them next to others that illustrate the same syllabication principle and pronounces the word.

5. Play the Spin a Word game with the learner. Make a spinner by making a circle out of oak tag, dividing it into pie shapes with multisyllable words printed in each section, and attaching a spinner in the middle. The student spins the spinner and pronounces the word it stops on. Progress is recorded by moving space by space along a gameboard.

6. Play a variation of Ball Toss with the learner. Post a list of multisyllable words nearby. The player with the ball must pronounce one of the words on the list. The child then tosses the ball to another student, who then has ten seconds to pronounce another word on the list. If the catcher is successful, he or she gets to throw the ball the next time. If he or she is unsuccessful, the ball goes back to the thrower, who gets another turn.

7. Play the Take-All game. Use a deck of cards that have multisyllable words printed on them. Place all the cards face down on the table. In turn, each player turns over one card and pronounces it. If the pronunciation is correct he or she keeps the card, but if it is incorrect the card is left on the table face up. The next student then turns over a new card. If the word is pronounced correctly, the student gets that card plus all the cards that are face up. If he or she is incorrect, the word must be returned to the table face up until someone can "take all." The person who has the most cards when all the cards on the table are gone is the winner.

8. A variation of a beanbag toss can be played. The materials include six 3- by 5-inch cards numbered in sequence from 1 to 6, beanbags, and cards with multisyllable words printed on one side and the numbers 1 through 6 printed on the other according to the difficulty of the word. The word cards are placed face down in six piles, each pile indicating a different degree of difficulty. The 3- by 5-inch cards are placed on the floor in a random pattern. When it is his or her turn, the player tosses the beanbag toward the numbers on the floor. If it lands on or near a number, the child draws a word from that pile and pronounces it. If correct, he or she gets that many points, with the winner being the first player to reach a predetermined score.

9. Play a motorcycle race game using toy motorcycles, a gameboard, and dice. Each space on the gameboard contains a multisyllable word. Each

player in turn throws the dice, moves that number of spaces, and pronounces the word printed there. If the word is pronounced correctly, the player stays; if not, he or she must return to the prior position. The first player to get to the end of the gameboard wins.

10. Play a variation of Scrabble in which the wood blocks are syllables and the object is to construct and pronounce multisyllable words.

## • THE POSTTEST

The pretest can also be used as the posttest. The procedure and criterion for mastery are the same.

## • ENSURING TRANSFER

Once the learner has practiced this syllabication skill, you must be sure that he or she is given reading material that calls for the pronunciation of unknown multisyllable words illustrating this principle and you must guide application of this skill in these situations. Suitable application situations include basal textbooks, library books, language experience stories, magazines, comic books, and any other reading material in which the learner encounters unknown multisyllable words illustrating this syllabication principle.

# VII•WA•2

## • THE PERFORMANCE OBJECTIVE

When given a known word containing the **ar** and **or** combination, the learner will pronounce other words containing these combinations.

## • THE PRETEST

Use the following words. The first vowel in each list has been previously taught as a sight word. Have the learner identify the first word and then ask him or her to pronounce the other words listed. The criterion for mastery is 22 out of 24 correct, with neither combination being missed more than once. *Note:* Some of the words listed are nonsense words, which are included so that the learner *must* use analysis rather than sight recognition.

|       | car    |       | for   |
|-------|--------|-------|-------|
| arm   | far    | hard  | corn  |
| bark  | part   | park  | horn  |
| farm  | farmer | lard  | north |
| barn  | jar    | star  | chort |
| dark  | garden | yard  | short |
| blark | flarb  | start | snort |

## • DIRECTING THE LEARNER'S ATTENTION

The purpose of this task is to teach the learner to pronounce words containing an r-controlled vowel. As such, it is a vowel generalization similar to storehouse module VI-WA-1. To teach this skill you should direct the learner's attention by stating exactly what he is to be learned and by highlighting the sound heard in the middle and the visual form of the **ar** or **or** combination. (For the word **bark,** for instance, you would circle the **ar** while simultaneously exaggerating the sound heard in the middle of the word.)

### • TEACHING ACTIVITIES

In teaching this vowel generalization you can use either the modeling technique or the discovery technique described in VI-WA-1, adjusting the suggestions to focus on **r**-controlled vowels.

### • SUGGESTIONS FOR RETEACHING

If, after having been taught with either the modeling or the discovery technique, the learner is unable to pronounce words containing **r**-controlled vowels, you should

1. Reteach the skill, using the alternate technique.
2. Reexamine your attenders to be sure that you are providing enough highlighting on the sound of the **r**-controlled vowel and on the **ar** or **or** letters.
3. Reteach the skill as a task of sound-symbol connection, using the suggestions provided in I-WA-9.

Do your pupils see you as an avid reader?

### • SUGGESTIONS FOR PRACTICE

Once the learner can pronounce words containing **r**-controlled vowels, create practice activities to solidify the skill, using the suggestions provided in VI-WA-1.

### • THE POSTTEST

The pretest can be used also as the posttest. The procedure and criterion for mastery are the same.

### • ENSURING TRANSFER

You should use the suggestions provided in VI-WA-1 to be sure that the learner uses the skills in pursuing daily reading activities.

# VII•WA•3

### • THE PERFORMANCE OBJECTIVE

When given a known two-syllable word ending in **–er,** the learner will correctly pronounce other two-syllable words ending in **–er.**

### • THE PRETEST

Use the following list of words. The first word in the list has been previously taught as a sight word. Have the learner identify the first word and then ask him or her to pronounce the remaining words. Criterion for mastery is nine out of ten correct.

**bigger**

| | | | | |
|---|---|---|---|---|
| sister | supper | letter | butter | blunder |
| summer | matter | better | dinner | winter |

### • DIRECTING THE LEARNER'S ATTENTION

The purpose of this task is to teach the learner to prouonce multisyllable words ending in –er. Although it includes both syllabication and a vowel principle, it is similar to storehouse module VII-WA-1. To teach this skill you must direct the learner's attention by stating exactly what is to be learned and by highlighting the number of syllables heard, the pattern of vowels and consonants, the sound value of the final –er, and the tying of the resultant pronunciation to a known word [in the word **sister,** for instance, you would first say the word, exaggerating the syllable break, then write the word showing the vowel-consonant–consonant-vowel arrangement and syllable division, then show the learner the sound of each vowel (particularly in the final –er syllable of the word), and finally help the child match his or her pronunciation with a word in his or her speaking vocabulary.]

### • TEACHING ACTIVITIES

In teaching this syllabication skill you can use either the modeling technique or the discovery technique described in VII-WA-1, adjusting the suggestions to focus on vowel-consonant–consonant-vowel words that end in –er.

### • SUGGESTIONS FOR RETEACHING

If, after having been taught this skill using either the modeling or the discovery technique, the learner is unable to pronounce words such as those tested in this objective, you should use the reteaching suggestions provided in VII-WA-1.

### • SUGGESTIONS FOR PRACTICE

Once the learner can pronounce multisyllable words ending in –er, create practice activities to solidify the skill using the suggestions provided in VII-WA-1.

### • THE POSTTEST

The pretest can also be used as the posttest. The procedure and criterion for mastery are the same.

### • ENSURING TRANSFER

You should use the suggestions provided in VII-WA-1 to be sure that the learner uses this syllabication skill in daily reading activities.

- **THE PERFORMANCE OBJECTIVE**

When given a known word composed of the –**ire** combination, the learner will replace the initial consonant with another consonant, blend, or digraph and correctly pronounce the new word.

- **THE PRETEST**

Use the following list of words. Have the learner identify the first word in the list and then ask for pronunciation of the remaining words. The criterion for mastery is 100 percent. *Note:* Some of the words listed are nonsense words, which are included so that the learner *must* use analysis rather than sight recognition.

| | | | |
|---|---|---|---|
| **fire**° | mire | wire | dire |
| tire | sire | hire | shire |

- **DIRECTING THE LEARNER'S ATTENTION**

The purpose of this task is to teach the learner to substitute initial consonants in the initial position of –**ire** phonograms and to pronounce the new words. This particular phonogram is taught separately since it fits neither the silent **a** principle or the **r**-controlled vowel principle the learner has previously mastered, although these words *look* like they would fit either of those principles. The most efficient technique is to teach the –**ire** as a letter substitution skill and, as such, it is similar to storehouse module II-WA-18. To teach this skill you must direct the learner's attention by stating exactly what is to be learned and by highlighting the varying initial consonants and the –**ire** combination. [In the word **tire**, for instance, you might circle the initial letter **t**, underline the –**ire** combination, and have the learner use the say-it-fast, say-it-slow technique (see I-WA-5) in pronouncing the word.]

- **TEACHING ACTIVITIES**

In teaching this letter substitution skill you can use either the modeling technique or the discovery technique described in II-WA-18, adjusting the suggestions to focus on words having the –**ire** phonogram.

- **SUGGESTIONS FOR RETEACHING**

If, after having been taught this skill with either the modeling or the discovery technique, the learner is unable to substitute initial consonants in –**ire** phonogram words and pronounce the new words, you should use the reteaching suggestions provided in II-WA-18, adapting them to fit this objective.

- **SUGGESTIONS FOR PRACTICE**

Once the learner can substitute initial consonants in –**ire** words and pronounce the new words, create practice activities to solidify the skill, using the suggestions provided in II-WA-18.

## • THE POSTTEST

The pretest can also be used as the posttest. The procedure and criterion for mastery are the same.

## • ENSURING TRANSFER

You should use the suggestions provided in II-WA-18 to be sure that the learner uses the skill during daily reading activities in the classroom.

# VII•WA•5

## • THE PERFORMANCE OBJECTIVE

When given compound words composed of two known words, the learner will correctly pronounce the compound words.

## • THE PRETEST

Print the following words on cards. Present each card to the learner one at a time, encouraging him or her to analyze each word and pronounce it. The criterion for mastery is 100 percent.

| | | | |
|---|---|---|---|
| afternoon | birthday | herself | outside |
| airplane | everything | himself | peanut |
| barnyard | grandfather | inside | policeman |
| bedroom | grandmother | milkman | sometime |
| sunshine | | | |

## • DIRECTING THE LEARNER'S ATTENTION

The purpose of this task is to teach the learner to pronounce compound words composed of two known roots. As such, this task is similar to storehouse module II-WA-15. To teach this skill you must direct the learner's attention by stating exactly what is to be learned and by highlighting both of the known words. (In the word **afternoon,** for instance, you might circle both **after** and **noon.**)

## • TEACHING ACTIVITIES

In teaching this structural analysis skill you can use either the modeling technique or the discovery technique described in II-WA-25, adjusting the suggestions to focus on compound words.

## • SUGGESTIONS FOR RETEACHING

Does your skill instruction help your pupils figure out what the "reading system" is all about?

If, after having been taught with either the modeling or the discovery technique, the learner is unable to pronounce the compound words tested in this objective, you should use the reteaching suggestions provided in II-WA-25.

## • SUGGESTIONS FOR PRACTICE

Once the learner can pronounce the compound words tested in this objective, create practice activities to solidify the skill, using the suggestions provided in II-WA-25.

## • THE POSTTEST

The pretest can also be used as the posttest. The procedure and criterion for mastery are the same.

## • ENSURING TRANSFER

You should use the suggestions provided in II-WA-25 to be sure that the learner uses this skill in pursuing daily reading activities.

## • THE PERFORMANCE OBJECTIVE

When given content words identified by the teacher, the learner will use each word correctly in an oral sentence.

## • THE PRETEST

The words to be tested are selected by the teacher. These may be words that appear in the basal text or in stories being read in class or that are associated with the study of a particular content area. To test for the meaning of such words, say each word out loud to the learner. Ask the child to make up a sentence or to "send a message" using that word. The criterion for mastery is 100 percent, since any word that is not used correctly will have to be taught.

The learner is asked to identify the following words in print in the next cluster of skills. You should include these words among those you test to be sure that the learner knows their meaning before having to pronounce them.

| wolf | carry | cover | brought | front | people |
| world | sign | across | enough | bear | log |
| worm | splash | bottom | head | calf | build |
| cried | spring | automobile | lie | deer | soft |
| pennies | station | buy | answer | eye | beautiful |
| cabbage | turkey | dear | balloon | vegetable | care |
| cage | soup | through | watch | left | year |
| heard | squirrel | thought | cross | minute | great |
| learn | wear | tomorrow | engine | monkey | picture |

## • DIRECTING THE LEARNER'S ATTENTION

The purpose of this task is to teach the learner the meaning of new words he or she will be encountering. This is similar to storehouse module I-IG-1 but different words are being taught. To teach this skill you must direct the learner's attention by (1) providing either a direct or a vicarious experience to form a basis for the concept, (2) identifying the characteristics of this concept, and (3) connecting the concept to its word label. *Note:* This objective focuses on meaning alone. The learner should not be asked to pronounce these words as they appear in print until after this skill has been mastered.

## • TEACHING ACTIVITIES

This is a word meaning skill similar to module I-IG-1, and you can adapt your teaching strategy from either the modeling or the discovery techniques described in that objective.

## • SUGGESTIONS FOR RETEACHING

If, after having been taught with either the modeling or the discovery technique, the learner does not understand the meaning of any word in this objective, you should adapt and use the suggestions in I-IG-1 to reteach the skill.

## • SUGGESTIONS FOR PRACTICE

After teaching the learner the meaning of these words, create practice activities to solidify the skill, using the suggestions provided in I-IG-1.

## • THE POSTTEST

The procedure and criterion for mastery are the same as for the pretest.

## • ENSURING TRANSFER

You should use the suggestions in I-IG-1 and reading comprehension activities such as those found in the final chapter to be sure that the learner applies the new word meanings during the routine daily language activities of the classroom.

# VII•IG•2

## • THE PERFORMANCE OBJECTIVE

When given words containing the suffixes –less, –al, and –ful, the learner will use each word correctly in an oral sentence.

## • THE PRETEST

Say each word to be tested out loud, asking the child to make up a sentence using the word you have just said. The criterion for mastery is 100 percent. Words such as the following can be used.

senseless   national   joyful   penniless   thoughtful

## • DIRECTING THE LEARNER'S ATTENTION

The purpose of this task is to teach the learner the meaning of the suffixes –less, –al, and –ful. This is similar to the storehouse module I-IG-2. To teach this skill you must be sure that the learner knows the meaning of the root word and you must direct his or her attention to the suffix, its meaning, and the way it alters the meaning of the root word.

## • TEACHING ACTIVITIES

This is a meaning unit task similar to storehouse module I-IG-2, and you can adapt your teaching strategy from either the modeling or the discovery techniques described in that objective.

## • SUGGESTIONS FOR RETEACHING

If, after having been taught with either the modeling or the discovery technique, the learner does not understand the meaning of the words in this objective, you should adapt and use the suggestions in I-IG-2 to reteach the skill.

## • SUGGESTIONS FOR PRACTICE

After teaching the learner the meaning of the words, create practice activities to solidify the skill, using the suggestions provided in I-IG-2.

## • THE POSTTEST

The procedure and criterion are the same as for the pretest.

## • ENSURING TRANSFER

You should use the suggestions in I-IG-2 and reading comprehension activities such as those found in the final chapter to be sure that the learner applies the new word meaning during the routine language activities in the classroom.

Does your reading skill instruction reflect a balance between the graphemic, syntactic, and semantic codes?

## VII•IG•3

## • THE PERFORMANCE OBJECTIVE

When given a sentence in which nouns are set off by commas in a series arrangement, the learner will identify the series of things referred to in the sentence in response to the teacher's questions.

## • THE PRETEST

Have the learner read sentences like the following and then ask him or her to answer the question you ask. The criterion for mastery is 80 percent. (Readability: Second grade.)

Mother went to the store to get apples, oranges, and milk.
What did Mother get at the store?

Sally took her paper, pen, and doll to school.
What did Sally take to school?

The cat, the dog, the boy, and the girl ran home.
Who ran home?

The woman went home with the baby, the ball, and the dog.
What did the woman go home with?

The car, house, and doll were wet.
What was wet?

## • DIRECTING THE LEARNER'S ATTENTION

The purpose of this task is to teach the learner the relationships signaled by commas in a sentence. This is similar to the storehouse module V-IG-4.

To teach this skill you must direct the learner's attention to the commas, the associated intonation pattern, and the meaning that the punctuation mark places upon the words around it.

### • TEACHING ACTIVITIES

This is an information-gathering task similar to the storehouse module V-IG-4, and you can adapt your teaching strategy from either the modeling or the discovery technique described in that objective.

### • SUGGESTIONS FOR RETEACHING

If, after having been taught with either the modeling or the discovery technique, the learner is unable to interpret the meaning signaled by the commas, you should adapt and use the suggestions in V-IG-4 to reteach the skill.

### • SUGGESTIONS FOR PRACTICE

After teaching the learner to interpret the meaning signaled by the commas, create practice activities to solidify the skill, using the suggestions provided in V-IG-4.

### • THE POSTTEST

The procedure and criterion for mastery are the same as for the pretest, although you may want to substitute new material.

### • ENSURING TRANSFER

You should use the suggestions in V-IG-4 and reading comprehension activities such as those included in the final chapter to be sure that the learner applies the understanding of the meanings signaled by commas during the routine language activities in the classroom.

# VII•IG•4

### • THE PERFORMANCE OBJECTIVE

When given a sentence containing a word unknown in meaning and in which a clue to the word's meaning is provided through the mood conveyed, the learner will state the meaning of the unknown word.

### • THE PRETEST

State the unknown word, telling the child that the word appears in the sentence he or she is going to read, together with a clue to the word's meaning. Using sentences like the following, ask the child to state the meaning of the word. The criterion for mastery is two out of three correct. (Readability: Third grade.)

invincible     The Black Knight was powerfully built. He was terribly stong. His horse was the quickest. His horse was the boldest. In addition, the Black Knight had strange, new weapons to fight with. No wonder all the other knights thought that the Black Knight was **invincible** in battle!

| lugubrious | The **lugubrious** wails of the witches matched the whistling of the wind in the lonely cemetery. |
| dreary | The clouds were black. Very little light came in the windows. Huge cobwebs were everywhere. The whole house was dark and **dreary**. |

### • DIRECTING THE LEARNER'S ATTENTION

The purpose of this task is to teach the learner to determine the meaning of an unknown word by using the mood conveyed by the surrounding context. This is similar to storehouse module II-IG-4. To teach this skill you must direct the learner's attention to the unknown word, to the words that explain the mood, and to that mood that gives clues to the meaning of the unknown word.

### • TEACHING ACTIVITIES

This is an information-gathering task similar to storehouse module II-IG-4, and you can adapt your teaching strategy from either the modeling or the discovery technique described in that objective.

### • SUGGESTIONS FOR RETEACHING

If, after having been taught with either the modeling or the discovery technique, the learner does not understand how mood can signal the meaning of an unknown word, you should adapt and use the suggestions in II-IG-4 to reteach the skill.

### • SUGGESTIONS FOR PRACTICE

After teaching the learner the skill of determining the meaning of an unknown word by mood, create practice activities to solidify the skill, using the suggestions provided in II-IG-4.

### • THE POSTTEST

The procedure and criterion for mastery are the same as for the pretest, although you may want to substitute new material.

### • ENSURING TRANSFER

You should use the suggestions in II-IG-4 and reading comprehension activities such as those included in the final chapter to be sure that the learner applies context clue definition by mood during the routine language activities in the classroom.

## VII•IG•5

### • THE PERFORMANCE OBJECTIVE

When given paragraphs each of which contains context clues for intonation patterns and ends with the same sentence, the learner will repeat the last sentence with the correct intonation pattern.

## • THE PRETEST

The material to be tested should be selected by the teacher to be sure that the learner's experience matches the content of the material. Direct the learner to listen to each story you read and to decide how to say the last sentence. The criterion for mastery is two of the three items correct. The following are examples of items that could be used.

> Dessert was ice cream. Mother planned to give everyone what they wanted. However, the further around the table she went, the more the ice cream disappeared. It looked like all the ice cream would be gone before she got to Jim. Jim finally said, "I really don't care if I get a smaller amount but . . . I want some ice cream."

> Mother asked who wanted ice cream. As she started to the kitchen she repeated, "Mary, Sue, Alice, and Joan want ice cream." Janet said, "Don't leave me out . . . I want some ice cream."

> When strawberry ice cream cones were handed out, Jake raised his hand. But he didn't get any. The same thing happened when chocolate ice cream cones were handed out. Finally, Jake thought there was only cake left. He said to his teacher. "I don't want cake, I . . . I want some ice cream."

## • DIRECTING THE LEARNER'S ATTENTION

The purpose of the task is to teach the learner how context can indicate relationships that result in various intonation patterns. Since intonation patterns reflect various relationships in our system of communication, this is a skill of contextual prediction that should be taught.

To teach this skill you must direct the learner's attention to the context clues since they signal the intonation pattern to be used. For instance, in the second pretest item, the context to be highlighted would be, **Don't leave me out.**

## • THIS IS A STOREHOUSE OBJECTIVE

The following instructional activities are your storehouse of techniques for teaching how context indicates relationships that result in various intonation patterns. This skill recurs in other forms later in the hierarchy. The activities that follow are to be adapted and used with each context-intonation objective as it occurs.

## • TEACHING ACTIVITIES

*The modeling technique.* Using the second item on the pretest as an illustration, you could teach this skill by following these procedures. Read the second pretest item aloud and emphasize "Janet said, 'Don't leave me out.'" When the last phrase, "I want some ice cream," is read, say it with no intonation. Then say, "I know how to read that last phrase because there is a clue earlier in the story. The clue is: "Janet said, 'Don't leave me out.'"

This tells us Janet thinks she's not going to get any ice cream. So the last phrase should be read "**I** want some ice cream." Can you say the last phrase the way I did?"

Repeat this procedure using other passages, gradually diminishing the auditory emphasis and modeling of the thinking process required to determine the correct intonation pattern until the learner is able to use correct intonation patterns with no assistance from you.

***The discovery technique.*** When using the discovery technique, you can still make use of passages with context that signals intonation patterns being highlighted. However, rather than being highly directive as you were in the modeling step, you can ask questions leading the learner to note the context that signals which intonation pattern to use. The dialogue, using pretest item 3, could be as follows:

"Listen to this passage. Now we need to figure out how to read the last phrase, **I want some ice cream.**"

What was happening to Jake?
What did he think was the only thing left?
How was he feeling?
He didn't want **cake.** What did he **want?** Right. He wanted some **ice cream.**

Continue this process using other passages. Gradually diminish the number of questions you ask as the learner formulates his or her own. When the learner can perform the skill with no assistance from you, you can assume the skill has been mastered.

- **SUGGESTIONS FOR RETEACHING**

If, after having been taught with either of the preceding techniques, the learner is unable to use context clues to determine how intonation patterns are used, you should:

1. Reteach the skill, using the alternate technique.
2. Provide role-playing situations in which the passages are acted out.
3. Exaggerate the highlighting techniques you provide when reading the material.
4. Be sure that the material used to teach the skill is part of the learner's background.

- **SUGGESTIONS FOR PRACTICE**

Once the learner is correctly using context clues as signalers for intonation patterns, adapt and use one or more of the following activities to solidify the skill.

1. Use passages such as the ones given for the teaching activities. The learner says the context clues and then uses the intonation pattern.

2. Use passages such as the ones explained earlier.
3. Act out situations, using context signalers for intonation patterns.
4. Allow learners to create their own situations, using context clues as signalers of intonation patterns.

### • THE POSTTEST

The procedures, directions, and criteria are the same for the posttest as for the pretest.

### • ENSURING TRANSFER

You should be sure that the learner's understanding of context clues as signalers for intonation patterns is used in the daily routine activities of the classroom. A good way to do this is during oral reading or silent reading of any material that contains context signals for intonation patterns. Simply ask the learners how to read phrases that have been signaled by context clues. Further, this skill should be incorporated into comprehension activities such as those in the final chapter.

## VII•IG•6

### • THE PERFORMANCE OBJECTIVE

When given a paragraph in which the details either precede or follow the main idea, the learner identifies the details and states how they support the main idea.

### • THE PRETEST

Direct the learner to read paragraphs like the following, to note the details, and to be ready to answer your questions about the details in the story. The criterion for mastery is 75 percent or better. (Readability: Third grade.)

> The people at the school worked hard to get ready for the open house. The teachers all put up new bulletin boards. They had folders ready showing each child's school work. The parents decorated the hallway and the office. The principal made a special note inviting everyone to come. Even the children helped by cleaning their desks.
>
>> What people helped to get the school ready for the open house?
>> How did the teachers help?
>> How did the parents help?
>> How did the principal help?
>> How did the children help?
>
> The pilot hurried toward his airplane. He looked at the tires. He put gas in the airplane. He made sure he had all the maps that he would need. He started the motor. He looked to see if the motor was working well. Then he called the control tower on his radio. He had done all that needed to be done to take off on his trip.

What was the pilot getting ready to do?
What was one of the first things the pilot did when he got to his plane?
What did he check when he got the motor started?
What did he do then?

### ● DIRECTING THE LEARNER'S ATTENTION

The purpose of this task is to teach the learner to recall details and state how they support the main idea whether it precedes or follows the details. This is similar to the storehouse module III-IG-6. To teach this skill you must direct the learner's attention to the facts in the paragraph, how they relate to the main idea, and what the main idea is.

### ● TEACHING ACTIVITIES

This is an information gathering task similar to storehouse module III-IG-6, and you can adapt your teaching strategy from either the modeling or the discovery technique described in that objective.

### ● SUGGESTIONS FOR RETEACHING

If, after having been taught with either the modeling or the discovery technique, the learner can not recall details and how they relate to the main idea, you should adapt and use the suggestions in III-IG-6 to reteach the skill.

### ● SUGGESTIONS FOR PRACTICE

After teaching the learner how to recall details and state how they relate to the main idea, create practice activities to solidify the skill using the suggestions provided in III-IG-6.

### ● THE POSTTEST

The procedure and criterion for mastery are the same as for the pretest, although you may want to substitute new material.

### ● ENSURING TRANSFER

You should use the suggestions in III-IG-6 and reading comprehension activities such as those included in the final chapter to ensure that the learner applies recall of details during the routine language activities in the classroom.

# VII•MT•1

### ● THE PERFORMANCE OBJECTIVE

When given a paragraph to read that has details that can be classified together, the learner will classify the details and select an appropriate title for the paragraph.

Direct the learner to look at four titles and then to read paragraphs such as the following, selecting the best title for each paragraph from the four choices offered. The criterion for mastery is 75 percent. (Readability: Second grade.)

The four titles follow:

The Tallest Animal in the World
The Life of the Elephant
All Kinds of Monkeys
The Beautiful Cockatoo Bird

The elephants in the zoo come from warm, wet jungles far away.

Elephants travel together. Many fathers, mothers, and babies follow an older elephant.

The elephants sleep under trees all day. At sundown, they go to a river to drink and wash.

At night the elephants look for food. They eat leaves of trees, wild fruits, seeds, bark, and grass. They must go far to find food for so many big animals.

Are you using highlighting devices to help direct your learner's attention?

The giraffe is the tallest animal in the world. He comes from a country that is warm and dry.

In the day the giraffe stays under some tall trees. His color helps him to hide.

The giraffe eats when the sun comes up and at sundown. He can reach leaves at the tops of the trees. He swallows leaves without chewing them. In this way he eats quickly. Then he brings the food back into his mouth and chews it.

The cockatoo is a beautiful bird. He may have pink or yellow feathers on the top of his head. Some cockatoos are white. Some are black. Some are red and black.

In his own country the cockatoo lives with many other cockatoos. He flies fast from tree to tree, looking for food. Cockatoos eat seeds, nuts, and fruit. They like the fruit on farmers' trees best of all.

Cockatoos are good pets for people who like beautiful birds.

There are different kinds of monkeys in the world. Some have long tails. Some have short tails. Some have no tails at all.

Some monkeys have hair on their faces. Some do not. Most monkeys are black or gray, but some monkeys are bright colored.

Many monkeys live in the tops of tall trees. They have four hands, not two hands and two feet, as people have. That is why monkeys are at home in the treetops.

• DIRECTING THE LEARNER'S ATTENTION

The purpose of this task is to teach the learner to select an appropriate title for a paragraph based on details that can be classified together. This is similar to storehouse module III-MT-2. To teach this skill you must direct the learner's attention to the facts in the paragraph, to the common denominator of these facts that allows them to be categorized together, and to that one title that reflects the category.

## • TEACHING ACTIVITIES

This is a manipulative task similar to storehouse module III-MT-2, and you can adapt your teaching strategy from either the modeling or the discovery technique described in that objective.

## • SUGGESTIONS FOR RETEACHING

If, after having been taught with either the modeling or the discovery technique, the learner cannot select the title that reflects the main idea, you should adapt and use the suggestions in III-MT-2 to reteach the skill.

## • SUGGESTIONS FOR PRACTICE

After teaching the learner to select the main idea by title usage, create practice activities to solidify the skill, using the suggestions provided in III-MT-2.

## • THE POSTTEST

The procedure and criterion for mastery are the same as for the pretest, although you may want to substitute new material.

## • ENSURING TRANSFER

You should use the suggestions in III-MT-2 and reading comprehension activities such as those included in the final chapter to ensure that the learner applies main idea thinking during the routine language activities in the classroom.

## VII•MT•2

## • THE PERFORMANCE OBJECTIVE

When given a multiparagraph selection in which the author's theme is implied but not stated, the learner states an appropriate theme.

## • THE PRETEST

Direct the learner to read a story like the following one and to state what the story teaches. The criterion for mastery is 100 percent. (Readability: Second grade.)

"Don't run away," panted a cat as he chased after a mouse. "I only want to talk to you."
But the mouse ran faster.
"Stop!" called the cat. "I want you to answer a question."
Still the mouse did not stop.
"Please wait," said the cat. "You're so handsome that I want to get a close look at you."

The mouse acted like a simpleton and stopped. Before she could say anything, the cat ate her up.

> We should allow others to enjoy things whether we enjoy them ourselves or not.
> Too many cooks spoil the stew.
> Those who tell us how fine we are often want something from us.

### • DIRECTING THE LEARNER'S ATTENTION

The purpose of this task is to teach the learner to select a theme that is implied. This is similar to storehouse module I-MT-2. To teach this skill you must direct the learner's attention to what the facts say, what his or her experience has taught the learner about such concepts and ideas, and how these experiences and facts relate to the theme.

### • TEACHING ACTIVITIES

This is a manipulative task similar to storehouse module I-MT-2, and you can adapt your teaching strategy from either the modeling or the discovery technique described in that objective.

### • SUGGESTIONS FOR RETEACHING

If, after having been taught with either the modeling or the discovery technique, the learner does not understand how to select an appropriate theme, you should adapt and use the suggestions provided in I-MT-2 to reteach the skill.

### • SUGGESTIONS FOR PRACTICE

After teaching the learner the skill of inferring the theme, create practice activities to solidify the skill, using the suggestions provided in I-MT-2.

### • THE POSTTEST

The procedure and criterion for mastery are the same as for the pretest, although you may want to substitute new material.

### • ENSURING TRANSFER

You should use the suggestions in I-MT-2 and reading comprehension activities such as those included in the final chapter to ensure that the learner applies selection of theme during the routine language activities in the classroom.

# VII•ET•1

### • THE PERFORMANCE OBJECTIVE

When given three reports of a happening, the learner will identify the writer of the report and describe how the author's use of biased words helped him or her to determine authorship.

## • THE PRETEST

Direct the learner to read paragraphs like the following three news reports from a mythical battle front and have him or her identify that which was written by a neutral observer, that which was written by a representative of the Blue army, and that which was written by a representative of the Green army. The criterion for mastery is 100 percent. (Readability: Fourth grade.)

> The forces of the Blue army attacked the Green again. They attacked the Green army in a savage way. After the fight the Blues moved back its front lines as they had planned.

> The forces of the Blue army threw itself at the Green army in vain. The Greens had solid lines. After the fight the Blues withdrew. They withdrew helter-skelter.

> The forces of the Blue army fought with those of the Green army. After the fight, the Blues returned to the position they had held before.

## • DIRECTING THE LEARNER'S ATTENTION

The purpose of this task is to teach the learner to assess word choice for clues regarding an author's position on a topic. This is similar to storehouse module IV-ET-1. To teach this skill you must direct the learner's attention to the key words that signal the author's position and to the connotation associated with those words.

## • TEACHING ACTIVITIES

This is an evaluative task similar to storehouse module IV-ET-1, and you can adapt your teaching strategy from either the modeling or the discovery technique described in that objective.

How would you rate the seatwork you assigned today?

## • SUGGESTIONS FOR RETEACHING

If, after having been taught with either the modeling or the discovery technique, the learner is unable to determine an author's position, you should adapt and use the sugestions in IV-ET-1 to reteach the skill.

## • SUGGESTIONS FOR PRACTICE

After teaching the learner to make judgments on the basis of author's word choice, create practice activities to solidify the skill, using the suggestions provided in IV-ET-1.

## • THE POSTTEST

The procedure and criterion for mastery are the same as for the pretest, although you may want to substitute new material.

## • ENSURING TRANSFER

You should use the suggestions in IV-ET-1 and reading comprehension activities such as those included in the final chapter to ensure that the learner applies making judgments based on author's word choice during the routine language activities in the classroom.

# CLUSTER VIII

**• THE PERFORMANCE OBJECTIVE**

When given a fraction of a second to examine flashcards having printed on them the following words, the learner will pronounce each within one second.

| post | quick | bowl | feather | honey | noise |
| already | both | breakfast | elephant | large | held |
| move | quite | country | kept | field | fire |
| paw | bump | circus | wonder | early | clothes |
| arrow | climb | warm | caught | floor | roar |
| hurt | war | board | egg | umbrella | roll |
| voice | always | uncle | else | piece | |

**• THE PRETEST**

Print each of the preceding words on a flashcard. Flash each to the learner, giving him or her less than one second to examine each word before pronouncing it. Criterion for mastery is 100 percent.

**• DIRECTING THE LEARNER'S ATTENTION**

The purpose of this task is to teach the learner to recognize instantly and pronounce the words contained in the pretest when they are presented on flashcards. This is a sight word recognition skill like that described in II-SW-6. To teach the skill you must make sure that the learner knows exactly what is to be learned, that the words being taught are in the child's speaking vocabulary, and that you have directed his or her attention by highlighting the unique visual characteristics of each word (such as the initial and final letters, length, shape, double letters, and so on).

### • TEACHING ACTIVITIES

This is a sight word recognition skill similar to that described in II-SW-6. If the learner does not recognize the word in print, adapt your teaching strategy from either the modeling technique or the discovery technique described in that objective. If the learner confuses the word with another word similar to it, adapt your strategy from the suggestions contained in I-SW-17.

### • SUGGESTIONS FOR RETEACHING

If, after having been taught with the suggested technique, the learner is unable to recognize instantly one or more of the words on the pretest, you should use the reteaching suggestions described in II-SW-6.

### • SUGGESTIONS FOR PRACTICE

After successfully teaching the learner to recognize instantly the words on the pretest, create practice activities to solidify the skill, using the suggestions provided in II-SW-6.

### • THE POSTTEST

The procedure and criterion for mastery for the posttest are the same as for the pretest.

### • ENSURING TRANSFER

To be sure that this skill is applied you must give the learner reading material containing the words now known at sight and have him or her read. You may guide the application by pointing out the words the child has just learned to recognize or, as he or she becomes more proficient, you can encourage independent reading of the newly learned words. Any material at the child's instructional reading level that contains the learned sight words would be appropriate. Additional suggestions for helping the learner use known sight words in context are contained in II-SW-6.

## VIII•SW•2

### • THE PERFORMANCE OBJECTIVE

When given a flash presentation of words that the learner frequently confuses, he or she will pronounce each word correctly within one second.

### • THE PRETEST

You will note whether the learner is confusing words any time you test on sight words or listen to him or her read. If, during either of these activities the learner says one word for another (such as **held** for **hold**), you should pair the words together and teach them using the suggestions provided in this objective. No specific list of words is provided, since various learners will confuse various words. As with other sight word objectives, the criterion for mastery is 100 percent with any pair of confused words being taught.

## • DIRECTING THE LEARNER'S ATTENTION

The purpose of this task is to teach the learner to recognize instantly pairs of words that he or she has tended to confuse in the past. As such, it is similar to that described in I-SW-17. To teach this skill you must be sure that the learner has mastered the previous visual training skills, that he or she knows exactly what is to be learned, that the words being taught are in the learner's speaking vocabulary, and that you have directed his or her attention by highlighting the discriminator that sets one word apart from another (such as the **e** in **held** and the **o** in **hold**).

## • TEACHING ACTIVITIES

In teaching this skill you can use either the modeling technique or the discovery technique described in I-SW-17, adjusting the suggestions to focus on the particular words that the learner is confusing.

## • SUGGESTIONS FOR RETEACHING

If, after having been taught this skill with either the modeling or the discovery technique, the learner continues to confuse the words, you should use the reteaching suggestions provided in I-SW-17.

## • SUGGESTIONS FOR PRACTICE

Once the learner can instantly recognize the words that he or she was previously confusing, create practice activities to solidify the skill, using the suggestions provided in I-SW-17.

## • THE POSTTEST

The procedure and criterion for mastery are the same as for the pretest.

## • ENSURING TRANSFER

Once the learner can recognize the easily confused words, you should immediately provide for application of this skill by giving the child reading material containing the words he or she now knows at sight. For specific suggestions regarding such application activities, see II-SW-6.

## VIII•SW•3

## • THE PERFORMANCE OBJECTIVE

When given the words he or she recognizes instantly, the learner will create and read a multiple-sentence story using these words.

## • THE PRETEST

Provide the learner with cards, each of which has printed on it a word he or she instantly recognizes. Say to the learner, "Today we are going to do something that is very hard. We are going to send messages. Look at the cards you have in front of you. Each card has a word on it that you know. Can you send me a message using the words you have there? If you want to send a message using a word you don't have on a card, tell me and I will make a card for you having that word on it." The criterion for mastery is the combination of any number of words in a way that is grammatically accurate and that makes sense. When the learner has formed the sentence, reinforce the value of his or her effort by reading it aloud yourself.

## • DIRECTING THE LEARNER'S ATTENTION

Do your practice activities reflect what was taught?

This is a language experience activity designed to teach the learner to produce and read messages using the individual words known at sight. As such, it is an application activity similar to that described in II-SW-8. To teach this activity you must make sure that the learner knows exactly what is to be learned and you must direct his or her attention to the idea he or she wishes to convey, to what the message would sound like when spoken, to what printed word cards the learner will need to "write" the message, and to the order in which the words must be placed. You might highlight by asking a series of questions such as, "What did you do yesterday after school that you could tell me about? Can you make a sentence about that and say it to me? What words did you use to say your sentence to me? How many of those words do you already have on cards and which ones will we have to make for you? What word will come first in your written message?"

## • TEACHING ACTIVITIES

This is a language experience activity similar to that described in II-SW-8. You should use the modeling and discovery techniques described in that objective as a basis for planning and teaching this task.

## • SUGGESTIONS FOR RETEACHING

If, after having been taught with either of the techniques described in the key objective, the learner is unable to create a single sentence message using his or her sight words, you should

1. Reteach the activity, using the alternate technique.
2. Be more specific in eliciting from the learner the idea he or she wishes to convey.
3. Be sure that the learner expresses the message first in oral form and that he or she understands that the written message will say the same thing as the oral message.
4. Be sure that the content of the message matches the learner's experience, changing the subject to match his or her experience if necessary.

5. Recheck the learner's mastery of the sight words, reteaching any that have not yet been completely mastered.
6. Return to the previous language experience objectives and make sure that the learner can do those simpler tasks before asking him or her to create entire sentences.

## • SUGGESTIONS FOR PRACTICE

Once the learner has been taught to use his or her sight words to create and read sentences, devise practice activities to solidify this skill, adapting the suggestions provided in II-SW-8.

## • THE POSTTEST

The procedure and criterion for mastery for the posttest are the same as for the pretest.

## • ENSURING TRANSFER

This objective is an application activity designed to help the learner use his or her sight words in context. In addition to the application specified here, however, you should use the suggestions in II-SW-6 to be sure that the learner uses his or her sight words in other contextual situations.

**VIII•SW•4**

## • THE PERFORMANCE OBJECTIVE

When given a fraction of a second to examine flashcards having printed on them the following words, the learner will pronounce each within one second.

| | | | | | |
|---|---|---|---|---|---|
| wolf | world | worm | cried | pennies | sign |
| splash | spring | station | turkey | across | bottom |
| automobile | deer | buy | dear | lie | answer |
| calf | learn | log | soft | beautiful | care |
| heard | year | carry | soup | squirrel | wear |
| cover | cross | through | thought | brought | vegetable |
| watch | monkey | engine | front | great | left |
| minute | | | | | |

## • THE PRETEST

Print each of the preceding words, on a flashcard. Flash each to the learner, giving him less than one second to examine each word before he pronounces it. Criterion for mastery is 100 percent.

## • DIRECTING THE LEARNER'S ATTENTION

The purpose of this task is to teach the learner to recognize instantly and pronounce the words contained in the pretest when they are printed on cards and flashed to him. This is a sight word recognition skill like that described in II-SW-6. To teach the skill you must ensure that the learner knows exactly what is to be learned, that the words being taught are in his or her speaking vocabulary, and that you have directed his or her attention by highlighting the unique visual characteristics of each word (such as the initial and final letters, length, shape, double letters, and so on).

## • TEACHING ACTIVITIES

This is a sight word recognition skill similar to that described in II-SW-6. If the learner does not recognize the word in print, adapt your teaching strategy from either the modeling technique or the discovery technique described in that objctive. If he or she confuses the word with another word similar to it, adapt your strategy from the suggestions contained in I-SW-17.

## • SUGGESTIONS FOR RETEACHING

If, after having been taught with the suggested technique, the learner is unable to recognize instantly one or more of the words on the pretest, you should use the reteaching suggestions described in II-SW-6.

## • SUGGESTIONS FOR PRACTICE

After successfully teaching the learner to recognize instantly the words on the pretest, create practice activities to solidify the skill, using the suggestions provided in II-SW-6.

## • THE POSTTEST

The procedure and criterion for mastery for the posttest are the same as for the pretest.

## • ENSURING TRANSFER

To be sure that this skill is applied you must give the learner reading material containing the words he or she knows at sight and have the learner read. You may guide the learner's application by pointing out the words he or she has just learned to recognize or, as the learner becomes more proficient, you can encourage him or her to read and apply the newly learned words independently. Any material that is at the learner's instructional reading level and that contains the sight words he or she has learned would be appropriate. Additional suggestions for helping the learner use his or her known sight words in context are contained in II-SW-6.

# VIII•SW•5

## • THE PERFORMANCE OBJECTIVE

When given a flash presentation of words the learner frequently confuses, he or she will pronounce each word correctly within one second.

## • THE PRETEST

You will note whether the learner is confusing words any time you test on sight words or listen to him or her read. If, during either of these activities, the learner says one word for another (such as **though** for **through**), you should pair the words together and teach them, using the suggestions provided in this objective. No specific list of words is provided, since various learners will confuse various words. As with other sight word objectives, the criterion for mastery is 100 percent, with any pair of confused words being taught.

### • DIRECTING THE LEARNER'S ATTENTION

The purpose of this task is to teach the learner to recognize instantly pairs of words he or she has tended to confuse in the past. As such, it is similar to that described in I-SW-17. To teach this skill you must make sure that the learner has mastered the previous visual training skill, that he or she knows exactly what is to be learned, that the words being taught are in his or her speaking vocabulary, and that you have directed the learner's attention by highlighting the discriminator that sets one word apart from another (such as the **r** in **through**).

### • TEACHING ACTIVITIES

In teaching this skill you can use either the modeling technique or the discovery technique described in I-SW-17, adjusting the suggestions to focus on the particular words that the learner is confusing.

### • SUGGESTIONS FOR RETEACHING

If, after having been taught this skill with either the modeling or the discovery technique, the learner continues to confuse the words, you should use the reteaching suggestions provided in I-SW-17.

### • SUGGESTIONS FOR PRACTICE

Once the learner can instantly recognize the words that he or she was previously confusing, create practice activities to solidify the skill, using the suggestions provided in I-SW-17.

### • THE POSTTEST

The procedure and criterion for mastery are the same as for the pretest.

### • ENSURING TRANSFER

Once the learner can recognize the easily confused words, you should immediately provide for application of this skill by giving the child reading material containing the words he or she knows at sight. For specific suggestions regarding such application activities, see II-SW-6.

## VIII•SW•6

### • THE PERFORMANCE OBJECTIVE

When given words he or she recognizes instantly, the learner will create and read a multiple-sentence story using these words.

● 433

## • THE PRETEST

Provide the learner with cards, each of which has printed on it a word the learner instantly recognizes. Say, "Today we are going to do something that is very hard. We are going to send messages. Look at the cards you have in front of you. Each card has a word on it that you know. Can you send me a message using the words you have there? If you want to send a message using a word you don't have on a card, tell me and I will make a card for you having that word on it." The criterion for mastery is the combination of any number of words in a way that is grammatically accurate and that makes sense. When the learner has formed his or her sentence, reinforce the value of the effort by reading it aloud yourself.

## • DIRECTING THE LEARNER'S ATTENTION

This is a language experience activity designed to teach the learner to produce and read messages using the individual words known at sight. As such, it is an application activity similar to that described in II-SW-8.

To teach this activity you must make sure that the learner knows exactly what is to be learned and you must direct his or her attention to the idea to be conveyed, to what the message would sound like when spoken, to what printed word cards he or she will need to "write" the message, and to the order in which the words must be placed. You might highlight by asking a series of questions such as, "What did you do yesterday after school that you could tell me about? Can you make a sentence about that and say it to me? What words did you use to say your sentence to me? How many of those words do you already have on cards and which ones will we have to make for you? What word will come first in your written message?"

*If they are interviewed 20 years from now, what will your pupils remember that you taught them about reading?*

## • TEACHING ACTIVITIES

This is a language experience activity similar to that described in II-SW-8. You should use the modeling and discovery techniques described in that objective as a basis for planning and teaching this task.

## • SUGGESTIONS FOR RETEACHING

If, after having been taught with either of the techniques described in the key objective, the learner is unable to create a single sentence message using his or her sight words, you should

1. Reteach the activity, using the alternate technique.
2. Be more specific in eliciting from the learner the idea he or she wishes to convey.
3. Be sure that the learner expresses the message first in oral form and that he or she understands that the written message will say the same thing as the oral message.
4. Be sure that the content of the message matches the learner's experience; change the subject to match his or her experience if necessary.

5. Recheck the learner's mastery of the sight words, reteaching any that have not yet been completely mastered.
6. Return to the previous language experience objectives and make sure that the learner can do those simpler tasks before asking him or her to create entire sentences.

## • SUGGESTIONS FOR PRACTICE

Once the learner has been taught to use his or her sight words to create and read sentences, devise practice activities to solidify this skill, adapting the suggestions provided in II-SW-8.

## • THE POSTTEST

The procedure and criterion for mastery for the posttest are the same as for the pretest.

## • ENSURING TRANSFER

This objective is an application activity designed to help the learner use his or her sight words in context. In addition to the application specified here, however, you should use the suggestions in II-SW-6 to make sure that the learner uses his or her sight words in other contextual situations.

# VIII•WA•1

## • THE PERFORMANCE OBJECTIVE

When given a known word illustrating the vowel-consonant-vowel principle of syllabication in which the first vowel might be either long or short, the learner will correctly pronounce other words that illustrate this principle.

## • THE PRETEST

Use the following list of words. The first word in the list has been previously taught as a sight word. Have the learner identify the first word and then ask him to pronounce the remaining words. The criterion for mastery is 13 out of 15 correct.

**never**

| river | seven | visit | ever | even |
| tiger | present | wagon | music | began |
| robin | become | finish | paper | over |

## • DIRECTING THE LEARNER'S ATTENTION

The purpose of this task is to teach the learner to pronounce words that illustrate the vowel-consonant-vowel principle of syllabication, in which the first vowel can be either long or short. As such, it is similar to storehouse module VII-WA-1. To teach this skill you must direct the learner's attention by stating exactly what is to be learned, and by highlighting the visual pattern of vowels and consonants, the sound value of each vowel phonogram, and the tying of the resultant pronunciation to a known word.

(In the word **river,** for instance, you would first say the word, exaggerating the syllable break; then write the word, showing the vowel-consonant-vowel arrangement and syllable division; then show the learner the sound of each vowel phonogram; and finally, help him or her to fuse the isolated syllables into the spoken word **river.**)

The learning key to analyzing multisyllable words that have only one consonant separating vowels is *flexibility*. The child must learn to divide the syllable by first placing the consonant with the vowel on the left (making it short) and then sounding the resultant vowel phonograms. If this approximation gives insufficient clues to the identification of the word, the single consonant is moved to the right of the consonant and the new syllables identified and sounded. One or the other syllabic divisions must give sufficient clues for the child to recognize the word, or the child must resort to asking someone for the identification. More syllable skill will not help. Either the word is nonanalyzable through syllable sounding or else it is not in the child's listening-speaking vocabulary and so he or she can have no way to know when it is correctly analyzed and sounded.

### • TEACHING ACTIVITIES

In teaching this syllabication skill you can use either the modeling technique or the discovery technique described in VII-WA-1, adjusting the suggestions to focus on vowel-consonant-vowel words in which the first vowel can be short or long.

### • SUGGESTIONS FOR RETEACHING

If, after having been taught this skill with either the modeling or the discovery technique, the learner is unable to pronounce words such as those tested in this objective, you should use the reteaching suggestions provided in VII-WA-1.

### • SUGGESTIONS FOR PRACTICE

Once the learner can pronounce multisyllable words such as those tested in this objective, create practice activities to solidify the skill, using the suggestions provided in VII-WA-1.

### • THE POSTTEST

The pretest can also be used for the posttest. The procedure and criterion for mastery are the same.

### • ENSURING TRANSFER

You should use the suggestions provided in VII-WA-1 to make sure that the learner uses this syllabication skill in daily reading activities.

# VIII•WA•2

### • THE PERFORMANCE OBJECTIVE

When given a known word illustrating the short y principle, the learner will correctly pronounce other two-syllable words containing the short **y.**

## • THE PRETEST

Use the following list of words. The first word in the list has been previously taught as a sight word. Have the learner identify the first word and then ask him or her to pronounce the remaining words. The criterion for mastery is 12 out of 14 correct.

| | | | | |
|---|---|---|---|---|
| **baby** | trappy | party | sleepy | dandy |
| candy | lady | bunny | story | hungry |
| city | grubby | puppy | cooky | pony |

## • DIRECTING THE LEARNER'S ATTENTION

The purpose of this task is to teach the learner to pronounce words containing a short y sound at the end. Although it involves both syllabication and a vowel principle, it is most similar to storehouse module VI-WA-1. To teach this skill you must direct the learner's attention by stating exactly what is to be learned and by highlighting the sound of the final syllable and the y at the end of the word. (For the word **candy**, for instance, you would first say the word, exaggerating the ending sound of the short y, and then write the word with the ending y circled.)

## • TEACHING ACTIVITIES

In teaching this vowel generalization you can use either the modeling or the discovery technique described in VI-WA-1, adjusting the suggestions to focus on the ending short y.

## • SUGGESTIONS FOR RETEACHING

If, after having been taught with either the modeling or the discovery technique, the learner is unable to pronounce words illustrating the ending short y principle, you should

How many of your pupils left your classroom today feeling both lovable and capable?

1. Reteach the skill, using the alternate technique.
2. Reexamine your attenders to be sure that you are providing enough highlighting on the final sound of each word and on the visual form of the final y.
3. Reteach the skill as a task of letter substitution, arranging the words according to common final endings (such as **candy** and **lady**) and using the teaching suggestions provided in II-WA-18.

## • SUGGESTIONS FOR PRACTICE

Once the learner can pronounce words illustrating the final short y principle, create practice activities to solidify the skill, using the suggestions provided in VI-WA-1.

## • THE POSTTEST

The pretest can be used also as the posttest. The procedure and criterion for mastery are the same.

• ENSURING TRANSFER

You should use the suggestions provided in VI-WA-1 to make sure that the learner uses the skill in pursuing daily reading activities.

# VIII•WA•3

• THE PERFORMANCE OBJECTIVE

When given a two-syllable word with an unaccented a in the initial position, the learner will correctly pronounce other two syllable words illustrating the same principle.

• THE PRETEST

Use the following list of words. The first word in the list has been previously taught as a sight word. Have the learner identify the first word and then ask him or her to pronounce the remaining words. The criterion for mastery is 100 percent.

**about** alone around asleep

• DIRECTING THE LEARNER'S ATTENTION

The purpose of this task is to teach the learner to pronounce words having an unaccented a in the initial position. Although it involves both syllabication and a vowel principle, it is most similar to storehouse module VI-WA-1. To teach this skill you must direct the learner's attention by stating exactly what is to be learned and by highlighting the sound of the initial syllable and the a at the beginning of the word. (For the word **afraid,** for instance, you would first say the word, exaggerating the beginning sound of the unaccented **a,** and then write the word with the beginning a circled.)

• TEACHING ACTIVITIES

In teaching this vowel generalization you can use either the modeling or the discovery technique described in VI-WA-1, adjusting the suggestions to focus on the unaccented a at the beginning.

• SUGGESTIONS FOR RETEACHING

If, after having been taught with either the modeling or the discovery technique, the learner is unable to pronounce words having an unaccented **a** in the initial position, you should

1. Reteach the skill, using the alternate technique.
2. Reexamine your attenders to make sure that you are providing enough highlighting on the initial sound of each word and on the visual form of the initial a.
3. Teach the words in the pretest as sight words, using the teaching suggestions provided in II-SW-6.

## • SUGGESTIONS FOR PRACTICE

Once the learner can pronounce words with an unaccented **a** in the initial position, create practice activities to solidify the skill, using the suggestions provided in VI-WA-1.

## • THE POSTTEST

The pretest can be used also as the posttest. The procedure and criterion for mastery are the same.

## • ENSURING TRANSFER

You should use the suggestions provided in VI-WA-1 to make sure that the learner uses the skill in pursuing daily reading activities in the classroom.

## • THE PERFORMANCE OBJECTIVE

When given a known word composed of the **−ew** combination, the learner will replace the initial consonant with another consonant, blend, or digraph and correctly pronounce the new word.

## • THE PRETEST

Use the following list of words. Have the learner identify the first word in the list and then ask him or her to pronounce the remaining words. The criterion for mastery is 100 percent. *Note:* Some of the words listed are nonsense words, which are included so that the learner must use analysis rather than sight recognition.

| | | | | |
|---|---|---|---|---|
| **new** | flew | stew | blew | chew |
| few | grew | crew | prew | slew |

## • DIRECTING THE LEARNER'S ATTENTION

The purpose of this task is to teach the learner to substitute initial consonants in the initial position of **−ew** phonograms and to pronounce the new words. As such, it is similar to storehouse module II-WA-18. To teach this skill you must direct the learner's attention by stating exactly what is to be learned and by highlighting the varying initial consonants and the **−ew** phonogram. [In the word **few**, for instance, you might circle the initial letter **f**, underline the **−ew** phonogram, and have the learner use the say-it-slow, say-it-fast technique (see I-WA-5) in pronouncing the word.]

## • TEACHING ACTIVITIES

In teaching this letter substitution skill you can use either the modeling technique or the discovery technique described in II-WA-18, adjusting the suggestion to focus on words having the **−ew** phonogram.

● **SUGGESTIONS FOR RETEACHING**

If, after having been taught this skill with either the modeling or the discovery technique, the learner is unable to substitute initial consonants in —ew phonogram words and pronounce the new words, you should use the reteaching suggestions provided in II-WA-18, adapting them to fit this objective.

● **SUGGESTIONS FOR PRACTICE**

Once the learner can substitute initial consonants in —ew phonograms and pronounce the new word, create practice activities to solidify the skill, using the suggestions provided in II-WA-18.

● **THE POSTTEST**

The pretest can also be used for the posttest. The procedure and criterion for mastery are the same.

● **ENSURING TRANSFER**

You should use the suggestions provided in II-WA-18 to make sure that this skill is used by the learner during daily reading activities in the classroom.

# VIII•WA•5

● **THE PERFORMANCE OBJECTIVE**

When given a stimulus word beginning with the **str** or **thr** consonant combinations and a group of three words of which one begins with the **str** or **thr** sounds, the learner will pair the two words beginning with the same sound.

● **THE PRETEST**

Using the following words, say to the learner, "Here are three words. Listen carefully. (Say the words.) "Which one sounds like (say the stimulus word) at the beginning?" Repeat the three words. The criterion for mastery is five out of six correct.

| | | | |
|---|---|---|---|
| saw | straw | shawl | Which one sounds like **street** at the beginning? Repeat the three words. |
| throw | mow | tree | Which one sounds like **three** at the beginning? Repeat the three words. |
| tall | this | threat | Which one sounds like **three** at the beginning? Repeat the three words. |
| stand | strand | chant | Which one sounds like **street** at the beginning? Repeat the three words. |
| strap | slap | swap | Which one sounds like **street** at the beginning? Repeat the three words. |
| mesh | tee | thresh | Which one sounds like **three** at the beginning? Repeat the three words. |

- **DIRECTING THE LEARNER'S ATTENTION**

The purpose of this task is to teach the learner to distinguish the **str** and **thr** sounds from other beginning consonant sounds. As such, it is similar to storehouse module I-WA-5. To teach this skill you must direct the learner's attention by stating exactly what is to be learned and by highlighting the beginning sound of the word as described in I-WA-5.

- **TEACHING ACTIVITIES**

In teaching this auditory discrimination skill you can use either the modeling technique or the discovery technique described in I-WA-5, adjusting the suggestions to focus on the **str** and **thr** sounds.

- **SUGGESTIONS FOR RETEACHING**

If, after having been taught this skill with either the modeling or the discovery technique, the learner is unable to distinguish the **str** and **thr** sounds from other beginning consonant sounds, you should

1. Reteach the skill, using the alternate technique.
2. Reexamine your attenders, making sure that the learner is listening to the beginning sound and that your highlighting is emphatic enough to help him or her distinguish the beginning sounds from other sounds.
3. Return to the previous auditory discrimination skills, making sure that the learner can perform them before requiring him or her to complete this objective.

- **SUGGESTIONS FOR PRACTICE**

Once the learner can distinguish the **str** and **thr** sounds from other beginning consonant sounds, create practice activities to solidify the skill, using the suggestions provided in I-WA-5.

- **THE POSTTEST**

The procedure and criterion for mastery are the same as for the pretest. Use the following words.

| | | | |
|---|---|---|---|
| through | thumb | tea | Which one sounds like **three** at the beginning? Repeat the three words. |
| sharp | start | stress | Which one sounds like **street** at the beginning? Repeat the three words. |
| stay | stray | steep | Which one sounds like **street** at the beginning? Repeat the three words. |
| theft | then | thrift | Which one sounds like **three** at the beginning? Repeat the three words. |

| | | | |
|---|---|---|---|
| thrive | tie | thimble | Which one sounds like **three** at the beginning? Repeat the three words. |
| stuck | strut | stub | Which one sounds like **street** at the beginning? Repeat the three words. |

### ● ENSURING TRANSFER

Although the learner will be applying this skill while learning to attach the sounds to the letter combinations in subsequent objectives, you should also use the suggestions provided in I-WA-5 to be sure that the child uses the skill during the routine daily reading activities of the classroom.

## VIII•WA•6

### ● THE PERFORMANCE OBJECTIVE

When given spoken words beginning with the **str** or **thr** sounds, the learner will identify the beginning letters in each word.

### ● THE PRETEST

Give the learner two cards, one having **str** printed on it and the other having **thr** printed on it. Say the following words, directing the learner to point to the letter card whose sound begins the word. The criterion for mastery is five out of six correct.

stride   throb   struck   strife   throng   thrush

### ● DIRECTING THE LEARNER'S ATTENTION

The purpose of this task is to teach the learner to establish a sound-symbol connection between the letter combinations **str** and **thr** and the sounds these combinations produce at the beginning of words. As such, it is similar to that described in I-WA-9. To teach this skill you must direct the learner's attention by stating exactly what is to be learned and by highlighting both the sound heard at the beginning of the word and the form of the letter combination it is to be connected with. (In the word **stride**, for instance, you might exaggerate the beginning **str** sound while simultaneously pointing to the cutout letters **str**.)

### ● TEACHING ACTIVITIES

In teaching this sound-symbol connection skill you can use either the modeling technique or the discovery technique described in I-WA-9, adjusting the suggestions to focus on the **str** and **thr** sounds.

### ● SUGGESTIONS FOR RETEACHING

If, after having been taught this skill with either the modeling or the discovery technique, the learner is unable to connect letters and sounds for the **str** and **thr**, you should

1. Reteach the skill, using the alternate technique.
2. Be more specific in directing the learner's attention, making sure that he or she is listening to the *beginning* sound while simultaneously looking at the letters.
3. Use more emphasis in highlighting the beginning sound, the letters, and the connection between them.
4. Return to the previous objective and make sure that the learner can distinguish between the beginning **str** and **thr** and other consonant sounds before requiring him or her to connect the sounds with letters.

● **SUGGESTIONS FOR PRACTICE**

Once the learner has successfully connected the **str** and **thr** letters to the sounds these combinations produce, create practice activities to solidify the skill, using the suggestions provided in I-WA-9.

● **THE POSTTEST**

The procedure and criterion for mastery are the same as for the pretest. Use the following words.

through   thresh   stray   stroll   thrive   strut

● **ENSURING TRANSFER**

Although the learner will be applying this skill in subsequent skills in the hierarchy, you should also use the suggestions provided in I-WA-9 to make sure that the learner uses the skill during the daily reading activities in the classroom.

# VIII•WA•7

● **THE PERFORMANCE OBJECTIVE**

When given a written sentence with one word missing and cued for the missing word by the letter combination with which that word begins, the learner will say a word beginning with that letter combination that fits the context of the sentence.

● **THE PRETEST**

Give the learner the following sentences. Say, "Each of these sentences has one word missing. Read the sentence, look at the letter combination that begins the missing word, and say a word beginning with that combination that will finish the sentence." Use the following sentences. The criterion for mastery is five out of six correct. *Note:* If a sentence fails to match a learner's experience background or does not provide enough context for him or her, you should alter the sentence accordingly. Sentence 1, for instance, could be changed to read, "In order to play football you must be big and str_____."

1. The football player was big and str_____.
2. The queen sat on her thr_____.
3. My mother fixed the rip with her needle and thr_____.
4. In the baseball game the umpire said, "Str_____ one!"
5. The man was fishing in the str_____.
6. The girl thr_____ the ball to me.

### • DIRECTING THE LEARNER'S ATTENTION

The purpose of this task is to teach the learner to use his or her knowledge of **str** and **thr** letter-sound correspondence and context to identify unknown words. As such, it is similar to that described in I-WA-14. To teach this skill you must direct the learner's attention by stating exactly what is to be learned and by highlighting the words in the sentence that provide clues to the identity of the unknown word, the letter combination that the unknown word begins with, and the sound associated with that letter combination. (In the first sentence of the pretest, for instance, you might highlight the words **football, player,** and **big**; direct the learner to look at the large cutout **str** and to get his or her mouth ready to say the sound of **str**.)

Think about your poorest reader. Have you given him or her any real reason to learn to read?

### • TEACHING ACTIVITIES

In teaching this context-letter-sound skill you can use either the modeling technique or the discovery technique described in I-WA-14, adjusting the suggestions to focus on the **str** and **thr** letter combination.

### • SUGGESTIONS FOR RETEACHING

If, after having been taught this skill with either the modeling or the discovery technique, the learner is unable to use context and the **str** and **thr** letter combinations to identify unknown words, you should use the reteaching suggestions provided in I-WA-14.

### • SUGGESTIONS FOR PRACTICE

Once the learner has successfully used the **str** and **thr** combinations and context to identify unknown words, create practice activities to solidify the skill, using the suggestions provided in I-WA-14.

### • THE POSTTEST

The procedure and criterion for mastery are the same as for the pretest. Use the following sentences.

1. When I use a ruler, I can draw a str_____ line.
2. The drink was hot and it burned my thr_____.
3. I lost my kite because the str_____ broke.
4. The jar was up high. I had to str_____ to reach it.
5. "Winning the game was my biggest thr_____," said the baseball player.
6. You only have one pet, but I have thr_____.

## • ENSURING TRANSFER

You should use the suggestions provided in I-WA-14 to make sure that this skill is used by the child during the daily reading activities in the classroom.

## • THE PERFORMANCE OBJECTIVE

When given words composed of the **str** and **thr** combinations and other phonetic elements known to him or her, the learner will correctly pronounce the words.

## • THE PRETEST

Put each of the following words on a card. Show the card to the learner and ask him or her to pronounce each word. *Note:* This is not to be a flash presentation. The learner may examine the words carefully before pronouncing the word. The criterion for mastery is 14 out of 16 correct. Some of the words listed are nonsense words, which are included so that the learner must use analysis rather than sight recognition.

| | | | |
|---|---|---|---|
| street | strong | three | throat |
| strap | strike | threw | thrash |
| string | strive | throw | thrig |
| strip | strobe | throne | thrust |

## • DIRECTING THE LEARNER'S ATTENTION

The purpose of this skill is to teach the learner to substitute **str** and **thr** letter combinations in the initial position of known vowel phonograms and pronounce the new words. As such, it is similar to storehouse module II-WA-18. To teach this skill you must direct the learner's attention by stating exactly what is to be learned and by highlighting the initial letter combination and the last part of each word. [In the word **street,** for instance, you might circle the initial **str** and underline the **eet,** having the learner use the say-it-slow, say-it-fast technique (see I-WA-5) in pronouncing the word.]

## • TEACHING ACTIVITIES

In teaching this letter substitution skill you can use either the modeling technique or the discovery technique described in II-WA-18, adjusting the suggestions to focus on the **str** and **thr** letter combinations in the initial position.

## • SUGGESTIONS FOR RETEACHING

If, after having been taught this skill with either the modeling or the discovery technique, the learner is unable to substitute the **str** and **thr** letter combinations in the initial position of known vowel phonograms and pronounce the new words, you should use the reteaching suggestions provided in II-WA-18.

## • SUGGESTIONS FOR PRACTICE

Once the learner can substitute **str** and **thr** letter combinations in the initial position of known vowel phonograms, create practice activities to solidify the skill, using the suggestions provided in II-WA-18.

## • THE POSTTEST

The pretest can be used also as the posttest. The procedure and criterion for mastery are the same.

## • ENSURING TRANSFER

You should use the suggestions provided in II-WA-18 to make sure that this skill is used by the learner during the daily reading activities in the classroom.

## VIII•IG•1

## • THE PERFORMANCE OBJECTIVE

When given content words identified by the teacher, the learner will use each word correctly in an oral sentence.

## • THE PRETEST

The words to be tested are selected by the teacher. These may be words that appear in the basal text or in stories being read in class or that are associated with the study of a particular content area. To test the words chosen say each word out loud for the child, asking him or her to make up a sentence using the word you have just said. The criterion for mastery is 100 percent, since any word not used correctly will have to be taught.

## • DIRECTING THE LEARNER'S ATTENTION

The purpose of this task is to teach the learner the meaning of new words he or she will be encountering. This is similar to storehouse module I-IG-1 but different words are being taught. To teach this skill you must direct the learner's attention by (1) providing either a direct or a vicarious experience to form a basis for the concept, (2) identifying the characteristics of this concept, and (3) connecting the concept to its word label. *Note:* This objective focuses on meaning alone. The learner should not be asked to pronounce these words as they appear in print until after this skill has been mastered.

## • TEACHING ACTIVITIES

This is a word meaning skill similar to module I-IG-1, and you can adapt your teaching strategy from either the modeling or the discovery techniques described in that objective.

## • SUGGESTIONS FOR RETEACHING

If, after having been taught with either the modeling or the discovery technique, the learner does not understand the meaning of any word in this objective, you should adapt and use the suggestions in I-IG-1 to reteach the skill.

## • SUGGESTIONS FOR PRACTICE
After teaching the learner the meaning of these words, create practice activities to solidify the skill, using the suggestions provided in I-IG-1.

## • THE POSTTEST
The procedure and criterion for mastery are the same as for the pretest.

## • ENSURING TRANSFER
You should use the suggestions in I-IG-1 and reading comprehension activities such as those found in the final chapter to make sure that the learner applies the new word meanings during the routine daily language activities of the classroom.

# VIII•IG•2

## • THE PERFORMANCE OBJECTIVE
When given a sentence containing a word unknown in meaning and in which a clue to the word's meaning is provided through a summary clue, the learner will state the meaning of the unknown word.

## • THE PRETEST
State the unknown word for the child and say that the word appears in the sentence the child is going to read, together with a clue to the word's meaning. Using sentences like the following, ask the child to state the meaning of the underlined word. The criterion for mastery is two out of three correct. (Readability: Fourth grade.)

When things are really going badly, singing camp songs with your pupils can do wonders.

misnomer  The fullback on the football team was huge. He weighed 250 pounds. He stood well over 6 feet tall. We called him Pee Wee, an obvious **misnomer.**

frantic  It was a frantic scene when the monster came in the front door. Children were screaming. Some people fainted; others were shouting to each other wildly.

minute  The missing piece to the machine was **minute.** When the worker dropped it, she had to use a magnifying glass to find it.

## • DIRECTING THE LEARNER'S ATTENTION
The purpose of this task is to teach the learner to determine the meaning of an unknown word by a summary of the context clues surrounding it. The task is similar to storehouse module II-IG-4. To teach this skill you must direct the learner's attention to the unknown word, to the words that explain the meaning of the unknown word, and to the summary of the known meanings as they relate to the unknown word.

## • TEACHING ACTIVITIES

This is an information-gathering task similar to storehouse module II-IG-4, and you can adapt your teaching strategy from either the modeling or the discovery technique described in that objective.

## • SUGGESTIONS FOR RETEACHING

If, after having been taught with either the modeling or the discovery technique, the learner is unable to use summary context clues, you should adapt and use the suggestions in II-IG-4 to reteach the skill.

## • SUGGESTIONS FOR PRACTICE

After teaching the learner to use summary context clues, create practice activities to solidify the skill, using the suggestions provided in II-IG-4.

## • THE POSTTEST

The procedure and criterion for mastery are the same as for the pretest, although you may want to substitute new material.

## • ENSURING TRANSFER

You should use the suggestions in II-IG-4 and reading comprehension activities such as those included in the final chapter to make sure that the learner applies summary context clues during the routine language activities in the classroom.

# VIII•IG•3

## • THE PERFORMANCE OBJECTIVE

When given a short paragraph in which a word in the last sentence should be stressed to obtain the exact meaning, the learner will identify the word to be stressed and emphasize that word when reading the paragraph orally.

## • THE PRETEST

Direct the learner to read silently paragraphs like the following and to decide which word should be emphasized. Then have the child read it out loud. The word to be emphasized is provided below each paragraph for the teacher's use only. The criterion for mastery is 80 percent. (Readability: Third grade.)

Ann's sister Susie was going to a doll show. Ann liked dolls too but she was sick and could not get out of bed. "I wish I could go," she said sadly.

the second **I** in the last sentence

The Tigers were very happy. They had won their first hockey game in six weeks. As they left the ice, Mike said, "The other team has been making fun of us but I wonder what they'll say now?"

**now**

Allen was getting his bike ready for the circus parade. He was putting ribbon on the wheels. It was noon and he still had only one wheel done "The parade will start at two o'clock," he said. "I just have to be finished by then."

**have**

Mrs. Jones liked Mrs. Smith's table. She liked it so much that she wanted to give Mrs. Smith fifty dollars for it. But Mrs. Smith said, "I wouldn't sell that table. Not for any price!"

**any**

Susan was in a hurry. Quickly she got her shoes and put them on. Then she started to tie her shoelace. Suddenly one of the shoelaces broke. "I knew this would happen sometime," she said.

**knew**

● **DIRECTING THE LEARNER'S ATTENTION**

The purpose of this task is to teach the learner how context can indicate relationships that result in various intonation patterns. This is similar to storehouse module VII-IG-5. To teach this skill you must direct the learner's attention to the context clues, since they signal the intonation pattern to be used.

● **TEACHING ACTIVITIES**

This is an information-gathering task similar to storehouse module VII-IG-5, and you can adapt your teaching strategy from either the modeling or the discovering technique described in that objective.

● **SUGGESTIONS FOR RETEACHING**

If, after having been taught with either the modeling or the discovery technique, the learner is unable to use context clues as a way to determine how intonation patterns are used, you should adapt and use the suggestions in VII-IG-5 to reteach the skill.

● **SUGGESTIONS FOR PRACTICE**

After teaching the learner the use of context clues as signalers for intonation patterns, create practice activities to solidify the skill, using the suggestions provided in VII-IG-5.

● **THE POSTTEST**

The procedure and criterion for mastery are the same as for the pretest, although you may want to substitute new material.

● **ENSURING TRANSFER**

You should use the suggestions in VII-IG-5 and reading comprehension activities such as those included in the final chapter to make sure that the learner applies his or her understanding of context clues as signalers for intonation patterns during the routine language activities in the classroom.

## VIII•IG•4

### • THE PERFORMANCE OBJECTIVE

When given a multiparagraph selection, the learner will recall details from each paragraph in response to questions from the teacher.

### • THE PRETEST

Direct the learner to read a story like the following one and to answer the questions you ask about the story. The criterion for mastery is 75 percent. (Readability: Second grade.)

One night at dinner Tom said, "Guess what I ate for lunch today, Mother."

"Why, I don't need to guess," said Mrs. Brown. "I fixed your lunch myself. I put a piece of pie, three chicken sandwiches, and an apple in your sack lunch."

"That's true. That's what was in my lunch," said Tom.

"What happened?" asked his mother. "Why didn't you eat the things I fixed? And if you didn't eat them, what did you eat?"

"Well," said Tom. "A group of us were sitting around the table at lunchtime. Dan sat next to me. He only had a sandwich and two hard-boiled eggs in his lunch. I like hard-boiled eggs, so I traded a sandwich for an egg.

"Sally had three peanut butter sandwiches. So I traded one of my chicken sandwiches for one of her peanut butter sandwiches.

"Will sat across the table. He had a cookie with white icing on it. I traded my piece of pie for his cookie."

"You're funny," laughed Mrs. Brown. Then she asked, "What became of your apple and the other sandwich?"

"Well, I traded my last chicken sandwich to Jane for a jelly one," said Tom. "And I traded my apple to Sam for a nickel. I bought some ice cream with that."

"Didn't anybody eat his own lunch today?" asked Mrs. Brown.

"I don't think anybody did," said Tom. "But I guess we'll eat our own lunches tomorrow. I don't think our teacher liked what we did very well.

"She laughed, but she said that she was glad that we didn't take the buttons off our coats and trade them."

What did Tom trade first?
What did Tom get in exchange for his piece of pie?
What did Tom do with the nickel he got from Sam?
What did Tom end up eating for lunch?

### • DIRECTING THE LEARNER'S ATTENTION

The purpose of this task is to teach the learner to recall factual information. This is similar to storehouse module III-IG-6. To teach this skill you must direct the learner's attention by setting specific purposes that serve as cues to the learner regarding what to note and remember while reading.

### • TEACHING ACTIVITIES

This is an information-gathering task similar to storehouse module III-IG-6, and you can adapt your teaching strategy from either the modeling or the discovery technique described in that objective.

### • SUGGESTIONS FOR RETEACHING

If, after having been taught with either the modeling or the discovery technique, the learner does not understand how to recall factual information, you should adapt and use the suggestions in II-IG-6 to reteach the skill.

### • SUGGESTIONS FOR PRACTICE

Once the learner is able to recall factual information, create practice activities to solidify the skill, using the suggestions provided in III-IG-6.

### • THE POSTTEST

The procedure and criterion for mastery are the same as for the pretest, although you may want to substitute new material.

### • ENSURING TRANSFER

You should use the suggestions in III-IG-6 and reading comprehension activities such as those included in the final chapter and make sure that the learner uses his or her factual recall skill during the routine language activities in the classroom.

# VIII•MT•1

### • THE PERFORMANCE OBJECTIVE

When given a paragraph containing details that can be classified into three categories, the learner will classify the details and state one title for the paragraph that reflects all three categories of details.

### • THE PRETEST

Direct the learner to read a paragraph like the following one, to categorize the details into three groups, and to make up a title for the paragraph that would fit all three groups of details. The criterion for mastery is 100 percent. (Readability: Third grade.)

> Jack and Betty had a busy day. First, they went to the lake to fish. They caught two fish and they ran after frogs that they saw along the edge of the lake. Then they went to the mountain. They climbed all the way to the top. On the way they surprised a deer who was eating grass. After they came back down, they walked all the way to the store. There they bought a soft drink and some candy because they were tired and hungry. They also talked to the man in the store and told him about their adventures. Finally they went back home. It had been a good day.

### • DIRECTING THE LEARNER'S ATTENTION

The purpose of this task is to teach the learner to find relationships between content words, to classify those details according to the relationships, and to determine a title that fits the classification. This is similar to storehouse module I-MT-1. To teach this skill you must direct the learner's attention by highlighting the concepts associated with each content word, to the common denominator that allows them to be classified together, and to a title that fits the classification systems.

### • TEACHING ACTIVITIES

This is a manipulative task similar to storehouse module I-MT-1, and you can adapt your teaching strategy from either the modeling or the discovery technique described in that objective.

### • SUGGESTIONS FOR RETEACHING

If, after having been taught with either the modeling or the discovery technique, the learner is unable to title the classification systems, you should adapt and use the suggestions in I-MT-1 to reteach the skill.

### • SUGGESTIONS FOR PRACTICE

After teaching the learner the skill of classifying or titling classification systems, create practice activities to solidify the skill using the suggestions provided in I-MT-1.

### • THE POSTTEST

The procedure and criterion for mastery are the same as for the pretest, although you may want to substitute new material.

### • ENSURING TRANSFER

You should use the suggestions in I-MT-1 and reading comprehension activities such as those included in the final chapter to make sure that the learner applies the skill of titling classification systems during the routine language activities in the classroom.

## VIII•MT•2

### • THE PERFORMANCE OBJECTIVE

Given a multiparagraph selection in which details are implied, the learner will supply such details in response to questions asked by the teacher.

### • THE PRETEST

Direct the learner to read a story like the following one and to answer the questions that you ask at the end. The criterion for mastery is 80 percent. (Readability: Fourth grade.)

> Long ago many pioneers traveled over the mountains to the Ohio River. They went in all sorts of wagons, but most of them went in covered wagons.

The bed or floor of the wagons was built high in front and back. This was to keep things from spilling out as the wagon went up and down over the steep hills and mountains.

Strips of wood were bent into half-circles. They then were fastened to the sides of the wagon. Over the strips of wood was stretched a thick white cloth, which was the cover. This cover was held firmly by ropes. At each end of the wagon it was pulled in toward the center. This was to protect the things inside from rain and dirt. In good weather the cloth could be pushed back.

The back wheels were almost as tall as a man. The front wheels were smaller. Iron bands went around the wheels. The bands were from four to six inches wide.

The wagons were big. They were about 15 feet in length. The cloth covering was high enough for people to stand under.

People stacked their belongings on each side of the wagon. They left a narrow path for the middle.

On the back of the wagon was a feed box for the horses. A tool box was usually fastened to the outside. Pails and kettles were hung on the sides or underneath.

The teams of horses that pulled the wagons had to be strong. They had to be well trained too in order to do the hard work that they did.


The questions to ask are the following:

Why did the team of horses have to be strong?
Why did the wheels have iron bands around them?
Why was the feed box put outside the wagon?
Why did they leave a narrow path down the middle of the inside of the wagon?
Why did they hang the pails and kettles on the sides and underneath the wagon?


## • DIRECTING THE LEARNER'S ATTENTION

The purpose of this task is to teach the learner to infer details implied in a passage. This is similar to storehouse module I-MT-2. To teach this skill you must direct the learner's attention to what the facts say and what his or her experience has taught him about such concepts and ideas.


## • TEACHING ACTIVITIES

This is a manipulative task similar to the storehouse module in I-MT-2, and you can adapt your teaching strategy from either the modeling or the discovery technique described in that objective.

Do you have a pupil who ends up in the principal's office almost daily? Could you be giving him or her reading tasks that are too difficult?


## • SUGGESTIONS FOR RETEACHING

If, after having been taught with either the modeling or the discovery technique, the learner is not able to infer implied details, you should adapt and use the suggestions in I-MT-2 to reteach the skill.

## • SUGGESTIONS FOR PRACTICE

After teaching the learner how to supply inferred details, create practice activities to solidify the skill using the suggestions provided in I-MT-2.

## • THE POSTTEST

The procedure and criterion for mastery are the same as for the pretest, although you may want to substitute new material.

## • ENSURING TRANSFER

You should use the suggestions in I-MT-2 and reading comprehension activities such as those included in the final chapter to make sure that the learner applies inferring details during the routine language activities in the classroom.

## VIII•ET•1

### • THE PERFORMANCE OBJECTIVE

When given two reports about the same event, the learner will identify which is factual and which is opinionated and will identify the words that signal opinion.

### • THE PRETEST

Direct the learner to read reports like the following and to identify which one is opinionated and which one is factual. The criterion for mastery is 100 percent. (Readability: Fifth grade.)

> In a recent speech to a private group, Mr. Smith analyzed the government's position in the war. This was done with precision and force. His statement is the most complete argument that has been made for continuing the war. He went to the very heart of our nation's interests. This was the basis for his position. He wisely ignored the carping of those who lack his vision.

> On November 14, Mr. Smith spoke to a group of citizens. They had gathered at the town hall. His topic was entitled "Our Government and the War." He stated that he agreed with the government's decision to continue the war. He listed his reasons for believing as he does. He gave the nation's best interests as one of his major reasons. He made no comment in his speech about the arguments put forth by people who disagree with the government's position on the war.

### • DIRECTING THE LEARNER'S ATTENTION

The purpose of this task is to teach the learner to judge whether material is fact or opinion. This is similar to storehouse module IV-ET-1. To teach this skill you must direct the learner's attention to whether the choice of words signals opinion or fact.

## • TEACHING ACTIVITIES

This is an evaluative thinking task similar to storehouse module IV-ET-1, and you can adapt your teaching strategy from either the modeling or the discovery technique described in that objective.

## • SUGGESTIONS FOR RETEACHING

If, after having been taught with either the modeling or the discovery technique, the learner does not understand how reports are opinions or facts, you should adapt and use the suggestions in IV-ET-1 to reteach the skill.

## • SUGGESTIONS FOR PRACTICE

After teaching the learner the skill of judging the content of the material, create practice activities to solidify the skill, using the suggestions provided in IV-ET-1.

## • THE POSTTEST

The procedure and criterion for mastery are the same as for the pretest, although you may want to substitute new material.

## • ENSURING TRANSFER

You should use the suggestions in IV-ET-1 and reading comprehension activities such as those included in the final chapter to make sure that the learner applies the skill of judging content of material as fact or opinion during the routine language activities in the classroom.

# AN ILLUSTRATIVE LESSON . . .

# ...ON APPLY-ING COMPRE-HENSION SKILLS IN CONTENT MATERIAL

Teaching a child to read includes more than teaching only the bits and pieces of reading skills. In a real sense it is the *application* of skills that produces readers, and this is especially true of comprehension. While comprehension skills can be defined and activities devised to teach a child these skills, they remain *situation-specific*; that is, although a child may be able to discover an inference in one reading selection, this does not mean that the skill will be available or used in all selections that he or she reads. Reading skills show a child how to learn how to read, but reading makes a reader.

The most obvious and logical way a teacher can help a child to use comprehension skill is through daily *content-area* reading. Problems in word meaning, main idea, inference, relationship, and so on, are found in the science book, the civics book, the arithmetic book, as well as in the basal reader. The teacher who ignores these instructional opportunities because "the skills program has already taken care of that," has missed the mark.

Teaching your children to think about and understand the variety of messages necessary for success in your classroom requires that you be both imaginative and flexible. You must accurately assess what your learners need to do or know in order to understand their schoolbooks and the kinds of comprehension operations that can best be taught from them.

In the first instance you are saying that you want your children to know and understand the content of your curriculum. If a reading assignment is made from a history book, then you expect them to know about history. In the second instance, however, you will be saying that you also want your children to learn to think! Now the history book becomes a vehicle with which you apply comprehension skills. A child can simultaneously learn a lesson about the American Revolution *and* develop skills in main idea or inferential thinking. These two considerations should guide you in planning all content lessons.

To illustrate the possibilities for applying comprehension skills to content-area reading assignments, we have chosen a short three-paragraph selection about whales, typical of most fourth or fifth grade science books. This selection is followed by a detailed analysis of the comprehension problems and instructional activities appropriate to learning about whales (the science content) and to learning how to comprehend (the applied comprehension skills). If this lesson is well taught, both goals can be achieved.

This analysis should not be viewed as a typical teaching model. It is much too long and detailed. Rather, it is offered in the hope that you will see how many opportunities there are in even a short reading lesson for helping children apply the informational, manipulative, and evaluative skills of comprehension. It should stimulate you to examine the content lessons you teach, so that you can discover ways to guide your students into active, appropriate comprehension activities. Use your content books to teach content, but use them also to teach applied comprehension skills.

The largest of all land or water animals is the whale. The great blue whale is sometimes over 100 feet long and weighs as much as 125 tons. Our largest elephants do not often weigh more than six tons, so the largest whale weighs more than 20 times as much as the largest elephant. Not all whales are as large as the great blue whale, however. The smallest whale, or dolphin, is seldom over four feet long

The whale can grow to such great size because it lives in water. The water supports its great weight and provides plenty of food for it. As the whale swims through the water, it sweeps bushels of food into its mouth at one time.

Although the whale is shaped like a fish, it is really a mammal. Its young feeds on the mother's milk. It has lungs instead of gills. It breathes air. The whale usually comes to the top of the water every five or ten minutes, but it can stay under water for 45 minutes. When it comes to the top of the water, the whale blows stale air from its lungs and takes in a supply of fresh air. Often when fishermen see the cloud of water vapor and air which the whale breathes out, they say, "There she blows."[1]

## COMPREHENSION QUESTIONS THAT COULD BE ASKED . . .

### • INFORMATION GATHERING–CONTENT WORD MEANING

1. How long is **100 feet**? Show me or tell me about something else that is 100 feet long.

[1]*Atomic Submarine Book*, McCormik-Mather Publishing Co., Wichita, Kansas, 1965, p. 72.

2. How much is **125** tons? What do you know about that weighs one ton? 125 tons?
3. How long is **four feet**? Point to something in this room that is four feet long.
4. What does **20 times** mean in sentence 3?
5. What does the word **supports** mean in paragraph 2? In sentence 2? Name two things that water provides to **support** the whale.
6. Give a synonym for the word **provides** in this same sentence.
7. **Sweeps bushels** has a strange meaning in this sentence. Explain it.
8. What is a **mammal**? Name three other mammals.
9. Give a synonym for **stale** in paragraph 3, sentence 5.
10. What are **gills**? What are **lungs**? Where are they found and what are their functions?
11. What is **water vapor**? What would it look like? Where might you see it besides whales?

### • INFORMATION GATHERING–SIGNALERS OF RELATIONSHIP

1. Reread the first sentence in the second paragraph. This sentence has two important pieces of information. What are they? How are they related? What is the key word that connects these two ideas?
2. Reread the first sentence in the third paragraph. This sentence contains two important pieces of information. What are they? How are they related? What is the key word that signals this contrastive relationship?

### • INFORMATION GATHERING–FACTUAL RECALL

1. What is the largest of all animals?
2. How long is it?
3. How much does it weigh?
4. Where does it live?
5. What is the smallest whale?
6. Is the whale a fish or a mammal?
7. What two things make a fish different from a mammal?
8. How long can the whale stay under water?
9. Do whales have gills?

### • MANIPULATIVE THINKING–CLASSIFICATION AND MAIN IDEA

1. What is the main idea in the first paragraph? The second? The third?
2. What would you name this selection: *Living in the Ocean, The Largest of All Animals,* or *Blue Whales and Dolphins*?

### • MANIPULATIVE THINKING–INFERENCES

1. A whale and an elephant are related to each other. Both are mammals. One lives on land, the other in water. Could a whale live on land? Why not?
2. Water supports a whale two ways: it provides plenty of food and supports its body. What does this mean? Explain.

1. Do you think the information contained in this story is true? Why?
2. What does the writer want us to have when we finish reading this material?
3. In paragraph 2, sentence 3, it is stated that the whale "sweeps bushels of food into its mouth." Does the whale have a broom and bushel basket? What did the author mean for us to think when he chose those words?

## DIRECTING THE LEARNER'S ATTENTION AND MODEL TEACHING ACTIVITY . . .

### • INFORMATION GATHERING—CONTENT WORD MEANINGS

For any depth of understanding of this selection the learner must have a sharp and specific meaning vocabulary. Key concepts are tested in the pretest and if any of these are unknown or if the meanings known are inappropriate to this selection, they must immediately be taught. In helping a learner develop these specific word meanings, you must do two things. First, you must structure an experience in which the concept is carefully examined and its conditions and parameters noted. As previously described in storehouse module I-IG-1, this can be done at four levels, each a little less powerful than the one that precedes it. First choice is a firsthand, hands-on experience with the actual concept that is being labeled. When this is impossible, vicarious or secondhand experience is tried. This might include pictures, diagrams, and so on, that capture the essence of the concept being learned. If this, too, is unrealistic, then the context of the material in which the word is found can be scrutinized for clues as to its approximate meaning. Finally, if these three fail or are not feasible, the dictionary can be used to explain the concept. This is, however, a case of words explaining words, and should be resorted to *only* if the preceding three techniques will not do the job.

Although the concept remains the same, attenders for learning the concept will differ according to the instructional technique being utilized. Take, for example, the concept *100 feet*. If firsthand experience is feasible, a typical exercise might be to have a student measure a hallway or playground with a 100-foot tape. This distance might then be visually examined by placing objects at either end. It might even be suggested that the learner imagine a whale between the markers. Obviously, such activity gives reality to the concept of a 100-foot linear distance. Attenders to such an activity would be the tape length, paces, and markers. These are the performances that serve to define "100 footness."

In similar fashion a learner might be given a diagram of a football field or some other familiar area that can be chopped into 100-foot segments. Now the *picture* is the experience and the various lines that compare it to 100 feet are the attenders. Context might permit accurate conceptualization of some words being examined but in the case of 100 feet, context is of no value and would not be used. Similarly, a dictionary would be of little help in developing this concept. Whatever words might be used to explain 100 feet would not be sufficient to create an accurate concept of this distance, for they would contain no attenders of sufficient quality to produce this concept.

Second, after the concept is examined, it is labeled: "This is 100 feet." Once the concept is clear, the label is easily attached.

Each of the concepts measured in the pretest has its own attenders that relate directly to the level of experience appropriate to or possible with the word or your classroom. Examine each word and try to determine the most useful level of experience: firsthand, vicarious, contextual, or dictionary. Then analyze the components of that experience that give the concept its dimensions. *These will be the attenders.* Determine the steps you will have the learner perform that put him in contact with these attenders. As he performs the necessary activities—physical or verbal—that highlight the concept, pair the word name or label with the defined attenders and the word has developed meaning. The following hints should help you with this task.

*One hundred twenty-five tons.* Like 100 feet, this is a measurement that needs some kind of physical reality if it is to be understood. You might arrive at an approximation of this concept by directing your learners to the fact that an average compact car weighs 3000 pounds. One hundred and twenty-five tons is 250,000 pounds. This would be how many cars? Such a comparison could be extended to the gross weight of all the children in the room. How many fourth graders would it take to equal the weight of one blue whale?

*Four feet.* The contrast between largest and smallest is needed for an understanding of this selection. Again, as in the concept 100 feet, measurement or comparison with a learner with a known height of four feet will create an understanding of this concept.

*Twenty times.* This is a computational concept and can best be understood by examining the ratio 6 to 120—elephant weight to whale weight.

*Supports.* This is a crucial concept for understanding the second paragraph. It can be dealt with in two ways. The sentence context should give adequate clues for a surface understanding. Simply direct learners to find synonyms for this term. In a very general way this will define the term. At a more complex level this concept relates to the effect of buoyancy on a floating or submerged object. To examine this concept from this position requires extended inferences and is described in detail under that category later in this section.

*Provides.* This verb can also be conceptualized through a search of the sentence context and development of synonyms. Should this not prove sufficient, a series of other sentences, such as "wind provides the energy necessary to move a sailboat," will highlight this concept.

*Sweeps bushels.* A discussion of the figurative use of the word **sweeps** would be both interesting and informative. However, although this appears to be solely a word meaning or concept problem, its instruction and attenders are more pertinent to the evaluative thinking area of comprehension skills. It is therefore described later in this section under that heading.

*Mammal.* A conceptual grasp of this term can be beautifully illustrated by teaching a classification activity. First direct the learners to read the first sentence in the third paragraph to discover what *things* are being compared. (The answer is **fish** and **mammal**.) Next make a chart on the blackboard. Direct the learners to search in the paragraph for qualities that belong in each column. *Note:* Some qualities are *implied* as opposites to those stated. This will become clear as your learners fill in the chart.

| **Fishness** | **Mammalness** |
|---|---|
| shape of fish | shape of fish |
| don't feed on mother's milk | feed on mother's milk |
| gills to breathe | lungs to breathe |
| breathes through water | breathes air directly |

The concept of *mammal* can then be stated as a generalization based on this classification. If you wish, it can be extended by adding other mammal qualities to the list.

*Stale.* Direct the learner to inhale and hold his breath. Count to 25. Tell him to exhale. Question to determine what happens to air that could change it from "fresh" to "stale." In both the whale and humans the body "burns" parts of the air to maintain life. Oxygen is converted to carbon dioxide and neither whales nor humans can live on this gas. A science experiment with a bell jar and candle would graphically illustrate this event. Each of these experiences, the holding of the breath and the candle, would be attenders for cueing the concept of *stale*.

*Gills and lungs.* A drawing or model of a fish and a mammal would serve to illustrate the two physical components gills and lungs. Their functions could be examined as part of the organism's need for oxygen and related to the definition of *stale* that has just been made. Comparative functions could be shown through either the drawing or model and the environmental conditions that determine the adaptation of gills or lungs could be discussed.

*Water vapor.* To develop this concept you could ask your learner to explain what happens when he breathes out on a cold winter's morning? Next ask for explanations of this phenomenon. Ultimately the understanding will be reached that moisture in the warmed air in the lungs is condensed when it strikes the colder outside air and becomes visible in the form of water vapor. This same event is triggered when the whale breathes in warm air and then dives deep into the cold ocean waters. The chilled air vaporizes and can then be seen when the whale returns to the surface of the ocean and breathes this condensation out.

The words chosen for this model lesson are probably the most critical for understanding the contents of this selection. However, you may discover other words that require equal attention from your learners. Whatever the case, you must be cognizant of both the comprehension demands of the selection and the verbal resources of your learners. The preceding examples should serve as sufficient models for developing other word meaning and concept exercises in this or similar material.

## • INFORMATION GATHERING–SIGNALERS OF RELATIONSHIPS

The first pretest question in this category is designed to measure the degree of understanding a child has regarding various meaning relationships, in this case, cause and effect. The sentence is indicating a cause-effect relationship between the whale's size and its water environment. These are the two information keys. They are linked by the word **because** which serves as the key attender to this relationship.

A model instructional activity to help a child grasp this relationship is to select the first—in this case, the effect condition—and cue it in its entirety. This could be done easily with simple underlining of the words "The whale can grow to such great size." Explain that this is one half of the important information in this sentence, and the other half is needed to make its meaning clear. Ask whether the learner can find the word or words that constitute the other half of this sentence. If this remains unclear and the child cannot see the other or causal half of this relationship, simply add the linking conjunction **because** to the first statement. Now ask for the second half of this relationship. The closure is obvious. Ask the learner to underline this second half of the relationship. Label the parts as information 1 and information 2; whales grow big and live in water. With these facts established, ask the child to examine carefully the **because.** Circle it to show its importance. Ask the question, "*Why* does the whale grow so big?" The answer will begin with the conjunction and set the relationship of water to size very clearly. See if the learner can then identify the word that signals the *why*. If he is still puzzled, replace **because** with **and.** Read the new transformation out loud. Ask whether the sentence still says the same thing as it does with **because.** Finally, introduce the terms *cause* and *effect*. Explain that when you look carefully at the two ideas in the sentence, you can see that one is a cause of the other. Say "Does the whale's size (idea 1) cause the other or does the water (idea 2) cause the whale's size?" Direct the learner to label each idea as cause or effect. To cement this relationship again, call attention to the key term **because.** Ask the child to create other sentences containing this word, to isolate the ideas in the sentences, and to decide which is a cause and which an effect.

In summary, key attenders to this relationship task are the ideas being related and the linking conjunction **because.** With these clearly highlighted, the causal relationship can be easily established.

Pretest question 2 in this category also measures a learner's skill in understanding a grammatical or meaning relationship and its component signals. In this case the child must identify and respond correctly to a *contrastive* signal. Instruction for this skill is essentially the same as that found in the preceding cause-effect situation, the only difference being the cue word **although,** which signals a contrastive structure. Attenders are the two ideas being contrasted and the signal word. Highlighting is again best accomplished by underlining, labeling, or circling these key components.

### • INFORMATION GATHERING–FACTUAL RECALL

At a literal level comprehension of this selection demands only three basic skills. First, does your reader have accurate concepts of the meaning of key words, second, does he understand the relationships signaled, and third, can he or she recognize and remember the factual information contained in the material. With just these skills the learner can acquire the basic information in the selection. This information serves two important functions. First, it is valuable in its own right. The child who can accumulate and assimilate concepts and facts *knows something* when he finishes his reading. What he knows is about whales and, although this may reflect only short-term memory, being able to acquire this sort of knowledge puts at his fingertips all kinds of factual information. This knowledge-gathering function is a primary component of reading comprehension. Second, and of more importance, is the *use* such factual information can be put to. Once a child knows something, he can think with and about it. Basic facts about whales become the vehicle for moving the child through all kinds of higher-level manipulation or thinking activities. The skill of factual comprehension supplies the material for thought.

Attenders for helping children recognize the factual content of this selection are the words that represent these facts. A key device for ensuring attention to these words is purpose setting, that is, giving the learner specific cues regarding what to look for before reading. Reading for factual detail is a memory task: The learner is rewarded not for thinking, but for remembering. The child will recognize and remember the things he or she knows you are looking for. Hence purpose-setting cues are essential.

Purpose-setting can be accomplished in many ways. For example, before reading the whale selection, you might put the following purpose-setting formula on the board:

Who?   What?   Where?   How many?   What happens?

Direct the learner to use this formula as a guide in his or her reading. Such a guide will invariably highlight the details of a selection. This activity could then be followed by assigning a color to each of the six formula keys, with words in the selection that match that key underlined with the appropriate color. This will unmistakably highlight the factual details.

Purpose can often be readily established by simply asking the reader to see how many things he can learn during his reading lesson. He then records his learning by making a tally mark on a piece of paper, each mark standing for something he learned during the reading. Such marks will usually represent the factual details of the selection.

In many classrooms reading to know the facts of a selection comprises the total comprehension process. When the child can memorize and then report back to the teacher all the facts of a passage, she or he is rewarded for being a good reader. Studies done on teachers' questioning tactics indicate this to be the overwhelming focus of reading comprehension instruction. Basically the fault with this instruction is not that it is done but that the information a child gathers through the identification of facts and details is not then put to further use as the basic building blocks for other, more cognitive, comprehension activities. Teach the child to see the trees in the forest, but follow this with activities that also show him the forest.

## • CLASSIFICATION AND MAIN IDEA

When you have established that the learner has accurate concepts for the specific vocabulary of this selection and a clear understanding of both the relationships signaled and the basic facts it contains about whales, you can then proceed to help her or him manipulate this information through higher-level and more difficult thinking skills.

The two pretest items on classification—main idea measured the child's ability to grasp the focus of each paragraph and the total selection. If the learner is not able to make these manipulations, the following teaching activity should be initiated.

Prepare either an overhead transparency or a copy of each paragraph. Direct the learner to watch as you underline the words **largest, animals,** and **whale** in the first sentence. Ask the child to read the second sentence and underline any word that he or she thinks belongs with the words you underlined in the first sentence. These should be **whale, 100 feet long, 125 tons.** If this pattern is not seen, underline these words and explain why they belong with the words in the first sentence. Continue to the third sentence, again asking for words that belong to the underlined words in the first sentence. Finish the paragraph in this manner, directing the learner to discover words that can be categorized with the three keys in the first sentence.

What you have done is cue the learner to the *key* details of the paragraph. Now you must help him generalize the focus or main idea of this information. You can do this by asking the question, "What are all these words talking about?" This should lead to the idea of whales and their size. If your learner is unable to classify the details in this fashion, you might follow the first question with a choice of three answers: "elephants and whales," "the size of whales," or "how whales grow so large." Now the learner does not generalize the paragraph focus, but simply recognizes it when you do. This is an easier task.

Finally, direct the child to reread the paragraph to find the sentence that best says this information. In each paragraph the first sentence is its topic sentence.

Continue to the second paragraph and cue the words **can grow** and **because.** Direct the learner to underline any other words or groups of words that belong to your key words. Continue to the topic sentence as described in the first paragraph.

Finally, direct the learner to read the third paragraph completely through and to find a word or two that seem to focus this content. Continue the exercise to the topic sentence identification.

Attenders for this main idea instruction are the individualized words that signal the overall focus of the paragraph. These words generate the mental act of grouping for common characteristics. From these signal-word cues the child develops the classifications necessary for understanding the focus or main idea of each paragraph.

Pretest question 2 asks for the same kind of manipulative activity as just described except that cues or highlights to this learning are the topic sentences of each paragraph rather than the key words within each paragraph. It therefore logically *follows* the recognition of each paragraph topic sentence. Instruction is done by underlining the topic sentence in each paragraph if this has not already been done. These sentences are the attenders to the overall point of the selection. After directing the learner to reread each of these underlined sentences, ask him to create a title that would best include them all. This can be a difficult task. Do not be surprised if your learner has difficulty with it. If much trouble is apparent (either no response or some unacceptable title), return to a recognition activity in which you provide three titles, one of which is obviously better than the other two. For example, you might say, "Look at three titles that I can put on the board. Which one best includes the topic sentences of each paragraph: *Hunting the Great Blue Whale; Whales, What They Eat; The Largest of All Mammals?*" Now the learner's job is to recognize the main idea as you have presented it. This is an easier task and one that will often be relied on in initial instruction to discover main ideas, whether in the paragraph or the selection.

### • DEVELOPING INFERENCES

Developing an inference requires the learner to think beyond the literal meaning found in a selection, asking: "What do the facts suggest? What implications do they contain?" You can best help learners make this leap from literal to inferential thinking by developing sophisticated questioning techniques. Such questions must require thought, not just memory. Their answers are subject to verification only through inductive reasoning and logic. When a learner has answered an inferential question and is asked to explain how he or she knew the answer, the usual response is "Well, it says *this* and it says *this*, and therefore, *that* has to be." (Given this fact and this fact, that result must follow.) The result is *not stated* on the page. It comes only after the learner has examined the facts, has been prodded by an inferential question, and has thought out an answer to the question that is logical in terms of the *facts* and *past experience*. This skill requires recognition of and memory for the facts of a selection, appropriate questioning skill, and past experience. In a general sense these three are the attenders to this task.

This selection is an excellent one for helping a learner develop the ability to infer. A fine way to initiate this activity would be to apply a variation of the SQ3R techniques in which the first two stages, S and Q (Survey and Question), are used to create a number of inferential "guesses." This is done as follows: Before reading the selection, put the title, *The Largest of All Animals,* on the chalkboard. Ask the learner to read it, saying, "This is the title of the reading lesson for today. I wonder if you can do something that is very hard. I wonder if you can guess what you are going to learn in this lesson just by reading and *thinking about* these five words. For example, can you make a question that you think will be answered as you read the rest of the lesson?" An obvious question is "What is the largest animal? You list any questions that will be answered through reading as an act of *inference*. The title is the basic factual content, and the questions and the inferences are generated by thinking about it. The value of these inferences can be discussed after the selection has been read and the questions reviewed. In this activity the attender is the title of the selection. With this and thought, inferences can be created.

Another fine opportunity for developing inferences is found in the second paragraph. This paragraph examines the relationships between a whale's size and the place where it lives. For example, the question "Could a whale live on land?" should lead to thinking far beyond the basic information found in the paragraph. The questioning dialogue might go something like the following:

*Class:* No, a whale can't live on land.
*Teacher:* Why not? They are mammals; they breathe air just as we do.
*Class:* They need water to keep their skins wet.
*Teacher:* All right. I'll wet the whale with a fire hose pumping water from the ocean. Now can he live on land?
*Class:* No, how would he eat? He'd starve to death.
*Teacher:* Then I will trap tons of food and pump it into his mouth and down his stomach. Now can he live on land?
*Class:* No, whales just can't live on land.
*Teacher:* Why not? Is there something special about water?

Although this looks like a stalemate, if you push hard enough and refer the class back to the word **supports** in the second sentence of the second paragraph, some learner will grasp the implications of this word and the dialogue will then continue:

*Class:* A whale can't live on land because water will support it, but land won't.

*Teacher:* What do you mean by support it?

*Class:* Well, a whale is so heavy that it just collapses on land; a whale in the water doesn't collapse.

*Teacher:* Why not?

*Class:* Water supports the whale.

Once again, this lesson needs additional facts before its inferential activities can be continued. If you are prepared, you can explore the concept of buoyancy. That is the key concept for continuing this line of questions. You can continue with a series of questions such as the following

*Teacher:* How many of you can swim? How many of you can float? What happens when you float? What does the water do?

Or you could have a pail of water, a spring scale, a brick, and some cord on hand to provide some additional facts with a simple demonstration of the effect of buoyancy on the weight of the brick. After illustrating the concept, you would continue in the following manner:

*Teacher:* What happens when I lower the brick into the water?

*Class:* It loses weight.

*Teacher:* Why?

*Class:* The water holds it up.

*Teacher:* Then why can't a whale live on land?

*Class:* Land won't support its great weight.

*Teacher:* What would happen?

*Class:* It probably wouldn't be able to breathe. All its fat would just squeeze it flat and it wouldn't get any air in its lungs. It would die.

*Teacher:* Why can it live in water?

*Class:* The whale has lots of food available that it can catch in the water. The water also supports its great weight, so that it can breathe. It doesn't weigh so much in the water (*buoyancy*).

Although you could choose to teach inferential skills from this selection in a slightly different manner, you can see that any instruction will demand imagination, flexibility, and superb questioning tactics. The success of your instruction will largely depend on the questions you ask and the facts these questions are drawn from. These, together with the learner's background, are your basic attenders to this task. When they are used properly, you will find that your learners develop high-level inferential skills.

### • EVALUATIVE THINKING

The final stage of comprehension of this selection involves the application of the skills of *evaluation*. As described in Chapter 2, these skills help the reader come to conclusions about what he reads by speculating on its usefulness, the author's motivations, and the author's point of view. Ultimately, developing such skills will produce a reader who can intuitively classify materials into such categories as fact-fiction or objective-informational-propaganda and who can critically examine what he or she reads for its argument, logic, or basis in fact, as opposed to merely reading for entertainment or recreation. Such a reader is able to judge the *validity* and *reliability* of what he or she reads. Without such critical skills, the reader is at the mercy of the writer.

To develop this critical skill is a long and often painful process. Many times there will be little opportunity to learn, practice, or apply this skill using normal classroom materials. Yet when the opportunity and materials are ripe for this comprehension activity, you will often find yourself walking a thin line between teaching children to be critical readers or doubting Thomases. The goal of this instruction is not to produce children who immediately disbelieve everything they read but, rather, to produce children who recognize that writers write for many reasons, some good and some bad—some to entertain, some to instruct, and some to control. Being able to differentiate one from another gives the reader both freedom and power.

The three questions found in the evaluative-judgment pretest will obviously not do all these things. Since this material is primarily informational, and the information is scientific and probably verifiable, there is little need to prove the motivations and biases of the author. With regard to question number 1, if a child feels the information is false or an outright lie, the fault is probably in the almost unreal sizes associated with the blue whale. An unsophisticated child's natural reaction would be "that can't be true; no whale could be that big." If this is a child's reasoning, the teaching tactics involve, first, the identification of those facts or inferences that are perceived as unreal and second, a series of questions such as:

*Teacher:* You feel that this story isn't true because whales can't be as large as this man says they are. Is there any way that we could prove that he is correct or incorrect in his information?

*Reader:* We could catch a whale and weigh and measure it.

*Teacher:* Correct. Then we would decide whether the author's information is accurate or exaggerated. But don't you think that other people have done this? Haven't other people weighed and measured a whale?

*Reader:* Yes, I suppose so.

*Teacher:* Well, then, why would this man exaggerate or lie when he knows that other people have information about whales?

*Reader:* I guess he'd be pretty dumb not to tell the truth.

*Teacher:* Is it possible to *verify*, that is, prove the size of whales, what they eat, where they live, how long they stay under water, that they are mammals, and so on?

*Reader:* I guess so.

*Teacher:* How could we check to see if this author's information is the same as other's observations?

*Reader:* We could look for information about whales in other books.

*Teacher:* Which books?

*Reader:* Encyclopedia? Science books?

*Teacher:* Now do you feel the information in this article is true or false?

*Reader:* It's probably true.

*Teacher:* Why do you think this?

*Reader:* Because information about whales can be verified. We can check what he says against real whales or other people's observations. Therefore, there is really no reason for this writer to tell us information that is not true. It would be too easy to prove that he is incorrect.

Question 2 has a parallel orientation toward judging the author's purpose and motivation in writing this selection. Here the focus is on identifying the type of communication and an inference as to why people write for this purpose. If a child is confused by these ideas and cannot give a reasonable explanation of the purpose of this material, your best instructional tactic is to direct him to this realization through questions:

*Teacher:* What did you learn about in today's reading lesson?

*Reader:* Whales.

*Teacher:* What did you learn about whales? (Notice that this selection is primarily factual in nature and intent, and this understanding will quickly lead to the author's purpose in writing it.)

Tell me as many things about whales as you can find in the lesson. (Here you would start a list of facts as they are discovered by your readers. When the list is agreeably long and impressive, direct the readers back to the original question.)

Now that we have all these things about whales that you have found in this lesson, can you figure out what the author wanted us to have when we read his story? Let's count and see how many things we have. One, two, and so on. (Here you could easily number the discovered information. It will be a rare instance when a reader will not see that this article is informative and its writer wanted to tell the reader all about whales. In that rare instance when the point is not made you can revert to a *recognition* rather than *discovery* task. Put these statements on the board.)

1. To know what men say when they spot whales.
2. To know a lot of information about whales.
3. To catch a whale and study it.

Now with these three intents or goals and the original list of information, pair the information with each goal in turn. Ask to see which goal best fits the list. This is as nearly foolproof as this instruction can get.

Attenders to this task will be the clarity of the questions you create and the listing of information found in the selection. These two factors lead the reader to understand the purpose of this material.

Finally, if a child is puzzled by the "sweeps bushels of food into its mouth" figure of speech, you must help the child to realize why writers use such literary devices. This too can be done through questioning.

*Teacher:* The writer has used this phrase to describe how a whale eats. He doesn't really have a broom or bushel basket, so why do you suppose the author chose these words to tell us about a whale's eating habits? What do you see or feel when he uses these words? Let's take the word **sweeps** first. What does this remind you of?

*Reader:* Well, when you sweep the floor, you move the broom. Maybe the author wanted us to get the idea that the whale doesn't just hang around waiting for his meal, but instead has to chase through the water gulping up his food on the run.

*Teacher:* That's a good answer. That's what **sweeps** says to me too. Now, how about **bushels.** What is a bushel?

*Reader:* It's a basket.

*Teacher:* Is every basket a bushel basket?

*Reader:* No.

*Teacher:* What makes a basket a bushel basket?

*Reader:* It's a special size.

*Teacher:* Would you call it a big or little size?

*Reader:* Big basket.

*Teacher:* Could you eat a bushel basket full of food?

*Reader:* No.

*Teacher:* Then what does this tell us about whales?

*Reader:* That they have big mouths and can eat a lot at one time.

*Teacher:* Correct. Now put the two words together and what do you see? Sweeps a bushel.

*Reader:* I see a whale splashing through the water after his food and swallowing great gulps of it.

*Teacher:* Correct. That is what the writer wanted us to see and that is why he chose those words to help us.

As you can see, questioning tactics are extremely important in helping children develop evaluative or critical reading skills. Attenders in this task will be the questions, so learn to ask good ones, and the facts, details, inferences, key words, and so on, that are used by the writer in exposing the reader to the material.

## • SUMMARY

While reading skills are essential, they are useless if taught in isolation and left there. Instead, skills must be applied; they must be used. Children will not always learn to apply skills by themselves; frequently, you must help them. The above is one sample of how application might be achieved. While the specific possibilities are as endless as the materials you will be using, you should be able to use the example as a model for teaching children to apply skills in the future.

# APPENDIXES

# SOURCES OF
# PRACTICE
# MATERIALS

The following is a list of programs, workbooks, games, references, and other commercial material that you can use to supplement the practice activities provided in this book. The list is selective, rather than exhaustive, including only those materials considered to be most useful in a reading skills program.

Two cautions regarding the use of this material are in order. First, do not use practice material as teaching material. Claims of the publishers notwithstanding, the materials included in this list do not *teach* the reading skills; they provide only the practice and repetition needed to make habitual a response taught previously. Directing the learner to use any practice material without first developing an understanding of what he or she is learning will result in partial learning at best and in total confusion at worst.

Second, do not give one or more of the following materials to a learner and direct him or her to complete the whole book. Such a strategy is both inefficient and dangerous. A learner seldom needs practice on all exercises in a particular book, and it is inefficient to demand that he or she do them all. Also, the skills practiced in many of these books are haphazardly or incorrectly arranged, so it is dangerous to demand that he or she do them in order. A far better practice is to clip the pages from workbooks and other materials, filing them according to the skills taught in this book. Then, when a learner needs practice on a particular skill, go to the file folder containing the workbook exercises for that skill and select one for use. By covering the page with acetate and directing the learner to write answers directly on the acetate with a grease pencil, you will be able to reuse the workbook page many times.

| PRACTICE MATERIALS | SOURCES |
|---|---|
| *Adventures in Discovery*<br>An early childhood education program using structured activities and books to develop concepts of time, size, and so on. | Western Publishing Company, Inc.<br>850 Third Avenue<br>New York, New York 10022 |
| Armstrong, Ruth, and William Merkelson. *Cards for Reading Response*<br>A self-directed individualized reading kit containing independent activities. | Creative Teaching Press, Inc.<br>Monterey Park, California 91754 |
| *Breaking the Sound Barrier*<br>An effective workbook approach to basic instruction in phonetics. | Macmillan Publishing Co., Inc.<br>866 Third Avenue<br>New York, New York 10022 |
| Burmeister, Leo. *Words—from Print to Meaning*<br>Has classroom activities for development of the word identification skills, sight words, context clues, morphology, and phonics. | Addison-Wesley Publishing Co., Inc.<br>Reading, Massachusetts |
| *Chandler Language-Experience Readers*<br>Individual pupil workbooks and paperback experience readers. | Chandler Publishing Company<br>124 Spear Street<br>San Francisco, California 94105 |
| Ekwall, Eldon. *Locating and Correcting Reading Difficulties*<br>Help in developmental, corrective, and remedial situations; gives concrete procedures. | Charles E. Merrill Publishing Co.<br>1300 Alum Creed Drive<br>Columbus, Ohio 43216 |
| Engelmann, Siegfried. *Preventing Learning Failure in the Primary Grades,* 1969<br>Contains valuable exercises for language and concept development and for sound-symbol drills. | Science Research Associates<br>259 East Erie Street<br>Chicago, Illinois 60611 |
| Farquhar, Carolyn, Bettye Jennings, and Elaine Weber. *Personalized Approach to Reading*<br>Provides a multitude of instructional strategies for specific reading skills. | Pendell Publishing Company<br>Midland, Michigan |

Forte, Imogene, Marjorie Frank, and Joy MacKenzie. *Kid's Stuff—Reading and Language Experiences—Intermediate—Junior High*
Provides many directed activities, plus ideas for individualized learning and learning centers.

Incentive Publications, Inc.
P.O. Box 12522
Nashville, Tennessee 37212

Forte, Imogene, Marjorie Frank, and Joy MacKenzie. *Kid's Stuff—Reading and Language Experiences—Primary Level*
Provides many detailed learning activities plus student activity pages for specific skills.

Incentive Publications, Inc.
P.O. Box 12522
Nashville, Tennessee 37212

*Frostig Program for the Development of Visual Perception*
A kit of exercises in five areas of perceptual development.

Follett Publishing Company
201 North Wells Street
Chicago, Illinois 60606

Hall, Nancy. *Rescue*
A collection of teaching suggestions and approaches. Geared for remedial reading.

Educational Services
P.O. Box 219
Stevensville, Michigan 49127

Herr, Selma. *Learning Actiivties for Reading*, Second Edition, 1970
Provides a multitude of directed activities in teaching selected reading skills.

William C. Brown Company, Publishers
135 South Locust Street
Dubuque, Iowa 52001

*Junior Listen and Hear Books*
Helps develop skills of auditory discrimination.

Follett Publishing Company
201 North Wells Street
Chicago, Illinois 60606

Kaplan, Sandra, JoAnn Kaplan, Sheila Madsen, and Bette Taylor. *Change for Children*
Excellent book for ideas and activities for individualized learning. Contains a step-by-step process for change.

Goodyear Publishing Co., Inc.
Pacific Palisades, California

*Macmillan Reading Spectrum— Spectrum of Skills*
Programmed books on various levels teaching selected reading skills.

Macmillan Publishing Co., Inc.
866 Third Avenue
New York, New York 10022

*The Magic World of Dr. Spello*
A workbook providing a useful review
of selected analysis skills.

Webster Division
McGraw-Hill Book Company
Manchester Road
Manchester, Missouri 63011

*Michigan Language Program*
Seventeen programmed workbooks for
the severely disabled reader.

Ann Arbor—Humphrey Science
Publishers, Inc.
Drawer 1425
Ann Arbor, Michigan 48106

*New Phonics Skill Texts*
Four workbooks with systematic
exercises and useful activities in
phonetics.

Charles E. Merrill Publishing
Co.
1300 Alum Creek Drive
Columbus, Ohio 43216

*New Webster Word Wheels*
A kit of word wheels emphasizing
beginning digraphs, blends, prefixes, and
suffixes.

Webster Division
McGraw-Hill Book Company
Manchester Road
Manchester, Missouri 63011

*Paper Bag Puppet Patterns*
Useful device for developing language
usage and placement of events in logical
sequence.

McGraw-Hill Book Company
1221 Avenue of the Americas
New York, New York 10036

*Peabody Language Laboratory*
This program teaches vocabulary
development and sentence structure to
young children.

George Peabody Teachers
College
Nashville, Tennessee

*Phonics Game Kit*
Games useful in practicing word
analysis.

Lyons & Carnahan
407 East 25 Street
Chicago, Illinois

*Phonic Lotto*
This and many other similar games are
available and can be used to practice
selected word analysis skills. Some of
the other games include *Group Word
Teaching Game, Group Sounding Game,
What the Letters Say,* and *The Syllable
Game.*

Garrard Publishing Company
1607 North Market Street
Champaign, Illinois 61820

*Phonic Quizmo*
This and other similar games are
available and can be used to practice
selected word analysis skills. Some of
the other games include *Phonetic Word
Wheel* and *Make-a-Word Game.*

Beckley-Cardy Company
1900 North Narragansett Avenue
Chicago, Illinois 60639

*Phonic Rummy*
This and many other similar games are
available and can be used to practice
selected word analysis skills. Some of
the other games include *ABC Game* and
the *Doghouse Game*.

Kenworthy Educational Service,
Inc.
138 Allen Street
Buffalo, New York 14201

*Phonics Workbooks*
A series of five workbooks containing
exercises for practice in phonetic
analysis.

Webster Division
McGraw-Hill Book Company
Manchester Road
Manchester, Missouri 63011

Series of workbooks on phonetic
analysis.
Useful if selected pages are used with
the appropriate skill taught in this book.

Lyons & Carnahan
407 East 25 Street
Chicago, Illinois 60616

Platts, Mary E. *Anchor*
Collection of games, activities and
projects to motivate language arts in
the intermediate grades.

Educational Services, Inc.
P.O. Box 219
Stevensville, Michigan 49127

Platts, Mary E. *Launch*
Contains games, activities and projects
to motivate the teaching of kindergarten
and preschool children.

Educational Services, Inc.
P.O. Box 219
Stevensville, Michigan 49127

*Programmed Reading*
A series of workbooks printed as
programs.

Buchanan-Sullivan Associates
and Webster Division
McGraw-Hill Book Company
Princeton Road
Hightstown, New Jersey 08520

*Reading Aids Through the Grades*
A listing of 300 reading activities.

Bureau of Publications
Teachers College
Columbia University
New York, New York 10027

*Reading Games*
A sourcebook of games to be used in
conjunction with reading instruction.

Teachers Publishing Corp.
22 West Putnam Avenue
Greenwich, Connecticut 06830

*Reading with Phonics*
A series of exercises useful in reinforcing
some of the skills taught in this book.

J. B. Lippincott Company
East Washington Square
Philadelphia, Pennsylvania
19105

*Resources in Teaching Reading*
Contains specific suggestions for
activities and exercises for reading.

Reading Laboratory
University of Florida
Gainesville, Florida 32601

| PRACTICE MATERIALS (*Continued*) | SOURCES (*Continued*) |
|---|---|
| *School Readiness Treasure Chest* Useful in developing oral language skills and ability to put events in sequence. | Harper & Row, Publishers 10 East 53 Street New York, New York 10022 |
| *Skilstarters* A personalized, game-oriented program of reading readiness. | Random House, Inc. 201 East 50 Street New York, New York 10022 |
| *Sounds I Can Hear* Records that help develop rudimentary auditory discrimination skills. | Scott, Foresman and Company 1900 East Lake Avenue Glenview, Illinois 60025 |
| *Source Materials for the Improvement of Reading* A reference list of sources of material. Request Bureau of Educational Research Bulletin No. 37 | Board of Education City of New York 110 Livingston Street Brooklyn, New York 11201 |
| Spache, Evelyn B. *Reading Activities for Child Involvement* Contains (571) stimulating, interesting activities for reinforcing skills. | Allyn & Bacon, Inc. 470 Atlantic Avenue Boston, Massachusetts |
| *Speech to Print Phonics* A strong program in auditory discrimination, useful in practicing tasks similar to many of those taught in this book. | Harcourt Brace Jovanovich, Inc. 757 Third Avenue New York, New York 10017 |
| *Spelling and Writing Patterns* A series of spelling workbooks stressing a multisensory, sound-symbol relationship approach. The activities can be easily and usefully adapted to reading tasks. | Follett Publishing Company 201 North Wells Street Chicago, Illinois 60606 |
| *Spice* A collection of reading-related activities. | Educational Service Box 112 Benton Harbor, Michigan 49022 |
| *SRA Basic Reading Series and Satellites* Reading selections useful in reinforcing instruction in phonetics. | Science Research Associates, Inc. 259 East Erie Street Chicago, Illinois 60611 |
| *Structural Reading Series* A series of workbooks and other materials useful in teaching decoding skills. | L. W. Singer Company, Inc. Division of Random House 201 East 50 Street New York, New York 10022 |

*Systems for Success*
A series of two workbooks designed for use with adolescent and adult illiterates.

Follett Publishing Company
201 North Wells Street
Chicago, Illinois 60606

Thompson Richard. *Energizers for Reading Instruction*
Contains teaching activities, games, transparencies, and chalkboard demonstrations to help individualization. Focuses on skill. Is illustrated.

Parker Publishing Company, Inc.
West Nyack, New York

*Vowel Dominoes*
A game useful in practicing vowel wounds. Other games are also available from this source.

Remedial Education Center
1321 New Hampshire Avenue N.W.
Washington, D.C. 20036

Weber, Elaine, and Jan Chappa. *Games That Teach Within Your Reach*
Provides many practice ideas that are keyed to fit specific reading skills.

Mott Institute for Community Improvement
College of Education
Michigan State University
East Lansing, Michigan 48824

# B

## SOURCES OF APPEALING READING MATERIALS

The following is a list of sources of appealing reading materials you can use to apply the skills that have been taught and to develop the reading habit among your learners. The list is divided into two sections. The first presents high-interest, easy-to-read books and where they may be obtained. The second gives sources of book lists that can be used as guides in selecting reading materials for your learners.

| HIGH INTEREST, EASY-TO-READ BOOKS | SOURCES |
|---|---|
| *Archway Paperbacks*<br>Large selection of paperback books ranging as low as third grade in difficulty. | Washington Square Press<br>Division of Simon & Schuster, Inc.<br>630 Fifth Avenue<br>New York, New York 10020 |
| *Aviation Readers*<br>A graded series of books on aviation. | Macmillan Publishing Co., Inc.<br>866 Third Avenue<br>New York, New York 10022 |
| *Basic Vocabulary Series*<br>Stories written by E. W. Dolch stressing the most common sight words. | Garrard Publishing Company<br>1607 North Market Street<br>Champaign, Illinois 61820 |

*Beginner Books*
A group of individually sold, easy-to-read
trade books on a variety of topics.

McGraw-Hill Book Company
1221 Avenue of the Americas
New York, New York 10036

*Break Through!*
Paperback series of high-interest, easy-
reading selections of a multiethnic
nature.

Allyn & Bacon, Inc.
470 Atlantic Avenue
Boston, Massachusetts 02210

*Button Books*
A series of easy-to-read stories about the
Button family.

Beckley-Cardy Company
1900 North Narragansett Ave.
Chicago, Illinois 60639

*Checkered Flag Series*
Classroom Reading Kit A and B (B)
Eight books about cars and motorcycles.
Has multicopies of same book.
Readability level is 2.4 to 4.5

Field Education Publications,
Inc.
2400 Hanover St.
Palo Alto, California 04304

*Childhood of Famous American Series*
Many titles of a low reading level.

The Bobbs-Merrill Co., Inc.
4300 West 62 Street
Indianapolis, Indiana 46268

*Cowboy Sam Series*
Easy-to-read ranch stories of special
interest to boys.

Beckley-Cardy Company
1900 North Narragansett Ave.
Chicago, Illinois 60639

*Deep Sea*
*Adventure Series (B)*
A series of easy-to-read books.
Readability is 1.8 to 5.0.

Field Educational Publications
2400 Hanover St.
Palo Alto, California 94304

*Discover Books*
A paperback book club associated with
*My Weekly Reader*.

Discover Books
Education Center
Columbus, Ohio 43216

*I Can Read Books*
Easy-to-read, attractive books for the
beginning reader.

Harper & Row, Publishers
10 East 53 Street
New York, New York 10022

*Know Your World*
Weekly newspaper for older students
who read at grades 3 to 5 level.

Xerox Education Publications
Education Center
Columbus, Ohio 43216

*Let's Find Out Books*
High-interest beginning reading books
about a variety of topics, including
biography and science.

Franklin Watts, Inc.
845 Third Avenue
New York, New York 10022

*Little Wonder Books*
Small booklets at low reading levels on topics of interest to children.

Charles E. Merrill Publishing Co.
1300 Alum Creek Drive
Columbus, Ohio 43216

*Paperback Classroom Library*
Collections of 100 paperback books for each of the six elementary grades and kindergarten.

Educational Reading Service, Inc.
64 East Midland Avenue
Paramus, New Jersey 07652

*Play the Game Series (B)*
Multiethnic books about great athletes. Readability level is 2.5 to 4.0.

Bowmar
P.O. Box 5225
Glendale, California 91201

*Pleasure Reading Series*
A series of well-known stories rewritten with special attention to vocabulary control.

Garrard Publishing Company
1607 North Market Street
Champaign, Illinois 61820

*Random House Reading Program*
*Rading Pacemakers (BO)*
A graded collection of hardcover books.

Random House, Singer School Division
P.O. Box 10075
Church Street Station
New York, New York 10049

*Reader's Digest Skill Builders*
High-interest, low-level materials modeled after the regular edition of *Reader's Digest.*

Reader's Digest Association
Pleasantville, New York 10570

*Reading Incentive—Part I (K)*
Sixteen kits on topics such as minibikes, snowmobiles, and horses. Readability level is 3.0.

Bowmar
P.O. Box 5225
Glendale, California 91201

*Scholastic's Reluctant Reader Library*
Paperbacks for students in grades 5 to 12, reading two or three grades below grade level.

Scholastic Book Services
50 West 44 Street
New York, New York 10036

*Target Books*
Contain biographies from sports and tall tales to current leaders.

Garrard Publishing Co.
1607 North Market Street
Champaign, Illinois 61820

*The True Books*
Informational books on a wide range of topics.

Children's Press
1224 West Van Buren Street
Chicago, Illinois

| | |
|---|---|
| *Aids in Selecting Books for Slow Readers* Lists both sources and criteria for selecting books for disabled readers. | American Library Association 50 East Huron Street Chicago, Illinois 60611 |
| Allen, Patricia (compiler). *Best Books for Children, Revised Edition,* 1964 A list of 3300 selected titled. | R. R. Bowker Company 1180 Avenue of the Americas New York, New York 10036 |
| *A Basic Book Collection for Elementary Grades.* An annotated list of essential books. | American Library Association 50 East Huron Street Chicago, Illinois 60611 |
| *A Bibliography of High-Interest, Low-Vocabulary Books for Retarded Readers* A valuable source list. | Colorado Department of Education Denver, Colorado |
| *A Bibliography of Reading Lists for Retardel Readers* A source of books suitable for disabled readers. Request Extension Bulletin, College of Education Series No. 37. | State University of Iowa Iowa City, Iowa 52240 |
| Carr, Constance. "Substitutes for the Comic Books," *Elementary English,* XXVIII (April–May, 1951), 194–200. Suggests books possessing much of the appeal of comics. | |
| Condit, M. A. *Trade Books for Beginning Readers,* 1960. Books for children in grades K through 3. | H. W. Wilson Company 950 University Avenue New York, New York 10452 |
| *Discovering Books* Paperback club for middle-age children. | Xerox Education Publications Education Center Columbus, Ohio 43216 |
| Dunn, Anita, Mabel Jackson, and J. Newton. *Fare for the Reluctant Reader,* 1964 A standard source for appealing reading material. | Capitol Area School Development Association State University of New York Albany, New York 12203 |
| Eakin, Mary K. *Subject Index to Books for Intermediate Grades,* 1963 | American Library Association 50 East Huron Street Chicago, Illinois 60611 |

Eakin, Mary K., and Eleanor Merritt.
*Subject Index to Books for Primary
Grades,* 1961
Cross-indexes the contents of nearly
1000 books.

American Library Association
50 East Huron Street
Chicago, Illinois 60611

*Elementaryl Paperback Collection*
Hundreds of books for all elementary
school children covering all interests.

E & R Development Co.
Vandalia Road
Jacksonville, Illinois 62650

Fry, Edward, and Warren Johnson.
"Booklist for Remedial Reading."
*Elementary English, XXXV* (October,
1958), 373–380
Includes approximately 100 books useful
with retarded readers.

*Good Time*
Paperback club for second and third
graders.

Xerox Education Publications
Education Center
Columbus, Ohio 43216

Kress, R. (compiler). *A Place to Start:
A Graded Bibliography for Children
with Reading Difficulties*

Reading Center
Syracuse University
Syracuse, New York

*Laurel Leaf Library*
Paperback book for upper elementary
age children.

Dell Publishing Co., Inc.
1 Dag Hammarskjold Plaza
New York, New York 10017

*Library Books for Retarded Readers*
A listing of high-interest, low-level
library books.

Illinois Reading Service
Box 277
Bloomington, Illinois 61702

*Library Materials for Remedial Reading*
A list of suggested materials. Request
Bibliography No. 3, Instructional
Materials Bulletin, June, 1959.

College Library
Iowa State University
Cedar Falls, Iowa 50613

Lundeen, Alma, and Margaret
Prendergrass. "Books for Retarded
Readers," *Illinois Library, XLIII* (April,
1961), 271–287
Provides a list of recommended books.

McConnell, M. L., and D. H. West
(compilers). *Children's Catalog*
A primary and essential source of
classified and graded lists of children's
books.

H. W. Wilson Company
950 University Avenue
New York, New York 10452

*Reading Shelf*
Designed for reading interests of all
children, grades 1 through 5.

Garrard Publishing Co.
1607 North Market Srteet
Champaign, Illinois 61820

Scholastic Paperback Library
Hundreds of books for all age levels.

Scholastic Book Services
904 Sylvan Avenue
Englewood Cliffs, New Jersey
07632

Spache, George, *Good Reading for Poor
Readers.* Revised Edition, 1966
A comprehensive list of printed materials
for poor readers.

Garrard Publishing Company
1607 North Market Street
Champaign, Illinois 61820

*Venture Books*
Large selection for beginning readers in
grades K through 3.

Garrard Publishing Company
1607 North Market Street
Champaign, Illinois 61820

*Viking SeaFarer Books*
A paperback collection containing
Caldecott and Newbury Award books.

The Viking Press
625 Madison Avenue
New York, New York 10022

*Weekly Reader*
Weekly newspaper for elementary
students. Five editions available.

Xerox Education Publications
Education Center
Columbus, Ohio 43216

*Yearling Books*
Contains award-winning children's book
for grades 2 through 8.

Dell Publishing Co., Inc.
1 Dag Hammarskjold Plaza
New York, New York 10017

# GROUP PLACEMENT TEST FOR WORD RECOGNITION SKILLS

## Teacher Test Items

### DIRECTIONS TO TEACHERS

*Procedures*

This test is designed for use with your total class. It is composed of word recognition skill tasks selected at random from each cluster. If a child performs within the criterion level established for each of the random samples in each cluster on this placement test, he probably possesses *all* the skills within that cluster. If the criterion level is not met for a particular cluster in the placement test, the learner should be pretested individually on *each* objective within that cluster to determine exactly where instruction should begin.

Your directions can be read directly from this appendix. The student answer sheets begin on page 499. Specific instructions for administering the test are found in Chapter 6.

In administering the test, timing is not critical except where noted in the teacher directions.

*Cautions*

This placement test is not a precision instrument. It will, however, guide you in placing your learners within a band of skills that you can quickly narrow by using the individual objective pretests. To be most effective, adhere strictly to the criterion suggested. It is better to be too careful than not careful enough.

Remember that the purpose of this test is to place the child within a cluster of skills. The purpose is *not* to diagnose *specific skill needs* and no decisions of this nature should be made until after you have pretested specific skills.

## CLUSTER I  SKILL SURVEY

If a learner makes more than two incorrect responses in this section he or she should be pretested on each objective in Cluster I.

*For test item 1*

**Teacher directions**  Direct the group to the first line. Tell them to circle the word that you show on the card, then move to the next card and have the group circle the word shown in the second line, and so on.

**Teacher shows**

a. **he**

b. **was**

c. **cat**

*For test item 2*

**Teacher directions**  Direct the learners to each line in turn. Flash a card (for a count of three) that matches one word in each line. Direct the learners to circle the matching word.

**Teacher shows**

a. **like**

b. **first**

c. **wants**

*For test item 3*

**Teacher directions**  Prepare cards having upper- and lower-case letters printed on them. Hold up the upper-case letter cards one at a time for a count of three and direct the learners to find the lower-case mate for each letter and circle it.

**Teacher shows**

a. **G**   b. **E**   c. **N**   d. **D**   e. **A**

*For test item 4*

**Teacher directions**  Direct the learners to each word in turn, telling them to circle the first or last letter as directed.

**Teacher says**

a. Circle the first letter

b. Circle the first letter

c. Circle the last letter

d. Circle the first letter

e. Circle the last letter

*For test item 5*

**Teachers directions**  Speak the following pairs of words, directing the learners to circle **Yes** if the words begin with the same sound and **No** if the words do not begin with the same sound.

**Teacher says**
a. shot    chew
b. pet    pit
c. stamp    champ
d. like    let
e. many    never

*For test item 6*

**Teacher directions**   Say the following list of words. Direct the learners to circle the letter-sound heard at the beginning of each word.

**Teacher says**
a. many
b. did
c. laundry
d. cabinet
e. scissors
f. hand

*For test item 7*

**Teacher directions**   Pronounce the following list of words, directing the learners to circle the pronounced word. Allow only five seconds for each response, then move on to the next item.

**Teacher says**
a. to
b. the
c. was
d. of

*For test item 8*

**Teacher directions**   Speak the following sentences to your learners, directing them to circle on their paper the word omitted from the sentence. Flash and remove a blank card to signal where the word is omitted as you say the sentence. These sentences may be repeated if necessary.

**Teacher says**
a. I took my pencil _____ school with me.
b. Can an elephant play the piano? _____
c. Can you find _____ coat?
d. I like to hide _____ the garage.

*For test item 9*

**Teacher directions**   Read the following list of words, directing the learners to circle the letter sound they hear at the beginning of each word.

**Teacher says**
a. keep
b. baker
c. tiger
d. rainbow
e. jump

*For test item 10*

**Teacher directions**  Read the following list of words, directing the learners to circle the letter-sound they *heard* at the end of each word.

**Teacher says**

a. **came**

b. **doll**

c. **place**

d. **lid**

*For test item 11*

**Teacher directions**  Direct the learners to circle the word in each group you pronounce. Allow only five seconds for each response and then move on the next time.

**Teacher says**

a. **down**

b. **help**

c. **fast**

d. **at**

e. **see**

*For test item 12*

**Teacher directions**  Read the following list of words, directing the learners to circle the letter-sound combination heard at the beginning of each word.

**Teacher says**

a. **shirt**

b. **shack**

c. **think**

d. **thistle**

## CLUSTER II  SKILL SURVEY

If a learner makes more than two incorrect responses in this section, he or she should be pretested on each objective in Cluster II.

*For test item 1*

**Teacher directions**  Say a word in isolation and then in a sentence, directing the learners to circle this word on the answer sheet. Allow only five seconds for each response and move on to the next item.

**Teacher says**

a. **girl:** The **girl** went home.

b. **after:** We will do it **after** dinner.

c. **who: Who** won the game?

d. **little:** He was a **little** boy.

e. **they: They** are going home.

f. **was:** She **was** going home.

*For test item 2*

**Teacher directions**  Read the following list of words, directing the learners to circle the letter-sound combination heard at the beginning of each word.

**Teacher says**
a. when
b. chip
c. this

*For test item 3*

**Teacher directions**   Direct the learners to each row in turn. Pronounce the first word in this row and have them circle the word you tell them to find.

**Teacher says**
a. The first word is **set.**      Now find and circle **tet.**
b. The first word is **cat.**      Now find and circle **lat.**
c. The first word is **but.**      Now find and circle **sut.**
d. The first word is **met.**      Now find and circle **seck.**
e. The first word is **cat.**      Now find and circle **lack.**

*For test item 4*

**Teacher directions**   Direct the learners to circle the word in each group that you pronounce.

**Teacher says**
a. wanting
b. wants
c. wanted

## CLUSTER III   SKILL SURVEY

If a learner makes more than two incorrect responses in this section, he or she should be pretested on each objective in Cluster III.

*For test item 1*

**Teacher directions**   Say a word in isolation and then in a sentence, directing the learners to circle this word on their answer sheets. Allow only five seconds for each response and then move on to the next item.

**Teacher says**
a. said: I **said** to sit down.
b. from: He came **from** his house.
c. surprise: I have a **surprise** for you.
d. door: He will open the **door.**
e. been: I have **been** at my house.
f. if: Do it **if** you can.

*For test item 2*

**Teacher directions**   Direct the learners to each row in turn. Pronounce the first word in this row and have them circle the word you tell them to find.

**Teacher says**
a. The first word is **pup.**      Now find and circle **drup.**
b. The first word is **cab.**      Now find and circle **crab.**
c. The first word is **bed.**      Now find and circle **slek.**
d. The first word is **rib.**      Now find and circle **clib.**

*For test item 3*

**Teacher directions** Pronounce each compound word, directing the learner to draw a line between the first part of the compound in column 1 and the second part of the compound in column 2.

**Teacher says**
a. any–one
b. with–out

## CLUSTER IV  SKILL SURVEY

If a learner makes more than two incorrect responses in this section, he or she should be pretested on each objective in Cluster IV.

*For test item 1*

**Teacher directions** Say a word in isolation and then in a sentence, directing the learners to circle this word on their answer sheets. Allow only five seconds for each response and then move on to the next item.

**Teacher says**
a. **please: Please** help me.
b. **song:** Let's sing a **song.**
c. **very:** This is **very** hard.
d. **guess:** I will **guess** the answer.
e. **there:** He is over **there.**
f. **were:** We **were** going home.

*For test item 2*

**Teacher directions** Direct the learners to each row in turn. Pronounce the first word in this row and have them circle the word you tell them to find.

**Teacher says**
a. The first word is **pick.**     Now find and circle **smick.**
b. The first word is **ham.**     Now find and circle the word **swam.**
c. The first word is **bat.**     Now find and circle the word **bast.**
d. The first word is **lug.**     Now find and circle the word **lust.**

*For test item 3*

**Teaching directions** Direct the learner to draw a line from the contractions in the left column to the words from which each contraction is formed in the right column.

**Teacher says**
(Directions only)

## CLUSTER V  SKILL SURVEY

If a learner makes more than two incorrect responses in this section, he or she should be pretested on each objective in Cluster V.

*For test item 1*

**Teacher directions** Say a word in isolation and then in a sentence, directing the learners to circle this word on their answer sheets. Allow only five seconds for each response and then move on to the next item.

**Teacher says**

a. give: I will **give** you a penny.

b. their: It is **their** house.

c. sure: I am **sure** it is right.

d. does: She **does** write well.

e. ready: I am **ready** to go.

f. what: **What** are you doing

*For test item 2*

**Teacher directions**   Direct the learners to each row in turn. Pronounce the first word in this row and have them circle the word you tell them to find.

**Teacher says**

a. The first word is **feel.**      Now find a circle **treel.**

b. The first word is **my.**        Now find and circle **ky.**

c. The first word is **day.**       Now find and circle **gray.**

d. The first word is **will.**      Now find and circle **skill.**

e. The first word is **ball.**      Now find and circle **skall.**

*For test item 3*

**Teacher directions**   Direct the learners to circle the word in each row that you pronounce.

**Teacher says**

a. newly

b. newer

c. newest

## CLUSTER VI   SKILL SURVEY

If a learner makes more than two incorrect responses in this section, he or she should be pretested on each objective in Cluster VI.

*For test item 1*

**Teacher directions**   Say a word in isolation and then in a sentence, directing the learners to circle this word on their answer sheets. Allow only five seconds for each response and then move on to the next item.

**Teacher says**

a. should: We **should** go home now.

b. believe: I do not **believe** your story.

c. heavy: That load you are carrying must be **heavy.**

d. tried: He **tried** very hard to win the game.

e. next: You are **next** in line.

f. where: **Where** are you going?

*For test item 2*

**Teacher directions**   Direct the learners to circle all the words in each row that say the word you pronounce.

**Teacher says**

a. Find and circle all the words that can say **boat.**

b. Find and circle all the words that can say **bout.**

c. Find and circle all the words that can say **bait.**

*For test item 3*

**Teacher directions**  Direct the learners to each row in turn. Pronounce the first word in this row and have them circle the word you tell them to find.

**Teacher says**
a. The first word is **sut.**    Now find and circle **sund.**
b. The first word is **thun.**    Now find and circle **thunk.**
c. The first word is **tin.**    Now find and circle **bint.**

*For test item 4*

**Teacher directions**  Pronounce each word, directing the learners to draw a line between the first part of the word in column 1 and the second part of the word in column 2.

**Teacher says**
a. dis–like
b. un–happy
c. dis–trust

## CLUSTER VII  SKILL SURVEY

If a learner makes more than two incorrect responses in this section, he or she should be pretested on each objective in Cluster VII.

*For test item 1*

**Teacher directions**  Say a word in isolation and then in a sentence, directing the learners to circle the word on their answer sheets. Allow only five seconds for each response and then move on to the next item.

**Teacher says**
a. **field:** They played ball in the **field.**
b. **clothes:** He was wearing his new set of **clothes.**
c. **early.** He got up **early** this morning.
d. **umbrella:** When it rains, we use an **umbrella.**
e. **always:** He is **always** happy.
f. **those:** He is going to eat **those** apples.

*For test item 2*

**Teacher directions**  Pronounce the first word in each list, directing the learners to circle all other words in the list that have the same middle sound.

**Teacher says**
a. The first word is **tooth.** Now find and circle all other words having the same middle sound as **tooth.**
b. The first word is **look.** Now find and circle all other words having the same middle sound as **look.**

*For test item 3*

**Teacher directions**  Direct the learners to look at each word in turn and to draw a line to separate the syllables in that word.

**Teacher says**
Directions only.

*For test item 4*

**Teacher directions**  Pronounce each compound word, directing the learners to draw a line between the first part of the compound in the first column and the second part in the second column.

**Teacher says**
a. **everything**
b. **afternoon**
c. **outside**

## CLUSTER VII  SKILL SURVEY

If the learner makes more than two incorrect responses in this section, he or she should be pretested on each objective in Cluster VIII.

*For test item 1*

**Teacher directions**  Say a word in isolation and then in a sentence, directing the learners to circle this word on their answer sheets. Allow only five seconds for each response and then move on to the next item.

**Teacher says**
a. **enough:** I have not had **enough** pie.
b. **build:** I will **build** a house.
c. **thought:** I **thought** you were at home.
d. **answer:** Did you get the right **answer?**
e. **engine:** The car has a big **engine.**
f. **must:** You **must** stay in the house today.

*For test item 2*

**Teacher directions**  Direct the learners to look at each word in turn and to draw a line to separate the syllables in that word.

**Teacher says**
Directions only.

*For test item 3*

**Teacher directions**  Direct the learners to each row in turn. Pronounce the first word in this row and have them circle the word you tell them to find.

**Teacher says**
a. The first word is **bop.**    Now find and circle **strop.**
b. The first word is **lang.**    Now find and circle **strang.**
c. The first word is **moat.**    Now find and circle **throat.**
d. The first word is **cresh.**    Now find and circle **thresh.**

*For test item 4*

**Teacher directions**  Direct the learners to lok at each word in turn and to cross out the letters in the word that are not sounded.

**Teacher says**
Directions only.

# GROUP
# PLACEMENT
# TEST FOR WORD
# RECOGNITION
# SKILLS
## Student
## Answer Sheets

NAME_____

*SCORES   Number wrong in each cluster of test.*

Cluster I      _____
Cluster II     _____
Cluster III    _____
Cluster IV     _____
Cluster V      _____
Cluster VI     _____
Cluster VII    _____
Cluster VIII   _____

*Cluster I*

1. a. he      it      it      it
   b. the     was    the    the
   c. come    come   cat    come

2. a. let      like    many    little
   b. first    fast    fun     fat
   c. want    was    weather   wants

3. a. p    b    o    g    t
   b. f    e    c    b    o
   c. u    m    a    v    n
   d. p    d    b    x    g
   e. a    v    u    k    r

4. a. elephant
   b. yes
   c. no
   d. top
   e. funny

5. a. yes    no
   b. yes    no
   c. yes    no
   d. yes    no
   e. yes    no

6. a. s    m    l    n
   b. d    t    o    b
   c. d    r    j    l
   d. e    r    s    c
   e. m    x    s    z
   f. h    d    f    w

7. a. ten      tot      told      to
   b. the      there    then    that
   c. as       saw     was     want
   d. of       over     fun     for

8. a. and     he       it       to
   b. in       my      no      a
   c. and     yes      I       the
   d. he      in       and    it

9. a. k       n       j       r
   b. p       t       l       b
   c. r       t       f       y
   d. m      d       f       r
   e. i       c       j       p

10. a. n      u       e       m
    b. f       j       t       l
    c. s       e       z       w
    d. t       d       p       s

11. a. don't    down    brown   doubt
    b. him     here     whelp   help
    c. fast     first     last     fist
    d. it       to       at      all
    e. sew     set      easy    see

12. a. sh      ch      s       wh
    b. ck      sh      h       sch
    c. t       dr      th     tl
    d. sl      wh     fr     th

*Cluster II*

1. a. get     fril     little     girl
   b. after     other     attic     Africa
   c. when     won     hoo     who
   d. letter     little     liddle     fitter
   e. then     the     they     thy
   f. saw     way     was     wasp

2. a. wh     th     ch
   b. wh     th     ch
   c. wh     th     ch

3. a. set     bet     wit     tet     tat
   b. cat     lat     fat     mat     tot
   c. but     sot     mut     cub     sut
   d. met     sack     sik     sect     seck
   e. cat     lick     lock     lack     lat

4. a. want     wants     wanted     wanting
   b. want     wants     wanted     wanting
   c. want     wants     wanted     wanting

*Cluster III*

1. a. sad     slap     said     sap
   b. for     frame     fun     from
   c. surprise     supper     search     soup
   d. doer     door     dock     poor
   e. ben     bend     been     bin
   f. it     is     ill     if

2. a. pup     dup     drip     drop     drup
   b. cab     crib     crop     crab     drab
   c. bed     sled     slik     sek     slek
   d. rib     kib     club     clib     cleb

3.  any       out
    some      body
    every     where
    with      one

<br>

*Cluster IV*

1. a. peas      place     please    breeze

   b. sing      sang      swing     song

   c. very      marry     weary     vary

   d. guest     guess     gets      guest

   e. where     their     there     wear

   f. were      where     wear      here

<br>

2. a. pick      smock     smalk     sick      smick

   b. ham       swam      swim      cam       slam

   c. bat       rast      beck      blast     bast

   d. lug       last      blust     lust      lost

<br>

3.  don't     let us
    I'll      do not
    let's     would not
    wouldn't  I will

<br>

*Cluster V*

1. a. dive      giv       live      give

   b. there     their     ther      they're

   c. sure      shure     chure     sur

   d. duz       dose      does      dos

   e. bread     reddy     ready     retty

   f. that      wat       what      wut

2. **a.** feel    treel    trell    freel    tree

  **b.** my    fly    ky    sky    by

  **c.** day    dray    tray    gray    they

  **d.** will    skell    skill    grell    grill

  **e.** ball    stall    still    skall    shall


3. **a.** new    newer    newest    newly

  **b.** new    newer    newest    newly

  **c.** new    newer    newest    newly


*Cluster VI*

1. **a.** should    could    would    showed

  **b.** beneath    believe    beehive    deliver

  **c.** heady    heavy    heave    levy

  **d.** tried    treed    trip    tried

  **e.** next    necked    net    mesh

  **f.** when    were    where    there


2. **a.** bote    boat    bot    boty    boate

  **b.** bote    bout    boit    bowt    bowl

  **c.** bait    bat    biat    bate    batty


3. **a.** sut    sunk    sund    sand    shut

  **b.** thun    thing    thunk    thonk    think

  **c.** tin    bent    bind    bent    bint


4.    dis    turb

     un    like

     an    happy

     un    light

     dis    trust

*Cluster VII*

1. a. field      felled      fielded      feeled
   b. close      clues      clothes      cloze
   c. ernestq      erly      pearl      early
   d. elephant      umbrella      underneath      umber
   e. all ways      almost      allowed      always
   f. these      those      their      toes

2. a. tooth    food    wood    book    room
   b. look    foot    stood    blood    took

3. a. after
   b. basket
   c. rabbit
   d. follow
   e. until

4.    each      man
         every      noon
         out       night
         home      side
         after      thing

*Cluster VIII*

1. a. every      enough      through      enuff
   b. build      built      bought      bilk
   c. through      thorough      though      thought
   d. anything      aniversary      answer      angel
   e. energy      engine      engineer      imagine
   f. much      most      must      mist

2. a. began
   b. open
   c. music
   d. never
   e. tiger

3. a. bop        stop        strup        stroke        strop
   b. lang       strang      stang        string       sang
   c. moat       trout       throw        thoat        throat
   d. cresh      thresh      tresh        thatch        threes

4. a. high
   b. knock
   c. crumb
   d. straight

# D

# DIAGNOSTIC CHARTS FOR CORRECTING COMMON SKILL DEFICIENCIES
## Keyed to Corrective Suggestions

The following chart will aid you in relating the observed reading hehavior of learners to specific instructional suggestions provided in this book. It is divided in terms of the observed behavior, the possible cause, and the sections in the book that provide helpful instructional suggestions. When you observe persistent learner deficiencies in reading and wish to locate specific corrective measures, check these charts for that particular behavior and refer to the objectives suggested.

You should be aware of several cautions, however, in using these charts. First, it is not possible for such charts to anticipate all the possible behaviors your readers may exhibit. These charts represent, instead, the most common types of problems you will encounter. Second, the cause listed for each chart is a *possible* cause; it is not possible to predict the actual cause without knowing the specific learner. You are urged to use your knowledge of the learner and his or her environment to supplement the possible cause listed on the chart. Finally, remember that any particular deficiency may exist because the learner has not mastered the prerequisites to that particular skill. Consequently, before using the instructional techniques suggested for a deficiency, check to be certain that the learner has mastered and retained the crucial prerequisite skills.

## IF THE LEARNER CANNOT READ AT ALL

| *When learner shows this behavior* | *The cause might be* |
|---|---|
| Fails to learn sight words at a normal rate. Confuses letters of the alphabet. | Poor visual discrimination. (See module I-SW-1.) |
| Cannot remember letter and word shapes. | Poor visual memory. (See module I-SW-2.) |
| Reverses words, e.g., says **was** for **saw**. Does not read from left to right and from top to bottom. | Has an orientation problem. Does not know how to look at words and the printed page. (See module I-SW-6.) |
| Does not hear the differences in sounds. Cannot rhyme. Letters do not have distinguishing sounds for the learner. | Poor auditory discrimination. (See module I-WA-5.) |
| Cannot provide the correct sound for specific letters. | Has not made the sound-symbol connection. (See module I-WA-9.) |
| Poor oral language. Limited vocabulary. Immature oral language patterns. | Few prior opportunities to express himself. Limited experience. (See all the comprehension modules in Clusters I, II, and III.) |
| Does not use context as a means for identifying unknown words. | Lacks sentence sense. Poor oral language background. (See above.) |
| Does not use the words he or she recognizes at sight to write sentences and stories. | Does not understand the thinking-writing-reading concept of language communication. (See module II-SW-8.) |
| Is not interested in learning to read. | Unfamiliar with books. Has not seen how books can be useful and/or enjoyable. (See suggestions in Chapter 4.) |

## IF THE LEARNER KNOWS SOME WORDS BUT DOES NOT READ FLUENTLY

| *When learner shows this behavior* | *The cause might be* |
|---|---|
| Has a limited stock of sight words. | Poor visual discrimination and/or memory or poor control of the associative process that pairs the visual with the auditory components of this learning. (See modules I-SW-1, I-SW-2, and II-SW-6.) |

Has mastered visual discrimination and visual memory prerequisites, but still has a limited stock of sight words.

Needs added practice on learning specific basic sight words or an increased incentive to read outside of reading class. (See modules II-SW-6 and II-SW-8.)

Failure to differentiate words somewhat different in spelling, as **where** and **there.**

Does not attend to the specific discriminator that contrasts the similar-looking words. (See module I-SW-17.)

Reads word by word. Lacks fluency and smoothness in reading.

Poor sight vocabulary as a result of lack of practice at reading outside of reading class. (See modules II-SW-6 and II-SW-8.)

Reversals in reading. Confuses **p** and **q, was** and **saw.**

Left-to-right orientation. (See module I-SW-6.)

Complete inability to sound out words. Inability to attack new or unfamiliar words.

Lacks the prerequisites for analyzing words. (See modules I-WA-1, I-WA-4, I-WA-5, and I-WA-9.)

Cannot blend together individual sounds or word parts in pronouncing unknown words.

Lacks understanding of how individual letters and word parts contribute to a word identification. Can't apply the principle of consonant substitution. Has not mastered aural fusion and clozure skills. (See modules II-WA-1 and II-WA-18.)

Does not understand the short vowel spelling patterns.

Lacks understanding of common word families and short vowel phonograms. (See module II-WA-18.)

Does not understand the long vowels principles.

Has not been properly taught these principles. (See module VI-WA-1.)

Cannot break words into syllables.

Does not know the principle upon which words are syllabicated. (See module VII-WA-1.)

Cannot analyze words in terms of word parts or structure.

Lacks understanding of compound words and/or of the root word-prefix-suffix structure. (See module II-WA-25.)

| When learner shows this behavior (Continued) | The cause might be (Continued) |
| --- | --- |
| Cannot analyze and pronounce contractions. | Does not understand the principle upon which contractions are formed. (See module IV-WA-9.) |

## IF THE LEARNER PRONOUNCES WORDS BUT DOES NOT UNDERSTAND

| When learner shows this behavior | The cause might be |
| --- | --- |
| The learner does not know the meaning of the content or referent words found in the passage. | Does not possess concepts for the words. Lacks experience background to match the content of the message. (See module I-IG-1.) |
| Does not perceive the relationships signaled by function words such as **it, meanwhile, and,** etc. | Does not understand the structured relationships signaled by such words. (See module I-IG-3.) |
| Substitutes words during oral reading that do not fit either the form class or syntactical function required in the sentence. | Overemphasis on sight recognition skills that are not accurately learned in the first place. Lack of practice in contextual prediction from either syntactic or semantic clues. (See modules I-WA-14, II-IG-4, and VII-IG-5.) |
| Cannot identify the facts and details of what is read. | Lacks direction and purpose for reading a selection. Teacher is asking the wrong questions. (See modules objective III-IG-6.) |
| Cannot classify or group concepts in terms of their relationships to each other. | Has not been taught to see and classify concepts in terms of their shared and common characteristics. (See module I-MT-1.) |
| Cannot grasp the main idea of a sentence or paragraph. | Does not apply classifying and relationship skills to contextual material. (See module III-MT-2.) |
| Does not make inferences based on the content of a message. | Lack of practice in "thinking" about a message. Poor questioning skills of the teacher. Does not apply background experience to what is read. (See module I-MT-2.) |

| When learner shows this behavior (Continued) | The cause might be (Continued) |
|---|---|
| Cannot use context to infer meaning for words that are both strange in print and strange in meaning. | Has not been taught to predict clozure by making a contextual guess based on the sense of the rest of the sentence. Has not been taught to trust and use his or her experience as a guide in predicting the meaning of a word that is not in his or her immediate meaning vocabulary. (See modules I-WA-14 and II-IG-4.) |
| Reads in a monotonous fashion without clear evidence of the spoken component of written language. | Overemphasis of sight vocabulary and flash card instruction. No systematic instruction in contextual guessing based on semantic and syntactic system. (See modules II-SW-8 and VII-IG-5.) |
| Is not able to describe or discuss an author's position or feeling about what he or she has written. | A child's belief that everything he or she reads must be true or it wouldn't be in the book. Lack of teacher direction to loaded words that reveal a bias or feeling that the author has toward the subject. (See module IV-ET-1.) |
| Cannot identify or describe irrelevant or anachronistic events or information that occur in reading materials. | See preceding statement and module I-ET-1. |

# THE SKILL OBJECTIVES AND THE LOCATION OF THEIR RESPECTIVE STOREHOUSE MODULES

CLUSTER I

| Module number | Skill description | Page No. | Storehouse module Page No. |
|---|---|---|---|
| I-SW-1 | Visual discrimination (geometric forms) | 89 | 89 |
| I-SW-2 | Visual memory (geometric forms) | 93 | 93 |
| I-SW-3 | Naming (geometric forms) | 95 | 95 |
| I-SW-4 | Naming (pupil's name) | 98 | 95 |
| I-SW-5 | Visual discrimination (name) | 99 | 89 |
| I-SW-6 | Visual sequencing (name) | 101 | 101 |
| I-SW-7 | Visual memory (name) | 103 | 93 |
| I-SW-8 | Visual discrimination (letters) | 104 | 89 |
| I-SW-9 | Visual sequencing (letters) | 106 | 101 |
| I-SW-10 | Visual memory (letters) | 107 | 93 |
| I-SW-11 | Naming (alphabet letters) | 108 | 95 |
| I-SW-12 | Visual discrimination (numerals) | 110 | 89 |
| I-SW-13 | Visual memory (numerals) | 111 | 93 |
| I-SW-14 | Visual sequencing (numerals) | 112 | 101 |
| I-SW-15 | Naming (numerals) | 113 | 95 |
| I-SW-16 | Visual discrimination (like letters) | 115 | 89 |
| I-SW-17 | Easily confused letters and words | 116 | 116 |

## CLUSTER II

| Module number | Skill description | Page No. | Storehouse module Page No. |
|---|---|---|---|
| II-SW-4 | Visual discrimination (like words) | 185 | 89 |
| II-SW-5 | Visual memory (words) | 187 | 93 |
| II-SW-6 | Sight-word recognition | 188 | 188 |
| II-SW-7 | Sight words | 194 | 188 |
| II-SW-8 | Language experience | 195 | 195 |
| II-SW-9 | Visual sequencing | 198 | 101 |
| II-SW-10 | Language experience | 199 | 195 |
| II-SW-11 | Sight words | 201 | 188 |
| II-SW-12 | Sight words | 202 | 188 |
| II-SW-13 | Sight words (upper and lower case) | 203 | 95, 188 |
| II-SW-14 | Sight words | 204 | 188 |
| II-SW-15 | Visual sequencing | 205 | 101 |
| II-SW-16 | Sight words | 207 | 188 |
| II-WA-1 | Auditory fusion | 208 | 208 |
| II-WA-2 | Auditory fusion | 211 | 208 |
| II-WA-3 | Auditory discrimination (ending **m, d, l, s**) | 212 | 128 |
| II-WA-4 | Sound–symbol connection (ending **m, d, l, s**) | 214 | 137 |
| II-WA-5 | Auditory discrimination (ending **b, f, g, n, p, t, v**) | 215 | 128 |
| II-WA-6 | Sound–symbol connection (ending **b, f, g, n, p, t, v**) | 218 | 137 |
| II-WA-7 | Auditory discrimination (**q, v, y, z**) | 219 | 128 |
| II-WA-8 | Sound–symbol connection (**q, v, y, z**) | 221 | 137 |
| II-WA-9 | Context/phonics (**q, v, y, z**) | 222 | 147 |
| II-WA-10 | Auditory discrimination (**sh** and **th**) | 224 | 128 |
| II-WA-11 | Sound–symbol connection (**sh** and **th**) | 226 | 137 |
| II-WA-12 | Context/phonics (**sh** and **th**) | 227 | 147 |
| II-WA-13 | Auditory discrimination (**ch** and **wh**) | 229 | 128 |
| II-WA-14 | Sound–symbol connection (**ch** and **wh**) | 231 | 137 |
| II-WA-15 | Context/phonics (**ch** and **wh**) | 232 | 147 |
| II-WA-16 | Auditory discrimination (short vowels) | 234 | 128 |
| II-WA-17 | Sound–symbol connection (short vowels) | 236 | 137 |
| II-WA-18 | Letter substitution (beginning consonant) | 238 | 238 |
| II-WA-19 | Letter substitution (final consonant) | 242 | 238 |

## CLUSTER III (*Continued*)

## CLUSTER IV

CLUSTER VI (*Continued*)

CLUSTER VII

## THE STOREHOUSE OBJECTIVES

| Module number | Skill description | Page No. |
|---|---|---|
| I-SW-1 | Visual discrimination | 89 |
| I-SW-2 | Visual memory | 93 |
| I-SW-3 | Naming | 95 |
| I-SW-6 | Visual sequencing | 101 |
| I-SW-17 | Easily confused letters and words | 116 |
| I-WA-1 | Auditory memory/sequence | 119 |
| I-WA-4 | Auditory closure | 125 |
| I-WA-5 | Auditory discrimination (say-it-slow, say-it-fast technique) | 128 |
| I-WA-9 | Sound–symbol connection | 137 |
| I-WA-14 | Context/phonics | 147 |
| I-IG-1 | Content word meaning | 162 |
| I-IG-2 | Affix meaning | 165 |
| I-IG-3 | Function words/relationships | 168 |
| I-MT-1 | Classification | 171 |
| I-MT-2 | Inference | 174 |
| I-ET-1 | Judging content | 177 |
| II-SW-6 | Sight word recognition | 188 |
| II-SW-8 | Language experience | 195 |
| II-WA-1 | Auditory fusion | 208 |
| II-WA-18 | Letter substitution | 238 |
| II-WA-25 | Structural analysis | 251 |
| II-IG-4 | Contextual prediction (context clues) | 259 |
| III-IG-4 | Contextual prediction (word position) | 294 |
| III-IG-6 | Factual recall | 298 |
| III-MT-2 | Main idea | 302 |
| IV-ET-1 | Assessing word choice | 335 |
| V-IG-4 | Contextual prediction (punctuation) | 353 |
| VI-WA-1 | Vowel generalization | 369 |
| VII-WA-1 | Syllabication | 403 |
| VII-IG-5 | Contextual prediction (intonation) | 417 |